THE SOCIOLOGY OF LAW AND THE GLOBAL TRANSFORMATION OF DEMOCRACY

This book provides a new legal-sociological account of contemporary democracy. This is based on a revision of standard positions in democratic theory, reflecting the impact of global legal norms on the institutions of national states. Chris Thornhill argues that the establishment of fully democratic, fully inclusive governance systems in national societies was generally impeded by inner-societal structural factors, and that inclusive patterns of democratic citizenship only evolved on the foundation of global legal norms that were consolidated after 1945. He claims that this process can be best understood through a transposition of key insights of classical legal sociology onto the form of global society. Extensive analysis of select case studies in different regions illustrate these claims. Thornhill offers a sociological theory of global law to explain contemporary processes of democratic integration and institutional formation and contemporary constructions of citizenship and political rights. This title is also available as Open Access.

CHRIS THORNHILL is Professor in Law at the University of Manchester. He is the author of several books on the sociology of law, especially on the sociology of constitutions. His books and other writings have been translated into many languages. He is a member of the Academia Europaea.

GLOBAL LAW SERIES

The series provides unique perspectives on the way globalization is radically altering the study, discipline and practice of law. Featuring innovative books in this growing field, the series explores those bodies of law which are becoming global in their application, and the newly emerging interdependency and interaction of different legal systems. It covers all major branches of the law and includes work on legal theory, history, and the methodology of legal practice and jurisprudence under conditions of globalization. Offering a major platform on global law, these books provide essential reading for students and scholars of comparative, international and transnational law.

Series Editors

M.E.A Goodwin *Tilburg University*
Randall Lesaffer *Tilburg University*
David Nelken *King's College London*
Han Somsen *Tilburg University*

Books in the Series

Intimations of Global Law Neil Walker
Legalized Families in the Era of Bordered Globalization Daphna Hacker
Transnational Sustainability Laws Phillip Paiement
The Sociology of Law and the Global Transformation of Democracy Chris Thornhill
Authority and the Globalisation of Inclusion and Exclusion Hans Lindahl

For Atina, Grace and John

THE SOCIOLOGY OF LAW AND THE GLOBAL TRANSFORMATION OF DEMOCRACY

CHRIS THORNHILL

University of Manchester

CAMBRIDGE
UNIVERSITY PRESS

CAMBRIDGE
UNIVERSITY PRESS

NOV 2 1 2019

University Printing House, Cambridge CB2 8BS, United Kingdom

One Liberty Plaza, 20th Floor, New York, NY 10006, USA

477 Williamstown Road, Port Melbourne, VIC 3207, Australia

314-321, 3rd Floor, Plot 3, Splendor Forum, Jasola District Centre, New Delhi - 110025, India

79 Anson Road, #06-04/06, Singapore 079906

Cambridge University Press is part of the University of Cambridge.

It furthers the University's mission by disseminating knowledge in the pursuit of education, learning and research at the highest international levels of excellence.

www.cambridge.org
Information on this title: www.cambridge.org/9781316649060
DOI : 10.1017/9781108186049

When citing this work, please include a reference to the DOI 10.1017/9781108186049

First published 2018

A catalogue record for this publication is available from the British Library

Library of Congress Cataloging in Publication data
Names: Thornhill, C. J. (Christopher J.), 1966- author.
Title: The sociology of law and the global transformation of democracy /
    Chris Thornhill, University of Manchester.
Description: Cambridge, United Kingdom ; New York, NY, USA : Cambridge
    University Press, 2018. | Series: Global law series | Includes
    bibliographical references and index.
Identifiers: LCCN 2018009340| ISBN 9781107199903 (hardback) | ISBN
    9781316649060 (paperback)
Subjects: LCSH: Sociological jurisprudence. | Law—Political aspects. |
    Democracy—Social aspects.
Classification: LCC K370 .T545 2018 | DDC 340/.115—dc23 LC record available
    at https://lccn.loc.gov/2018009340

ISBN 978-1-107-19990-3 Hardback
ISBN 978-1-316-64906-0 Paperback

CONTENTS

ACKNOWLEDGEMENTS

Research for this book was very generously funded by the European Research Council (ERC) (Advanced Grant 323656-STC). I owe a great debt of gratitude to the ERC for this funding, which made it possible for me to conduct extensive research in different countries and in some of the world's great cities, notably Bogotá, Brasilia, Frankfurt, La Paz, London, Moscow, Nairobi and Saint Petersburg. Additionally, I wish to thank everyone who has assisted me with my research in connection with this book. In particular, my thanks are due to Maria Smirnova and Carina Calabria, who for several years provided both excellent company and extensive information concerning Russian law and the legal systems of different Latin American countries. All analysis of Russian law set out in the book is indebted to Maria Smirnova, who has been a truly magnificent co-researcher over recent years. Some aspects of Chilean and Colombian case law were explained to me by Rodrigo Cespedes, and Dominic Dagbanja and Elizabeth O'Loughlin helped me with questions concerning Ghanaian and Kenyan law. In Bogotá, Juan Barrero, Jorge González and Julieta Lemaitre showed great generosity in taking time to clarify for me the finer points and broader implications of Colombian constitutional law. Colleagues at the Institute of Legislation and Comparative Law under the Government of the Russian Federation in Moscow were extremely helpful in sharing their knowledge of the complexities of Russian public law. Also very fruitful were discussions in which I participated at conferences and colloquia held in Aarhus, Bogotá, Bremen, Cardiff, Edinburgh, Moscow and Tel Aviv, and I am grateful to all participants in these events. Discussions in my postgraduate seminars at the University of Brasilia in October 2016 will stay in my mind for a long time, and I am grateful to all the students there for their intellectual company. Students who took my course on the Sociology of Law at Manchester University in 2017 also contributed immeasurably to the book, as their questions forced me to rethink many of my claims. In November 2016, I spent a month at the

Max-Planck-Institut für europäische Rechtsgeschichte in Frankfurt, where I wrote some of the historical sections of the book. The Institute in Frankfurt was always a wonderful place to work, and I am grateful for the opportunities it offered me over many years, up to 2016. More informal discussions with Guilherme de Azevedo, Paul Blokker, Hauke Brunkhorst, Emilios Christodoulidis, Jean d'Aspremont, Pierre Guibentif, Gorm Harste, Poul Kjaer, Aldo Mascareño, Ben Morris, Jiri Priban, Darrow Schecter, Gunther Teubner and Neil Walker were also very enlightening, and they fed into the book indirectly. Atina Krajewska discussed many of the ideas in the book with me, and she put me right on many points. As ever, I am extremely grateful to Finola O'Sullivan and other colleagues at Cambridge University Press for supporting my research.

Introduction

This is a book that is concerned with democracy. It aims to contribute to the defence of democracy, and to achieve this goal it aims to contribute to the broad understanding of democracy – that is, to enhance comprehension of the historical processes through which democracy developed, of its social foundations and of the expectations that people who live in democratic societies can reasonably entertain. In particular, a key objective of this book is to set out an analysis of democracy that responds to currently widespread reactions against established democratic arrangements, which are evident, in different expressions, across Eastern and Western Europe, the USA and parts of Latin America. A characteristic of these reactions is that they commonly involve a rejection of the transnational normative elements that typically underpin contemporary democratic systems, and they advocate a renationalization of democracy. Such reactions have of course not yet come close to reversing the great successes in global democratic formation that have been witnessed since the 1980s. But they demand extreme vigilance. For this reason, this book aims to account for democratic government in terms that are immune to both populist and nationalist impulses and to inflationary ideas of democratic representation, which inform many such reactions.

With these objectives in mind, this book renounces the normative terrain of much democratic theory, and it does not attempt to assess either the relative value of different models of democracy or the normative grounds for commitment to democracy. Instead, it seeks to alter the focus and the vocabulary of debate about democracy, observing democracy as a reality brought into life by quite contingent events, precarious circumstances and highly improbable – often clearly undemocratic – processes. As a result, it implies that much of the formal normative defence of democracy, which sees democratic institutions as justified by clear normative principles, has limited value. This book questions the idea that obligations expressed through democratic government can be attached to the primary concepts, such as self-legislation, reasonable freedom and collective autonomy, that are used in classical democratic analysis.[1] It argues, at one level, that the defence of democracy has been made unnecessarily difficult because democracy is often explained and justified in historically unreflected, sociologically ill-construed categories. Democracy is often conceived and legitimated in conceptual forms that have little to do with the actual reality of democracy, and this burdens democratic institutions, in their factual structure, with expectations that are hard to satisfy. In fact, the terms in which democracy is usually defended acquire a spurious plausibility, and they can easily be turned against democracy as a social given reality, leaving democratic institutions vulnerable to internal criticism. In response to this, this book attempts to provide a more cautious and realistic account of democracy as a governance system, rejecting much of the classical conceptual apparatus of democratic theory, and it then defends democracy on this revised, more cautious and contingent basis. In so doing, it indicates that much of the common critique of democracy, demanding a return to nationalized, immediate experiences of participation, results from a miscomprehension of democracy, which is partly induced by the terms in which democracy is explained and advocated. Overall, this book tries to show that democracy has been misunderstood by those who defend it, and this misunderstanding is proving detrimental to its chances of continued consolidation. On the account offered here, democracy is both more and less than commonly assumed, and it needs to be vindicated as such.

In setting out this defence of democracy, this book also proposes a particular defence of sociology, and in particular of legal sociology, as a method for interpreting the rise of democracy, and for assessing the demands that we can channel towards democratically authorized institutions. Indeed, it defends the sociology of law as the most appropriate source of a plausible defence of democracy. It claims that democracy is most accurately understood and most effectively – i.e. realistically – defended if it is approached from a legal-sociological perspective. That is, democracy is best comprehended if categorical normative claim-making is renounced, if its functions are traced to underlying social processes, if its normative foundations are located within broad societal contexts and – above all – if the claims to obligation and legitimacy made by democratic

---

[1] See pp. 17–8 below.

institutions are observed in a perspective that probes at the social realities underlying legal-normative constructs. A sociology of democratic normativity is required to explain and, ultimately, to vindicate democratic organization – indeed, the more sociological analysis of democracy is, the more robust the defence of democracy is likely to be.

In this respect, this book makes the distinctive methodological claim that the sociology of law is the original and eminent science of democracy. The sociology of law, it is claimed here, first developed as an ambivalently affirmative inquiry into early democratic institutions, and, in its rejection of the simplified registers of classical democratic theory, it still provides the perspective in which democracy can be most accurately explained and protected.[2] To be sure, this book argues that the sociology of law has followed many stray paths along its historical course. However, this has usually occurred when it has digressed from the basic principles of the legal-sociological outlook. Consequently, this book attempts to consolidate the position of the sociology of law as a basic science of democracy by restating its core principles, and by applying a distinctive legal-sociological focus to processes of democratic formation in different parts of contemporary global society.

Before this book addresses its major questions, however, this introduction attempts to establish a definition of democracy, to identify the core conceptual elements of democracy and, above all, to account for the social and institutional implications of the categories in which democratic government is usually envisaged. In so doing, it aims to provide a framework in which, in subsequent chapters, the factual development of democracy can be analysed. Using this framework, later chapters in this book explain how democracy assumed a form that deviated from its classical construction, and they show how classical ideas of democracy contained internal normative constructs that inevitably steered democratic formation onto unpredicted pathways.

I.1   What Is a Democracy?

For the sake of simplicity, democracy is defined here, in relatively uncontroversial, practical terms, as follows. At an institutional level, democracy is *a societal condition in which individual members of a population or a*

---

[2] Law was a very important focus in early sociology, and the deep connection between legal analysis and sociology has often been noted (see Parsons 1977: 11; Gephart 1993: 86). Later, law's importance as a core object of sociological study declined.

designated political group, acting in the role of citizens, are included in a system of political representation, in which they have an equal participatory (that is, usually, electoral) role in constructing the general order of governance and in authorizing the particular laws that regulate their actions. At a normative level, thus, democratic institutions are defined and legitimated by the fact that they conduct processes of collectively endorsed legislation, so that citizens recognize the laws by which they are obligated as expressions of collective commitments.[3] On this basis, shared obligation, often understood as shared freedom, lies at the normative core of democracy. The original principle of modern democracy was formulated in the political philosophies of the Enlightenment. This principle was, namely, that democracy is a political system in which laws acquire legitimacy because they publicly express reasonable freedoms – freedoms

---

[3] My definition of democracy is close to that proposed by Rosanvallon, stating that: 'Equality in the polling station' is the 'first precondition of democracy, the most elementary precondition of equality, and the indisputable foundation of the law' (1992: 11). For a variation on this basic claim see Böckenförde (1991: 291). One recent analysis makes this point most clearly, stating that democracy presupposes a 'people, which is politically self-governing' and which 'is able to interpret the decisions of state as its own' (Haack 2007: 303). Iris Marion Young claims simply that the 'normative legitimacy of a democratic decision depends on the degree to which those affected by it have been included in the decision-making process' (2000: 5–6). My definition is also close to that of Tilly, who sees democracy as involving 'broad, equal, protected, binding consultation of citizens with respect to state actions' (2007: 34), and as presupposing 'broad citizenship, equal citizenship', and 'protection of citizens from arbitrary action by government officials' (2000: 4). My definition also overlaps with Dahl's theory of polyarchy, claiming that in a democracy: 'Citizenship is extended to a relatively high proportion of adults, and the rights of citizenship include the opportunity to oppose and vote out the highest officials in the government' (1989: 220). Like my account, Dahl also states that 'democracy is uniquely related to freedom ... It expands to maximum feasible limits the opportunity for persons to live under laws of their own choosing' (1989: 89). See also Dahl's insistence on full inclusion as one of the criteria of democracy, such that '[t]he citizen body ... must include all persons subject to the laws of that state except transients and persons proved to be incapable of caring for themselves' (1998: 78). Similarly, Beetham defines democracy as a 'mode of decision-making about collectively binding rules and policies over which the people exercise control', adding that a democracy is most perfectly realized 'where all members of the collectivity enjoy equal rights to take part in such decision-making directly' (1993: 55). Shapiro's definition of democracy (2003: 52) as a political system designed for 'structuring power relations so as to limit domination' is also compatible with mine. For the classical Hellenic definition of democracy, which also contained a presumption of equal participation of citizens, see Meier (1970: 37). The values of equality and freedom are also central to more recent attempts to calibrate the degree of democracy that exists in different polities (see Lauth 2015: 7; Munck 2016: 11). The norm of freedom as an element of democracy has been proclaimed most boldly by Goodhart, who observes democracy as resting on a 'political commitment to universal emancipation' (2005: 150).

that reasonable subjects (citizens) are likely to exercise.[4] In fact, democracy rests normatively on a *double obligation*, in which citizens accept their obligation towards political institutions because these institutions recognize their obligation to express reasonable freedoms and to translate these freedoms into law. In realized form, both institutionally and normatively, democracy inevitably means more than this. Clearly, democracy can assume a multiplicity of forms – it can appear as direct democracy, parliamentary democracy, presidential democracy, council democracy, economic democracy, industrial democracy or even commissarial democracy. But democracy cannot easily mean less than this. Of course, democracy has been widely reconceived in recent years, especially in light of the supposed diminishing importance of national political institutions.[5] Owing to the increasingly transnational form of contemporary society, the assumption that members of the single national people should act as the sole source of governmental legitimacy has become questionable.[6] In fact, even at the origins of modern national democracy, national sources of constitutional agency were not fully separated from global normative orders.[7] However, the above definition contains some necessary conditions that a political system – that is, *the mass of institutions in society responsible for producing legislation* – must satisfy in order to be qualified as democratic.

First, in order for a political system to be classified as democratic, there must be an ongoing practical authorization of the governmental order by its citizens. That is, there must be a *chain of communication*, reflecting both contestation and consent over the sources of legitimate

---

[4] In the early construction of democratic theory, however, this claim was developed to imply that freedom is a condition in which the human being behaves in accordance with generalized maxims of practical reason: in which the human being finds a source of obligation in its own rationality, and acts in accordance with this. The legitimate state, then, is a state that externalizes the rational self-obligation of the citizen, so that the person acquires an objective obligation to the state as a legal guarantor of his or her subjective self-obligation. The freedom provided by the state is thus primarily not freedom, but obligation. We can find this argument in Rousseau and in the theorists of the French Revolution, who viewed freedom and virtue as coterminous and implied that citizens possessed an enforceable obligation to be free, in virtuous fashion (see p. 78 below). This argument finds the most distilled expression in Kant. For Kant, the human capacity for 'inner freedom' is linked to the fact that the human being is a 'being that is capable of holding obligations'. Human freedom is thus an obligation 'toward oneself', and the human being enters a 'contradiction to itself', violating its own inner freedom, if it acts in breach of generally obligatory laws (Kant 1977b [1797]: 550).

[5] See examples below at pp. 195–8, 201.

[6] See analysis below at pp. 432–3.

[7] See the impact of global norms in the French Revolution, reflected in Abbé Grégoire's draft for a *Declaration of the Rights of Nations* (1793). This is reprinted in Grewe (1988: 660–1).

legislation, that connects citizens with different organs of the political system, and this communication must be institutionally entrenched, so that it cannot be unilaterally abrogated. This is an ineradicable part of a democracy.

Second, to be defined as democratic, a political system must be centred around a construction of the citizen as an individual person, capable equally of reflexively responsible and politically implicated decisions that impact on acts of legislation, processes of inclusion and the distribution of goods in society. This cannot be left out of any definition of democracy.[8] Indeed, democracy revolves around a construct of the citizen as a basic focus of legitimacy or as a basic *subject of democracy*, and the recognition of the citizen as a source of law's obligatory force is foundational for the democratic political system as a public order.[9] Democracy, therefore, is a mode of government in which the citizen forms the core *legitimational figure* for the political system. From the first emergence of the basic elements of modern democracy, the political system explained its legitimacy and authorized its functions on the basis both of the legal-normative recognition of rights of citizens and of the translation of the interests, commitments and freedoms of citizens into legal form.[10]

On this basis, third, to be considered democratic, a political system cannot, except perhaps on grounds of age, incapacity or avowed hostility to democracy, exclude distinct sectors of society from the factual exercise of citizenship rights.[11] As discussed below, democracy presupposes the

---

[8] See Seyla Benhabib's definition: 'Popular sovereignty means that all full members of the *demos* are entitled to have a voice in the articulation of the laws by which the *demos* is to govern itself. Democratic rule, then, extends its jurisdiction in the first place to those who can view themselves as the authors of such rule' (2004: 20). See the definition of the citizen as a person 'associating with other persons to have voice and action in the making of our worlds' in Pocock (1995: 52). See Habermas's claim that 'citizens of a democratic legal state understand themselves as the authors of the laws, which they, as addressees, are obliged to obey' (1998: 152).

[9] The American Supreme Court has stated accordingly: 'This Government was born of its citizens, it maintains itself in a continuing relationship with them, and, in my judgment, it is without power to sever the relationship that gives rise to its existence. I cannot believe that a government conceived in the spirit of ours was established with power to take from the people their most basic right. Citizenship *is* man's basic right, for it is nothing less than the right to have rights.' *Perez* v. *Brownell* 356 U.S. 44 (1958).

[10] I agree with Charles Tilly's claim that citizenship is a necessary but not sufficient condition of democratization (2004: 8).

[11] Representative government, therefore, is not necessarily democratic, and it may often be the opposite of democracy. Representative government does not presuppose factual inclusion of citizens. See for this argument Schmitt (1928: 2009); Pitkin (1967: 190–1). Both the French and the American Revolutions were driven in part by hostility to pure

equality of citizens as a precondition of legitimate legislation, and it contains an essential disposition towards full political inclusion of citizens, so that as many people as possible in society participate in creating laws and recognize legislation as expressing their own claims to liberty.[12] Political systems that make it impossible for some social groups who are affected by law to participate in making law belong outside the category of full democracy.

In the definition of democracy set out above, it is clear that democracy is, above all, a system of inclusive and authoritative legislation. In this definition, laws only become legitimate to the degree that they are passed by a legislative body, whose acts originate in procedures for collective participation, expressed most essentially in elections. Notably, in the eighteenth century, when the conceptual basis for modern democracy was first established, it became an article of faith that personal freedom could be most effectively guaranteed by a legislature, representing the people or the nation as a whole. The direct correlation between personal freedom and the collectively mandated legislature thus became a defining feature of early democratic theory. At different global locations, the legislature was conceived as the dominant organ of government, in which collective freedoms could be enforced as the foundation for society's legal order.[13] Early in the American Revolution, James Otis saw

---

representative government, and some of their protagonists saw the democratic exercise of popular or national sovereignty as an alternative to inherited ideas of representative government. The French Revolution reacted – initially – against established ideas of representative government (see Rosanvallon 2000: 19–21). During the Jacobin period, notably, Saint-Just claimed that government spoke directly for the people (see Jaume 1997: 133). In the American Revolution, there was less hostility to representation than in the French Revolution, but, ideologically, it renounced the English doctrine of virtual representation (see Pole 1966: 54; Wood 2008: 8, 26). For an early critique of virtual representation in America, see the claims in Otis (1769: 28). Rousseau's theory of national sovereignty, which gave conceptual impetus to the French Revolution, was based on a critique of democracy as representation (1966 [1762]: 134).

[12] Amongst early proto-democratic theorists, Rousseau argued that citizens all become 'equal through the social contract' (1966 [1762]: 137). Kant argued that citizens (*Staatsbürger*) are the members of a particular society – a state – and they are defined by the fact that they are 'unified for legislation'. For Kant, the essence of citizens resides in their equality, and it is expressed in the exercise of political rights: in 'the capacity for participation in elections constitutes the qualification for citizenship'. Crucially, for Kant, a citizen is not obliged to show obedience to a law to which he or she has not 'given approval' (1977b [1797]: 432–33).

[13] Of course this principle was stimulated by Locke. It was then elaborated by Blackstone (1765: 143). It later became an article of faith in revolutionary France. In the USA, early constitutional rebellions were deeply marked by insistence on 'the colonial right to control of legislative power' and early state constitutions clearly placed the legislative branch at the centre of the constitution (Pole 1966: 29–31).

the 'supreme legislative' power as the 'sovereign power of a state' (1769: 4), and he claimed that 'supreme and subordinate powers of legislation should be free and sacred in the hands where the community have once rightfully placed them' (1764: 52). The 1776 Constitution of Maryland declared simply that 'the right of the people to participate in the legislature is the best security of liberty, and the foundation of all free government'. One account argues that the French Revolution witnessed the birth of a 'unique conception of legislative authority', capable of radically transforming society as a whole (Achaintre 2008: 21). Accordingly, during the French Revolution, Saint-Just stated that the 'legislative body is like the unmoving light that distinguishes the form of all things ... It is the essence of liberty (1791: 102).

The primacy accorded to the legislature in democratic theory means that laws not created through inclusive popular participation in legislative acts have questionable, contestable legitimacy. Moreover, this means that laws created through popular participation have higher-order status, they override other laws, or other legal norms, that a society may contain, and, above all, they have primacy over laws created in other institutions. This latter fact possessed particular importance in the historical rise of democratic institutions, as, in most pre-democratic societies, legislation was not a dominant source of law, much law existed in piecemeal informal normative orders and there was no clear hierarchy between different normative structures in different parts of society.[14] Consequently, popular participation in law making evolved as a norm that allowed governments to centralize society's law-making powers and to establish strict hierarchy between different laws. As a result, legislation is the central element of democracy, and the legitimacy of democracy depends on its claim to channel the will of the people or the nation, through the legislative organs of government, into law.

Of course, this is not to say that in a democracy participatory acts are channelled without filtration into law. It is necessarily the case that democracies establish constitutional systems, centred on human rights guarantees, to ensure that all citizens in society can participate adequately in political will formation. Indeed, the common theoretical claim that democracy presupposes rights is perfectly sustainable, and it is not

---

[14] Before the French Revolution, governments did not monopolize powers of legislation, and, thereafter, they did so only notionally. In medieval societies, law was not made, but found in local sources in conventions, and even monarchical attempts to bring order to such conventions caused friction between central institutions and local elites (see Grinberg 1997: 1021, 1025).

contradicted here.[15] On the contrary, it is argued throughout this book that there is little sense in imagining a modern democracy without also imagining the citizen, defined as a holder of general and temporally secure rights, as the basic point of legitimational reference for the political system.

Nonetheless, in a strictly constructed democracy, basic rights – for instance, rights regarding personal inviolability, freedom of movement and expression, access to justice – obtain value to the extent that they underpin the participatory dimension of democracy, securing and maximizing access to the procedures required for electoral authorization of law. Such rights, therefore, must be rights that shape democratic procedure, which prevent exclusion of social actors from collective decision-making processes, and which stabilize a general, equal and inclusive construct of the citizen as a participant in legislation. Democracy always presupposes that the citizen, as an equal participatory agent, stands at the origin of law making, and law is created by acts of citizens oriented towards legislation. In consequence, democracy contains the normative implication that rights are willed by citizens as principles that promote equal inclusion in legislative processes, and that rights obtain legitimacy because they act to ensure that the citizens retain a position at the origin of laws. Guarantees for rights lose democratic legitimacy if they obstruct their origin in democratic choice making. In a strictly constructed democracy, it is legitimate to assume that basic rights themselves are designed by constitution-making decisions, or at least by practical consensus between citizens, such that any normative or procedural constraint placed on acts of popular will formation possesses a clearly political origin.[16]

I.2 The Citizen

In this definition, the idea of the citizen is central to the norms, the practices and the obligations that support modern democracy. Notably, the period in which the modern democratic state began to take shape, the revolutionary period of the late eighteenth century, implanted in society the idea that the state and the citizen are integrally connected, and that the state is formed and legitimated as an entity that stands in an immediate and directly constitutive relation to the persons that it integrates – that is,

---

[15] For different expressions of this theory see Habermas (1994: 88–9); Beetham (1999: 93); Benhabib (2009); Benvenisti and Harel (2017: 40).

[16] See this claim in Bellamy (2007: 51); Loughlin (2010).

to citizens (see Bendix 1996 [1964]: 89–90). Democracy, in consequence, is originally a system of legislation that is created by, and remains centred around, citizens. In Europe, this association between state and citizen is underlined most symbolically by the Declaration of the Rights of Man and the Citizen in France in 1789. In the USA, the positive state-founding implications of citizenship were defined in equally forceful fashion.[17]

During the early rise of democracy, first, the state consolidated itself – functionally – as a public order by defining and legally demarcating the persons subject to its power, by bestowing, variably, certain equal rights upon them, and, in so doing, by removing them from alternative local affiliations (Gosewinkel 2001: 138; Gironda 2010: 70, 343). This involved the recognition of persons as citizens. In some states, in fact, the concept of the citizen was constructed quite instrumentally by political actors in order to weaken the power of aristocratic estates, to create a vertical hierarchy – that is, a 'rational order of rank' – in society, and so to establish 'closer relations between the nation and the constitution of state'.[18] The construction of the citizen was thus integral to practices of institutional formation and territorial integration that underpin modern statehood.[19] In close connection to this, in its early emergence, the modern state was formed, normatively, as an entity that was authorized through the voluntary commitment of single persons, and it extracted legitimacy and legislative power from the generic construct of the citizen – by granting extended rights of participation, and by establishing preconditions for civil and political inclusion.

In both these respects, the modern state was formed as an entity that was correlated with the citizen as a *claimant to rights*, and the state acquired public authority for its functions by including citizens in this capacity. The modern state was elaborated as a system of shared rights, allocated to citizens, in which political institutions were able to incorporate their constituents and authorize legislation on the basis of these rights. Consequently, Shklar argues – quite persuasively – that there is 'no notion more central in politics than citizenship' (1991: 1). Similarly, Dahrendorf states that the

---

[17] On the American Revolution as reflecting a strong positive ethic of political foundation see Wood (1992: 325); Edling (2003: 4).

[18] This was the plan in Hardenberg's designs to reform the Prussian state after its military defeat by Napoleon (1931 [1807]: 316–18).

[19] The modern construction of the citizen was of course linked to earlier structural processes. It accelerated and consolidated pre-existing processes of territorial state formation, in which the increasing unity of legal order had already stimulated the growth of centralized, territorially concentrated political institutions (see Brunner 1942: 261).

entire 'revolution of modernity' can be summarized in one word: 'the citizen' (1965: 79). Gosewinkel adds to this by defining citizenship as the core concept underpinning the 'patterns of development of modern statehood' (2016: 37).

At the historical centre of the concept of the citizen, and of the modern state more generally, are two principles: *individual decision* and *collective equality*. First, modern citizenship was conceived as a condition that is freely and reflexively elected by individual persons. On this basis, it contains the expectation that it will enhance personal freedom. At least formally, second, the condition of citizenship implies that all citizens, having decided to be citizens, are equally included in a shared system of public rights, by means of which they are able to shape legislation and define the objective conditions of personal freedom and obligation. The combination of these two principles underpins the basic form of the modern state.

In revolutionary France, for example, the idea of the citizen assumed importance as the localized corporate structure of society under the *ancien régime* dissolved. A modern concept of the citizen developed in France as a body of persons began to identify and promote a common set of interests, which were opposed to the corporate power of the Bourbon monarchy, but which, in their relative consistency, detached individual persons from their more private societal locations in guilds, professional corporations and estates, which were defined by status-related privileges and immunities.[20] Citizenship was thus linked to a twofold process of *individualization* and *collectivization*, in which single members of society decided, separately, to become members of an extended national community, and their exercise of singular rights led, collectively, to the formation of a generalized, extensive, national society, with authority to override the legislative edicts of any corporate entity, including the monarchy. Even before 1789, some advocates of national membership had suggested that the institutional structure of the *ancien régime* already contained commonly binding basic laws, which expressed and protected the shared interests of all members of the citizenry, overriding particular or local privileges.[21] During the revolutionary period, the decisive rejection of particular legal privileges,

---

[20] See discussion of the individualizing impact of the dissolution of the guilds in France in Garaud (1953: 11); Fitzsimmons (2010: 58). On the transformation of citizenship through the dissolution of estates in other European societies see Koselleck (1979: 109); Boli (1989: 43).

[21] See relevant analysis in Bickart (1932: 1–2, 73, 103, 133); Duclos (1932: 30–31); Echeverria (1985: 3); Vergne (2006: 263).

and their replacement with generally applicable obligations, became a core article in thinking about citizenship.[22] During the Revolution, in fact, the elements of voluntarism and collectivism in the figure of the citizen assumed acutely intensified form as the citizen, literally, was mobilized in the process of nation building. At this time, military engagement in defence of the Republic became a core determinant of citizenship, and the first Republican governments made the ascription of rights of citizenship conditional on the personal willingness of members of society to serve in the army. As a result, the exercise of political citizenship was integrally fused with the concept of the *citoyen-soldat*.[23] Notably, attempts in revolutionary France to provide a constitution for the nation were closely connected with attempts to provide a constitution for the army, and early draft military constitutions stated that the *soldat* and the *citoyen* should remain as closely connected as possible.[24] In some declarations, the personal experience of death in combat for the revolutionary polity was viewed as the most concentrated expression of equal citizenship. During the Revolution, Billaud-Vaurenne described the experience of death in defence of the Republic as a 'recall to equality', distilling an essentially formative – elective/collective – aspect of Republican existence (Billaud-Varenne 1794: 31).

In revolutionary America, analogously, national citizenship was projected as the result of an elective personal decision, and the construct of the citizen was closely linked to military engagement. American citizenship was originally associated with service in anti-colonial militias, and the initial expansion of citizenship in the early years of the Revolution was driven by a need for citizens to accept conscription in the struggle against colonial rule. This created a body of persons claiming citizenship as a distinct legal category, electively positioned outside the royal franchises created in England, and decisively committed to the American revolutionary

---

[22] German historiography still differentiates between society based on estates and society of citizens (*altständisch* or *staatsbürgerlich*) to determine the division between early modern and modern society, such that the concept of the citizen expresses a great historical caesura. On the semantics of this see Weihnacht (1969: 41).

[23] The 'valeur de nos soldats républicains' was described by Robespierre as a distinctive bastion of the Republic (1793d: 2). The *citoyen-soldat*, one historian claims, condensed a 'new type of political subjectivity' (Hippler 2006: 89). See also Boli (1989: 11).

[24] See Art XXXXIIII of the projected military constitution for revolutionary France in Lacuée, de Cessac and Serva (1790: 12). If we accept Hintze's claim (1962: 53) that every 'constitution of state is originally a military constitution', the concept of the citizen-soldier that evolved in the age of revolution can be placed at the core of a new comprehension of public authority.

cause.[25] Accordingly, an early commentary on American citizenship, by David Ramsay, explained that, through the revolution, the 'political character of the people' had been transformed 'from subject to citizen': the relation of the citizens to the state resided in the fact that they were united, through a voluntary personal act, such that the citizen possessed 'an individual's proportion of the common sovereignty' (1789: 3–4). Slightly later, the Supreme Court declared, in strikingly military language, that:

> *Citizenship*, which has arisen from the dissolution of the feudal system ... is a substitute for allegiance, corresponding with the new order of things. Allegiance and citizenship, differ, indeed, in almost every characteristic. Citizenship is the effect of compact; allegiance is the offspring of power and necessity. Citizenship is a political tie; allegiance is a territorial tenure. Citizenship is the charter of equality; allegiance is a badge of inferiority. Citizenship is constitutional, allegiance is personal. Citizenship is freedom; allegiance is servitude. Citizenship is communicable; allegiance is repulsive. Citizenship may be relinquished; allegiance is perpetual. With such essential differences, the doctrine of allegiance is inapplicable to a system of citizenship; which it can neither serve to controul, nor to elucidate.[26]

In both early revolutionary settings, in consequence, the citizen was the fundamental lynchpin in the emergent political system. As such, citizenship was conceived as the result of an equal and voluntary political decision, of the choice to identify with a particular, integrative community, often of a military or partially militarized nature, through which the citizen could raise claim to certain collective rights and freedoms. This decision separated the community of citizens from traditional patterns of government founded in coercion and dependence or from traditional patterns of affiliation based on involuntary obligation (Rosanvallon 1992: 72–3).[27] Voluntary collectivism, expressed in concentrated form in military obligation, formed the centre of the volitionally constructed

---

[25] See Kettner (1978: 127); R. Smith (1997: 87); Kestnbaum (2000: 21). One account argues that the 'citizen soldier' was institutionalized in the French and American Revolutions (Janowitz 1980: 14). In Kloppenberg (2016: 360), the argument is proposed that war against England created an ethic of citizenship in America, based on autonomy and equality.

[26] 3 U.S. 133 *Talbot* v. *Janson* (1795).

[27] The connection between citizenship and military identity goes back a long way, and it was famously formulated by Machiavelli. In revolutionary America, rules of citizenship had to be defined at an early stage in the revolutionary wars, as laws had to be established to regulate persons not loyal to the Republican cause and to disarm potential traitors. See for example Articles 27–8 of the Articles of War of the Continental Congress, 1775. In France, citizenship clearly also hinged on a willingness to take up arms. Indeed, military service was an intensified experience of citizenship (Hippler 2002: 16). See generally on the link between military service and citizenship rights Janowitz (1976: 190–1); Sanborn (2003: 4–5).

acter—

national state.[28] Indeed, the linkage between citizen and soldier formed a key precondition for the longer rise of democratic citizenship, and, throughout modern history, the militarization of society has recurrently led both to the solidification of existing patterns of political enfranchisement and demands for enfranchisement by hitherto marginalized citizenship groups.[29]

This association between democracy and citizenship is not meant to indicate that, within a democracy, citizenship is a simple or static construct, or that democratic institutions can gain legitimacy through the simple and immediate substantiation of the will of citizens. Like democracy, the citizen is definable in multiple categories, and some aspects of citizenship do not, by necessity, give rise to democratic government.[30] Moreover, clearly, the contours and obligations of citizenship cannot be neatly drawn (see Isin 2002: 272). It is ingrained in the democratic construction of the citizen as a legitimational figure that, in establishing general rights, it contains multiple meanings and stimulates multiple, often conflicting, claims to rights, and it reflects socially variable demands for legal recognition and political participation. In particular, the concept of the citizen can easily be taken to project a generalized, homogeneous

---

In both cases, citizenship resulted from a clear and decisive choice. See important discussion in Kettner (1974: 218, 241); Zolberg (2006: 86–7).

[28] This thread runs through all research on democracy. See for discussion Turner (1990: 211).

[29] On this principle see Tilly (2004: 89–90). An important example of this is the experience of African Americans in the USA, where military mobilization repeatedly led to push-back against racist citizenship laws. On this process in the late 1860s see Berry (1977: 92). Tilly's general claim is that the centralization of government originating in extraction for military purposes creates basic conditions of citizenship (1990: 83, 115–20).

[30] The normative concept of citizenship is deliberately reflected here in wide and encompassing terms. The contemporary idea of citizenship comes in all theoretical sizes. This concept can be phrased in semi-classical terms, as practical worldly engagement (Arendt 1958: 257). It can be focused on deliberative interaction (Habermas 1992: 649). It can imagine civil society as a primary locus of citizenship (Arato 2000; Alexander 2006: 34). It can place emphasis on social conflict (Touraine 1994: 24, 113). It can accentuate the importance of shared identities and engaged social membership (Walzer 1994: 54). It can prioritize political participation (Pateman 1970: 105; Barber 1984: 132). It can include participation in market activities, alongside more classical arenas of political agency (Somers 2008: 279). It can assume radical, experimental features (Brunkhorst 1998: 10). It can be seen as a pattern of exclusion and contestation (Isin 2002: 35–6). It can accentuate the transferability of national citizenship to the global level (Linklater 1998: 36; Bosniak 2000: 508). It can imagine a reality of citizenship that transcends national membership (Soysal 1994: 165; Benhabib 1999: 734). It can even envisage cosmopolitanism and community membership at the same time (Delanty 2000: 145). In each formulation, however, the idea of citizenship is unified by the fact that it implies that the citizen is a *political transformer* of societal interests into legally generalized norms.

pattern of inclusion, which cannot simply accommodate multiple groups existing in society at a given moment. As discussed below, the connection of citizenship to dominant social groups of necessity means that, to become reality, citizenship must acquire a pluralistic institutional form. In consequence, the citizen necessarily forms a centre of contest, and, simultaneously, it pushes at the historically given boundaries of societal in- and exclusion, legal recognition and non-recognition. As one theorist has observed, citizenship always refracts the fault lines between membership and non-membership, participation and absence of participation (Barbalet 1988: 97).

Nonetheless, even in its most ambiguous and contested dimensions, democracy depends on citizenship, and citizenship is fundamental to democracy and the obligatory force of democratic laws.

First, in the original emergence of modern national societies, citizenship contained several layers of rather distinct meanings, which were not fully differentiated, and which still in fact partly overlap. Initially, during the first period of national revolution in the eighteenth century, early nation states began to define members of society as holders of certain general legal titles, which meant that they were protected by national laws. At this level, citizenship was defined as possession of a general body of thin protective rights, linked to legal membership in a nation. Moreover, at this time, nation states began to allocate political rights to their members, which meant that some members of society appeared as citizens in the sense that they were entitled to participate in the political life of the national community. At this level, citizenship was defined as possession of general rights to shape legislative processes, linked to national membership. This meaning of citizenship eventually became the cornerstone of democracy. In establishing these two sets of rights, however, states were also forced to decide which members of society were to be assigned such rights, in order to determine the legal qualifications of persons assuming national membership and seeking access to legal protection and political influence. This was clearly the case in revolutionary America, where it was necessary to distinguish American citizens from Britons. This was also the case in revolutionary France, where the new Republic was quickly threatened by foreign intervention and intrigue, and citizenship presupposed Republican loyalty. For this reason, as soon as they began to allocate inclusive constitutional rights, states also began to establish more exclusionary, identificational principles of citizenship, or nationality, to determine affiliation to a particular polity and to justify and regulate access to centrally allocated rights.

From the outset, therefore, citizenship possessed quite divergent normative implications: it implied rights to claim membership in a nation, or nationality (however defined); it implied rights to passive legal protection in a national community; it implied entitlement to the active exercise of certain primary rights of political participation. In some settings, these meanings have been elided. In the French Revolution, notably, the separate meanings of the terms citizenship and nationality were not clearly distinguished (Schönberger 2005: 23). In other linguistic contexts, the vocabulary capturing the distinct senses of the citizen as a legally protected member of a people and of the citizen as a participant in public life, and indirectly also in legislative processes, is not fully elaborated.[31] As a result, different aspects of citizenship contribute to democracy in different ways, and not all principles of citizenship fully and unambiguously endorse a participatory political ethic.

Despite these ambiguities, however, each aspect of citizenship is vitally formative of democracy. Indeed, even more technical, reduced definitions of citizenship that simply address qualifications for national membership are not devoid of democratic implications. From the eighteenth century onwards, even the simple construction of citizenship as a set of formal rights belonging to co-nationals contained the implication that being a citizen implied a status that was distinct from private or feudal allegiance. Even this primary legal definition of citizenship created generalized rights for members of the nation, as it conferred a publicly ordered form on rights that had previously been dependent on objective membership in guilds, families and associations. Even in its reduced aspects, therefore, citizenship was premised in primary notions of legal equality and equal freedom (Fahrmeir 2000: 19). Indeed, the concept of the citizen in this basic legal sense contributed greatly to the legal formation of the nation state as a system of inclusion, and it played a core role in expanding a legal order across society that was decisively separated from the residual private attachments that had underpinned feudalism (Gosewinkel 2001: 11). Even citizenship in the sense of simple nationality thus involved implicit legitimational claims about the essentially egalitarian nature of the community to which a citizen belonged.

---

[31] In German, *Staatsangehörigkeit* denotes membership of a people, with consonant legal rights, and *Staatsbürgerschaft* approximates to (but does not fully cover) the sense of the citizen as political participant (Gosewinkel 1995: 545). On the slow transformation of the concept of the citizen in late-Enlightenment Germany see Schlumbohm (1975: 158); Stolleis (1990: 337–8).

Second, clearly, the concept of the citizen is not constitutively linked to the collective commitment to democratic rule, and citizenship can be defined in ways that contradict democratic ideals. In societies of classical antiquity and in medieval Europe, rights of citizenship were the exclusive property of particular social strata, and they implied duties and obligations specific to socially privileged groups.[32] Moreover, a distinction is often made between the traditional Republican concept of the citizen as an active, public participant in political community and the traditional Liberal concept of the citizen as a relatively passive holder of private legal rights, linked to individual freedoms.[33] Accordingly, some concepts of citizenship see citizenship as an actively politicized process of contested engagement, and some concepts of citizenship view citizenship as linked primarily to the enjoyment of certain protected rights.[34] In many contexts, a more reduced, liberal definition of citizenship as a legal condition, in which certain prior entitlements are preserved, has been accepted, and this does not of itself provide a basis for robust democracy. Indeed, hypothetically, citizenship as a condition of private rights holding is entirely possible in societies that are not easily qualified as democracies.[35]

Despite this, however, in the late Enlightenment, a new and enduringly resonant figure of the citizen was constructed, whose normative implications cannot be eradicated from political-legitimational debates about democracy. During the Enlightenment, first, the citizen was constructed as a singular legal person, with certain private legal rights attached to membership in a national community. This idea of the citizen was clearly articulated in the legal theories of Locke and Kant. At the same time, however, the citizen was imagined not solely as a single or private person, but as the political articulation of *nationhood*: that is, as a *collective singular* person, claiming rights and freedoms of a collectively binding nature, and expressing the interests of the nation as a whole. This idea of the citizen was clearly expressed in the legal theories of Rousseau and Sieyès.

---

[32] Of course, Aristotle did not accept an encompassing model of citizenship. Exclusion was also embedded in the culture of citizenship in ancient Athens (Manville 1990: 11). In medieval Europe, membership in corporations, such as guilds or cities, was a typical precondition for the possession of citizenship rights.

[33] See Young (1989: 252–3); Kymlicka and Norman (1994: 353); Hutchings (1999: 7–8); Miller (2000: 43–4); Bellamy (2011); Carter (2001: 149).

[34] For the former approach see Lipset (1960: 84–5) and for the latter see Marshall (1992 [1950]).

[35] In fact, for much of the nineteenth century, European states possessed legal systems based on private rights, but they did provide expansive political rights until around 1870.

These two dimensions of the citizen flowed together in the revolutionary culmination of the Enlightenment, and they formed an essential foundation for the later growth of democracy. In the revolutionary period, in fact, the two faces of the citizen – the liberal face of passive or protective private rights, and the Republican face of active public duties – were galvanized. This produced an idea of citizenship that entitled the citizen both to legal protection for private rights and to legal-political participation in the exercise of public rights. Above all, this entailed an idea of citizenship in which the exercise of political rights often conflicted with laws intended for the preservation of more passive protective rights, and political rights were often focused on renegotiating the scope of personal rights.

Through this fusion, the citizen emerged in the late Enlightenment as a legal figure combining *singular private subjective rights* and *collective public subjective rights*, whose actions mediated between the domain of private interaction and the realm of public authority, and in which inchoate personal/societal demands were articulated with public institutions.[36] Through this construction, the citizen became a line of communication between government and society, and rights became the diction of this communication. The establishment of the citizen as legitimational figure for the political system created an abiding and often unsettling impulse for the political system of modern society, as it connected the public-legitimational form of the polity to deep-lying private or societal interests. At one level, the construct of the citizen established citizenship as a political form of interaction, based on rights to participate in creating collectively binding laws. Yet, the construct of the citizen also tied the polity at the most integral legitimational level to private claims, prerogatives and conflicts. This meant that a distinctive form for the citizen was created, in which the citizen engaged with the political community through claims to rights and through the exercise of rights, and in which the political system acquired information from society, mediated through the citizen, in the form of rights. Through this dual form, the citizen became the *primary environment* of the national political system, acting as a *line of transmission* through which social demands, in the medium of rights, could be directed towards the political system, and processed by the political system.

---

[36] Habermas explains this by claiming that citizens of state and citizens of society are physically identical persons, but appear in 'complementary roles' (1992: 442). For a claim, close to mine, that the 'substance of citizenship' is rights, and that 'rights of citizenship' refract lines of contest of social in- and exclusion, see Isin (2009: 376–7).

From the Enlightenment onward, the citizen could not be imagined as a purely passive holder of allocated private rights, and citizenship necessarily implied a condition in which members of society were implicated in, or at best challenged for access to, the legislative system of the polity. Indeed, it is fundamental to the modern concept of the citizen that it translates claims to rights and freedoms into political form, it demands political recognition for rights, and it cements rights as elements of public order and public obligation, shared equally by all society and demanding recognition in all aspects of legislation. A democratic citizen is constructed through a process in which political institutions acquire obligations towards persons in generalized legal form, so that citizens are legally implied and recognized as holders of rights that underpin all acts of legislation. As the environment of the political system, the citizen appears as a broad aggregate of rights, allocated to all members in society, and subject to general expansion, which form the basis for the legitimacy of the political system as a functional order. The ability of a citizen to insist on rights that are enacted in all law, even in law that does not specifically concern each particular citizen in each moment of her or his life, might easily be seen as the basic criterion of a democracy, separating democracy as a political form from a simple corporation. The citizen, thus, is only imperfectly constructed if its actions are solely expressed as demands for fulfilment of momentary interests or enactment of private commitments. Instead, a democratic political system is defined by the fact that citizens seek common recognition of rights, so that rights become ingrained in the public constitutional fabric of society: a modern, geographically expansive democracy is difficult to envisage without a structure of public law of this kind.

On this basis, the democratic political system is defined by the fact that it reacts to claims to rights expressed by citizens, who constitute its societal environment, and it translates such claims into generalized form, giving recognition to the citizen as an agent of an eminently *public* character – that is, as an agent *who is normatively co-implied in all legislation*. In this capacity, the citizen becomes a central part of the political structure of society, articulating the norms that all laws must recognize. To this degree, the modern citizen is categorically separated from the private actor, seeking localized or punctual endorsement or protection for particular interests. In a democracy, by consequence, the citizen becomes a socially transformative figure, both legitimating and challenging the contours of the political system through new demands for rights, and expressing rights at consistently heightened degrees of inclusivity. This process of claiming and gaining recognition for rights is primarily institutionalized through democratic elections. Clearly, it was through suffrage extensions that modern democracies were created; widening of electoral franchises reflected, historically, the 'acceptance of the concept of *unit citizen* of the nation state', distinct from private or lateral associations, as the basic source of public authority (Rokkan 1970: 27). However, this also presupposes other patterns of subjective mobilization outside and in parallel to elections.

Of necessity, third, the idea of citizenship contains exclusionary implications, and the process of accessing rights inherent in citizenship refracts manifold social conflicts, both ethnic and socio-economic in nature. These implications also sit uneasily with democracy.

The initial early-democratic construct of the citizen as an embodiment of the nation inevitably led to the exclusion or marginalization of some groups; in fact, this occurred as soon as this construction was confronted with a factually existing, pluralistic society. In most early national societies, rights pertaining to citizenship were initially withheld from minority groups, who were often defined on ethnic grounds. In some cases, citizenship rights have only been expanded in gradual, measured, circumspect and prejudicial fashion to non-dominant ethnic sectors, such that the granting of rights to some ethnic groups has widely implied the withholding of rights from other social groups (Kymlicka 1995: 74). Moreover, early prototypes of modern national democracies also restricted rights of citizenship on socio-economic grounds. Tellingly, the discovery of the citizen in revolutionary France led almost immediately to the imposition of restrictions on the groups allowed to exercise full rights of citizenship (see Grandmaison 1992: 88, 239; Rosanvallon 1992: 72). The idea of citizenship entailed both the exclusion of some social groups seen as threatening to the Republic, and the subdivision of the body of designated citizens into different categories of political entitlement, calibrated by degrees of activity, passivity and entitlement to legislative participation.[37] Such distinctions between different grades of citizenship were typically based on income or wealth, as, in many post-1789 societies, only persons with a certain level of ownership were deemed actively implicated in national affairs.[38] This principle was established early in the French Revolution,

---

[37] On the first point see Wahnich (1997: 81) and on the second see Rosanvallon (1992: 87). The distinction between active and passive citizens is discussed in Sieyès (1789: 12).

[38] In the French Revolution, income-based calibration of citizens was theoretically constructed by Sieyès. But this principle soon became widespread. For instance, Kant retained the distinction made by Sieyès between active and passive citizenship, determined by

as rights of active citizenship were founded in birth, age, domicile, fiscal contribution and employment.[39] Similar processes were reproduced in many new nations created in the longer wake of 1789, and it was common for national populations to be divided *de facto* into passive citizens and active citizens, of which only the latter had full suffrage rights.[40]

As a general point, it can be observed that, across all societies, there exists a close correlation between the early rise of democratic citizenship and the emergence of class conflicts. The rise of the citizen was closely linked to, and in fact causally implicated in, the rise of social class as a focus of agency. As discussed, the principle of citizenship was originally connected to the socio-geographical expansion of national societies, and it reflected the construction of societies as aggregates of individuals with similar rights and duties, distinct from local status hierarchies. Owing to its connection with nationhood, the citizen necessarily assumed central importance in the societal order of the nineteenth century. In particular, citizenship created a condition in which social groups were increasingly separated from their historically localized positions, and conflicts between groups were transferred from the local/sectoral settings typical of *ancien-régime* structures onto the more extended territorial conditions of national society. In this setting, different individuals recognized individuals in other locations as possessing similar interests and problems, and members of particular social groups inevitably began to identify themselves as *classes*, possessing relatively uniform and unifying collective motivations across different social locations.[41] As soon as people perceived themselves as citizens, therefore, they necessarily perceived themselves as members of classes, and they used rights attached to citizenship to advance claims attached to class interests. This is expressed both in the fact that, through the expansion of national societies, some class groups mobilized for increased citizenship rights and in the fact that some status groups mobilized to exclude other groups from enjoyment of such rights.[42]

---

property ownership (1977b [1797]: 432–33). Notably, Robespierre challenged this principle, stating that to deprive persons of rights of active citizenship was 'the greatest of all crimes', and it was wholly incompatible with the abolition of privileges at the core of the Revolution (1791: 21).

[39] See the presentation of this plan by Sieyès to the National Assembly in (1789: 72).

[40] See general discussion of early franchise restrictions at pp. 134–7 below. The distinction between active and passive citizens was widespread, not only in Europe, but also in Latin America (see Guerra 1992: 372–3).

[41] On the connection between nation-building, citizenship and class formation see Bartolini (2000: 180).

[42] See discussion below at pp. 287–90.

Overall, from its first emergence as a political concept, citizenship implied varying degrees of inclusion and political privilege, and it released inter-group conflicts that had been less generally articulated in the political order of pre-modern society. It cannot, therefore, simply be assumed, in the manner of T. H. Marshall, that rights of citizenship have a necessarily 'homogenizing effect', leading seamlessly to more consistent integration of population groups (Gosewinkel 1995: 536). On the contrary, some rights of citizenship are necessarily conflictual, and citizenship and class conflict express a common process of societal formation.

As discussed below, however, citizenship has proved more power-ful as a norm of inclusion than of exclusion, and the claim to equality implied in citizenship has recurrently provided a robust internal meas-ure by which exclusionary constructs of citizenship have been chal-lenged.[43] From the outset, citizenship spelled out a powerful logic of inclusion, and, once established as a principle of legitimacy, citizenship contained an unmistakeable orientation towards full and comprehensive inclusion. Indicatively, Robespierre stated in the French Revolution that under a constitution based on popular sovereignty '[a]ll citizens, who-ever they may be, have the right to lay claim to all levels of representa-tion ... and [e]ach individual has the right to contribute to creating the law by which he is obligated ... If not, it is not the case that all men are equal in rights, or that each man is a citizen'.[44] Likewise, in private cor-respondence in the early stages of the American Revolution (1776), John Adams clearly perceived the emphasis on full inclusion in the concept of the citizen, stating that the result of the principle of citizenship would be as follows:

> There will be no End of it. New Claims will arise. Women will demand a Vote. Lads from 12 to 21 will think their Rights not enough attended to, and every Man, who has not a Farthing, will demand an equal Voice with any other in all Acts of State. It tends to confound and destroy all Distinctions, and prostrate all Ranks, to one common Levell.[45]

After the revolutionary era, Tocqueville apprehended this point equally clearly, explaining that, once separated from status, citizenship releases an

---

[43] See on this Dahrendorf (1965: 79); Janoski (1998: 147). See the claim in Münch that 'the development of rights of citizens' necessitates 'inclusion of all social groups in membership in the social community and in equal exercise of civil rights' (1984: 297).

[44] See Robespierre (1789). This is a speech held in the National Assembly in October 1789.

[45] This correspondence is reprinted in Adams (1979: 211).

unstoppable inclusionary momentum. He explained: 'This is one of the most invariable roles that govern society. The further electoral rights are extended, the greater is the need of extending them. After each new concession, the strength of the democracy increases, and its demands increase with its strength' (1866 [1835]: 89).[46]

Above all, citizenship contains two principles that create an overriding matrix of inclusive social recognition. On one hand, it contains the core principle of equality. On the other hand, it ties public rights to private rights. On this joint basis, citizenship emerged as a term in which social agents were able both to challenge political exclusion (by claiming equal rights of electoral participation) and to demand social inclusion (by claiming an equal entitlement to collective freedoms).[47] Of course, these processes are always incomplete and inherently conflictual. Both normatively and factually, however, the citizen linked society's political system to a multi-level contest over the terms of legislative inclusion, and through this the system that we now call democracy was able to evolve.

I.3   The Citizen as Inclusion

The principle of inclusion projected by the idea of the citizen has vital implications in the normative, legitimational dimension of the political system. To speak in terms close to those used by Hauke Brunkhorst, the rise of the modern citizen in the American and French Revolutions in the late Enlightenment produced a distinctive transformation in the content of law itself. From this time, law was integrally legitimated by its claim to represent the reasonable freedoms of all citizens, and the law could not silence demands for inclusion without silencing the grounds of its validity (Brunkhorst 2010: 15). In polities defined by a commitment to citizenship, therefore, attempts to diminish, or to bar persons from, the exercise of the rights of citizens have usually shown recognition of their own perversity, and such polities have enacted exclusionary measures in furtive,

---

[46] For similar processes in classical democracies, see the account of the growth of Greek citizenship in Meier (1980: 87, 127). For more recent statements of this point see Przeworski (2008); Goodin (2010: 199).

[47] As one account has aptly stated: 'Citizenship defines membership of a political community, and so invites the excluded to struggle for inclusion' (Foweraker and Landman 1997: 31).

clandestine or openly ideological form.[48] As one theorist states, once the principle of equal citizenship is established in a polity 'no acceptable reason can be given to justify unequal distribution of citizenship in violation of the formal idea of equality' – any such unequal distribution must *de facto* acknowledge its own lack of legitimacy (Thompson 1970: 179). At core, the citizen articulates a teleological idea of national society, in which the founding principle of equality steers and directly regulates processes of contestation and inclusion.

In most polities defined by a commitment to citizenship, in consequence, the concept of citizenship has been used either immediately or incrementally to extend democratic integration to social groups prohibited from exercising full rights of political participation. This applied, first, to marginalized or to incompletely represented social groups, such as members of the working class in nineteenth- and early twentieth-century Europe and Latin America. However, it also applied to more systematically excluded social groups, such as women in polities with only male suffrage, people of colour in classical apartheid regimes (for example, pre-1964 USA, pre-1994 South Africa), and indigenous populations living in incompletely decolonized states (pre-1991 Colombia, pre-2009 Bolivia). All these groups have claimed the normative substance of civil and political citizenship as a focus for extending their socio-political inclusion.[49] In such instances, conflict over citizenship laws and legal interpretation of citizenship formed the structuring principle for intensified democratization:[50] citizenship generated a norm of contestation by

---

[48] One example is the restoration monarchy of France initiated in 1814, which preserved a parliamentary chamber for symbolic reasons, although this chamber was strategically designed so that it scarcely possessed representative powers (Bastid 1954: 219; Sellin 2001: 240). An extreme example is the disfranchisement movement in the Southern States of the USA around 1890, which deployed a combination of open fraud and manipulation and great subterfuge and oblique techniques to suppress electoral rights of black citizens (Kousser 1999: 32–6; Riser 2010: 14, 46). See Balibar's comment that, once articulated, the equality implied in citizenship 'is not limitable' (2011: 58). See also Lockwood (1996: 542).

[49] See discussion below at pp. 437–42.

[50] Note that in early concepts of citizenship in revolutionary America black people were described as 'inhabitants, but not citizens' (Ramsay 1789: 2). Think, then, of the *Dred Scott* ruling (1857) in the USA. *Dred Scott* flatly denied that black Americans could obtain rights of federal citizenship. This triggered the Civil War – a war about citizenship – and resonated though long processes of civil struggle, which were not completed until the 1960s. Note also the franchise reforms in the UK, which began in the nineteenth century. The first of these, in 1832, was specifically designed *not to create* a democracy. However, as discussed below, the Great Reform Act stimulated a process of suffrage reform, completed in the twentieth century, which eventually constructed most people in society as citizens.

which patterns of exclusion could be challenged and processes of inclusion expanded and intensified. This is lucidly exemplified by the female suffrage movement in the French Third Republic, in which suffrage activists focused their energies on posing the simple question: Did the legal terms *citoyen* and *français*, which constructed clear general rights for French people, also include women? (Hause 1984: 11). Moreover, the concept of citizenship formed a mainspring for democratic inclusion in societies without typical representative systems of governance. This is evident, in particular, amongst members of colonized populations in territories subject to imperial rule, where the ideal of citizenship has been widely utilized to mobilize people against dominant colonial regimes.[51] In such cases, citizenship provided the basis for the formation of new governmental institutions. Overall, citizenship sets out a universal norm, which is relatively indifferent to polity type, and which can be articulated as a demand for inclusion *wherever there is a political system*.

The principle of inclusion projected by the idea of the citizen also has implications in the systemic, structural dimension of the political system. Indeed, as mentioned, this concept often underpins the practical processes in which national political systems gain an expanded integrational hold on society, bringing actors in different parts of society into proximity to the political system, and supporting practical/systemic trajectories of nation building and societal formation. In particular, this is reflected in the fact that societies founded in constructs of citizenship have typically witnessed a multi-level process of institutional formation, in which citizenship has been broadened to include more social groups, and in which, consequently, the number of rights exercised by citizens has also increased. Through their longer-term evolution, most modern political systems built up a three-level corpus of citizenship rights in their societies, containing *private economic rights, political rights* and some *social rights*. These rights evolved through the contested practices of citizenship, and they marked the widening of citizenship across society. However, these rights also acted institutionally to embed the political system within a given regional or national society. Notably, the consolidation of each stratum of rights involved the elimination of local power, it intensified the immediacy of

---

[51] This began in revolutionary America. In the Spanish colonies in Latin America, the figure of the citizen was fundamental to the 'break with colonial order' and 'the construction of new national communities' (Conde Calderón 2009: 13). This continued through decolonization in Africa. Note the telling comment that in South Africa 'African intellectuals' fought the legacies of colonialism by 'using liberalism's egalitarian proclivities to their advantage' (Halisi 1997: 65).

the link between citizens and government, and it led to a reinforcement of governmental infrastructure – e.g. increase in judicial control of society, centralization of public bodies, rising fiscal penetration of the state and increasing welfare responsibilities.[52]

In consequence, the concept of inclusion projected by the idea of the citizen underpins the material-institutional structure of the modern political system, and it has proved a key element in the creation of political systems with extensive socio-geographical reach. The construct of the citizen, claiming and enacting rights, is integrally linked to a process of societal nationalization, in which society as a whole is increasingly underpinned by reasonably uniform norms, and central institutions penetrate deep into society. Indeed, the fact that the citizen is defined by a claim to rights of equality means that the more a society is defined by citizenship practices the more it tends towards nationalization and societal convergence around central legal and political institutions, and the less important private, regional and sectoral affiliations become.[53] The citizen forms a link between the political system and its society which impels both the political system and society as a whole towards a condition of higher integration, more compact centralization, and deeper nationalization.

On each of these counts, not surprisingly, leading texts in general sociology have identified the citizen as a matrix of *inclusionary modernization* in contemporary society. In this perspective, the citizen of democracy is perceived as a core element in the creation of national societies and national institutions. In this perspective, in fact, citizenship allows, or in fact renders essential, the removal of structural variations in society. Moreover, it allows, or renders essential, the generalized expansion of societal membership beyond localized, segmentary or private affiliations.[54] Most paradigmatically, Weber argued that the modern state

---

[52] See examples of the voluminous literature on the link between the expansion of citizenship and progressive nationalization in Schattschneider (1988: 89–90); Bendix (1996 [1964]: 90); Bartolini (2000: 180); Caramani (2004).

[53] Of course, this process of centralization does not preclude federalism or even ethno-federalism. However, it implies legal uniformity. For examples of federalism obstructing legal uniformity see discussion of the USA below at pp. 289–93.

[54] For example, Durkheim saw the rise of citizenship as replacing local and particular identities, playing a key role in the expansion of governmental consciousness through society: as such, he saw citizenship as 'what constitutes democracy' (1950: 120). Of course, Marshall viewed citizenship as a focus of inclusion which mediated and supplanted class antagonisms. This idea is taken up in Honneth (1992: 191). Parsons saw the expansion of rights-based citizenship as reducing the weight of particularistic identifies and affiliations (1965). Habermas viewed citizenship practices as a category of interaction capable of liberating persons from unreflected attachments, and empowering them to establish universally

is characterized by the fact that, in contrast to the internally privatized political order of pre-modern society, it extracts its power from, and explains its power in relation to, *the citizen*. For Weber, the 'concept of the citizen' is central to the legitimacy of the modern state, and the state owes its legitimacy to the fact that it is authorized by the people *qua* citizens. As a citizen, the members of the people are uniquely extricated from their 'particularization in professional and familial positions' and they are abstracted against 'distinctions of material and social circumstances' – the 'unity of the people', in contrast to the 'dividedness of private life spheres', is reflected in the citizen, and the state acquires legitimacy through its focus on the citizen as a fully generic source of inclusion (1921: 266). Above all, for Weber, this legitimating reference to the citizen coincides with the nationalization of the state – with its functional expansion across national society. The citizen accompanies and supports the state in this process, and it allows the state to legitimate its power, in relatively depersonalized general form, across the divisions that separated the personal power structures of pre-modern society.

In its different implications, in short, the principle of citizenship has converged around a basic construction of the person as an equal addressee of law, correlated by necessity with an inclusive legal order, and able to claim rights of participation in this order.[55] Indeed, in the modern definition and comprehension of citizenship, it is difficult fully to separate the three different categories of rights that, with variations, coalesce around this term – (1) the right of affiliation to a community; (2) the right to recognition, protection and private freedom under law; (3) the right to participate in collective deliberation and law creation in a community. Different theories and different legal models may of course give privilege to one or other of these sets of rights. But a theory of citizenship cannot easily exclude any one of these three groups of rights.[56]

---

valid normative agreements. This underpins Habermas's orientation of citizenship away from ethnic and cultural backgrounds towards rational political participation (1992: 636). Luhmann observed citizenship as a generalized form of social inclusion, which at once underpins the differentiation of the political system, and establishes a 'generalized relation' between the person and the state, creating complex, non-coercive lines of communication between the political system and those persons that it addresses (1965: 15–56). See important discussion in Turner (1993: 4).

55 Pocock defines this as the sense that 'human social life' resides in 'universality of participation' (1975: 75).

56 See for example Benhabib's overlapping triadic definition of citizenship, including collective identity, privileges of membership, and social rights and benefits (1999: 720–2).

In all its variations, moreover, the concept of the citizen as claimant to rights formed a core foundation for the rise of democracy from the eighteenth century to the present. Democratic systems are defined by the fact that they confer institutional form on the rights and practices attached to citizenship, by which means they extract legitimacy from the citizen as a basic general fulcrum of public order. In exercising their rights, citizens construct and revise the terms of their obligation towards public institutions, and rights stabilize generalized obligations both for the government and for citizens throughout society. Essential to this construction of obligations through rights is that democratic systems avoid extreme disparities in the construction of citizenship, and they project the citizen, from which they derive legitimacy, in relatively general terms, as an agent that is able to claim similar rights, that is equally recognized in legislation, and that is implicated in similar fashion in the production of legislation. Democratic systems can easily tolerate cultural, regional and interest-dependent variations in citizenship. For example, democracy may be enhanced by the establishment of mechanisms to ensure minority representation, whose interests cannot easily be captured under national models of citizenship.[57] Moreover, it is perfectly possible to imagine, at least, a democratic system that is not attached to a national community – in essence, citizenship is a hallmark not of a democratic nation state, but of a democratic political system. However, democratic polities cannot easily survive great unevenness or acute variations in political affiliation, at least if this affects the extent to which citizens perceive the political system as a focus of social and legal obligation. More categorically, democratic polities cannot tolerate disparities in the distribution of rights, at least rights of procedural and political character. As discussed below, states unable to institutionalize a general construct of the citizen, possessing equal and generalized rights, have struggled to establish democracy as a socially meaningful form.

I.4   The Citizen and the Political

Overall, from the late eighteenth century onward, the state–citizen nexus became the core formative dimension of public authority. The basic legal construction of citizenship cements a series of subjective rights at the core of public order, which define the legitimacy of government as correlated

---

[57] This point is made expertly in Young (1989).

with the fulfilment of certain collective obligations.[58] Implicit in the state–citizen nexus is the principle that it articulates certain bilateral obligations between the citizen and the polity, which separate the state both from privatistic or patrimonial patterns of social organization typical of pre-modern structures, and from momentary processes of government and the persons momentarily exercising governmental power. As a result, the citizen, or the fact that the political system is correlated with the citizen, allows a society (of citizens) to see some institutionalized norms as entirely public, in which the freedoms of all persons are implicated, and which cannot be derived from single private interests.[59] In this respect, vitally, the citizen underpins a distinct domain of strictly *public law*, in which certain laws, rights and norms of recognition are firmly stabilized as the substructure of government.[60] As a result of its general recognition of citizenship, in turn, the state assumes a clear higher-order position in society, with primacy amongst other institutional systems, and it is authorized to implement laws with higher validity than other sources of obligation, slowly eradicating other repositories of power.[61] In consequence of this, then, the state becomes an immediate presence for persons in society, and social relations are increasingly directed through the state.[62]

In this respect, the citizen is deeply constitutive of what we now perceive as the categorically *political* dimension of society, and the normative dimension of classical democratic theory contains an emphatic

---

[58] Subjective rights are usually seen as indicators of interests in private law. But the concept of citizenship clearly means that some subjective rights, relating to procedures for participation and legal recognition by administrative bodies, are also established in public law, reflecting interests directed towards public persons. For a classification of subjective rights in public law see Kelsen (1911b: 630). For Kelsen, there exists expressly a 'right to vote in the subjective sense', which results from a subjective interest in the 'result of an election' (2007 [1906]: 318).

[59] This concept of the citizen is expressed, paradigmatically, in the theory of public opinion set out diversely by Carl Schmitt and Jürgen Habermas. For Schmitt, a political order depends for its political quality on the fact that citizens engage with each other as public actors, which occurs through participation in the public sphere. This condition is always threatened by the danger that citizens may lapse back into a condition determined only by private interests; indeed, he saw this danger as specifically institutionalized in parliamentary government (1928: 245–7). For Habermas, in partial analogy, the legitimacy of a democracy depends on engagement of citizens in public debate (1990 [1962]: 142).

[60] See for related ideas Balibar (2008: 525).

[61] In France, citizenship replaced the power of the aristocracy. In America, it replaced colonial power. In other societies, it replaced other traditional power structures; for example, it replaced the power of the cities in the Dutch Republic (see Prak 1997: 416).

[62] See Tilly's simple claim: 'Strong citizenship depends on direct rule' (1995: 228).

construction of society's political domain.[63] Indeed, the determination of a certain part of society as distinctively political was of fundamental importance for early democratic practice and reflection. At an overarching symbolic level, both of the early democratic revolutions made expansive claims about the political substance of society. In both revolutions, it was expressly argued that revolutionary (democratic) government was legitimated by the fact that it possessed a categorical political quality, and its legitimacy was derived from the fact that it originated in clearly political acts, possessing both a generally inclusive foundation and collectively binding implications. In both revolutions, moreover, a political vocabulary was devised to distinguish political exchanges from exchanges in the rest of society, and to consolidate the political domain as a generic sphere of interaction. Notably, in the early democratic vocabulary of the revolutionary era, the political system was constructed in terms that accorded to it a distinct *origin*, a distinct pattern of *agency* and a distinct mode of *communication*, each of which possessed an inherently political character. Each of these elements was closely tied to the concept of citizenship, and each element acted to consolidate and reproduce the political system as a distinct societal domain.

In the revolutionary period, first, the *origin* of the political system was constructed through the development of the revolutionary doctrine of the *pouvoir constituant*, which became central to the constitutional thought of the French Revolution. In the French context, this doctrine claimed that a polity obtains legitimacy if it is created through the collective decision of the sovereign nation of citizens, establishing – *ex nihilo* – a constitutional order to determine the content of legislation to which members of the people owe obligation, and to bind acts of public officials and holders of delegated power.[64] This doctrine placed the aggregated will of the citizens at the origin of the national polity, and it stated that all law had to be legitimated through reference to an original, binding political decision. In revolutionary America, the authority of the emergent Republic was also, clearly, imputed to founding collective acts of constitution making, which ensured that an original political decision formed the legitimational core

---

[63] The correlation between citizenship and the distinctive characteristics of the political dimension of human life has been widely noted. See for example Touraine (1994: 121); Arendt (1958).

[64] The classical expression of this principle is in Sieyès (1789). But most theorists that insist on an emphatic political dimension in society have replicated this view. See for example Schmitt (1928: 76).

of the polity.[65] In both settings, the theory of constituent power projected an idea of the political system as higher-order social domain, with inclusionary authority across all society, and it anchored this authority in a primary collective political decision.

In the revolutionary era, second, the *pattern of agency* characteristic of the political system was constructed through the development of the concept of the citizen as political participant. As discussed, the ideal of citizenship supported a distinctive construction of the political system, and it marked out the political arena as a domain in society that is quite distinct from other functional spheres. In the first instance, citizenship described a set of voluntary commitments standing at the origin of the political system, constructing the political system as a unique societal space, which is structurally detached from local and private sources of authority. Once established, citizenship evolved as a set of practices in which the political system organized its interactions with other parts of society, translating social demands into public political form. In particular, the citizen helped to form a location in which legislation could be created for all society, and engagement in law making helped to produce legitimacy for laws as they were applied across all parts of society. As a result, most importantly, the citizen instilled a principle of general higher authority in the political system, constructing the political system as a social domain with a disposition towards *necessary inclusion*, enabling the political system to extend its authority at an increasing degree of penetration across society.

Less visibly, third, the *mode of communication* that defines the political system was established in the revolutionary era through the importance attached to rights in the figure of the citizen. As a legal construct, the idea of the citizen expressed the principle that a legitimate political order is based on a series of commonly exercised, equally applied rights, and it articulated the formative connection between the political domain and the exercise of rights.[66] Through this connection, the principle became widespread that contests about the form of public order are to be transmitted through claims to rights, and the widening boundaries of the political domain and the shifting contours of political legitimacy are traced and challenged through claims to rights. On this basis, then, laws are justified

---

[65] This theory was repeatedly set out in the *Federalist* (Madison, Hamilton, and Jay 1987 [1787–8]: 327). It underlies the entire doctrine of constitutional sovereignty, which forms the centre of the USA as polity.

[66] In agreement see Linklater (1996: 93).

through their recognition of rights, and they are authorized across society as enactments of rights. General rights of the citizen, thus, became the dominant, *eminently political* vocabulary of society, in which deep-lying legitimational conflicts could be refracted, vindicated and stabilized, and in which the political system could generate collectively plausible explanations for its functions. Indeed, rights institutionalized channels of politicization in society, and they created a medium in which the cycle of communication between government and society could be structured. On this basis, the political system began to communicate with the citizen through rights, and processes of expansionary inclusion within the political system were focused around the positive consolidation of rights.[67] In this respect, rights allowed the citizen to act as the social environment for the political system.

These three political elements, each of which was connected to the figure of the citizen, created the foundation for the modern democratic political system. On the basis of these three elements, the modern political system was defined by the fact that (a) it possessed an inclusive construction of its legitimacy, incorporating all society in the production and legitimation of law; (b) its legitimacy was of a higher-order nature, and it was able to authorize legislation across all parts of national society; (c) it was functionally distinct from other systems, and it did not rely for its authority on any source that was not founded in political communications and acts of political inclusion. On this basis, the growth of democracy was inseparably associated with the basic emergence of a distinct, differentiated political domain in modern society. The rise of democracy and the rise of a strictly delineated political system were two parts of the same process.

Since the French Revolution, many attempts have been made to isolate the specific political dimension in modern society. Strikingly, many theorists have identified *conflict* as the irreducible political component of society.[68] At the formative core of the modern political system, however, lie three elements – constituent power (origin), the citizen as participant (agency) and rights (communication). Characteristic for the political system, constructed by these three elements, is that it separates the law from private or personal relations, and it extends across society a system of norms which, by their inner telos, place all members of society

---

[67] For a similar claim, namely that the 'politicization of citizenship' was the first step in a process in which statutory form was conferred on subjective rights, see Colliot-Thélène (2010b: 104).

[68] See for salient claims in this lineage Schmitt (1932a); Weber (1921: 506); Lefort (1986: 51); Mouffe (2005: 9).

an equal footing. Central to this system is the translation of social claims into rights, which are then applied as the general legitimational basis for legislation. Although access to these norms may be dependent on singular experiences of conflict, the basic normative fabric of the political system is defined not by conflict, but by an implied universality and by a normative logic of extending inclusion.

1.5   Conclusion

Democracy can be defined as a condition marked by some ongoing production of consent through a line of norm-generating communication, articulated through rights of citizenship, between the people and the organs of governmental legislation. In its normative substance, the concept of democracy, based on the idea of the individual citizen as a practical and general source of legitimacy, contains an ineradicable presumption in favour of *equal and comprehensive inclusion* in the production of law. Once articulated, the idea of a political order founded on democratic citizenship implies that any selectivity in the representation of the people falls below the normative expectation inscribed in democracy. Any societal inequality in the distribution of rights of political participation contradicts the defining principle of democracy, and so reduces the obligatory force of law. Once democracy is established as a norm, systems of representation that do not give effect to equal and comprehensive inclusion are, if judged by democracy's own inner criterion, merely partial and incomplete, and the obligations that citizens possess towards their institutions are also partial and incomplete.[69] Full democracy implies full citizenship: the less people act as citizens, exercising equal rights to obtain shared freedoms, the less democratic a society is.

The ideal foundations for democratic governance were originally established in the short revolutionary interim in France and the USA in the late eighteenth century. Tellingly, one leading political thinker has stated that 'thinking of democracy today means that we have to think about the convergence of the two revolutions at the end of the eighteenth century' (Gauchet 1995: 178).

Naturally, there were great distinctions between the French and the American Revolutions in the conception of the citizen by which they were determined. Notably, the constitutional lineage of the USA placed greater emphasis on the fact that government acquires legitimacy if

---

[69]   See discussion of this in the USA in Kaczorowski (2005: 17).

citizens exercise and gain recognition for private rights; the French lineage placed more emphasis on the immediate exercise of popular sovereignty as a source of legitimacy.[70] Of course, further, neither the French nor the American Revolution was centred around a unified idea of citizenship or a unified idea of popular self-legislation. The divergences between revolutionary factions in France and between the individual constitutions created in France in 1791, 1793 and 1795 have been widely examined. One recent authoritative account claims that the French Revolution was split between three rival models of government – one based on democratic Republican citizenship, one based on a mixed constitution or limited monarchy and one close to twentieth-century authoritarianism (Israel 2014: 695). One alternative account states that political reflection in the Revolution oscillated between the 'relatively passive' concept of representative government and 'more audacious vision' of sovereignty as the factual exercise of power by the people (Rosanvallon 2000: 20). The American Revolution was perhaps even more polarized in its conception of the citizen. The division between Federalist and Anti-Federalist ideas of the Republic, based on divergent approaches to the relative authority of the national government and the separate states, persisted long after the Founding.[71]

Moreover, both Republics quickly deviated from the construction of citizenship on which they were founded. As discussed below, the early American Republic was initially based on a restricted, semi-aristocratic idea of political participation, but it became more socially inclusive through the nineteenth century. In France, by contrast, democratic formation followed a reverse trajectory. During the Revolution, democracy was often envisioned in maximalist terms, based on the ideal of the immediate presence of the people in government. For example, Robespierre accepted the practical need for delegation of competence in government functions. He observed that 'democracy is not a state in which the people, in continual assembly, regulate by themselves all public matters', and he saw democracy as a type of polity in which the people rely on 'delegates' to do 'what they cannot do by themselves' (1793b: 5–6). However, Robespierre tried to ensure that governmental organs were placed as close to the people as possible, and that the people should be able to scrutinize the actions of

---

[70] See Rosanvallon (2000: 49–100). By 1795, notably, Sieyès tried to limit the absolute concept of sovereignty by proposing a theory of judicial review, or by establishing a 'jury constitutionnaire' (Sieyès 1795: 1311).

[71] For the Federalist idea of citizenship see Sinopoli (1992: 131). See discussion below p. 289.

their representatives and that government was open to public observation (1793a: 22). At the same time, Saint-Just declared that popular representatives are bound directly by the indivisible will of the sovereign people, and any assembly of representative 'deliberates in place of the people' (1793: 17): any constitution loses legitimacy if 'the general will is not applied exactly to the formation of laws' (1793: 18). Of necessity, such conceptions were quickly abandoned. After the revolutionary period, political theorists in France soon elaborated a very nominal concept of democracy in which the representative body of government was separated from any claims to direct identity with the people, such that democracy was increasingly founded on a strict functional distinction between the factual people and the governmental power.[72] The functionally divided conception of democracy as representation was in fact already evident in some theories of representative government elaborated in the revolutionary era, such as those of Sieyès and Condorcet.[73] Across Europe, however, it was soon accepted after 1789 that democracy had to be constructed on a representative design, which some earlier democratic theories originally perceived not as a form of, but as an alternative to, democracy (see Manin 1997: 4).[74]

In the longer wake of the revolutionary period, in fact, the ideal of the common self-legislation of citizens implied in democracy was subject to a series of fundamental revisions, and it was re-imagined as one element of a governance system combining elements of popular will formation and elements of limited constitutionalism. Often, democratic ideas were assimilated into models of monarchical constitutionalism, in which constitutional rule, expressed in some basic charter or constitutional document, was established through the prerogative acts of sitting dynasties, and the assumption that citizens could exercise sovereign power was suspended.[75] In fact, the creation of a constitution by fiat remained the most common pattern of constitution making until the late nineteenth

---

[72] For varying reflections on this process in different contexts see Carré de Malberg (1920/2: 203, 504); Duguit (1923b: 128); Constant (1997 [1819]); Wood (2008: 8); Tuck (2015: 249). As Dahl has explained, this fusion of democracy and representation entailed a 'transformation of democratic theory and practice' that underpins the essential structure of all modern democracies (1989: 29).

[73] See Sieyès (1789: 20). See for comment Rosanvallon (2000: 16, 65).

[74] Rousseau, notably, stated that representative government could not be seen as government by the general will. This idea was later articulated by Schmitt (1928: 218).

[75] For discussion of this process in different countries see Kirsch (1999: 24, 53); Schmidt (2000: 111); Laquièze (2002: 67).

century. Naturally, these doctrines could not easily accommodate simple democratic ideals.

As discussed below, in sum, the ideal structure of democracy that began to take shape in the revolutionary era was not followed by its concrete realization, and the normative claims of revolutionary democracy filtered only very marginally into political practice. In most cases, as Brunkhorst has stated, it was only the memory of these claims that persisted into the nineteenth century, and these claims acted primarily as grounds for performative contestation, in which social groups articulated opposition to existing power structures.[76]

Despite these restrictions, however, both early revolutionary settings produced a concept of the democratic political system, which, although in its details superseded, still casts a normative paradigm for contemporary democratic politics and democratic reflection. Central to both revolutions of the late Enlightenment was a conception of a political system based, as discussed, in the three elements of citizenship – that is, in the claim that a polity obtains legitimacy (a) through primary constitution-making acts; (b) through the inclusionary participation of politically implicated citizens and (c) through the ongoing assertion of basic rights.

From a contemporary perspective, of course, aspects of the classical conception of the political system appear redundant. Above all, the factual exercise of constituent power appears an improbable criterion of democratic legitimacy. Some theorists have resolutely insisted that democracy must trace its legitimacy to a founding constituent act.[77] Other theorists are more inclined to adjust this concept to given societal realities (Ahlhaus and Patberg 2012: 25; Lang 2017: 23). Normatively ineradicable from the core elements of political democracy, however, is the claim that some active presence of the people in framing the legal order of government, some active exercise of citizenship in upholding government and some factual claiming of political rights are original and essential aspects of democratic practice. Normatively ineradicable from these elements, further, is the claim that, in a political system claiming democratic legitimacy, the *people stand at the beginning of law*. In a legitimate democratic polity, the people exist, originally, outside the law: the people form a political

---

[76] For Brunkhorst the norm-founding claims of great revolutions form deep-lying 'normative constraints', which, once established, become ungrained in society and shape subsequent processes of social development (2014: 38, 467). See discussion below at pp. 196–7.

[77] See Carré de Malberg (1920/2: 490–1); Schmitt (1928: 72); Böckenförde (1991: 294–5); Müller (1995: 47); Möllers (2000: 199–200); Colón-Ríos (2010: 242); Grimm (2012: 223); Loughlin (2014).

entity that is external to law, and the government must enact the prior will of citizens through its laws. The original revolutionary idea of democracy presupposed that the people, as citizens, are incorporated in a line of communication, access to which is determined by inclusive rights, in which popular demands and claims to rights are translated into legislative acts. In this conception, the people cannot be reduced to an actor without agency, and the popular agency of citizenship cannot be reduced to a simple legal dimension or to a process that occurs within the legal system: this concept implies, fundamentally, that law refers outside itself, to basic political acts of citizens, to obtain legitimacy. Still today, this part of the classical construction of democracy persists: *the idea of the active citizen cannot be effaced from the concept of democracy, and it cannot be eliminated from the origin of democratic law.* Democracy, thus, contains two quite distinct implications: one primarily legal and the other primarily political. It is a system of rights-based legal integration, in which citizens themselves, in their political capacity, create the rights in, and by means of which, they are integrated.

The concept of the citizen underpinning modern democracy came into being as a central figure in a number of collective social processes. This concept was at the centre of the social process that created nations, performing attendant functions of integration. It was at the centre of the social process that created political systems, performing attendant processes of centralization. The association between the democratic citizen and wider social processes has instilled particular, emphatic normative expectations in the conceptual structure of modern democracy. The citizen appears as the subject of law, demanding full legal inclusion in a system of rights. Further, the citizen appears as a subject of law demanding full inclusion as a distinctively *political* agent, in a categorically *political* system, in which rights originate in categorically *political* actions and demands for freedom.[78] The combination of these principles necessarily means that democracy appears as a political system created by citizens assuming the form of distinct political subjects, actively authorizing the norms by which they are integrated. It means that, after the construction of democratic citizenship in the revolutionary era, theorists of democracy were invariably required to look for a political subject (citizen) to which they could attribute the formation of democratic systems, and by which such systems were brought into being. Political theorists typically looked for the citizen

---

[78] On the deep linkage between law and politics in the concept of the democratic citizen, see Peters (1993: 208–9, 322).

as a rational agent, capable of translating reasonable freedoms into laws. Moreover, it means that theorists of democracy were required to observe the political system, created by society's political subject, as the dominant institutional focus of society. As discussed below, however, these expectations may have reflected impulses in deep-lying social processes, but the actual subject around which they coalesced (the people, as an aggregate of citizens) is not easy to find. Indeed, the dual assumption attached to the democratic subject – that the citizen demands legal inclusion and political participation – created contradictions that most democracies struggled, functionally, to overcome.

1

The Paradox of Democracy and the Sociology of Law

1.1 Political Democracy as Theory and as Fact

There are a number of deep historical misapprehensions surrounding the institutional consolidation of political democracy. Indeed, the actual emergence of democracy as a system of governance, centred around the exercise of participatory political rights by the citizens of a particular society, appears to be a particularly elusive historical phenomenon. When we examine the historical formation of democratic institutions, therefore, a certain amount of myth-breaking work is required.

1.1.1 Late Democracies

A striking fact in the development of political democracy is that it first became widespread considerably later than is usually indicated. In fact, typical analyses of democracy are marked by a peculiar blind spot when trying to identify the point at which democracy was commonly consolidated as a governance regime. Histories of modern democracy usually indicate that the central features of democracy, which were conceptually articulated in the late eighteenth century, became reality through the nineteenth century. By way of illustration, one recent book on Russian history, written by an eminent historian, begins with the following sentence: 'The model of the nation that emerged in Europe after the French Revolution and the Napoleonic Wars was founded on the principles of citizenship and civil rights' (Engelstein 2009: 1).[1] In this narrative, much of Western Europe already possessed a basic system of political inclusion in the earlier nineteenth century, and this is taken as a standard with which patterns of political development in Russian history, supposedly marked by a pathological delay in the formation of democratic institutions, need to be contrasted. One important historian has identified the beginning of

---

[1] For a more nuanced account of the divergent evolutionary pathways of Russia and Western Europe, see Burbank (2003: 422–4).

democracy at mid-century, describing the national uprisings of 1848 as the 'hour in which representative democracy was born in Western and Central Europe' (Best 1990: 13). One widely influential account of democratic formation has identified the period 1828–1926 as comprising a *first wave* of democratic consolidation, in the course of which, by 1900 in particular, a number of countries had developed democratic institutions (Huntington 1991: 13–16).[2] Similar ideas are evident in the works of distinguished sociologists, who date the advent of universal political citizenship, at least in countries seen as possessing strong democratic traditions, to the earlier nineteenth century.[3] Even more sceptical interpreters observe 1918 as the date at which, at least in progressive countries, democracy was generally instituted.[4]

It is difficult to be sure how such interpretations of modern political history have arisen, and why such assumptions are so widely accepted, even amongst otherwise excellent scholars and intellectuals. Perhaps, we might speculate, such assumptions result not from analysis of actual social or historical reality, but from a theoretically inflected construction of social reality, or from a tendency amongst historical interpreters to conflate socio-political reality and theoretical debates.

As discussed, the basic conceptual architecture of democracy was surely outlined in the revolutionary period at the end of the eighteenth century, especially in the USA and France. Central to the revolutionary construction of democracy was the claim that democracy enabled individual people to give legislative expression to basic freedoms, creating binding obligations on this foundation. After the revolutionary époque, then, the conceptual repertoire of democratic revolution retained defining importance, and it shaped theoretical reflection on politics in a number of ways.

---

[2] Even more rigorous observers accept the idea of a first wave of democratization, occurring in the nineteenth century (Ziblatt 2006: 337).

[3] See the assertion, common amongst sociologists in the USA, that 'Britain gave citizenship to the workers in the early or mid-nineteenth century' in Lipset (1959: 93). Such exaggerated views seem to result from the assumption that core elements of American democracy were originally imported from Britain (see Lipset 1963: 93). However, inflationary constructions of British democracy are widespread amongst even the most admirable American scholars, often leading to absurd claims. See – as an egregious example – the assertion that, unlike in many post-colonial states in Africa, democracy survived in India after 1950 because 'Indian elites were often trained in Oxford and Cambridge during the colonial period, and may have imbibed commitments to democracy from the English' (Shapiro 2003: 87).

[4] For example, Dahl argues that the 'main centers of successful democratization' had created democracies by 1920 (1989: 216). More accurate is Parsons, who stated that the 'form of democratic association ... was nowhere complete, if universal adult suffrage is a criterion, until well into the present century' (1964: 353).

In the earlier nineteenth century, first, the enactment of shared freedoms became a criterion of governmental legitimacy at most points on the political spectrum. Amongst advocates of revolutionary transformation, as discussed, it was widely argued that a government acquires legitimacy if it reflects the collective will of citizens, and that the legitimacy of law presupposes the maximization of personal freedom for as many people in society as possible. However, the protection of shared freedoms was also perceived as a core function of the state amongst more gradualist theories of socio-political change.[5] In this respect, the French Revolution instilled a deep caesura in political reflection. From this point onwards, early modern theories which, in paternalist fashion, had typically argued that the state or the prince acquired authority through the preservation of peace, order and security, lost traction. Instead, collective liberty became a key gauge of state legitimacy.[6] Throughout the nineteenth century, second, political controversy in Europe tended to polarize around reactions to the claims of the French Revolution, so that Conservative, Liberal and Radical lines of political reflection were all determined by a distinctive reaction – respectively, critical, cautiously affirmative or consolidating – to the theoretical legacy of the revolutionary era. Throughout the nineteenth century, political opinions were dominated by a memory of the French Revolution, and the conceptual caesura that marked the Revolution was recalled, either with horror or with enthusiasm, as the beginning of democracy. Tocqueville explained this accurately in 1835, stating: 'A great democratic revolution is occurring among us. All of us can see it, but not all judge it

---

[5] This is exemplified by the thought of Hegel, who, although clearly not a radical, argued that law must be founded in the attempt to create a concrete institutional form for human freedom (1970 [1821]: 46). See semantic discussion of changes in the meaning of 'freedom' in the later eighteenth century in Schlumbohm (1975: 55, 66).

[6] The paternalist theory of the state became central to post-Reformation political thought. In fact, at the conceptual centre of the Reformation was the claim, against the scholastic natural-law theories imputed to Roman Catholicism, that government is merely the worldly regiment, which is fully distinct from the regiment of freedom and faith – order and freedom are thus quite separate. The world of government and the world of faith have entirely distinct functions: the state must take responsibility for maintaining 'external peace', and the church must help 'make people pious' and oversee spiritual well-being (Luther 1883a: 252). Above all, Luther argued the laws of the worldly regiment cannot bring freedom, and compliance with worldly law is not a path to freedom. A 'Christian person,' Luther explained, 'has enough in faith, so that he does not need works to be pious', and whoever has faith is 'delivered from all commandments and laws' (1883b: 25–6). Central to the revolutionary era, however, was a desire to reconnect freedom and law, and to re-imagine the law as a sign of virtue. The legal theories of the French Revolution were much closer to Calvinism, which accorded law a more constitutive role on human salvation (see Calvin 1939 [1536]: 150).

in the same fashion'. Some people, he mused, think that democracy is new or even an accident and they 'still hope to stop it', whereas others think that it is 'irresistible' (1866 [1835]: 2). To this degree, the democratic ideals promoted in the revolutionary period obtained a certain enduring reality.

In fact, many leading thinkers who lived through the longer aftermath of the French Revolution appeared to be convinced that the evolving form of the nation state in nineteenth-century Europe was enduringly shaped by ideals of citizenship and civil rights. As a result, the perception that the early nineteenth century was an era defined by the emergence of demo- cratic politics was quite widespread, even amongst contemporary observ- ers. This perception was most clearly articulated, in alarmist fashion, on the more reactionary fringes of European political debate, where the idea of popular rule was a common spectre, giving rise to great anxiety. Conservative philosophers and social theorists of the earlier nineteenth century often painted an appalled picture of their societies. They implied that the democratic ideals of the revolutionaries in 1789 were approach- ing full implementation, and, as an alternative, they demanded a return to the inherited, purportedly natural, order of authority based in estates and religion.[7] In some respects, however, Radical social and political theorists shared aspects of this analysis, and they replicated some ideas of their reactionary adversaries. Naturally, these theorists argued that the principles of 1789 had provided insufficient emancipation for the socie- ties in which they took shape. However, Radical theorists of the earlier nineteenth century opted for a historical standpoint that reflected more Conservative views, assuming that at least partial democratization had become a historical reality.

Such claims were expressed, for example, by Proudhon, who set out a critique of post-1789 social formation in Europe, claiming that it was based on a system of formal individual rights (1967 [1840]: 76), and dominated by centralized government under party-political institutions (1936 [1852]: 266). These claims were further emphasized by Karl Marx, who, in *The Jewish Question* and the *Manifesto of the Communist Party*, reflected in highly influential fashion on the contradictions inherent in

---

[7] See for example Bonald (1843 [1796]: 118–19); De Maistre (1847 [1797]: 81); Gentz (1979 [1819]: 219). In this context, Bonald emerged as an important Conservative forerunner of legal-sociological theory, arguing both that legitimate law presupposes a religious foun- dation (1847 [1802]: 41), and that popular government leads to societal disaggregation 1847 [1802]: 51). He also claimed, like later sociologists, that a legitimate constitution is an 'intrinsic order' or the 'soul of society' (1847 [1802]: 161). After 1815, Chateaubriand famously declared that Europe was 'rushing towards democracy' (Hamerow 1983: 285).

early constitutional democracy. In these writings, he suggested that the national societies emerging after 1789 were defined by centralized state institutions and moderately elaborated patterns of democratic representation. Consequently, Marx indicated that the basic objectives of the revolutionary era, especially the demands for some form of political-democratic citizenship and some guarantee of legal protection for civil rights, had been widely instituted after 1815 (1956 [1844]: 364).

Whatever the legacy of the revolutionary era in theoretical debate, however, the image of accelerating democratization projected both by reactionary opponents of the French Revolution and by radical commentators on its legacy did not even come close to being a reality until after 1870. Even the most superficial survey of European societies in the decades after 1815 reveals that the prevalent model of statehood at this time showed little or no recognition of civil rights or political citizenship.

For instance, France did not have a fully competitive male franchise until after 1870. From 1851, France had continuous male suffrage, but electoral rights were initially exercised within a controlled, Bonapartist system. Great Britain began to move towards democracy in 1832. But it initially had a small property-based franchise, and, until 1918, its government was never elected by more than approximately 30% of the population (roughly 60% of men, and no women). Of course, many people have claimed that the UK was a democracy by 1900. Even some expert historians date the advent of mass democracy in Britain to the 1880s.[8] One commentator, without contradiction, reflects that it was commonplace in the early twentieth century to claim that Britain was 'the most stable and mature democracy in Europe' (Scally 1975: 10). In 1905, Dicey himself declared that it was impossible to doubt that 'the English constitution had been transformed into something like a democracy' (1962 [1905]: 48). Even critical observers stated that, by 1900, England, in terms of franchise membership, was 'practically a democracy' (Porritt 1899: 628).[9] However, the words 'something like' and 'practically' might be seen as having an operative

---

[8] Rosanvallon, who is surely one of Europe's leading political historians, claims that, at least for men, 1884 brought the 'realization of political equality' in the UK (1992: 131). One author acknowledges that in the 1880s 'sizeable proportions of the male electorate' remained 'unenfranchised', yet this same author still claims that 'mass democracy was real enough' (Joyce 1994: 192). In their otherwise highly critical analysis of political liberties in the UK, Ewing and Gearty argue that the 'principle of universal suffrage' was established around 1900 (2000: 22).

[9] The leading early history of the British franchise also states that after 1885 the British electoral system was a 'democracy in its main lines' (Seymour 1915: 523). This misapprehension was seemingly widely shared. Prominent figures as unalike as Henry Maine and Kier Hardie

importance in these commentaries. Britain did not resemble a full democracy until 1918.[10] Even the electoral reforms of 1867 and 1884, which extended the male franchise in Britain, merely established, not the single democratic (male) citizen, but a patriarchal model of the household as the basic source of political legitimacy and as the primary unit of social interaction with government.[11]

Comparably, Prussia had no national representative body until 1847. Thereafter, under the constitutional order established in 1849/50, Prussia possessed a restrictive, weighted electoral system, in which voting rights were allocated to separate fiscal classes on the basis of their contribution to public revenue. After 1871, the German Empire (*Reich*) instituted universal suffrage for male citizens over 25 years of age, so that Germany had a universal male franchise, and from 1918, a universal female franchise, until 1933. Yet, although most of the male members of the German population were allowed to vote, they could not vote for a parliamentary assembly that was fully authorized to introduce legislation. Government by a democratically elected legislature, was not established nationally in Germany until 1919. The USA developed a selective democratic franchise earlier than most European states; after all, unlike European states, the American polity was expressly based in the concept of popular sovereignty. However, the American Revolution did not lead to full manhood suffrage, either in the states or in the Republic as a whole, and it did not separate political rights from socio-economic privilege. In the USA, either partial or complete exclusion of black voters was almost universal

---

considered Britain a democratic state after 1884 (see Maine 1886: 8; Hardie 1894: 375). For an account of this widespread error, see McKibbin (1990: 68).

[10] Indicatively, in 1912, the Conservative Party headquarters calculated that the introduction of universal male suffrage would lead to the loss of 103 seats in England and Wales (McCrillis 1998: 12). This fact alone demonstrates that, even in the consciousness of political leaders, the UK was not a democracy at this point.

[11] For claims close to this view see Biagini (1992: 313). There is little truth in the assumption, underpinning much American sociology of political evolution in the UK, that the nineteenth-century reforms in Britain 'resulted in relatively early manhood suffrage and the full attainment of parliamentary government' (Almond 1991: 473). Dicey himself admitted this, describing household suffrage as a sign of the 'moderation' (which we might take to mean incompleteness) of British democracy (1962 [1905]: 253–4). The fact that the embellishment of the British tradition of 'democracy' is so common might be the result of Marshall's evident overestimation of the extent of citizenship in nineteenth-century Britain. Marshall's work contains a mixed message on political citizenship in the UK. Close to the approach advanced in this book, he argues that until 1918 the franchise was a 'group monopoly'. But he also argues 'that citizenship in this period was not politically meaningless' (1992 [1950]: 12–13).

through, and beyond, the nineteenth century, and it remained common in many states in the South until the 1960s. Many states, in both North and South, imposed generally discriminatory qualifications for the right to vote throughout the nineteenth century.[12] Moreover, even the exclusion of the most privileged stratum of the people (white men) from electoral participation was widespread until the 1820s.[13] Many states barred recipients of public assistance (known as *paupers*) from the franchise for the whole nineteenth century (see Steinfeld 1989: 335).

Overall, throughout the nineteenth century, democracy evolved, if at all, as a system of political administration that was strategically intended to demobilize core sectors of society, typically on grounds of class, ethnicity or national provenance. Of course, female suffrage was not widespread until after 1918, so most political systems automatically demobilized a large sector of society (50 per cent of the adult population) on gender grounds. Of all major states, France had the most democratic franchise for men in the nineteenth century. But France did not establish electoral participation for women until 1944. Democracy only existed in the nineteenth century, at most, in the *form of a rather crude, selective approximation*. In this condition, the basic inclusionary implications of democratic citizenship were selectively controlled and widely deactivated.

Although it obtained a preliminary conceptual definition in the late eighteenth century, therefore, democracy assumed concrete shape very slowly. Even in its most minimal definition, it did not take hold until after 1870. It was not broadly in evidence until after 1918, and it was not consolidated as a norm of governance until after 1945. In Europe, after 1815, the legacy of the political institutions briefly created in revolutionary France remained of marginal organizational significance for almost a century. Typically, as mentioned, the ideas of national self-legislation promoted in the revolutionary era were assimilated into very limited doctrines of political Liberalism, in which the rule of law, with guarantees for certain limited rights, was allowed to stand in for democracy.[14] A far more

---

[12] One account claims that between 1889 and 1913 nine states outside the South imposed a literacy qualification for voting, thus excluding many blacks, poor whites and immigrants (Kousser 1974: 57–8). Between 1890 and 1904, seven ex-Confederate states imposed similar restrictions.

[13] One historian argues that in 1790 fewer than 50% of the original 13 states of the USA approached an electoral system based on equal manhood suffrage (i.e. without freehold qualifications) (Wilentz 2005: 27, 201). By the early 1820s, most states in the Union (now expanded) had at least partly separated electoral participation from property ownership. On the persistence of freehold qualifications, however, see Chute (1969: 301, 311).

[14] See above p. 35

important legacy of the revolutionary interlude was the fact that monetary rights, enabling free market practices, in contrast to political rights, enabling free electoral practices, obtained increased legal protection across large parts of Western Europe.[15] Indeed, for much of the nineteenth century, and in fact beyond, only private rights approached a condition of legal consolidation, and many states made relatively robust provisions for the general rule of law; for many observers, private rights remained the primary guarantor of human liberty.[16] This has led a number of sociologists, historians and legal theorists to observe that nineteenth-century Europe was dominated, in form, by the evolution of two strictly differentiated social spheres – a semi-autonomous domain of political administration and a semi-autonomous domain of early capitalist civil society, expressed legally in the freedoms of singular subjective rights holders.[17] In fact, however, in most nineteenth-century societies, the basic political apparatus was not strongly consolidated or constitutionally formalized. In the constitutional domain, the revolutionary concepts of political democracy had very limited impact until the final third of the nineteenth century, and it was only after circa 1870 that general political rights were widely exercised.

1.1.2   Unwanted Democracies

A second salient complication in the development of political democracy is that the actual process of its construction found very few unequivocal advocates, and it ultimately evolved in an institutional form that diverged greatly from its initial conception.

Democracy is now viewed as a general norm of political organization, and it is often depicted as the outcome of an almost teleological process of institutional development. Clearly, early models of political democracy grew on the foundation set by social contract theory, which saw the

---

[15] Most states in Europe and the USA saw a widening of capitalist markets in the earlier part of the nineteenth century. In all cases, this was expressly based on the solidification of private rights of ownership, exchange, contract and movement.

[16] As late as the 1890s, Rudolf Sohm declared, in debates on the drafting of the German Civil Code (in force from 1900), that the 'Magna Carta of our public freedom resides in private law. What we call freedom is much more strongly tied to civil law than to the constitution of the state' (Mugdan 1899: 909). Earlier, Gerber also argued that public-law rights have private-law origins (1852:35). Most famously, Savigny had earlier claimed greater importance for private law than for public law, and he viewed private law as law in which the full subjectivity of the people found expression (1840a: 14, 22).

[17] See for varying descriptions of this Hegel (1970 [1821]: 343); Marx (1956 [1844]); Freyer (1935: 134); Menke (2015: 266–71).

formation of the modern state as the result of a collective rational demand for freedom under law. Underlying much contractarian theory of government is a conviction that freedom under law is an existential condition, in which human beings collectively enact laws to secure general freedoms that reflect a realization of their innate capacities: the contract appears as an act of rational voluntarism, in which laws are established that all people, individually, recognize as conditions of their reasonable liberty. This idea was clear in the thought of Rousseau, who saw the forming of the social contract as an act in which people separated themselves from their natural particularity, and enacted a pure will as the foundation for the polity.[18] Similarly, Kant argued that where human beings deduce categorically compelling laws, human reason assumes for itself the obligatory role originally ascribed to God: that is, to the 'highest legislator', whose 'will is the law for all people' (1977b: 334). On this account, a state based in collective self-legislation enacts the will of the *whole person*, giving expression to deeply constitutive human freedoms and correlated obligations.[19] Today, some contemporary theories still express similar claims in their accounts of democracy, viewing it as a political order that reflects an ingrained, *constitutively human* desire for emancipation, rational autonomy and collective freedom from coercion.[20] Even in less substantialist theories, the idea prevails that democratic government is not separable from inner processes of human self-realization.[21] Even empirical sociological analysis of democratic formation tends to imply that democratization is impelled by collective actors, motivated by collective demands for freedom and held back by entrenched, anti-emancipatory social forces.[22] Moreover, the rise

---

[18] Rousseau stated that the will of the person, as a natural being, may well, in some instances, be 'contrary or dissimilar' to the collective contractual will by which the person is rationally bound in the polity (1966 [1762]: 246).

[19] On the connection between freedom and obligation in early democratic freedom see pp. 4–5 above.

[20] This idea is reflected in high-level theoretical sociology – for example, in Habermas (1968: 350); Touraine (1994: 306); Brunkhorst (2017: 128). This idea is reflected in some anthropological theory. For instance, Boehm argues that processes leading to modern democracy are shaped by anti-hierarchical emphases that are imprinted, through early evolutionary formation, in general human dispositions (2001: 4–5, 253). See similar claims in Knauft (1991: 395). For discussion, see Howell (2002: 226–8).

[21] See expressions of this idea in theories of deliberative democracy, for example Gutmann and Thompson (2004: 3); Fishkin (2009: 6); Goodin (2010: 209). In fact, even critiques of the rationalist preconditions of deliberative theory argue that people are collectively drawn to democracy because of its 'constitutive commitment to nondomination' (Shapiro 2003: 147).

[22] See notes 34 and 38 at pp. 51–2 below.

of political democracy is often linked to the formation of distinctively national societies, in which populations demand collective freedom and unification under shared systems of self-legislation. This condition is viewed, both nationally and in international law, as an immutable right.[23]

Throughout the early history of democracy, however, it is difficult to identify any universal propensity for democratic formation, and it is difficult to identify the emergence of democracy as the result of collective demands for political freedom. In many instances, democracy was created in highly contingent fashion, often quite strategically, for anti-democratic motives. On this basis, the elevation of democracy to the standing of a universal right is not founded in a historical process, and it does not derive from a collective demand for this right.

Tellingly, the earliest theorists of popular sovereignty, whose works stand at the origins of modern democracy, were hardly fervent advocates of democracy as a form of popular self-rule. As mentioned, the conceptual substructure of modern democracy was largely established in the late eighteenth century by theorists such as Rousseau, Sieyès and Madison. In different ways, these theorists argued that institutions assume legitimacy by expressing the will of the people, in appropriately rationalized, general form, and by ensuring that the popular will is channelled through acts of governmental legislation. However, these early architects of democracy were not democrats. Rousseau may have been the principal early theorist of democracy. But he was expressly hostile to democracy as practice (see Fralin 1978: 96). Sieyès, a leading author of two of the constitutions of revolutionary France, was only prepared to champion a very restricted, elite-led form of democracy (Lowenstein 1922: 215–16; Grandmaison 1992: 88). The government of the early American Republic, which provided a much more enduring basis for the evolution of democratic institutions than revolutionary France, was expressly devised as a political system that excluded the people from government functions.[24] It was conceived as a Republic, and, as such, it was sharply differentiated from a democracy. The normative dignity now widely accorded to democracy is not found amongst early democratic thinkers.

---

[23] See discussion at p. 163 below.

[24] In *Federalist* 10, Madison described democracy as a form of government that endangers 'both the public good and the rights of other citizens'. He concluded that 'popular government' could only exist if governmental power was entrusted to popular representatives who were not the people. He advocated the 'delegation of the government ... to a small number of citizens' (Madison, Hamilton and Jay 1987 [1787–88]: 125–6).

In the longer wake of 1789, then, Liberal thinkers and politicians of the nineteenth century normally expressed muted enthusiasm for some kind of popular inclusion. Many theorists, including – to some extent – Marx himself, have asserted that the Liberal bourgeoisie was a primary agent of democracy.[25] Yet few Liberals showed much support for fully inclusive democratic representation. Across the canon of Liberal inquiry, there were few endorsements of mass enfranchisement, and most theorists of a broadly Liberal persuasion in the nineteenth century were not willing to sanction the degree of popular integration required by democracy.[26]

In many cases, the commitment of Liberal theorists to the introduction of political democracy, as far as it existed, was driven by the fact that they saw mass-political integration as a key to successful and efficient economic expansion or imperialism: full political inclusion of the proletariat appeared to provide a basis for concerted national economic mobilization and external colonization.[27] Just as the need for military mobilization underpinned the extension of citizenship in the late Enlightenment, the need to mobilize members of society for foreign wars and for economic

[25] This idea has its origins in Aristotle's thought. See prominent variants on this claim in Lipset (1959); Moore (1973 [1966]: 413); Marx and Engels (1987 [1848]); Habermas (1990 [1962]: 115).

[26] Much early nineteenth-century Liberalism was dedicated, strategically, *to not being democratic*. Indicatively, the tone for anti-democratic elements of Liberal theory was consolidated in post-1815 France, where Guizot eventually defined the 'sovereignty of reason' as an alternative to the sovereignty of the people (Rosanvallon 1985: 88). See also the distinction between popular sovereignty and national sovereignty in Sismondi's thought (1836: 66). For discussion of reticence about democracy or 'anti-egalitarianism' amongst German Liberals in the mid-nineteenth century see Backes (2000: 5000). In the UK, Mill was of course relatively enthusiastic about franchise reform. However, paradoxically, he claimed both that it is unjustifiable that there should be 'any arrangement of the suffrage' in which 'any person or class is peremptorily excluded' and that some type of 'plural voting' should be established to ensure a 'counterpoise to the numerical weight of the least educated class' (1861: 1559–60, 171). He also notoriously stated: 'As soon as any idea of equality enters the mind of an ordinary English working man, his head is turned by it. When he ceases to be servile, he becomes insolent' (1864: 149). As discussed below, Weber, Germany's leading Liberal intellectual, endorsed parliamentary democracy in very uncertain terms.

[27] In the UK, such ideas are often associated with Joseph Chamberlain (see Searle 1995: 50). But social reform and imperialism were quite diffusely combined in Liberal politics. See for discussion Semmel (1960: 13, 90); Matthew (1973: 236); Scally (1975: 26). On similar tendencies in Germany, see Winkler (1964: 77); Wehler (1969: 492; 1973: 176); Mommsen (1975: 128, 137); Schnorr (1990: 148). For examples of social-liberal imperialism in different European countries, see Naumann (1990: 65), claiming that 'political-economic democracy' creates stable governmental systems, promoting national expansion; Weber, advocating parliamentarization in Germany as a means for training national leadership elites for external expansion (1921: 343).

expansion overseas had a similar impact in the nineteenth century.[28] Affirmation of political democracy amongst Liberals was thus, in key respects, closely linked to the pragmatics of inter-state economic rivalry, and the evolution of democracy in Europe was usually accelerated in societies in a process of, or aspiring to, imperial expansion. Even in the early twentieth century, partly in consequence, many European societies found themselves without a strong democratic political bloc that was fully committed to the implementation of comprehensive democratic reform.[29] In many cases, in fact, democratic systems of representation were institutionalized not by Liberals, but by Conservatives, and the establishment of democracy was often shaped by the designs of Conservative politicians, which were only marginally related to the endorsement of democracy as a normative institutional order. In some instances, mass-enfranchisement was effected to promote a clearly anti-Liberal strategy, and it was conceived, often successfully, as a means to shore up support for Conservative policies.[30] Notably, in the UK, the 1867 Reform Act, rightly or wrong regarded by many as 'the most important single step in the establishment of British democracy' (Herrick 1948: 175), was crafted by the Tory Party. While helping to engineer the 1867 Reform Act, Prime Minister Disraeli declared that it would 'never be the fate of the country to live under a democracy'.[31] In Germany, a mass franchise was introduced by Bismarck, who saw the creation of a semi-Bonapartist variant on democracy as a means for securing Conservative dominance in the newly founded Empire.[32] Significantly,

---

[28] Notably, Bismarck granted universal suffrage during the wars of German unification, evidently to mobilize support for the emerging national state. Later, the linkage between citizenship and imperialism became more programmatic. On democracy and imperialism in France, see Freeman and Snidal (1982: 324). Most notably, Giolitti established something close to full male suffrage in Italy in 1912, to consolidate support for the annexation of Libya.

[29] See for example Bollmeyer (2007: 69, 315–16).

[30] Analysis of this phenomenon is central to the recent, very noteworthy interventions in Ziblatt (2017: 109–110). One key claim in Ziblatt's work is that the emergence of an organized Conservative Party, able to link its prerogatives to the democratic system, was a common precondition for democratic stability (2017: 358).

[31] See for analysis Saunders (2011: 9). Gladstone himself, like other Liberals around him, was hardly a fully converted democrat. Gladstone portrayed himself as an 'inequalitarian', who rejected the demand 'either for manhood suffrage or for household suffrage' (Vincent 1976: 224–26). For further discussion of Liberal reticence about reform prior to 1867, see Himmelfarb (1966: 135). One account, with which I agree, argues that it was not until the franchise reform of 1918 that an expressly 'democratic, as distinct from merely increasingly popular' agenda became dominant in the UK (Garrard 2002: 69). Even in 1918, the UK fell well short of democratic government. See discussion below p. 328.

[32] See Anderson (2000: 401). Most Liberals in Imperial Germany, at least in the earlier decades, showed strong support for the more reactionary anti-democratic parts of the

female suffrage was often instituted by Conservative politicians, and, as is well documented, it often led to a reinforcement of the position of Conservative parties.[33]

Additionally, amongst social groups in the nineteenth century who seemingly had the most to gain from the introduction of full political democracy, enthusiasm for democratic institutions was not unequivocal. Evidently, the early European labour movement possessed an official ideology that claimed that it possessed unified interests, and it was capable of promoting these within democratic institutions.[34] Moreover, many theorists have defined the working class as the driving force behind democratization.[35] Practically, however, the political parties representing organized labour in Europe were originally marked by a deep scepticism in face of political democracy.

First, theorists of the radical Left, whether Communist or Anarchist, were typically driven by their conflict-based theory of politics to deny that the institutions of liberal democracy could provide anything but selective representation, cementing the prerogatives of a dominant economic class, and they refused to work within existing representative institutions.[36]

---

constitution, notably the weighted franchise in Prussia (see Gagel 1958: 104). The accusation of Bonapartism is often directed at Bismarck (see Wehler 1969: 459–60). However, this description is often rejected (see Gall 1976: 631).

[33] In Europe, full female suffrage was introduced in the UK by Baldwin, in France by De Gaulle, and in the USA by Wilson. Naturally, many Conservatives may well have seen propertied women as a solid source of political protection against the male working class. For example, there was clear Conservative support for selective female suffrage in the UK (see Auchterlonie 2007: 83). Notably, in most countries, female enfranchisement did not lead to a shift to the Left. One analysis calculates that it often led to a decline in left mobilization (Bartolini 2000: 231). In the USA, famously, the female suffrage movement was, by the late 1860s, 'deeply tinged with racism' (Dudden 2011: 9), and its leaders saw black enfranchisement as a threat to its own success. One observer argues that in the Civil War era 'some key woman suffrage activists embraced racism as a political tool' (Free 2015: 6). Woodrow Wilson introduced the Nineteenth Amendment against firm opposition from some states. However, Wilson's national-integrationist attitude to government did not extend to black Americans, and he even encouraged federal segregation (see Wohlgemuth 1959: 163). One excellent analysis states that Wilson's policies 'undermined the claims to citizenship and economic security of all African Americans' (Yellin 2013: 4).

[34] In their classical programme for the Communist Party, Marx and Engels argued that the labour force had been unified in its interests by conflict with the bourgeoisie, and that the proletariat had become organized as a class and as a party. On this basis, they claimed that the proletariat was called upon to assume 'political domination' by 'conquering democracy' (1987 [1848]: 42, 52).

[35] See note 38 below.

[36] This attitude stretched from anarchism, to Bolshevism, to Sorelian syndicalism, and ultimately to fascism, the last major theoretical offshoot of Marxist conflict theory.

Second, the more moderate leadership cadres of organized labour, even when sympathetic towards democratic reformism, were often unsure about the ways in which they should position their organizations within established governance systems. For this reason, leaders of organized labour habitually lacked confidence in their ability to manage existing institutional structures, often preferring to work in tandem with more established elite groups (Miller 1964: 37). This ambiguity is distilled in the thought of Ferdinand Lassalle, a leading figure in the early German labour movement. Lassalle viewed the constitutional order of high-capitalist society as a mere expression of given power relations (1892 [1862]: 19). However, he also stressed the need for constructive accommodation with the existing legal/political order. Throughout the nineteenth century, therefore, the early labour movement did not converge around a clear political subject.[37] In fact, it is highly debatable whether the organized working class was a leading actor in the creation of democratic govern-ance systems.[38] Notably, in most of Europe, the working class only became a potent political factor after armistice in 1918, and, once incorporated in the political system, many members of the working class soon turned against democracy.

On these grounds, it is difficult to see the historical formation of democ-racy as a process involving the triumph of a formal idea, or even of a widely held desire for collective freedom and self-determination. Although, in Europe at least, some rudimentary elements of democracy were gradu-ally institutionalized through the late nineteenth century and the early twentieth century, its realization was, in most instances, not impelled either by powerful organized forces or by powerful ideologies. It is dif-ficult to identify a major European democracy that was constructed on the basis of a powerful ideological consensus or a simple and generalized demand for political self-determination. Importantly, as mentioned, pro-cedures for democratic representation only began to become widespread in Europe around 1870. This process, however, was normally underpinned by the promotion of positivist constitutional theories, whose primary

---

[37] Eley's culturalist account of the European Left generates an impressively articulated account of the working class as a transnational collective sovereign, acting with 'collectivist élan' and born from a 'shared working class experience' (2002: 85).

[38] This is of course a disputed point. But, in agreement with my assertion, see the claim in Collier that 'democracy has hardly been a "popular" victory in the sense that the lower classes were responsible for bringing it about' (1999:191). More emphatic in claiming a formative role for working-class movements in creating democracy are Aminzade (1993: 19); Przeworski (2008: 313). Rueschemeyer, Stephens and Stephens claim that the working class was 'the most consistently pro-democratic force' (1992: 8).

exponents gave only very muted recognition to popular sovereignty and democratic legitimacy, and who wished to create democratic institutions not expressly legitimated by collective will formation.[39]

Tellingly, the French Third Republic, legally founded in 1875, which was much the most democratic major state in Europe until 1918, was strongly shaped by positivist outlooks, and it was based on a few briefly worded and undemonstrative constitutional laws (Nicolet 1982: 1965). The constitutional laws of the Third Republic grafted provisions for universal male suffrage onto an existing system of limited parliamentarism, but they did not express a full commitment to popular sovereignty, and the institutional structure of the polity remained partly based in earlier monarchical ideals.[40] Leading spokespersons for the Republic tended to downplay the importance of democratic mobilization for the legitimacy of the polity, and they opted for a sharply reduced positivist idea of citizenship.[41] Indeed, one core claim in positivist thinking was that the citizen expected to underpin the political system *did not actually exist*, and citizens needed to be educated to assume the practical functions that the legitimational function of democratic citizenship presupposed (see Garrigou 2002: 109).[42] During the foundation of the German *Reich* in 1870–1, analogously, general man-

---

[39] This is exemplified in German positivism by Gerber. On the importance of positivism in the founding of the Third Republic in France see Nicolet (1982: 156).

[40] See for this view Esmein (1903: 464); Barthélemy (1904: 1); Deslandres (1937: 447); Mayeur (1984: 57); Rosanvallon (1994: 11; 2000: 248–49). On the 'modest beginnings' of the Third Republic, see Bury (1973: 227).

[41] See for example Esmein (1903: 248–49). Duguit saw national citizenship as a condition of solidarity to which persons pertain by virtue of complex memberships in orders, professional groups, etc., but he rejected the idea that a nation, or a nation of citizens, could possess a simple 'national will' (1923b: 10, 16). On the impact of positivism on the founding of the Third Republic see Ponteil (1968: 397); Aminzade (1993: 51).

[42] Indicatively, Émile Littré was one of the leading positivists at the foundation of the Third Republic, and he accounted for the legitimacy of the Republic on a thin theoretical basis. Citing positivist sociology as a premise for his political views, he advocated Republican government as a pattern of elite-led polity, in which government 'must belong to the enlightened', and in which due regard must be shown for the 'slowness with which public spirit is transformed, the danger of metaphysical and absolute concepts in social questions' (1880: 144, 388). Tellingly, Littré was also a prominent educationalist. In different settings, the education of citizens to be citizens assumed central significance in the growth of democracy. This was already implied in the works of Rousseau and Condorcet. It also assumed central importance in societies in Latin America, where centralized nation states had to be created through the nineteenth century – here the linkage of education and nation building was very strong. See the discussion of the pedagogy of the 'imagined nation' in Colombia (Márquez Estrada 2012: 309). See more recent sociological analyses that stress the role of mass schooling in creating and integrating national citizens in Boli (1989: 44); Meyer, Ramirez and Soysal (1992); Ramirez and Moon (2012: 191).

hood suffrage was introduced by the constituent parliament (*Reichstag*) of the North German Federation in almost casual fashion, despite a lack of advocates for its implementation.[43]

This absence of a unifying normative commitment to popular sovereignty meant that democracy, as it slowly became reality, diverged strikingly from its first conceptual design. As discussed, democracy was originally projected as a system of collective self-legislation, in which citizens channelled acts of collective volition through constitutionally ordered legislatures. The primacy of the legislature was an almost universal article of faith amongst early democrats, both in the USA and in France. Early state constitutions in post-1776 America accorded high authority to legislatures, a tendency which was weakened before the drafting of the Federal Constitution (Lutz 1980: 68). In revolutionary France, as mentioned, the primacy of the legislature was almost a sacred matter of doctrine, and executive institutions were conceived as subsidiary organs of the legislature (Troper 1973: 35; Jaume 1989: 19–20; Rosanvallon 2008: 196). As democracy took shape, however, it became clear that it was not the legislature but the executive that would form the dominant branch of democratic government, and, as a general norm, the larger the franchise represented through the governmental system, the more preponderant the executive would become.

Indicatively, the early rise of democratic institutions often owed more to Bonapartism than to more classical liberal-democratic ideals, and early democracy developed on a distinctively authoritarian, executive-led pattern, hardly embodying a collective demand for freedom (Rosanvallon 2000: 200). In its original design, the French Empire created by Napoleon Bonaparte contained some democratic elements, and, in its first conception, it cannot be classified as fully authoritarian. Initially, Bonapartism was established as a political regime type that selectively utilized some aspects of constitutionalism as instruments to consolidate the power of the state and to centralize the state administration (Thiry 1949: 105; Kirsch 1999: 212). Later, the Second Empire in France established one of the first enduring mass male franchises in Europe, albeit for a legislature with limited competences, and for elections that were only semi-competitive.[44] Arguably, in fact, a full franchise was established in the

---

[43] In parliamentary debates on this question, the introduction of general manhood suffrage in Germany had only two vocal supporters (Meyer 1901: 239–40). The *Reichstag* of the North German Federation was itself elected by universal manhood suffrage.

[44] See discussion of the authoritarian constitution, the legislature incapable of political action, and controlled electoral processes in the Second Empire, in Berton (1900: 83); Price (2001: 42, 54).

Second Empire precisely because it provided support for a counter-revolutionary imperial regime (see Freeman and Snidal 1982: 324). Male democracy was eventually consolidated in France after 1870 in a system that rejected Bonapartism. However, Bonapartism played a central role in establishing the bedrock for popular government in France, and it was under a Bonapartist regime that broad electoral participation was first institutionalized. As mentioned, similarly, in Imperial Germany the first mass franchise was incorporated in a political system with, arguably, a semi-Caesaristic executive (Stürmer 1973: 473). Switzerland introduced universal male voting in 1848. However, the two major European states which first enduringly institutionalized universal male voting were France and Germany, and, in both these cases, mass-electoral engagement was integrally linked to the institutionalization of governance structures centred around powerful executives.

Ultimately, as political systems with mass-democratic characteristics became more widespread, legislatures were rapidly displaced as the leading branch of government, and core legislative functions migrated to the executive. By the end of the nineteenth century, it was widely noted by political theorists and sociologists that progressive democratization had led not to the creation of popular legislatures, but to executive-dominated governance.[45] Robert Michels eventually concluded that 'democracy leads to oligarchy' and that 'democracy has an inherent preference for the authoritarian resolution of important questions' (1911: viii, 363). By World War I, even observers who supported democracy observed parliamentary institutions as mere training grounds for executive elites.[46] Even in societies marked by particular hostility to executive rule, the executive slowly became the dominant political organ.[47] This means, simply, that legislatures were originally conceived as the institutions with responsibility for expressing democratic impulses, and for giving reality to democratic freedoms. Yet, as soon as democracy approached consolidation, legislatures lost influence.[48]

---

[45] Representing this view in different national settings, see Godkin (1903: 11). Weber (1921/22: 862); Michels (1911: 363), Low (1904: 6); Bryce (1923: 374)

[46] See below p. 92.

[47] See the excellent analysis in Roussellier (2015: 43). Roussellier states that the Third Republic was founded in a spirit of 'fierce hatred' towards the executive, but that parliamentary organs eventually, by the 1920s, entered deep decline (544).

[48] See the claim in Woodhouse that the British parliament, supposedly a strong legislature in a stable democracy, was losing its position as the fulcrum of political life by circa 1900 (1994: 17). See observations on this process in both the USA and the UK in Craig (1990: 168). In such cases, the causal connection between the *growth of democracy* and the *decreasing*

On balance, positivism and Bonapartism, as much as any normative demand for collective freedom, underpinned the slow factual emergence of democratic government. The material form of early democracy in Europe had little relation to the normative constructions that appeared in theoretical reflections expressed in the French Revolution.

1.1.3   Misunderstood Democracies

A third striking fact in the development of democracy is that its primary ideological basis resides in a historical misconstruction. It is commonly argued – indeed, it has almost become part of a myth of democracy – that the early constitutional form of representative democracy was created as part of a popular reaction against a political system characterized as *absolutism*.[49] This view of course widely replicates the self-comprehension of eighteenth-century revolutionaries on both sides of the Atlantic, who considered themselves engaged in revolt against absolutistic policies, and who saw their pursuit of freedom as a pursuit of freedom from absolutistic rule – or despotism.[50] On this account, early democratic constitutions were designed by increasingly unified national populations as they sought to impose restrictions on excessively powerful monarchical executives, and so to maximize opportunities for collective self-determination.

In fact, however, the first incipient rise of democracy was not primarily shaped by a movement against monarchy, and it was certainly not driven by a rejection of an already existing, over-powerful order of state. More realistically, the early growth of political democracy should be seen as directed against *corporatism*. It was not the monarchical features of government but the corporations and semi-autonomous intermediary institutions standing between citizens and monarchical institutions in European societies, which were superseded by the first emergence of elements of political democracy. Corporations, of course, had a long tradition in Europe, reaching back to the medieval period. Through the first emergence of modern state-like

---

influence of primary democratic organs (legislatures) is commonly observed (see Craig 1983: 94).

[49] See for example Böckenförde (1958: 20); Schmitt (1969: 88); Grimm (1972: 491); Rosanvallon (1992: 71; 2000: 14); Markoff (1999a: 665); Alexander (2006: 228). For nuanced discussion, though still seeing Absolutism as the prime cause of the revolutionary crisis, see Guerra (1992: 23).

[50] The Declaration of Independence in 1776 was designed to secure liberation of the American states from 'absolute Despotism'. Thomas Paine saw himself fighting against 'hereditary despotism' (2003 [1791]: 145). Robespierre declared that 'human reason marches ... against thrones' (1794c: 3).

institutions, corporations were positioned between the state and the citizen, providing, in some cases even well into the nineteenth century, a semi-political administrative structure, in which many questions and conflicts of day-to-day politics were regulated and adjudicated (Neuburg 1880: 5). Originally, many corporations contained elements that would now be seen as democratic, at least in localized form, and they allowed some popular participation in decision making regarding matters of public concern, especially relating to economic organization.[51] To some degree, corporations permitted modes of sectoral citizenship, in which persons exercised private and public rights in specific functional domains. Ultimately, however, the expansion in the power of national political institutions, originally promoted by central monarchies, led to the erosion, and eventually the abolition, of such intermediary institutions. In this respect, the initial appearance of national democracy as a governance system was usually rooted in the same developmental processes that had previously defined and created monarchical government, which was also focused on eradicating corporatist institutions. Rather than uprooting the institutional order of monarchy, early democratic institutions typically accelerated and intensified the formative trajectories, designed to eliminate corporations, which had previously underpinned the rise of monarchical rule.

This was clear enough in the French Revolution. The French Revolution was partly caused by the failed endeavours of the Bourbon monarchy to suppress the remnants of medieval corporations that still persisted in French society. Notably, the last decades before 1789 had seen repeated attempts on the part of the monarchy to abolish or at least to weaken guilds and corporations. Such policies were intended, in particular, to intensify the government's powers of fiscal extraction, and to impose a uniform, centralized legal order across society. Ultimately, however, these policies proved unsuccessful, and guilds and corporations were able to preserve some of their functional independence.[52] The fact that the monarchy failed in these policies meant that its already chronic fiscal weakness was exacerbated, and it was vulnerable to sabotage both by antagonized representatives of older corporations and by newly radicalized political groups. Indeed, a coalition between traditional holders of corporate privilege and new political elites was at the causal centre of the revolution of 1789 (see

---

[51] See the discussion of guilds as representative organs of public legal formation in Najemy (1979: 59).

[52] Most importantly, the French monarchy attempted to abolish corporations in 1776, but it was not able to do so. In many respects the French monarchy was itself merely one corporation among others (Sewell 2008: 37).

Egret 1970: 89). However, far from negating the centralizing policies of the monarchy, the revolutionaries of 1789 immediately continued and reinforced the anti-corporatist strategies that had marked the *ancien régime*. Laws prohibiting corporations were introduced in the early months of the revolution and reinforced in subsequent constitutions.[53] In fact, the revolutionaries promoted a far more stringent centralization of government and a far more efficient system of fiscal extraction than their monarchical predecessors. One description of this process has stated how the Revolution, in causing the 'destruction of orders and corporations', suppressed 'everything that placed material limits on the exercise of sovereign power', creating a 'society of legally equal individuals' who were directly 'exposed to the immediate action of the state' (Gueniffey 2000: 59). Charles Tilly, tellingly, has described the French Revolution as 'the most sensational move' towards political centralization in modern history (1990: 107).

At an obvious level, the growth of early democratic institutions led to the abolition, or at least to a dramatic weakening, of corporations. The emergence of early democratic polities meant that, as the state claimed to extract legitimacy from all members of society, state institutions acquired an increasing monopoly of social and legal power, and local and status-defined obligations embedded in corporations lost social purchase. At a more submerged level, however, it was the monarchical suppression of corporations that in itself caused the first expansion of democracy in the eighteenth century. The slow decline of corporations in early modern Europe meant that the local judicial and administrative structures, in which many social questions had been adjudicated and regulated, disappeared. Moreover, the decline of corporations was flanked by a broader individualization of society, in which persons were released from local and personal structures of authority and forced to act as autonomous agents, especially in economic interactions.[54] In this situation, centralized monarchies were not able, on their own, to sustain the regulatory functions required by increasingly expansive societies. Monarchies, in fact, were originally in themselves little more than corporations, and, once positioned at the centre of their societal environments, they usually lacked the infrastructural authority required to impose a legal order across all social

---

[53] See the account of the assault on guilds as bastions of 'disgraceful privileges' in the Revolution in Vardi (1988: 717).

[54] One account states that in pre-1789 France social interaction was defined by 'corporate identity' and the 'individual had essentially no standing' (Fitzsimmons 1987: 270). A different interpreter argues that the global *ancien régime* was a societal condition in which there were 'corporations and estates instead of individuals' (Guerra 1992: 25).

fields, marked by rising levels of individualization.[55] In consequence, political democracy, based in socially generalized constructions of political authority and reliant on some idea of national citizenship, first began to take shape as part of a societal order created by monarchies. In fact, democracy first emerged as a system of regulatory administration that performed functions required by monarchical societies and necessitated by the rise of monarchies, which monarchical institutions, in themselves, were not able to perform adequately.

In other words, democracy first began to emerge as a political system in which broadly mandated institutions replaced localized corporations as the dominant centres of societal inclusion and regulation. For the first time in modern history, early political democracy instituted an organizational form for governmental institutions, in which they were able to produce laws, which could be justified and enforced across all domains of society, above the sectoral partitions in society's structure, which had originally been created and entrenched by medieval corporations. The idea of the single person as a citizen, voluntarily conferring authority to rule on national institutions, formed a core term of inclusion for societies marked by simultaneous processes of economic and geographical expansion and social individualization. Far from reducing the power of established states, however, the system of early democracy constructed a political order that penetrated more deeply into society and that was much more effective than monarchies in establishing central authority and reasonably uniform legislative control within the national societies in which they were located (Bendix 1996: 113). Indeed, in many settings, controlled experiments in democratization were encouraged by sitting elites as techniques for managing society after the dissolution of the traditional social order, and for forcing social agents, released from local power structures, into convergence around state institutions, thus solidifying central political authority.[56] In key respects, therefore, democracy evolved through a bundle of processes, linking patterns of elite-initiated societal administration, strategies of national centralization, and structured institutional differentiation. The reaction against political authoritarianism possessed limited importance in these processes.

Democracy is usually observed, normatively, as the result of the demands of national populations in the exercise of their sovereignty. However, it is

---

[55] On the general weakness of early modern monarchies see Lousse (1958: 92); Gueniffey (2000: 59).

[56] See on this Rokkan (1961: 138; 1975: 572); Caramani (2004: 2).

more historically accurate to see democracy as a legal artefact that was used to galvanize the nations from which democratic political institutions purported to extract legitimacy. Democracy emerged as an administrative form that expanded the power of the political system through national society, occupying and regulating the social domains once filled by local or corporatistic structures of authority. One brilliant analysis of early democracy explains how the institutionalization of political elections was used mainly to promote social integration of different groups and different classes, to establish a national frame of reference for political order and to consolidate organs of national regimentation (Kühne 1994: 34–7).[57] The formation of early democratic institutions was thus driven by a transpersonal logic of political centralization. If viewed systemically, this process marked, in many respects, a continuation and intensification of the centralizing functions of monarchical polities. Not surprisingly, Weber placed great emphasis on the centralizing impact of democratic mobilization, which he saw as forming a stark counterpoint to feudal or patrimonial patterns of social integration (1921/2: 862).

In these respects, the founding concepts of democracy, and, in particular, the underlying idea that democratic institutions extract their legitimacy from their original authorization by citizens, should not be taken literally. In fact, these concepts were intrinsically interwoven with the deep-lying processes of social formation discussed above. The early rise of democratic concepts coincided closely with a process of societal nationalization, in which societies and their institutions expanded beyond their historical local and professional structures. At a manifest level, the concepts of democracy spelled out a basic normative model for the legitimization of political authority. This model is generally reproduced in more contemporary theory: it reflects the idea that a *chain of legitimation*, running from the people (or nation), acting as citizens, through the constitution, transfusing organs of state, and returning to the people in the form of positive laws, is the condition of all political legitimacy.[58] At the same time, however, these concepts did not spell out a normative model of democratic governance in which existing political subjects obtained representation. They served, more vitally, to create the national political system and even the modern nation itself. Functionally, these concepts acted to estab-

---

[57] See also Gironda (2010: 70). This is corroborated in Caramani (2003: 436). For early theoretical comment on the deep link between citizenship practices, especially voting, and the nationalization of the political system, see Ariel (1964: 35).
[58] See the articulation of this theory in Böckenförde (1991: 299).

lish a distinctive political domain in society, in which political interactions were clearly abstracted against the privatistic patterns of local/corporate power that characterized early modern social order, and by means of which political actors were able to exercise expanded control of society as a whole. Although the early democratic imagination placed emphasis on concepts of *popular sovereignty, citizenship, participation* and *collective freedom*, these concepts were not reflections of factual subjects or factual demands for freedom. In their most essential dimensions, these concepts formed a normative apparatus through which the modern political system began to elaborate itself, through which a system of essentially public order was solidified in society, and through which national society was itself created. In many respects, in fact, the primary concepts of national democracy came into being before the putative subject of national democracy (the people, acting as citizens) actually existed. When these concepts first emerged, the people did not exist as a collective subject, bound by the laws of repressive monarchies; people existed in diffuse pre-national locations, bound by multiple, patchwork legal orders. The original subject of national democracy was, in short, a fiction, which *generated itself* through the doctrine of national democracy.[59] Most importantly, this process of democratic self-imagination did not contradict preceding, typically monarchical, patterns of political-systemic formation. It established an alternative, more effective foundation for the consolidation of the national, centralized political system.

The early rise of democracy, in sum, was centred on a deep paradox.

As discussed, the concept of democracy has undergone many transformations. However, at the core both of classical democratic theory and of classical democratic institutional practice is the assumption that democracy is a political system in which laws are created and acknowledged as legitimate by a collective political subject. According to classical democratic theory, this subject acts prior to law, and the law acquires obligatory force as it reflects the choices and reasonable freedoms of this subject – usually circumscribed as the *people*, the *nation* or, more properly, the *citizen*. On this basis, early democratic theory contained a clear monopolistic claim, indicating that law that is not supported by the will of sovereign citizens cannot claim legitimacy. Originally, this idea underpinned proto-democratic contractual theories,[60] and it was given full expression during

---

[59] On the 'founding fiction' of democracy see Rosanvallon (2008: 11).

[60] Rousseau did not actually argue that the citizens stand prior to and create the state. But his theory of contractual legitimacy, stating that the government destroys its authority

the revolutions in France and America.[61] Later, this idea assumed central importance in democratic reflection, as it became more pervasive and diffuse in the twentieth century. To be sure, recent thinking about democracy has weakened the association of the people with a territorial nation, and rights of participation in political processes are not now invariably attached to national membership.[62] Yet, as discussed, an essential principle that underlies all democratic theory is that citizens, often observed simply as *society*, stand outside the legal-institutional form of the polity, and they construct this form, in accordance with collectively demanded or acceded norms, in order to establish conditions for their freedom and self-determination. In contemporary democratic thought, the people are still configured as an active self-legislating aggregate of persons, demanding particular political freedoms, and acting prior to the legal form of their public order.[63]

Despite such global theoretical consensus, however, the actual development of political democracy appears not as the result of a deliberate collective choice by a collective subject, but as an essentially contingent occurrence. As a historical phenomenon, the rise of democracy was linked to certain deep-lying social processes, and it facilitated the deepening extension of the political system into national society. But it was not constructed or propelled by any obvious necessity, rational design, moral-theoretical consensus, collective mode of agency or shared demands for freedom. Only rarely did democracies result from a collective push for emancipation by agents within national societies. The growth of democracy was in fact deeply enmeshed in the processes of institutional centralization that pre-existed the first emergence of democratic institutions, and to which early democratic practice was – in its overt normative self-conception – opposed. Moreover, the conceptual subjects whose freedoms were used to give normative support to early democracy did not possess a material existence, and, in many cases, they only acquired reality

---

wherever it derogates from the terms set in the 'primitive act' of contract formation, can easily look like a theory of constitution-making (1966 [1762]: 53). Similarly, Kant did not argue that the social contract is a real constitutional object, which citizens agree before they create the state. He argued that the process of constitution-making is a moral process in which not the practical organization of government power, but the idea of the social contract, acquires a regulative function, as a 'mere idea of reason' (1977c: 153). However, this view has a certain analogy to constitutional theory.

[61] Thomas Paine claimed that all hereditary government is 'a species of slavery', while 'representative Government is freedom' (2003 [1791] 312).

[62] See below p. 414.

[63] See for instance Habermas (1992: 607); Bellamy (2007: 154); Webber (2009: 19).

subsequent to their normative construction. It is widely noted, historically, that reasonably uniform national peoples only came into being a long time after their first construction as the original authors of democratic polities.[64] In many cases, as discussed in Chapter 4 below, the ideal of democratic citizenship only came close to material realization through long processes of social construction, often with little foundation in democratic agency. Overall, the basic assumption that democratic law originates in reflexive acts of existing societal constituencies can only be very partially substantiated. Democratic government was not primarily created for reasons that we would now recognize as democratic.

1.2   The Sociology of Democracy

1.2.1   Early Social Theory

The contingent nature of democracy was not reflected in the classical self-explanations, or the classical critiques, of democratic polities. As discussed, much early democratic theory in the eighteenth century was marked by a literal approach to democracy, and it actively promoted the fictitious concepts around which democracy was paradoxically cemented. In some respects, however, certain lines of political reflection that gained momentum during the nineteenth century showed appreciation of the paradoxical asymmetry between the ideas of national self-legislation promoted in the Enlightenment and the factual realities of emergent post-revolutionary polities. In varying ideological guises, many theorists expressed the suspicion that early democratic ideas projected a fictitious reality, which was not linked to factual patterns of agency, and which could not become a material political form. Running through some lines of theory in the nineteenth century, in fact, was a pervasive sense that the revolutions of the eighteenth century had attempted to create a political system whose content, substance and legitimacy had only been simplistically articulated by its advocates. Throughout the nineteenth century, early democratic theory was recurrently exposed to the criticism that it reposed on a sequence of societal fictions, and it was incapable of establishing enduring and objectively legitimate institutions.

To illustrate this, first, through the earlier nineteenth century, the group of theorists now known as *historicists* argued that the experiments in revolutionary-democratic constitutionalism in France had proved

---

[64] See important pronouncements on the fictionality of nationhood in Dahl (1989: 3); Linz (1993: 361); Beetham (1999: 82).

short-lived because constitutions created at this time were founded in a fictional construction of the sovereign people. In particular, historicists claimed that, in the early democratic revolutions, legal orders had been abstractly implanted in society, and they were not able to presuppose historically embedded motivations amongst their populations.[65] This perception was initially reflected in the works of Burke, who dismissed the idea that formally imposed institutions could secure political legitimacy, and he emphasized instead the historical, organic premises of political obligation (1910 [1790]: 58). This critique was visible in the writings of Savigny, who rejected rational or contractual constructions of law, and implied that law acquired authority through its attachment to local customs and affectual norms. Savigny especially accentuated the 'organic connection of the law with the essence and character of the people'. He claimed that law guaranteeing freedom is law that proceeds 'from the innermost essence of the nation itself and its history' (1850: 113), and he saw in the reception of Roman law in the German states a vital enactment of traditional freedoms (1840b: 11). Underlying the historicist approach was the basic claim that members of a national population could not be separated from their local historical form, and the construction of the people as a single rational agent, able electively to transform and legitimate society's political structure, was always projective. At the origins of historicism, tellingly, Gustav Hugo argued that the 'legal truths' of a particular people cannot be defined *a priori* as 'pure, general, or necessary'.[66] Instead, he explained, valid laws can only 'be learned historically, from facts' (1823: 19); they are 'empirical', and they are 'different depending on time and place' (1823: 55).

Second, over a longer period, the group of theorists now categorized as *positivists*, many of whom were initially close to historicism, also opposed the voluntaristic theories of state legitimacy and legal authority espoused by early democrats. Positivists broadly accepted the defining moral-philosophical claim of the Enlightenment that the modern state must operate under formally binding law, and they rejected the more obviously reactionary constructions of the state as a legally unbound actor, acting in analogy to a private person (see Albrecht 1837: 1496). To this degree, most early positivists were located in the more Conservative margins of

---

[65] See for example Ranke (1833: 794); Savigny (1850: 113). Historicism was not intrinsically Conservative. Its critique of constitutional rationalism in the name of historically integrative experience was central to later patterns of liberal constitutionalism. To illustrate this, see Droysen (1846: 426).

[66] Gustav Hugo might in certain respects be viewed as the precursor of both historicism and positivism (Eichengrün 1935: 113–14).

early constitutionalism. From Hugo, to Puchta, to Gerber, to Laband, to Jellinek, the positivists argued that the modern state necessarily required a legal form, and the basic legitimacy of the state could only be conceived in legal/constitutionalist terms. However, unlike more mainstream theorists of the Enlightenment, positivists were resistant to the idea that the laws of state could be produced through acts of popular-rational legislation, or through any external patterns of will formation. Indeed, they indicated that this idea originated in metaphysical constructions of the state as a collective person, which could not provide a reliable foundation for political order.[67] As a result, the positivists observed the formation of the law of the state as a simple positive exercise, engendered either through legislative acts, or, at most, through societal processes of institutional evolution (see Jellinek 1900: 323, 392).

On one hand, the positivist outlook gave rise to quasi-Hobbesian constructions of legal authority that defined the law as a simple structure of command. This idea was first spelled out in English positivism, and it then migrated into German positivism, where legal authority was eventually construed, in principles derived from Roman private law, as the manifestation of the sovereign volitional power of the state, acting as a formal legal person.[68] By the middle of the nineteenth century, the leading exponent of German positivism defined the state as the 'highest juridical personality', defined by the attribute of the 'power to command' (Gerber 1865: 3). On the other hand, however, the positivist outlook gave rise to formalistic constructions of the law, claiming that, once created, the law possesses free-standing obligatory force, and that questions of legal validity and political legitimacy need to be resolved through purely legal analysis, without reference to external factors, be these political, sociological or normative.[69] These two lines of thinking were not categorically distinct,

---

[67] See Kelsen's argument that positivism is defined by its 'conscious opposition to metaphysical speculation' (1962: 316). See the additional claim in Ott that legal positivism is determined in its essence by 'the refusal to take recourse to metaphysical presumptions' (1976: 104).

[68] For the English theory see the following claim in Austin: 'Every positive law, or every law simply and strictly so called, is set, directly or indirectly, by a sovereign person or body, to a member or members of the independent political society, wherein that person or body is sovereign or supreme' (1832: 267–8). For important historical commentary on Germany see Schönberger (1997: 52).

[69] This principle was fundamental to positivism. This culminated in Kelsen's claim that law is simply *pure law*: it is a 'logically closed complex of norms', and these norms regulate legal questions and dilemmas without any external direction (1920: 114). In consequence, Kelsen explained, 'juridical knowledge' need concern itself with 'legal norms' and nothing else (1920: 109).

and they flowed together in the thought of most positivists. Generally, positivists argued that the state first makes the law, but is then bound by it. Laband, for example, who was widely regarded as the proponent of the most baldly statist version of positivism, defined the constitutional order of the state as the result of an 'act of will of the state', but he still imputed to the constitution a 'binding force', which even state agencies could not easily ignore (1911: 39).

On this foundation, positivists opted for a largely apolitical concept of law, and they endeavoured to account for law's authority by isolating the law against political forces and specific acts of volition in society (Böckenförde 1958: 211–12). Above all, positivists argued that the legal foundations of the state should be interpreted in a purely formalist perspective, and they should not be confused with collective demands or rationally articulated moral objectives.[70] As a result, although positivists typically favoured some pattern of constitutionalism as a model of legal/political order, they did not endorse expansive ideals of citizenship, imagining democracy as the self-enactment of popular visions of freedom or autonomy. In particular, they rejected the idea that the political system could derive its legitimacy from a manifestly political, external will, expressed by actors in society at large. Instead of this, they claimed that the political system obtains its legitimacy through a circular relation with the law, in which the law, of itself, imposes constraints on the use of political power, and the law internalizes and satisfies the demands for legitimacy directed towards the political system (see Häfelin 1959: 95).

The line of positivist reflection eventually culminated in the works of Hans Kelsen, who both transformed positivist ideas, and developed these ideas to a high degree of refinement. Notably, Kelsen argued that law should be examined as a pure system of norms, occluded against all extra-legal factors, and that analysis of law is distorted by theories which dualistically separate the source of law's authority from the law itself. For example, he claimed that natural-law arguments falsely bind the law to a realm of ontological facts or subjective values; they originate in a 'solipsistic epistemology', which mistakenly presumes that particular value-deductions can form a reliable foundation for objective legal norms (1925: 37). Similarly, he asserted that contractarian claims that the law must express agreements of principle, which then provide a scheme for

---

[70] For example, the young Jhering argued that legal principles are 'abstracted from observation of the conditions of life' (1852: 25). In his later work, he turned categorically against this view and opted for a utilitarian construction of law.

the 'legitimation of the state', make both the law and the state dependent on external values or moral notions, which the law cannot meaningfully articulate (1934: 128). Further, he insisted that questions of legal validity should be categorically detached from all material sociological analysis of law's authority and efficacy (1911a: 10). In particular, he concluded that the sources of legal authority cannot be founded in distinct acts of the state. For Kelsen, there is no voluntaristic foundation for law, and law possesses no source of volitional authority outside itself. Even the norms contained in a constitution, he observed, should not be construed as outcomes of collective-voluntaristic decisions about the order of state. The constitution, although authorizing law, is merely an objective fact or a self-reference of the law, which law creates *for itself*: it is an original norm, or a 'point of departure for a procedure', and its sole function is to create a normative frame of reference, in which legal questions can be formally processed, and in which law can refer to objective principles to regulate the exercise of political power (1934: 64).

On this basis, Kelsen argued that theories of democratic legitimacy premised in substantial/material or voluntaristic processes of norm formation should be viewed as expressing a metaphysically contaminated account of the law. To be sure, Kelsen was a committed democrat, and one reason for his hostility to political voluntarism was that he perceived this as a source of anti-democratic thinking.[71] However, he viewed democracy, in essence, as a normative order in which not the people or the demos, but the constitution on its own determines formal principles of legitimacy for the polity. In consequence, he concluded that the classical-democratic idea that the people could act as an immediate presence in government was a 'meta-political illusion', resulting from a misguided understanding of the foundations of legal-constitutional validity (1929: 21–2). In this respect, Kelsen brought to a pithy conclusion the longstanding line of argument amongst positivists, who, through the nineteenth century, had implied that attempts to legitimize the modern democratic state through reference to collective political subjects rested on unreliable and chimerical metaphysical principles.

Such cautious responses to early democratic theories became especially evident amongst theorists in the nineteenth century who examined the politics of early democracy from a more *sociological* angle. Of course, sociological thinking did not develop in a vacuum, and many sociologists

---

[71] Kelsen saw metaphysical legal thinking, premised on the idea of extra-legal substance, as inherently authoritarian (1933: 25).

have perceived their methods as deeply indebted to theorists working during the Enlightenment, notably Montesquieu, Adam Smith and David Hume.[72] In the nineteenth-century context, however, sociology evolved as a conceptual lineage which reflected deep democratic scepticism, and it combined elements of historicism and positivism, galvanizing these to enunciate a distinctive critical account of early democratic ideas found in the Enlightenment.[73] To be sure, sociology eventually differed from early historicism and positivism in that it accepted democracy as a reality – even as a necessary reality. Gradually, sociologists sought not to suggest counter-models to the democratic state, but to explain the grounds for the emergence of democracy, and to interpret its distinctive benefits. Sociology thus slowly staked out a particular position in a wider endeavour, in Pierre Rosanvallon's words, to 'give flesh to democracy' (1998: 133), and to place democracy on more adequate conceptual foundations. However, the attitude of early sociology to democracy was always ambiguous. In particular, early sociological thinking was distinctively defined by a concept of society that separated societal dynamics from the conscious lives and interests of individual human agents, and which observed society as a phenomenon *sui generis*. This *discovery of society*, which was formative of sociology as an intellectual orientation, created the basis for a sharp reaction against formal-rational, formal-individualist or simply voluntaristic comprehensions of political subjectivity in early democratic thinking (see Bouglé 1896: 119; Gauchet 2007: 156).

The early growth of sociological theory was, in general, very closely linked to the early rise of democratic ideals of freedom and equality, and the academic discipline which we now understand as sociology evolved, in some respects, as a commentary on the first emergence of democracy as a form of political organization. Tellingly, Siegfried Landshut observed in a very important work that early sociology constructed its basic unit of analysis – society itself – by examining the impact of the 'ideas of freedom and equality' on the 'demands and expectations' of human beings (1969: 85). In particular, early sociology placed its primary focus on structural questions relating to the transformation of political order after the collapse of the *ancien régime*. The most important theorists who contributed

---

[72] Durkheim saw Montesquieu as a founder of modern sociology (1953). In similar spirit, see Duguit (1889: 492); Esmein (1903: 44–5); Gurvitch (1939: 625). On the origins of sociology in the Scottish Enlightenment see Small (1907); Lehmann (1930).

[73] Both early positivism and historicism contained clear sociological assumptions about the grounds of legal validity. See for example Puchta (1828: 141). For comment see Brockmöller (1997: 58, 116).

to the first emergence of sociology sought to comprehend the dynamic forces underlying the formal abstraction of the modern state, and the correlated growth of an individualized market-based civil society, in which social agents increasingly laid claim to distinct economic and civil rights. In the earlier twentieth century, tellingly, Hans Freyer argued that sociology in its entirety evolved as a discipline that was engaged with the 'history of civil society', and that the 'dissolution of society from the state' formed the primary and abiding 'object of sociology' (1935: 134). As a result of this emphasis, early sociology was deeply concerned with the normative foundations of the modern state, as its position in relation to societal actors and organizations was reconfigured. In consequence, sociology first took shape as a discipline that examined the lines of articulation between centralized political institutions and diffuse agents through society, and which endeavoured to explain the motivations that linked these institutions to different societal domains. In contrast to more classical philosophical inquiries, however, early sociology promoted an analysis of the emergent modern state, which tried to account for the collective preconditions of institutional legitimacy and the social and motivational grounds for acceptance of laws in modern society without reliance on rational or individualistic ideas of human self-legislation. Notably, sociological theory approached these themes in a spirit of tentative relativism, sceptically interrogating the foundations of public authority and observing the claims for collective rationality and collective freedom that shaped early democratic institutions with interpretive semi-positivistic caution.

In the first instance, many thinkers who might now be grouped together as forerunners of sociology analysed the formation of early democratic institutions in harshly critical fashion. For all their great differences, many early sociologists were united by a rejection of the notion, identified with the French Revolution, that democratic political institutions could simply be grafted onto the existing structure of society, or that appeals to formal or universal principles of freedom could provide adequate *motivational* or *obligational* support for these institutions. In this respect, most specifically, early sociological theorists questioned the assumption that a rationalized aggregate of persons known simply as 'society' could be objectively isolated from the state as a source of legitimate law, and that this society could rationally organize itself as a distinct constituent power, giving expression to simple, universal ideas of freedom, to be transmitted through the state. As an alternative, early sociologists began to develop the idea that the increasingly differentiated form of the state was not simply detached from society, but in fact obtained its legitimacy through complex, embedded social phenomena, which connected it, in fundamental ways, to underlying processes in society as a whole. On this basis, in effect, early sociological theorists denied the existence of the people as *an aggregate of contract-forming subjects*, standing opposite the state as a collective rational actor, and they rejected the assumption that a society could be centred in one single mode of rational or contractual subjectivity, or one single vision of collective freedom, reflected through the political body of the state. On this account, rational ideas of freedom could not produce adequate motivational force to stabilize the position of government in society and to legitimize government in face of those subject to its power. Instead, early sociologists gradually formulated the idea that a political system is always legitimated by complex, half-submerged motivations, many of which evade rational analysis, and which can only be disclosed through contextually refined interpretation. To this degree, early sociology was clearly hostile to the idea that the political domain could be seen as a discrete, volitionally constructed part of society, enshrining formal liberties for all persons. The sociological challenge to early democratic reflection was expressed from a perspective that accused early democratic theory of being inattentive to the intricately formed social foundations of political legitimacy and of failing to recognize the socially diffuse, often subliminal, impulses that move different agents to show compliance with political directives.

To illustrate this, for example, Bentham set out an early sociological critique of the normative principles that supported democratic ideals in revolutionary France (2002: 30). Likewise, Burke ridiculed the 'metaphysic rights' championed by the revolutionaries of 1789, preferring instead the 'real rights of men', based in civil society and convention, as the premises of political order (1910 [1790]: 56–8). The sociological critique of early democracy, phrased as an analysis of the consequences of the French Revolution, was then later expanded in the works of Tocqueville. Tocqueville viewed democracy as an inherently fragile political form, whose factual reality depended not on the collective exercise of sovereign powers, but on socially distinctive behaviours. He argued that the 'democratic revolution' of 1789 had only occurred in the material dimension of society, and it needed to produce a transformation in the 'laws, ideas, habits and customs' of the people to become real and useful (1866 [1835]: 10). Similarly, Comte viewed both the 'dogma of universal law' and the 'dogma of the sovereignty of the people' expressed in the revolution as performing an 'indispensable' function in terminating the decadence of the *ancien régime*. Yet he also observed these concepts as the results of 'revolutionary metaphysics', and so as incapable of stabilizing an enduringly balanced social order (1975: 28–32). Analogously, Saint Simon argued that revolutionary democratic principles had been founded in 'vague and undefined desires', determined, importantly, by the fact that revolutionaries had been 'ignorant of politics' (1966: 158). Overall, theorists in the early lineage of sociological reflection proposed a way of thinking about the claims of democracy which insisted that governmental orders presuppose more than subjectively rational institutions to prove enduring and legitimate. In particular, they argued that institutions need to be deeply correlated with societal structure.

This early sociological critique of ideas of democratic freedom found its most important articulation in the works of Hegel. Vitally, Hegel accepted the basic legitimational principle of the French Revolution. One leading commentator has argued that the French Revolution forms the defining 'event' in Hegel's philosophy (Ritter 1957: 15). Above all, his political thought was centred around the principle that modern society presupposes the existence of a state, embodying rational freedoms able to penetrate across society. He thus clearly endorsed the Rousseauian claim that a legitimate state is a public-legal order, enabling rational social freedoms for all members of society.[74] To be sure, Hegel argued against popular government, and he claimed, instead, that general freedom could be most effectively realized under a constitutional monarchy, supported by an enlightened and educated civil service (1970 [1830]: 468–9, 473). However, he strictly rejected all reactionary ideals of state power, and he insisted that a state is only legitimate if it creates public-legal conditions for the realization of the consciousness of liberty and the exercise of social freedom.

In defending the rational state, however, Hegel opted for an approach that expressed a distinctive sociological caution about the core principles of early democratic theory, and he opposed both individualism and the voluntarism of classical democratic reflection.

First, Hegel rejected the claim that a rational state could be created through simple acts of popular foundation, on terms dictated by the formal or contractual will of the people.[75] In fact, he rejected the claim that laws with claim to generalized authority could be imputed to reflex-

---

[74] Hegel described the legal system as the 'realm of realized freedom', or, like Kant and Rousseau, as the domain of 'second nature' (1970 [1821]: 46), giving material expression to otherwise only inchoate rational human freedoms.

[75] Hegel was always critical of the contract as a form of agreement, seeing it as an expression of particular wills and particular interests, without a substantial ethical content (1970 [1821]: 172, 400).

ive acts of a simply formed political subject – *the people, the nation* or *the citizens*. Crucially, he argued that the power 'to make a constitution' is not an abstract or volitional power, to be exercised by a self-designated constituent body (1970 [1830]: 336). The freedoms enshrined in a constitution cannot be seen as the results of simple choices or rational decisions, emanating from articulated interests in society. On the contrary, he stated that constitutional freedoms only become meaningful if they are underscored and sustained by robust positive institutions, which provide an integrating bedrock for the particular freedoms exercised in society. All subjective freedoms, for Hegel, presuppose the presence of positive institutions, capable of casting a consolidated rational form for society, on the foundation of which single freedoms can be exercised. Ideas of freedom that are simply imposed on society always contain the risk of causing a fragmentation of society, and of undermining the positive institutions that freedom requires for its enjoyment. In fact, institutions ensuring freedom necessarily pre-exist and determine the rationality of subjects claiming constitutional freedoms. Accordingly, he indicated that legitimate institutions reflect an encompassing condition of society, which is embedded in the historically formed 'spirit of the people' (1970 [1830]: 336), and their authority is constructed through objective processes of legal norm formation and rationalization.

Second, Hegel claimed that agents in modern society were not able immediately to construct an idea of their freedoms capable of sustaining a fully legitimate state. Central to Hegel's work was the insistence that modern society had become irreversibly differentiated into a plurality of legal-normative spheres, each reflecting distinct experiences and distinct legal constructions of freedom.[76] Modern society, he explained, contains a 'great breadth' of liberties, of both public and private nature (1970 [1830]: 333).

[76] Notably, Hegel argued that the modern economy distils certain ideas of freedom, based in the self-interest of individual parties (1970 [1821]: 340). These freedoms have substantial value and need to be protected, but, as they are based in formal, unilateral freedoms, they cannot establish the obligatory basis of government. Moreover, he argued that the human being as a whole could be divided into distinct characters, with distinct needs and ideas of freedom, depending on the societal sphere in which they operate. These characters were 'person' (in law); 'subject' (in morality); 'family member' (in the family); 'bourgeois' (in the economy). In each of these substantiations, the human being necessarily pursues different needs, and it cannot arrive at a comprehensive experience of freedom (1970 [1821]: 348–9). Freedom must incorporate, yet also be distinct from, such functionally selective freedoms, and it can only be guaranteed by the state. Even within the state, Hegel argued that different ideas of freedom needed to be institutionalized, and he viewed the state as a total entity comprising a number of 'particular spheres' (1970 [1821]: 477). These spheres included corporations, civil service, representative organs and, of course, executive and legislature.

In particular, modern society was increasingly dominated by formal freedoms engendered in the emergent capitalist economy, or civil society. However, he argued that such freedoms were only ever partial freedoms, pertaining to a particular set of intrinsically instrumental social interactions, with an intrinsically instrumental nature. Owing to the differentiation of society, individual people ordered their lives around selective, sectorally determined ideas of freedom, and they could not extract all-embracing ideas of freedom from their own singular interests. Notably, Hegel viewed freedoms 'in the European sense', as sanctioned by the French Revolution, as freedoms of the 'subjective will', the will of isolated individuals, which cannot amount to a conclusive experience of freedom (1970 [1830]: 312). Modern society, therefore, could not be forced to converge around the dictates of simply formed collective subjects, or around simply constructed ideas of rationality, freedom and institutional legitimacy. Democratic doctrines suggesting that a people, at a given moment in history, could project universal rational norms of governmental legitimacy, entailed, for Hegel, a deep simplification of the motivational, functional and historical structure of society. Indeed, such doctrines resulted from simplified constructions of reason, which were ill-adapted to society in its complex existing form.[77]

For Hegel, in consequence, it was illusory to think that the people might appear in society as identical citizens, with simply generalized ideas of freedom and equality. All citizens, he indicated, may be free and equal at a level of formal abstraction (1970 [1830]: 332). In concrete reality, however, citizens appear in society in many roles and many functions, each of which may entail rather different, often multiple, ideas and experiences of freedom. Importantly, moreover, individual persons may hold dear experiences of freedom that cannot be easily generalized across different parts of society, and which pertain to particular social histories and locations. In fact, individual persons may be alarmed by the formal freedoms created through the processes of social differentiation and economic individualization that shape their lives. For Hegel, therefore, a government able to produce deep obligational force for law needs to encompass, to moderate and to protect the multiple rationalities and the multiple freedoms that modern society contains. In fact, a legitimate government might need

---

The idea of freedom, thus, could only appear through the institutionalization of a wide range of particular claims to liberty.

[77] Hegel described the concept of the 'people' as an 'inorganic totality', which could not, in immediate form, bring legitimacy to a state (1970 [1821]: 473).

to combine many different legal institutions, proportioned to different spheres of social interaction, permitting, within certain rational constraints, the exercise and the institutionalization of a plurality of individual liberties across society.[78] For this reason, Hegel argued that some institutions of the *ancien régime*, especially corporations and estates, retained an important function in modern societies. Most especially, he claimed that such institutions have a role in mediating between the economy and the polity, in obviating the excessive dominance of the prerogatives of particular sectoral interests, and, to some degree, in shielding people from the consequences of individualistic economic freedoms.[79]

Overall, in asserting that there is no one simple subject in society from which state institutions can claim legitimacy, Hegel placed himself squarely against revolutionary individualism and rational natural-law theory (see Riedel 1982: 93, 114). As stated, he centred his political philosophy around the claim that the state needs to embody a higher rationality or a higher consciousness of freedom for society. However, this rationality might only appear in perspectivally differentiated form, meaning different things to different people in different social locations, functions and institutions.[80] For Hegel, the legitimacy of government institutions depends on their ability, not blankly to impose generalized ideas of freedom, but to uphold, to balance and to secure a variety of societal liberties, within an overarching construction of a free rational society. For Hegel, it is not the case that all persons in a society governed by a legitimate state will be free in the same way, or that they will experience their freedoms in identical fashion. Indeed, crucially, a legitimate state, intricately enmeshed in society's own structure, will promote the balanced legal institutionalization of a range of freedoms. In such a state, the provision of institutional security quite different freedoms, as much as any formal constitutional declaration of freedom, will act as the source of governmental legitimacy. In this latter respect, Hegel struck a note that remained vital for subsequent sociological reflection.[81] His suggestion that legitimate government presupposes the

---

[78] A legitimate state for Hegel is 'the reality of the substantial will', in which freedom obtains its highest expression (1970 [1821]: 399). This state cannot be confused with the particularized interests that determine interaction in 'civil society' (the economy).

[79] For Hegel, estates and corporations form a 'mediating organ' between the government and the people, who are factually 'split up into particular spheres and individuals' (1970 [1821]: 471).

[80] For Hegel, the state is a 'living spirit' differentiated into 'particular modes of efficacy' (1970 [1830]: 331).

[81] Close to my account, Jonas argues that questions concerning the exercise of free will and the process of institutional formation are not separable for Hegel (1980: 156). For other

measured institutionalization of a range of freedoms, often preventing the volatile revolutionary expression of simple emancipatory claims, became a core characteristic of sociological reflection. In this respect, Hegel implied, in a claim with far-reaching sociological implications, that, in a legitimate state, freedom must be seen as the freedom of real people, and freedom is only freedom if people actually desire it for themselves. This implies that there may exist many experiences of freedom, each of which may require distinct modes of institutionalization.[82] Underlying this claim is the sense that in a modern, pluralistically formed society the law is not legitimated by the freedoms of simple citizens, and the law acquires a partly autonomous role in establishing social conditions of constrained pluralism.

After Hegel, a more strictly sociological critique of democracy emerged in more radical sociological theories. For example, this critique is visible in the works of Proudhon, who argued that the rational individualism of early democratic theory had eradicated more authentic, substantial patterns of liberty from society (1966 [1840]: 225).[83] In particular, Proudhon condemned the processes of institutional centralization linked to early majoritarian democracy, which he saw as reflecting a violation of essential human liberties (1927 [1861]: 40). This critique is also visible in the works of Karl Marx. To be sure, Marx was not an anti-democratic theorist; he clearly supported a Rousseauian construction of the legitimate political system as an expression of collective freedom (species being), self-legislation and citizenship. Yet Marx proposed a political critique of democracy which indicated that early representative democracy had been abstractly imposed on society, and it failed to establish basic liberties that pierced deeply into society or that meaningfully emancipated social agents (1956 [1844]: 364, 366). For Marx, modern democracy was constructed in a spirit of blindness towards existing objective relations in society, and the early architects of modern democracy were uninterested in creating a condition of genuine equality – or genuine citizenship – to support their institutions. In fact, Marx's

---

accounts of Hegel as a sociologist, see Willke (1992: 20); Zalten (2006: 225). Very importantly, Freyer argued – in my view, entirely accurately – that Hegel's philosophy of law was the 'origin of German sociology' (1930: 213).

[82] Notably, one account has argued that the Jacobin period of the French Revolution witnessed a 'deinstitutionalization of politics' (Rosanvallon 2000: 74).

[83] Proudhon clearly belongs to the class of early sociologists. His work had the distinctive sociological feature that he observed society as possessing a reality distinct from the single agents that it contains; tellingly, he viewed the triumph of individuated property ownership as 'suicide of society' (1966 [1840]: 307). On Proudhon as a sociologist, see Gurvitch (1940: 58); Bouglé (1910); Hall (1971: 35).

critique centrally addressed the concept of the citizen in early democracy. He argued that the model of the citizen formalized in most post-1789 legal orders expressed an idea of citizenship based in a thin stratum of generalized atomistic liberties, focused on the realization of economic prerogatives, and it actually obstructed the genuine fulfilment of the ideals of equality first attached to revolutionary doctrines of citizenship. He claimed that, in early democracies, legal citizenship had been established as an instrument for preserving existing property relations, so that, far from realizing a condition of substantial equality, the citizen became 'a servant' of the capitalist economy. This meant that the 'bourgeois' replaced the 'citoyen' as the essential focus of society's legal/political structure (1956 [1844]: 366).

For Marx, modern constitutional democracies were always afflicted by a deep contradiction: they purported to offer general legal freedoms to their citizens, yet in fact they only offered economic freedoms, which could only benefit a small sector of society. Existing democratic systems presupposed that the claim to general freedom, from which they derived their formal legitimacy, remained at the surface level of society, and that it did not penetrate deeply into societal interaction, inducing demands for equal material and economic freedom. Early democracy, in other words, always presupposed that its founding normative principles did not become sociologically real. Marx argued that if citizens exercised their democratic rights in a deep sociological dimension, this would jeopardize existing economic relations, and, as backlash, democratic institutions would inevitably assume authoritarian features; elite groups would utilize the apparatus of democracy not to establish general freedoms, but to protect their select economic privileges (1960 [1852]: 194–6). Consequently, Marx concluded that political democracy could only acquire full legitimacy if it possessed a sociologically effective constitution, establishing rights and freedoms for the citizen as a *completely societal agent*, in the totality of its relations, including rights of socio-material equality. In this respect, Marx expanded the implication of early democratic theory, to claim that government is only democratically legitimated if citizens are able to live in material conditions in which they recognize their freedoms, not only in their laws, but in their *labour*: legitimacy, thus, presupposes equality in law and equality in labour at the same time (see 1962 [1932]: 568).

Overall, many of the classic texts in which sociology began to assume methodological shape as a distinct way of examining modern society were based on the claim, implicitly, that the modes of proto-democratic political organization resulting from the French Revolution and the American

Revolution were undermined by *an absence of society*.[84] That is to say, these texts indicated that the institutional design projected in early democratic theory was not correlated with *objectively manifest* social conditions, or with an *objectively visible* social agent. In particular, the argument was common amongst early sociologists that the democratic ideal of the modern state was based on the positing of a simplified distinction between state and society, in which the state was formally counter-posed to the collective will of subjects in society, from which the state was expected to extract its legitimacy. Sociology reflected a deep sense of the fictionality of common concepts of political subjectivity, and it implied that democracy was only able to proclaim legitimacy by falsifying the subjects to which it imputed its legitimacy. For the early sociological outlook, the subjects conferring legitimate obligatory force on legal and political institutions could not simply be projected in the form of an abstract collective singular personality (a nation of citizens), and acts of rational self-legislation, imputed in like manner to all persons, could only provide a fictitious, simplified point of attribution for the legitimization of public authority. On this account, the *forgetfulness of society* in the early democratic state had produced a deeply reductive model of political agency and political subjectivity to support its claims to legitimacy. Central to such sociological critiques was the claim that early theorists of democracy had constructed their models of the legitimate state on dualistic premises, borrowed from the *rationalist metaphysics* of the early Enlightenment, which posited *absolute rationality*, singularly incarnated in the subjects of individual citizens, as the basic principle of legitimate law. Underlying the early sociological attitude to the modern state was a deep scepticism concerning *political metaphysics*, and critical reactions to early democratic ideals tended to question democracy, not only because of its sociological vacuity, but because it substituted *metaphysical subjects* for *material/historical subjects* in attempting to articulate the sources of legal freedom and legal obligation in modern society.

The sociological apprehension about the metaphysical subjectivism underpinning the ideas of freedom in the modern democratic state was evidently not without justification. In placing the identity of government and collective freedom at the centre of political legitimacy, early theories of democracy clearly took recourse, in part, to metaphysical ideas of authority, which used residually metaphysical concepts to conceive the inner

---

[84] For this reason, some commentators on the theoretical beginnings of sociology argued that it 'arose in the first instance as a deeply conservative movement' (Nisbet 1943: 161). See also Strasser (1976: 27).

legitimational connection between order and freedom.[85] In particular, these theories utilized ideas of political subjectivity inherited from classical metaphysics, and they viewed the institutional order of democracy as legitimated not by its realization of the freedoms of given persons, but by its realization of freedoms inhering generically in human nature – that is, *species freedoms*. For this reason, early democratic theory made extensive use of natural-law theory, and it constructed the human subject of democracy in categories derived, at least implicitly, from classical natural law. In fact, for many early democrats, the realization of abstract or natural freedom appeared more important than the practical institutionalization of democratic government.

To illustrate this, Rousseau's idea of the general will was manifestly extracted from a tradition of religious thinking, which identified the will of *virtuous citizens* as the foundation for legitimate government. His theory of the social contract premised political legitimacy in a purified construction of the human will and human freedom: the will underpinning legitimate government, he argued, was the will, not of factually existing citizens, but of citizens as rationalized metaphysical abstractions of their existing subjectivity.[86] Citizenship appeared to Rousseau as a moral condition, reflecting a 'remarkable change' in the human spirit, in which all agents in society are placed under and protected by a binding civil law (1966 [1762]: 55–6). Citizenship, on this account, is a moral choice, a calling, which elevates the political community into a transfigured ethical state (Rosenblatt 1997: 246). Famously, therefore, Rousseau concluded that a political system acquires legitimacy partly through its pedagogic functions in educating people to be citizens: that is, in separating them from their natural selves – in forcing them to be free. On this account, the political system was required, circularly, to create the virtuous citizens that it presupposed for its legitimacy as an institution guaranteeing collective liberty (1966 [1762]: 54). During the French Revolution, Condorcet followed Rousseau in opting for a pedagogic account of citizenship (1994 [1791]: 81). Indeed, Condorcet argued that there is a 'large gap between the rights which the law recognizes in citizens and the rights of which they have real enjoyment': this gap had to be bridged by education (1797 [1795]: 344).

At the beginning of the French Revolution (before France had become a Republic), similarly, Robespierre declared his objective to 'guide men towards happiness by virtue, and towards virtue by legislation founded on

---

[85] See p. 96 below.
[86] See relevant discussion in Riley (1986: 62); Urbinati (2006: 91).

the immutable principles of universal morality' (Hamel 1865: 80). Later, he argued that a democracy is a type of polity, in which the 'citizen is subordinate to the judge, the judge to the people, and the people to justice'. On this basis, he declared: 'In our country, we want to replace egotism with morality ... the tyranny of fashion with the rule of reason ... vanity with magnanimity' (1793b: 4). Ultimately, he observed legitimate government not as a state of practical order, but as a condition of shared virtue, in which people, as citizens, are severed from their factual dispositions and factual motivations, and brought under the simple law of virtue. He stated simply that the 'soul of the Republic is virtue' (1794: 7). He added to this the claim that the 'mainspring of popular government in peace is virtue', but 'the mainspring of popular government in revolution is, simultaneously, *virtue and terror*': without terror 'virtue has no power' (1794: 13).[87]

Both Rousseau and Robespierre founded their idea of the citizen in a radical dichotomy between inner virtue and outer depravity. They assumed that a government could only assume legitimacy if it reflected the condition of virtue inherent in the interior moral life of the species, and, where needed, if it deployed terror to give expression to such virtue (Blum 1986: 241). Terror, thus, was essential for making people virtuous, and for ennobling them into a state of democratic freedom and citizenship. By implication, in fact, both Rousseau and Robespierre suggested, real people may feel terror in face of the virtues and freedoms which they are supposed to experience as free citizens in a democratic Republic. In these respects, classical theories of democracy were marked by a metaphysical resentment towards the actual material subjects of democracy. They defined democracy as legitimated by its realization, not of freedoms that people wanted for themselves, but of prior, necessary, virtuous freedoms: the realization of genuine freedom appeared more important than the factual experience of freedom. Like earlier natural-law theories, moreover, early democratic theorists were prepared to endorse intense authoritarianism as a path to freedom.[88] This metaphysical construction of freedom

---

[87] One important commentary has explained how the Jacobins understood 'virtue' as a condition of elevated freedom and justice, forming a strict bond of 'solidarity' between people and government (Jaume 1989: 322).

[88] Leibniz, Wolff and, to some degree, Kant, had all expressed respect for rational authoritarianism. Wolff distinguished quite clearly between monarchy and tyranny, but, within the minimal constraints of natural law, he saw subjects of monarchies as persons who had pledged to 'allow the will of persons in authority to be their own will' (1756: 173–4). He also argued that obedience is still necessary when laws are unjust (1756: 424): 'subjects have to obey persons in authority' because 'subjects are not always able to judge what is in their interest' (1756: 460).

did not end with the end of the French Revolution. As mentioned, after the French Revolution, Kant argued that valid laws had their origins in divine intelligence, close to divine reason, through which human subjects elevated themselves above their natural-material lives (1977b [1797]: 334).[89]

Across the spectrum of early democratic thinking, therefore, democratic legitimacy and metaphysical constructions of human subjectivity were closely connected. Laws able to obtain and command legitimacy were usually imputed to acts of rationality and concepts of liberty standing above human agents in their factually given reality, which may inspire terror in merely material human beings. As a result of this, the leading legal and political theorists of the late Enlightenment placed particular emphasis on the claim that laws assuming validity for one state must also necessarily assume validity for a number of states, and each legitimate state must be subject to *the same laws*. Early theorists of democracy tended to express enthusiasm for international law, and they developed a notion of the democratic subject which encompassed many peoples and many nations at the same time.[90] Moreover, the metaphysical emphasis of early democratic theory was reflected in the fact that its exponents generally saw democracy as a *total condition*, identifying collective self-legislation as the sole and

[89] This analysis revolves around an anthropological recasting of the legal metaphysics proposed by Leibniz. Leibniz asserted that legitimate law is defined by teleological reference to an ideal political order, or to a condition of human perfection: to the City of God. For Leibniz, law deserving to be called natural is not based in anthropological observation. It is law that is identical with the 'laws of the best republic', and which guides human society towards the 'idea' of unity with God's own law: that is, with laws which God might freely give to himself (1885: 6). Leibniz thus saw natural law as constitutive of and deducible from a condition of human perfectibility, and he saw human perfectibility as a condition of possible likeness between humanity and God. Similarly, Wolff argued that order and perfection are internally correlated, concluding that rationally ordered government is a sign of perfectiblity (1751: 448).

[90] Kant was an early theorist of international law, endorsing an idea of transnational moral 'federality' (1977b [1797]: 211). In the French Revolution, as mentioned, Abbé Grégoire also drafted a Declaration of the Rights of Nations, which was presented in the National Convention in June 1793, at almost the same time as the Jacobin Constitution. This document tied the theory of national sovereignty to a rights-based construction of international society. It insisted that only governments 'based in equality and liberty' had claim to legitimacy (Art 8), and that constituent actors were bound to create constitutions in conformity with international law (Grewe 1988: 660–61). In 1793, Robespierre compared international abuse of rights by states to the exercise of private violence by brigands and bandits (see Redslob 1916: 286). The reciprocity between national rights and international rights was also central to the thought of Condorcet (1847: 527). In the USA at the same time, the Supreme Court stated in *Chisholm v. Georgia* (1793) that the 'national judiciary' had in part been designed to supervise the 'conduct of each state, relative to the laws of nations' (*Chisholm v. Georgia* 2 U.S. 419 (1793)).

necessarily exclusive form of human freedom. This principle was formulated by Rousseau (1966 [1762]: 54), who saw political freedom as entailing a total transformation of the human being. This was also expressed in the 1789 Declaration of the Rights of Man, stating that a society that does not guarantee general laws does not have a constitution. However, Robespierre expressed this most clearly, stating that the Revolution did not 'recognize any other legitimate government' and it rejected all polities not 'founded on liberty and equality' (1793a: 30).

In contrast to such ideas, the more sociologically oriented theorists, whose work evolved, diffusely, in the wake of 1789, began to elaborate the principle, albeit on very divergent foundations, that obligatory authorization for law must be engendered through the acts of real political subjects, formed by determinate patterns of social interaction, and seeking concretely embedded liberties. The basic impetus towards the growth of sociology as a discipline came from the idea that the generic, absolute freedoms envisioned in the Enlightenment had to be translated into real, experienced freedoms, into the freedoms of real subjects, in order to provide a foundation for political order. If freedom and social order were to be closely linked, social order needed to offer freedoms with an objectively identifiable core. More Conservative opponents of classical democracy, such as Burke and Savigny, viewed the historically existing people, defined by ancient customs and traditions, as the primary political subject, whose motivations and desires for freedom needed to be reflected as legitimate law. From a less overtly Conservative perspective, Hegel argued that the laws of the legitimate state needed to reflect ideas of liberty discretely embodied in all separate spheres of society. From a Radical standpoint, Marx accepted Rousseau's claim that legitimate laws reflect total freedoms. However, he rejected the belief that such laws could be created by simple rational subjects. He saw the collective subject of the human species, freed from economic self-estrangement, as the necessary substrate of political order (1962: 593–4).

Across the great ideological distinctions between these outlooks, early sociological criticism of revolutionary democracy converged around the claim that, at least under current conditions, society could not authorize its laws in simply unitary form. For the sociological outlook, the existing subject of society inevitably assumed a complex, historically constructed shape, and its interests and liberties could not easily be distilled into single subjects or simply binding or universally generalizable norm-giving acts. On this account, any attempt to construct a unitary subject to support society's laws relied on simplified metaphysical preconditions.

As a result, early sociological theorists implied that the institutional form of early democracy should be observed as a work of legal artifice, lacking deep-lying obligatory force, and the universalized laws of the democratic state could not be expected to find genuine compliance amongst factually existing human subjects.[91] The core sociological challenge to early democracy was that, instead of proclaiming absolute formal freedoms, it needed to find and then to institutionalize real freedoms.

1.2.2   Classical Sociology

Similar approaches to early democratic theory and early democratic institutions appeared, later, in the primary works of classical sociology, written as sociology was becoming established as an academic discipline. These works were also shaped by the idea that standard accounts of democratic government possessed only precarious social foundations. In the classical era of sociology, between circa 1880 and 1920, sociologists began to articulate the claim, inchoate in earlier social theories, that the subject of democracy could not be formally separated from society, and democracy assumed value only as it provided freedoms that reflected not metaphysical capacities, but genuinely desired societal experiences. Sociology thus coalesced around an attempt to separate human society from the formal projection of human species, and to account for society and its freedoms without relying on abstracted constructs of liberty.

The sociologists of the classical epoque also proposed a sceptical interpretation of political democracy and its legal apparatus. However, sociologists of the classical period tended to revise the more critical aspects of earlier social theorists. On one hand, sociologists of the classical era retained a broadly relativistic approach to democracy, and they insisted that the legitimating potentials of political democracy could only be explained through analysis of their multiple, contingent social foundations. On the other hand, however, such sociologists recognized that democracy was gradually emerging as an enduring system of mass integration, which reflected deep transformative processes in society. While proto-sociological theorists in post-revolutionary Europe had rejected the claim that democracy and democratic laws possessed strong sociological foundations, classical sociologists began to probe in more nuanced, affirmative fashion at the social bases of democratic law, and the freedoms which such laws articulated. As a result, classical sociologists eventually

---

[91] This view is distilled in Marx (1956 [1844]).

proposed theories of democracy that, despite their underlying relativism, clearly acknowledged the emancipatory forces in democratic politics. Combining these two impulses, classical sociologists began to account for the rise of the modern state by reconstructing democracy as a political form that afforded and institutionalized qualified liberties for social agents, yet which had developed through submerged, non-rational historical processes, and which produced freedoms and obligations in ways that lacked hard normative or rational necessity. At the core of classical sociology, in fact, was a memory of the terror of freedom in the French Revolution. Following Hegel's path, classical sociologists attempted to graft together the recognition of subjective freedom as a core element of modern society created by democracy and the attempt institutionally to insulate persons against the anxieties – the terror – which they often felt in face of this freedom. In particular, legal sociology evolved around a concept of modern law, and especially the rights contained in modern law, that observed the law as a medium for the promotion of human freedom and social integration, yet which separated the law from the strict normative demands of revolutionary thinking. Early sociology thus endorsed democracy as the political form of subjective freedom, but rejected monopolistic claims to freedom contained in much earlier democratic theory.

This fragile, contingent endorsement of democracy is apparent in the works of Durkheim.[92] Famously, Durkheim interpreted the development of the modern liberal-democratic state, accompanied by the rise of a rights-based democratic legal order, as a process caused by underlying trajectories of social differentiation. This process, he argued, was shaped by an incremental division of labour in society, and it reflected the emergence of a societal order determined by contractually constructed patterns of integration, reflecting a condition of *organic solidarity*. In this respect, Durkheim argued that the legal form of democracy was established through the incremental diminution of vertical, coercive structures of political authority; by the growing reliance of political institutions on relatively autonomous, contractual legal norms; and by the increasing moral individualization of social agents subject to the power of political institutions (1902: 28–9). He viewed the rise of the modern state and the simultaneous emergence of the individual person as a holder of rights of personal dignity and equality as correlated evolutionary characteristics of modern society (1928: 93–4).

---

[92]   On the critique of Enlightenment in Durkheim see Horowitz (1982: 354).

The modern state, Durkheim argued, had been constructed through the emergence of the contractual patterns of integration that typify modern society more widely. The modern state evolved as a set of institutions that, no longer based in vertical authority or repressive patterns of collectivity, necessarily engaged with and constructed persons in society as holders of contractual rights, and it was not strictly separable from the patterns of lateral contractual engagement that defined interpersonal interactions in society as a whole. As a result, the state necessarily generated a legal order that acknowledged all persons subject to power as holders of distinct rights and that facilitated individual exchange between persons and government bodies.[93] In this regard, democracy appears not as a simply realized political order, but as an ongoing *process of integration*, in which the form of the state is closely linked to, and shaped by, the autonomous differentiated functions of the legal system and the autonomous patterns of integration in society more generally. The rights-based, relatively uncoercive legal order of the early democratic state had developed through a historical process, in which the impetus of functional differentiation had made the centration of society around mechanical patterns of solidarity and coercive authority improbable, and in which the state was only able to function by interacting with persons on premises implying their recognition as rights holders. In each respect, Durkheim argued that the political order of modern society was formed by the fact that the law acted as a relatively informal medium of integration, and, in both their private-societal and public-political interactions, citizens were integrated in society through the exercise of legal rights, generated spontaneously by the underlying transformation of society.

Importantly, to be sure, Durkheim's functional-evolutionary account of the state did not entail any devaluation of the ethical content of the modern democratic order, and it manifestly did not imply that democratic institutions were not legitimated by broad-based societal motivations. Durkheim's thought may have been critical of the methodological rationalism that shaped the earlier revolutionary conception of democracy. Yet, as one important commentary has observed, his analysis of democracy reflected a decisive and affirmative 'sociologization of the principles of 1789', designed to place the formal-rational demands for autonomy expressed in revolutionary France in a more sociologically plausible perspective

---

[93] This is reflected in Durkheim's sociological view of administrative law, which he viewed as typical of societies that belong to a 'more elevated type' (1902: 200).

(König 2002: 37).[94] He observed the rise of democracy as the result of a process of common deliberation, in which governmental organs are linked to and legitimated by the common consciousness of individual agents through society. He acknowledged this discursive aspect of democracy quite clearly. He argued that the democratic state 'communicates by full necessity' with 'the mass of the nation', such that democracy 'appears as the political form by means of which society obtains a purer consciousness of itself' (1950: 123). In this respect, he distinguished the collective consciousness of modern society from the collective consciousness of less differentiated societies, and he claimed that modern democracy rests on the presence of a refined reflexive moral consciousness in society, able perhaps to balance out dysfunctional patterns of individualization and institutionally to preserve individualism as a source of moral integration (Cotterrell 1977: 248). As a result, he concluded, a 'society is more democratic to the degree that deliberation, reflection and critical intelligence play a more considerable role in the course of public affairs' (1950: 123). Indeed, he argued that the 'true characteristic of democracy' is twofold: it is based in 'the greatest extension of governmental consciousness', and in the 'closest communications between that consciousness' and the people as a whole (1950: 122). In these respects, he demonstrated a deep commitment to democracy as a source of moral order. Indicatively, he argued that modern society is defined by two deep emancipatory processes, which together form a 'double movement'. These processes are the formation of a 'strongly constituted' state and the growth of individualism (1928: 93). Although he viewed the institutionalization of individual freedoms primarily as an autonomous function of the law, he concluded that the law alone could not complete this process, and government was required to promote elevated patterns of solidarity.

At the same time, however, Durkheim's theory of the state was based in the conviction that the people only became the subject of democratic governance, not through direct demands for freedom, but through longer processes of reflection, collective consciousness formation and transpersonal social evolution. Democracy, he explained, could not be simply conceived as a 'discovery', which had occurred or taken shape in the nineteenth century. On the contrary, democracy could only be made explicable through

---

[94] Close in spirit to Durkheim, see the argument in Ferneuil that 'the influence of metaphysical principles' on the French Revolution had blinded its protagonists to the foundations of legitimate government and valid law (1889: 20). In a review of this book, Durkheim affirmed its attempt to explain the revolutionary principles as social facts (1890). Durkheim's critique of metaphysics is set out in Durkheim and Fauconnet (1903: 466).

analysis of its deep, socio-reflexive foundations (1950: 123). The processes underlying the rise of democracy, he concluded, were linked to embedded structural conditions – to the widening of society through the decline of feudalism, to the rise of monarchy, to the emergence of moral individualism as the dominant interactive pattern, and ultimately to the penetration of moral ideas across all society (1950: 122).

Important in this respect, in particular, is the fact that Durkheim claimed that the legal rights and liberties acquired by single persons in democratic societies had evolved as the relatively incidental results of wider processes of individualization and political differentiation, which had little to do with formulated collective interests, demands or rational constructions of freedom (1902: 403; 1950: 92). The construction of persons as rights holders was connected to the differentiation of the political system, and the liberties that arose through this construction were liberties of transpersonal nature, and they were not willed through single acts or choices. For Durkheim, to be sure, citizens have an important role to play in society, which they discharge in performing voluntary duties and in assuming individual offices in intermediary organizations and institutions (1950: 76, 87, 116). However, citizens do not necessarily appear as agents demanding or effectively giving rise to abstract general liberties, and individual persons do not assume primary responsibility for setting the basic political form of society, or for legislating broad conditions of moral order. On the contrary, citizens are likely to assume their functions in relatively localized moral-contractual settings, and they are not expected to project macro-structural liberties for all society.[95] At times, in fact, individual persons may experience alarm and alienation in face of the general rights and liberties which modern society has attributed to them. In some cases, consequently, citizens may require institutional protection for the singular life spheres in which their own particular liberties are located, and these life spheres may require specific, variable patterns of institutionalization to protect them. Like Hegel, Durkheim insisted that the corporatistic institutional residues of pre-democratic society still had an important role to play in preserving social cohesion.[96] He viewed corporations and professional groups as bodies that could cushion the subjects of democratic society against unmitigated exposure to the consequences of individualism (i.e. unmitigated economic competition), and which

---

[95] See p. 97 below.
[96] For analysis of the relation between Durkheim and Hegel close to my own see Colliot-Thélène (2010a: 82).

facilitated communication between state and society (Gautier 1994: 839). Indeed, he suggested that in modern society corporations might need to be integrated within the political system (1902: xxxi).

A similar tone of equivocating scepticism regarding democratic formation is audible in the political-sociological works of Weber. Like Durkheim, Weber focused the legal and political aspects of his sociology on examining broad processes of centralization, differentiation and individualization, triggered by the socio-economic transformations of the eighteenth century. To an even greater extent than Durkheim, however, Weber condensed his political sociology around core questions of democratic legitimacy formulated in the Enlightenment. Accordingly, he sought to explain first, why democratic institutions had developed; second, how these institutions secured legitimacy to sustain the transmission of laws across society and third, how these institutions and their legitimacy might prove to be enduring. To each of these questions, however, Weber provided somewhat ambivalent answers, reflecting a distinctive sociological construction of democratic politics.

In assessing the reasons why democratic institutions had developed, first, Weber explained that democracy had become prevalent, in part, because of demands for mass incorporation in the political system. Owing to the growth of the modern capitalist economy, the closely related dissolution of the local estate-based structure of European society and the resultant individualization of personal life horizons, modern society was marked by a deep need for institutions able to integrate diffuse, geographically expansive populations.[97] It was in this context, Weber argued, that the modern democratic state had developed. The modern state had emerged, initially, as a collective association whose formally rationalized structure meant that it was able to apply political power in a consistent, apersonal manner across society, and whose extensive bureaucratic apparatus and uniform legal order allowed it to perform integrational functions for political communities detached from their traditional historical locations (1921/2: 825). In this process, the formalization of the law played a core role in promoting integration in the state, and the emergence of a depersonalized legal system underpinned the societal expansion of state power. Ultimately, the growing institutionalization of the bureaucratic state had also led to the emergence of democracy as a pattern of government.

---

[97] For Weber, democratization and the formation of bureaucracy are always closely linked (1921/22: 567). Both processes occur as a result of the decline of estates as governance structures (1921/22: 129).

As a polity type whose institutions were able to draw together populations across large social and geographical divisions, democracy showed a particular adequacy to the extended form of modern society.[98] Indeed, parliamentary institutions, based in recognition of personal legal equality, rational uniformity and official professionalization, were distinctively proportioned to the structure of modern society, and they were able to conduct processes of social integration at an appropriately high level of abstraction and geographical extension.

For Weber, consequently, the development of parliamentary institutions was inseparably connected with the increasing bureaucratic organization of the state, and democracy usually took hold in contexts in which social integration presupposed a differentiated system of formal law and impersonal administrative rule (1921/2: 571).[99] Notably, Weber viewed the prevalence of general subjective rights that support modern democracies as linked to the bureaucratic expansion of government, and he examined subjective rights as institutions that underpin political orders in settings in which individual status claims and personal privileges have lost purchase as sources of political power. The basic construction of persons as holders of rights had been caused by the administrative expansion of the state and the depersonalization of society's political structure (1921/2: 419).[100] Overall, Weber indicated that modern society had evolved in a fashion that presupposed the existence of relatively free-standing political/administrative institutions, able to construct motivations for and uniformly to integrate society in its extended, materially divided structure. Democracy generally developed as a system of legitimation and as a pattern of organization for institutions of this kind.

Despite this acceptance of the necessary correlation between modernity and democracy, however, Weber claimed that the factual foundations of the institutions of modern democracy were often obscured by normative theoretical illusions. Indeed, his description of democracy as a mode of administration adapted to mass society did not reflect a full

---

[98] Democracy is associated with mass mobilization through parties and with integrative appeals of powerful leaders, both modes of integration typical of geographically and economically expansive societies (1921/22: 568).

[99] Bureaucratic institutions, Weber argued, are produced by the reduction of economic differences in society (1921/22: 567). Both democracy and bureaucracy are linked to the rise of capitalism (1921/22: 142).

[100] Weber wrote quite extensively about the intellectual origins of basic rights, which he associated with natural-law doctrines (see 1921/22: 498–501). But the material cause of basic subjective rights lies in the inclusionary expansion of government and the diminution in the significance of social variations in the use of government power.

affirmation of democracy. To be sure, Weber saw some practical benefits in parliamentary democracy. One benefit that he identified in constitutional democratization, clearly, was that it provided a relatively stable integrated apparatus for the ordered development of social forces. One further benefit was that, in institutionalizing mass-political participation, it helped to prevent revolutionary overthrow of government.[101] Yet Weber was also clear that democracy had evolved through processes that had little to do with the demands for shared liberty usually associated with democracy.

As a functional response to pressures of societal integration, democracy, for Weber, did not imply a form of government that presupposed the rational engagement or the meaningful participation of citizens in political processes. On the contrary, he claimed that 'the modern concept of the citizen' had been created by the 'inescapable domination of the state bureaucracy' (1921: 266–8). That is to say, persons had been legally constructed as citizens because this legal form facilitated their interaction with the state administration, and it simplified the integrational processes that had brought the state into being. Moreover, he argued that 'modern parliaments' had developed primarily because they help to generate and demonstrate the 'minimum of internal agreement' amongst persons who are 'dominated by the instruments of bureaucracy' (1921/2: 851). In both respects, he viewed the political form of democracy not as a focus of collective freedom, but as an effective instrument of social coordination, defined primarily by administrative functions. Consequently, he claimed that the legal obligations imposed by democratic institutions are not to be seen as expressions of shared liberties or rational reflection.[102] He observed the growth of parliamentary institutions as part of a wider formalistic pathology of social rationalization, which actually eradicated experiences of particular freedom and autonomy. He construed the condition of 'rational life-conduct', which he associated with modern democracy, as an experience, not of elected liberty, but rather of fateful subjection (1920: 203). Contra the basic normative emphases of democratic theory, therefore, Weber suggested that democratic institutions had evolved without a deep foundation in deliberated human interests or in an articulated human will. Moreover, the legitimacy of democratic institutions was of a fragile nature, and the claim of democracy to protect common freedoms

---

[101] He saw the threat of the 'democracy of the street' arising in situations where parties are weak and weakly rationalized (1921/22: 868).

[102] For Weber, modern law is integrally connected with capitalism, and it creates a legal order that satisfies needs for legal security in a widening monetary system (1921/22: 506).

and to generate substantially binding legal obligations was illusory. Above all, therefore, the primary association of democracy and collective freedom was not sociologically tenable.

In discussing how democratic institutions secure legitimacy for laws, second, Weber claimed that laws obtain legitimacy in democratic systems primarily because of the rise of rule-determined rationalism, which he viewed as expressed, most prominently, through the consolidation of formalized legal systems and the expansion of the bureaucratic apparatus of modern states (1921: 339). Modern parliaments, he claimed, are able to presume legitimacy for the laws that they impose because they are created and implemented in highly formalized procedures, on tightly regulated foundations, which means that, at different locations in society, persons subject to law can be persuaded that these laws are formally authoritative.[103] In this respect, however, Weber also identified a deep paradox in the structure of parliamentary democracy.

On one hand, as discussed, he argued that parliamentary democracy first developed because of the fact that modern mass societies depend on institutions capable of integrating populations in environments in which the local and intermediary institutions of premodern societies have disappeared (1921/2: 519). Accordingly, parliamentary democracy had stabilized itself by producing a formal system of legality, in which laws were legitimated by technical procedures and professionalized judiciaries, that did not rely on personal chains of command. As a technical, impersonal order, parliamentary democracy was able to secure motivations for the economically disparate classes and regionally diffuse groups whose emergence characterized modern social order. In fact, Weber claimed that the 'belief in legality', separate from local, familial or personal loyalties and affiliations, and compliance with procedurally correct statutes, constituted the 'most frequent form of legitimacy' in modern society, and this pattern of legitimacy was reflected in the growth of parliamentary democracy (1921/2: 19).[104] Parliamentary democracy, in sum, distils the wider rationality of modern society, and it cements a formal, depersonalized legal order as the basis of its legitimacy. As a result, the formalization of the law plays a key role in the institutionalization of the political system.

---

[103] On the essentially bureaucratic nature of parliamentary representation see Weber (1921/22: 330, 339).

[104] As Andreas Anter has observed, 'the belief in legality' underscores the rise of modern political institutions, and the confidence of members of society in legal institutions is foundational for the stability of modern social order (1995: 95).

On the other hand, Weber was always sceptical about the capacity of formalized democratic procedures to integrate complex, materially divided modern societies. He argued that the formal techniques used in parliamentary democracies for generating and legitimating laws were, in some circumstances, insufficiently robust to draw together the polarized classes and factions that modern society contains.

First, Weber claimed that the integrational power of formal law itself is always subject to certain limits. Notably, law does not originate in formal procedures. It is only in relatively recent historical periods that law has been created by rational, professional means (1921/2: 505). In fact, although crucial to the legitimacy of modern society, formal law can be seen as reflecting a diminished mode of social association, in which individual agents are forced into compliance with insubstantial normative imperatives and trapped in cycles of purposive action that are not inherently valuable. The legitimacy of formal law is always a necessary but depleted mode of legitimacy, in which human action is structured by instrumental purposes and more authentic expressions of human autonomy and human freedom are suppressed (1921/2: 439). Moreover, in periods of social upheaval, refoundation or normative uncertainty, formal law alone is unlikely to construct a cohesive integrational order for society. In such situations, Weber indicated, alternative patterns of legal formation are likely to evolve, implanting stronger, affectual motivations into law (1921/2: 497). Despite the central importance of rational positive law for modern society, the law cannot entirely renounce all reliance on personal substances, and in some situations the law requires immediate personal authorization. Although democracy had evolved as a mode of integration distinctive of modern societies, it could not always rely on its own apersonal formalism to perform its inclusionary functions.

Second, Weber argued quite generally that the institutions of parliamentary democracy were always overstrained by the legitimational/ integrative demands channelled towards them from the complexly fissured societies, in which they were situated, and whose inhabitants they were expected to integrate and to unify (Anter 1995: 74). For Weber, as discussed, the primary function of parliamentary institutions lay in the fact that they were required to integrate large societal constituencies. As a result, in parliamentary polities, political parties necessarily assumed particular importance as organizations for incorporating society into the political system. Parties, in fact, first developed in parliamentary systems as core organs for solidifying broad support for the political system, and for linking social agents to the political centre of society. Indeed, wherever an elected parliament became the focus of social integration, political parties acquired new dimensions and new obligations, and they were transformed into large-scale mechanisms for producing electoral results, for recruiting support for governments, and for coordinating exchanges between state and society as a whole. For Weber, the shift from the patronage-based party to the modern political party, acting as a highly mobilized electoral 'machine', was central to the rise of the modern political system (1921/2: 862). As parties assumed more expansive integrational functions, however, the formal-legal order of parliamentary institutions lost some of its force as a primary system of integration. In fact, as they expanded, party-political organizations relied increasingly on strong leaders to mobilize support, and they always tended towards the promotion of 'plebiscitary democracy', so that purely parliamentary bodies and parliamentary procedures assumed a more secondary position in the overall integration of society. Weber argued that such leadership was exemplified by Gladstone in England, who, during the franchise reforms of the late nineteenth century, appeared as a 'dictator of the electoral battlefield', able to maintain support in his party by winning votes across the country (1921/2: 843–5).

On this basis, Weber expressed a deep scepticism about modern democracy. He concluded that the essential functions of mass-integration that are accorded to parliamentary organs necessarily mean that parliamentary democracy generates functional demands that its institutions are unable to satisfy, and it inevitably assumes authoritarian, Caesaristic characteristics (1921/2: 862). Indeed, he stated that, in modern parliamentary democracies, parliamentary institutions do not form the centre of the political system, and their primary function is not the immediate democratic representation of social actors. On the contrary, the main function of parliamentary institutions is to provide a forum in which political leadership elites can be trained, and it is such elites, not parliament itself, that assume the pivotal role in integrating society as a whole. If parliament is to fulfil its integration functions, in short, it must be oriented towards the formation of national political elites, able to reach out to constituencies in society and to integrate different social actors through qualities of leadership. Consequently, the formation of elites must be the primary objective of parliamentary institutions, so that the representative responsibilities of parliament lose emphasis. Eventually, in his direct interventions in constitutional debate, Weber expressed great enthusiasm for presidential democracy, and he viewed the office of President as assuming vital integrational functions for society as a whole (1921: 468, 482).

Overall, Weber identified two reasons why parliamentary democracy did not possess adequate inclusionary power for modern society. First, he claimed that parliamentary institutions could not always satisfy the legitimational demands and the requirements for cohesion that characterized rapidly evolving, increasingly pluralistic and differentiated mass societies. Ultimately, he implied, parliaments only played on a secondary role in integrating their populations, and they contributed to this process, primarily, through elite formation. Second, he claimed that the formal legal order of democracy was itself too weak to galvanize entire populations, and it needed to be supplemented by more vital patterns of obligation, command and motivation. The impersonality of modern law resulted from the fact that it was required to secure integrative motivations for large, extensive societies. But, in some conditions, this objective could only be achieved by law that was suffused with a deeply personal, mobilizing appeal (1921: 508). In this second respect, Weber reiterated the long-standing sociological critique of democracy – namely, that laws produced in democratic states do not have a strong obligatory power, that the legitimacy of democratic law is always rather fictionalized and abstracted, and that it is illusory to think that democratic laws reflect the interests of actually existing societies, or factually manifest collective subjects. In fact, he concluded, the legal order of parliamentary democracy was unable to capture and fully to express the complex claims of factually existing populations, whose will it was supposed to represent. For Weber, the legal order of democracy was produced by social pressures caused by the original differentiation of modern society. Yet, in some circumstances, this legal order was unable to incorporate the multiple sectors existing in mass society in one unifying, integrational structure.

In considering the question of how democratic institutions might endure, third, Weber claimed that, if democracy were to survive, it required stronger foundations of legitimacy than those created solely by parliamentary bodies, by typical democratic procedures and by formal legal systems. For democracy to become fully solidified, it was essential for democratic institutions to supplement formally abstracted resources of legitimacy by promoting deeper, more visceral or affectual appeals than those produced through rationalized or rule-determined legal procedures. The functions of legitimation and integration attached to democratic institutions, including legal institutions, could only be accomplished if they were governed by powerful charismatic leaders, capable of embodying *charismatic rationality* – that is, leaders who possessed the ethical responsibility required to identify the long-term interests of the polity, and to motivate diverse societal actors to pursue these interests (1921: 554, 558).[105] On this account, the democratic political system could only cement its integrative position in society to the extent that its legitimacy was sustained by motivations based not in the primary norms of democratic procedure, but in the extraordinary appeals of charismatic leaders (1921/2: 140). In this respect, Weber implied that the charismatic rationality of leading politicians can generate collectively recognized purposes, which possess higher, more categorical value than the formal, instrumental purposes on which the rationality of parliament is founded.

In each aspect of his analysis of democracy, Weber came to an aporetic conclusion. He argued that democracy was not constructed on the basis of deep-lying human emphases or demands for freedom. On the contrary, it evolved as an order of integration, through the relatively autonomous expansion of the political system, caused by the underlying transformation of society more widely. However, he also argued that the political system of democracy was inherently unstable, and it relied on affectual, non-rational, at times intensely politicized motivations in order to perform its basic integrational functions.

The two great classical sociologists arrived at some rather similar conclusions about democracy. Both argued that democracy is a mode of political-systemic organization, which has evolved as the consequence of deep-lying formative dynamics in society, and which resides on fragile foundations. Durkheim was significantly more affirmative about democracy than Weber, and he argued that democracy reflected a morally elevated pattern of social integration (see Prager 1981: 938). Self-evidently, however, both perceived very distinctive advantages in democracy, and both saw democracy as a necessary response to wider patterns of individualization and social transformation. Neither showed strong affection for theoretical positions that obviously rejected democracy. Nonetheless, both Durkheim and Weber indicated that parliamentary democracy was a highly uncertain political order, which evolved for reasons that had little to do with conceptual constructions of human freedom, and both saw the democratic ideal of governance by acts of a subjectivized popular will as illusory.

It is no coincidence, in consequence, that many sociologists who followed Durkheim and Weber accentuated their sociological scepticism in the face of democracy. Notably, the main backbone of sociological reflection from the late nineteenth century up to 1945 intensified the more

---

[105] See for comment Breuer (1991: 175).

critical components of classical sociological reflections on democracy. Subsequent theorists concluded that modern democracy was incapable of making good on its promises of human freedom, and that it did not provide stable foundations for social cohesion and legitimacy. These ideas resonated through the thought of Michels, Freyer and Gehlen.[106] As discussed below, it was only after 1945 that sociological theorists began to adopt a less sceptical attitude to democratic formation.

1.3 Legal Sociology and Analysis of Democracy: How Was It Different?

From the aftermath of the French Revolution onwards, sociology evolved as a discipline with certain common attitudes to the rise of democracy, and with certain common claims concerning the social premises of law's legitimacy and obligatory power. In fact, it is possible to identify an outlook close to a distinctive legal-sociological approach to the early democratic state, elements of which can be found at all points across the political spectrum.

First, earlier sociological analysis of democracy usually approached democratic political systems from a perspective that was sceptical about formally generalized claims regarding legal validity and formally generalized concepts of political legitimacy. Inherent in the earlier sociological approach to democracy was the sense that societies obtain integrity, and political institutions obtain legitimacy, through complexly structured motivations, and that, consequently, laws can acquire and presume legitimacy in a multiplicity of ways: there is no categorically binding, essentially rational source for law's obligatory force. For early sociologists, the idea that the law is supported by a unitary citizen, seeking unified and general freedoms, always appeared improbable and fictitious. On the sociological view, the primary indicator of the legitimacy of a law is not the extent to which it enshrines rationally acceded collective liberties, but the extent to which, in a given conjuncture, it generates sustainably cohesive

---

[106] As discussed, Michels argued that democracy necessarily had a tendency to create oligarchy. Gehlen claimed that the bureaucratic character of the state undermined its claim to consensual legitimacy and forced it to extract legitimacy from pure economic strategy – the 'dictatorship of the standard of living' (1963: 262). Freyer concluded that democracy should be seen as a condition, not 'of government of people by people' but rather of 'the administration of things' (1955: 101). He also argued that the rational constitutional formation of political power in the sense of modern democracy destroys political legitimacy (1955: 68).

social structures, which usually results from law's function as a *medium of normative integration*. As a result, thinkers in a recognizably sociological lineage proposed a theory of legitimacy in law and governance that was deeply committed to the *idea of contingency*: that is, such theories indicated that the legitimacy of laws is always contextual, dependent on broader societal circumstances, lacking fully binding foundations, and also inherently precarious. For this reason, classical sociology converged around the claim that law acts on its own as a primary source of democratic formation. Across a range of early sociological perspectives, the law appeared not as the expression of collectively reflected freedoms, but as a relatively autonomous, differentiated sphere of society. From this perspective, modern society relied on law for positive functions of social integration, which drove the construction of democratic institutions. The positive autonomy of law thus emerged as a core element in sociological analyses of early democracy.

Second, earlier sociological analysis of democracy commonly implied that the obligatory force of law is the result, in part, of the experiential aspect of human society. On this perspective, law acquires legitimacy through its interwovenness with dimensions of lived historical consciousness, which cannot be captured in simple normative formulae. Indeed, one implication of the sociological approach is that law can construct liberties in many different ways, and freedom in law can be experienced very differently by different agents, at different times and in different places. There is no one citizen whose freedoms provide a basis for all legitimate laws, and, above all, it cannot be assumed that freedoms are rationally prior to the actual experience of them. For early sociology, freedom lies not in the compliance with a pre-existing norm, but in the experience of freedom – freedom must be an experience that people *actually want* and freedoms must be freedoms that people *actually wish to exercise*: in this respect, early sociology reacted critically against metaphysical thinking and early democratic thinking at the same time. Early sociological understandings of democracy often implied that democracy's claim to possess a monopoly of legitimacy, excluding alternative accounts of human liberty, could itself be seen as authoritarian, or at least as unreflectingly oppressive.

As exemplified by Durkheim and Weber, sociological theories of democracy have widely indicated that the formation of democratic society might release freedoms that members of society may easily, in some settings, find *unbearable*. For this reason, the inhabitants of societies in a process of democratic formation may require some institutional protection from the experiences of atomized liberty and customary disintegration generated through, or in conjunction with, the rise of the democratic state (see Durkheim 1930 [1897]: 439). The governmental system has an obligation to secure the institutionalization of individual liberty, which is just as powerful as any obligation to secure liberty itself. In fact, liberty only becomes liberty through its institutionalization: for much early sociology, it is not the abstract collective manifestation but the stable institutional organization of liberty that forms the primary indicator of governmental legitimacy. Durkheim, in particular, made this point emphatically clear in claiming that the institutionalization of singular spheres of liberty, within localized parts of society, is of the most vital importance in modern differentiated societies. This was reflected in his analysis of professions, and the patterns of contractual institutionalization that, he argued, characterize professional associations in societies marked by highly developed organic solidarity (1902: 206). This was also articulated in his assertion that social liberties are most adequately realized when individuals take steps 'to concentrate and to specialize' their freedoms, and to seek realization of freedoms within a small organizational horizon: such specialization of freedom becomes necessarily more refined the more elevated and differentiated society becomes (1902: 396–7). For Durkheim, consequently, one core function of the state is to ensure that individual liberties are given adequate institutional support and protection (1950: 99).

For these reasons, classical sociology was strongly committed to the avoidance of revolutionary conflicts unleashed by the growth of individualistic economies, polarized societies, and categorical constructions of freedom. Tellingly, Durkheim was clear that individualistic patterns of association do not always have beneficial outcomes. He argued that sociology needed to concern itself with finding 'moral brakes' to 'regulate economic life' (1928: 267).[107] Similarly, Weber was deeply preoccupied with

---

[107] See the correlation between individualization, economic pressure, and despair in Durkheim's analysis of suicide (1930 [1897]: 283). On the function of organized corporations in palliating individual exposure to economic pathologies, see Durkheim (1902: vii, xvii). In this respect, Durkheim showed great enthusiasm for a corporatist variant on classical parliamentary democracy. He implied that it was necessary to reinforce the role of intermediary organizations, such as corporations and professional bodies, located 'outside the state, but submitted to its actions', in order to provide robust institutional protection for persons in a state of individual economy freedom (1930 [1897]: 437–9). Consequently, he saw a widening of the organizational periphery of the state as a means of institutionalizing individual liberty. See comment on the sociology of loneliness in Schluchter (1979: 251). In similar spirit, Freyer argued that 'alienation' was the 'secret concept of the nineteenth century', around which social theory evolved. Freyer saw charismatic legitimacy as the quality

finding ways to soften the antagonisms of modern society. Indeed, his idea of democracy as a system of elite-led integration was intended, in part, to ensure that democracy did not assume radicalized revolutionary form. Importantly, he observed charismatic leadership as possessing a distinctive revolutionary quality, standing outside and subverting established legal orders and helping to preserve social integration in settings in which formal law did not exist (1921/2: 142). He thus viewed the creation of plebiscitary government as a means both to preserve the vital, motivational force of charisma, yet also to reduce its revolutionary volatility, using revolutionary legitimacy to instil integrational powers in the political system that might help avert revolution (1921/2: 156–7).[108] Both Durkheim and Weber implied that extreme societal unrest could only be avoided if the government, aided by sociology, showed full regard for the experiential realities of those subject to its power. Weber, in particular, claimed that the legal order of democracy could only perform its integrational functions if sustained by non-legal, affectual sources of integrative power.

On this basis, third, the early sociological analysis of democracy implied that democracy is always a rather improbable form. From the standpoint of classical sociology, the legal foundations of democracy had developed through essentially contingent processes, and there is no absolutely compelling subjective reason to presume that the institutional order of democracy must remain unchanging. For this perspective, democracy developed through the differentiated geographical and functional widening of society, deeply linked to the differentiation and expansion of the modern economy, and concepts of democratic rule evolved to stabilize society in its extended form. However, this outlook implied that there is a strong likelihood that, if democracy persists as a generalized mode of social organization, its actual institutional structure will be subject to variation. It is no coincidence, for example, that the theories of democracy proposed by classical sociologists, notably Durkheim and Weber, endorsed a system of democratic rule whose organizational pattern differed markedly from classical parliamentary or representative systems. As discussed, Durkheim retained a strong corporatistic element in his preferred model of the democratic polity.[109] As discussed, similarly, Weber incorporated a pronounced symbolic dimension in his theory of democracy. In each

---

of a political system in which social integration occurred through archaic, deeply affectual appeals, able to establish more solid structures of inclusion than rationally driven integration processes (1976 [1957]: 206).

[108] In agreement see Breuer (1994: 145).

[109] See p. 86.

instance, the variance from a more standard template of democracy was due to the fact that both Durkheim and Weber showed concern for the lived experiences of persons and the conditions of institutionalization under democracy. In each respect, they suggested that the human subject of democracy could not be captured or represented in standardized legal norms, and it may necessitate atypical institutions and atypical patterns of inclusion.

In addition to these points, classical sociological accounts of democracy contained a further distinctive feature, which was less expressly or intentionally formulated, but which throws very important light on the rise of democratic institutions. As discussed, the constitutional doctrines of the Enlightenment were normally supported by the principle, formalized most paradigmatically by Rousseau and Kant, that, as an aggregate of citizens, *the nation* is the essential foundation of legitimate rule, and that a polity acquires legitimacy if it is founded in laws that a nation gives to itself. On this model, a polity becomes legitimate if persons (citizens) in a given society (nation) recognize the law as law which, if they adequately exercised their moral and rational faculties, they would be inclined to give to themselves: if those persons to whom laws are applied can rationally identify their own subjective freedoms in these laws. As mentioned, this idea was reconstructed as constitutional doctrine by Sieyès, and other early constitutionalists who claimed that a legitimate polity must be founded immediately in the rational will of the nation, and that the laws of this polity must translate the will of the people into objectively binding norms.[110]

Quite fundamentally, however, the discipline of sociology evolved as a body of inquiry that challenged the *societal abstraction* of the ideas of collective political subjectivity in classical models of democracy. Early sociology expressly refuted the idea that human freedoms could be concentrated around the form of the nation, defined as a simply existing collective subject. In this regard, sociology fixed squarely on the central paradox in the conception of national democracy.

On one hand, for example, Durkheim argued that democratic political systems, defined by collective inclusion in government and distribution of legal rights through society, began to emerge as a legal-political form as societies were released from relatively authoritarian, pre-modern organizational structures. To this extent, Durkheim identified a close correlation between the formation of democracies and the formation of nations. Indeed, he saw the figure of the citizen as a figure that promoted

---

[110] See pp. 17–8.

the expansion of national society, separating the governmental consciousness of society from local or sectoral particularities.[111] Simultaneously,
however, Durkheim argued that the rise of democratic legal and political
institutions should not be seen, in some classical normative fashion, as the
result of acts in which persons in society collectively laid claim to rights
and freedoms, to which they possessed inherent shared entitlements. On
the contrary, he described the growth of democratic institutional forms
as the result of a progressive functional expansion of the political system,
shaped by the growing autonomy of law, in which the political system constructed the persons affected by its functions in less coercive terms.[112] The
expansion of the political system, thus, was causally prior to the formation
of nations and national citizens, and the political subject of democracy
developed as the political system extended its functions into society, linked
to more general processes of institutionalization. The growth of democracy was in fact, in part, a result of the evolutionary dimensions of the
political system itself. Of course, Durkheim possessed a distinctive confidence in modern society, and he observed the emergence of democratic
institutions as sustained and necessitated by wider processes of moral
integration. Nonetheless, the growth of a society based on liberal social
and political values could not be conceived as the outcome of deliberately
determined processes (1918: 143). In consequence, Durkheim argued that
the people, supposedly the central agent in democratic order and the central producer of democratic freedom, was not a strongly implicated actor
in the actual rise of democracy. On the contrary, the national people often
figured as a relatively marginal apparition in the emergence of democratic
society, which was created by deep-lying functional processes.

This complex dialectic of national democracy is still more visible in the
works of Weber.

First, Weber was quite evidently a nationalist. He manifestly viewed
the formation of nations, in which social agents structured their actions
outside local environments and organizations, as a defining hallmark of a
modern society, integrally linked to the emergence of integrated exchange
economies. Moreover, he identified affiliation to a given nation as a (if not
the) defining source of motivation in modern society, clearly assuming
greater force than affiliation to any other social grouping characteristic

---

[111] For Durkheim, the fact that citizens take part 'from afar' in political deliberations and government measures is the fact that 'truly constitutes democracy' (1950: 120).

[112] He argued that democracy and individual rights develop in parallel as the state experiences
a 'growing extension of its responsibilities' (1950: 99).

of modern society (including economic class), or than any other source of social obligation.[113] In fact, to the extent that he felt a strong sympathy for democracy, he advocated an expansion of democratic institutions, and particularly of democratic constitutional norms, because he viewed this process as vital for reinforcing the unity of the nation and for drawing members of national societies into more immediate experiences of cohesion.[114] He thus saw the integration of the nation as the basic function of the law. Indicatively, for example, in late-Imperial Germany, Weber declared strong support for the political integration of the German people through internal democratic reforms (1921: 247). He did this for many reasons, some ethical, some more functional. One vital reason for this, however, was that he perceived such integration as a precondition for the consolidation and reinforcement of the German nation in the system of global political-economic competition: internal political integration appeared as a crucial precondition for external political and economic expansion.[115] To this extent, Weber clearly shared common ground with earlier theorists of classical democracy, and he proposed a functionalist theory of popular sovereignty, viewing a political system in which members of the national people are able to express their most dynamic forces as an ideal system.

At the same time, however, Weber indicated that the system of national cohesion created by parliamentary democracy was not very strong, and parliamentary democracies could not always generate enduring obligations amongst national citizens. Structurally, as discussed, he argued that democracy was often undermined by its failure to bind together the populations of national societies in robustly constructed identities. Importantly, at the very core of Weber's work is the implication that modern society itself does not of itself actually exist as a unified structural order: for Weber, there is no material reality that can simply be defined as *society* – society

---

[113] At one level, Weber's idea of the politician, endowed with strong integrative characteristics, is intended as a figure with nationally unifying force. Generally, Weber made no secret of his nationalism (1921: 25). However, he took pains very strictly to differentiate national belonging from ethnic belonging (1921/22: 528).

[114] Repeatedly, for example, Weber expressed concern about the fact that in Germany the process of nation-making, linked to the rise of the middle class as a dominant social group, was being held up by the undemocratic political system. Democratization was needed, therefore, as part of a nation-making process, enabling the 'bourgeois classes' to assume their rightful position as 'bearers of the national political interests' (1921: 23).

[115] Weber often associated democratization and democratic culture with reinforcement of Germany's status as a world power (1921: 23). In particular, this was why the role of parliament as a training ground for elites, which could promote Germany's interests in the international arena, seemed so important to him (1921: 475).

only exists as a set of dispositions in the minds of the distinct subjects who, individually, constitute society.[116] There are of course, he indicated, certain commonly observable tendencies in society, revealed for example in patterns of nation building, institutional consolidation and political centralization. However, society does not exist as a collective/material entity, with a collective/material structure. As a result, society is originally and essentially founded, and it can only gain cohesion in, individual subjective motivations, and it only assumes perceptible structural form as the motivations of diverse subjects converge in coordinated expectations, in shared patterns of action and in overarching institutions, commonly recognized as legitimate (1921/2: 19).[117]

On this basis, Weber concluded that the legitimacy of a political system depends on its ability to solidify shared integrational motivations in the minds of persons at different positions across society. Democracy is only formed as a distinct social phenomenon under circumstances in which members of society, subjectively, are prepared to recognize the laws of democratic institutions as binding (see Anter 1995: 154). Indeed, democracy only evolves as it solidifies a particular set of motivations in the minds of social actors, binding them together in democratic patterns of political behaviour. However, as discussed, Weber was always of the view that parliamentary democracy was undermined by its inability to produce an arresting mass of motivations for the factionalized populations of modern society. In consequence, he advocated that a system of democracy should be established in which a strong presidential executive stands alongside parliamentary institutions, and in which supplementary functions of integration are performed by particularly selected leadership elites. As discussed, he observed the democratic parliament, primarily, as a school for training national elites, who, on acceding to high-ranking offices, would be responsible for integrating the nation domestically and for securing and advancing the interests of the nation in international politics (1921: 343). The most distinguished members of such elites would be figures in possession of distinct *charismatic* qualities, able to instil cohesion in, and to mobilize, national populations by appealing to and shaping their motivations at an affectual, deeply emotional level.

---

[116] This radical subjectivism is at the methodological core of Weber's sociology (1921/22: 16–17). See discussion of the implications of this in Gurvitch (1940: 19); Tyrell (1994).

[117] For Weber, sociology is the science of correlated social action. Social action only occurs through the 'comprehensible orientation' of the behaviour of one or more 'individual persons' (1921/22: 6).

On this foundation, Weber interpreted parliamentary democracy as a fundamentally paradoxical political system. On one hand, he indicated, democracy had been born as societies assumed the form of nations, and its integrational functions were determined by this context. On the other hand, however, he implied that parliamentary democracy could not actually presuppose the prior material existence of a people, acting in nationally unified form. In appealing to the classical ideas of national self-legislation resulting from the philosophical traditions of the Enlightenment, democracy could only fabricate a very artificial account of itself. In fact, the primary function of democratic institutions, for Weber, was not to translate the demands of an existing national people, or an existing group of citizens, into a unified system of law, but rather *to create the people*, and to imprint onto post-traditional society a powerfully unifying and integrative ethic of nationhood (Weichlein 2007: 107). He perceived democracy as a political system, not of *collective self-legislation*, but of *collective integration*, which is itself required to engender the people – the nation – through acts of visceral, charismatic motivation.

In this respect, like Durkheim, Weber inverted the classical ideal of national democracy: instead of endorsing a system in which the people, as sovereign citizens, construct their own representative institutions, he endorsed a system in which representative institutions construct the people from which they extract their legitimacy. In diametrical opposition to early democratic theory, he argued that democracy cannot be formed by a pre-existing people, acting as the primary law-giving subject of the political system. The people can only provide legitimacy for the political system in a socio-psychological dimension, which is specifically not expressed in collective acts of rational self-legislation, and which must be strategically generated, by charismatic leaders, within the political system. On Weber's view, parliamentary democracy always remained deficient, and it failed to bind together members of the nation as a solidly unified subject. It was only as a machine for establishing charismatic leadership elites that democracy could fulfil its integrative functions. In effect, Weber argued that democracy could only become real if its subjective foundation were created by collectively constructed, partly affectual, non-democratic motivations: democratic society could only become real if its laws were sustained, in part, by unreflected experiences of subjective unity, and the basic function of democracy was to sustain such experiences of unity. Democracy, in short, is not legitimated by the people – *it is legitimated by its construction of the people*.

In the key positions of classical sociology, in sum, the idea of democracy as a reflected condition of national-subjective self-legislation was dismissed, or at least strongly relativized. Most particularly, these outlooks converged around the claim that the essential normative core of democracy – the idea of the people as a body of self-legislating citizens, seeking shared liberties – is not an objectively given presence in modern society, and modern society necessarily contains many peoples, with often sharply counterposed political interests, that cannot be condensed into a unitary model of citizenship. To be sure, classical sociologists admitted the presence of the citizen as a legally protected construct, engaging in some public practices.[118] But the leading outlooks in classical sociology observed that most democracies developed without or before the people, and they were required either to fictionalize the existence of the people, or even to address the *absence of the people* as their most fundamental problem.[119] On this basis, early sociological theory appreciated, at least intuitively, that the normative apparatus of democracy was not a reflection of a factual reality, and that democratic norms of governance such as national sovereignty and participatory citizenship appeared as formulae that sustained the emergence of the national political system, yet which were not correlated with a given societal condition. Over a longer period of time, it became a commonplace in political sociology and in more sociologically reflected lines of constitutional theory that modern parliamentary democracy was centred around a fiction, an *absent people*, and the primary obligation of democratic institutions was to translate this *absence* into a material form.[120]

1.4   Legal Sociology and the Paradoxes of Democracy

In many respects, sociological analysis of democracy proved far more accurate in its accounts of democratic institutional formation than earlier or concurrent normative discussions of the early democratic state. In

---

[118] As mentioned, Durkheim argued that the citizen has an important role to play in different institutions, for example of a professional or educational nature, which allow citizens to participate in governmental deliberations, and link the citizen to governmental consciousness (1950: 76, 116, 120). Marshall clearly perceived the importance of the active aspect of citizenship – which he saw as including the 'right to participate in the exercise of political power' (1992 [1950]: 8). However, this aspect was not in the forefront of his inquiry, and he conceived the citizen more generally as part of a process of social integration (28). Parsons accentuated the importance of political rights of citizens as elements of social integration (1965).

[119] See recent reiteration of this view in Colliot-Thélène (2010b: 162).

[120] For example, Duguit described the idea of the state as a 'sovereign collective person' as a construct based 'in worthless metaphysical concepts' (1923: 49). At the same time, Schmitt argued that parliamentary governments were sustained by fictitious, metaphysical constructions of their citizens as harmonious collectives (1923: 45).

fact, analyses of democracy in classical sociology came close to grasping the basic historical paradoxes of democracy set out above. Clearly, both Durkheim and Weber intuitively perceived that the evolution of democracy was necessarily a slow process, and it could not be made reality in a single historical event, based in some collective voluntaristic act. Moreover, both Durkheim and Weber were aware that democracy was not a political system whose realization could be propelled by single political theories, or which could be sustained by static, rational normative designs. Both argued, quite expressly, that classical theories of democracy, assuming that constitutional democracy reflected generalized ideas of liberty, were simplified and misguided, and that much of the legitimating substance of democracy was concentrated at a socially submerged, non-articulated level. In addition, both Durkheim and Weber claimed that most accounts of the rise of democracy, which tended to construe democracy as a strategy for restricting the authority of monarchical states, were historically erroneous. Central to their comprehension of the modern democratic state was the claim that democracy had evolved as a legal/political order that intensified an already pervasive process of socio-political centralization, which manifestly heightened the authority of political institutions,[121] and which replaced the localized, acentric, corporatistic structure of early modern society. For both theorists, the rise of democracy was part of a broader process of functional differentiation, in which the political system cemented itself above the functionally diffuse conditions of pre-modern order. In each respect, classical sociological theories perceived the essential contingency of democracy, and this insight clearly provided a paradigm for comprehension of the actual emergence of democratic institutions.

The importance of classical legal sociology for capturing the rise of democracy became most visible in its appreciation of the deepest paradox of democracy – the fact that democracy is defined as government by the people, but it in fact assumed material form largely in the absence of the people, or through its own systemic construction of the people. This insight was central to the basic emergence of sociology as an interpretive method, standing against the more deductive reflections of the Enlightenment. As sociology reacted against the formal constructions of the Enlightenment, it necessarily began to perceive that the most central political assumption

---

[121] Notably, Durkheim claimed repeatedly that the rise of democracy, and the emergence of constitutional rights structures attached to democracy, greatly increased the power of state institutions (1950: 93). By this, he implied that state power expanded as it interacted with persons in society on a complexly articulated, contractual basis. Obviously, Weber's theory of the convergence of democracy and Caesarism has parallel implications.

of the Enlightenment – the idea of the national people as a self-legislating body of citizens – was projected in chimerical fashion, and that it relied on an essentially metaphysical reduction of the people in its factual-historical form. At the centre of classical sociology was a denial that legitimate normative order can radiate from a universally imputed human consciousness, concentrated around the single idea of the citizen. Instead, normative order appeared as the result of relatively autonomous legal functions. The citizen appears in the sociological lineage as a paradoxical fictional construct, which the governing order invariably presupposes, yet which is actually materialized by the governing order itself.

Nonetheless, if early sociological theory was defined by its intuitive appreciation of the paradoxical elements in the modern democratic state, sociological inquiry itself also evolved, quite centrally, around a series of unusual and enduring paradoxes. In fact, sociology took shape as a discipline that, in the final analysis, shied away from the implications of its most central definitional insights and intuitions. In its key formulations, classical sociology was ultimately marked by the decision to accept and to re-articulate the constructions whose fictitious formality it had identified. Strikingly, classical sociology itself finally reaffirmed many of the core fictions of democratic political order.

1.4.1   The Dream of Political Society

At an obvious level, as early sociology repudiated many of the claims of the Enlightenment, it rejected the principle that the modern state was created by simple acts of popular authority. As a result, it dismissed the semi-metaphysical construction of the state as a dominant centre of rational liberty. In particular, early sociological reflection tended to reject the volitional-universalist conception of political system as a primary focus of social freedom, and it accentuated ways in which freedoms were linked to formative processes outside politics, in different social spheres.

In this respect, however, early sociology itself reflected and re-articulated a persistent paradox. This paradox was manifest in the fact that, despite its own intuitions, sociology was not willing to renounce the central position accorded to the political system in society. Despite interpreting the historical formation of the state on the basis of a theory of differentiation, early sociologists usually ascribed a particular societal dominance to the political system, and they typically viewed modern society as a distinctively *political society*. Of course, there are exceptions to this amongst classical and post-classical sociologists. For example, Proudhon was clearly not a statist theorist. Eugen Ehrlich set out a sociology of law that expressly relativized the importance of the state as a source of law (1989 [1913]: 124). Very importantly, later, Georges Gurvitch imagined a democratic order in which the rule of law penetrated into society through pluralistic organizational forms, situated in different sectors of societal exchange and production (1929: 420–22). More generally, however, early sociology retained a clear and often emphatic *political* focus. Most notably, early sociology retained the idea that the political system was supported by patterns of political experience, motivation and compliance that were relatively constant across different societal domains, suggesting that all parts of society depended on the political system for their cohesion. Moreover, early sociology argued that law acquires legitimacy as it is infused with political content. In fact, early sociologists even echoed the classical claim that a democratic polity has the particular distinction that it can promote social cohesion and social freedom more effectively than other types of polity: that a democracy possesses an eminently political substance, and its integrational force is heightened by this fact.

This emphatic political dimension in classical sociology was closely linked to the relation between early sociology and positivism. As mentioned, alongside its opposition to early democratic theory, classical sociology was marked, methodologically, by an equally intense opposition to the legal and political implications of positivism. Of course, early sociology was itself close to positivism, and Durkheim in particular is usually placed in the positivist category (see Durkheim 1928: 132). However, both Durkheim and Weber rejected the idea, specific to legal positivism, that governmental legitimacy could be seen as the mere result of a formal system of legal rules. Both dismissed the claim that legal analysis could, in pure form, produce legitimacy for the exercise of political functions. In fact, classical sociologists generally asserted that law could only obtain legitimacy through its correlation with embedded societal reflexivities, and, albeit in a fashion distinct from that typical of the Enlightenment, they insisted that law's legitimacy presupposed a social conjuncture in which the legal system was bound to a broad political will, existing in society at large. As a result, early legal-sociological theory was centrally marked by a quite distinct *political attitude*. This attitude relativized the moral power of the state. Yet this attitude nonetheless saw the state as a central focus of human liberty in society, founding an overarching system of public law, and formed through a deep articulation between the political system and wider processes of social volition and collective patterns of motivation.

This emphatic political dimension in sociology was clear enough in the pre-sociological works addressed above. For example, although he framed his analysis of the modern political system within an empirical theory of social differentiation, Hegel perceived the state as an aggregate of institutions required to radiate and secure universal ideas of liberty across all parts of society.[122] Hegel argued that the modern state forms a rational ethical order on which other liberties in society, be these the market-proportioned liberties of early civil society or the distinctive status-defined liberties of familial or professional life, are structurally reliant: no rights or liberties can exist outside the objective-rational order of the state.[123] Consequently, he claimed that the modern state must be correlated with a complexly constructed societal-political will, and it draws its legitimacy from its ability to balance different societal freedoms and to protect the most generalized, rationally necessary freedoms against merely particular unilateral interests and prerogatives. Notably, he concluded that in a legitimate state a constitution reflects 'the spirit of the entire people', and, although it enshrines particular liberties, it gives strict expression to the freedoms of the people in 'self-consciousness of their rationality', and it cements preconditions for higher-order liberties across the separate, differentiated spheres of freedom that society incorporates (1970 [1830]: 336). The state, consequently, stands at the centre of society, and all social liberties are finally underpinned by the generalized rationality embodied in the state.

As discussed, later, Durkheim concluded that the modern democratic state derives its legitimacy from its refined embodiment of the collective moral consciousness of society, and, on this basis, it assumes a clear ethical, public-legal authority in relation to other societal domains.[124] He argued that the state is 'a special organ which is required to elaborate certain representations which are valid for all people' (1950: 87). It has the duty to

---

[122] For Hegel, the state cannot be 'confused with civil society', and it provides for rational freedoms that cannot be restricted to protective economic rights (1970 [1821]: 399–403).

[123] He followed Rousseau's idea of the social contract in accepting that the state is founded on an absolutely general will. Yet, he rejected the principle underlying contract theory that collective freedoms are authorized by persons on an individualist basis, seeking freedoms for particular motives (1970 [1821]: 400).

[124] Durkheim argued that the modern state acts as a point of crystallization for collective beliefs and collective representations, and democratic institutions obtain legitimacy by consolidating general moral order and reflexivity in society (see Marx 1974: 340–2; Sintomer 2011). As a result, the state is able to exercise a distinctive directional power for all society, overseeing and providing for the integration of otherwise fragmented, laterally contractual processes of social integration (Lacroix 1981: 240).

guide citizens 'towards the sentiment of common solidarity' (1902: 207), at times protecting citizens from extreme pressures of individualization and contractual differentiation. Like Hegel, in fact, Durkheim supported a political order capable of binding the contemporary ethics of individualism to an objective system of 'moral unity', based in the restriction of personal egotism (1898: 8).

In some ways, Weber proposed an essentially materialist, instrumental theory of the state, closely related to Marx's idea of the state as pure superstructure.[125] Yet, equally clearly, he argued that the state is legitimized by its functions of national integration, and it owes its legitimacy to its ability, as a focus of public law, to hold together the otherwise intensely polarized groups that national mass democracy releases, producing compelling motivations across the functional domains that modern society comprises. Distinctively, Weber defined the state as a set of institutions that, uniquely, can claim a *monopoly of legitimate power* in society, or which even act as the 'final source of all legitimate physical violence', imposing directional authority on all social domains (1921/2: 519). In fact, Weber claimed that politics itself is an anthropologically privileged domain of human exchange and volitional interaction, which, as it is focused on a contest over the means of *legitimate violence*, possesses a particular distinction and primacy *vis-à-vis* other patterns of interaction (1921: 556).[126] In this context, Weber's preference for democracy over other polity types becomes explicable; he saw democracy as a polity that institutionalizes inter-party competition, breeding tough-minded and integrative politicians, which ensures that those who gain access to the means of legitimate coercion are equipped to deploy them for the national interest (1921: 558). As a result, he came close to explaining the legitimacy of the modern political system as defined by distinctive attributes of rational voluntarism, which, in their more conventional normative formulation, he rejected as simplistic.

Although born from an anti-universalist attitude towards the state, therefore, sociology soon developed as a singularly statist mode of social analysis, which attached very distinct, socially encompassing objectives to the modern political system. In many cases, in fact, classical sociology moved close to the ideas of the Enlightenment, which it otherwise

---

[125] He argued that the development of the modern bureaucratic state is integrally connected to 'modern capitalist development', and the modern state sustains legal conditions that promote 'the strictly rational organization of labour', which defines capitalism (1921/22: 826).

[126] For expert comment see Zängle (1988: 5); Kalyvas (2008: 39).

criticized, and it interpreted the political system as a guarantor of over-arching liberties, even species liberties, underwriting patterns of cohesion for all members of society. Above all, sociology developed as a discipline that observed the political system as a *dominant system of inclusion*, which was able to absorb conflicts triggered by the emergence of mass society, and to preserve a basic overarching structure of societal integration. At the centre of this idea was the principle that the political system can be correlated, albeit contingently, with the materialized political will of society, and, in refracting this will, it assumes the power to resolve or at least palliate conflicts created by wider processes of social differentiation. Although early sociology might easily be seen, in its entirety, as a *science of social differentiation*, its exponents generally refused to accept the politi-cal implications of this scientific outlook, and they preserved what was at core a mono-rational account of modern society's political domain.[127] Indeed, early sociologists widely perceived the political system, although itself constructed through differentiation, as an antidote to societal pres-sures caused by society's wider functional disaggregation and geographi-cal extension, and by the problems of class tension, individualization and despair induced by this process.

Of particular significance in this regard is the fact that early sociological theory opted for a sharply critical view of the possible differentiation of politics and law. Indeed, although they based their models of democratic formation around the idea that the law supports democracy as a relatively autonomous and differentiated medium of integration, classical sociolo-gists also argued that law's integrational functions are never completely autonomous, and these functions presuppose simultaneous acts of cat-egorically political integration.

At one level, both Durkheim and Weber examined the evolution of modern law as a process of differentiation, implying that modern law, sep-arate from religious and other substantial residues, could be examined as a simple medium of positive social integration. For Weber, modern law was a system of positive norms produced by overarching patterns of ration-alization, integrating society because of its formal rational content. For Durkheim, modern law was a relatively autonomous, pluralistic system of norms, reflecting the growing fluidity of social exchanges and the rise of organic solidarity, integrating society on a lateral, contractual basis.[128] In

---

[127] See similar claims in Gephart (1993: 109).
[128] Modern law is based in contract, and contract is a 'basic norm' that can act to sustain mul-tiple legal arrangements (1902: 192).

both cases, positive law is formative of democracy, and the rise of democratic institutions depends on the integration of social agents through law, separate from strictly political imperatives.

Ultimately, however, neither Durkheim nor Weber accepted the full implications of this approach to modern law. Both concluded that, in a legitimate political order, the law must be suffused with, and then societally transmit, a distinctive political ethic, such that the law gains authority from the fact that it is linked to the political system and to the integrational values and motivations that are concentrated in the political system. On both accounts, the political system is required to imprint higher norms within the law to support its integrational functions. As discussed, Weber proposed an account of modern law in which law on its own, as a system of differentiated positive norms, is unable to meet the demands for legitimacy in modern secular society. Law, thus, presupposes a personal or an expressly *non-legal* political residue to sustain its obligatory, integrational force.[129] Similarly, Durkheim argued that both politics and law perform universal ethical functions for society, and the legal order of a society based in organic solidarity, founded in non-coercive norms and subjective rights, is correlated with the expansion of state power, the extension of governmental consciousness and the broadening of ethical authority. To be sure, Durkheim insisted that the powers of the state are always limited, especially in the regulation of 'economic tasks', which are 'too specialized' for political regulation (1902: xxxvi). However, he also concluded that, as society becomes more differentiated, the 'points at which we are in contact' with the state multiply, and the 'dependence' of people on the state as an organ that elevates them to a consciousness of their solidarity necessarily increases (1902: 207). Despite emphasizing the essentially differentiated form of modern society, therefore, Durkheim reserved a particular importance for the general moral functions of the state and the integrative force of governmental consciousness, implying that the state may embody a principle of moral order above the contractual organizations in society at large.

The theories of democracy proposed by classical sociological theorists, in sum, were marked by a disposition that evaded some core implications of their own sociological insights. At one level, early sociologists argued

---

[129] For Weber, the charismatically integrated community is close to the religious commune, *Gemeinde* or *Ekklesia* (1921/22: 141). It closely mirrors Sohm's account of the inspired or organically integrated religious community, which, tellingly, Sohm viewed as a community defined and constituted by *non-legal* means (1892: 22).

that the political system was not founded in acts of collective human self-legislation and experiences of rational freedom, and it could not presuppose that its power was authorized by identical agents in different parts of society. However, they also accorded to the political system a dominant position in society. At a different level, they observed modern society as structured by a pervasive logic of differentiation, bearing in particular on the systems of politics and law and requiring the law to perform core functions of integration. Yet they also concluded that law acquires its highest legitimacy through its distinct capacity for transmitting powerfully integrative ethical-political substances through society. Indeed, it was a characteristic attitude of many early sociologists that they claimed that legitimate law presupposes a distinctively *political* content, and it is only as law refracts interests defined by a clearly political will, and as it connects different wills across society, that it acquires genuine legitimacy, distinct from the mere formal laws propagated in the Enlightenment.[130] Classical *legal* sociology was, in essence, *political* sociology, and it constructed the social functions of law by examining them in relation to politics. In these respects, sociological theories of democracy clearly retained aspects of the deep political voluntarism which characterized early democratic theory, and they construed the legitimate political system as a *correlated aggregate of societal wills*.[131] In fact, these theories echoed the view that democracy is sustained by collective subjective freedoms, of a higher order than the partial freedoms selected by persons in their singular natural lives.

1.4.2   Re-imagining the People

This paradox in classical legal sociology persisted into more contemporary legal sociology. In fact, the legacy of classical legal sociology is deeply reflected in the fact that recent legal sociology has retained a core focus on political substances, and it still preserves a certain proximity to the political-philosophical ideas of the Enlightenment.

---

[130] Weber elevated politics to a distinctive anthropological position. He asserted that the political is a dominant realm of human practice in society, formed by human conflict (1921: 340), and that societies marked by a weak sense of the political suffer low levels of political integration and dynamism (1921: 309). Later, Schmitt argued that the integrity of society as a whole depends on its ability to secure a strong political ethic, also based in conflict (1932a: 28–9).

[131] Leading sociologists have of course argued that sociology results from a resolute critique of the Enlightenment. See, most famously, Luhmann (1967).

Notably, after 1945, when political democracy became more globally widespread as a realized governance system, legal-sociological theory tended to abandon its original sceptical attitude towards democratic norm construction. Broadly, most post-1945 legal-sociological accounts of democracy have endeavoured to perpetuate and to re-formulate the ideals of democracy and citizenship promoted in the Enlightenment. Indeed, the leading positions in more contemporary lineages in the sociology of law and democracy remain, in essence, attempts to identify how the people, as a mass of citizens, can be made present within institutions in which public authority is vested, so that persons, as citizens, can envision themselves, however remotely, as authors of the laws that are applied to them. In particular, legal-sociological accounts of democracy promoted after 1945 have usually attempted to imagine distinctive models of democratic subjectivity, reflecting, on one hand, the societal conditions that shape the construction of democratic law, yet insisting also that democratic legitimacy presupposes some degree of rational-subjective consensus. As a result, many prominent legal-sociological theories of democracy that developed after 1945 sought to establish a synthesis between classical sociological ideas and more classical philosophical models of democratic will formation. Overall, the main positions in the sociology of law that acquired influence after 1945 have tended to cross the boundary that originally separated normative and sociological thinking, and they have disavowed many of the more critical impulses of classical legal and political sociology. A deep rapprochement with political philosophy underlies much legal sociology after 1945.

To be sure, some lines of legal-sociological research after 1945 remained close to classical sociological analyses of democratic institutions. Even such theories, however, tended to opt for an expressly normative approach to the political system.

For example, Talcott Parsons clearly assumed a position close to Durkheim in his analysis of democracy. Like Durkheim, Parsons saw the question of democracy primarily as a question of normative integration, concerning the secure institutionalization of the patterns of individualism that characterize modern society.[132] In this respect, he viewed the law as a core medium in the processes of institutional integration on which

---

[132] On the centrality of the concept of institutionalized individualism in Parsons see Parsons (1977: 53). In his earlier work, he argued that the question of the 'legitimacy of institutional norms' depends on a 'common value system', capable of sustaining the 'integration of individuals' (1949 [1937]: 768). For comment see Mayhew (1984: 1290). For an important account of Parsons's sociology, explaining it as an attempt to combine 'the objectivity

modern society relies, acting to incorporate individual persons as participants in the wider democratic society. Like Durkheim, further, although he was optimistic about the capacity of democracy for integrating individual persons in an ordered society, he did not link democratic formation to specific social demands, or to concrete acts of collective self-legislation. Instead, he centred his reflections on the claim that, owing to their internal functional pressures and exigencies, modern differentiated societies will tend to gravitate towards democratic patterns of political interaction and organic norm formation.

In the first instance, Parsons claimed that the emergence of democracy was linked to the fact that modern geographically expansive societies, containing large populations, are required to produce and dispose of political power in flexible organizational forms, at a high degree of generalization. Any complex system of organizational coordination, he explained, relies on the abstraction of political power, not as a source of immediate coercion, but as a 'symbolically generalized and legitimized' resource, with symbolic functions akin to those of money in the economy (1969: 366). For Parsons, such abstraction of political power is not possible in societies in which political organization does not possess a 'consensual element', based in 'structured participation in the selection of leaders' (1964: 255). As a consequence, he concluded that only polities with an 'institutional form' close to 'the democratic association' are able to 'legitimize authority and power in the most general sense' and to 'mediate consensus in its exercise by particular persons and groups' (1964: 355–6). Only democracies, in other words, can generate power in a form that can be generally legitimated in modern society. On this account, democracy is a political system that is produced through an evolutionary logic of equilibration in society, in which the utilization of political power can be supported by complex consensus, such that it is distilled into a form that can be easily mediated and recognized across differentiated societal domains (1969: 371). A democratic polity is defined by the relative depersonalization of power, and accordingly it has the distinction that it is able to ensure that society contains sufficient power to promote collective and commonly beneficial services.[133] As power is granted to leaders through a generalized mandate, all society is implicated in the production and deployment of power, enhancing the 'totality of commitments made by the collectivity as a whole' (1969:

---

of order' and the 'activity of individuals' in a theory of institutional individualism, see Bourricaud (1977: 22).

[133] On the critique of zero–sum models of power in Parsons see Bourricaud (1977: 164).

390): through democracy, society acquires more power, and it is able to accomplish more with this power. On this basis, democracy appears as the institutionalized form likely to be assumed by the political system in a balanced differentiated society.

Throughout his work, Parsons argued that the construction of a separate and universally oriented legal system, with professionalized judicial institutions, is vital for the evolution of advanced democracies. Generally, he implied that the primary functions of law are not intrinsically linked to the political system. Instead, he placed the role of law in the functional domain of 'social integration' (1977: 52), at least partly separate from the directional actions of the political system. In this respect, he argued that democracy depends on the fact that social agents are connected with the wider societal community through the law, or through rights that are generated within the law, and the exercise of legal rights is central to the overall integration and the functional balance of democratic society in its entirety. In this respect, he concurred deeply with Durkheim in indicating that individual agents are integrated in society through autonomously constructed, often informal, legal rights. Notably, he saw the informal institutionalization of the law as most effectively realized in the 'development of English Common Law, with its adoption and further development in the overseas English-speaking world'. He observed the Common Law as 'probably decisive for the modern world' and 'the most important single hallmark of modern society' (1964: 353).[134] The distinctive importance of the Common Law in the evolution of democratic institutions is attached to the fact that it provides an independent normative system that connects individuals in their particular life settings to the societal community more widely, and it constantly promotes effective integration by facilitating the informal exercise of legal rights.[135]

Parsons added to this analysis the claim that democratic governance performs distinctive integrational functions in modern society, especially in societies with pluralistic national populations, containing multiple 'subcollectivities within the societal community' (1965: 1015).[136] In this respect, he argued along lines close to those traced out by Durkheim and Weber, defining the legitimational value of democracy through its contribution to social integration (1949 [1937]: 768). Indeed, he claimed that it

---

[134] Parsons thus insisted on the 'analytical distinctness of the legal from the political', and he concluded that the functions of the legal system have a decentralized nature (1962: 563).

[135] For comment see Rocher (1989: 150); Gephart (1993: 243–4).

[136] See also Parsons (1970: 33).

is particular to democracies that they permit the simultaneous integration of many sub-national groups within the political system (1965: 1014), and they open rights of citizenship to a range of socially affiliated collectives in pluralistic, non-exclusive fashion. To this degree, Parsons followed T.H. Marshall in proposing an integrational theory of citizenship. He claimed that democracy has the legitimating benefit that it institutionalizes multiple domains of citizenship, in which social actors can claim rights of citizenship in the general political sphere without forfeiting other sectoral identities or group affiliations, thus allowing a society to preserve cohesion but to maintain sectoral pluralism at the same time.[137] Accordingly, he argued that democratic institutions are sustained by complex, non-hierarchical patterns of inclusion, and, as a result, they generate multiple layers of rights, in which different social constituencies are integrated more evenly in the political system. In this regard, notably, Parsons ascribed distinctive importance to the role of civil rights in the constitutional order of democratic society. He claimed that rights form core media of inclusion for the national community, and the spread of rights through society leads to an 'emancipation of individuals of all categories' from 'diffuse particularistic solidarities', facilitating their integration in national society as a whole (1965: 1039). For Parsons, thus, in addition to its character as a system that effectively produces political power, democracy needs to be seen as a system of pluralistic legal inclusion, capable of integrating the multiple constituencies of a national society. In this regard, he again emphasized the importance of the law in promoting the patterns of integration required in a democracy, and he implied that formative democratic processes take place as individuals exercise rights that are informally allocated through law. The non-coercive form of democratic government is closely linked to the fact that the law provides access to rights as autonomous instruments of social integration. Indeed, strong democracies are clearly defined by the fact that the law – relatively informally – facilitates pluralistic, organic patterns of rights-based inclusion. In each respect, democracy is defined as a political system that institutionalizes a plurality of freedoms.

Despite this emphasis on law's informal quality, Parsons also indicated that a distinct legal structure is essential to the political system of a democracy. In his early writings, he emphasized the claim that effective use of

---

[137] Parsons argued that there are different particular collectivities within society, but full citizenship creates a system of integration that allows people to exist in single collectivities, with particular expressive contents, while claiming equality at an overarching level (1951: 77–8). See the comments on this in Lechner (1998: 182, 185).

power presupposes the institution of 'a rational-legal system of authority and democracy' (1942: 155). Eventually, he arrived at the conclusion that a 'highly generalized universalistic legal order is in all likelihood a necessary prerequisite for the development of the ... democratic association with elective leadership and fully enfranchised membership' (1964: 353). Moreover, he argued that advanced collective organizations necessarily require laws of a constitutional nature, based on the principle of 'equality before the law', which preclude the exercise of authority by informal means, and which contribute to the maximization of the resources of power available to society (1969: 377). Importantly, he claimed that the effective production of power presupposes a 'firm institutionalization of the normative order', in which the distribution and allocation of power to particular persons are always subject to formal constraint and the 'legality of actual uses of power can be tested' (1969: 371). On these grounds, Parsons approached a description of democracy based in a theory of organic legal norm formation, arguing that evolutionary processes in society, driving the political system towards maximum inclusion and most effective goal attainment, impose a distinct normative (i.e. constitutional) shape on the political system.

In this affirmation of democracy, Parsons was clear that analysis of democratic formation could not explain democracy through reference to the simple choices and decisions of the members of national populations. On the contrary, he argued that inclusive democracy is a social condition that typifies highly evolved, balanced societies, marked by distinctive patterns of differentiation and normative integration. The function of a democracy, thus, is not to encapsulate overarching ideals of liberty, but rather objectively to institutionalize freedoms for individual social agents, and integratively to equilibrate the freedoms pursued by different social groups. Law plays a key integrational role in realizing this condition. In this context, the citizen is accommodated in the political system not as rational author of laws, but as a pluralistically institutionalized actor. In this respect, Parsons reiterated sociological principles first enunciated by Hegel, Durkheim and Weber, arguing that adequately proportioned institutionalization is the core precondition of democracy.

At the same time, however, the theory of democracy outlined by Parsons clearly contains a very strong normative dimension, and he came close to proposing a categorical model of the legitimate political system. This aspect of his theory sits uneasily alongside the more informal construction of law's role in democratic formation. In effect, he implied that modern society depends on a specific polity type for its equilibrium, and that a political system not assuming a relatively generalized normative form, with a differentiated legal system and protected basic rights, is likely to lack the 'political and integrative capacity' to perform its functions (1964: 356). On this basis, Parsons effectively postulated a universalized concept of societal evolution to explain the rise of democracy, substituting the evolutionary propensities of society as a whole for the political species freedoms of human agents as the basic paradigm for explaining democracy. As a result, he also moved close to classical, normative theories of democracy. In this account, the people do not form a simple subject of democracy. However, society itself, in its evolutionary processes, creates a democratic system in which people acquire and recognize general freedoms under generalized rational laws. The people thus re-enters democracy as a political subject, whose social integration presupposes certain norms and is tied to a political system with a relatively uniform normative order. As a result, the informal integrative power of law relies on the fact that it is underpinned by a strictly defined normative model of the state.

More typically, the period after 1945 saw a shift amongst legal/political sociologists towards clearly neo-classical theories of democracy.

This shift can be observed, first, in the critical sociological theory that developed in the Federal Republic of Germany (FRG) after 1949, especially from the early 1960s onwards, which engaged closely with the contradictions of modern democracy. This line of sociology, formed through a fusion of Marxist anti-capitalism and Rousseauian republicanism, was first articulated in the works of Franz Neumann and Wolfgang Abendroth.[138] Subsequently, it culminated in the works of Jürgen Habermas.

In his earlier works, Habermas set out a theory of democracy that approached in spirit the ideals of the high Enlightenment, and which reproduced classical convictions concerning the rational content of legitimate laws. Central to Habermas's theory, in its initial formulation, was the claim that in a fully legitimate democracy laws are established that create conditions of freedom, in which citizens recognize in law the possibility of exercising their personal autonomy in a rational, generalized fashion, and thus accept legal obligation on that foundation. For this reason, he explained, democracy presupposes the existence of a public sphere, arising from the separation of state and society in the eighteenth century, in which

---

[138] See the seminal critique of the formalization of social liberties in late-capitalist legal systems in Neumann (1937: 553). Abendroth supported a radical social-democratic conception of democratic constitutionalism, envisaging the constitutionalization of all society on the basis of the social rights contained in the constitution of the FRG (1967: 113–14, 133).

members of different social groups can freely engage in public communi-cation, and discursively mediate separate interests into publicly acceptable laws (1990 [1962]: 152–3, 327). For the early Habermas, consequently, democracy depends on a deep correlation between the public sphere and the law, and, in an evolved democracy, agents in the public sphere trans-mit discursively formed agreements into the political system, where they acquire legal form, constituting the foundations for objectively recognized collective liberties and obligations. In this regard, he viewed the positiviza-tion of the law as a central precondition of modern democracy, and he saw democracy as caused and eventually defined by the opening of the law to discursively formed, positively contingent social agreements. In an ideal democracy, the citizen acquires a central position as a focus of critique, discursive mediation and legal justification, and justificatory interactions between free citizens establish premises for universally obligatory laws (1973: 138). Later, Habermas paid great attention to law's instrumental functions, and he argued that the modern legal system acquires regulatory functions that close it to consensual orientations in society. However, he retained the claim that the rise of modern law cannot be separated from processes of justification that underpin rational social integration more widely. Throughout his work, he stated that society depends for its cohe-sion on the rational integration of social agents, and this function is per-formed and reflected, in part, by law, or by the system of legal liberties (rights) contained in a democracy (1976: 266–7). Like Parsons, he argued that the legal institutions of society are connected with broader patterns of social integration, and the law reflects the more informal discursive pro-cesses required to integrate persons, as citizens, in the societal community underpinning democracy (1976: 267).

Against this ideal-typical model, Habermas claimed that European democracies created after 1945 were founded in a primary distortion, or even a depoliticization, of the public sphere (1973: 55). As a result, the essential function of democracy in engendering shared legal freedoms had been deeply undermined. On one hand, he argued, the welfare states of post-1945 Europe constructed their legitimacy through the mediatization of social agents in structured interest-based organizations, so that state and society were fused together, and free discursive exchange between citizens was necessarily limited. The welfare state, of necessity, generated legiti-macy not by reflecting communicative agreements regarding deep-lying conflicts, but by allocating resources to materially disadvantaged groups to pacify them and to prevent communication about social divisions. As a result, the welfare state suppressed the public sphere, and it stabilized the political system around select material interests and processes of strategic compensation (1990 [1962]: 336). Moreover, post-1945 states relied on instruments of mass manipulation to control public opinion, and, in this respect too they greatly eroded the functions the public sphere. As a result of these factors, the states of post-1945 Europe had established political institutions with little democratic legitimacy, and their legal components typically reflected the prerogatives of dominant organized groups in society (1990 [1962]: 275; 311–12). Above all, Habermas argued, the legal order of such states had been severed from its deep legitimating connection with the democratic people (citizens), and law had been deprived of its primary role as a transmitter of societal values, agreements and rational freedoms from society into the political system. In contemporary democracy, he concluded, it had become possible to have 'affluence without freedom'. But the 'fundamental interest' that citizens have in 'self-determination and participation' had been suppressed, and the democratic idea of 'political equality' involving the 'equal distribution of political power' and the actual opportunity to exercise power had been renounced. 'Elite pluralism' had replaced 'the self-determination of the people' as the basis substructure of democracy (1973: 170). In such societies further, the law had been widely transformed into a mere medium of social steering and control, designed not to articulate freedoms in the public sphere, but externally to stabilize and to regiment social interactions. As a result, Habermas concluded that modern law possesses a dual function, acting both as a medium for discursive social integration and for constructing collective freedoms and as an instrument of 'systemic rationality' (1976: 265), serving to stabilize the instrumental basis for the economic system and the administrative system in society.[139]

In this respect, Habermas centred his theory of democracy, on one hand, around the claim that, in contemporary society, the people are always strategically excluded from democratic government, which, as a result, is inevitably supported by compensatory or ideological functions. On this account, the rational-integrational functions of law are deeply suppressed in contemporary society, and the political system sustains its position through strategic control of the law, closing itself against the normative residues contained in discursive processes of integration. On the

---

[139] In his earlier works, Habermas paid more attention to the repressive or systemic functions of law. His later works were strongly concerned with the possible configuration between law and 'communicative power' (1992: 182).

other hand, he implied that the ideal of discursive will formation should be used as the normative premise for a critique of contemporary democracy. Sociological reflection on democracy, thus, has the deepest responsibility for examining the reasons why the people remain absent in modern political systems, and how this can be rectified (1973: 196). Sociological reflection on law has the primary responsibility to mobilize the law as a bearer of rational liberty.

Ultimately, this neo-classical shift in legal sociology became visible in the rise of *procedularist* theories of democratic legitimation and democratic law production in the 1960s and 1970s. These theories accepted a basic sociological account of the differentiated, pluralistic design of democratic society, and, contra more classical normative theories, they centred their analyses on the precondition that the will of the people cannot simply be articulated as a foundation for legitimate political institutions. Rather than dismissing the normative claims of democracy, however, such theories developed the claim that, in the complexly structured conditions of modern society, democratic will formation must necessarily occur in multi-centric fashion. Accordingly, democracy relies on the presence of *multiple procedures* to construct the popular will of citizens, and, objectively, to transmit this will, through the political system, into general legal form.

The turn towards proceduralist theories of democracy became visible, first, in more classical normative analyses of national democracies. Outside the field of sociological research, for example, this turn can be seen in the works of Lon Fuller, who identified a series of procedures required to produce validity for law (1969: 39). This turn can also be seen in the thought of John Rawls, who viewed the establishment of fair procedures, within a counterfactually constructed reasonable community, as a precondition for defining the objectives of government, and as a constituent source of law's binding authority (1971: 86, 136). However, the proceduralist model of democratic legitimation acquired particular importance for sociological inquiry in the works of Habermas.

Like Rawls, Habermas tried to devise a theory of proceduralization in order to revitalize classical-democratic doctrines of collective self-legislation in contemporary society. Centrally, he proceeded from the precondition that, in complex differentiated societies, it is not possible to presume either final justification for laws, or unified patterns of subjective will formation to legitimate the practices of government (see Sciulli 1988: 385). Indeed, both the law and the subject of law are highly contingent and socially constructed. Consequently, he argued that the establishment of deliberative democratic procedures, open to all citizens in equal manner, is essential for creating formal rational consensus to inform and bring legitimacy to legislation, and it is only in procedural form that the popular will can be articulated. On this basis, Habermas opted for a theory of deliberative procedure as a means of securing 'the rationally motivated recognition' of legal norms, which, he claimed, was required to support the generally legitimized use of public power (1973: 148). He eventually concluded that the doctrine of popular sovereignty itself should be reconstructed as a theory of a multifocal political subject, generating legitimacy for laws in multiple acentric discursive procedures (1992: 649). The sovereign people, he explained, should be observed as a mass of proceduralized communication processes, no longer 'concretely concentrated in the people', but institutionalized as a source of political legitimacy through the diffuse 'communication network of political public spheres' (1992: 362–5). In consequence, he indicated, citizens could only become subjects of democracy as participants in discursive procedures, in which not the establishment of absolute values or categorically binding norms, but rational consensus between equally entitled fellow communicative actors, forms the primary foundation for legitimate law.

In this respect, Habermas's work stands as an attempt to combine the essential sociological insight into the underlying reality of differentiated pluralism in modern society with the essential philosophical endeavour to explain the normative principles presupposed by valid democratic law. In attempting this theoretical synthesis, on one hand, he clearly held closely to the classical philosophical view that legitimate laws produced by the political system need to be seen as containing and communicating rationally generalizable freedoms and obligations for all members of society. On the other hand, he held closely to the classical sociological view that laws acquire legitimacy when they generate motivations for persons in positive fashion, in their factually given societal conditions. Notably, he observed engagement in deliberative procedure as a distinctive, and relatively informal mode of citizenship practice, able to produce rationally generalized norms in locally embedded contexts, and, in consequence, creating a personally reinforced motivation for the acceptance of such norms (1992: 169). In this respect, he clearly followed the core sociological claim that law performs functions of integration as a positive medium, largely decoupled from the political system, reflecting more widely given patterns of social integration. In this respect, in fact, he constructed the figure of the citizen in a form designed to mediate between philosophical and sociological views of democracy. He argued that, as law is tied to the deliberative acts of citizens, law's positive embeddedness in society actually heightens its force as a rational medium, so that law is able to function both as an informal and as a rational means of integration. Accordingly, he viewed legitimate government as integrally linked to participatory citizenship practices, in which legislation is legitimated by the fact that laws are distilled from the vital 'communicative power' of citizens, constructed through deliberative procedures across different societal locations (1992: 182). In this perspective, citizens produce laws through discursive political practices, and they recognize the general validity of the laws because these laws express a rationality articulated through quite diffuse acts of factual engagement (1992: 187). In a legitimate polity, in other words, the rationally binding dimensions of law are not easily separated from the positive processes of law's formation. On the contrary, law assumes rational form through the participatory practices of political citizenship, and it acquires full integrational force through the same practices.

Despite this attempt at methodological synthesis, Habermas's theory clearly privileged the philosophical construction of legitimacy over the sociological construction of legitimacy. His definition of legitimacy rearticulated, albeit with sociological nuance, the classical principle that rational universality or rational volition acts as an indicator of legitimate law. In this respect, crucially, Habermas's thought on democratic legitimacy traced the most extreme contours of the paradox of legal sociology. He insisted, on one hand, that legitimate laws cannot be simply dictated by a rational democratic subject, and that the legitimacy of laws must be interpreted as a result of multiple societal practices, located deep in the life horizons of social agents. There is no factual sovereign subject that can simply authorize laws. Like Hegel, however, he argued that, even in its societal dispersal, it is possible to reconstruct the rational democratic subject of democracy, which appears as a diffuse, multi-local, yet ultimately also generically constructed source of legitimate legislation, underpinning the validity of all democratic functions. He thus insisted that the layers of social determination and even communicative distortion that have formed modern society cannot fully obscure the presence of a socially generalized political subject, seeking socially generalized freedoms. Society is always able to converge around the norm-generative acts of the democratic people, whose rationality is expressed in communicative acts of consensus production. Implicitly, moreover, the political system is able to connect itself with rational processes of integration in society, which are expressed through law. The integrative function of law depends thus, ultimately, on the presence of a rational political subject, expressed through a rational political system, to inform its content. Despite his earlier emphasis on the repressive functions of the state and the informal rationality of law, he ultimately arrived at the more positive assessment that the political system is able to integrate society on the basis of rational legal norms.

As an alternative to more obviously neo-classical theories of democracy, Niklas Luhmann also developed a legal-sociological theory to account for the growth of democracy and the nature of democratic legitimacy in contemporary society.

At the heart of Luhmann's political reflection is the claim that modern society is not determined in its entirety by any simple form of reason, imputable to obviously identifiable human subjects. Instead, modern society is shaped by a radically pervasive logic of functional differentiation, which means that society is divided into a series of distinct social systems, all of which conform to their own internal mode of rationalization. In consequence of this, society consists of multiple systems and multiple patterns of *systemic rationality*, each of which is expressed in a particular internal code: for example, the system of law is coded *lawful/non-lawful*; the system of politics is coded *subject to power/not-subject-to-power*; the system of the economy is coded *payment/non-payment*. Amongst these systems, no one rationality can be privileged above others as a bearer of particularly elevated values, and no rationality can be generalized across society, *trans-systemically*, as a source of universally applicable norms or freedoms (1993: 416). As a result, for Luhmann, the rationality of society is not the shared rationality of persons, extracted from some universal substrate of human interest, reason or will. Society is multi-rational, and each of its rationalities is a rationality of a particular system.

For this reason, Luhmann's work forms the most radical critique of the political humanism of the Enlightenment, and he squarely rejected universal subjectivistic constructions of rationality as outmoded residues of metaphysical thinking (1993b: 255). For Luhmann, the people, as a set of rational actors, cannot be identified as the central focus of society – society is a mass of systemic communications, which are not distinctively human. For this reason, further, Luhmann suggested that it is sociologically untenable to define the political system as a rational centre of society, expressing principles of generalized freedom or consensual volition, and it is improbable to imagine that laws passed by the political system assume legitimacy through their correlation with factual human subjects, acting, across all society, as rational authors, or rational addressees, of law. The political system has responsibility for producing *collectively binding decisions* for society, but such decisions originate in highly contingent inner-systemic communications. In fact, Luhmann claimed that society in its modern differentiated form cannot converge around, or assume defining imperatives from, its political system, and the legitimization of the political system is not a process that entails the establishment of legal or political norms that are recognized as obligatory for all actions in society. On the contrary, the rationality of the political system is merely one mode of systemic rationality among others, with no claim to any primacy for society as a whole, so that the legitimacy of the political system does not depend upon its projection of general values or general liberties for all members of society. In this sense, Luhmann warned against constructions of society that conceptually inflate the power of the political system. Generally, he claimed that political systems that promote normative or programmatic ideals for society in its entirety, such as socialist states or even Keynesian welfare states, are prone to assume unmanageable responsibilities, and they even threaten the differentiated fabric of modern society as a whole (1981b: 48). In this respect, he stated that the 'use of politics for purposes of the shaping of society' is likely to give rise to 'ineffective decisions' (1981a: 82–3). Consequently, he implied that the legitimacy of politics depends, not on the representation of encompassing norms in all parts of society, but on the self-restriction of political functions, recognizing that politics is simply one differentiated system amongst others, in the context of an acentric society. As a result, he concluded emphatically that it is not possible to 'centre a functionally differentiated society on politics without destroying it' (1981b: 22–3).

On this basis, Luhmann claimed that it is not plausible to presume that the democratic political institutions of modern society have been created and legitimized by simple acts of rational selection or reasoned self-reflection. On the contrary, like Durkheim and Parsons before him, he argued that the rise of democracy had been caused by a broader process of functional differentiation, in which different social systems had become focused on quite distinct spheres of societal exchange. In this context, democracy had emerged as a prevalent pattern of political-systemic formation because the democratic organization of the political system allowed society's political functions to acquire a form that was adequate to the wider reality of functional differentiation in which the political system was located.[140] Democracy, in other words, evolved as the institutional form of the adequately differentiated political system.

In this respect, in particular, Luhmann placed great emphasis on the increasing autonomy of the law in the emergence of democracy. He explained that democracy had developed as the prevalent type of political system because of the *positivization of the law*, such that the formation of democratic politics was in part observable as the result of a process of transformation *within the law*.[141]

In modern society, Luhmann explained, the differentiation of the law as a social system means that the rationality of law is necessarily detached from substantial values, and it is founded in positive decisions and placed on highly contingent foundations. On this basis, the law obtains a key role in modern society as a medium that can easily be altered, that permits adaptive systemic reactions to rapidly changing circumstances, and that allows other systems to authorize their functions in positive, contingent fashion. The positivization of law, its adaptation to contingent societal realities, is fundamental to modern society as a whole, and it makes it possible for society's different systems to reproduce themselves in their highly uncertain environments. Indeed, the evolution of the modern legal system as a simple system of positive norms, whose function is to stabilize sequences of legal expectation, plays a vital role in allowing society as a whole to secure itself against the extreme contingent occurrences that it contains.

For Luhmann, this significance of legal positivization has particular implications for the rise of democracy. Democracy evolves as a political system that is distinctively legitimated by the fact that it can adapt to its unpredictable environments, and which is able to produce and authorize political decisions in highly contingent, positive fashion. It owes this character to the fact that it is able to assimilate and utilize the positive form of modern law to conduct its exchanges, deploying positive law to generate flexible forms its functions and to translate its decisions easily into a socially adequate medium of exchange. Democracy, in other words, can

---

[140] Luhmann argued that democracy is a form of politics that reflects the nature of modern society – a 'society without a centre'. In its ability to generate flexible reserves of power, democracy avoids the destructive tendency to force society into convergence around the political system (1981b: 23).

[141] In Luhmann's earlier work, the claim appears that 'the actual impetus' to the growth of democracy was the positivization of law: that is, the 'full positivization of the normative premises of collectively binding decision making', in which 'law is released from residual religious and natural-legal attachments' (1971: 37).

only exist because of the positivization of law, and democratic politics constantly reflects and augments the essentially positive form of modern law. Democracy results from an evolutionary process in which both law and power respond, adaptively, to the need for uncertain decision making, and law and politics interlock as a systemic order for generating authoritative decisions in highly insecure social contexts, in a highly differentiated society. Like other legal-sociological theories, therefore, Luhmann viewed democracy as integrally linked to the transformation of the legal system, and the structures of democracy emerge as the political system adapts to the contingent reality of modern society by ordering itself around law's positive form.

At an intentional level, Luhmann set out a hyper-contingent theory of democracy. He argued that democracy cannot be conflated with substantial values, acts of will formation or rationally selected processes. Indeed, even the basic idea that democracy can be tied to particular human interests, human demands or human subjects should be viewed as deeply misconstructed and reductively metaphysical. For Luhmann, democracy is simply driven by the positivization of law, and it evolves as a political system that is adapted to the contingent nature of society. In this respect, Luhmann showed deep awareness of the fictionality of the figures of legitimacy proposed by classical democratic theorists. He conceived the idea of the collectively self-legislating people as a mere *semantic form*, which allows the political system to project a grounding for its functions, but which cannot be attached to a concrete set of agents in society (1984a: 102; 2000: 319–71). Elsewhere, he defined the central constitutional-democratic principles of basic norms, natural rights, democratic consensus, collective freedom, popular will-formation and national sovereignty as mere *hyper-fictitious self-descriptions*, which a political system generates and utilizes to underpin its inner coherence, yet which cannot be attached to real social subjects (1990: 184–5, 191). In fact, he even viewed the basic principle that a political system presupposes legitimacy as an inner fiction of the political system, serving to bring symbolic plausibility to otherwise contingent political communications (2000: 123). Above all, he claimed, the reality of democracy cannot be extracted from the idea of a citizen claiming distinct shared freedoms or acting as the origin and source of legitimacy for laws. For Luhmann, democracy may well generate certain freedoms for social agents, and it is probable that it will institutionalize political practices associated with citizenship. But these freedoms are contingent outcomes of the evolutionary processes underlying democracy, and they cannot be statically defined as the deliberate outcomes of democratic design. Like

Helmut Schelsky, he implied that democracy only guarantees freedoms in society if it is allowed to evolve in a relatively unstrained, limited and balanced fashion, permitting the plural exercise of freedoms in other systemic dimensions.[142] If democracy is conceived as a mechanism for the imposition of general freedoms, perhaps including far-reaching participatory freedoms or even material freedoms (welfare), through society, it is likely to lose efficacy as a guarantee of freedom (1994: 157).

In this respect, Luhmann took up a most advanced position in the legal-sociological critique of democracy, implying that the core constructs around which democracy is stabilized are fabricated to simplify systemic functions.

Despite this emphasis on political contingency, however, Luhmann also offered some more concrete-institutional descriptions of the democratic political order, and the processes through which it generates legitimacy. In this dimension of his theory, his account of modern democracy still moved, persistently, within the terrain of classical theories of democracy. Indeed, he resisted the conclusive implications of his own thought.

First, Luhmann argued that democracy involves the triadic sub-differentiation of the political system into three institutional sub-systems, *politics, administration* and *public*, all of which interact with each other to create and legitimate legislation (1971: 62). The interactions between these components of the political system take place through a circular mass of political-systemic procedures (for instance, elections, parliamentary recruitment processes, policy hearings, lobbying negotiations, civil-service briefings, public debates, grass-roots consultation, legislative drafting), through which the political system tests and constructs legitimacy for its legislative outputs. Each point in this triadic order obstructs the excessive concentration of power in any other part of the political system, and each point forms a source of counter-power, recursively checking the power stored in other elements of the political system. This three-cornered institutionalization of political power allows the effective production of power as a societally communicable form, and it maximizes the chances that power will find compliance in the processes of its societal distribution (1981b: 45–7). Like Parsons, Luhmann claimed that complex societies need to generate political power as an expansionary, fluid, yet also generalized, medium of exchange, serving to facilitate the multiple patterns of inclusion that these societies, in their differentiation, contain,

---

[142] During the social-democratic experiments of the 1970s, Schelsky argued that it was necessary to choose whether to pursue 'more democracy or more freedom' (1973: 47, 63–4).

presuppose and necessitate (1981b: 44–5; 1988: 68). To generate power in this fashion, modern societies depend on the construction of a political system that is able to avoid the excessive concentration of political power in one set of institutions, and which can construct many different procedures for distributing power through society. As a result, modern societies tend to evolve a political system that produces power through a process of *recursive circularization*: that is, through procedures in which the transmission of power is always checked by institutions able to exercise counter-power, so that the simple build-up of power at one point in the political system becomes improbable. In such systems, the reserves of power that society can use and make available for its exchanges are necessarily augmented, expanded and internally differentiated – society acquires *more power*. Democracy, thus, evolves as a type of political system that is able effectively to produce power for a modern society.

In explaining this, Luhmann argued that the internally differentiated construction of the democratic political system is determined by the fact that the political system presupposes a running exchange with the legal system, so that political decisions can be procedurally translated into law. In fact, he claimed that the democratic organization of the political system should be construed as a mass of inter-institutional arrangements for establishing a 'mutual dependency' between law and politics, making it possible for political decisions to be distilled into positive legal form, so that they can be reliably and consistently mediated across society (1981c: 164). In the triadic order of the political system, legislation is concentrated in the administration, and other parts of the system form articulations with the administration to transpose rough political exchanges into legal form. As a result, the political system is always likely to evolve in a form which increases its compatibility with the legal system. The inner triadic structure of the democratic political system thus reflects an adaptive intelligence within the system itself, which facilitates its articulation with the law.

On these grounds, second, Luhmann claimed that it is only where power can be proportioned to, or configured around, generalized legal criteria, that it can presume effective compliance amongst its addressees. It is only through its 'self-referential juridification' that power can be transmitted through society (1997: 357). In explaining the relation of power to law, in fact, Luhmann stated repeatedly that, for its effective transmission, power must be *coded as law*, and law must imprint a distinct normative code into the structure of power. In its inclusionary transmission through society, he claimed, the power conserved and produced by the political system needs to be constructed through the binary code: *lawful/non-lawful*. The 'pure code of power' is insufficient for the effective distribution of power, and power only becomes usable – that is, it undergoes an 'enormous expansion' – if it is translated into the code of law (1984b: 41).

What this means is that, in order to generate and circulate power through society, the political system is obliged to code its inner communications *twice*: once for itself (as *subject-to-power/not-subject-power*), and once for those exchanges subject to power in society (as *lawful/nonlawful*). For Luhmann, politics relies integrally on law: collectively binding decisions formed in the political system cannot be radiated across society without utilizing the normative apparatus of law as a *generalized medium of inclusion*. For this reason, Luhmann indicated that, while other social systems contain entirely distinct codes by which they reproduce their functions, law and politics exist in a relation of *second coding* (1997: 357). In consequence, the political system is likely to accept legal self-restriction as a condition of its societal transmission, and, to simplify its effective mediation, it is likely to acknowledge legal checks on the use of coercion. Above all, the political system is likely to promote recognition of persons as holders of general legal rights, so that persons cannot be included in simply coercive fashion within its communications (1965: 25). The person as general rights holder appears, for Luhmann, as a core form for the effective transfusion of political power through society, and recognition of power's addressees as rights holders is central to the legitimation of the inclusionary functions of the political system.

On this basis, Luhmann retreated from the deepest implications of his own democratic theory. Although he proposed an avowedly contingent or hyper-sociological theory of democratic order, he implied, ultimately, that the political system is shaped by a particular inner, evolutionary reflexivity, which orients its communications towards a specific legal/normative form. On Luhmann's account, political power relies on the presence of a systemically (not reflexively) generalized rationality to perform its functions through society, and general compliance with political decisions, although not normatively determined, is likely to depend on the ordering of power in a legally generalized form. The legitimacy of political power, therefore, requires the construction of a distinctive, adaptive intelligence in the political system, and this intelligence expresses itself in the distribution of political power in rationalized legal form. Luhmann eventually expanded this theory of second coding to incorporate a theory of the modern political system as operating necessarily as a *legal state* or as a *constitutional state*. He concluded that the political system can only effectively generate power if it is internally checked by a constitution, which transforms (i.e. *second-codes*) political power into legal power (power coded as lawful/non-lawful) (1990: 201; 1993a: 426). Indeed, he explained the organization of the political system as a legal-constitutional state leads to an 'increase in the freedom' of both the legal system and the political system at the same time (2000: 391). Although based in positive law and reflective of deeply contingent societal premises, therefore, the democratic state necessarily assumes a particular normative shape, and it condenses a broad rationality into legal/political form.

In these respects, Luhmann moved from a radically sociological perspective towards a semi-classical theory of political democracy. Overall, he attempted to construct a model of democratic legitimacy without a political subject and without recourse to any static humanistic notion of legal authority. However, both at an institutional and at a normative level, he adopted a quite standard model of the democratic political system. Ultimately, he came very close to the original democratic claim that the legitimate political system is the legislative embodiment of a rational will that condenses society's political power into an overarching order, which persons across society are likely to recognize as generally valid, obligatory and even as likely to secure relative social liberty (lack of vertical coercion). Central to the emergence of democracy, for Luhmann, is the fact that national political systems acquired legitimacy by adaptively configuring their reserves of power with the law, and, in so doing, by acquiring a medium of communication proportioned to a differentiated society. The political system, consequently, obtains legitimacy as it is correlated with the differentiated structure of society as a whole, and it articulates this correlation in a particular normative order: *society's differentiated form becomes the subject of the political system.* In proposing this theory, to be sure, Luhmann did not see the legitimate political system as an embodiment of constitutive human freedoms, and self-evidently he did not see the legitimate political system as a reflection of human rationality. But he did see the legitimate political system as an embodiment of a societal rationality, permitting the collective exercise of liberty through society. He implied that democracy is legitimated by the fact that it translates power into a limited, socially transmissible form, which society as a whole, in its differentiated structure, is likely to recognize as legitimate, for which the political system presupposes a particular normative grammar and a particular medial form, or a particular medial rationality. The rationality of the political system is articulated through the distillation of power into law, and the legitimate political system is always oriented towards legally codified democracy.

1.5 Conclusion

Legal sociology has a very distinctive qualification for examining the character and preconditions of modern democracy. As discussed, classical legal sociology first unmasked the contingency of democratic formation, which it observed as driven by wider societal processes of differentiation. Generally, both early social theorists and classical sociologists argued that the legitimation of the modern political system was caused not by the generalized demands of citizens, but by intricately formative patterns of social construction. On this basis, early legal sociology articulated the core insight that the legal form of democracy is the outcome, not of collective demands for self-legislation, but of systemic differentiation. In particular, the law plays a vital role in promoting the processes of integration that underpin democracy. *Democracy, thus, is produced through a process of spontaneous apersonal integration and institutionalization. The primary outcome of such differentiated political institutionalization is the preservation of partial, particular liberties.* On this account, democracy is not a finally realized political condition, but a continuing process of integration, closely linked to the autonomous functions of the law.

Despite its eminent qualifications for examining the realities of democracy, legal sociology always struggled to consolidate and even to accept the implications of its own essential intuitions. As stated, in the classical period, sociologists of law retained the idea, contrary to their deep theoretical impulses, that the political system is the dominant system of integration in society, that the political system assumes founding significance for the legitimacy of law, and that the political system is articulated with a generalized subjective substructure through society. Central to these assumptions is the idea that legislation is the core political function, and that, in its legislative actions, the political system produces legitimacy by condensing aspects of society's basic self-comprehension. Moreover, early legal sociologists repeatedly looked for collective sources of political agency, experience, motivation and *embedded voluntarism* to sustain the functions of the political system and the legal system. Although early legal sociology identified the fictional character of the claims of classical democratic theory, sociologists persisted in looking for the popular will, or the trans-systemically manifest citizen, as the source of law's authority. Much classical legal sociology devoted itself, however awkwardly, to projecting a recentralization of society around categories of political experience and norm formation, and it viewed the legitimacy of law as the consequence of law's collective-volitional, essentially political character. This resulted primarily from the classical sociological critique of positivism, which imputed a simple circular relation between law and politics as the legitimational premise of the political system.

After 1945, then, legal sociology widely aligned itself to more conventional normative or rational-volitional theories of democratic law, persistently imagining law as the expression of general political freedom. Most contemporary legal sociology still imagines the people as the subject of political order, and it has not yet fully digested the paradoxical perspective which appears in the works of Durkheim and Weber. Even in theories, such as that proposed by Luhmann, that programmatically disavow the idea of politics as a system of rationally determined human action, some aspects of classical democratic theory persist, often in rather curious, oblique fashion. Overall, sociological analysis has struggled to outline the societal substructure of the differentiated political system (democracy), and it still looks for an underlying rational order with which democracy must be correlated.

This book is an attempt to re-examine the development of modern democracy by using a framework based on the deepest, primary conceptual insights of legal sociology. In particular, it takes very seriously the recurrent (and recurrently ignored) intuition in legal sociology that democracy is only a contingent, incidental occurrence, whose reality is only obliquely linked to the ideals of rational generalized freedom and external will formation, in which its common normative justifications are articulated. Moreover, this book argues that, empirically, the original insights of classical legal sociology are deeply and distinctively corroborated in contemporary society, and it views the emergent legal form of democracy as the result of positive processes of legal integration that have little to do with democratic rationality. On this basis, the book examines how the rise of democracy has been driven by deeply contingent factors, that are most effectively interpreted by the sociology of law – *if* the sociology of law holds true to its own founding insights. The book tries to show that democracy is most accurately understood if we abandon constructions of democracy as a condition of realized human self-legislation or realized citizenship, and if we decisively renounce constructions of the political system as a dominant system of integration and legitimation. *The sociology of law holds the key to explaining democracy if it thinks not as the sociology of politics, but as the sociology of law: if it accepts the insight that law acts as a free-standing medium of integration.* On this basis, therefore, this book takes the core perceptions of classical legal sociology as the foundation for a global sociological analysis of contemporary democracy.

National Democracy and Global Law

2.1 The *People Introuvable* and the First Crisis of Mass Democracy

As discussed above, even if defined in minimalist terms, the factual development of democracy initially followed a very fitful path. Before 1914–18, no European societies had constructed political systems even close to the institutional design and integrational reach of full democracies. To be sure, by this time, most countries in Europe, and some countries in Latin America, had evolved polities with some partial democratic features. None, however, could plausibly claim to extract legitimacy to support their legislative acts from an equally and comprehensively included national population. Generally, *strategically selective democratization* was the dominant pattern of political organization from the midway into the nineteenth century until midway into the twentieth century. One of the most persuasive analysts of the history of modern democracy states simply that 'suffrage discrimination' was the normal principle of political citizenship for most of the nineteenth century, and that electoral franchises were created, not as mechanisms of popular inclusion, but as 'extraordinarily effective instruments of political repression' (Goldstein 1983: 334).

To illustrate this, for example, in the longer wake of the Great Reform Act of 1832, the UK progressively developed a constitutional order based on the idea that the elected chamber of Parliament was the core organ of state. As a result, the period after 1832 saw a progressive widening of the authority of the House of Commons within the parliamentary order as a whole, which culminated in its acquisition of evident superiority in 1911. However, until the establishment of full male suffrage in the Representation of the People Act of 1918 and the stepwise enfranchisement of women from 1918 to 1928, the British government had very restrictive electoral laws. From 1884, the last franchise reform prior to 1918, gender, age and housing tenure were still the primary determinants of the right to vote.[1] Moreover, general elections before 1918 were marked by entrenched protection of plural voting for privileged groups; in fact, multiple enfranchisement persisted residually until 1950, when the first general elections without plural voting were held.[2] Additionally, through the late nineteenth century, and, even after 1918, elections in the UK were not always fully competitive. After 1918, tellingly, weak electoral competition was most pronounced at critical political junctures. This was evident in late 1918, when, after World War I and the electoral reforms of 1918, the Liberal and Conservative parties campaigned on the same platform. It was again evident in 1931, when, after the Wall Street Crash, the Labour Party split and its more Conservative elements formed a coalition government that effectively eliminated electoral competition until after 1945. Before 1945, in consequence, there were only two years – from 1929 to 1931 – in which, albeit still with plural voting, Britain had a government elected by a full franchise in fully competitive elections. Strictly, in fact, throughout the entire process of democratization up to 1950, British governments were selected by a number of separate electoral franchises, based on different admission criteria.[3] Unlike electoral systems defined by fully constitutional principles, franchise membership in the UK had its origins in private qualifications, and voting rights were initially allocated on grounds of status or group affiliation.[4] The British political system was historically not underpinned by a generalized idea of subjective voting rights or by general ideals of political citizenship.[5] Naturally, selective enfranchisement left a powerful impression on British politics. Owing to franchise restrictions,

---

[1] In fact, 1918 did not bring an end to electoral exclusion. On one calculation, after 1918 still only 93 per cent of adult men were enfranchised in the UK (Tanner 1990: 387). Moreover, 1918 did not bring an end to the principle of franchise variation, as it established different age qualifications for admission to the franchise for civilians and military personnel, and it created a robust property qualification for female voting.

[2] The extent to which plural voting privileged wealthy voters is illustrated by electoral statistics from Glasgow. Around 1910, the wealthy urban wards in Glasgow, which mainly voted Tory, had over 250 per cent enfranchisement (i.e. more electors than residents, because of plural registration). By contrast, poorer wards often had less than 50 per cent enfranchisement (see Smyth 2000: 12–13).

[3] One account describes the existence of seven separate franchises in the 1910 elections Blewett (1972: 358). See also Hanham (1959: 191).

[4] The existence of multiple, overlapping franchises in the UK in the early twentieth century can be seen as a remnant of earlier regalian systems of representation, in which electoral rights resulted from private grants, privileges and acknowledged interests.

[5] See discussion below at pp. 332–3.

class interests did not become openly politicized until after 1918,[6] which meant that organized labour was weakly integrated in the political process, and the emergence of a strong and nationalized Socialist party was impeded. Consequently, the Labour Party was essentially an adjunct to the Liberal Party until 1918 (Wrigley 1976: 43–4; Packer 2001: 177).[7]

After unification in the 1860s, analogously, Italy had a moderately powerful parliament, but until 1912 its franchise was very small, and electoral rotation of office was not fully competitive (Webster 1975: 14; Romanelli 1979: 217). Before 1948, Italy only had a government created by competitive and fully democratic elections (albeit still without female voting) in the years from 1919 to 1922. After 1871, Imperial Germany had a large male franchise, in which, unlike in Britain, the political system was expected to address divergent organized class interests at a relatively early stage, certainly from 1890 onwards. However, up to 1918, members of the German parliament (*Reichstag*) elected by this franchise had only limited authority: they did not possess full powers to initiate legislation, and members of the Reichstag could not assume ministerial positions. After the formation of the Third Republic, France, which was by some distance the most democratic major European state in the nineteenth century, had a settled full male franchise and competitive elections. In fact, the basis for full male suffrage had been established as early as 1848.[8] However, the Third Republic was created through the annihilation of radical political opposition in the Paris Commune. Throughout the Republic, governmental executives were unstable, governments were sometimes extremely

---

[6] On the rise of 'class-based electoral politics' in the UK after 1918 see Hart (1982: 820).

[7] Note the following analysis of the political position of organized labour before 1914: 'Labour was operating on the basis of a highly restrictive franchise, and one which was probably peculiarly unfavourable to it. It is difficult for a mass working-class party to be politically successful when about half the working-class is voteless' (McKibbin 1974: 87). Even accounts that stress the growing importance of the labour movement in the UK before 1914 recognize the very limited political representation of labour, even in its industrial heartlands (Laybourn and Reynolds 1984: 64, 94). Organizationally, before 1918, the Labour Party was a 'federation of affiliated trade unions and socialist societies with no official means of individual membership and no set political programme or ideology', which remained in 'the shadow of the Liberal Party' (Worley 2005: 4).

[8] France had a full male franchise in 1848, which was briefly suspended. It again had a full male franchise from 1851, albeit for elections of plebiscitary nature, which were not fully competitive. The 1871 elections seem a good point at which to identify the stabilization of male democracy in France. Some observers would claim it was established earlier (Rosanvallon 1992: 24–5). Some observers claim that it was established later (Rueschemeyer, Stephens and Stephens 1992: 85; Collier 1999: 42).

short-lived, and their powers were not fully anchored in parliamentary elections. Women were not allowed to vote until after World War II.

The USA of course had a relatively large male franchise from the 1820s onwards. Yet, large sectors of society were excluded from participation in elections on grounds of ethnic group membership until well into the second half of the twentieth century, and access to electoral rights varied greatly across regional divides. Notably, the exponential growth of white democracy in the era of President Jackson was flanked by very repressive policies towards non-dominant social groups, such that from this time American democracy acquired a clearly and deeply imbued racist hue.[9] Indeed, in the Civil War and the franchise experiments during Reconstruction, the USA experienced an unusual process of enfranchisement and disfranchisement in which the black population was briefly incorporated in, and then, in many states, once again excluded from, the electorate. Even during Reconstruction, however, enfranchisement of the black population was not uniform. At this time, many northern states did not establish African-American suffrage (see Gillette 1979: 7–10), and the Fifteenth Amendment was needed to secure voting rights for the black population in the north (Gillette 1965: 165).[10] In 1865, there were only five states in which blacks and whites had equal voting rights (McPherson 1964: 333).

Overall, throughout the nineteenth century, national societies were not very effective in creating democratic governance systems. The early processes of citizenship formation and socio-political nationalization that ran through the nineteenth century did not culminate in the consolidation of national democracies. Through the nineteenth century, as mentioned, it was widely claimed – by both advocates and opponents of democracy – that, once established, national citizenship would inevitably give rise to more egalitarian patterns of political-systemic formation, broadly aligned to electorally preponderant social and political interests in society.[11] In

---

[9] One important account explains that Jackson's presidency was 'radically libertarian', 'militantly republican' and 'openly racist' (Smith 1997: 201).

[10] Gillette calculates that up to late 1868 'no northern state with a relatively large Negro population had voluntarily accepted full Negro suffrage' (1965: 27). A different account calculates that, in 1840, only 7 per cent of free slaves in the northern states were fully enfranchised (Litwack 1961: 75).

[11] See above pp. 22–3. This was intermittently implied by Marx and Engels. This theory was implicit in the *Communist Manifesto*. Notably, Marx saw full enfranchisement, under some conditions, as an alternative to revolution. He stated that universal suffrage in England was a 'socialist measure' that would lead to 'the political supremacy of the working class' (1852). He also argued that in England 'universal suffrage was the direct content of the

reality, however, it was not the progressive elaboration of citizenship or gradual political enfranchisement that led to the establishment of mass democracy as a general political model. Ultimately, mass-political democracy was jolted into life in unpredicted fashion, and it was initiated, not by acts of national will formation, but by factors linked to exogenic events – by the intense militarization of nationhood and international challenges to national legal systems caused by World War I. The war proved to be the great catalyst for mass politicization in most of Europe, and most European states underwent a process of intensified democratization either during or in the years that followed the period of conflict (1914–18). World War I therefore triggered the first process of large-scale, cross-polity democratization.

The rise of democracy at this juncture was not universally linked to military mobilization. Spain and Sweden became democracies at this time despite the fact that they were non-belligerent in World War I, although full democratization in Spain was delayed until 1931 because it was not directly involved in the war.[12] France already had male mass democracy before 1914. Moreover, intensified democratization also occurred in Latin America at this time.[13] In most cases, however, democratic political systems were created around 1918 in societies in which populations had been acutely affected by the experience of warfare. In each case, the rise of democracy was inseparable from the fact that state structures had been subject to extreme duress by pressures linked to military mobilization, and populations had experienced intensified national integration through military conflict and psychological adversity. In the period around World War I, therefore, conditions close to mass democracy typically came into being through one of three different processes: (1) existing monarchical or imperial governments were replaced by abrupt regime transformation

---

revolution' (1855). This view later became an article of faith for Eduard Bernstein and other revisionists (1899: 127). This principle was also declared by Proudhon, albeit from a position hostile to centralized democratic systems. Proudhon stated that in democracies, in which the 'right to vote is inherent in the man and the citizen', there will be a national tendency towards 'economic equality' (1865: 270). See the later version of these claims in Kautsky (1918: 5). In the interwar period, the Austro-Marxist Max Adler was still able to argue that 'for the proletariat, political democracy is an indispensable weapon, a powerful means to exert influence in the state' (1926: 11).

[12] Sweden had near complete male suffrage in 1909 and female suffrage in 1921. However, until 1917, the government was not fully democratically accountable. Spain's democratization in 1931 was not directly caused by the war, but it was a longer-term consequence of social forces (class mobilization, industrial agitation, nationalism) released by the war.

[13] In Argentina, for example, expanded, but still very incomplete, male suffrage was introduced in 1912, leading to greatly increased popular participation in elections.

(e.g. Germany, Austria); (2) existing governments implemented hasty reforms, establishing a more equal electoral franchise to permit extended participation in politics (e.g. Italy, UK, Belgium, Netherlands); (3) new states came into being through the collapse of former multi-national Empires (e.g. Czechoslovakia, Poland, Hungary, Yugoslavia), which also established political systems with a large franchise.

The fact that the expansion of democracy was impelled by military conflict throws very distinctive light on its normative foundations, indicating that mass-democratic institution building was first driven by very contingent factors. In fact, this link between war and democracy had important consequences for the eventual construction of democratic institutions in different European societies. Most democracies created around and after 1918 reflected the impact of the war in six separate respects.

First, the rise of full democracy around 1918 was closely linked to Imperialism and the struggle for military expansion. Through the nineteenth century, as mentioned, democracy was often advocated as a mode of political organization which, in helping to motivate the population to support the government, might prove conducive to external expansion, both through economic production and military combat. This reasoning obtained pressing relevance during World War I, which for many combatants was not clearly distinct from an imperial war. In some societies, in fact, governmental executives repeatedly promised reform of domestic suffrage laws as a means of solidifying support for the military effort.[14] As a result, the accelerated path towards democracy after 1914 was tied to considerations of military efficiency and success, and political reform was strongly shaped by strategic calculations, which had little to do with democracy as a normative good.

Second, in the new democracies created around 1918, governmental power was not captured, either in full or incrementally, by organized democratic actors or constituencies. Of course, to some degree, political reform was triggered by the democratizing impact of military conscription, which had levelled out social distinctions on the battlefield and drawn inhabitants of different regions into close proximity to one another, promoting an intensified nationalist pattern of citizenship and political affiliation.[15] Indeed, as in the revolutionary era in the late eighteenth century, warfare,

---

[14] Famously, at Easter 1917, the German Kaiser promised constitutional reforms, after which a cross-party reform commission was established (see Bermbach 1967: 52–3).

[15] Importantly, like Hobbes before him, Weber saw the shared experience of equality in face of violent death, intensified in the years 1914–18, as formative for democracy (1921: 268).

incubated nationalism, and democratic enthusiasm became inseparable in World War I.[16] However, such experiences did not result in a situation in which newly nationalized societal constituencies, motivated by claims for collective freedom, actually gained hold of power. On the contrary, in most cases, power was given to populations by government elites for a number of different reasons, few of which reflected a deep commitment to democracy and few of which proved propitious for enduring democratic institution building. In some cases, governmental executives in 1918 were extremely anxious about the inflammatory, potentially revolutionary, mood of their (often still armed) populations, caused by long periods of deprivation in military combat, and exacerbated by the revolution in Russia in 1917. Under such circumstances, new democracies were created very quickly, and they were designed not to secure collective freedom, but to prevent complete revolution: their motivation was essentially protective and counter-revolutionary. In some cases, power was partly transferred to national populations because political elites felt a sense of obligation towards their populations for their sufferings in the war, and they granted democratic citizenship as a political right because of a sense of duty.[17] In this respect, however, political elites often noted that their nations had become Conservative and patriotic through military incorporation, such that the gift of democracy appeared relatively risk-free.[18] In these respects, the expedited growth of democracy after 1918 was shaped by a range of quite conflicting motivations. Clearly, however, this most intense wave of democratic formation did not result from simple acts of collective self-legislation.

Third, most democracies established after World War I reflected a very strained definition of their primary constituent subjects.

In most societies, notably, the push for mass political and economic inclusion around 1918 was not supported by a clear construction of the people or the citizens that were to be included in government, and no unified faction of the people was able to present itself as a secure source of

---

[16] Weber also identified the deep nexus between democracy and nationalism, forged in World War I (1921: 246).

[17] This was the stance, for instance, of Lloyd George, who stated that soldiers had a 'right to a voice in choosing the Government sends them to face peril and death' (Pugh 1978: 51). Weber, writing in 1918, claimed that enfranchisement of soldiers ('returning warriors') was almost a moral command. He viewed electoral reform as the 'only means' to secure the future of German national society (1921: 308).

[18] In the UK, for example, franchise extension was partly based on assumptions regarding the Conservative orientation of the soldiers' vote (Pugh 1978: 51). Female suffrage movements also became less radical during the war (Hause and Kenney 1984: 213).

authority for government. In many cases, the advent of national democracy occurred in a political reality in which institutions were unable to stabilize a unifying model of citizenship around which their functions could be concentrated, and they were incapable of producing a legitimational bedrock for their functions.

Paradigmatic for these problems was the Weimar Republic, the most important of the new democracies established after World War I, which replaced the semi-constitutional order of Imperial Germany in 1918–19.

The Weimar Republic was founded – although ambivalently – in the name of the German proletariat, and it was established in a context marked by the extensive mobilization of radical political factions against the imperial executive, which culminated in the collapse of the Empire's ruling Hohenzollern dynasty in late 1918. Moreover, the legal foundation of the Weimar Republic was a constitution that was clearly committed to the construction of a nationally unified model of citizenship, able to pull together diffuse factions in German society. For example, the German constitution of 1919 was intended to reduce the exercise of separate authority by different regional governments, and to establish the national state as the highest focus of legal authority (Art 13). Moreover, it was committed to the renunciation of pure liberal capitalism as the dominant economic principle. As a result, the constitution espoused strong ideals of material or economic citizenship, and it provided for representation of the workforce in labour councils, placing the political system in close proximity to the people in their everyday life contexts (Art 165). However, despite these integrative ambitions, the Weimar Republic immediately appeared as a democracy without a clearly identifiable subject, which was unable to gravitate around a fixed order of citizenship, and whose stability was deeply undermined by this absence.

This lack of solidity in the construction of the people was reflected, for example, in the bitter hostility between the left-wing factions that initially assumed government functions in Germany after World War I. Notably, the German political left had been divided during the war and the faction of the political left that took control of government after the war, the Majority Social Democrats (SPD), had, by late 1918, already accomplished the reformist ambitions that its leadership had previously pursued. As a result, many leading members of the SPD would probably have preferred to avoid the foundation of a completely new democratic regime, and they were not convinced of the necessity of uprooting the monarchical system of the Empire (Matthias 1970: 22; Mühlhausen 2006: 99). Moreover, by 1919, the claims of the SPD to represent the German people had been badly undermined by the fact that leading party members had authorized the murders of other important figures on the political left (members of the Communist Party, including Rosa Luxemburg and Karl Liebknecht), who had in fact previously been attached to the left wing of the SPD itself. This lack of cohesion at the core of the Weimar Republic was already evident on the day of its foundation. On this day, symbolically, different factions of the German labour movement made separate proclamations concerning the foundation of the new Republic, so that, initially, two different Republics were created, one by the Majority Social Democrats and one by the Communists, formerly in the SPD.

This lack of solidity in the construction of the people was also manifest in the inter-group agreements that underpinned the Weimar Republic. Indicatively, the Republic was partly instituted because figures attached to the old elites of the Imperial government, especially the more progressive sectors of the military and heavy industry, decided to cooperate with the SPD in establishing the new democracy. These groups were prepared to sanction the creation of a democratic order with mixed liberal and social-democratic features, not because of any deep commitment to democracy, but because they saw this as a means to avoid full-scale revolutionary overthrow and full-scale transformation of the existing economic system (Schieck: 1972: 155; Albertin 1974: 660; van Eyll 1985: 68). This meant that the new Republic resulted in part from pragmatic contrivance, and it lacked deep-set foundations. Moreover, the Weimar Republic was actually constituted by three political parties, forming the Weimar Coalition, which comprised the SPD, the left-liberal German Democratic Party, and the Zentrum (the Roman Catholic Party). These parties had drifted out of their customary political orbit during World War I, in which some of their members had collaborated in cross-party committees to promote constitutional reform (see Patemann 1964: 86; Bermbach 1967: 67–9). The ability of these parties to form a coalition in 1918–19 to support the foundation of the Republic was largely the result of the personal relations, and resultant willingness to enter compromise, that had developed between members of the different parties during the war (Mommsen 1990: 28). Soon, however, it became clear that these personal relationships were insufficiently strong to sustain an enduring cross-party popular-democratic consensus, and the objectives of the founding coalition rapidly lost influence after the creation of the Republic. The Zentrum, notably, avoided pledging loyalty to the new Republic altogether (Morsey 1966: 613). As a result of this, the democratic constitution, drafted by leading members of the Weimar Coalition, did not find strong support amongst subsequent governments, and some of its core provisions were ignored and then partly suppressed.[19] In fact, the primary elements of the founding constitutional text of the Weimar Republic possessed a shadowy reality through the course of the Republic, as few politicians felt any great inclination to put its policy commitments into practice. Most notably, the material provisions of the Constitution, reflecting corporatist/welfarist ideals of citizenship, were only partially realized, and they were increasingly suspended by the end of the 1920s.[20]

To be sure, the German democracy was a rather extreme example of a democracy without an underlying democratic subject, based on a highly fractured construction of democratic citizenship. The fragmentation of democratic agency in the Weimar Republic was especially manifest because of the accelerated democratic transition from semi-representative to mass-democratic government in Germany. To some degree, however, this phenomenon was common to most interwar democracies, few of which were underscored by a normatively integrated model of democratic citizenship. In the UK, for example, democracy was specifically consolidated in and after 1918 in a form designed to prevent the assumption of government by parties representing the increasingly radicalized labour movement. As mentioned, in the first post-armistice elections, in December 1918, the Liberals and the Conservatives campaigned on a joint platform to obstruct the electoral advance of the Labour Party. Subsequently, an anti-Labour 'equipoise', often entailing strategic coalitions between capitalist parties to eliminate the political threat posed by organized labour, remained the dominant principle of British government until after 1945 (McKibbin 2010: 64).[21] In Italy, the newly democratized political system that emerged from World War I was chronically hamstrung by the fact that its leading democratic parties (the Socialists and the People's Party) found each other ideologically abhorrent and could not agree on principles for collaboration (Knox 2007: 362). In Austria, leading theorists of the political Left endeavoured to construct a model of cross-class sovereignty to cement the foundations of the post-1918 democratic system (see Bauer 1980: 62). However, this system was blocked by anti-labour factions (Gerlich 1980: 245).

---

[19] See on these points Weisbrod (1975: 243); Petzina (1985: 63); Schaefer (1990: 38); Meister (1991: 189); Lepsius (1993: 81).

[20] See the classic studies in Kahn-Freund (1932: 168–9); Kirchheimer (1981).

[21] On the motives for the creation of a broad anti-labour coalition in 1918, integrally linked to the expansion of the electorate in the same year, see Turner (1992: 3–7). Turner describes this process as an 'alignment of the governing parties against Labour', which 'undercut historic Liberalism' (1992: 448).

Across Europe, in other words, the first factual integration of the people into the national political system was not carried forward by a wave of mass mobilization or by any real expression of a conclusively unified demos. On the contrary, it was determined by an uncertain push-and-pull process between different actors, different organizations and different interests, which hardly shared common principles of democratic self-government, and many of which accepted democracy on a very contingent, pragmatic basis.

Fourth, new democracies created after 1918 were centred around intensely contested, and internally unsettling, constructions of citizenship.

During World War I, for example, most states had passed legislation identifying and making provision for the treatment of enemy aliens, promoting strictly exclusive ideas of citizenship (King 2000: 90; Gosewinkel 2016: 124–30). Democracy was thus implanted in societies marked by virulent nationalist aggression. Further, owing to the military context, democracies created after 1918 were required to incorporate populations marked by recent experience of complete mobilization for, and comprehensive incorporation in, national war machines. Consequently, these new democracies were generally shaped by the conviction that their institutions were required to derive legitimacy from the continued deep inclusion of their constituencies in governmental functions. The military environment surrounding mass democratization, meant that democratic institutions were often expected to integrate the national people at a high degree of intensity, providing both political and material compensation for recent sacrifices in combat and establishing collectivist organs of economic administration for peacefully reincorporating the population in civilian life.[22] As a result, many political observers after 1918 advocated the creation of corporatist systems of political-economic coordination, which were supposed to construct an immediate relation between state institutions and social agents, and in which government organs were required to assume extensive responsibilities for social administration and material distribution. These constitutional models placed only partial emphasis on the recognition citizens as holders of personal subjective rights, and

---

[22] Notably, the democratic settlements after 1918 included, with variations between polities, expanded social rights for working classes, new powers for trade unions (e.g. co-determination, freedom to create collective wage agreements), labour tribunals to regulate disputes and some mechanisms of social protection. This was most advanced in Germany, where protective rights for workers were established in the constitution of 1919, and some provisions were made for nationalization of leading industries.

instead they constructed state legitimacy as a condition dependent on the integration of citizens as holders of collective material rights.

Such enthusiasm for comprehensive political integration was common on the radical political left in post-1918 Europe, as Marxist theorists sought to redefine democracy on the basis of enhanced material unity between state and society.[23] One broad line of Marxist orthodoxy around 1914, based on a fusion of late-liberal statism and Marxist economic-democratic theory, devised a theory of *organized capitalism* to explain the conjuncture of democracy at this time. Proponents of this theory argued that, owing to its increasingly central position in the national economy, the state could assume a steering function in coordinating large-scale monopolistic enterprises, guiding the economy towards socialism in accordance with a popular political mandate.[24] An alternative, reformist line of corporatist socialism advocated the creation of economic councils at the workplace as part of plan for a broad-based consensual transition to socialism.[25] In some countries, more socially conciliatory representatives of organized labour saw corporatism as a strategy for economic cooperation with employers, aimed at realizing industrial harmony.[26] More moderate welfarists, of course, viewed social provision and basic social rights as means for establishing a deepened connection between state and society, and as a result most interwar states created rudimentary welfare systems. However, corporatist outlooks were also common amongst political Conservatives, who often projected a semi-corporatist polity model in which corporatist deputations in the economy were expected to reinforce the coordinating power of the political system, and to stabilize the position of economic elites.[27] Eventually, such outlooks culminated in the policies of ultra-Conservative, or Fascist corporatist theorists, which were generally based

[23] Famously, in Italy, Gramsci saw egalitarian democracy as a state of proletarian hegemony (1996: 61). In Austria, the Austro-Marxists saw the materially consolidated national community as the basis for a legitimate state (Adler 1922: 33, 49, 196).

[24] This outlook was especially widespread in Germany. On the impact of these ideas on interwar Social Democratic politics see Könke (1987: 101). On the broad spectrum of support for such theories, ranging from Marxists to liberals, see Zunkel (1974: 31, 51–2, 63). For the economic theory underlying this see Hilferding (1910: 295).

[25] This approach assumed greatest impact in Germany (see von Oertzen 1976: 67). But provisions for collective bargaining were widespread across Europe after World War I; in fact, most countries established fora for cross-class mediation during the war. See comments on this in Lorwin (1954: 50); Middlemas (1979: 151); Horne (1991: 15); Turner (1992: 12, 52, 334–5, 369).

[26] For an analysis of corporatism on this pattern, see discussion of the Mond-Turner talks in Britain in the late 1920s in Currie (1979: 134).

[27] See brilliant contemporary analysis in Landauer (1925: 192)

on repressive models of material citizenship, designed to subordinate the labour movement to macro-economic policy making.[28] After 1918, therefore, a material conception of democracy became widespread at different points on the political spectrum, and this conception was centred on an idea of the citizen as an agent endowed with strong claims to material integration in the political system.[29]

Fundamental to corporatist constitutionalism was the fact that it integrated many political and economic actors directly into the political system. Indeed, it premised the legitimacy of the state on an intricately articulated and highly mediated construct of citizenship, based on the principle that the state should allocate political and economic rights to a range of actors across society in order to reduce inter-class conflicts and to solidify its own foundation in society. In this respect, World War I in fact led to an intensified realization of principles of inclusion embedded in the basic normative construction of national citizenship, and the corporatist political systems created after 1918 embodied attempts, initially, to ensure that national political institutions extracted their legitimacy from the full inclusion of the citizen. At the same time, however, corporatism integrated diverse social actors into the political system in their quality, not solely as formal citizens, but as adversaries in the industrial production process, and it sought to produce legitimacy for the political system by mediating the conflicts between citizens in the material, productive dimension of their lives. Owing to their widespread corporatist bias, European states after 1918 were forced to balance sharply divergent ideas of citizenship, and actors in different sectors of national society utilized their position within the political system, assigned to them under corporatistic arrangements, to demand very different entitlements and very different patterns of inclusion. Across Europe, organizations representing the labour movement viewed corporatistic citizenship as an opportunity to demand extended material rights. By contrast, leaders of organized business used corporatism to entrench more limited, monetary rights. As Marx had anticipated, therefore, the first emergence of mass democracy created a situation in which different social factions used rights inherent in citizenship to claim quite distinct, often logically opposed, sets of rights, and society as a whole became deeply polarized through the deep politicization of rival rights claims.

---

[28] Fascist corporatism began in economic and labour legislation introduced by Mussolini in the mid-1920s. But aspects of this were duplicated in most fascist states.

[29] For still illuminating reflection on this, see Halévy (1938: 95–133).

In most instances, national political systems in post-1918 Europe were not able to resolve conflicts between conflicting constructions of citizenship. Most states were unsettled, usually fatally, by the fact that they institutionalized conflicts between counter-posed sets of rights and interests, articulated with different models of citizenship. Before 1918, as discussed, most governments only possessed rudimentary systems of democratic representation, which were not equipped to conduct the far-reaching processes of class mediation, societal transformation and economic redistribution, to which the material conception of democracy realized after 1918 committed them. As a result, most democracies established after 1918 lacked a stable organizational form in which the national people could be integrated into newly expanded governmental functions. In most cases, the democratic experiments commenced around 1918 were unsettled after just a few years, as governing coalitions failed to establish consensus on the relative weight of socio-economic rights (welfare) and monetary rights (investment, accumulation rights). This became acutely visible as governments were split apart by controversies over fiscal arrangements after the Wall Street Crash of 1929, when, owing to capital withdrawal, governments lost the capacity to balance out rival claims and rival rights in relatively pacified manner.[30] At this point, the inherent tendency in national citizenship to expose society to a process of inclusive politicization, translating originally private rights claims into volatile political conflicts, became strikingly and acutely manifest, with systemically debilitating outcomes. At this point, most European states renounced the attempt to sustain cross-class coalitions and cross-class models of citizenship, which had originally informed their constitutional designs, and they dramatically switched preference towards the economically dominant actors in these coalitions.[31]

Fifth, despite the prognoses of more evolutionary theorists of democracy, the first emergence of the national population as a political agent around 1918 did not result in the more consolidated integration of the people, or even in the steady solidification of representative-democratic institutions.

[30] In Germany, the cross-class Grand Coalition collapsed in 1929/30 over differences in fiscal policy between constituent parties. This led to the end of democracy. On plans for reduced public spending and reduced taxation amongst Conservative elites in the UK, which were reflected in the formation of the semi-dictatorial national government of 1931, see Ball (1988: 156); Ewing and Gearty (2000: 237). As in Germany, the national government of 1931 in Britain was legitimated, even on the moderate Left, by claims that 'national crisis' required 'national retrenchment' (Currie 1979: 140).

[31] A notable exception is Sweden, where inter-group bargains, crossing lines of traditional class adversity, proved relatively solid (see Gourevitch 1984: 116).

On the second point, notably, the expansion of mass democracy around 1918 did not lead to the reinforcement of elected legislatures. On the contrary, it led to the transfer of directive power from legislatures to executives, and to the concentration of executive power in the hands of relatively closed political elites. As Weber and his followers had prophesied, mass-democracy, defined as a system of governance led and legitimated by popular parliamentary legislatures, did not long survive the transition to fully inclusive representation. In fact, the democratic widening of the electorate and the concomitant growth of government functions around 1918 almost invariably meant that the executive soon became the dominant branch of government.[32]

On the first point, further, the expansion of mass-democracy did not lead to the promotion of laws reflecting the wider social and economic interests of the majority of the population. Of course, some experiments in interwar democracy did yield important legislation for the promotion of material redistribution and broad economic amelioration. In the years following 1918, the basic structure of later welfare states was established in a number of societies, including Germany, Sweden and the UK.[33] More pervasively, however, the primary outcome of the first experiments in mass democracy was that large sectors of national populations were prepared to mobilize, often using military or paramilitary force, for political and economic initiatives that clearly favoured the interests, not of newly enfranchised social strata, but of historically dominant minorities. New post-1918 democracies in Austria, Germany, Italy and Spain (after 1931) all rapidly came under attack from intensely militarized social factions (widely associated with *Fascism*), which aimed to sabotage democracy and to replace it with extremely coercive governmental orders. These factions

---

[32] By 1925, executive prerogative had become a core instrument of legislation in Germany, and, by 1930, executive prerogative was the essential constitutional foundation of government. Notably, key economic legislation introduced by President Ebert in the economic inflation was introduced by executive fiat. In the UK, interwar elections were primarily designed not to represent the people, but to broker an inter-party mandate to support executive authority, a pattern which culminated in the suspension of competitive government in 1931. In Italy, the legislature was effectively eliminated as an independent organ of government in 1922. After 1933, government in Austria was placed on prerogative foundations, based on emergency legislation introduced in 1917. The authoritarian constitution of 1934 was introduced by decree. Across Europe, in fact, the interwar era was defined by the rapidly rising dominance of the executive branch.

[33] On Lloyd George's social policies as the basis of the British welfare state see Morgan (1979: 107–8). On the early development of a welfare state in Germany after 1918, see the standard account in Preller, discussing rising average income (1949: 155), introduction of the eight-hour day (1949: 210), and rising social insurance investment, up to 1930 (1949: 463).

served the protection of barely camouflaged elite prerogatives, but they nonetheless recruited heavily from working-class constituencies. After 1918, therefore, democratization brought a swift and radical turn away from democracy amongst social groups who supposedly stood to benefit most from democratic rule. Even countries that preserved some (partial and thin) vestige of democracy through the interwar era, such as the UK, veered away from conventional systems of representation, and they partly abandoned the competitive component of fully democratic politics.[34]

In addition, sixth, early mass-democratic societies typically lacked overarching national organizational structures, they were still largely dominated by local centres of authority and obligation, and their capacities for integration of mass-political forces were not strong. At one level, World War I brought a great leap forward in the nationalization of democratic political systems, linked to exponentially heightened governmental coordination of the economy and to the intensification of democratic competition between national political organizations.[35] Indeed, the military environment greatly intensified the basic nationalization of society. However, few societies in this period possessed political institutions that were robust enough to contain the politicization and polarization of society caused by mass-democratic mobilization and mass-democratic contestation over different rights. In most democracies that emerged around 1918, political institutions soon began to resort to more personalistic techniques of administration and consensus formation. In fact, the authoritarian polities that were established in the 1920s and 1930s usually reverted in part to a pre-modern polity type, and their leadership structures often relied on older patterns of patronage and favour to generate societal support. Under these regimes, political parties were only able to connect the different population groups in national societies to national institutions by co-opting local and traditional elites, and by entrusting these elites with responsibilities for social coordination between national institutional centres and regional constituencies.[36] As discussed, democracy first began to evolve

---

[34] See p. 329 below.

[35] For empirical analysis to support this claim see Caramani (2004: 197).

[36] This was especially the case in the authoritarian regimes created in the 1930s in Southern Europe. One commentator on Italy under Mussolini has observed that government was primarily conducted by 'para-state bodies' tending to coalesce with dominant economic and local actors (Bonini 2004: 101). Speaking of Spain under Franco, one important commentary explains how the fascist regime structure converged with ancient, local patronage-based modes of governance (López and Gil Bracero 1997: 137). Generally, interwar authoritarian regimes loudly proclaimed nationality as a founding principle of government. Indeed, the idea of the people as an entity transcending all internal divisions was crucial for

after 1789 through the ideological mobilization of the nation, and early democratic institutions invariably established their authority by invoking the nation as the author of public power. Factually, however, even after 1918, most early mass-democratic societies were only patchily nationalized, and they did not possess either the organizational mechanisms or the institutional infrastructure to consolidate the national people as a unified basis for government. In most societies, political institutions were unable to absorb the pressures triggered by the nationalization of political integration processes and political conflict, and they were not able to project a stable model of national citizenship to encompass and mediate the full set of conflicts existing in national society. As a result, early-modern localism soon reappeared beneath the surface of the democracies created in Europe after 1918, and it remained a dominant political influence until after 1945.

After 1918, in short, national political democracy emerged in Europe, for the first time, as a system of mass-political inclusion. Few societies reached a condition close to full democracy at this time, but most advanced markedly towards democracy. Although paradigmatically exemplified in Europe, in fact, similar processes of political construction can be observed in Latin America. The early processes of democratization and nationalization, which began around 1789 and which ran, at varying degrees of articulation, through the nineteenth century, gained sudden expression, explosively, in the political experiments initiated in and after 1918. Almost immediately after this expression, however, these processes were suspended. By approximately 1940, democracy had virtually disappeared from the global map. Democratization occurred around 1918 in a context marked by multiple, often mutually exclusive, patterns of citizenship, which directed acute social antagonisms towards newly constructed national democratic institutions. Moreover, democratization occurred in contexts in which states lacked organizational forms to absorb the intensified, often intensely conflictual, demands of enfranchised citizens. This meant that institutions struggled to withstand the national articulation of societal conflicts, and they collapsed in face of the pressures caused

---

the initial emergence of fascism as a movement, which occurred in Italy during and after World War I (see Procacci 1968: 165; De Grand 1978: 159). However, fascist states actually undid long-standing processes of socio-political nationalization. For example, one interpreter of Nazi Germany explains how the societal reality of the regime was determined by the endeavour of regional authorities to solidify their own positions, thus creating a highly centrifugal apparatus (Rebentisch 1989: 265). Democratic governments have usually been much more effectively in promoting the construction of nationalized societies. Indeed, the nationalization of society presupposes the existence of deep-reaching participatory organs.

by the integration of social groups with nationally politicized economic rivalries. Although the figure of the *citoyen* had acted as the construct that first underpinned the differentiation of the modern political system, after 1918, the *citoyen* appeared in an acutely politicized form that could not easily be incorporated in national political systems, and which prevented the stabilization of the political system as an integrative social domain. The impetus towards inclusion of the citizen that shaped the first rise of national societies ultimately culminated in a process that simultaneously accentuated both the particularistic and the homogenizing elements in citizenship, and which resulted in both the stabilization of the position of societal elites and the (often violent) eradication of non-dominant social groups. The intensification of national political inclusion through World War I was the primary explanation for each of these problems.

On these grounds, the period of accelerated democratization in inter-war Europe, caused by military mass-mobilization in World War I, brought into sharp relief the essential insight of classical sociological theory concerning the nature of democracy: namely, *that democracy could not, without deep reduction, be centred around the will of the people.* This basic insight of early sociology acquired intensified relevance in post-1918 Europe, where national governments found themselves lacking unifying patterns of citizenship to support their already precariously balanced institutions. After 1918, most states were obliged to manufacture a construction of the citizen strong enough to transcend the acute divisions, linked to class-based, inter-party and regional distinctions, which existed between newly integrated social groups. In this setting, however, states were visibly unsettled by their endeavours to correlate their institutions with a deep-lying popular will and to make the people materially palpable in acts of government. Then, as mass democracies collapsed into authoritarianism, the patchwork form of elite pluralism typical of pre-modern, pre-national, socio-political structure became clearly visible beneath the inclusionary orders established through early national democracy. At this time, many national political systems renounced ideas of national citizenship altogether, reverting to reliance on more traditional local modes of coercion to galvanize societal support. Although interwar polities were based on the attempt to construct complexly mediated patterns of citizenship to support government, they were soon defined by the disappearance of the national citizen as a focus of legitimacy. Throughout interwar Europe, states were unable to construct modes of integration that allowed the people to act as a relatively stable subject, as legally included citizens, through the institutional organs of government. The more the political system was centred on the people as a factually existing group of citizens, the more unstable democracy became, and the less securely the people were integrated in government. The original sociological intuition about the paradox of democracy thus became reality.

The underlying weakness of political subject formation in post-1918 democracies was clearly observed by legal theorists situated at the sociological end of interwar legal analysis. The primary claim in the works of Carl Schmitt, for example, was that post-1918 parliamentary democracy revolved around a fictional construction of the political subject of society.

For Schmitt, this projective aspect of democracy was expressed in the fact that theorists of parliamentary-democratic representation necessarily resorted to political idealism to support their claims. Such theorists, he argued, only managed to justify their model of democracy by constructing it around an imaginary people, endowed with fictitious ethical-consensual orientations and metaphysical propensities for rational behaviour, which could not be found in the conflictual reality of a modern class society (1922: 46). Above all, Schmitt argued that advocates of parliamentary democracy were forced to presume that members of national populations were naturally inclined towards relatively harmonious coexistence, and that their interests and prerogatives could be peacefully mediated into generalized legal form, facilitating their integration in the political order (1923: 45). When confronted with nations in their objectively existent, materially pluralized shape, however, parliamentary-democratic institutions struggled to produce objective laws that could assume general acceptance amongst all actors in their populations. These institutions typically proved incapable of resolving conflicts between the societal factions, which they had sought to integrate, and they merely provide an organizational form for rival social and economic interest groups (1923: 11). For Schmitt, in consequence, parliamentary-democratic institutions were invariably prone to crisis as they attempted to palliate the real social antagonisms that they internalized as they tried to secure legitimacy through inclusion of their national populations.

In addition, Schmitt argued that the projective, fictional aspect of parliamentary democracy was displayed in the fact that, although parliamentary institutions purported to derive legitimacy immediately from the will of the people, the organizational forms particular to parliamentary democracy in fact served actively to disaggregate this will. Such institutions – for example, delegatory chambers, parliamentary factions, political parties – were incapable of incorporating the will of the people in its cohesive totality, and they inevitably obstructed the integration of the people as a unified political agent (1923: 19–20). Indeed, he claimed, such institutions had the unavoidable consequence that the people were subject, usually along fissures determined by class affiliation, to pluralistic division, parcellation and fragmentation, before they could be integrated into the political system. Parliamentary democracy, in short, could not be premised in the enactment of the will of a national people, and it could only ever give partial, unmediated expression to the interests of a given population.

On this basis, Schmitt came to the conclusion that the people could only be represented as an *absent force* in the parliamentary-democratic system (1928: 209–10), and a democratic system obtained greatest proximity to the will of the people if it renounced the attempt organically to represent the people through delegatory institutions. Accordingly, he decided that the legal apparatus of parliamentary representation had to be subordinated to provisions for plebiscitary elections, and only direct popular acclamation of political leaders could allow the actual will of the people to become visible (1928: 243, 1932b: 85–7). At times, in fact, he claimed that a system of commissarial dictatorship, legitimated by the symbolic approval of the people for a ruler, could be seen as more democratic and more democratically legitimate, than parliamentary democracy (1919: 136, 1927: 34). In other legal-sociological constructions of this time, the view also prevailed that emergent parliamentary systems lacked the institutional capacity to draw society together in a unified whole, and that democratic political subjectivity had to be constructed by means distinct from the typical institutions of democracy. In such cases, it was argued that democracies were required strategically to materialize the people to whom they attached their claims to legitimacy.[37]

2.2   The Transformation of Democracy

If the experiments in nationalized mass-democracy that began around 1918 met with catastrophic failure, political democracy finally – albeit still gradually – became a more securely established and increasingly widespread political form after 1945. Indeed, the underlying, socially formative trajectories of nationalization and democratization, which had been suspended in most societies after 1918, recommenced after 1945, and, in this setting, these processes experienced much more robust institutionalization.

---

[37] In 1928, Smend argued that the state obtains legitimacy partly through the 'integrational force' of political symbolism (1955: 163).

To be sure, in the immediate wake of 1945, democratic states still formed a minority grouping in the international community. Self-evidently, the influence of the Soviet Union in Eastern Europe until the 1980s prevented the emergence of regular democracies in this region. Moreover, many new states created after 1945, especially in post-colonial Africa, were initially founded as nationalized democracies, but, as in Europe in the interwar era, their institutions lacked deep-lying social foundations, and they collapsed into one-party systems, almost invariably dominated by local elites or privileged social groups.[38]

To an increasing degree, nonetheless, after 1945, democracy gradually became a norm by which nation states were measured and legitimated, and there evolved a growing presumption that, in order to presume legitimacy, states should take democratic form. As a result, most states that were reconstructed, or which came into being, after 1945, were designed, at least officially, as democracies. This began in the immediate aftermath of 1945, with the foundation of new democracies in the FRG, Japan, India and Italy. This continued through decolonization in the 1950s and 1960s, and through the transitions in Southern Europe in the 1970s. Democracy then eventually became a global norm through the Latin American transitions of the 1980s, the Eastern European transitions of the 1990s and the African transitions of the 1990s and the first decade of the twenty-first century. These different processes of transitional polity building induced an effective *globalization of democracy*. Naturally, this does not mean that democracy exists everywhere. Clearly, non-democratic governance is currently prevalent in much of Central and East Asia, and many states classified as democracies contain authoritarian features. However, democracy is a global political form, and polities with no democratic features are rare.

There are several factors in the process of democratic globalization that began after 1945 which require particular attention, and which, like the failure of democracy after 1918, throw broad light on the essential foundations of contemporary democracy. Analysis of these factors again calls into question more classical explanations of democracy. However, it allows us to understand democracy in a global sociological perspective.

2.2.1   Full Inclusion

First, the years after 1945 witnessed the growth of political systems in which collective participation of citizens in the foundation of government,

---

[38]   See for discussion of one example below pp. 402–5.

and the ongoing inclusion of popular representatives in political processes, unmistakably increased. In fact, for the first time in world history, after 1945 national populations, acting as equals citizens, were able, step-by-step, enduringly to claim some responsibility both for the founding laws of their polities and for laws passed at a day-to-day level.

At the level of constitution making, this process varied from society to society. Some new democracies were created with only minimal popular consultation about the form of government. In many democracies created in the immediate aftermath of World War II, constitutional laws were imposed by external actors, often by occupying forces or organs of territorial administration.[39] In many post-colonial states, departing imperial actors were keen to ensure a pacted transition to democratic rule, and they only negotiated the terms of constitutional transfer with small coteries of hand-picked elite players.[40] The model of pacted transition reappeared later in Spain after 1975, and, by contagion, in different Latin American states (see Weyland 2014: 60). In some democracies established at a later stage, by contrast, democratic constitutions were created through wide-ranging consultation, linking the process of constitution writing to the participation of different societal groupings, and even to civil-society organizations.[41] Across the spectrum of democratic re-orientation, however, polities created through these separate processes made at least some claim to originate in the interests of a national people.

Most importantly, this period solidified the presumption that democracy should be a system of *full inclusion*. After 1945, few new democracies were created that endorsed franchise restrictions. Similarly, most polities that had already evolved partial democratic features prior to 1945 revised their electoral laws to ensure that full suffrage became commonplace, and economic privileges in voting allocations or constitutional influence were widely abolished. Examples of this are electoral reforms in the UK in 1948–50, removing all remaining electoral privileges, reforms in France in 1944–5 that guaranteed female suffrage, and constitutional reforms in Denmark in 1953, limiting the impact of established social privilege on legislation. Moreover, crucially, overt racial or ethnic discrimination in electoral provisions became unusual, and it was subject to broad censure.

---

[39] See below p. 312.

[40] For instance, the insertion of bills of rights in post-colonial constitutions was often promoted as a means to facilitate the peaceful transfer of power to new elites, guaranteeing protection for established interests. See general discussion in Parkinson (2007: 273).

[41] See pp. 434–7 below.

Such discrimination survived in Canada until 1960, Australia until 1962, the USA until 1964/5 and South Africa until 1991–4; it was also fundamental to the state of Rhodesia created in 1965. However, such states formed a minority, and they were widely exposed to international pressure, of different kinds, to reform their electoral policies.[42]

2.2.2   Full Nationalization

Second, most democracies created in the processes of polity building beginning after 1945 witnessed the beginnings of a process of *political nationalization*, in which political authority was divided more evenly across the constituent memberships of national societies, and political institutions obtained inclusionary support from a widened range of social groups.[43] As discussed below, the globalization of democracy inevitably meant that new patterns of democracy began to emerge, some of which fell clearly short of the criteria normally used to define democracy. Political nationalization, giving rise to the even inclusion of national citizens, rarely became a fully consolidated reality. Nonetheless, most new democracies established in the decades after 1945 developed national political parties, articulated with social groups consolidated at a national level, and they were increasingly founded in reasonably uniform processes of collective national will formation, political integration and general representation.

Alongside this, further, societies that converted to some form of democracy during the waves of post-1945 transition usually experienced a process of *structural nationalization*. Through the nationalization of political institutions, the historically localized structure of societies was increasingly eroded, and societies tended, to an increasing degree, to converge around centralized institutions, such that private centres of authority lost their influence. This phenomenon is discussed more extensively below.[44] Suffice it to say here, however, that, in new post-1945 democracies, constitutions or high-ranking laws were introduced that limited the remnants of local, feudal traditions, and which made the legitimacy of legislation

---

[42] On the destabilizing impact of international censure in Rhodesia, whose legitimacy following its unilateral declaration of independence from the UK was very thin, see White (2015: 116).

[43] Note that Caramani identifies 1918 as the point in which, in Europe, political systems became nationalized (2004: 197). I agree with this, but my claim is that the moment of nationalization in 1918 resulted in institutional collapse, and states were not able to maintain stability in the face of their own nationalized structure and environment until after 1945.

[44] See p. 162.

contingent on nationally established normative systems. This was evident in political systems created in societies as diverse as Japan (1945–7), Italy (1948), the FRG (1945–9), India (1947–50), Bolivia (1952), Ghana (1957), Kenya (1960–3), each of which had historically been marked, to varying degrees, by low levels of structural unity.[45] In societies with older democratic lineages, local points of intersection between the governmental apparatus and members of society also became weaker.[46]

On this last point, certain variations need to be observed. In many cases, the institutionalization of national democratic representation after 1945 was only possible because democratic political systems were organized on a diffusely decentralized or federal model, permitting the coexistence of different regional groups beneath the normative order of the national legal system. In extreme cases, in fact, democratic political systems were only able to take root because they conferred high degrees of autonomy on regional groups defined by minority ethnic affiliation. This was especially common in Latin America, in which, as discussed later, eventual democratic consolidation often depended upon the recognition of multiple constitutional subjects, with distinct collective rights.[47] Nonetheless, such decentralization was usually linked to a parallel process of societal formation, in which political authority was attached to uniform legal norms, and the ability of regionally embedded actors and local elites to monopolize public power for purposes not formally sanctioned by national law was diminished.

Overall, the processes of democratization that occurred after 1945 gradually began to establish a basic condition of nationalization in domestic societies. That is to say, these processes began to construct a societal order in which national laws were created by national subjects, and different domains of national societies were integrated, relatively evenly, in the same legal system and the same political system. In these processes, consequently, a relatively solid and geographically stable model of the citizen became the defining source of legislation.

---

[45] See discussion of Germany and Kenya in Chapter 4 below. For other examples, measures introduced in Japan after 1945 removed the feudal 'house system' of family authority (Oppler 1976: 113). Measures introduced in Bolivia in 1952 removed feudal land tenure and created a national system of trade-union-based organization, which constructed a national pattern of citizenship (García Linera 2014: 198). Measures introduced in Ghana in the 1950s and early 1960s were designed to abolish chieftaincy and to create a unified national order (Rathbone 2000: 140).

[46] See for instance discussion of the USA below at p. 295.

[47] See p. 439.

2.2.3   International Law and National Sovereignty

Third, importantly, these overlapping dynamics of democratic inclusion and systemic nationalization took place in a broad legal environment, which profoundly reconfigured the concepts of national sovereignty and national citizenship developed through the earlier history of democratic theory and democratic practice. The emergence of national populations as powerful actors in the political system usually occurred through a process in which more classical ideas of national political agency were replaced by new patterns of primary legal norm formation. Indeed, secure democratization typically occurred in settings in which the assumption that the acts and demands of national citizens form the essential source of legitimate political order was strongly relativized. After 1945, most significantly, the global reproduction of democracy was closely tied to the growing power of international law and international organizations, and the importance of international law had a deeply consolidating impact, both normatively and systemically, on the emergent global form of democratic government. Particularly prominent in this context is the fact that the period after 1945 saw the promulgation of a number of instruments of international human rights law (with either global or regional reach), and these instruments promoted a distinct definition of democracy, which discernibly shaped the emergent constitutional form of both new and old democracies. Indeed, in many cases, these instruments constructed a meta-normative order for national democratic constitutions, providing for extensive cross-fertilization and normative interpenetration between the national and the international legal domains (see Shany 2006: 342).

For example, the primary documents of international human rights law introduced after 1945, notably the Charter of the United Nations (UN Charter), the Universal Declaration of Human Rights (UDHR) and later the International Covenant on Civil and Political Rights (ICCPR), all fostered a constitutional presumption that legitimate states should recognize the persons in their territories as holders of certain generalized rights. All these documents implied that states had a duty to provide protection for the singular/subjective rights of individual citizens. To some degree, these documents implicitly affirmed 'the participation of the individual in international law' as an agent 'possessing rights and freedoms directly rather than through the State as a conduit of individual protections' (Weatherall 2015: 190). In addition, more mutedly, these documents promoted rights-based government as a political ideal. At the very least, these instruments implied a global model of the citizen, in which citizens were viewed as endowed with the same rights, across all borders, and which conferred legitimacy on acts of law in necessarily generalized fashion, insisting that laws of national states were to be proportioned to a global idea of the citizen as a holder of fixed rights. Together, these documents reflected the rise of a global legal system in which certain normative principles acquired legitimacy above national jurisdictions, originating in norms whose existence was increasingly independent of different nation states, national governments and national societies. Indeed, the original impetus towards the expansion of human rights law after 1945 was driven in part by the proceedings against war criminals in Japan and Germany, in which it was decided that certain norms had globally immutable authority, and individual persons representing their governments had singular responsibility in cases of egregious human rights abuses. On this basis, governments were imputed strict obligations regarding the promotion of human rights for individual members of their societies. From this time on, very slowly, it became accepted that national legal orders were, at least in principle, overarched by a system of higher norms, largely extracted from human rights law, by which states were morally obligated as constitutional subjects, and by which, in some cases, individuals were permitted to seek redress against their own governments.

Self-evidently, the international legal norms formalized after 1945 did not immediately become a global reality. The penetration of such norms into national societies was slow and fitful. Still today, clearly, this process remains incomplete. Moreover, these norms did not immediately construct a foundation for national democracy. It was not until the 1970s that human rights protection and democratization were clearly and unreservedly correlated.

One reason for the limited impact of international human rights law on democratic formation was that the realization of the democratic potential of international human rights law was decelerated by the intensification of the Cold War in the early 1950s. A further reason for this was that the wave of decolonization in Africa had a very ambiguous effect on the political effects of international human rights law. Over a longer period, the global consolidation of international human rights law was clearly induced, partially, by anti-colonial actions – especially by protests against apartheid in the 1960s, backed by UN Declarations and (eventually) by rulings of the International Court of Justice (ICJ).[48] However, during the period

---

[48] Legal Consequences for States of the Continued Presence of South Africa in Namibia (South West Africa) Notwithstanding Security Council Resolution 276 (1970), Advisory Opinion, 1971 I.C.J. 16 (June 21).

of decolonization itself, newly mandated heads of African states were usually (quite justifiably) very protective of their sovereignty, and they rejected external interference in their domestic politics. This tendency was underlined in quite simple terms by the Declaration issued by the summit conference of the Organisation of African Unity (Cairo 1964), which emphasized both the categorical nature of the right to national sovereignty and the inviolability of national borders. This sovereigntist outlook inevitably created a (still persistent) tension between the relative authority of collective rights to national sovereignty, exercisable by governments, and the singular rights of individual persons, located within national societies (Burke 2010: 26). Indeed, this outlook clearly weakened the domestic impact of international human rights, especially those of a political nature. At the end of decolonization in the 1970s, consequently, human rights law reached, globally, a singularly low ebb, as many African states refused to protest against atrocities in Uganda. At the same time, dictatorships were established in much of Latin America. Although constructed as systemic principles after 1945, therefore, human rights, especially those relating to collective political freedoms, did not acquire global political authority for roughly 25 years.

A further reason for the limited impact of international human rights law on democratic formation was that international human rights declarations and conventions did not immediately contain a full and unequivocal endorsement of democracy. In fact, owing to the democratic crises in interwar Europe, these documents expressed scepticism about the unrestricted exercise of popular sovereignty.[49]

In the first instance, most international human rights documents were focused on the rights of single citizens, and singular rights were promoted as the most essential focus of governmental legitimacy. The rise of human rights law, consequently, did not imply an unequivocally binding right to democracy. Importantly, the Council of Europe viewed human rights and democracy promotion as integrally linked. The European Convention on Human Rights (ECHR) did not initially contain an express right to democracy, but it was marked, programmatically, by a commitment to furthering political democracy, and by the assumption that the necessities of democratic society should act as guidelines in the implementation

---

[49] Tellingly, Lauterpacht, one of the leading theorists of the post-1945 human rights system, argued both that global human rights necessarily implied a 'limitation of the sovereignty of states' (1945: 211) and that the right to 'national self-legislation' was not 'rigid or absolute' (1945: 145). Instead of self-legislation, he saw the 'primary right of freedom', meaning single freedoms for individual agents, as the goal of international human rights law (1945: 145).

of ECHR norms. Article 3 of the First Protocol to the ECHR then declared a right to free elections. The Charter of the Organization of American States (OAS) also declared a commitment to promoting democracy (Art 2(b)). By contrast, however, the right to democracy in the UN Charter was – at best – more implicit, and the extent to which the UN instruments established a right to democracy is open to dispute. Art 21 of the UDHR declared a right to democracy, with full and free elections. However, this right was not expected to be enforceable. It was only later, in the ICCPR of 1966, that it was stated, in Art 25(b), that electoral participation is a binding basic right, and the ICCPR set out a series of further rights which prescribed, if not democratic, then at least liberal government structures, with rights-conscious legislatures, free judiciaries, gender equality and equality before the law.[50] Even in the ICCPR, however, the actual definition of democracy was rather vague (Fox 1992: 55).[51]

A particular complication surrounding the initial relationship between international human rights law and democracy arose from the fact that, as decolonization gathered global momentum, the UN emphatically proclaimed a categorical right to *national self-determination*. This right was expressed in the UN Charter, and it was more forcefully declared in the General Assembly in 1960.[52] Indeed, in 1980, the right to self-determination was described in the UN as part of international *jus cogens*.[53] The right to self-determination has obvious implications for democratic self-government, and promotion of self-determination is not strictly separable from the promotion of democracy. Classically, however, self-determination was usually interpreted, primarily, as a right to territorial sovereignty: that is, as a right to be exercised by nations within recognized state boundaries, and to be enacted by governments. This state-focused construction of the right to self-determination was largely shaped by the

---

[50] Note the initially relaxed interpretation of these provisions by the UN Human Rights Committee, which accepted that single-party states could meet global standards of democracy (Cassese 1995: 63).

[51] One account explains how the diversity of governmental orders amongst states in the UN 'precluded consensus on the specifications' of the right to political participation (Fox and Roth 2001: 327).

[52] General Assembly Resolution 1514 (XV) of 14 December 1960.

[53] Report on the Right to Self-Determination, E/CN.4/Sub.2/405/Rev.1 (1980). See discussion in Parker and Neylon (1989: 440). This idea had already appeared in earlier opinions in the ICJ. See the 1971 opinion of Judge Ammoun in the Advisory Opinion, Legal Consequences for States of the Continued Presence of South Africa in Namibia (South West Africa) notwithstanding Security Council Resolution 276. In this opinion, the 'right of peoples to self-determination' is 'not merely "general" but universal' (75).

fact that it was formulated in terms designed to stabilize newly formed post-colonial governments, and, above all, to avert minority secession in such contexts.[54] As a result, the right to self-determination expounded as *jus cogens* is most essentially, not a right to electoral participation, to which single persons lay claim, but a right of collective sovereignty, or even as a right to territorial decolonization (Burke 2010: 37). As such, the right to self-determination is not identical with a right to democracy.[55] Tellingly, the UN Declaration on self-determination in 1960 provided an entitlement for colonial peoples to form their own states, but it did not protect single or collective political rights for persons within newly formed territories (see Macklem 2015: 170).

It was only rather gradually and tentatively that the increasingly protected right to self-determination was interpreted internationally as containing, at least implicitly, a right to some degree of popular-democratic self-legislation. For example, in resolutions concerning apartheid in South Africa and Rhodesia, the UN closely linked self-determination, democracy and human rights. In 1965, the UN issued a resolution condemning the 'usurpation of power by a racist settler minority' in Rhodesia, which clearly implied that self-determination necessarily implied majority-based government.[56] The UN continually voiced criticism of South Africa, and it expressly supported the 'legitimacy of the struggle of the oppressed people of South Africa in pursuance of their human and political rights, as set forth in the Charter of the United Nations and the Universal Declaration of Human Rights'.[57] The General Assembly then suspended representation of South Africa in 1974.[58] In fact, in Art 1(3), the ICCPR itself (1966) declared that self-determination should be exercised 'in conformity with the provisions of the Charter of the United Nations'. The probable democratic nature of self-determination was again implied in the UN in 1970, in the statement

---

[54] After 1945, recognition of collective rights of minority peoples within established state borders was initially very cautious. See the general discussion of the attempt to avoid secessionist movements in early UN norms on self-determination in Thornberry (1989: 874, 882).

[55] These two meanings of self-determination were always kept separate (see Laing 1991: 240–2). One important observer states that in early instruments promoting national self-legislation the democratic aspect of consensus-based self-government was 'totally disregarded' (Cassese 1995: 72). A different account argues that the democratic implications of self-determination were 'abandoned' through the course of decolonization (Musgrave 1997: 97).

[56] Security Council Resolution 217 (1965).

[57] Security Council Resolution 311 (1972).

[58] On the status of apartheid-era South Africa as 'international outcast' see Geldenhuys (1990: 269).

that 'all peoples have the right freely to determine, without external interference, their political status'.[59] Later, the advisory opinion of the ICJ in
Western Sahara (1975) might be taken to indicate that self-determination
has democratic implications. This opinion construed self-determination
as the right of a people 'to determine their future political status by their
own freely expressed will'.[60] In some settings, the UN endorsed democracy more actively. For instance, UN bodies monitored pre-independence
electoral participation in a number of African countries (Franck 1994:
86). The UN also prepared the foundations for democratic government in
Namibia (Fox 1992: 577). By the 1980s, the UN Commission on Human
Rights declared that popular participation in political decision making is
a right.[61] By the 1990s, it was declared in organs of the UN that democratic self-legislation had become 'one of the essential principles of international law', with *erga omnes* force.[62] Notably, in Resolution 940 (1994)
concerning Haiti, and Resolution 1132 (1997) concerning Sierra Leone,
the UN Security Council demanded restoration of democratic government. Moreover, UN peacekeeping mandates increasingly often involved
oversight of elections (Joyner 1999: 342). Later still, the ICJ pushed its reasoning further in the direction of the recognition of a right to democracy,
implying that states are required to promote democracy under international human rights law.[63] As a result of these developments, some authors
have argued that there now exists a *global right to democracy* (Cassese 1979:
157; Franck 1995: 85, 139; Benhabib 2012: 207).[64]

---

[59] Declaration on Principles of International Law concerning Friendly Relations and
Co-operation among States in accordance with the Charter of the United Nations, Res.2625
(XXV) (24 October 1970). One interpreter argues that the UN declarations concerning the
'internal aspect of self-determination' covered 'all elements of democracy' (Wheatley 2002:
231).

[60] Western Sahara, Advisory Opinion, ICJ GL No 61, [1975] ICJ Rep 12, ICGJ 214 (ICJ 1975).

[61] UN Commission on Human Rights, Resolution 1983/14 (22 February 1983).

[62] ICJ, East Timor, Portugal v Australia, Jurisdiction, Judgment, [1995] ICJ Rep 90, ICGJ 86
(ICJ 1995), 30 June 1995.

[63] Legal Consequences of the Construction of a Wall in the Occupied Palestinian Territory,
ICJ Advisory Opinion, 9 July 2004.

[64] Such claims imply that national government obtains recognition and legitimacy through
satisfaction of norms endorsed by the international community, which actively promote
democracy (Franck 1992: 91). Some observers claim that the right to democracy has existed
since 1948, with the passing of the UDHR (Cerna 1995: 290). Some observers even claim
that democracy is now established as a norm with *jus cogens* status (Ezetah 1997: 509).
These claims are surely exaggerated, and it is improbable to imagine that the international
community as a whole might enforce sanctions against a state falling below common
standards of democracy. Here I agree with Cohen (2008: 585). Yet, it is beyond doubt that
the spirit of international human rights law, impelled by a sense of horror at the results

On these grounds, international law has only provided a rather uncertain imperative for democratic polity building. Despite these qualifications, however, in the longer wake of 1945, international human rights law became increasingly prominent as a basis for democratic institutional construction, and eventually it was only through the impact of international human rights law that democracy became globally widespread.[65]

First, the link between international human rights and democracy was due, simply, to the growing presumption in favour of democracy in international law. As discussed, even if such provisions are difficult to enforce, the right to electoral participation is set out in a number of international instruments. Although it is doubtful that we can identify a binding global right to democracy, moreover, some hard provisions of international law generate the presumption that legitimate government will approximate to the model of democracy. Some principles of international law with clear *jus cogens* authority, especially concerning racial equality, almost of necessity create a presumption in favour of political equality, which is typically realized in a democracy.[66] At the very least, therefore, international human rights contains an emphatic *orientation towards democracy*. Even if it falls short of *jus cogens* status, democracy is widely viewed as a precondition for the international legitimacy of governments.[67]

Second, the link between international human rights and democracy was due to the fact that different international instruments constructed a series of personal rights that, taken together, strongly implied a right to democracy. These rights included rights contained in the UDHR, such as rights to free expression, rights to justice, rights to free movement and rights to legal and procedural equality, which cannot easily be accessed outside a national political system with some resemblance to a democracy. In these respects, international law implied a norm of citizenship likely to be found in a democracy, and it promoted rights likely to be exercised under political systems ensuring relative legal and political equality.

---

of combined authoritarianism and racism in the 1930s, implied a strong endorsement of democracy as a governmental ideal (see Bradley 2016: 49).

[65] As Przeworski has noted, most models of democratization do not consider this fact (2008: 305). Przeworski himself argues that international norms were of 'overwhelming' importance in the enfranchisement of women. My claim is that effective enfranchisement for both genders required international norms.

[66] On the particular significance of the global anti-apartheid movement as a driver in democracy promotion in the UN see Klotz (1995: 45).

[67] Apart from UN practices, this is reflected *inter alia* in the Helsinki Accords (1975), the 1990 Charter of Paris, the EC Guidelines on Recognition of New States in Eastern Europe and in the Soviet Union (1991).

International human rights law gained democratizing effect partly because it became enforceable through international organizations, so that human rights principles impacted widely on patterns of democratic formation. By the 1970s, the system of international law was relatively consolidated, and it had begun to assume material results. The major UN human rights covenants were approved in 1966 and took effect in 1976. Notably, the 1970s saw the intensification of monitoring by UN bodies, the establishment, ultimately of vital significance, of the Inter-American Court of Human Rights (IACtHR) (1978–9), and the propagation of the Helsinki Accords (1975), which provided important normative directives in Eastern Europe. At this time, the ICJ also began more consistently to develop jurisprudence with direct human rights implications.[68]

However, the democratizing effect of human rights law also became palpable in more diffuse processes, in which a broader range of actors endorsed international norms as a framework for democratic reorientation.[69] As mentioned, for example, the impact of international human rights was visible in the creation of post-authoritarian democracies after 1945, such as the FRG, Italy and Japan, in which international legal principles played a key role. This was also visible in the construction of post-colonial polities, such as India and Kenya, which, initially, were keen to signal their legitimacy through the domestic reproduction of international norms. Few democracies evolved in the decades after 1945 which did not to some degree adhere to the model of rights-based democracy promoted under international instruments. This tendency was then greatly reinforced in the transitions in Latin America and Eastern Europe in the 1980s and 1990s and the transitions in Africa in the 1990s and the early twenty-first century. In such cases, international law was not strictly imposed as a pattern of democratic formation. However, states possessed strong incentives to absorb global norms concerning democracy, and external norms

---

[68] In the *Tehran Hostages* case (1980), the ICJ based its ruling in part on human rights considerations.

[69] Yuval Shany provides an important account of some of the ways in which international and national legal norms intersect. He particularly mentions local remedies, complementarity, enforcement of arbitral agreements, and margins of appreciation (2007: 27–37). This is a helpful start, but it is not extensive enough. For other lines of transnational legal articulation, see Chapter 5 below. However, I agree with Shany's basic claim that these processes bring about an internationalization of national norms (2007: 9). See the classical discussion of this in Jessup (1956: 136). On the generally intensifying fusion between domestic and international law see Nollkaemper (2009: 75).

provided an immediate matrix for constructing the legitimacy of new governments.[70]

In conjunction, these processes had distinctive implications for the basic form of contemporary national democracy. In fact, these processes had the outcome that the most essential basis for democracy – the power of national self-legislation – was, in most of the world, pre-configured by the system of international law. Indeed, democracy only became globally widespread as the right to democracy was promoted by global norm setters. This transformed the basic theoretical architecture of democracy, as the determinant normative motivation for constructing and justifying democracy was reoriented from *freedom* to *compliance*. In this process, a model of citizenship was imposed on societies by external norm setters as a *remedy* for the crises of citizenship caused by national democratic formation after 1918, and it was deeply marked by its remedial content. Through the processes of post-1945 democratic formation, the extent to which the domestic political acts of national populations could assume founding significance for the institutional order of their society was restricted, and acts of national populations were subject to increasingly powerful prior normative limits by principles of international law. Progressively, in fact, international norms came to set a basic, widely reproducible normative template for democratic institutional construction. Indeed, basic institutions of national democracy were often expected to assume a pre-defined form, giving priority to particular rights of persons as the most essential preconditions of democracy (see McCorquodale 1994: 865, 876). As a result, the rising prominence of international human rights laws undermined certain classical principles of democracy. In particular, the prior authority accorded to international human rights law meant that democracies were generally stabilized around a clear, uniform normative design, in which the law-making capacities of the national people were subject to external construction. Of course, it is also widely noted that international law is not of itself inherently democratic, and organizations that create international law operate in tension with classical norms of democracy.[71]

On each of these counts, contemporary democracy has the paradoxical feature that it is not created democratically. In some respects, it originates in norms and norm-setting actions that are intrinsically undemocratic.

---

[70] To explain this see select literature on norm diffusion at note 109 below.

[71] James Crawford has sketched some of these points, noting *inter alia* that international law has weak democratic credentials because it privileges domestic executives; it dictates prior principles to national legislatures; it allows states to bind future legislatures; and it is difficult to apply to international organizations (1994: 117–18; 132).

2.2.4   *International Law and the Sovereign People*

One outcome of these processes, fourth, was that in many cases of democratic polity building after 1945, national populations only became sovereign citizens in their own societies as a result of externally imposed norms,
and on the foundation of external constructions of legitimate sovereign
power. The achievement of democratic sovereignty, classically conceived
as the free act of the collective body of national citizens, was widely realized as the consequence of international normative directives and expectations. In fact, national populations only became sovereign actors under
conditions in which sovereignty was exposed to constraint by prior global
norms, and the content of sovereign legal acts was partly predetermined.
International human rights instruments become the founding norm of
most national polities, and they assumed the functions of primary authorization originally imputed to acts of sovereign populations.

In these respects, the correlation between the solidification of international law and the growth of democracy meant that national communities lost some autonomy in their domestic political acts. National
democracy was gradually consecrated as a global legal form as part of a
process in which external organizations imposed tighter normative controls on nation states in their domestic legislation, both constitutional and
statutory, and nation states increasingly aligned their internal normative
systems to internationally extracted directives.[72] In fact, in most societies, citizens became full citizens of nation states and citizens of global
order at the same time, and democratic citizenship became widespread as
national citizenship internalized principles declared in international law.
In this respect, citizens themselves acted as points of filtration, through
which global norms entered national legal systems, often heightening the
obligations placed on national political actors. As discussed below, this
process of transnational democratization followed a variety of paths.[73]
Broadly, however, after 1945 legal norms ordained by acts of national will
formation were necessarily relativized. Where such norms deviated from
shared human rights constructions, they slowly became open to challenge by individual citizens on grounds provided by higher-order international norms.

---

[72] See discussion of Germany below. Note, similarly, that drafters of the Indian Constitution
were strongly influenced by post-1945 international discourses on human rights (see
Chaube 2000: 159).
[73] See Chapter 4 below.

2.2.5   International Law and Democratic Institutions

A further result of these processes, fifth, was that, in the institutional architecture of new democracies, the classical relation between branches of government was revised, and the institutions conventionally intended to give expression to the will of the national people lost some of their importance.

In the early democratic experiments of the eighteenth century, the idea was prevalent that democratic self-rule was most effectively guaranteed through the separation of powers within the state, and that in any political system centred on the separation of powers all branches of government needed to emanate directly from the people. In general, this theory was not very effectively realized, and it was subject to great variation in different societies. For example, the separation of powers in the USA followed a quite specific course, and the judiciary played a much more powerful role in the construction of American nationhood than in post-1789 Europe (Lacroix 2010: 201). In the French Revolution, however, great care was taken to promote the supremacy of the legislative body, which was emphatically proclaimed as the primary organ of the sovereign people (see Troper 1973: 35, 58, 92, 176, 205; Achaintre 2008: 329). The constitutions of revolutionary France were designed, in particular, to ensure that the judicial branch operated within strictly defined normative parameters, and it could not arrogate powers and enact interests that pertained to the legislative branch (Lafon 2001: 102). As discussed, moreover, democracy eventually took shape, after 1918, on a pattern that very greatly privileged, not the legislature, but the executive branch of government. To be sure, this period saw a gradually increasing interest in the judiciary as an apparatus able to bring additional protection to democratic institutions. This was reflected in the constitutions of Austria and Czechoslovakia established after 1918, both of which provided for Constitutional Courts, albeit still with limited competences. A rudimentary system of judicial control was also established in the German constitution of 1919. Generally, however, the constitutions of this period remained defined, at least conceptually, by the notion that the vertical linkage between a parliamentary legislature and a strong executive was the most secure pattern of democratic organization, giving full expression to the principle of popular sovereignty.

After 1945, the basic principles regarding the separation of the powers in classical democracy, rooted in the strict idea of national sovereignty, experienced far-reaching revision, which was integrally determined by the rise of international human rights law. Overall, the rise of a global system of human rights, which pre-constructed sovereign legislative acts, meant

that legislatures gradually lost influence as primary organs of legal formation. In particular, domestic judicial institutions acquired greatly increased
importance, as they were required to give effect to norms contained in, or
at least extracted from, the global legal system, and they acquired greatly
increased importance on this basis. Indeed, in post-1945 polities, domestic courts often evolved as structural links between national law and the
international legal system, locking the national constitutional order into a
wider, internationally overarching legal order, and proportioning domestic legislative practices to internationally pre-defined norms.

   This institutional transformation of democracy was most evident in the
fact that, in the longer wake of 1945, most new democracies established
constitutions granting far-reaching powers to institute Constitutional
Courts, with authority to review legislation for compliance with constitutional norms. This meant that, in some cases, Constitutional Courts
acquired the position of *co-legislators*, policing the acts of democratically
mandated assemblies, and ensuring that legislative and executive powers were exercised within strict procedural and normative limits. The
rise in the authority of Constitutional Courts was strongly connected to
the growing importance of international law, and such courts were often
assigned the duty to ensure that norms defined at the international level
were recognized and reflected in domestic legislation. This tendency is
clearly exemplified in the new democracies created after 1945 in the FRG,
Italy, Japan and India. In these settings, typically, constitutions were created which internalized international human rights law in domestic law.[74]
Moreover, such new Constitutions established a strong independent judiciary, and Constitutional Courts, or powerful Supreme Courts, quickly
assumed the power to hold other branches of government to account in
light of international norms.[75]

   In this context, the basic model of contemporary democracy, and,
indeed, the basic model for democracy as a globally sustainable institutional order, was first fully consolidated in the allied-occupied Western
zones of Germany. Here, tellingly, a pattern of democracy was created in
which the people *did not* create the essential order of the state, and the
people *did not* act as a constituent power. On the contrary, after 1945,
constitution-making acts in Western Germany were formally limited by

---

[74] See below pp. 312–4.
[75] In post-1945 West Germany, for example, the drafters of the *Grundgesetz* were clear that a
   strong independent judiciary, able to scrutinize laws and to protect individual rights, was
   prescribed by the allied powers (Säcker 1987: 268).

certain normative ground-rules, set out by external military bodies and based on international preconditions. Further, the emergent corpus of international human rights law formed a de facto pre-constituent power in this setting, pre-structuring individual decisions regarding the design of the constitution of the nascent state of the FRG, and pre-defining the over-all scope of constitutional authority.[76] The impact of external norm provid-ers was especially evident in the presumption that the new constitution of the FRG would establish a powerful Constitutional Court, with powers of constitutional review, and that the competences of the court would be linked to the ongoing protection of internationally defined human rights. Of course, Germany is usually seen as a late democracy, with an ingrained tradition of hostility to democracy.[77] In fact, however, Germany actually set the parameters, globally, for most effective processes of democratic state building. It was only when the German model of democracy – based on internationally pre-formed constituent power, strong obligations to international law, and robust judicial authority – was consolidated that democracy became a global political form.

The pattern of democracy building that developed in the decades after 1945 was marked by important variations. In some new democracies, international law was allowed to assume direct effect in national judi-cial rulings, even to the degree that it could shape the content of national constitutions.[78] Few states created immediately after 1945 ascribed such authority to international law. However, by the 1980s, many countries had witnessed a broad judicial arrogation of authority, in which courts typically based rulings, often of a transformative nature, on international law. Ultimately, in some societies, the functions of Constitutional Courts in overseeing compliance between domestic and international law were transferred to distinctive non-judicial institutions, which were designed to prevent conflicts between these two legal domains before they become manifest in open judicial controversy. In Brazil, indicatively, the depart-ment of the Federal Attorney General has established representatives in all federal ministries to ensure that all new acts of legislation are compatible

---

[76] The authority of international human rights law in the FRG was established before the *Grundgesetz* was written, and the principle that 'the general rules of international law' would form an 'integrating component of federal law', creating 'immediate rights and duties for all inhabitants of the territory' was settled prior to constitution making. The same applies to the principle that the Constitutional Court would be the 'Guardian of the Constitution' (Constitutional Commission of the Conference of Minister Presidents of the Western Occupation Zones 1948: 23).

[77] See lengthier discussion below p. 326.

[78] See below p. 342.

with international law and, by extension, with rulings of international courts. Moreover, this department scrutinizes decisions citing international law in state courts to prevent conflicts with internationally accepted norms. Special officers are therefore positioned at many institutional levels of the federal polity to ensure that international human rights law is consistently applied. In Russia, some new laws and draft legislation are scrutinized by a separate academic institution, the Institute of Legislation and Comparative Law under the Government of the Russian Federation, one of whose functions is to ensure compliance of domestic legislation and executive acts with international law.

2.2.6   *International Law and Domestic Sovereignty*

In addition, sixth, a further consequence of these processes is that states lost their monopolistic position in defining the basic normative grammar for their societies in which they were located. Increasingly, states operated within contexts in which high-ranking norms entered society from multiple sources, some based on national authority, some based on international law, some based on mediated exchanges between national bodies and international courts. Of course, historically, national states had always been situated in complex, pluralistic legal orders, and the claim of national states to determine the entire legal structure of society was always aspirational.[79] After 1945, however, it was increasingly accepted that sources of authoritative law could penetrate national societies from many points, and that inner-societal actions were structured through a broad range of norms. Public law was no longer anchored in unifocal constructions of the citizen, and citizens could claim rights and freedoms from many different sources.

On each of these counts, the spread of democracy as a mode of national political organization after 1945 depended on the attenuation of some key principles of classical democracy and classical democratic constitutionalism. Generally, in fact, it was only after the renunciation of the core institutional assumption of democracy – namely, that the will of the people, acting as an aggregate of citizens, sets the foundations for national political order, and is then continuously enacted through an elected legislature – that

---

[79] As discussed, this was due to the fact that, historically, states were always components within a pluralistic social landscape. However, it was also due to the fact that states operated in legal environments in which much law, especially in the realm of private law, was made by actors outside the state (Jansen 2010: 49).

democracy became a broad, consolidated, and ultimately *global* political form. Beneath the emergent process of global democratic formation after 1945, it became visible that the growth of democracy was driven by factors that were not envisaged in earlier democratic theory, and the primary categories of classical democratic theory were not easily able to account for the modes of agency which underpinned democracy in its eventual global character. Democratic systems that actually became reality after 1945 deviated substantially from classical constructions of democratic formation. In particular, the global emergence of democracy after 1945 was most strongly determined, not by popular political activism or citizenship in national societies, but by the *incremental rise of a global legal system*, and the constitutional basis for democracy resulted from interaction, not between factual citizens, but between national and global law. Democracy, in other words, developed for reasons that were not primarily connected with democracy, and it was created by patterns of agency that acted, essentially, as functional equivalents to the constructs of political subjectivity in classical democracy.

2.3   National Democracy and the Global Legal System

After 1945, a legal system began to evolve which was produced through interactions between organizations, often with either judicial or legal norm-setting functions, located at different points in global society. This legal system disconnected itself from national legal-political orders, and it acquired a relatively invariable form both within and across different national societies, increasingly overarching and incorporating different national legal systems. After 1945, moreover, a legal system began to emerge which was capable of producing justification for legal rulings and legitimacy for political institutions on global legal premises, which were located above national structures of legitimacy. In particular, after 1945, a legal system progressively developed which attached particular legal authority to individual human rights, which were imputed to all singular persons in all societies, simply as subjects of law, and which were applied as sources of authority for actions and decisions by institutions in different parts of global society. In its centration on human rights, the legal system as a whole entered a process of *intensified differentiation, intensified inclusion*, and *intensified global extension*. The legal system expanded beyond the limits of national societies by extracting a source of legitimacy from single persons, located in all spheres of global society, and it began to assume global authority, uniformity and extension by isolating individual persons – as rights holders – as its primary point of reference. Eventually, this reference to singular rights holders meant that the global legal system internalized a relatively autonomous source of legitimacy for legal norms, and it was able to assume a broadly consistent form, to presume broadly analogous principles of legal validity, and to produce broadly similar binding norms in different regions of the world. In this process, the primary reference for the production of law was, not the citizen as political agent located in national society, but the generic singular citizen, constructed as a holder of universal rights. Once it began to construct its authority around this generalized model of the citizen, the legal system was separated, globally, from more classical, nationally embedded sources of legitimacy, and it acquired a norm for authorizing laws that was not attached to particular decisions, to particular locations or institutions, or to particular patterns of agency and participation. Of course, the global legal system did not become a globally differentiated entity in a short period of time, and it took decades until the legal system, integrating institutions and assuming authorization at national and supra-national level, was fully formed and fully autonomous as a global order. The switch from the national citizen to global human rights as the primary source of legitimacy for law which occurred after 1945, however, clearly marked the moment of take-off in a longer process of global legal-systemic differentiation.

This rights-based differentiation of the global legal system can be observed in a number of different processes.

2.3.1   Jus Cogens

The differentiation of the global legal system can be seen in the projection of certain human rights as principles with *jus cogens* authority, placed above other norms of international and national law. The construction of norms with this rank in a global legal hierarchy began in effect shortly after 1945 – notably, in the Convention on the Prevention and Punishment of the Crime of Genocide (adopted 1948). This process was then implicitly solidified both through rulings of the ICJ in the 1960s and the early 1970s. Importantly, the ICJ did not develop a conventional body of human rights jurisprudence until much later than this, and the extent to which it can pronounce on human rights questions is still subject to limits. However, at least in a standard-setting dimension, the ICJ articulated human rights norms from an early stage, and, soon after its establishment, it began to develop the idea that there are human rights that reflect an international 'community interest' (Simma 2013: 589).[80] As early as 1949, the ICJ declared that certain general normative obligations were to be derived from 'elementary considerations of humanity'.[81] Subsequently, judges on the ICJ began to propose the theory that norms with *jus-cogens* standing formed something close to a global constitution, which cannot be changed, in positive fashion, through inter-state agreements, and to which the 'law concerning the protection of human rights may be considered to belong'.[82]

Defined strictly, human rights comprehended as *jus cogens* may be quite limited in nature. For example, such norms may clearly be seen to incorporate the rights of protection from torture, slavery, racial oppression or apartheid, use of force, aggressive war, piracy and crimes against humanity (see Bassiouni 1996: 68).[83] However, *jus cogens* has been widely subject to increasingly expansive construction. As discussed, *jus cogens* norms are widely seen to include rights of self-determination. Many courts now argue that the right of access to court is part of international *jus cogens*.[84] Some human rights courts have deliberately expanded the interpretation of *jus cogens*, asserting, for example, that 'a person's dignity and physical integrity' are protected by *jus cogens*,[85] and that the 'fundamental principle of equality and non-discrimination has entered the realm of *jus cogens*'.[86] Such claims are not fully realistic; even the most basic principles of *jus cogens*, such as the prohibition of torture, are not robustly

---

[80] For an ICJ ruling stressing the status of human rights as principles with *erga omnes* force see Case Concerning Barcelona Traction, Light, and Power Company, Ltd [1970] ICJ 1.

[81] *Corfu Channel, United Kingdom v. Albania*, Judgment, Merits, ICJ GL No 1, [1949] ICJ Rep 4, ICGJ 199 (ICJ 1949), 9 April 1949.

[82] Judge Tanaka (Dissenting Opinion), *South West Africa, Ethiopia v. South Africa, Second Phase*, [1966] ICJ Rep 6, ICGJ 158 (ICJ 1966), 18 July 1966.

[83] Judge Dugard expressed the separate opinion in the ICJ in 2006 that norms with *jus cogens* standing are a 'blend of policy and principle'. He claimed that they 'affirm the high principles of international law', including 'the right to be free from aggression, genocide, torture and slavery and the right to self-determination'. These norms 'enjoy a hierarchical superiority to other norms in the international legal order': Armed Activities on the Territory of the Congo (New Application: 2002). (*Democratic Republic of the Congo v. Rwanda*), ICJ Reports 2006, Separate Opinion Dugard.

[84] See ECJ, Joined Cases C-402/05 P and C-415/05 P. *Yassin Abdullah Kadi and Al Barakaat International Foundation v. Council of the European Union and Commission*.

[85] IACtHR, Case of *Caesar v. Trinidad and Tobago*. Judgment of 11 March 2005.

[86] IACtHR, Case of *Yatama v. Nicaragua*. Judgment of 23 June 2005. Other courts have asserted a long catalogue of rights with *jus-cogens* standing, including rights to property and religious freedom. See the Greek Supreme Court case, *Prefecture of Voiotia v. Federal Republic of Germany* 11/2000 (288933) (4.5.2000).

protected, and they have often not stood up to state immunity challenges.[87] Nonetheless, the catalogue of rights understood as having *jus cogens* status extensive potential reach, and it implicitly contain some rights of individual and collective autonomy and dignity. In an early authoritative discussion of *jus cogens*, it was claimed that breaches of such norms 'refer to cases where the position of the individual is involved, and where the rules contravened are rules instituted for the protection of the individual' (Fitzmaurice 1958: 40).

Especially important in the concept of *jus cogens* is the fact that it is conceived as a normative order standing separate from the legal systems of national states, and requiring elaboration through jurisprudential methods and perspectives that states do not possess. In other words, *jus cogens* is law, not of states, but above states, to which all states are subordinate. To some degree, of course, this can be said of all international human rights law. For practical purposes, obligations set out in the UN Charter are often considered to have, if not *jus cogens*, then at least *erga omnes* force, and fulfilment of such rights is a precondition of membership in the international community of states (MacDonald 1987: 144; Van der Vyver 1991: 26; Weatherall 2015: 105). As early as 1948, in fact, the ICJ declared that, to be a member of the UN, a state needs to 'accept the obligations of the Charter', implying that the Charter has *erga omnes* force.[88] More recently, however, the principle that *jus cogens* lies in a normative domain that is categorically distinct from the law of states has acquired emphatic support in different judicial fora.

For example, the Inter-American Commission on Human Rights has proposed a definition of *jus cogens* as a 'superior order of legal norms, which the laws of man or nations may not contravene' and as the 'rules which have been accepted, either expressly by treaty or tacitly by custom, as being necessary to protect the public morality'. On this account, it is distinctive for such norms that they possess 'relative indelibility'. Indeed, on this account, norms of *jus cogens* 'derive their status from fundamental values held by the international community, as violations of such peremptory norms are considered to shock the conscience of humankind and therefore bind the international community as a whole, irrespective of protest, recognition or acquiescence'.[89] In a recent report on the meaning

---

[87] See ECtHR, *Al-Adsani* v. *the United Kingdom* [GC] – 35763/97. Judgment 21.11.2001; ECtHR, *Jones and Others* v. *The United Kingdom* Nos 34356/00 and 40528/06 14 January 2014.

[88] Conditions of Admission of a State to Membership in the United Nations (Article 4 of the Charter), Advisory Opinion of 28 May 1948, I.C.J. Rep. (1948).

[89] *Domingues* v. *United States*, Case 12.285, Report No. 62/02, 22 October 2002.

of *jus cogens*, the UN Special Rapporteur clearly separated such norms from inter-state acts, explaining that 'the existence of a *jus cogens* norm' is mainly to be determined 'on the basis of customary international law' instead of on the grounds provided by treaties.[90]

Implicit in these accounts is the claim that *jus cogens* is best interpreted by courts and quasi-judicial bodies with an international perspective, able to perceive and interpret the highest norms of global society. Paradigmatic for this construction of *jus cogens* is a declaration of the IACtHR, which defined its own role in the following terms:

> It is the courts that determine whether a norm can be considered *jus cogens*... Such norms establish limits to the will of States; consequently, they create an international public order (*ordre public*), and thus become norms of enforceability *erga omnes*. Owing to their transcendence, human rights norms are norms of *jus cogens* and, consequently, a source of the legitimacy of the international legal system. All human rights must be respected equally, because they are rooted in human dignity; therefore, they must be recognized and protected based on the prohibition of discrimination and the need for equality before the law.[91]

At the heart of this interpretation of *jus cogens* is a direct and systematic link between global law and individual persons, which implicitly cuts through and relativizes the powers of sovereign nation states.[92]

2.3.2   Human Rights Courts

The differentiation of the global legal system has also become visible in the increasing facility with which individual persons are able to present cases before international human rights courts and commissions. By the last decades of the twentieth century, individual persons in most national societies in Europe, Latin America and Africa were able, with some reasonable hope of success, to appeal directly to international courts and commissions in cases of human rights violation.[93] In other parts of the

---

[90] See Special Rapporteur on *Jus Cogens* (2017:30).

[91] IACtHR, Advisory Opinion OC-18/03, 17 September 2003, Requested by the United Mexican States. For a theoretical position close to this see Brudner (1985: 253–4).

[92] See overlapping discussion in Weatherall (2015: 135, 172).

[93] See widening of rules on individual standing in the Latin American system in IACtHR, Case of the *Pueblo Bello Massacre* v. *Colombia*, Series C No. 140, Judgement of 31 January 2006; Case of the *Saramaka People* v. *Suriname*, Judgment of 28 November 2007 Case of the *Saramaka People* v. *Suriname*. Judgment of 28 November 2007. One judge on the IACtHR even claimed that 'effective recourses under domestic law, to which specific provisions of human rights treaties refer expressly, are part of the international protection of

world, access to global human rights law was more difficult, but still possible through international monitoring bodies and other norm setters. Moreover, most international courts endeavoured to create wide rules of standing to link global law immediately to single persons in national societies. Of great significance in this process was the creation of the International Criminal Court, which, although not created by a general binding UN regulation, acquired powers of jurisdiction relating specifically to individual citizens in national societies. In each instance, there emerged a direct and systematic legal nexus between global law and the national citizen.

2.3.3   Human Rights Corpus Juris

The differentiation of the global legal system is also manifest in the fact that the courts attached to the UN system and the courts linked to the ECHR and, later, to the American Convention on Human Rights (ACHR) were able to produce norms in self-authorizing fashion, typically from within a general canon of human rights law. As a result of this, the system of global law experienced a substantial extension, and international legal bodies were able to produce and reproduce law on independent foundations. Naturally, different courts developed separate bodies of jurisprudence. However, various international courts contributed in distinct ways to the establishment of a free-standing global legal order, typically extracting authority from human rights.

As mentioned, tellingly, the ICJ, although not created as a human rights court, has utilized human rights as important elements in its rulings.[94] Indeed, at a very early stage in its operations, it implicitly construed some human rights as reflecting a common global interest, and as separate from the interests and motivations of individual states.[95] Importantly, in 1971, in a case with important human-rights implications, judges on the ICJ stated that they had a duty to contribute interpretively to the broad formation of a canon of international law, stating that an 'international instrument

---

human rights', Separate Opinion of Cançado Trindade in IACtHR, *Case of the Dismissed Congressional Employees. (Aguado-Alfaro et al.) v. Peru.* Judgement of 24 November 2006.

[94] One informed observer has stated that the ICJ now has 'no competition' in the 'international protection of human rights' (Simma 2013: 601). For examples see Armed Activities on the Territory of the Congo (*Democratic Republic of the Congo v. Uganda*). Judgment of 19 December 2005; Advisory Opinion Concerning Legal Consequences of the Construction of a Wall in the Occupied Palestinian Territory, 9 July 2004.

[95] Reservations to the Convention on the Prevention and Punishment of the Crime of Genocide, Advisory Opinion of 28 May 1951.

has to be interpreted and applied within the framework of the entire legal system prevailing at the time of the interpretation.[96] Analogously, the European Court of Human Rights (ECtHR) has commonly defined itself as the promoter of a 'public order' for Europe, and it conceives human rights as binding constitutional principles for all Europe.[97] The IACtHR has repeatedly presented itself as a creative participant in the interpretation of the 'corpus juris of the International Law of Human Rights', and it has shown distinctive freedom in establishing principles with international authority.[98]

2.3.4　Treaties

The differentiation of the global legal system can be seen, further, in the fact that some human rights, as part of *jus cogens*, are defined as an inviolable normative horizon for the establishment of inter-state treaties. This was reflected in the Vienna Convention on the Law of Treaties (1969), in force from 1980, in which the expectation was expressed that all inter-state treaties should comply with certain general norms of international law. Although not expressly formulated as rights, these norms include the higher-ranking principles constructed in UN instruments. This meant that treaties were authorized on grounds independent of the states that were party to them, and all states that were signatories to treaties were expected to recognize binding obligations regarding human rights.

2.3.5　Domestic Courts

In addition, the global differentiation of the legal system is evident in the fact that courts within many national polities have acquired the authority directly to apply human rights norms, partly based on international instruments, in order to act against the executive branches of their national governments. This means that many national governments are increasingly subject to appeal by individual citizens, using international law either directly or indirectly. In fact, owing to the increasing force of international human rights systems after 1945, domestic courts have

---

[96] Legal Consequences for States of the Continued Presence of South Africa in Namibia notwithstanding Security Council Resolution 276.

[97] See for example *Loizidou v. Turkey (Preliminary Objections)* – 15318/89. Judgement 23.3.1995.

[98] The IACtHR construes itself as the guardian of a 'corpus juris of international human rights law', which, on its own account, 'comprises a set of international instruments of varied content and juridical effects (treaties, conventions, resolutions and declarations'. This view is set out in IACtHR, Advisory opinion OC-16/99 of 1 October 1999).

often been required to collaborate with international courts in creating and giving reality to different international instruments. This means that courts at both levels gradually became co-players in the formation of a broad transnational legal order.[99] Eventually, many domestic courts promoted the presumption that they had an obligation to contribute to the development of international law, at least within the horizon of their own societies, so that both national and international courts acted together to lock national states into a legal structure, a diffuse *corpus juris*, which was not created by national norm setters.[100] In consequence, national courts acquired responsibility for interpreting international law in their own societies, and for measuring the acts of coordinate branches of government against principles originally derived from international treaties and conventions. As a result of this, in turn, the acts of elected legislatures became increasingly proportioned to norms stored in and prescribed by judicial bodies, and actors within national judicial systems were able to project strict normative constructions for the acceptable use of political power. This again meant that national will-formation was intrinsically limited by fixed legal principles of non-national derivation. In this process, notably, national courts increasingly took notice of rulings in other national courts, and inter-judicial borrowing became a common practice, induced partly by the underlying jurisprudential congruence of national legal systems based on shared expectations regarding human rights.[101]

Through these processes, human rights law was formed as a set of recursive principles, by means of which the global legal system was able to assume and to sustain its extended and differentiated position in global society, marked by increasing inclusionary authority. The growing salience of human rights law meant that the global legal order acquired a relatively autonomous normative basis, constructed by a number of loosely connected norm setters, and it was able internally to generate higher norms to regulate interactions that occurred above, between and, eventually, *within* national states. By the 1980s, it was widely accepted that international law, founded in human rights, was normatively independent of the states that created it, and it was produced primarily by actors within the global legal

---

[99] For different accounts of this see Scelle (1932); Jessup (1956); Koh (1999: 1411); Roberts (2011: 68, 69, 80).

[100] One early account states that domestic courts operate 'at a peculiarly sensitive point where national and international authority intersect', constructing law from two sources (Falk 1964: 170).

[101] See examples below at pp. 244–8.

system.[102] By the late 1990s, the direct connection between international legal order and the individual citizen had become increasingly robust, and international norms were solidly institutionalized within national societies. Sociologists of human rights institutions have documented the exponential growth of bodies protecting human rights at a national level in the late twentieth century, which they describe as a 'human rights revolution' (Koo and Ramirez 2009: 1326).

Overall, the core principles of post-1945 international law – namely, that the individual person stands as a point of imputation for some inviolable rights, and that all persons have a right to an effective remedy in cases where such rights are abused – meant that a clearly global legal system was able to develop, which did not rely solely on individual treaties or formal acts of state for its existence and enforcement. Within this global legal framework, today, international courts and semi-judicial bodies routinely sanction national states in order to protect certain core individual rights, and, although not always successful, the protection of individual rights is widely accepted as a global legal function. One leading judge on the IACtHR has spoken extensively of the creation of a global legal order that leads to an 'emancipation of individuals from their own State'. This legal order is seen as resulting from the fact that the 'right to access (lato sensu) international justice has finally crystalized as the right to have justice really done at the international level'.[103] To be sure, this claim is overstated. Yet, it is not devoid of truth. Moreover, domestic courts routinely interact with international courts to configure the normative fabric of their own societies. After 1945, therefore, the lateral transnational nexus between single human subjects, defined as holders of rights, formed a central impetus for the evolution of a global legal system. This system was gradually constructed as a relatively autonomous, self-reproductive order of norms, distinct from classical political institutions, positioning national citizens immediately within a transnational legal-normative order.

This process of legal formation, defined by the disembedding of the law as a global system, had deep and pervasive consequences for the development of national democratic institutions. In fact, the globalization of democracy and the global differentiation of the legal system emerged, temporally and causally, as two closely linked occurrences.

---

[102] This is reflected in the increasing presumption in favour of a right to democracy discussed above, which implies that states have to create themselves in a form that fits an overarching normative order.

[103] IACtHR, Case of the *Sawhoyamaxa Indigenous Community* v. *Paraguay*. Judgment of 29 March 2006.

As mentioned, the defining features of democracy after 1945 were integrally shaped by the fact that national political institutions became partly fused with institutions in the global domain, and partly, at a fundamental level, legitimated by norms originating outside national societies. Although physically situated in national societies, in fact, national legal and political institutions were increasingly defined by interaction with global legal bodies, and they formed integral parts of the global legal system. Decisions of national bodies could not easily be separated from norms distilled from their interaction with international bodies. Above all, citizens of national societies were increasingly pre-defined by international law, and they held rights, and assumed legal form, which were originally defined under international law. Indeed, in more extreme cases, the consolidation of national democracy was only possible because persons and institutions extracting authority from the international system assumed responsibility for overseeing the formation of democratic institutions.[104]

This general transformation of democracy has led many observers to suggest that the period after 1945 began to witness the rise of a *world polity*, or even that it created the rudimentary foundations for a global political system or a global state, assuming regulatory authority for exchanges in global society as a whole. In fact, the idea has become widespread in certain avenues of political inquiry, especially in international relations, cosmopolitan political theory, and some lines of global sociology, that national democracies are integrated into a global political order.[105] The global transformation of democracy, however, was not induced by the emergence of a world *polity*. On the contrary, this process was shaped by a relative diminution of the importance of strictly political institutions in relation to legal institutions, and it meant that political institutions forfeited their claims to primacy in the global ordering of society. In fact, the period after 1945 witnessed, not the rise of *world politics*, but the rise of *world law*. At the core of this process was the fact that national states

---

[104] See discussion in Chapter 3 below.

[105] For different versions of this position see Meyer (1980: 131), arguing for the existence of a 'world polity' as a 'decentralized polity', based around a system of rules dictating state behaviour; Wendt (2003); Held (1991: 165, 1996: 354, 1997: 97); Boli and Thomas (1997: 187); Linklater (1998: 36, 2007: 93), identifying first steps towards a global polity; Goodin (2010: 179); with greater reservations, Beck (1998: 65); Höffe (1999: 426); Schmalz-Bruns (1999: 237); Shaw (2000: 255); Young (2000: 271); Archibugi (2008: 97); Brunkhorst (2007: 101); Koo and Ramirez (2009: 1329); Albert (2014: 517), recognizing some polity-like features in global society; earlier Albert claimed that 'the development of world-statehood' is 'not in sight anywhere' (2002: 322).

were increasingly obliged to recognize human rights norms as inviolable sources of legitimacy for domestic law. Through the rise of single human rights, national democratic institutions were locked into the global legal system, into the *system of world law*, and, both internally and externally, their legitimacy was made contingent on their enactment of human rights norms, enshrined in global law. As national states defined their legitimacy through reference to human rights law, they became increasingly porous to global norms, they proportioned their laws to norms that were replicated across the divides between national societies, and they established the architecture of democracy on relatively generic foundations, as part of a global legal system. Above all, national states usually became democracies as they constructed their citizens in accordance with norms established in the global legal system, and as they adapted their laws to the idea of the person (the citizen) as a holder of a globally acknowledged set of subjective rights. Through these rights, national law and international law entered an increasingly deep coalescence, and both formed correlated parts of a global legal system.

At an institutional-sociological level, this correlation between the solidification of global human rights law and the generalization of democracy as a national mode of political organization can be ascribed to a number of factors, in different functional domains.

On one hand, it is often claimed that the global emergence of democracy after 1945 and the global consolidation of democracy since the 1980s were connected, even causally, to the expansion of a hegemonic brand of liberalism, linked to patterns of capitalist individualism.[106] On this account, the connection between democracy and human rights law results from inter-elite interactions, promoting human rights law partly because it creates conditions that are favourable for global capitalism (see Dezalay and Garth 2002: 15; Guilhot 2005). These arguments clearly have a certain weight, as waves of democratization have usually, although not always, followed international macroeconomic shifts. However, the globalization of democracy cannot be seen as a process that simply provided global entrenchment for neo-liberalism. Most democracies created since 1945 have been less committed to depredatory capitalism than their authoritarian precursors. Indeed, with the exception of those created in Eastern Europe after 1989, most new democracies created since the 1980s

---

[106]   On the post-1945 period see Ruggie (1982). On the 1980s see Conaghan and Malloy (1994: 99, 261); Wylde (2012: 33).

specifically replaced governments that embodied booty capitalism.[107] In some cases, notably Brazil under Lula, Argentina under Kirchner, Bolivia under Morales, relatively new democratic systems have been solidified that performed wholesale processes of capital transfer to disadvantaged social groups.

In fact, the most important cause of the link between the global legal system and national democracy is that, as they connected their legitimacy to formally defined external norms, national states usually underwent a process of more robust and enduring institutionalization in their domestic environments. Paradoxically, the linkage between national law and international law meant that national political institutions became more resilient in face of pressures caused by the nationalization of the societies that surrounded them, and by the political constituencies contained in these societies. Aspects of this paradox are discussed more extensively below, in examples given in Chapter 4. Broadly, however, where they acquired support through international human rights law, state institutions were able to gain a certain degree of structural autonomy against their own constituencies, and they were less likely to be unsettled by the endemic social conflicts that, as national democracies, they were forced to internalize. That is to say – as state institutions internalized principles of legitimacy from international law, they acquired the capacity to legislate without refracting deeply embedded societal conflicts, and they were less likely to experience the crises of the type that afflicted European States in the period from 1918 to 1939, when they extracted legitimacy immediately from the resolution of conflicts between national citizens. In particular, the assimilation of international law helped to establish a construction of the citizen to underpin democratic governments, and it facilitated the legitimation of legislation around a stable, and stabilizing, model of the democratic citizen.

As discussed above, national democracies created after 1918 had struggled to solidify a model of the citizen from which they extracted their legitimacy. Some states pursued deep incorporation of their societal constituencies, constructing citizens as holders of pervasively integrative

---

[107] For example, the dictatorships in Brazil, Chile and Argentina embodied extremely aggressive forms of monopoly capitalism, characterized by virulently oppressive policies towards organized labour. One observer describes the regimes in the Southern Cone as based on a 'marriage of convenience' between military repression and economic liberalization (Ramos 1986: 7). Some pre-transitional African states paid lip-service to non-capitalist ideals. But most embodied a strongly patrimonialist variant on booty capitalism. This is acknowledged even by observers who are deeply critical of the economic background to the democratic reforms (Fatton 1992: 26; Shaw 1993: 87).

rights of political participation and material co-ownership. However, almost without exception, these states failed to stabilize a unitary, enduringly legitimational idea of the citizen, and they were deeply unsettled by the adversity between the groups of citizens which they had internalized: they failed securely to institutionalize the citizen as a source of legal authority. Importantly, this failure to solidify the citizen revealed a deep paradox at the core of national citizenship itself. As discussed, the idea of the national citizen promoted a general pattern of social inclusion. However, as this pattern of inclusion was extended to integrate social actors in their material dimensions, it triggered intense inter-sectoral conflict around the state, leading to the fragmentation of citizenship and national society. In its generality, moreover, the concept of the citizen was focused on legislative institutions as organs of integration. However, as these institutions encountered conflictual tensions in society caused by the material fragmentation of the citizen, they were prone to locate power in the hands of dominant social factions, ultimately excluding minority groups from effective access to political rights. From the outset of modern democracy, the high generality of the concept of the citizen contained the risk that it excluded minorities, it surrendered authority to elite interests and particular powerful factions, and it weakened the general cohesion of national society as a whole. Each side of this paradox became starkly visible in the collapse of democracy in the interwar era.

After 1945, by contrast, the model of the citizen was displaced from the inner-societal domain, and it was increasingly patterned on norms derived from international human rights law. In this form, the citizen gradually emerged as a relatively secure, static source of legitimacy for governmental acts, and it was less prone to generate volatile inter-group conflict or to perpetuate entrenched elite monopolies around the state. The national citizen had originally formed the basis for the growth of national democracy. In fact, however, national democracies had only been able to incorporate the citizen in partial, selective form. When the citizen was integrated in national political systems in its full material complexity, national state institutions could not incorporate it as a stable focus of legitimacy for legislation, and they collapsed in face of the social antagonism that citizenship generated. National democracy was only stabilized, eventually, on the foundation of the citizen extracted from global law, in a form not burdened by inter-party, class-determined and regional distinctions. In this construction, the external abstraction of the citizen helped to avert the systemic crises that characterized purely national democracy, producing a form of legitimation that was less susceptible to deep and volatile politicization. As discussed below, this meant that organs of political democracy were less likely to be dislodged by the societal conflicts with which they were confronted, they were less vulnerable to elite colonization, and they typically became more robustly institutionalized at a national level.[108]

On these counts, as international law entered the fabric of national society, it made it possible for democratic institutions in national societies *structurally to adapt* to the pressures with which they were confronted within their societal constituencies, and it alleviated their exposure to pressures caused by their own nationalization. The global construction of the citizen as universal rights holder was conceived, internationally, as reaction to the endemic violence, the institutional implosion, and the ultimate multiple genocide, that accompanied the first wave of democratization after 1918. However, it entered national societies as a source of *structural adaption*, around which national institutions began to configure their legitimational processes in more sustainable procedures. *International* law, thus, played a key role in cementing democracy as a *nationalized* political order. In other words, national states only completed their inner trajectories of democratic nationalization as they became intricately enmeshed in the system of global law, and the legitimational figure of the citizen, around which the nationalization of state institutions was configured, was only cemented through the domestic incorporation of international norms. Both formative processes of modern statehood – nationalization and democratization – only became sustainable because of the domestic internalization of global law.

It is often argued that a precondition for the full recognition of globally defined legal norms is that they are recognized through patterns of contention, through which they acquire reality and vitality (Brunnée and Toope 2000: 70–4; Wiener 2014: 7). Seen over a longer period, this claim probably has some justification, as founding democratic norms have entered national societies through multiple lines of diffusion. However, it is a fundamental aspect of modern democracy that its foundations were imprinted in national society by exogenic processes and external acts.[109]

---

[108] The claim that the insertion of nation states in transnational systems reinforces processes of societal nationalization may seem counterintuitive. However, it is also implied, from a different angle, in research on educational sociology and human rights institutions. See for examples Meyer, Ramirez and Soysal (1992: 134); Koo and Ramirez (2009: 1334).

[109] The time has long passed in which it was possible to claim that 'regime transitions' are 'the outcome of a domestic political process that is not influenced by actors outside the nation-state' (Pevehouse 2002: 517); Pevehouse's argument contains an early rejection of

Indeed, one core reason why democracy was able to take hold in different societies after 1945 was, specifically, that it did not originate in objective societal contests, it partly closed national political systems against intensified conflicts, and, above all, it was structured around an external definition of citizenship rights.

Of course, such processes of national democratic institutionalization after 1945 did not always occur in the same ways, or for the same reasons, in different societies. Moreover, these processes did not always create fully, or equally, functioning democracies. In broad terms, as examined in Chapter 4, the linkage between the growing authority of international law and the institutionalization of national democracy took several different forms. First, this link can be seen in societies with longer-standing democratic elements, such as the UK and the USA, in which, owing to the interpenetration between national and international law, the democratic constitutional order became more effectively generalized (nationalized). Second, this link can be seen in societies which historically possessed weakly institutionalized and weakly nationalized democratic systems. In such societies, typically, the rising power of judiciaries, mediating international law into domestic law, played a core role in the relative stabilization of democracy, standing alongside and supplementing functions of other branches of the governance system. Paradigmatic for this is the case of the FRG after 1949. But, in the contemporary world, Colombia and some other Latin American states exemplify this model. Third, this link can be seen in societies, in which a full democracy has not been established, but in which elements of democracy are reinforced by interaction between national institutions and the global legal system. Russia is perhaps the key example of this. Fourth, this link can be seen in societies in which historic ethnic rivalries between different population groups impeded the

---

the nationalist view of democracy claiming that interaction with international organizations with a higher democratic intensity is a salient cause of democracy (2002: 529). For an assertion of a direct causal link between the standing of international law and the growth of democracy see Simmons (2009: 55). For alternative examples of theories of externally triggered norm diffusion as a source of contemporary democracy see Gourevitch (1978: 911), offering an early account of the importance of the international system in domestic politics; Weyland (2014: 222), stressing the importance of 'external stimuli' and external models in creating democracy; Greenhill (2010: 129, 141), arguing that norm-constructive socialization, linked to membership in intergovernmental organizations, is a key factor leading to democratic formation; Keck and Sikkink (1999) and Park (2006), emphasizing the role of transnational advocates in promoting democracy; Risse and Sikkink (1999), accentuating interest of the international community as a key determinant of democratization; Gleditsch and Ward (2006: 925, 930), explaining how the regional proportion of democracies impacts on processes in particular states.

formation of a national political system, drawing legitimacy from national citizens. Kenya is an important example of this model. These categories are ideal types, and many states show features that could be included in more than one of these types. Generally, however, the interpenetration between global law and national law, especially in the dimension of human rights, has played a vital role in democratic institutionalization and broader systemic nationalization across the whole range of polity types, shaped by a range of resistances to democratic citizenship. The inscription in national law of the features of generic citizenship, defined under global law, has proved indispensable in permitting the emergence of national citizenship, exercised in a democratic order. Indeed, this interpenetration has often (in fact, almost invariably) facilitated processes of national democratic institution building which national societies themselves were not able to achieve.

None of this is meant to imply that the growth of democracy did not entail the strengthening of representative institutions, or that it did not require an expansion of concrete citizenship practices. However, democracy finally evolved, globally, on a pattern in which the functions of representative institutions were subject to normative influence, pre-formation, and constraint by pre-determined global norms. In this pattern, representative institutions became one part of an institutional/legitimational mix, and their functions were clearly limited by some higher elements of global human rights law. In this pattern, further, representative institutions acquired legitimacy, not by integrating real citizens, but by displaying compliance with norms attached to global definitions of citizenship. This meant that legislative processes of social inclusion were subject to prior normative filtration, and governments were not required to internalize conflicts between social actors in order to show legitimacy.

Likewise, none of this is meant to imply that, in some settings, the global rise of national democracy after 1945 was not impelled by inner-societal struggles, by the politicization of specific inner-societal conflicts, or by the mobilization of national political subjects, as activist citizens. Clearly, the growth of democracy after 1945 resulted from concerted mobilization by social groups against, depending on location, class-based, imperialist, or dictatorial structures of domination. To deny this, evidently, would be absurd. Even in such cases, however, the rise of democracy was in part attributable to the prior expansion of a global legal system; the global rise of rights created an overarching order in which democratic struggles and patterns of citizenship could be articulated and legitimized. In many cases, the global legal system promoted a universal political vocabulary, in which specific social struggles could be easily translated into political practice.[110] Even in highly conflictual settings, institutions created within national democracies after 1945 were not fully separable from the global legal system: such institutions normally defined their legitimacy in relation to this legal system, they acted within constraints imposed by this legal system, and, importantly, they played a core role in perpetuating and reproducing the content of this legal system within national environments.

In certain respects, on this basis, the global rise of democracy after 1945 can be observed as a *secondary process*, or even as a *process of secondary constitutionalization*, in which the increasingly dense interrelation between the legal structures of national societies and the global legal order as a whole set the basic legal-constitutional form of democracy at a national level. Of course, as mentioned, it took decades until this democratic form became a fully evolved reality. After 1945, nonetheless, human rights law increasingly became the dominant criterion for the organization of actions in the global legal domain, and human rights norms rapidly came to act as *primary constitutional* principles, which framed and legitimated actions of institutions and organizations in the inter-state arena. Incrementally, moreover, the institutions of national democracy began to mirror this process, and, in different settings, national democratic institutions evolved as subsidiary components of the higher constitution of the global legal system. In consequence, national democracy was instituted as the result of *secondary constitutional acts*, in which processes of legal foundation within national societies, often mediated through judicial interactions, transposed the constitutional norms of the global legal system into the norms of national legal systems.

Whereas in the classical concepts of democratic constitutionalism citizens were defined as agents that create the law, after 1945 a model of the citizen was implanted within national society by the global legal system, and constitutional laws were consolidated on that basis. The citizen itself became the product of a global legal system. National societies did not create the conditions of national citizenship; instead, they assimilated constructions of the citizen from the global legal domain. Of course, national societies retained a distinction between citizens and non-citizens. Yet, basic rights of national citizens were only formed through the admixture of global rights to national rights. In each respect, the institutional system of national democracy generally evolved as a *secondary constitution*, integrated within, and giving effect to, the *primary constitution* of global law.

[110] See pp. 402–3 below.

If viewed closely, the global rise of democracy after 1945 can be viewed as a process that occurred, in part, *within the law*, which, at that time, was beginning to evolve as an increasingly autonomous and differentiated system. As discussed, the classical doctrine of national democracy had suggested that the establishment of democracy is an eminently *political* process, reflecting the translation of a distinct political will into legally generalizable form. Ultimately, however, democracy eventually became a global factual reality, not as the expression of any political will or any aggregate of political practices, but rather as the objective articulation of principles already constituted and preserved within the global legal system. In the decades that followed 1945, democracy became more prevalent and more entrenched as more societies were locked into the global legal order, and as the global legal order, based on subjective human rights, pre-structured the production of law, the generation of legitimacy, and the practice of citizenship within national societies. By the 1990s, most national societies were integrated within a global legal system, and most national societies had acquired at least partially democratic institutions, pre-constituted by the normative order of global law. The slow penetration of the global legal system into national societies, and its resultant integration of national institutions within a global legal order, widely created the *constituent foundation* for national democracy. In this setting, global law became, of itself, the primary subject of democracy.

2.4   Global Democracy and the Sociology of Law

The global rise of democratic polities in the decades after 1945 displays three of the deepest paradoxes in the history of modern society.

First, this process demonstrates the paradox that, with few exceptions, modern national states were only institutionalized as such as they were integrated into a post-national legal order: the construction of nation states as stable political units, within effectively nationalized social systems, did not occur within a legal/political order created by nations, or their populations, themselves.

Second, this process demonstrates the paradox that democracy only became a globally enduring political form as it began to assume an institutional reality that was not centred on the people (the *demos*) as the dominant focus of political agency and norm formation. As discussed, after 1945, democracy was gradually established as a globally acknowledged and endorsed system of governance. However, by this time, the primary and most essential norms of democratic constitutionalism were no longer solely extracted from the decisions of a particular people or the actions of particular citizens. The citizens of populations that experienced the growth of democracy, in fact, were defined a *priori* within an overarching system of public-legal norms, centred on human rights, and their demand for democracy was constructed as an element of international law. Through this process, essential functions of legitimacy production and legal norm construction classically imputed to national citizens were absorbed and reproduced *within* the global legal system.

In fact, third, this process demonstrates the paradox that most societies did not develop a stable, *political* system until domestic institutions coalesced with the global *legal* system. As discussed, the basic legitimational vocabulary of democratic politics was focused, not solely on establishing the democratic political system, but also, less manifestly, on abstracting a political system for society more generally. However, few societies achieved this on purely national political premises. Before 1945, most political systems were inherently unstable. Indeed, they were rendered unstable by the fact that they were democratic: by the fact that they were forced to incorporate complex, rival models of citizenship, which they were unable to sustain at a national level. In most cases, it was only as political exchanges were underpinned by, and even performed *as*, law that societies were able to consolidate and sustain stable political systems. The basic idea of classical democracy – namely, that democracy is the product of a democratic subject, acting pre-eminently, and in eminently political fashion, as a citizen – proved to be a fiction.

In sum, nations first became nations *after nationhood*. Likewise, democracy first became democracy *after the demos*. Polities became political *after politics*.

The factual formation of democracy after 1945 relates in complex manner to the approaches to democracy found in classical legal sociology.

On one hand, democracy finally developed on a pattern that clearly verified the defining insights of legal sociology. As discussed, the insight into the absent subject of democratic politics had assumed great importance in sociological reflection on the initial development of democratic organizations. This insight clearly captured the contingency of early processes of democratic institution building. Then, as, after 1945, democracy became a factual reality, this founding sociological insight slowly began to acquire relevance for a deeper, more structurally enduring, problem of democratic formation, which early sociologists could not have begun to envision. What became clear through the long process of democratization in the twentieth century is that the classical sociological analysis of democracy did not only comprehend the paradoxes underlying the first tentative emergence of national democracy in the nineteenth century – it also showed great prescience in intuiting the paradoxical form that democracy would eventually assume in the twentieth century. In focusing on the absence of the people as a core feature of democracy, classical sociology clearly anticipated, in unforeseen ways, the paradigm shift that underpinned the stabilization of democracy after 1945. Ultimately, the legal-sociological relativization of democracy was strongly substantiated by the fact that democracy emerged, globally, as part of a secondary constitution, in which the *displacement of the factual citizen* from the institutional focus of democratic governance was a pronounced, indeed *necessary* feature. The original sociological perception of the illusions of democracy, intimating that democracy could not be centred in any factual reality of collective human agency, was, therefore, fully corroborated. Democracy was established, globally, through a process, in which the actual, existing citizen was, not located at the centre of, but evacuated from the process of public norm production. The citizen was replaced by the socially abstracted form of global human rights. In this respect, as earlier sociologists had indicated, the law itself acted as the primary medium of democratic integration.

Early sociologists had argued repeatedly that the initial cult of democracy was founded in chimerical constructions of human agency and human legal subjectivity, which only managed to project authorship for law by relying on formal-metaphysical accounts of popular agency. After 1945, this claim was vindicated by the fact that national democracy was stabilized on abstracted normative foundations, in which national acts of self-legislation were strictly determined by a pre-stabilized, external constitutional system. The primary constitution of international law, within which national democratic constitutional systems eventually evolved, formed an intensified analogue to the metaphysical constitution of rational law, posited by early theorists of popular government in the Enlightenment and then criticized by sociologists. This constitution translated the uncertain figure of popular sovereignty into an entirely fictionalized idea of the citizen: the citizen was projected as a formal holder of rights, defined within a global legal order, positioned outside objective spheres of social interaction. Indicatively, in fact, theorists of international law, who played a role in creating the international legal order after 1945, often conceived of international human rights on foundations derived from the classical tradition of natural-legal philosophy (see Lauterpacht 1945: 25). This was not an invariable attitude, and some architects of the international legal order after 1945 were sceptical about the renewal of interest in 'the doctrine of natural law' (Kelsen 1962: 319). National democracy, however, was widely realized on a model that formally admitted the fictionality of the people, and which translated the will of the people into a formatively structured normative domain. Indeed, democracy was established within a global order that specifically acknowledged that the democratic subject could only be substantiated in a fictitious design. In this process, international law expressly *stood in for, supplanted,* and *evaded the conflicts inherent in* the patterns of political subjectivity constructed in national societies.

On the other hand, however, the factual development of democracy also contradicted some basic analyses of early legal sociologists, and it provided evidence that demanded a revision of some core legal-sociological claims. As discussed, earlier legal sociology had showed a deep unwillingness to accept the implications of the paradoxes that it identified in democracy. Leading classical legal sociologists had remained intent on explaining democratic legitimacy as a condition in which the political system reposes on deeply embedded political-volitional substructures. In fact, sociologists commonly persisted in looking for the people as a subject of democracy, and they imagined that democracy could only obtain legitimacy if the volitional motivations of the people could be identified at its core.

Notable in this respect is the fact that classical proponents of legal sociology had tended to be dismissive of international law, which they often saw as a normative order constructed outside the realm of everyday socio-legal practice and motivation, such that it could not be viewed as an objective source of legal or political obligation. For many early legal sociologists, international law appeared as a particularly implausible outgrowth of rationalist or formalistic conceptions of legal validity, and as an extreme example of the forgetfulness of society in the legal traditions resulting from the Enlightenment: some leading early sociologists of law simply denied that international law could be seen as law (Ehrlich 1989 [1913]: 19; Weber 1921/2: 221). In the interwar years, then, many legal-sociological observers claimed that the inherent fragmentational tendencies in mass democracy were greatly exacerbated by the fact that, during their transition to mass-democracy, democratic states had ascribed increasing authority to international norms, and, in some of their functions, they accepted the jurisdiction of international organizations. At this time, it was increasingly claimed amongst sociological theorists that the slowly growing force of the international legal order, focused from 1920 on the League of Nations and the Permanent Court of International Justice (PCIJ), obstructed the formation of political systems based on national self-legislation. Amongst legal theorists concerned with domestic democratic processes, the gradual rise of international law was often viewed as a process that fractured the presence of the people at the centre of government, and at the centre of national law-making processes. Indeed, amongst interwar constitutional theorists with strong sociological sensibilities, it was widely asserted that international law, at least insofar as it constrained domestic institutions, was not easily compatible with national statehood and national self-legislation.[111] Paradigmatically for this critique, Carl Schmitt set out the sociological claim that 'the people, not humanity, is the central concept of democracy', and the factual interests of the people could not sublimated into a set of external norms (1928: 160). Across different lines of earlier legal-sociological analysis, therefore, the first rise of international law was perceived as one of the primary challenges to democracy.

In this respect, however, early sociological analyses were clearly inaccurate, and their insistence on finding a real political subject to support democracy led them onto stray paths. Democracy, as it finally emerged, did not need to be centred on the people: it was centred on international human rights law precisely because this law intruded on the national material life of the people. Although derided by sociologists, Kelsen's claim that democracy presupposed, not an actively engaged people, but a pure system of norms, proved more sociologically accurate than the common sociological critique of positivism. In fact, long before 1945, Kelsen had clearly foreseen the necessary primacy of international law in the legal systems of democratic states (1920: 215). Democracy, in short, took hold as it replaced the people with an abstracted concept of humanity as its central point of reference.

Overall, the actual globalization of democracy after 1945 both substantiated and contradicted certain basic insights of legal sociology at the same time. Classical legal sociologists had clearly observed that democratic government was not underpinned by a real political subject. This view was eventually corroborated by the factual shape of democracy. Yet, the ultimate global form of democracy also underlined the inability of sociology to accept the implications of its founding insights. Classical sociologists had been right in their critical reflections on the paradoxical fictions of popular sovereignty. But they had been wrong in thinking that real democracy

---

[111] Notably, Schmitt deplored the imposition of international-legal constraints on national states. In his more polemical moments, however, he saw international norms, not as an apolitical system, but as the results of highly political acts, backed by extensive resources of physical violence (1932a: 77).

necessitated foundations deeper than this paradox. Democracy ultimately struck root as an abstracted figure of popular sovereignty, which early sociologists diagnosed, rejected and endeavoured to reconfigure, was formally institutionalized as the basis of government. The formation of the subject of democracy within international law implied that fictitious constructions of legal authority were necessary and inevitable preconditions for democracy. Without such fictions, there was no democracy.

After 1945, in consequence, legal sociology found itself confronted with a position similar to that which it addressed in the wake of the Enlightenment. At this juncture, legal sociological reflection was once again confronted with democracies with no manifest subjects from which to claim authority, reliant on metaphysically abstracted constructions of their sovereign peoples. Indeed, the period of democratic re-orientation after 1945 can be seen as a period of *second Enlightenment*, in which the rise of global democracy was flanked by the promotion of universal normative principles, defined, now not on openly metaphysical foundations, but on the basis of international law. After 1945, indicatively, the main assumptions of classical Liberalism once again became commonplace, and many of the formalist principles of early Liberalism – especially regarding the essentialist foundation of rights, the universal-rational basis of legal obligations, and the natural-legal origin of democracy – were re-established as orthodox perspectives in legal and political theory. This was expressly stated in the constitution-making processes in both FRG and India, both of which were paradigmatic for later constitutional acts. In both cases, ideals of natural law were expressly debated during the writing of the constitution.[112]

After 1945, however, legal sociology once again struggled to accept the implications of its own basic insights, and it re-commenced its attempt to discover a distinctively political source of authority for the increasingly globalized system of democracy. As discussed, at this time, the reaction amongst sociological theorists of law to the *second Enlightenment* differed from their reactions to the *first Enlightenment*. Whereas sociological theorists who reacted to the first Enlightenment had approached the normative construction of democracy with scepticism, sociological theorists who reacted to the second Enlightenment assumed a stance that was more

---

[112] Lauterpacht's influence was felt in the Indian Constituent Assembly (Chaube 2000: 159). Early decisions of the Constitutional Court in the FRG argued that the moral basis of the Constitution could be traced, among other sources, to the 'great philosophers of state in the Enlightenment' (BVerfGE 5, 85 (85) 1). On the importance of ius-natural ideals amongst drafters of the *Grundgesetz* see Otto (1971: 199–200).

overtly and sympathetically committed to promoting the global process of democratization. Indeed, whereas early legal sociology had responded to the first Enlightenment by focusing its gaze, critically, on the metaphysical content of democratic theory, sociological theory responded to the second Enlightenment by devoting itself to explaining how, in global society, real substance could be infused into the existing order of democracy. After 1945, sociological theorists gradually accepted that democracy had to be perceived as a global or transnational form, in which patterns of legitimation fused elements of national and global law. Sociological theory thus became centred, slowly, on the idea that the national people had lost their monopoly in the production of democratic legitimacy. In recognizing this, however, sociological theory persisted in its search for the democratic people, and it reacted to the increasingly global form of democracy after 1945 by attempting to explain how concepts of classical democracy, already fragile in purely national political systems, could be made to acquire meaning in the global legal order. Indeed, in the longer wake of 1945, legal-sociological accounts of democracy began to project ways in which the presence of the people, hard enough to find in national society, could be reconfigured in global society. Even as the people visibly faded from the centre of legal/political organization, sociological theorists tried to reconstruct new models of democracy in the global setting, attempting to place global institutions on a continuum with national democratic systems. At the centre of legal-sociological democratic theory after 1945, therefore, was a re-initiation of the earlier attempt to imagine the political content of democracy, and to reconnect the legal system of democracy with manifestly political motivations. But this approach was now framed within a much less sceptical account of democracy as governance system.

Such approaches to post-national democracy appear in an almost endless sequence of variations, and they cannot be exhaustively canvassed here. However, some theoretical positions have an exemplary quality in this regard.

Most obviously, the attempt to transfer the (absent) people of national democracy into global society is observable in cosmopolitan theories of democratic institutions. Such analysis is shaped by the sense that national democracies are part of a wider institutional order, in which national institutions interact formatively with global norm setters. In such theories, nonetheless, political institutions, both national and global, are expected to extract and to display legitimacy in much the same way as in classical democracies. Indeed, cosmopolitan theories generally seek to illustrate how originally national patterns of self-legislation can be re-envisioned as the source of institutional legitimacy for global society as a whole.

At one level, this re-envisioning of the national people appears in the work of sociologically oriented cosmopolitan thinkers who argue that supra-national political systems, for example the UN and the European Union (EU), generate globally valid reserves of legitimacy. Underlying such theories is the claim that the sources of legitimacy required by trans-national bodies are not discontinuous with national-democratic process of legitimate will formation. This is also reflected in lines of global sociology, which have begun to identify preliminary contours of world statehood in contemporary society (Schmalz-Bruns 1999: 237; Brunkhorst 2007: 101; Habermas 2012: 22–3; Albert 2014: 517).[113] This re-envisioning of the people is clearly manifest in more activist/pluralistic theories of cosmopolitanism, which claim that the rise of global society creates new modes of radical political agency, based on border-crossing legal norms.[114] It is also perceptible in the insistence, amongst some sociological theories of transnational law, that legal community, albeit constructed across geographical boundaries, remains the source of law's authority (Cotterrell 2008). Even cosmopolitan theories that are reluctant to claim that contemporary society contains fully global political institutions have accentuated the emergence of new forms of transnational citizenship, articulated around international legal norms (Benhabib 2009: 699; Cohen 2012: 217).

This re-imagining of the people is especially salient in the most refined theory of cosmopolitan democracy, that set out by Hauke Brunkhorst. Brunkhorst's theory of democracy hinges on the claim that there is a *co-evolutionary* relation between the legal norms that underpin national democracy and legal norms of a transnational, cosmopolitan nature. On this basis, he argues that national democracy and transnational norms, although historically separate, are always correlated with each other, and global institutions acting to protect democratic legal rights are inevitable consequences of the historical orientation towards democracy in national societies. To explain this, Brunkhorst asserts that national democracy is based on certain shared demands for self-legislation and freedom, which, in their essence, have an egalitarian content that reaches beyond national boundaries and beyond the confines of purely national citizenship laws, implying a process of legal inclusion and recognition that always exceeds the constraints of purely national politics (1994: 231). In this respect, he

---

[113] For examples of such claims see note 105 above.
[114] See the varying expressions of this theory in Sousa Santos (2002: 437, 2012: 19).

proceeds from the assumption that democratic citizenship is driven by experiences of *solidarity*, oriented towards collective liberty, and the normative content of solidarity, in principle, is universal. By definition, solidarity is not restricted to national fellow citizens, and it creates globally inclusive norms that, for their final realization, require global institutions for their realization and enforcement. Underlying this theory is an implied assumption that human social experience necessarily generates patterns of shared liberty and non-instrumental coexistence, and that solidarity is a *universal species quality*, articulated primarily in the normative foundation of citizenship (2017: 101–2). As a result, the citizen of a nation state and the citizen of the world are always situated in the same 'normative horizon' (2002: 110), and the rights claimed by national citizens are commensurate with, and they in fact objectively pre-construct, rights of a global nature, of global citizens.

Overall, for Brunkhorst, democracy inevitably contains both national and global elements, and claims to rights asserted at a national level often both co-imply and presuppose rights declared at a transnational level. In this formulation, however, the co-evolution of national and global democratic rights is phrased in essentially neo-classical terms, and the rise of global democratic institutions is examined as an extension of the original self-expressions of popular sovereign agency.[115] In this respect, Brunkhorst's theoretical gaze turns on the paradigmatic question of classical sociology, and he seeks to translate the normative political legacy of the French Revolution into an objectively meaningful contemporary reality. In this focus, the global citizen appears in the same form, articulating the same normative processes, as the national citizen, and the growth of transnational democracy brings to fruition the moral potentials that were always implicitly inherent, although often factually suppressed, in national democratic citizenship.[116] Importantly, for Brunkhorst, both nationally and transnationally, norms of freedom and equality are created and expressed through discursive practices of popular protest and moral contestation (2017: 119).

The sociological transposition of classical ideas of democratic governance onto the dimensions of global society is also evident, second, in proceduralist theories of democracy, which attempt to account for democratic legitimation processes at a transnational level. For example, Habermas's theory of procedural democracy was first conceived for national societies

---

[115] See the major statement of this theory in Brunkhorst (2014).
[116] See also Habermas (2005: 240).

and their institutions. Eventually, however, he arrived at the conclusion that the theory of democracy as a system of deliberative procedures can be translated to the transnational domain, and that, through this, the 'conceptual association of democratic legitimation with familiar state organizations' can be loosened (1998: 166).

The most important, and most conceptually challenging, attempt to construct a proceduralist theory of global patterns of democratic legitimation appears in the legal-sociological research of Gunther Teubner.

At one level, most obviously, Teubner turns away from any attachment to classical ideas of democracy, and he accentuates the core insight of legal sociology that the political system of society cannot simply extract authority for its functions from a given people, defined as a factual aggregate of citizens. He advances this argument, first, by arguing that contemporary globalized societies cannot be centred around national or international political institutions, in which collective agreements can be represented in stable, binding fashion. Globalization, for Teubner, is reflected in 'the worldwide realization of functional differentiation', one consequence of which is that classical political institutions no longer construct regulatory norms for all functional domains (2004: 14). One key outcome of global functional differentiation, thus, is that state institutions lose their primacy. He develops this analysis, second, by proposing a theory of societal constitutionalism, based on the claim that, in global society, individual functional sectors – for instance, media, health, sport, the economy – generate their own sources of constitutional and democratic agency, and they evolve constitutional norms, to regulate and create regime-like structures for their specific exchanges, in quite distinct, contingent ways (2011: 9). In particular, owing to the relative weakness of state authority, it is vital for modern society that different social spheres preserve capacities for 'inner constitutionalization' (2011: 51), or self-constitutionalization, especially in situations in which their communications collide with, or threaten to unsettle, communications in other systems (2011: 51, 2017: 333).

On Teubner's account, the constitutional order of global society is necessarily pluralistic and acentric, resulting from auto-constitutional potentials residing in different social spheres. In particular, the constitutional reality of society cannot be imputed to unifying acts of a given people: there is, in fact, no people – national or global – that can underlie and bring unity to different areas of institutional practice and law production. The most important norms that structure societal exchanges are produced, not by deliberate acts of single or collective actors, but by the inner reflexivity of different media of communication, and they are not articulated with formal political processes of norm production (2012: 121). As a result, the normative order of each social sector retains a conclusively pluralistic character.

Self-evidently, Teubner's theory of global society and global law cannot be linked to more neo-classical attempts to press political institutions into an immediate relation to some single, originating, self-legislating people. Indeed, his work reflects a remarkable endeavour to articulate an irreducibly contingent model of legal/political order, especially in the global setting, and to comprehend patterns of legal construction without simplified reference to primary agents. At the core of Teubner's work is a deep attentiveness, closely continuous with the core insights of classical sociology, to the pluralistic form of social freedom. Despite this, however, he centres his theory around ideas of politics and proceduralization, in which, in some respects, a trace of more classical ideas of democracy is still perceptible.

On one hand, in the micro-sociological dimension of his theory, Teubner claims that, within the different sub-systems of society, constitutional norms are generated by the distinct exercise of constituent power, in which forces specific to a given social sector spontaneously generate constitutional norms. To be sure, the constituent power in this sense cannot be captured by any 'anthropomorphic identification' of such power with the strategic acts of a people, community, or collective. On the contrary, such power articulates the 'social potentials' and 'energies', or even the 'communicative power', which is formed in distinct sectors of society, and which gain expression in acts of sectoral self-constitutionalization (2012: 62–3). On this basis, Teubner concludes that different social sectors afford opportunities for distinct modes of democratic norm construction, in which 'decentralized collective actors' assume a role in shaping the normative order for a given social domain (2012: 122–3). Indeed, he is very clear that each sector of society possesses its own specific mode of politicality, and every partial system of society remains a realm of contest, in which different actors or stakeholders challenge each other to participate in structural formation or in the creation of 'regime rules' (2018). Nonetheless, he imputes a distinctive political content to such processes of self-constitutionalization and sectoral democratization, claiming that each transnational regime contains functionally specialized aggregates of contested agency. The self-contestation of transnational regimes thus supplants the political representation of national peoples as the core energy of democracy (2018). To account for the political substance of constitutional formation, then, he employs a dual concept of the political, implying that different social sectors possess a political force that cannot be captured in conventional categories of institutional politics, and which is worked out through contextually embedded contests over the legal/structural form of different societal domains (2012: 121). Although shifting the politics of society onto highly contingent procedural foundations, therefore, the idea still endures in Teubner's thought that there are certain primary political-democratic substances in society. Albeit in delineated social sectors, the distillation of political energy in constitutional norms remains a core process in global society, and *political self-legislation* remains a distinctive emphasis of social agents. As implied, a core concern in Teubner's later work is to translate the dominant semantics of classical democratic politics into categories that can be identified in the plural regimes of global society. In this setting, the classical *demos* may be replaced by a range of actors, such as social movements, stakeholders, professional bodies, standard setters, all of whom contest the form of a particular regime. These actors, however, exist as remote equivalents to the classical *demos*.

On the other hand, in the more macro-sociological focus of his theory, Teubner argues that society as a whole is capable of obtaining an overarching normative balance, and even of securing reasonable freedoms that traverse different social sectors. In this respect, his work moves close to more classical pluralist claims, similar to arguments set out by Hegel, that even in the most differentiated societies highly particular modes of liberty can co-exist and generate complementary rationalities (2018). In his earlier work, he indicates that the legal system of society is able to institutionalize procedures through which different social systems can be sensibilized to each other, and in which adaptive learning processes can be stimulated in different social systems (1983: 28). In some cases, this means that destabilizing expansionary impulses in one social system that risk unsettling society as a whole can be checked by normative claims in other social systems, such that society as a whole preserves a political configuration adapted to the separate rationalities of different systems. This might mean, for example, that, faced with expansionary economic energies, political forms of agency in other systems (say, social movements, protest groups, professional associations) might instil their micro-political prerogatives into the normative structure of society as a whole. In his later work, this idea re-appears in the assertion that, from inside their own reflexive intelligence, the different sectoral constitutions of society can, and in fact necessarily must, construct 'principles of an *ordre public transnational*'. That is to say – different social sectors can articulate principles of a unified meta-constitution, in relation to which each social domain, in its own constitutional perspective, 'evaluates its own norms', and configures its norms with the meta-normative form of society as a whole (2017: 330). At no point, categorically, does this theory imply that society as a whole possess a unitary macro-constitution or unifying patterns of political agency, based on demands of socially encompassing subjects. However, residually, it holds out the possibility that conflicts between different constitutional orders might be balanced in a 'transnational meta-constitution', and that different sectoral constitutions might evolve internal conflict rules to avoid collision with other constitutions (2017: 329). In this respect, even in the most resolutely acentric analysis of modern society and its law, an echo is heard of a lament for overarching political rationality and trans-sectoral democratic norm formation.

In general, more contemporary legal sociology has opted for a view of democracy which is more immediately affirmative than that set out by classical sociologists, and which moves on a continuum with classical democratic theory. As discussed, classical legal sociology viewed democracy as inherently paradoxical. At the same time, however, legal-sociological theory widely internalized this paradox in its own conceptual structure. As a result, *legal sociology remained fixated on the people, defined as a collectively self-legislating agent, as a source of legitimacy, although it clearly explained that this people cannot be constructed as a source of legitimacy.* This legal-sociological paradox is commonly intensified in more recent analysis of the conditions of global democracy. In the realities of globalized democracy, in which the existence of a people as the basis for democratic political organization is difficult to identify, legal-sociological research has not been able fully to capitalize on the insights that were inherent in legal sociology in its classical years. Sociological analysis persistently looks for continuities between contemporary and classical democratic processes. Indeed, as the absence of the people (citizens) in democracy becomes an almost incontrovertible fact, sociological inquiry becomes increasingly resolute in its desire to find this people (citizens), and to locate the political agency of the people, in some form, at the centre of social life.

The remainder of this book is designed to demonstrate that, in order to understand democracy in contemporary society, we need more resolutely to follow the implications of classical legal-sociological arguments. As the requirement for a global sociology of legal formation becomes more pressing, the greater becomes the relevance of the primary insights of classical legal sociology into the fictionality of democratic subjectivity. Classical legal sociology contains two claims that profoundly illuminate the reality of contemporary democracy.

First, simply, classical legal sociology claimed that democracy was created without a people. In contemporary society, democracy now appears as a mode of political organization, which is specifically not centred around the people or the citizen, and whose evolution and legitimization are not dictated by specifically political patterns of normative agency. As a result, contemporary society fully reflects one core original claim of legal sociology. More tellingly, second, classical legal sociology claimed that democracy should be observed as the result of a process of *apersonal institutionalization*, and the conceptual forms of democracy underpin this process. In much early sociology, the societal expansion of democracy was attributed to the autonomous functions of the legal system in promoting social integration, often through the distribution of basic rights to individual agents. Using this insight, we can now see that, within national societies, the process of national-democratic institutionalization failed, and national democracies were not reliably stabilized around national constructs of citizenship. On this basis, we can see that democratic integration and institutionalization began to approach completion when the political citizen, to which the political system owes its legitimacy, became fully apersonal: when it was transferred from the national-political to the global-legal domain, so that the core legitimacy of political institutions was disarticulated from national constructs of political agency. Both central claims in the legal-sociological theory of democratic contingency contain a key to understanding democracy. To understand democracy, we need to move beyond the underlying paradox of legal sociology, we need renounce the search for the people or the political subject at the core of democratic law, and we need to observe the formation of democratic law as shaped by a fully contingent process of institutional construction.

It is an error to seek the origins of contemporary democracy in national democracy, national democratic subject formation, or even in distinctively political sources of agency. Democracy presupposes, not continuity with national citizenship practices, but *a deep and incisive rupture with more classical national democratic systems and more conventional patterns of political subject formation*. Explaining contemporary democracy means explaining the process through which external, global modes of norm production have supplanted more classical sources of political agency, and it demands that we renounce all attachment to conventional constructions of citizenship and political subjectivity. Explaining contemporary democracy means explaining the ways in which law's autonomy shapes democratic integration and legislation.

3

Before the Law?

3.1 Introduction

The classical theory of democracy revolves around the assumption that legal and governmental institutions acquire legitimacy to the extent that they are willed by the people. This assumption is supported by two primary presuppositions.

Most obviously, as discussed, classical democratic theory presupposes that, in a legitimate political system, persons expected to abide by laws must be fully and equally implicated, by electoral means, in the making of these laws, and they must recognize these laws as having some claim to represent interests in which, either materially or rationally, they have a share. To this degree, the persons who originally give authority and legitimacy to laws are seen as actors who pre-exist the laws, and who have pre-legal capacities and certain pre-legal motivations that dictate the substance of the laws. Central to this idea of democratic governance is the principle that the people, centred on the acts of the citizen, is a subject that has some kind of political existence *prior to and outside the laws*, and principles agreed by this subject in its original pre-legal form become the foundation for the laws of the polity as a whole.

This idea was anticipated in the early tradition of social contract theory. Of course, the more refined early theorists of the contractual origins of legitimate government emphasized that, before entering a social contract, the people does not exist as a fully formed, articulate actor. Some theorists of the social contract clearly denied that the people could meaningfully lay claim to any particular rights outside an ordered system of civil law.[1] Yet, the idea that the laws of the legitimate polity must be attributable to pre-legal actions remained pervasive through the tradition of social contract theory. Indicatively, Rousseau argued that people possess no rights

---

[1] Similar to Rousseau after him, Hobbes argued that, under the social contract, people must 'lay down certaine Rights of Nature' and that all persons are required to renounce 'such Rights, as being retained, hinder the peace of Mankind' (1914 [1651]: 74–80).

outside the polity formed by social contract. However, he argued that the contract confers positive force on rights that attach innately to all human beings – indeed, in entering a polity, people are placed in a condition in which their innate rights acquire real and effective form (1966 [1762]: 56). These ideas were later crystallized in revolutionary theories of national sovereignty and constituent power, which were closely related to models of contractual legitimacy. Central to such theories, as discussed, was the claim that the people, as a sovereign presence, exists outside the law, and the law obtains legitimacy to the degree that it is wilfully enacted by the people, in accordance with primary rational interests or agreements articulated by the people prior to their self-submission to the law. In the revolutions of the eighteenth century, such principles were applied in the first instance in early constructions of constitutional legitimacy, and they acted to legitimize new constitutions in France and America. But, by extension, these principles imply that all laws with claim to general validity have to be imputable to particular choices of collectively engaged political subjects (citizens).[2] As discussed above, the classical concept of democracy has undergone innumerable mutations since the revolutionary époque. However, the idea of the *original externality* of the people remains an abiding component of democratic freedom. This is reflected, in essential form, in the works of Habermas, for whom, in its basic conception, the democratic constitutional state is 'an order which is wanted by the people themselves and legitimated by the free formation of their will and their opinion' (1998: 100). In fact, for many observers, the doctrine of constituent power is still a precondition of democracy.[3]

Alongside this, the essential core of democratic theory is supported by the principle that, as an organizational system based on collective decisions, democracy has an indisputably *political* character, and it elevates and dignifies a distinct political domain above other parts of society. In different ways, the concept of democracy as a system of collective political inclusion is deeply interwoven with the emergence of a concept of the political.[4]

On one hand, at a factual-sociological level, the original evolution of democratic ideas occurred in social settings in which centralized monarchies, assuming some state-like attributes, had already assumed a dominant position *vis-à-vis* more private sources of authority. In early modern

---

[2] See above p. 37.
[3] See p. 36 above.
[4] See the important historical studies of this phenomenon in Meier (1980: 288–91).

Europe, indicatively, democracy began tentatively to take root in a context in which central legislators had begun to clear away the pluralistic legal residues of feudalism, such that the legal order of society, originally embedded in local legal customs and corporate conventions, was powerfully shaped by monarchical directives. The seventeenth and eighteenth centuries, notably, had seen far-reaching processes of legal codification, in which monarchical decisions increasingly formed the foundation for the enactment of law (see Jansen 2010: 13). In the revolutionary period, then, the powers of sovereignty originally attached to monarchies, expressed in the authority to define the law, were in many respects simply transferred to early democratic institutions (Böckenförde 1991: 95; Beaud 1994: 245). Notably, the first years after 1789 in France were marked by quite vigorous policies of legal codification, in which executive bodies assumed new powers of legal organization.[5] Early democracy, therefore, was defined by a distinctive presumption that the political system possessed primacy amongst societal institutions, and the core principles and practices of early democracy reflected, above all, a subordination of law to politics.

On the other hand, at a conceptual level, the concept of politics in the contemporary sense of the word evolved in conjunction with constitutional ideas regarding constituent power, national sovereignty and national citizenship, spelled out in the French and American Revolutions. Importantly, to be sure, the epithet *political* had been used to describe institutions with collectively founded authority long before institutions even remotely resembling modern states had developed. In mediaeval Europe, for example, a body was construed as *political* if it was defined by principles of collective accountability, if it was designed to resolve problems having implications for all members of society[6] and if it could not be seen as the mere extension of a private person or a set of private interests.[7] Indeed, societies of antiquity had also constructed a distinct category of the political, based on ideas of collective self-determination (Meier 1980: 277).

---

[5] This was exemplified in France by the rural code (1791), the penal code (1791), draft civil codes of 1793, 1794 and 1796, and finally the Napoleonic civil code (1804).

[6] The concept of *Quod omnes tangit ab omnibus approbari debet* was thus applied to define matters of a political nature, requiring broad consensual resolution. On the application of this concept in different medieval societies in Europe, see Najemy (1979: 59); Maddicott (2010: 227–8). Importantly for this study, this maxim began as a principle of procedure in medieval corporations, but it became a constitutional principle of government through the late-medieval expansion of political institutions (see Congar 1958: 213, 243, 258).

[7] In late medieval England, for instance, Fortescue argued that, as it was partly based on consent, English government had a distinctive and unusual 'political' character (1942 [c. 1470]: 79).

However, the idea of the political as a distinct social domain acquired particular prominence in the eighteenth century, a period in which concepts of antiquity were often reconfigured.[8] During the revolutionary era, a concept of the political gained broad purchase, which perceived the determinant of politics in the fact that it reflected patterns of will formation that could not simply be reduced to private authority, and which construed one part of the social order as formed by, and in turn promoting, collective motivations, with a certain binding dignity in relation to other social spheres.

This distinction of the political was reflected in core concepts of the revolutionary era.

As discussed, for example, the idea of the citizen played a central role in creating a distinct political domain in society. In France, the figure of the *citoyen* as a focus for collectively structured action, based on *sui generis* affiliations and obligations, and committed to producing a legally defined public order, acquired socially transformative force both before and during the revolutionary period (Gruder 1984: 351). In the American Revolution, the quality of citizenship was construed specifically as a *political tie*, forming a volitionally constructed, categorically political community, creating a distinct authority for the governmental order.[9] In both settings, the citizen distilled a particular construct of the political, based simultaneously on individual choice and collective action, conferring an unprecedented degree of legitimacy and authority on the political system.[10] In both settings, moreover, actions of citizens served to impute a particular authority to the law, such that the citizen, claiming a position within a politically structured community, formed a higher-order, distinctively public source of authority for legal acts. In this respect, the concept of the political played a key role in elevating the relative authority of legislatures. As discussed, further, the doctrine of constituent power proposed in the French Revolution acquired key importance in the construction of a relatively autonomous category of the political, implying that the law presupposes a categorically political reference for its legitimacy, and that the legitimacy of law cannot be founded on law alone (Böckenförde 1991: 91). On these conceptual foundations, politics was imagined as a higher

---

[8] On similarities between Hellenic concepts of the political and the transformative processes in the eighteenth century, see Meier (1980: 278).

[9] As mentioned, this idea was spelled out in the Supreme Court. See in particular *Talbot* v. *Janson*, 3 U.S. 133 (1795).

[10] See Schmitt's argument that 'the citizen, the citoyen' is the 'specifically democratic, that is, political figure' (1928: 245).

mode of interaction and agreement, which exists before other elements of the polity, and which generates the primary source of legitimacy for law.

In addition to this, in the revolutionary era the constitution of state itself was envisioned as a distinctively political construct. Both revolutions converged around the idea that the constitution stands at the beginning of the polity, marking a radical caesura with previous political institutions, and creating a system of laws to determine subsequent legal and political acts. In this respect, the constitution pre-eminently symbolizes the political origin of law, and the political origin of the legal system. At the centre of classical constitutionalism was the assumption that law must be supported by an original, collectively acceded political act, which separates the political order from pre-political conflicts, and this act is cemented in the constitution. Of course, it has been widely noted that constitutionalism is not necessarily democratic, and it can impose norms on processes of political will formation that do not always have a majoritarian foundation and may easily constrain public deliberation.[11] As an element of democracy, however, the constitution forms a political declaration of rights. Its essential function is to define the procedures through which society's political contests and disagreements can be articulated and mediated, ensuring that acts of legislation, and the ongoing production of rights, are supported by a public, political will.[12] Under the political constitution, rights act as instruments for the deepening inclusion of society, and conflict over rights gives solid reality to the will declared in the constitution. For some constitutional theorists, the constitution is the essential fulcrum of society's political domain.[13]

---

[11] Jefferson himself made this point, saying that a constitution falsely stabilizes governmental conditions against the will of the people. He expressed this by arguing that

> each generation is as independent as the one preceding, as that was of all which had gone before. It has then, like them, a right to choose for itself the form of government it believes most productive of its own happiness; consequently, to accommodate to the circumstances in which it finds itself, that it received from its predecessors; and it is for the peace and good of mankind, that a solemn opportunity of doing this every 19 or 20 years, should be provided in the constitution, so that it may be handed on, with periodic repairs, from generation to generation (1899: 43).

This claim, in different forms, is widely considered in some more recent theory (see Sunstein 1993: 329, 352; Bellamy 2007: 1–2).

[12] See discussion of these core preconditions of the political constitution in Goldoni (2012: 928, 929, 937).

[13] See Carl Schmitt's claim that a constitution contains a decision about the historical order of a people, which pertains to the ontological level of the 'concrete political existence' of the people (1928: 23).

In different constructions, in sum, the revolutionary period gave birth to the modern idea of the political, and the passage from feudal society to modern society was surrounded by concepts that emphasized the political as a category of practice. The political emerged as a mode of subjective association, in which people were separated from the private ties ingrained in pre-modern social structure, and they were required to generate collective solutions for contingent, generally troubling problems of social organization (Meier 1980: 194). In fact, it was only through the evolution of an administrative order founded in the generalized concept of the citizen that society began to obtain structures and institutions that we would now recognize, systemically, as *political*, distinct from the private, aristocratic origins of social control.[14] Notably, in France the revolutionary concept of the political led to the accelerated centralization of a state domain, focused on legislation, fully separate from corporate and local conventions, and able to situate law-making power authoritatively within one set of institutions. Similarly, in the USA, state institutions, based on voluntary allegiance, acquired greatly expanded, generalized powers, including the power to eliminate old jurisdictions, to reform fundamental laws, to abolish ancient legal prerogatives and to impose national taxes (Nelson 1975: 90–2; Edling 2003: 225; Bradburn 2009: 47). In both situations, the rise of political citizenship led, immediately and by direct cause, to a growth in the power of the body politic, to the extension of evidently political institutions across society, and to the general suffusion of society with political content. Citizenship produced a concept of the political that imposed a basic national shape on society. In both settings, the rise of political citizenship meant that individual interests and conflicts were, at least incipiently, transferred to a national level, released from local structures, and governments acquired the obligation to project their legitimacy through reference to national society as a whole.

Through the factual institutionalization of democracy, as discussed, these core principles of democracy presented intense and destabilizing challenges to the architects of democratic polities. However, the idea that in a democracy the people, as a group of collectively implicated citizens, is an external political subject, and that a democracy is founded in distinctive external patterns of political association and decision-making remained central to the semantic parameters of democratic thinking. Democratic thinking – both affirmative and critical – was galvanized,

---

[14] On the general anti-privatistic, and therefore anti-aristocratic, impulse contained in the political as social category *per se*, see Meier (1980: 210, 257).

historically, around the idea that government owes its legitimacy to a will that is located outside the law, and which determines political institutions in accordance with generalized popular prerogatives.

In recent years, the underlying form of democracy has undergone a deep transformation. Through this process, first, it is observable that democracy was not established by the people in their capacity as external actors, and the people do not materially precede the laws that they authorize. On the contrary, the primary laws of the democratic polity, which claim to derive authority from the people, typically pre-exist the people, and they are determined by the global legal system. Similarly, second, democracy did not develop as an eminently political form, in which citizens created the political order through acts of external association, prior to the laws by which they are bound. In fact, the idea of democracy as an intensely and intrinsically *political* system of organization has lost some of its plausibility. Beneath the symbolic level of public debate, democratic rule is now sustained by concepts that are only marginally related to classical principles of democracy, and the political concepts of democratic citizenship no longer act as adequate constructions of the essential substance of democratic organization. What is striking in the transformation of modern democracy is that *the law itself* produces authority for democratic norms, and many ideally political sources of norm construction have been supplanted by concepts that are internal to the law: *the legal system itself, in its globally overarching form, becomes the subject that underlies democracy*, and there is no external political subject to support the law. This is especially striking in the essential political form of the constitution, which, in most societies, simply results from inner-legal acts. Indeed, *the law itself widely internalizes the classical functions of citizenship*, and exchanges between citizens about the form of the polity and the form of the law mainly occur within the law, as a relatively autonomous system. As a result, the essential political substance of democracy has become precarious.

This chapter observes the ways in which the conceptual structure of democracy has been modified in recent years, and it attempts to outline the core concepts and legal constructions around which democratic institutions are now consolidated. In particular, the analyses set out below show that, conceptually, the distinctively pre-legal, *political* origin of law has been eroded, so that law is now mainly formed, in intricately self-referential fashion, by law. Contemporary democracy is built around *functional equivalents* to classical patterns of democratic citizenship, and these equivalents are primarily constructed within the law: law's reference to law emerges as an equivalent to classical concepts of political voluntarism and subjectivity. These functional equivalents create a distinct line of communication between the political system and society, in which the legal citizen becomes the primary, underlying basis for democratic construction. To be sure, the citizen can still enter the law-making process through normal democratic procedures, but this engagement occurs only at the secondary level of societal norm formation. The primary level of norm construction – that is, the construction of the basic and irreducible residue of legitimacy – occurs within the global legal system, expressed through equivalents to political will formation. Indeed, the basic political figure of the citizen can only appear, in its essential form, as a construction of the law, so that citizenship itself is translated into a series of functional equivalents.

3.2   The New Fabric of Democracy

3.2.1   Human Rights and Democracy Promotion

As discussed above, the increasing prevalence of democracy since 1945 has been deeply shaped by the fact that democratic government is implied as an optimal governance form in international human rights instruments. The expectation of democracy is formalized in regional instruments, such as the ECHR or the ACHR. It is also prescribed in the founding documents and subsequent human rights instruments of the UN. Indeed, the basic recognition of a state depends, in part, on its membership in the UN, which necessarily implies some acceptance of democracy as a desirable mode of governance.[15] To some degree, therefore, democratic government is required under general international law.

In considering this, it is essential to repeat the qualifications set out above that, after 1945, most international human rights instruments and conventions did not immediately assume great constitutional influence. Initially, moreover, some international legal orders did not unequivocally promote democracy. The ECHR was designed to consolidate a system of human rights law necessary for democratic society. By contrast, the UN initially endorsed democracy in slightly more reserved fashion. Equally importantly, the formal pronouncement of human rights as core legal-political norms often did little to prevent the growth of harshly anti-democratic governments. To some degree, the privileging of self-determination as a primary political right actually provided legitimacy for authoritarianism, as it often took shape in the form of one-party, presidential or plebiscitary

---

[15]   See an illuminating discussion of this, and of the wider impact of the UN on states ostracized, partly or fully, from the international community in Geldenhuys (1990: 124).

systems (see Miller 2003: 609). Furthermore, the regional system of international law created in Latin America after 1945 placed the greatest emphasis on human rights, including democratic rights.[16] Yet, this system did not obstruct the emergence of extreme authoritarianism in the 1960s and 1970s, usually directly or indirectly supported by the USA. In Latin America, democracy was a rare and precarious phenomenon until the 1980s. It was only through a longer trajectory of international legal consolidation, therefore, that democracy was effectively supported by international law.

Despite these reservations, the global extension of democracy in the decades after 1945 was, at least in part, the result of the solidification of international legal norms, beginning in 1945. In some cases, there was a clearly discernible connection between the rising power of international human rights norms and the growth of democracy. As mentioned, this can be seen in the first democratic transitions of the late 1940s, which were initiated by occupying forces and strongly determined by UN human rights instruments. This connection can also be seen in democratic transitions that began in the 1980s in Latin America and Europe, which were impelled, in part, by the rising salience of international human rights law, including rights linked to democratic government.

The transitions that occurred in some parts of Latin America in the 1980s were marked by the fact that, by the 1970s, organs of the UN had become increasingly critical in their responses to political circumstances in some societies with authoritarian regimes.[17] In parallel, the IACtHR, which began to hear contentious cases in 1987, was founded in the late 1970s. Ultimately, the early period of democratization saw deep domestic penetration of global human rights discourses in different Latin American societies. For example, the move towards democracy in Argentina, commencing in 1983, was strongly linked to the national enforcement of international legal instruments, which were used as points of domestic orientation during democratization.[18]

---

[16] See Articles XX and XXXII of the American Declaration of the Rights and Duties of Man.

[17] The Chilean regime under Pinochet was several times condemned for human rights abuses in the UN General Assembly in the 1970s, which had a direct impact on the policies of the regime (Hawkins 2002: 62, 77). In 1978, the UN adopted Resolution 33/173, recognizing enforced disappearance as a major violation of international human rights. This had implications for Chile, Argentina and other Latin American states. In 1986, the UN adopted Resolution 41/161, which prescribed a series of measures required to restore the rule of law and democratic government in Chile.

[18] This is discussed extensively in Merry (2006: 58); Sikkink (2011: 64).

In Europe, the transitions of the late 1980s were informed by the fact that the authority of human rights law was reinforced by the Helsinki Accords and by the implementation of the ICCPR in the 1970s. These documents did not dictate an unambiguous right to democracy, but they expressed a strong presumption in favour of principles likely to be guaranteed under democratic government. Together, these developments created a wide grammar of legal expectation, in which sitting regimes became vulnerable to internal and external pressure. In the more open Eastern European societies, the subsequent trajectory of democratization was shaped, in part, by the fact that politically engaged groups identified the importance of international human rights law, and they mobilized social and political organizations around such norms.[19] Even in Russia, the Helsinki Accords had a mobilizing effect (see Nahaylo and Swoboda 1990: 196; Snyder 2011: 57; Smith 2013: 229). After the full onset of the democratic transitions in Eastern Europe in 1989/90, ultimately, international human rights norms assumed powerful directive implications. These norms performed a clearly orienting function in defining the path for new democracies, enabling new states to gain legitimacy very quickly, both before their own populations and before the international community.[20] Indicatively, the Vienna Declaration and Program of Action was agreed in 1993, and it acquired great importance in the context of the democratic transitions in Eastern Europe. This Declaration stated that there existed a strict link between democratic formation and observation of human rights law. It declared: 'Democracy, development and respect for human rights and fundamental freedoms are interdependent and mutually reinforcing ... The international community should support the strengthening and promoting of democracy, development and respect for human rights and fundamental freedoms in the entire world'.

Analogously, in the African transitions that began in the 1990s the passing of African Charter on Human and Peoples' Rights, in force from 1986, provided important direction for democratic polity building. This Charter did not establish a categorical right to democracy, but, in Art 13(1), it set out a right to participate freely in government. Moreover, the African Commission on Human and Peoples' Rights proved outspoken in

---

[19] In Poland, it was widely noted that the Helsinki Accords were important background factors in the political transformation of the 1980s (see Snyder 2011: 230).

[20] This motivation is widely addressed, but see, for one exemplary account, Wotipka and Tsutsui (2008: 749–50).

its insistence on the establishment of competitive democracy as political norm.[21]

Very importantly, regional international organizations, such as the African Union, the European Union, and the Organization of American States have either made democracy a condition of membership or they actively promote democracy (Wheatley 2005: 132).[22] In some cases, states have converted to democracy as part of an express strategy to gain such membership.[23]

During the processes of democratic institution building in recent decades, therefore, the basic form in which national populations were first able to insist on, exercise and realize their democratic agency was, to some degree, pre-defined by a system of international human rights. The diction of rights created a normative order, identifiable across the globe, in which political demands within national societies still subject to authoritarian governments could be articulated and globally recognized. Indeed, in voicing political demands as claims to rights, populations were able to draw attention to their demands amongst organizations in the international domain, for example NGOs, advocacy groups and UN bodies, who were able to attract additional support outside national societies. This was especially widespread in the democratization processes in Latin America, where international human rights organizations played an important role in generating support for democracy. In some Latin American transitions, in fact, international human rights law was ultimately enforced as a proxy for political agency, and the alignment of governmental conditions to international law replaced constituent action as the focus of democratic re-orientation.[24] However, this is also visible in Africa. Even in more recent cases of institutional re-orientation, for example in the uprisings in North Africa in 2011, appeals to international human rights law assumed striking constituent force.[25]

Once established, then, new democratic systems in national societies have usually immediately constructed their populations as rights holders.

---

[21] See ACHPR/Res.10(XVI)94: Resolution on the Military (1994).

[22] See Protocol of Amendments to the Charter of the Organisation of American States ('Protocol of Washington'); African Union Declaration on the Principles Governing Democratic Elections in Africa, AHG/Decl.1 (XXXVIII), 2002

[23] Notable is the case of Spain in the 1970s, where democratic reform was advocated in large part because it provided a path towards EU membership (see Thomas 2007: 58).

[24] In Chile, for example, Pinochet's 1980 Constitution was amended before the transition to accommodate human rights, and the revised constitution recognized the authority of international law.

[25] See discussion of this in El-Ghobashy (2008); Odeh (2011: 996).

Indeed, where democracy has proved enduring, political actors have typically created constitutions which acknowledged persons as holders of rights defined, either directly or indirectly, under international law.[26] In some cases, transitional constitutions have been partly fleshed out through the rulings of judicial actors, who based their decisions on international norms.[27] In most democratic transitions, states have accepted the jurisdiction of international courts during the process of democratic restructuring, and they have signalled compliance with international law, or at least with regional human rights conventions, as a precondition of their legitimacy. As a result, new democratic states have founded substantial parts of their domestic public law on international law, such that international law has acted as an autonomous constituent element in the domestic legal order.[28] In extreme cases, international courts have taken pains to ensure that their jurisprudence is assimilated in the public law and the legal procedures of the states over which they have jurisdiction.[29] As discussed, in some settings, this incorporation occurs at a pre-judicial level, as legislative processes are covered by advisory bodies that prevent conflict between new laws and international norms.[30] In each respect, in short, democratic formation is barely distinguishable from the implementation of international legal norms.

The role of international human rights in promoting democracy has had a series of consequences for the global reality of democracy in modern society.

First, the significance of international human rights has meant that, in most processes of post-authoritarian democratization, the basic subject of

---

[26] Of course, not all states with new constitutions have emerged as stable democracies. But no states have emerged as stable democracies without constitutions, and few constitutions have failed to give some recognition for human rights law. The diffusion model of constitutionalization used by Elkins (2010: 996) to explain constitution making in Europe can be applied globally. I agree with Elkins that it is 'nearly unthinkable' that a 'state could achieve full democracy without a constitution' (2010: 972). On my account, this is deeply linked to the fact that new constitutions cannot easily be separated from international human rights law.

[27] Before the final establishment of democratic rule, judges engaged in important acts of law making inter alia in transitional Poland, South Africa and Hungary, in each instance using international human rights law as the basis for judgement.

[28] See discussion of the block of constitutionality in some Latin American courts below at p. 245.

[29] See as an important example IACtHR, Case of *Ticona Estrada et al.* v. *Bolivia*. Judgment of 27 November 2008, endorsing the block of constitutionality in Bolivia.

[30] A key example of such a body is the Departamento Internacional da Procuradoria Geral da União in Brazil.

national democracy was, at key stages in its expression, constructed not as a factual volitional agent, but in externally projected and defined legal categories. In most new democracies, the fundamental design of constitutional law was originally proportioned to a *pre-formed legal subject*, whose political expectations, which determined the substance of democracy, were first constructed through principles of international law, within an existing external legal corpus. For this reason, in many cases of democratic transition, the democratic people emerged in a form that was clearly separated from more embedded traditions of popular will formation, and the democratic institutions that were created to satisfy the people were produced in a generalized form, partly defined by human rights norms. This was reflected, most obviously, in the high degree of convergence between newly created constitutions.[31]

Second, the role of international human rights in the formation of new democratic polities has had the result that political actors in national societies often had only limited freedom to define the content of their laws. In some cases, of course, conflicts have occurred between models of political subjectivity proposed in international law and models of political subjectivity existing in domestic society. Examples of this are most obvious in societies with large indigenous populations, for example in Latin America; in societies with religious legal cultures, notably in North Africa; and in societies with deeply ingrained paternalist traditions, such as Russia. But, in most cases, the construction of democracy has been driven by an international model of citizenship. The content of laws generally acknowledged as democratic is now widely determined not by the degree to which laws represent interests of a national political subject, but by the degree to which they protect the interests of a subject defined in international law. On this basis, although rights-based democracy has become the standard model of popular governance, it is clear that human rights and democracy can easily be in tension.[32]

Through these processes, most particularly, the basic source of democratic legitimacy has been profoundly transformed. The basic source of

---

[31] Most constitutions now have uniform features. Very few democratic constitutions do not contain a catalogue of rights, possessing some degree of entrenchment. Very few establish fully sovereign legislatures. Very few do not create courts without at least some powers of constitutional judicial review.

[32] For this claim see Donnelly (1999: 619). Susan Marks's analysis of democracies arising from global normative presumptions has similarities to the more critical elements of my analysis here (see Marks 2000: 96). As discussed below, however, my eventual conclusions are very different.

legitimacy no longer resides in the national constituent power. Instead, it resides in a threefold relation between actors at different points in the global legal system. That is, it resides in a relation between first, persons in national society; second, governmental institutions in national society and third, norm providers in international society. This relation has replaced the national constituent power as the essential political axis or mainspring of democracy. In many cases of objective democratization, the basic constitutional structure of the democratic order has been produced not through the primary voluntary or political acts of a people, but through a moderated interaction between these three points in the global legal system.[33]

In more classical concepts of democracy, as mentioned, the normative force of democracy resided in the idea that there exists a chain of legitimation, which connects the people as an original constituent actor with the particular acts of government. Of course, historically, the actual institutionalization of this chain was subject to deeply polarized debate, but the presumption that the exercise of governmental power must be directly linked to the sovereign acts of the people remained an inalienable core of democratic thinking. However, in recent democratic transitions, the classical concept of democracy has been supplanted by a *cyclical, three-point model* of democratic formation. In the current model of democratic formation, first, the people typically formalize their will against the existing government by demanding human rights, largely based on and recognized under international law. Second, governments react to such demands by acknowledging the existence of the people, in their capacity as claimants to rights, in accordance with international norms. Third, international human rights organizations and judicial bodies then provide constructions of legitimacy for the state in question, based on acknowledgement of persons as holders of rights. Through this process, the original chain of legitimation in more classical ideas of democracy is broken, and the presence of the people as a real aggregate of citizens is symbolically translated into an idea of the people as a holder of rights, internalized and cyclically reproduced within the law. The chain of legitimation becomes a chain that connects not real people to the organs of government, but different elements of the global legal system, each of which converges around human rights norms.

The articulation of this democratic model, with variations, is common to most recent democratic transitions, especially in Latin America and Eastern Europe. In this model, the eminently *political* matrix of democratic

---

[33] On the internationalization of constituent power see Wheatley (2010: 245).

legitimization is constrained, and the extent to which the people are able to appear, before the law, as an active political subject is limited.

3.2.2   Persons Not People

In classical conceptions of democracy, the people, the nation or the citizen was posited as the primary subject of public law, and democracy was typically explained as a system in which the nation forms a corporate body, creating laws claiming political primacy over the interests of single individuals and other associations. Indeed, at the core of early democratic theory was the claim that democracy acquires legitimacy as a form of *political association*, whose political content reflects the essentially associational fabric of human societies.[34] Of course, in the very early period of liberal-democratic thinking, the ideal form of government was sometimes imagined as a system for protecting the inalienable natural rights of single human subjects.[35] Some more recent theorists have still retained this view (Nozick 1974: 26–7). Yet, from the Enlightenment to World War II, the development of democracy both as doctrine and as institutional practice was driven by the idea that democracy institutionalizes a mode of political will formation, in which collective interests are articulated that are not reducible *a priori* to the simple single interests of individual persons, and in which citizens engage in collective political practices and collective demands to create law. As mentioned, it is fundamental to the idea of the citizen that it translates private interests into collective patterns of contestation and recognition, and it forms a deep cycle of communication around the political system. In recent decades, however, the focus of democratic legitimation and organization has shifted paradigmatically *from the people to the person* as the primary source of legitimacy for legislation. Accordingly, the legitimacy of legislation is increasingly constructed not as a result of its authorization by a collective actor, but as the consequence of its adequacy to, and its recognition of, certain rights ascribed, within the law itself, to *single persons*.

This redirection of democratic legitimacy was promoted, originally, in the aftermath of World War II, as the instruments that underpinned the

---

[34] This connection between democracy and political association is of Aristotelian origin. But it also runs through early precursors of democratic theory. See for salient examples Althusius (1614: 169); Rousseau (1966 [1762]: 67).

[35] See Locke's claim that government is created to protect and preserve already existing rights (1999 [1690]: 48).

emerging global legal system crystallized individual human rights as the normative premise of democratic governance. Through this period, first, it was implied in the major documents of international law that the defining measure of a government's legitimacy is that it does not violate the protected human rights of its particular subjects, and that it passes laws showing recognition of persons subject to laws as singular holders of rights.[36] As discussed, in the post-1945 corpus of international human rights law, the right to democratic participation was rather tentatively protected, whereas the separate individual rights acquired increased exponentially in importance. On this basis, it was increasingly assumed that international organizations could monitor levels of democratic legitimacy in different societies, and that such monitoring should focus, primarily, on evaluating degrees of human rights abuse and on ensuring the integrity of single persons, *qua* rights holders, within national states. Indeed, even in cases where international organizations addressed the situation of large population groups, they tended to focus on these groups as collective holders of singular rights.[37] As a result of this, the single person as a holder of rights, separated from its embodied corporate location in the nation, became a pivotal point in the global legal order. Initially, as mentioned, this was offset by the focus on self-determination in early UN norms concerning decolonization. To a large degree, however, the basic legal order which sustained the growth of democracy after 1945 was condensed around the legal concept of the single person as a formally isolated citizen, and the global system that evolved after 1945 increasingly produced laws in order to safeguard the rights of single persons, in relative isolation from other members of their national populations. Of course, rights were accorded to persons universally, such that all persons were construed as members of a large human collective. However, the allocation of rights depended on recognition of each person as a separate rights-holding agent, with separate legal claims.

The singularization of the citizen throughout this period was reflected, tellingly, in the fact that international law attached rights and liberties to

---

[36] Alongside the UN Charter and the UDHR, the Convention on the Prevention and Punishment of the Crime of Genocide (1948) clearly spelled out the principle that individual subjects have rights under international law.

[37] For example, the provisions for trusteeship of former colonies in the UN Charter focus on non-self-governing populations as rights holders, stating, in Art 76(c), that former colonial powers with duties under the trusteeship system are expected 'to encourage respect for human rights and for fundamental freedoms for all without distinction as to race, sex, language, or religion, and to encourage recognition of the interdependence of the peoples of the world'.

persons constructed in highly generic fashion. In particular, international law detached the rights-holding subject from the objective political personalities – that is, from the concrete associational structures and collective groupings – manifest in real societies, and early post-1945 instruments of international law were muted in the recognition of rights of factually existing collective actors. Notably, for example, post-1945 international law gave relatively weak recognition to the rights of minority population groups, the protection of which was usually subsumed under general human rights law (law giving rights to all individual persons). In fact, it was not until the 1990s that international human rights law was widely extended to cover sub-national social groups.[38] Equally importantly, post-1945 international law was reticent in establishing rights of economic or industrial collectives, such as trade unions or syndicates. Although the main international-legal instruments after 1945 recognized certain basic labour rights, the interests of persons in their corporate capacity as workers or employees were not strongly prioritized. Similarly, in early national constitutions created after 1945, emphasis was placed on the protection of single human rights, partly at the expense of rights contested and constructed by collective associations. In the first wave of democratization after 1945, newly founded states usually applied rights to persons in society that strictly separated these persons from the collectives in which their claims were constructed, and they generally perceived rights as singular institutions, attaching to singular persons as invariable subjective

---

[38] Historically, the International Labour Organization (ILO) was a pioneer in promoting international standards to address the claims of indigenous and tribal peoples. In 1957, the ILO adopted Convention 107, which concerned the protection of indigenous and other tribal or semi-tribal populations in independent countries. ILO 107 received 27 ratifications, and it formed the first endeavour to codify indigenous rights at the level of international law. In 1989, the ILO adopted the Indigenous and Tribal Peoples Convention, 1989 (No. 169) (hereafter, ILO 169), which reflected a vital change in attitude towards indigenous populations in international law, and it promoted a doctrine not of assimilationism, but of solidarity, as the premise for their legal recognition. ILO 169 entered into force in 1991, giving formal international protection to a number of collective rights for indigenous peoples. These rights included rights to cultural integrity, to consultation and participation in relevant decision-making processes, to certain forms of self-government, to land occupancy, to territory and resources, and to non-discrimination in the social and economic spheres. Despite the fact that only 22 states, most of them in Latin America, have actually ratified ILO 169, the norms embodied in the Convention have been developed by other bodies and courts. It has achieved wide-ranging impact beyond the states that have ratified it. In addition, in 2007, the UN Declaration on the Rights of Indigenous Peoples was formally adopted by 143 Member States of the UN. Although only accorded the status of soft law, the Declaration strongly affirms the rights to self-determination of indigenous peoples.

entitlements.[39] This tendency was then reinforced in later processes of democratization. From the middle of the 1980s, democracy promotion was often expressly associated with the relativization of collective rights, and possession of rights was construed as an alternative to membership in political organizations based on collective modes of economic organization.[40] Overall, human rights were initially constructed, both in international law and in domestic constitutions that assimilated international law, as rights that persons possessed independently of the concrete organizations in which their lives were positioned. Throughout the post-1945 period, it was widely assumed that interwar experiments in democracy had failed, not least, because of the insufficient individualization of legal subjects under the corporatist systems created at this time. This had meant that generalized personal rights could easily be deprioritized by momentarily dominant social groups.[41]

To some degree, therefore, the process of democratic consolidation after 1945 revolved around an idea of democracy in which the normative form of democratic law making was stripped away from real existing persons, and the concrete agency of democratic citizenship was diminished. As an alternative, a mode of generalized legal subjectivity – formally individuated citizenship – was superimposed across the factual structure of national populations, and democratic laws were projected as laws applied to fictionally universalized individual subjects. Indeed, the essence of democracy was constructed around static apolitical subjects, centred on single human rights claims, originating within the global legal system itself.

This formal reconstruction of the basic subject of democracy necessarily had far-reaching implications for the role of citizenship in contemporary democratic systems. As discussed, central to the construction of the citizen as a legitimational figure for the political system is the fact that citizenship, attached to claims for rights, gives rise to a contestation and renegotiation

---

[39] For example, in the constitutions of newly democratized states in Germany, Italy and Japan earliest collectivist provisions were abandoned, and new democratic constitutions did not promote collective economic rights.

[40] Argentina is the classic example of this. From the 1940s Argentina had a highly collectivist tradition, which gave extensive recognition for trade-union rights. The 1980s brought a reorientation towards singular rights. Similar processes occurred across Latin America, notably in Bolivia.

[41] For instance, anti-corporatist measures were widely implemented in Western Germany after 1945. This began with decisions of the American occupying forces to reject regional constitutions that contained corporatist elements. It culminated in legislation introduced in 1949 to limit trade union collectivism. In Japan, a series of anti-corporatist laws were implemented after 1945.

of the boundaries of inclusion and legitimation in society. Indeed, citizenship can be defined, paradigmatically, as a condition in which society as a whole is *exposed to politicization by actors claiming rights*, through which transformative processes in society are articulated towards the political system. This process presupposes that the citizen is embedded in concrete life structures, in which common experiences create claims to rights, which are then directed towards the political system. The fixing of the construct of the citizen around an externally defined set of norms, however, means that the rights that can be activated by citizens become more formally determined, externally circumscribed and partly separated from social experience. Indeed, the external construction of the citizen means that, in most settings, citizens acquire the same rights, defined by a uniform model of citizenship, and the rights to which citizens can lay claim formally pre-exist the acts in which they demand them. Above all, in contemporary democracies, the citizen assumes rights not primarily by articulating conflicts within its own society, but by reaching out into the global normative system, and demanding inner-societal recognition for rights that already exist. Rights claimed by one person, therefore, do not require trans-sectoral collective mobilization, and they do not necessarily transform collective life structures. In consequence, the extent to which claims to rights challenge the boundaries of the political system is limited, and most claims emanating from national society can be absorbed through existing sets of rights, which are already stored in the global legal system.

In these respects, international human rights law imposed a more restricted spectrum of political subjectivity on society, and it effectively pre-defined the forms in which political subjects could be constructed, limiting the societal volatility attached to rights claims. Society's potentials for political subject formation were, in part, generated by the law: indeed, society is partly de-subjectivized. Of course, the rise of international law did not bring an end to social mobilization, and, as discussed below, it did not bring an end to the claiming of new rights. However, rights were increasingly formed through an immediate nexus between the single person and global law, and they could be constructed relatively discretely, without requiring the unsettling politicization of all society.

3.2.3 *Margin of Appreciation*

The two processes described above led, gradually, both to an externalization and to a formal abstraction of the essential subject of democracy. One result of this is that socially embedded practices lost some importance in

the reinforcement of democracy, and democracy could easily be solidified around a small set of formal norms. Accordingly, democracies could
be established on relatively thin normative foundations, and they did
not presuppose the mobilization of deep-lying, complex constituencies
or the broad-based experience of citizenship.[42] One further result of this
was that the legitimacy of democratic institutions and the acts of legislation performed by democratic institutions became increasingly measured
by abstracted, external standards, not identified with a factually existing
subject. Democratic institutions were increasingly defined as legitimate
through reference not to aggregated acts of real self-legislating citizens,
but to criteria present within an existing legal system.

Importantly, this reconstruction of democracy after 1945 is reflected
not only in patterns of democracy promotion, but in the judicial structure
of global society, and especially in the interactions between national government organs and principles of inter- or supranational jurisprudence.
This can be seen in the fact that many national states began to construct
their legislative acts within supranational legal orders. Increasingly, states
explained the validity of their legislation, at least in part, by the extent to
which single laws tracked or mirrored established higher-order principles,
enshrined in international law. In particular, human rights obligations
under international law became a measure by which, either implicitly or
expressly, all domestic legislation had to be assessed and interpreted. This
meant, most notably, that the legitimacy of democratic legislation was
partly defined by principles external to the legislative process, external to
the factual purpose of any given act of legislation, and external to any *factual subject* that participated in legislation. As a result, in most democracies, at least one component of the legitimacy of law was constructed not
by acts of will formation reflected through the law, but by norms stored in
a global legal system, to which law, and acts creating law, had to be proportioned. Just as the concrete volitional form of the people became marginal to democracy as a whole, therefore, it also became marginal to single
legislative acts, and acts of law began to acquire and signal legitimacy not
through the political motivations or demands of citizens, by which they
were shaped, but through the international norms to which they were
proportioned.

---

[42] Many enduring democracies created after 1945 were constructed through inter-elite pacts,
in which agreement about recognition of international human rights norms had central
importance. Important examples of this are the FRG, Japan, Spain, Chile, Ghana and South
Africa.

In some cases, the obligations of national legislators under international law are defined very tightly.[43] For example, in Latin America, since the establishment of the IACtHR, domestic law is certified as legitimate if it is in compliance with the ACHR, and the principle of compliance is formulated in the doctrine of the *control of conventionality*. According to this doctrine, the ACHR must be integrated as higher law in the normative hierarchy of the legal systems of states party to it (see Dulitzky 2015: 57, 60). Consequently, legislators in national states are rigidly bound by the ACHR, and domestic judicial actors, and in fact all public authorities, have the duty to ensure full compatibility between 'internal legal norms' – the laws of national societies – and the ACHR. In fact, national courts are expected to evaluate domestic legislation both by considering its compliance with the ACHR and by assessing it in light of the 'interpretation of the treaty provided by the Inter-American Court'.[44] Some Latin American courts, notably the Colombian Constitutional Court, have adopted the technique of devising a *block of constitutionality* – that is, of directly incorporating some international treaties in domestic constitutional law. These treaties include the ACHR, and, by extension, the rulings of the IACtHR, which means that the jurisprudence of the IACtHR has a position in Colombian law similar to constitutional rank. In establishing this principle, the Constitutional Court aims both to avoid referral of cases to the IACtHR and to obtain semi-legislative power for itself.[45] In the Latin American setting, generally, domestic courts have a salient role in constructing democracy, and in many states law is legitimated, at least in part, through its correlation with the international normative system.

Outside Latin America, the role of judicial bodies in assessing the validity of national legal norms is less strictly guaranteed. Nonetheless, courts are widely assigned responsibility for establishing the legitimacy of law by assessing its conformity with international law, and especially with international human rights provisions. In other supranational jurisdictions, this procedure is most obviously formalized in the doctrine of the *margin of appreciation*. That is to say, most states now accept that domestic laws can only be legitimate insofar as they are aligned to global normative

---

[43] IACtHR, Exceptions to the Exhaustion of Domestic Remedies (Arts. 46(1), 46(2)(a), and 46(2)(b) American Convention on Human Rights), Advisory Opinion, OC-11/90 (10 August 1990).

[44] See the first statement of this in IACtHR, Case of *Almonacid-Arellano et al v. Chile*. Judgment of 26 September 2006. See also Colombian Constitutional Court C-410/15. I am grateful to Carina Calabria for lengthy discussion of these points.

[45] See a leading discussion of this in T-1319/01.

standards, and that, with qualifications, international courts can supervise domestic law to ensure that it does not deviate too far from overarching principles. Nonetheless, domestic law is allowed to deviate from international norms in cases in which a particular legislative act either meets a pressing need within the national society in question, or where it is singularly justified as a reflection of a more local legal convention.

The doctrine of the margin of appreciation is implied in most supranational legal orders. As mentioned, the IACtHR usually requires strict recognition of international norms within domestic law. However, it has at times applied a doctrine close to the margin of appreciation.[46] This doctrine has been used, more implicitly, by the UN Human Rights Committee.[47] However, this doctrine has greatest importance in the jurisprudence of the ECtHR. Typically, in the ECHR system, the margin of appreciation has been promoted as a means to make supranational human rights protection workable, and it reflects a compromise between the demands of separate national states and the autonomy of the supranational system as a whole. Nonetheless, the margin of appreciation doctrine clearly limits democratic volition in states that are parties to the ECHR, and it curtails the extent to which law is legitimated by popular political decisions. Clearly, this doctrine places national legislation in a subordinate, or at least normatively circumscribed, position within a transnational legal order, and it implies, centrally, that national laws are formed and justified within a discretionary sphere, the boundaries of which are dictated by international legal norms and bodies interpreting such norms.

At a most obvious level, one consequence of the doctrine of the margin of appreciation is that democratic legislation within national societies is always subject to restrictions by higher-ranking international norm providers. As a result, judicial bodies outside national states are authorized to scrutinize public acts within national societies to ensure that they do not exceed the limits of a sanctioned sphere of national legislative autonomy. In addition, however, this doctrine implies that judicial actors within national states are allowed to assess the actions of their own governments through reference to the margin of appreciation, and they are authorized to evaluate laws and legal rulings not solely on intrinsic substantive grounds, but in light of their position within the international legal order.

---

[46] IACtHR, Proposed Amendments to the Naturalization Provisions of the Constitution of Costa Rica, Advisory Opinion OC-4/84, 19 January 1984.

[47] *Shirin Aumeeruddy-Cziffra and 19 other Mauritian women* v. *Mauritius*, Communication No. 35/1978, (9.4.1981). U.N. Doc. CCPR/C/OP/1 at 67 (1984).

Although not originally conceived as a doctrine to be applied by national public bodies,[48] in fact, the principle of the margin of appreciation creates a certain latitude in which national judicial bodies can examine domestic acts of legislation and determine whether they fall within or outside acceptable discretionary limits. As a result, national courts interpret international norms to define the sphere of discretion within which national legislative acts can assume legitimacy.

The principle that domestic courts can establish the margin of appreciation was formally stated in one of the main ECtHR rulings applying this doctrine, *Handyside* v. *UK* (1976). First, in this ruling, the Court set out the basic concept of the margin of appreciation. It recognized that, although all parties to the ECHR are bound by common norms, the Contracting States had 'fashioned their approach in the light of the situation obtaining in their respective territories' and they were qualified to reflect and address 'the demands of the protection of morals in a democratic society' within their own territories.[49] On this basis, the Court noted that the doctrine of the margin of appreciation implies a supervisory relation between supranational and national courts, and that the primary duty of the ECtHR is to protect higher-ranking norms. Second, however, in this ruling, the Court developed a two-pronged method for protecting human rights. It stated that it itself possessed responsibility for ensuring that the rights required for democratic governance were protected in signatory states, and deviations from Convention standards could only be accepted to the degree that they did not derogate from an overarching commitment to democracy. Yet, it also declared that national courts had a designated responsibility for ensuring that domestic public agencies act within a margin of appreciation, and, to this degree, the supervisory functions of a supranational court are less important than those of national courts. In this instance, it was decided that national courts were authorized to apply a margin of appreciation in their own rulings, and they could decide on the legitimacy of public acts by balancing these acts against international human rights standards. The Court ruled that the margin of appreciation 'is given both

---

[48]   One commentator states that the margin of appreciation is 'fundamentally a transnational device' and it can 'have no direct domestic application' (Greer 2000: 34). To support this, see the claim, in an ECtHR case, that: 'The doctrine of the margin of appreciation has always been meant as a tool to define relations between the domestic authorities and the Court. It cannot have the same application to the relations between the organs of State at the domestic level': *A. and Others* v. *the United Kingdom [GC]* – 3455/05. Judgment 19 February 2009 [GC], at para 184.

[49]   *Handyside* v. *The United Kingdom*; - 5493/72. Judgement 7 December 1976 para 57.

to the domestic legislator ... and to the bodies, judicial amongst others, that are called upon to interpret and apply the laws in force'.[50] Indicatively, the ECtHR stated that 'the machinery of protection established by the Convention is subsidiary to the national systems safeguarding human rights'.[51]

In key respects, this ruling reflected a basic reconfiguration of democratic theory. In this articulation, democracy was defined as a political system founded in a discretionary relation between national political organs and overarching normative dictates, in which legislative acts had to be proportioned *a priori* to pre-defined legal norms. In this relation, national courts and other public bodies were accorded a primary role in giving reality, within a discretionary margin, to human rights norms situated in the international domain, ensuring that acts of legislative bodies did not exceed constraints resulting from these norms. The essential substance of democracy, thus, was construed not as the enactment of a political will, but as an inter-institutional discussion about the variable enforcement of human rights law. A concept of democracy as a *formal process of compensation between existing legal-normative principles*, in which different courts balance legislative imperatives against implied human rights standards, became evident in this process. In this conception, the originating subject of the democratic system was translated into an abstracted construction of the person as rights holder, defined in international conventions. Accordingly, this subject gained political expression not through primary political acts, but through an inner-legal relation between judicial actors and international norm setters.

Over decades, many variations have been added to the classical doctrine of the margin of appreciation. In some countries, the doctrine has justified guarantees for human rights in domestic law that may be at variance with those promoted in international law.[52] However, in some cases, courts have adopted a reverse practice, and they have posited a wide spectrum of appreciation, in which they are entitled to offer more robust protection for certain rights than provided by international courts. Examples of this are found in Europe, where some national courts have accentuated their independence from the Strasbourg court by claiming the authority to entrench human rights more fully than the ECtHR.[53] This is in fact notable

---

[50] Ibid para 48.
[51] Ibid.
[52] This is the principle in *Handyside*.
[53] In one UK case the Supreme Court claimed to go 'rather further than the evolving jurisprudence of the European Court of Human Rights has yet clearly established to be required':

in Russia, whose superior courts have in a several cases fleshed out a body of case law that, in some instances, establishes rights above Strasbourg thresholds.[54] In some cases, national courts have argued that they are not bound by Strasbourg jurisprudence. Yet, in stating this, they have claimed new powers and envisioned new rights in their own domestic systems.[55] Examples of similar reasoning are also found in Latin America, where some courts have given to some rights a more expansive protection than guaranteed at the supranational level, by the IACtHR.[56]

In such examples, the basic content of democratic law is formed and explained within a relation of balances, and the interaction between national and supranational legal norms becomes an effective wellspring for democratic, even constitutional, legislation. As a result, the basic position of political agency is reconfigured, and primary legal norms are created, transnationally, without reference to any real existing subject. In some cases, in fact, the contested balancing of rights between different courts becomes – of itself – a source of new legal principles. Through each of these processes, the fact that courts conserve an image of the person as an original rights holder partly replaces the democratically engaged people (citizen) as a basic source and reference for legitimate legislation. As a factual agent, the citizen is subsumed within a set of inner-legal exchanges.

Rabone and another v. *Pennine Care NHS Foundation Trust* – [2012] 2 All ER 381 (Brown SCJ). See also the Norwegian ruling, Decision HR-2011-00182-A, 26 January 2011, in which the Supreme Court expanded ECHR rights concerning self-incrimination. I follow the analysis in Andenaes and Bjorge (2013: 245).

54   In Russia, in 2016, the Russian Constitutional Court (RCC) ruled, with reference to Convention on the Elimination of all Forms of Discrimination Against Women, that women have the formal right to be judged by a jury trial (RCC Ruling on Merits No. 6-P of 25 February 2016). The Russian Criminal Procedure Code (Article 31) requires a trial by jury for defendants that committed a crime punishable by lifelong sentence. At the same time, Arts. 57 and 59 of the Criminal Code state that women are exempt from lifelong sentence in general. In theory, this means that women accused of committing crimes potentially resulting in a life sentence are not allowed to be tried by jury. The RCC has altered this situation and recognized the formal right of women to be tried by jury.

55   See the claim that the courts may possess the right to oppose franchise restrictions in *Moohan and another* v. *Lord Advocate* [2014] UKSC 67 (Hodge).

56   See the expansive reading of the right to *vida digna* in the Colombian Constitutional Court (T-009/13). Central to the jurisprudence of the Colombian Constitutional Court is the claim (see T-406/92) that, where appropriate, it can establish rights above the thresholds set out in domestic constitutional law and above levels of protection provided by the ACHR and general international human rights law.

3.2.4   Proportionality

The abstraction of democratic subjectivity through the concept of the margin of appreciation is intensified through the growing judicial application of the doctrine of *proportionality* as a measure of the legitimacy of legislation. In its currently common form, the doctrine of proportionality implies that public bodies can only pass laws that restrict the established basic rights of particular subjects if such restriction is dictated and justified by the fact that it engenders a collective benefit or value that is proportionate to the consequences of the restriction. In applying principles of proportionality, in particular, courts are expected to decide whether a particular law or a particular administrative decision restricting human rights shows due recognition of the rights of the person affected by the act or decision, or whether any disadvantages experienced by affected parties may exceed justifiable limits. In most cases, intrusion on subjective rights is only seen as warranted as it can be construed as necessary for *upholding a democratic society*.[57]

Of course, the principle of proportionality is not of itself new, and basic concepts of balancing have long been familiar in most legal systems. The doctrine of proportionality originated in administrative law and police law, as a principle to obviate the use of unnecessarily harsh measures by public bodies.[58] In recent years, the spread of proportionality has intensified its meaning and broadened the scope of its application. The contemporary use of proportionality reasoning began – in part – in national legal systems as a means of resolving conflicts between constitutionally guaranteed rights and public interests. The use of proportionality was then expanded in international organizations and international human rights systems, in which proportionality began to cover questions of subsidiarity and derogation from international norms in supranational legal orders.[59] More recently, the application of proportionality has been widened to the

---

[57] This principle is set out in the ECHR and in case law of the ECtHR. It is subject to variable interpretation, allowing states considerable latitude on limiting internationally defined human rights. In *Handyside*, the ECtHR allowed this term to cover censorship intended for 'the protection of morals in a democratic society' (para 57). This principle is also expressed in the American Declaration of the Rights and Duties of Man (Art XXVIII).

[58] It was already formulated in the Prussian Land Law of 1794, which stated that 'laws and edits of the state' should not 'restrict the natural freedom of citizens any more than was required by the common purpose' (Remmert 1995: 27).

[59] In the EU, the principle of subsidiarity contains proportionality implications. In the ECtHR, proportionality is implied in the margin of appreciation doctrine.

degree that many courts use proportionality without fixed reference to a formalized body of constitutional law or human rights law, and courts often simply evaluate acts of domestic public bodies through reference to loosely implied transnational human rights standards. Notable examples of this can be found in Canada, in which proportionality assessment of public acts is intensified where international norms and values have relevance to a case.[60] Important examples can also be found in Chile, where courts have used proportionality reasoning to ensure that rights protected under international law are accorded higher entrenchment in domestic proceedings.[61] In such cases, proportionality has formed an important sluice through which general international norms have assumed constitutive effect in domestic law.

Significantly, the use of proportionality has led to a relativization of classical patterns of legislative agency, and it has imposed on national legal systems a construction of democratic obligation, and so also of the underlying democratic subject, which is projected in highly abstracted, innerlegal fashion.

One clear implication of the use of proportionality is that the legitimacy of a law or other public act can be established through judicial balancing of two sets of rights: the right of an individual affected by a decision and the rights of the democratic community as a whole. This means that a judge is required to assess which of the competing rights weighs most heavily in a given situation, and which of these rights warrants the most urgent protection in the act in question. Through this process, the legitimacy of a law emerges not as the result of a substantial public decision, but as a judicially constructed relation between rival principles, which are already articulated and stored in the legal system. Indicatively, one tribunal which actively promotes proportionality has stated that the use of proportionality reasoning entails a 'concrete harmonization of rights', in which law's legitimacy becomes measurable not by any substantive value that it contains, but by the fact that it mediates equally between rival rights claims.[62]

One further implication of the use of proportionality is that, ultimately, courts assume the power to define the broader normative fabric of society, and the extent to which the authority of binding legal norms can be traced to primary political acts or even substantively defined collective

---

[60] *Slaight Communications Inc* v. *Davidson*, [1989] 1 S.C.R. 1038.
[61] See Corte Suprema, 28/01/2009, 4691-2007.
[62] Bolivian Constitutional Court 2621/2012.

preferences is reduced. In assessing the proportionality of acts of public bodies, courts are expected not only to scrutinize the content of a particular act of a legislative or administrative body, but also both to assess the impact of this act on persons affected by it, and to evaluate whether its benefits for the democratic community are sufficiently great to warrant this impact. In so doing, courts increase the burden of justification that is imposed on public bodies, in their legislative and administrative functions. In fact, courts impose expectations on public bodies that are established, literally, by an anticipation of the social consequences of laws and administrative acts, and by a projection of the ways in which such laws and acts may or may not affect the rights of persons held and exercised, under constitutional law or even under international law, throughout society. In applying proportionality, courts must presume a broad understanding of society as a whole, and make far-reaching decisions about its constitutional nature and its democratic form.

Through the expansion of proportionality, the role of the factual citizen is diminished in democracy, and it is replaced by a more formal inner-legal construction of society's political subject. This occurs, first, because, where laws are authorized on proportionality grounds, judges acquire greatly expanded authority in assessing the validity of acts perpetrated by public bodies, so that the competence of courts often exceeds the limits implied under classical separation of powers arrangements. This occurs, second, because, in applying proportionality, judges become defenders of democracy, and they are charged with responsibility for assessing the normative requirements of democratic society as a whole. Judges are required to authorize law not because it is created by democratic subjects, but because it is proportioned to democratic subjects, defined through a judicial construction of society as a whole. This occurs, third, at a more fundamental level, because proportionality envisages legitimate law not as law that people have willed, but as law that adequately balances different rights. Through this process, implicitly, the citizen is no longer defined as the factual or original legitimating author of law. Instead, law acquires authority as the citizen is transposed into a model of rights-holding legal subjectivity to which laws need to be purposively aligned, and laws are only allowed to restrict recognition of this subject on strictly controlled discretionary premises. In this process, the legitimacy of law is constructed retroactively, through its adequacy to the formal rights of the democratic citizen. In this process, thus, *the citizen moves from the beginning to the end of law*: the citizen brings legitimacy to law not as law's author, but as a judicial construction of law's addressee, often implicitly based on international human rights law. Courts internalize the figure of the citizen, which is translated into a movable legitimating norm for legislative acts, positioned at the end of law.

Particularly significant in this respect is the fact that, in some societies, superior courts have adopted a distinctive constitutional practice, which is based on proportionality reasoning, but which uses proportionality not only to place normative limits on the acts of state bodies, but to prescribe positive obligations to them. This is especially prominent in Colombia, whose judicial system is in many respects a laboratory for the creation of principles of global democratic law. In Colombia, proportionality is now widely used across a range of cases. However, it has a distinctive importance in cases relating to mass displacement and civil violence, as a result of which large population groups have been deprived of access to basic rights. In such cases, the Colombian Constitutional Court has developed a line of jurisprudence which argues that some social groups are placed at a *disproportionate level of vulnerability* because of their exposure to internal displacement and violence, and the resultant endemic violation of their rights. These groups usually include women, children, elderly persons and indigenous groups; in some cases, in fact, indigenous women and children are classified a particular sub-group of doubly jeopardized, ultra-vulnerable persons.[63] On this basis, the Court has argued that the state has a series of intensified obligations towards such groups, and it must promote *proportionate affirmative action* to ensure that their rights are raised to the same level as those of other, less vulnerable groups. The Court has recommended that extensive programmes of action should be initiated, whose implementation it claims authority to monitor, in order to ensure that affirmative action provisions are put into practice.[64]

In each of these examples, proportionality leads to a clear transfer of law-making force from a materially given demos to an abstracted rights-based concept of the human subject. In this process, the factual authorship for law is transferred from the active political citizen to citizen qua legal rights holder. As bodies designated to protect the inner-legal construct of the citizen, then, courts become both custodians of democracy and the source of democratic laws, and legislation is enacted and justified because of a construction of democratic citizenship articulated within the law.

[63] A-092/08.
[64] Ibid.

3.2.5   Inter-legality

The expanding role of the legal system in establishing the basic elements of democracy means that judicial bodies are often positioned in the interstitial domain between legal orders situated at different parts of global society. In this position, courts create laws by presiding over an interaction between principles stored in different locations of the legal system, and they promote primary legislation, and even perform basic acts of democratic citizenship, through their *inter-legal* position.

Most commonly, this *inter-legal* position of courts is expressed through the fact that they are required to oversee the subordination of domestic law to international law, or at least to ensure the accommodation of these two dimensions of the global legal system. More infrequently, the inter-legal position of courts is expressed in reactive fashion, as courts defend domestic legal principles against international legal norms, often under the banner of national sovereignty. Cases of this kind are frequent in the USA, the UK and Russia, where courts are often reticent to give immediate effect to international law.[65] In these settings, to be sure, there are obvious examples in which courts simply reject norms contained in international law.[66] In such contexts, however, international law more generally acquires an osmotic effect, as outward rejection of the application of international law by national courts typically – over time – softens into a position in which domestic legal principles are aligned to the basic expectations of international law.[67] In some cases, the inter-legal position of courts is expressed more delicately, as courts consider expectations in different dimensions of the global legal system at the same time, and they ultimately construct basic norms on a fluid, hybrid, intrinsically transnational foundation. The use of law of varying provenance to reach verdicts with far-reaching significance

---

[65] In a recent case, the RCC ruled on the supremacy of the Russian Constitution above conflicting rulings of international courts and tribunals (RCC Ruling on Merits No. 21-P of 14 July 2015). Later in 2015, a federal constitutional law was adopted solidifying the right of the RCC to rule, essentially, on the constitutionality of a Strasbourg judgement (Federal Constitutional Law No. 7-FKZ of 14 December 2015). On 19 April 2016 this federal law was used for the first time when the Ministry of Justice requested the RCC to assess the constitutionality of an ECtHR judgement on the question of prisoners' voting, handed down by the ECtHR in *Anchugov and Gladkov v. Russia* (Applications nos. 11157/04 and 15162/05, Judgment of 4 July 2013). See RCC Ruling on Merits No. 12-P of 19 April 2016. Also, the RCC has declared that it is an 'impossibility' to implement the ECtHR Yukos judgement (OAO *Neftyanaya Kompaniya Yukos v. Russia* (Application no. 14902/04, Judgment of 15 December 2014)) (see RCC Ruling on Merits No. 1-P of 19 January 2017).

[66] ICJ, LaGrand case (*Germany v. United States of America*). Judgment of 27 June 2001.

[67] See general discussion of the USA and the UK in this respect below at pp. 296–9, 343–5.

is observable in the UK courts.[68] In such instances, national democratic agency is not the basis of law. National law is configured around the interaction between different parts of the global legal system.

In some contexts, the function of inter-legal law making by courts results from the fact that courts are required to balance the norms contained in different dimensions of the legal system that exist in their own societies. In this position, courts acquire very far-reaching sociological significance in promoting overarching processes of social integration. In such environments, courts at times assume responsibility for harmonizing the legal claims of different communities, especially indigenous communities, and they are required to construct a generate legal order to facilitate coexistence between them. Inter-legality, thus, becomes a precondition of objective social inclusion, promoting patterns of citizenship able to integrate diverse factual populations. Indeed, the basic construction of citizenship becomes a central function of judicial bodies.

The assumption that courts need to play a role in ordering plural legal communities as a means of effecting societal integration was pioneered, to a large degree, in Colombia, where the higher courts established a model of inter-cultural and inter-legal balancing to define and address the legal position of indigenous groups. Under this principle, it was accepted that, under most circumstances, indigenous groups should be allowed to assume a certain degree of legal autonomy in their own territories, and they were recognized as holders of a distinctive legal personality, with distinctive, although circumscribed, rights and entitlements. The Constitutional Court, notably, declared *legal pluralism* a basic fact of Colombian society, acknowledging that the national legal order as a whole contains multiple legal domains, as a result of which certain group-specific rights exist alongside each other. In particular, the Court declared that 'the cultural survival of indigenous people' is a constitutional value of great importance, which requires that indigenous communities should be granted a 'high degree of autonomy'. Consequently, it stated that the 'maximization'

---

[68] See opinions in *R Osborn* v. *Parole Board* [2013] UKSC 61. Here, common law principles and ECHR principles were fused. It was stated (Reed SCJ) that 'protection of human rights is not a distinct area of the law, based on the case law of the European Court of Human Rights, but permeates our legal system'. Moreover, it was stated that the ECHR does not 'supersede the protection of human rights under the common-law or statute, or create a discrete body of law based upon the judgments of the European court'. In other words, it was implied that UK courts have a distinct collaborative function in creating European human rights law, to which common law reasoning also contributes. See related discussions in *Kennedy* v. *Charity Commission* – [2014] 2 All ER 847.

of their autonomy and 'the minimization of restrictions' on this autonomy should be taken as guiding norms in cases concerning indigenous justice.[69]

In establishing these principles, however, the Colombian Constitutional Court argued that the pluralistic quality of the national legal system was necessarily subject to some constraints. In particular, it ruled that the exercise of pluralistic rights by indigenous communities had to be limited by the fact that in some circumstances courts might be required to protect a higher constitutional principle, normally related to basic (international) human rights, to which the pluralistic demands of inner-societal legal orders are necessarily subordinate. As a result, the Court concluded that restrictions on legal pluralism could be legitimated, on proportionality grounds, in cases where judges were called upon to 'safeguard' norms of the highest constitutional prominence.[70] Following this principle, indigenous liberties and powers of autonomy required limitation in cases in which they entered conflict with a small 'hard nucleus' of essential human rights with obvious higher-order standing: that is, in particular, the right to life, the right not to be tortured, right to due process and minimal rights of subsistence.[71] Accordingly, judges addressing cases in which claims to indigenous legal autonomy posed a risk to the standing of other rights were required to apply standards of inter-legal proportionality – of 'rational evaluation' – to assess which rights and which elements of legal order should, in a given case, 'enjoy greater weight'.[72] Ultimately, this approach culminated in the principle that the 'imperative legal norms' of Colombian public law should be accorded 'primacy over the usages and customs of indigenous communities when they project a constitutional value that is superior to the principle of ethnic and cultural diversity'.[73] Overall, the legal personality of indigenous populations was constructed through the balancing of the demands for indigenous autonomy, which were clearly recognized as *rights*, against the most high-ranking essential norms, declared in national public law and international human rights law.

The use of the concept of inter-legality in Colombia meant that the cultural rights of indigenous communities could be extended, and it created legal grounds to support a condition of multiple inner-societal citizenships. But it also meant that the rights claimed by different groups of

[69] T-349/96.
[70] Ibid.
[71] T-903/09.
[72] See T-254/94; SU-510/98.
[73] T-009/07.

citizens could be subject to prior constraint and inner-legal control, and that the attribution of such rights could be managed within the legal system itself. Indeed, this concept expressed the overlying principle that the people has one defining higher will, which, in some circumstances, must prevail over pluralistic or factional interests. The balancing function of the Court meant that the Court was given responsibility for establishing a collective legal form for the people, and for deciding which norms should express the sovereign will of the people in its entirety, above its factually pluralistic, fragmented form. Notably, internationally protected rights played a core role in this process, and the highest will of the people was usually constructed through reference to the citizen as a rights-obligated agent under international law. The people, thus, appeared, in the most essential form, through inner-legal acts, and their legal-political reality was pre-defined by norms within the global legal system.

The superior courts in Bolivia, a society marked by much greater ethnic complexity than Colombia, have gone still further in developing a pluralistic method of inter-legal or inter-cultural constitutional practice, to promote multiple citizenship and to secure conditions of national legal inclusion. In this respect, an important distinction has to be made between patterns of constitutional pluralism in Bolivia and Colombia. The Constitutional Court in Bogotá has much greater structure-building importance in Colombia than the (generally much weaker) Bolivian Constitutional Court in Sucre,[74] and the Colombian Court has used its influence to impose a stable, vertical and relatively hierarchical system of norms on society.[75] In Bolivia, the political executive is currently more authoritarian, and courts are less likely to act against governmental directives. In Bolivia, moreover, pluralistic movements in society, especially those tied to the politics of indigeneity, have greater *transversal* force than in Colombia, and they can create normative orders that are more strictly separated from the central legal system.[76] Notably, Art 9(1) of the Bolivian constitution states that the constitution is designed to create a 'just and harmonious society', based on decolonization, providing 'full social justice' and consolidating 'plurinational identities'. In fact, the legal system as a whole is designed on a model that notionally places indigenous justice on a level of parity with ordinary justice. Unlike Colombia, where the Constitutional Court has acted to reinforce public institutions at all

---

[74] See below at pp. 363–6.
[75] See below at pp. 446–8.
[76] See below at pp. 440–2.

societal levels,[77] social mobilization around collective rights in Bolivia has led to a transformation, and even to the partial replacement, of conventional public-legal bodies. For example, some local governments and autonomous indigenous regions have begun to experiment with new patterns of democratic representation, and they have acquired far-reaching freedoms in recasting the form of democracy at a local level (Bazoberry Chali 2008: 153).[78]

As in Colombia, nonetheless, the Bolivian Constitutional Court has developed an approach that acknowledges the pluralism of domestic legal orders as a 'founding element of the state'. The Court both sanctions, and actively attempts to preserve, the coexistence of multiple legal orders, multiple parallel citizenships and multiple systems of justice within the national polity. In fact, the Constitutional Court has established a distinct principle for maintaining harmony between the multiple legal orders contained in society. It has argued that the term, *vivir bien* (living well), supposedly based on the culture of the Aymara people, and designating recognition of harmony in diversity, forms a matrix for incorporating divergent normative expectations in one overarching legal system.[79] On this principle, attempts in the Constitutional Court to balance the claims to rights arising in different legal orders are intended to guarantee conditions of good life for as many groups within society as possible.[80] In adopting this approach, however, the Court has assumed a balancing function in relation to different legal orders in society, and, as in Colombia, it promotes a jurisprudence that is intended to transmit higher-order integrative norms across society. Notably, the Court has stated that acts of balancing linked to recognition of 'legal pluralism' and 'inter-legality' serve to uphold the 'jurisdictional unity' of society, and they are to be seen as 'structuring elements' of the political order.[81]

In promoting inter-legality, the Bolivian courts clearly intend to protect and to give expression to the factual pluralism of interests within Bolivian society. However, in the doctrine of inter-legality, courts also acquire supreme authority over the pluralistic expressions of the people, and the pluralistic model of judicial control does not imply that all modes of legality

---

[77] See below at p. 367.
[78] See below at p. 441.
[79] This concept is officially based on socio-anthropological analysis of the moral values of the Aymara people. See for discussion Yampara Huarachi (2011: 13).
[80] Bolivian Constitutional Court 1023/2013.
[81] Bolivian Constitutional Court 1422/2012.

have equally valid status, in all circumstances.[82] On the contrary, courts assume a pivotal role within the multi-structural legal order of society, and they have responsibility for the 'weighing up' (*ponderación*) of the relative validity of the rights and claims inscribed in different legal domains.[83] Significantly, the Constitutional Court has interpreted the concept of *vivir bien* as a norm that enjoins different communities not to deviate too far from generalized constitutional principles, and not to challenge in disproportionate manner the 'axiomatic guidelines' of the Constitution.[84] Such guidelines are also strongly linked to international law.[85] This implies that the principle of inter-legality is employed to ensure that indigenous legal customs and expectations should remain circumscribed by, and, in cases of conflict, *subordinate to*, higher constitutional norms, including internationally defined rights. *Vivir bien*, accordingly, is closely assimilated to a logic of proportionality. In these respects, Bolivian public law follows Colombian law in recognizing that the principle of inter-legality is to be guided, ultimately, by the recognition of normative hierarchy, in which certain basic human rights have primacy. As in Colombia, the judiciary has the duty to decipher the higher sovereign will beneath the plural legal orders of society, and this will is widely constructed through the use of international human rights law.

In Colombia and Bolivia, the commitment to legal pluralism is intended to bring the factual form of the (highly pluralistic) national people into close proximity to the political system, and so to guarantee a high degree of sensitivity between the legal/political order and different material groups in society. This concept is understood as the foundation for a multi-centric, multi-normative democracy, based on multi-centric citizenship, adapted to the post-colonial legal landscape. In this process, however, the essential form of the people is constructed through judicial interpretation, partly through reference to international human rights norms. In their functions at the centre of a complex order of inter-legality, courts clearly stand in for, and in fact give final embodiment to, the people as a national collective actor, or as a legally meaningful aggregate of citizens. The people only

---

[82] In some cases, the Bolivian Constitutional Court has used international law to overrule local justice. See discussion below at p. 441. For comment on these points see Attard Bellido (2014: 41–2).

[83] This expressed paradigmatically in Bolivian Constitutional Court 1422/2012.

[84] Bolivian Constitutional Court 1422/2012.

[85] Art 410, II of the Constitution establishes a doctrine of the block of constitutionality for Bolivia, which means that immediate domestic effect is accorded to international human rights treaties.

become visible above their factual pluralism through the interpretive acts of courts, which establish the most essential components of the will of the people on the basis of human rights norms. In fact, although claiming to give articulation to the pluralistic will of the people, courts actually envision this will through the principle of proportionality, so that this will, in the final analysis, is defined by uniform external norms. The essential core of the popular will is extracted from acts of judicial balancing, and, as such, it assumes a reality above the particular normativities in society. In this respect, above all, the processes of integration that underlie democracy are conducted within the law.

3.2.6   Open Constitutional Jurisprudence

Alongside such specific functions, institutions within the legal system form the primary norm-giving subject of democracy in other, more general, ways. In many cases, the basic legal-political order of democracy is now often defined not by political decisions, but by constructive use of the law by advocates and judges, often piecing together a patchwork of national, international and comparative legal sources. Of course, use of comparative and international legal sources to resolve questions of national public law, or even to articulate primary constitutional norms, is not new. Even in relatively established democracies, key constitutional problems have been addressed through citation of international norms.[86] In some societies, however, constructive judicial citation from international sources has reached a very high level, and it now, at times, fills the gaps in, or even supplants, domestic law. For different reasons, in fact, such citation even replaces or supplements popular sovereign acts in creating, de facto, new constitutional norms. Often, the founding norms of democratic government are established through the emergence of a model of open statehood, or open constitutionalization, in which courts establish constitutional jurisprudence that integrally connects national and international law. In some cases, the basic political form of the people is constructed as an inner-legal hybrid, fusing national and international legal elements.

The importance of open constitutional jurisprudence is observable, in particular, in the legal systems of relatively new democratic states, where national constitutional law is only partly consolidated. In such settings, decisions in controversial matters are often reached on amalgamated

---

[86] See the case in the American Supreme Court, Lawrence v. Texas, 539 U.S. 558 (2003).

grounds, constructed from national and international law. In fact, in such settings, courts often resolve cases marked by particularly intense constitutional contest by reading domestic law together with international law, and they seek to generate legitimacy for law in disputed areas by borrowing authoritative principles from international law, or from other jurisdictions. Such jurisprudence is often used where the national will is uncertain, or consensus cannot easily be established, and it insulates the legal/political system against the need to identify or to incorporate the real will of citizens. Through these processes, the construction of basic legal norms results from an interaction between legal orders, and cross-penetration between norms stored at different points in the global legal system forms a primary law-creating agency.

Some of most extreme examples of such jurisprudence can be found in the wake of democratic transitions in Eastern Europe. In Hungary, for example, a new constitution was not written following the systemic upheavals of 1989. Instead, senior jurists adopted a doctrine of the *invisible constitution*, which they used to flesh out amendments to the existing constitution by claiming that elements of national law had to be aligned to international law. Indeed, the Constitutional Court used Strasbourg jurisprudence to shape domestic law before Hungary had acceded to the ECHR (see Sajó 1995: 260). Similar patterns of jurisprudence were also used in Poland after 1989. In Poland, international law was used in courts as surrogate constitutional norms until the first democratic Constitution was written in 1992.

Particularly illuminating examples of open constitutional construction, however, can be found in post-transitional public law cases in Africa, especially in cases that address issues with high public sensitivity.

In post-apartheid South Africa, the Constitutional Court welded aspects of domestic law and aspects of national law to address deep-lying constitutional problems, and to create nationally binding constitutional norms. In fact, the Court developed the doctrine that, in highly controversial cases, the national will of the people must be made visible through constructive integration of domestic and international law. For example, in one of the most famous South African cases, S v. *Makwanyane and Another* (1995),[87] which was heard under the interim transitional constitution of 1993, the new Constitutional Court ruled against the constitutionality of the death penalty. In this ruling, the judges observed that it was their duty to rule in

---

[87]   S v. *Makwanyane and Another* (CCT3/94) [1995] ZACC 3; 1995 (6) BCLR 665; 1995 (3) SA 391; [1996] 2 CHRLD 164; 1995 (2) SACR 1 (6 June 1995).

deeply contested matters by establishing legal norms giving expression to the will of the entire South African people: 'to articulate the fundamental sense of justice and right shared by the whole nation as expressed in the text of the Constitution.'[88] Distinctively, they claimed that, in establishing principles of national jurisprudence, they were required to show regard for the multiple legal orders inherent in domestic society, and to elaborate 'indigenous value systems' as a basis for the national legal order.[89] In particular, the Court argued that it was obliged to develop the indigenous value of *ubuntu*, defined as an attachment to human dignity,[90] as a legal foundation for the national community. In the transitional setting, therefore, the Constitutional Court observed itself as obliged both to express the collective will of the people and to show due recognition for the indigenous law of different peoples in South African society, and so to galvanize a characteristically heterogeneous yet unified normative will to support democratic constitutional law. Implicitly, the Court saw itself as responsible for creating a trans-sectoral ethic of national citizenship to support the law, and for projecting a unified constitutional subject to support the new democracy.

In pursuing this nation-forming objective, however, the Court argued that the values inherent in domestic law should be elaborated and reinforced through constructive assimilation of international law.[91] Accordingly, it implied that the values inscribed in the given legal patchwork of indigenous South African law did not of themselves provide a sustainable collective will, and they needed to be systematically interpreted in light of international human rights law. The Court declared that 'public international law and foreign case law' should be cited as a means fully to articulate a meaningfully national system of legal norms.[92] The constitutional subject of national democracy, thus, could only be created within the law; in fact, the formation of this subject specifically presupposed its abstraction against the factual subjects in society. It was only on the basis of this will that the death penalty, which probably enjoyed majority support, could be declared illegal.

In post-transitional Kenya, further, the superior courts have promoted the constructive hybridization of national and international legal sources in cases touching upon sensitive questions in society, especially questions

[88] Ibid para 362.
[89] Ibid para 304.
[90] Ibid para 225.
[91] Ibid para 373.
[92] Ibid.

relating to inter-population conflicts. In this regard, they have attempted to craft norms for all citizens, in all ethnic memberships, overarching the conflictual fissures between different social groups. This is visible, for example, in cases concerning land law and evictions, matters which had historically provoked deep social and constitutional controversy,[93] and which had been exacerbated through internal population displacements during the long process of democratic transition, starting in the early 1990s.

In one important High Court case, the Petitioners for the affected parties used the UDHR and the ICCPR to give weight to rights of protection from forcible eviction.[94] Moreover, the trial judge relied on international and comparative legal sources, especially the UDHR and relevant South African case law, to establish a right to housing.[95] In so doing, the Court rejected, as not being 'good law', previous rulings that had placed international law below domestic law in court proceedings,[96] stating that it was 'proper and good practice to seek guidance from international law where our laws are silent or inadequate' on an issue of great societal importance.[97] In addition, the court referred extensively to rulings of the African Commission to create a legal framework for addressing evictions.[98] Moreover, standing for the applicants was asserted on the basis of Indian case law, *Shetty* v. *International Airport Authority*. Through this fusion of legal sources, the court was able, ultimately, to overturn established dualistic principles concerning 'the rule of paramountcy' of the written Constitution in Kenya, and it was able constructively to elaborate new constitutional principles on a transnational basis. As a result, the court was able to establish transnational principles to 'direct the Government towards an appropriate legal framework for eviction based on internationally acceptable guidelines'.[99] In a later eviction case, the High Court presumed 'relevance and

---

[93] For background see Harbeson (2012); Manji (2014).
[94] *Satrose Ayuma & 11 others* v. *Registered Trustees of the Kenya Railways Staff Retirement Benefits Scheme & 3 others* Petition 65 of 2010, at para 25.
[95] Ibid at para 66.
[96] Ibid para 79.
[97] Ibid.
[98] See for example relevant judgements in the African Commission in *Free Legal Assistance Group and ors* v. *Zaire*, Communication 25/89; *Centre for Housing Rights and Evictions (COHRE)* v. *Sudan*, Communication 296/2005; *Centre for Minority Rights and Minority Rights Group International on Behalf of Endorois Welfare Council* v. *Kenya*, Communication 276/2003.
[99] *Satrose Ayuma & 11 others* v. *Registered Trustees of the Kenya Railways Staff Retirement Benefits Scheme & 3 others* at para 109.

applicability of the general rules of international law and treaties or conventions ratified by Kenya'.[100] Additionally, the court placed restrictions on government evictions by quoting the *UN Basic Principles and Guidelines on Development-based Evictions and Displacement* (2007) and other international guidelines,[101] thus establishing international soft law norms as applicable principles in domestic law. In one case in the High Court, the court, basing its authority on UN Guidelines on evictions,[102] instructed the government to assist victims by introducing legislation to give effect to social and economic rights, and it demanded more robust protection for such rights than for formal property.[103]

In Kenyan law, therefore, judicial hybridization of legal sources has developed into a process of deep constitutional construction, contestation, and effective political will formation. Indeed, some of the most intensely unsettling historical disputes in Kenyan society, especially those concerning land, have been translated into interactions between different legal domains and legal institutions. Notably, such hybridization is not uncontroversial. One leading ruling of the High Court was ultimately overturned by the Court of Appeal, where it was argued that the courts were not entitled to re-engineer property relations, or to usurp functions of the political branch.[104] However, the contested nature of such open jurisprudence indicates that it acts as a conflictual site for the construction of citizenship.

A similar, yet more enduring process of primary norm production through open constitutional jurisprudence is visible in some societies in Latin America, most especially Colombia, where open jurisprudence has clearly been used to define the basic subject of national democracy. From the early 1990s onwards, the Colombian Constitutional Court committed itself to a strong doctrine of open jurisprudence, with far-reaching implications for the basic structure of the state. First, the Court declared that it had authority to create constitutional law by integrating international norms into domestic constitutional law: as mentioned, it assumed the power to construct a *block of constitutionality*, adding supplementary

---

[100] *Kepha Omondi Onjuro & others* v. *Attorney General & 5 others* [2015] eKLR at para 67.

[101] Ibid para 144.

[102] *Mitu-Bell Welfare Society* v. *Attorney General & 2 others* [2013] eKLR at para 63.

[103] Unfortunately the verdict was undermined by legal flaws, notably that the Court devolved authority to non-judicial bodies to supervise adequacy of implementation. *Mitu-Bell Welfare Society* v. *Attorney General & 2 others* [2013] eKLR at para 79.

[104] *Kenya Airports Authority* v. *Mitu-Bell Welfare Society & 2 others* [2016] eKLR at para 112.

norms and rights to the existing system of public law. In this respect, the Court ruled that international treaties with *jus cogens* standing had to be directly incorporated in domestic law. Second, the Court argued that the state had an obligation 'to adapt norms with inferior standing in the domestic legal order to the content of international humanitarian law',[105] so that high-ranking international norms were to be used as leading values in constitutional interpretation. This approach was underpinned by the axiom that an international norm should become part of domestic law if it offered greater protection for human rights than any conflicting domestic norm.[106] Eventually, the Court extended such approaches to establish a series of rights not immediately guaranteed by the constitution, including rights to education,[107] and rights of cultural integrity and ethnic diversity.[108] The Court even declared that the block of constitutionality is itself *open*, and that the higher-order norms of national society can be revised retroactively by judicial institutions, if relevant international law changes.[109] Notable in this respect is the fact that the Court has declared itself responsible for defining the persons to whom international *jus cogens* is applicable; it insisted, in particular, that all persons in society, occupying different positions in the ongoing regional civil war, are subject directly to international norms with *jus cogens* rank.[110] Further, the Court decided that international soft-law norms regarding treatment of forcibly displaced persons should be domestically integrated as *jus cogens*.[111] It also stated that international norms were to be used to determine rights to truth, justice and reparation; it thus constructed a doctrine of international *jus cogens* to regulate transitional justice provisions resulting from the civil war.[112] On this basis, the Court effectively produced its own definition of *jus cogens*, and it even incorporated principles into the normative ambit of the national constitution whose authority in the hierarchy of international law was unclear.

In these respects, the Colombian Constitutional Court dictated the underlying normative grammar for Colombian society, and it promoted a creative model of open jurisprudence to assume primary

---

[105] C-225/95.
[106] T-1319/01.
[107] T-306/11.
[108] T-907/11.
[109] C-500/14.
[110] C-225/95.
[111] C-753/13.
[112] C-250/12.

constitution-making functions for society, in a context of deep societal division and intense conflict. In Colombia, in fact, such inner-legal supplanting of primary political functions has assumed quite extreme dimensions. In the above examples, the Constitutional Court devised a method of higher norm formation in which it, of itself, acquired clear sovereign responsibility, freely deciding the content of constitutionally binding norms for all society, and freely configuring the sovereign political form of the people. In fact, the Court openly asserted that it possessed greater higher-order norm-setting authority than the government. It decided that the essential sovereignty of the state had to be adapted to the reality of a global constitution, articulated through higher-ranking international norms, and that old-fashioned static ideas of national sovereignty had become unsustainable.[113] Later, the Court claimed that the sovereign power of government was restricted both externally by international norms and internally by 'the rights of persons'. This conception of sovereignty, it argued, was perfectly consonant with the idea of sovereignty expressed by the national constitution, promoting respect for popular self-determination and inalienable rights.[114] The assimilation of international law played a central role in this process of political construction. In consequence, open jurisprudence quite literally *stood in for* sovereign political authority.

3.2.7   Legal Exports and Symbolic Legitimacy

In some settings, patterns of open jurisprudence have obtained particular legal authority because certain courts have acquired symbolic regional pre-eminence, and their jurisprudence confers high prestige on processes of norm formation when utilized in other courts. Indeed, in some global regions, certain courts enjoy much higher regard than courts in neighbouring or regionally connected countries. As a result, their rulings are widely borrowed by other national courts to give strength to their decisions, especially in questions surrounded by great constitutional controversy. This gives rise to a very distinctively transnational system of norm production or jurisprudential transplantation, in which courts are able to secure constitutional, or at least high-ranking, authority for their judgements by basing them in the jurisprudence of other courts endowed with transnational influence. In such cases, the borrowing of norms replaces

[113]   C-574/92.
[114]   C-225/95.

national or regional political authorization as a foundation for legal formation, and inter-judicial exchanges acquire powerful constituent force.

This pattern of constitutional transplantation can occur for many
reasons.

Of course, such transplantation sometimes simply occurs for linguistic
reasons, because rulings are published and made available in languages
that can be accessed in courts developing new lines of reasoning. For
example, the doctrine of the block of constitutionality, which has proved
so influential in Latin America, was initially borrowed from rulings of
the Constitutional Court in Madrid.[115] At a more structural level, however, such transplantation typically occurs when, for embedded societal
reasons, there are deep overlaps between different national legal systems.
Historically, such transplantation was common in the relation between
colonial states and former colonial powers. Obviously, in many former
colonial states, the law of former colonial rulers initially possessed high status, and it still retains influence. Increasingly, however, this post-colonial
relationship can have a converse effect, and many post-colonial states now
widely borrow normative principles from other, non-metropolitan legal
systems in order to build up a store of jurisprudence that is severed from
the case law of the original metropolitan legal order.[116] More commonly,
legal transplantation across jurisdictions occurs when one legal system is
partly designed on the template of the other. For this reason, German case
law is widely used in Eastern Europe, Russia and Central Asia.[117] Indeed,
recent legal and procedural reforms in Russia are widely based on the

---

[115] See early use of this term in the Spanish Constitutional Court (10/1982, 23 March 1982).

[116] Use of Indian law in Anglophone Africa is striking in this regard. Noteworthy is reliance
on Indian law in the Kenyan High Court to enhance social rights guarantees and to impose
human-rights duties on non-public bodies. See *Satrose Ayuma & 11 others* v. *Registered
Trustees of the Kenya Railways Staff Retirement Benefits Scheme & 3 others*. In this case,
South African jurisprudence was also used to construct human dignity as a principle that
informs adjudication. Through these links, we can see the emergence of an informal jus
commune in formerly common-law states. See the excellent discussion of this phenomenon in O'Loughlin (2018).

[117] The practice of the German Constitutional Court was referred to in one of the landmark
RCC rulings, the Ruling on Merits No. 21-P of 14 July 2015 on the supremacy of the
Russian Constitution over conflicting judgements of international tribunals. Also, RCC
Justices Gadjiyev, Yaroslavtsev, and Bondar often refer to German legislation and case law
in their dissenting opinions. For example, see the RCC Ruling on Merit No. 11-P of 14 May
2012 on seizure of a debtor's housing; RCC Ruling on Merits No. 26-P of 2 December 2013
on fair taxation of private vehicles; RCC Ruling on Merits No. 10-P of 28 March 2017 on
adequate justification of draft legislation by its initiator; RCC Ruling on Merits No. 12-P of
19 April 2016 on prisoners' voting.

appropriation of norms from German public law.[118] Analogously, rulings of Indian and South African courts are widely internalized by courts in states with constitutions that are declaredly programmatic in their enforcement of social rights.[119] In such cases, family resemblance between legal systems, based on similar constitutional objectives, underpins the transplanting of authoritative rulings.

In addition, such constitutional transplantation occurs because some courts have already extensively addressed sensitive problems with which other states in the same region are confronted. In such examples, courts export and borrow jurisprudential norms that are applied to specific questions, when one court has developed an important body of case law in questions of rising general significance. One obvious example of this is the position of the Colombian Constitutional Court in Latin America. Notably, rulings of this court form influential authorities in states whose judiciaries engage with legal questions pertaining to indigenous communities and their rights of access to resources.[120] For similar reasons, South African rulings on rights to medicine and housing also permeate other jurisdictions in Africa, which are required to examine cases on similar questions, and authoritative decisions in South Africa are replicated in other courts.[121] Notably, German rulings on rights of personality, extended to incorporate rights to protection of, and access to, personal information and genetic data, have been transplanted widely from one legal system to another.[122] In some such acts of borrowing, original German rulings have not even been cited, but lines of reasoning first developed in Germany provide an implied basis for the solidification of rights in other states.[123]

---

[118] The German Administrative Procedural Code and other relevant laws were translated into Russian. They were used by the drafters of the Russian Administrative Litigation Code adopted by the Duma on 8 March 2015. On the recent use of German law in Russia see Starilov (2005: 36); Lapa (2010).

[119] See p. 241 above.

[120] See use of Colombian case law in the leading ruling of the Bolivian Constitutional Court on indigenous rights, 300/2012.

[121] See use of South African case law on the right to shelter in the Kenyan High Court, *Kepha Omondi Onjuro & others* v. *Attorney General & 5 others* [2015] eKLR.

[122] For example, German rulings regarding the right of information regarding family background have been extended in the Chilean Constitutional Court, creating a right to identity, so adding a new right to the Chilean Constitution. See Rol N° 834-2007-INA (13 May 2008).

[123] See the case concerning protection of genetic resources of indigenous peoples in Brazil: TRF-1. AC 4037 RO 2002.41.00.004037-0. Desembargadora Federal Selene Maria de Almeida. Julgamento 17/10/2007. QUINTA TURMA. Publicação: 09/11/2007 DJ p. 137.

This constitutional transplantation also occurs, importantly, because some courts are situated in states whose compliance with international law is high, or which have constructively grafted international norms onto domestic case law, and whose jurisprudence acquires prestige on that basis. This can be seen in Indian rulings on social and economic rights, which are often constructed through use of international law, and which have high impact in other countries, especially in Africa.[124] At a general level, this is again exemplified by the Colombian Constitutional Court whose wide influence in Latin America is partly attributable to its effective internalization of international law. In recent years, notably, the Chilean Constitutional Court has cited from the Colombian Constitutional Court to construe protective rights for children.[125] It has also used Colombian rulings, in decisive fashion, to establish rights to personal identity.[126] Most importantly, the doctrine of the unconstitutional state of affairs, which has been used by the Colombian Constitutional Court to implement legislative remedies for displaced persons, has migrated into Peruvian and Brazilian constitutional jurisprudence. In Brazil, albeit as yet only injunctively, this concept has been employed to claim remedies for deep-lying structural problems in Brazilian society, notably relating to prison conditions and human rights violations amongst prison populations.[127] In each regard, rulings of the Colombian Court have obtained an authority close to that assumed by higher-ranking international law, and they are accorded persuasive force in other courts. Tellingly, the doctrine that supports the authority of international law in Colombia, the block of constitutionality, has been incorporated by other courts in Latin America, where the Colombian formulation of this doctrine has often acquired a status close to that of precedent.[128]

Owing to these processes of transplantation, it is not only international law that assumes primary norm-setting functions across national boundaries. In some respects, quite distinctive transnational legal communities are being formed, connecting different national states, without any immediate foundation in international law. In such instances, some national courts act as authoritative norm providers, which are able to construct firm precedents or even to generate new rights within other national

---

[124] See note 117 above.
[125] Rol N° 1683-10 de, 4 January 2011.
[126] See discussion in Nogueira Alcalá (2013).
[127] Brazilian Supreme Court, Arguição de Descumprimento de Preceito Fundamental (ADPF) 347. At the time of writing, this case has not yet been judged.
[128] See use of his doctrine in the Bolivian Constitutional Court in 0110/2010-R.

judicial systems. To some degree, therefore, the law of some national courts is in the process of evolving as a *de facto* system of international law, and it assumes a degree of transnational, semi-precedential authority otherwise enjoyed only by international law. This process is usually driven by the fact that the courts with such influence have established high or distinctive protection for human rights in their legal systems, which facilitates and promotes the borrowing of their rulings across societal divisions. In each respect, the law itself obtains powerful, quasi-sovereign functions, and law-giving processes occur without any authorization by external political acts.

3.2.8   Living Constitutionalism/ Transformative Constitutionalism

The emergence of relatively autonomous patterns of legal norm construction is also visible in the proliferation of the doctrine of *living constitutionalism*. This doctrine implies that judges have a distinct responsibility for expanding the text of national constitutions, and they do this by concretely identifying and articulating the will of the people, at a given historical moment. This doctrine further enhances the powers of judicial bodies in creating new laws and in establishing the form of national democracy, often in conjunction with an increase in the force of international law.

The theory of living constitutionalism has acquired distinctive prominence, on one hand, in controversies about constitutional interpretation in the USA. In this context, this doctrine is related to the rivalry between judges and legal theorists adopting an originalist theory of the constitution and judges and legal theorists claiming that the letter of the constitution needs to be adapted to prevalent social conditions. In the USA, originalism has recently emerged as an influential doctrine.[129] More traditionally, leading judges strongly endorsed the principle that living judicial interpretation and reconstruction of the constitution is a core aspect of democracy,

---

[129] It is persuasively argued that originalism is an ideologically generated doctrine, caused by a backlash against the realist impulse of the Supreme Court in the 1950s and 1960s (J. O'Neill 2005: 30).

and that the Constitution must be adapted to changing conditions.[130] Over a long period, in fact, judicial constructions of the law in the USA have produced a number of new rights, which have been effectively added to the constitution. Since 1945, these rights have included both negative or protective rights against segregation and discrimination, widened rights of human dignity, rights to privacy, and more positive rights regarding reproductive decisions and equality rights for women (Strauss 2010: 12–13). In addition, the doctrine of living constitutionalism has a long history in Canadian constitutional law, in which judges originally used constructive constitutional interpretation to define a distinctive body of Canadian public law, separate from English law.[131] In this context, judges have systematically pursued enhancement of human rights law as a means to consolidate the democratic structure of the constitution.

Variants on the doctrine of living constitutionalism have been promoted in many societies in recent years. This doctrine became very influential in the FRG in the 1950s, where constitutive interpretation of the *Grundgesetz* was promoted to reinforce a democratic political system that originally had limited societal support.[132] First, the catalogue of basic rights in the

---

[130]   See the most famous formulation of this idea, by Wendell Holmes:

> [W]hen we are dealing with words that also are a constituent act, like the Constitution of the United States, we must realize that they have called into life a being the development of which could not have been foreseen completely by the most gifted of its begetters. It was enough for them to realize or to hope that they had created an organism; it has taken a century and has cost their successors much sweat and blood to prove that they created a nation. The case before us must be considered in the light of our whole experience, and not merely in that of what was said a hundred years ago

> *Missouri* v. *Holland*, 252 U.S. 416 (1920). An expanded variation on this doctrine is at the core of what is probably the most famous recent articulation of American constitutional philosophy: Ackerman (1991). In some respects the doctrine of the living constitution was already anticipated by John Marshall who argued that a 'provision is made in a Constitution intended to endure for ages to come, and consequently to be adapted to the various crises of human affairs': *McCulloch* v. *Maryland*, 17 U.S. 316 (1819).

[131]   See the classic account of this doctrine in *Henrietta Muir Edwards and others (Appeal No. 121 of 1928)* v. *The Attorney General of Canada (Canada)* [1929] UKPC 86 (18 October 1929). Note the observation that a constitution is 'drafted with an eye to the future' and must be 'capable of growth' in *Hunter* v. *Southam Inc* [1984] 2 S.C.R. 145. Likewise, note the view that '[n]arrow and technical interpretation' can 'stunt the growth of the law and hence the community it serves' in *Law Society of Upper Canada* v. *Skapinker* [1984] 1 S.C.R. 357. For comment see Waluchow (2001).

[132]   See below p. 317.

Grundgesetz was especially conceived as a set of directives for the broad elaboration and expansion of constitutional values. During the drafting of the *Grundgesetz*, Carlo Schmid declared in the Parliamentary Council that basic rights should be interpreted not as a supplement to the constitution, but as its leading and most fundamental principles (see Jestaedt 1999: 8). After the enforcement of the *Grundgesetz*, then, the Constitutional Court promoted a construction of basic rights that insisted that constitutional norms should permeate through all society, allowing the content of basic rights to radiate into all areas of law.[133] This expansive construction of constitutional rights, of course, was reflected in very different lines of interpretation, and the widening of rights was expressed in very different doctrinal outlooks. One of the most significant interpreters of the basic rights provisions in the *Grundgesetz* argued that basic rights should be seen as objective institutions, creating an injunction for both judicial figures and legislators continuously to bring them to realization (Häberle 1972: 165). In this argument, the society of the FRG in its entirety was observed as a community of constitutional interpreters (Häberle 1975). An alternative influential account of basic rights argued that the enforcement of basic rights actually freed different societal domains from the immediate control of the state, enabling parts of society covered by basic rights to develop a relatively separate, autonomous constitutional order, especially a *communication constitution*, a *labour constitution* and an *economic constitution* (Scholz 1971: 294, 1978: 219). Yet, across such interpretive variations, the early basic rights jurisprudence of the Constitutional Court clearly impacted transformatively on the constitution, allowing it to assume meanings and to concretize rights not fully envisaged in the text of the Constitution itself.

Significant examples of the doctrine of living constitutionalism can be found in India, where Article 32 and Article 226 of the Constitution authorize the judiciary to issue special directives to protect the rights contained in the constitution. The Supreme Court has interpreted Article 32 to augment its own authority, and it has assumed direct responsibility for the interpretive expansion of constitutional law (see Ray 2003: 147).[134] This began in the 1960s and 1970s with the elaboration of the concept of the *basic structure* by the courts, which authorized the judiciary to insist

---

[133] This technique, tellingly, has been seen as 'constitutional expansion' (Aulehner 2011: 48).

[134] One description of this explains that the authors of the 1950 Constitution in India did not anticipate that the judiciary would be frequently concerned with cases 'between citizens and government' and they foresaw an independent but limited role for the courts (Dhavan 1994: 313).

on the inviolability of a hard core of constitutional rights against parliamentary encroachment.[135] Later, the Supreme Court opted for a more programmatic commitment to living constitutionalism, assuming power to widen rights enunciated in the Constitution. In particular, the Court stated that it was under obligation 'to expand the reach and ambit' of any fundamental rights under scrutiny, and to avoid approaches that might attenuate the 'meaning and content' of fundamental rights. Accordingly the Court declared that it was required to ensure that constitutional provisions are interpreted and enacted, 'not in a narrow and constricted sense, but in a wide and liberal manner ... so that the constitutional provision does not get atrophied or fossilized but remains flexible enough to meet the newly emerging problems and challenges'.[136]

The Indian Supreme Court used this approach to flesh out a new range of substantive rights, such as, for example, the right to education,[137] and protective rights against discrimination.[138] In some public interest cases, in fact, Indian courts have put in place supervisory arrangements to ensure implementation of their rulings, to intensify judicial presence in policy-making, and even to ensure the impact of judicial interventions in legislation. In such cases, notably, the Supreme Court has broadened the classical reach of mandamus to establish control over some discretionary powers of the government.[139] For example, the Supreme Court has issued mandamus in cases where hospitals have failed to provide emergency medical care,[140] and in response to petitions for the education of the children of prostitutes.[141] The practice of living constitutionalism, thus, substantially extended the reach of bodies situated in the legal system, and, in some respects, it became a material part of the policy-making process.[142] In one notable public interest case, the Supreme Court even outlined draft judicial

---

[135] See the famous articulation of the basic structure doctrine in *His Holiness Kesavananda Bharati Sripadagalvaru and Ors. v. State of Kerala and Anr.* ((1973) 4 SCC 225).

[136] *Francis Coralie Mullin v. Administrator Union Territory of Delhi and others,* (1981) 1 SCC 608.

[137] *Mohini Jain v. State of Karnataka* (1992 AIR 1858).

[138] *Madhu Kishwar and others v. The State of Bihar and others* (AIR 1996 5 SCC 125).

[139] See *Vineet Narain v. Union of India,* AIR 1996 SC 3386 and *Bandhua Mukti Morcha v. Union of India & ors.* (1997) 10 scc 549.

[140] Paschim Banga Khet Mazdoor Samity & Ors v State of West Bengal & Anor. [1996 4 SCC 37].

[141] *Gaurav Jain v. Union of India & Ors.* (1997) (8) SCC 114. For this and the above information I am indebted to Sathe (2001: 80).

[142] For example, the Court has acquired legislative functions regarding environmental policy and food provision. See *T.N. Godavarman Thirumulkpad v. Union of India & Ors.* [(1997) 2 SCC 267]; *PUCL v. Union of India and Ors.* 2007 (12) SCC 135.

legislation, based on unincorporated international treaties, in order to remedy lack of effective legal provisions concerning sexual harassment.[143]

In some African countries, especially South Africa, judges have devised a yet more radically purposive approach to constitutional interpretation. As mentioned, in *S v. Makwanyane and Another* (1995), judges in the South African Constitutional Court argued that they have a duty to give effect to certain transnational values in their constitutional jurisprudence, and they applied such jurisprudence as a transformative ethic through society. In other cases, the Constitutional Court interpreted the Constitution, jointly with international law, to create distinctive sets of rights, including rights to housing, rights of access to medicine, and rights of privileged access to land.[144] Moreover, as in India, judges in South Africa have made wide use of supervisory orders, to ensure that judicial provisions are implemented.[145] Indian and South African contributions to the model of living constitutionalism have been widely appropriated in other parts of Southern Africa, where a purposive approach to constitutional law has acquired central importance in processes of constitutional consolidation. In Botswana, for example, the principle has been proposed that 'the primary duty of the judges is to make the Constitution grow and develop in order to meet the just demands and aspirations of an ever developing society which is part of the wider and larger human society governed by some acceptable concepts of human dignity'.[146]

In these examples from India and Africa, the basic idea of the living constitution, constructed through judicial interpretation, has been expanded to form a doctrine not only of living, but in fact of *transformative* constitutionalism. Indeed, in some societies, the primary tenets of living constitutionalism have established a quite distinct constitutional model, in which judges assume extensive powers of societal transformation. In this model, judges extract from basic norms set out in the constitution the authority to read new meanings into the constitution and to expand the societal obligations generated by the constitution, using a broad construction of constitutional law to shape social relations. In this, strong impetus is provided

---

[143] *Vishaka and others* v. *State of Rajasthan and others* (1997) 6 SCC 241.

[144] *Alexkor Ltd and another* v. *Richtersveld Community and Others* (CCT 19/03) [2003] ZACC 18.

[145] *Sibiya and Others* v. *Director of Public Prosecutions: Johannesburg High Court and Others* (CCT 45/04) [2005] ZACC 16.

[146] *Sesana and Others* v. *Attorney-General* (2006) AHRLR 183 (BwHC 2006).

by international law. In fact, it is now possible to identify a distinct family of transformative constitutions, in which judges have arrogated interventionist powers to control the political branches, to oversee acts of government, and to instil jurisprudentially configured human rights norms into the structure of society. Notably, transformative constitutions are usually reflected as highly political constitutional systems, designed to provide not only a normative order, but a solid organizing form for popular democracy.[147] Yet, in most such constitutions, the responsibility for implementing democracy is ultimately attributed to the judicial branch, and high-ranking judges promote constructive jurisprudence as a primary force in the realization of transformative democratic values.

In Kenya, which clearly belongs to this constitutional family, the promotion of transformative jurisprudence by the superior courts has assumed unusual dimensions. During the process of constitutional transition, first, the Kenyan courts adopted a living tree approach to constitutional interpretation.[148] Later, however, this approach was expanded to generate a constructive reading of the social rights contained in the 2010 Constitution. In particular, judges in the Kenyan Supreme Court have commonly argued that they are entitled to reach rulings by taking non-legal facts and non-legal phenomena into consideration, and by showing regard for the sociological context of cases brought to court.[149] As a result, judges have looked beyond settled positivist constructions of the law, and they have decided cases for reasons intended to promote the programmatic transformation of society as a whole. This transformational approach of the courts is partly based on the Constitution itself, notably in Art 20(2) and 20(3)(a) and (b), which implicitly authorize judges to expand existing human rights provisions. However, this approach is more firmly grounded in Section 3 of the Supreme Court Act (2011). This Section states that it is the responsibility of the court to 'develop rich jurisprudence that respects Kenya's history and traditions and facilitates its social, economic and political growth'.

This provision has provided the cornerstone for the development of transformative jurisprudence. Notably, in an important ruling, the former Chief Justice, Willy Mutunga, declared that 'this provision grants the Supreme Court a near-limitless, and substantially elastic interpretive

---

[147] See discussion below at p. 357.
[148] In Re Estate of Lerionka Ole Ntutu (Deceased) [2008] eKLR.
[149] *Communications Commission of Kenya & 5 others* v. *Royal Media Services Limited & 5 others* [2014] eKLR at para 357.

power', and it creates an 'interpretive space' in which the Court can shape the normative form of society.[150] In the same ruling, Mutunga also stated:

> Each matter that comes before the Court must be seized upon as an opportunity to provide high-yielding interpretive guidance on the Constitution; and this must be done in a manner that advances its purposes, gives effect to its intents, and illuminates its contents'. As a result 'constitution making does not end with its *promulgation;* it continues with its *interpretation.*[151]

In a different Kenyan case, the strategy of transformative constitutionalism was fleshed out further, and the Supreme Court posited an integral relation between the founding will of the constitution and the interpretive will of the judiciary, stating that: 'Transformative constitutions are new social contracts that are committed to fundamental transformations in societies ... The Judiciary becomes pivotal in midwifing transformative constitutionalism and the new rule of law'.[152] In this setting, overall, Kenyan judges have increasingly renounced classical political-question doctrines concerning the judicial branch. Instead, they have construed the judiciary as a co-legislator, or even, at times, as a co-constituent force, using interpretive acts to transfuse society with constitutional norms, and to shape societal relations on this basis.[153]

In the Kenyan context, it is notable that, at the time of writing, the promotion of transformative jurisprudence by the superior courts remains contested. In fact, political parties and governmental leaders have demonstrated only a qualified interest in implementing the democratic constitution. As a result, the judiciary has been placed in an at times isolated normative position, and judges have been obliged to exercise discretion in their consumption of public and governmental confidence. In fact, senior judicial appointments remain susceptible to political pressures, such that the recent body of progressive case law is susceptible to being overturned.[154] This problem is intensified by ethnic biases within leading political parties, which mean that political influence on judicial appointments often reflects a privileging of one ethnic group. In Mutunga's judicial work, however, the

---

[150] *Senate & another v. Attorney-General & 4 others* [2013] eKLR at para 157.

[151] Ibid at para 156.

[152] *Communications Commission of Kenya & 5 others v. Royal Media Services Limited & 5 others* [2014] eKLR at para 377.

[153] Notably, these policies have been accompanied by more day-to-day policies, intended to improve access to justice, to raise the quality of judicial services, and, above all, to reduce judicial corruption. This was initiated through the Judiciary Transformation Framework, led by Joel Ngugi.

[154] As an indication that this might be happening, see *Kenya Airports Authority v. Mitu-Bell Welfare Society & 2 others* [2016] eKLR.

strategy of transformative constitutional analysis was designed to establish the Supreme Court as an elevated bearer of the national will, able to detach the basic structure of national democracy from the factual, parcellated interests of society, and to galvanize it, in manifest form, for all citizens.[155] Underlying this approach was an endeavour to consolidate a fully national jurisprudence, in which Kenyan citizens, historically divided into ethnic sub-communities, could interpret their interests and direction in generalized form. This in turn underpinned a conception of the state as a discursively created organic national community, in which interpretation and enactment of the founding substance of the constitution, centred around judicial actions, binds together the people as a national whole.[156]

Importantly, Mutunga's nationalizing construction of the judicial role was underpinned by extensive use of international law, and in fact by the insistence that, under Art 2(5,6), Kenyan constitutional law had to be interpreted in monist fashion (Mutunga 2015a). In other words, the construction of a distinctively *national* jurisprudence, separated from private or ethnic interests, was seen to presuppose *international* law as its foundation. The essence of the national citizen, distinct from the particular interests of sub-national populations, was projected through inner-judicial acts, partly involving an internalization of international law.

The most extensive willingness of judges to engage in transformative application of the constitution is evident in some Latin American states. Most notably, some Supreme Courts and Constitutional Courts in Latin America have decided that they are authorized to implant new norms in domestic constitutional law, often giving heightened protection to principles declared in international human rights conventions. In some cases, this occurs in relatively predictable fashion, as courts simply place international treaties and conventions within the hierarchy of domestic norms, following clear constitutional directives. As mentioned, some Latin American courts, led by Colombia, have assumed responsibility for developing a doctrine of the block of constitutionality, in which they decided that some international treaties should be viewed as parts of the domestic constitution.[157] In Colombia, this doctrine is loosely authorized by Art 93

---

[155] In the Matter of the National Land Commission [2015] eKLR.

[156] In Re the Matter of the Interim Independent Electoral Commission [2011] eKLR at para 86.

[157] The theory underlying this concept states that the constitution is a block of higher-ranking norms that is subject, where appropriate, to expansion by the courts. It can include 'norms and principles which, without appearing formally in the articulated sense of the constitutional text, are utilized as parameters for the constitutional review of laws' (C225/95).

of the Constitution, which provides for the direct effect of international law. In parallel, however, the Colombian Constitutional Court has developed this doctrine in a direction not foreseen in the Constitution itself, and it has applied it as part of a broader strategy of transformative constitutional concretization, designed to craft solutions for the most pressing problems of domestic society by reinterpreting basic constitutional provisions.

Central to this transformative approach to the Constitution in Colombia is the principle, established by the Constitutional Court, that the list of rights formally set out in the 1991 Constitution is not exhaustive,[158] and that these rights can be purposively adapted to the changing demands of society. As a result, when faced with cases with human rights implications, Colombian judges are able to widen the substance of existing rights, and even to establish new rights, with constitutional authority. A live constituent power thus remains vested in the Constitutional Court. This process is guided by the fact that judges take the commitment to protecting the dignity of the human person as the defining, overriding value expressed by the Constitution, and they apply this as an interpretive norm that authorizes them to adapt existing rights to changing conditions or exigencies or to crystallize new rights (López Cadena 2015: 67, 81). Judges are thus required to pursue 'systematic' and 'axiological' interpretation of individual cases, to determine whether they potentially give rise to new rights.[159] In one key early case, notably, the Constitutional Court stated that the Constitution had initiated a 'new strategy for realizing the effectiveness of fundamental rights': this depended on the assumption that judges, not the public administration or the legislator, had primary responsibility for giving effect to them.[160] On this basis, the Court decided that judges were authorized to identify and establish new rights, as long as such rights could be viewed as 'inherent to humanity', and as necessarily connected with the basic values elaborated in the constitution.[161] This meant, in particular, that judges were able to interpret commitments to social and economic rights proclaimed in the constitution as key determinants in the concretization of rights. In fact, judges claimed that they were placed under a particular injunction to translate social rights into reality, and even to treat them as a precondition for the effectiveness of primary civil and political

---

[158] For background see López Medina (2004: 443).
[159] T-002/92.
[160] T-406/92.
[161] Ibid.

rights.[162] As discussed below, further, the Colombian Constitutional Court has developed an extensive monitoring system in cases addressing large-scale human rights abuses, and it has assumed material responsibility for the implementation of new constitutional rights. In each respect, the Colombian Constitutional Court has defined itself as a constituent organ of societal transformation, which welds together a robust body of human rights law to recast the basic normative structure of society. In each respect, the Court defines the essential form of the national citizen, and it constructs the rights to which citizens can lay claim, in conformity with which it then develops its jurisprudence.

Overall, the idea that constructive or transformative judicial interpretation can produce the basic legal architecture of democracy has become a dominant idea in many legal/political systems. Widely, in fact, the doctrine of living or – in intensified form – transformative constitutionalism is seen both as a proxy and as a supplement for the exercise of democratic sovereignty by the people.

Three points have particular importance in the growth of the doctrine of living constitutionalism.

First, in its classical form, the doctrine of living constitutionalism is typically associated with the attempt, articulated especially by judges and legal professionals, to make sure that a given national society does not become trapped in the past by its constitution. Accordingly, it is intended to guarantee that the idea of popular sovereignty originally articulated in the constitution can be re-expressed and re-enacted, within the broad constraints of the original constitutional text, in a form adjusted to contemporary societal conditions.[163] The living constitution is construed as an evolving expression of the primary sovereignty of the people, in which courts and judicial bodies act in conjunction with other political institutions to express moments of deep transformation in the popular will, and in the legal-political form of the citizen (Ackerman 2007: 1758, 1791). At the core of this doctrine is an endeavour to balance objective legal obligations with the changing expectations of the national population, and judges assume a coordinating position in deciding which momentary demands of the people should be allowed to impact on the factual structure of the constitution. In some quite extreme cases, in fact, judges have

---

[162] Ibid.

[163] One exponent of living constitutionalism in the USA declares himself 'dedicated to the elaboration of the original understanding of We the People at one of the greatest constitutional moments in American history' (Ackerman 2014: 329).

openly expressed the opinion that they are qualified, or even *obliged*, to read new constitutional norms into a given constitutional text, and spontaneously to align a constitutional order, parts of which they perceive as redundant, to existing societal circumstances.[164]

Through this doctrine, the essential constitutional idea of popular sovereignty is transformed into a practice of judicial interpretation. In many cases, the theory of the living constitution rests on the presumption that society as a whole is constantly in the process of expressing a changing constitutional will, which is articulated through everyday political procedures such as elections, legislation and even seismic shifts of opinion. The task of the courts, then, is to adapt the existing text of the constitution to the manifest will of society, and to translate the will of society into constitutional formal provisions. In some cases, in claiming authority to interpret the will of the people, judges clearly assume the entitlement to replace the constituent power as the originating source of legal norms.

Second, in many cases, the theory of the living constitution is closely linked to public interest litigation, or cause lawyering. Indeed, the practice of judicial constitutional transformation is often flanked by a willingness of judges to encourage litigation by groups representing interests to which they impute public significance, but in which their immediate interest is limited. Accordingly, this doctrine often goes hand in hand with a relaxation of laws on standing, through which the range of persons able to initiate litigation is broadened, and groups acquire personality if they can claim to express interests of general constitutional importance.[165] As a result, the doctrine of living constitutionalism reflects the presumption that judges are authorized not only to interpret the will of the people, but to open new channels of articulation between government and society, and even to define the emergent interests in society warranting constitutional recognition. Examples of this can be seen, most famously, in the USA, in which the transformation of constitutional law during the era of the Civil Rights Movement was shaped by the strategies of politicized advocacy groups.[166] In India, the transformative judicial elaboration of the constitution is difficult to separate from the growing liberalization of rules on standing and from the resultant recognition of new subjects in public interest cases. In Latin America, the consolidation of the block of constitutionality has been integrally determined by litigation initiated by strategic

---

[164] *Ghaidan v. Godin-Mendoza* [2004] UKHL 30 (21 June 2004) 24.
[165] See below at pp. 466–8.
[166] See below at pp. 303, 468–9.

litigators.[167] In each case, courts have claimed an entitlement to designate and integrate new constitutional subjects and new modes of citizenship, presuming to express the will of the nation more clearly than the text of the constitution itself. In so doing, and they have allocated *de facto* constituent power to new holders of constitutional agency, or to persons assuming distinctive citizenship roles.

Third, the growth of purposive reasoning encouraged by the theory of the living constitution is closely linked to the wider rise in the authority of international law. The exercise of purposive constitutional construction by judicial actors typically entails an adjustment of existing constitutional or administrative norms to reflect common standards of international human rights law. This is clearly observable in Canada, the homeland of living-tree constitutionalism, where constructive constitutional interpretation takes place within a normative framework partly determined by international law.[168] This is also visible in African polities, where the alignment of domestic law to international standards forms a powerful impetus for purposive judicial interpretation. In some African courts, purposive readings of the constitution clearly extract supplementary authority from norms declared in the international domain.[169] This is most evident in Latin America, especially Colombia, where, as discussed, the fusion of international law and domestic law is at the centre of transformative constitutionalism.

In each of these respects, courts apply the doctrine of living constitutionalism to claim authority to speak *as the will of the people*, in conditions

---

[167] See Colombian Constitutional Court T-967/09 (here, the court incorporated new rights in the block of constitutionality relating to displaced persons); C-753/13 (here, the court established certain rights of transitional justice not based on, but loosely extracted from, international treaties).

[168] After the passing of the Canadian Charter of Rights and Freedoms (1982), it was declared in the Supreme Court that the proper approach to the interpretation of the Charter of Rights and Freedoms is a purposive one: *R. v. Big M Drug Mart Ltd.*, [1985] 1 S.C.R. 295. To realize this, it was also argued that domestic and international human rights should be interpreted together: that international obligations should be a 'relevant and persuasive factor in Charter interpretation'. Notably, it was also argued that 'the Charter should generally be presumed to provide protection at least as great as that afforded by similar provisions in international human rights documents which Canada has ratified'. In other words, domestic human rights protection should be at a higher level than protection granted under international law. See Reference Re Public Service Employee Relations Act (Alta), [1987] 1 S.C.R. 313.

[169] See most famously *Government of the Republic of South Africa and Others* v. *Grootboom and Others* (CCT11/00) [2000] ZACC 19; 2001 (1) SA 46; 2000 (11) BCLR 1169 (4 October 2000).

where the existing legal order of popular sovereignty is contradictory, inadequate and unable to accommodate, or adapt to, societal pressure. In such cases, the courts construe the living constitution to create a unified popular will, typically underwriting their authority to construct the *national* will by referring to norms inscribed in *international* law. The growth of the doctrine of living or transformative constitutionalism reflects a process, quite emphatically, in which democratic agency is internalized within the legal system, which projects the basic form of the citizen to support legislation. Moreover, it reflects a process in which the law itself generates new laws, even of a founding/constitutional nature, and the interpretive interaction between laws established at different points of the global legal system is able to define society's basic political substance. In these respects again, the underlying form of the citizen is imprinted in national society by the legal system, and the sovereign citizen is constructed by courts on premises at least partly established in international law. In some cases considered here, in fact, the sovereign population only assumed legal form because it was aligned, by acts of constructive jurisprudence, to a global model of the citizen, based on international human rights.

Importantly in this respect, the doctrine of living constitutionalism has also been translated into a doctrine that is applied in international courts. For example, the ECtHR has defined the ECHR as 'a living instrument' which 'must be interpreted in the light of present-day conditions'.[170] Both in advisory Opinions and rulings, judges on the IACtHR have claimed authority to construct the ACHR as part of an 'international human rights corpus juris' or a 'corpus juris of international human rights law', reflecting the fact that the international community has the right to develop new concepts and new norms.[171] On this basis, the IACtHR has assumed the power to promote 'an evolutionary interpretation of international rules on the protection of human rights' and to generate expanded rights from already formulated international norms.[172] The Court thus perceives itself not merely as an actor in a regional human rights system, but as a participant in the creation of global human rights law. Moreover, like national courts, judges on the Court have asserted that the Court is authorized to determine which international norms have *jus cogens* rank, and to add

---

[170] *Tyrer* v. *The United Kingdom*-5856/2 25 April 1978.
[171] IACtHR, Juridical Condition and Rights of the Undocumented Migrants, Mexico, Advisory Opinion, Advisory Opinion OC-18/03; IACtHR, Case of the *Yakye Axa Indigenous Community* v. *Paraguay*. Judgment of 17 June 2005.
[172] IACtHR, Case of the *Yakye Axa Indigenous Community* v. *Paraguay*. Judgment of 17 June 2005.

new norms to the list of those with *jus cogens* force.[173] Even the international norms from which domestic constitutional jurisprudence extracts political authority are produced through judicial norm construction, as part of the relatively autonomous system of international law.

3.2.9 *The Right to Rights*

This transformation of national democracy and national citizenship is also visible in the fact that the power of courts widely leads to a reinforcement of rights relating expressly to judicial functions. Indeed, courts typically place particular emphasis on the protection of rights of access to courts, and they often define the right to judicial remedy as a right of distinctive importance, or as a parent of other rights. It was lamented by Hannah Arendt in the aftermath of World War II that rights were inalienably attached to national citizenship, and that persons could easily be deprived of the 'right to have rights': this could be effected through displacement, expulsion or other modes of coercive disfranchisement (Arendt 1951: 296). In fact, Arendt placed this observation at the centre of a critique of human rights. In contemporary society, however, the purely nationalized model of citizenship is increasingly eroded or at least supplemented by a more transnational construction of citizenship, which is generated within the law, and which stretches beyond nationally allocated rights. Of course, some persons are selectively excluded from rights holding, and, self-evidently, human rights do not form a universally binding grammar. Clearly, the access to rights is still determined by laws of national citizenship. Communities falling outside territorial limits have weakly protected access to rights, and migrants within national societies have relatively reduced rights. Moreover, in some states, communities of marginalized or displaced persons lack access to rights.[174] In extreme cases, persons are deprived of access to rights by torture or incarceration. Increasingly, however, at different levels of the global legal system the presumption has hardened that there is a relatively robust *right to judicial hearing*, implying that there is no situation, globally, in which people can legitimately be deprived of the right to have rights.

In international human rights instruments and conventions, first, the right of access to justice is subject to intensified legal protection. In international human rights courts, denial of effective access to courts has

---

[173] IACtHR, Case of *Yatama v. Nicaragua*. Judgment of 23 June 2005.
[174] See below at pp. 462–3.

frequently been taken as grounds to delegitimize sitting governments. Important examples of this are found in the case law of the IACtHR, where, owing to a long history of political manipulation of the judiciary in Latin America, the Court has strongly censured states restricting access to courts.[175] In one leading case, access to justice was described as 'an imperative of jus cogens'.[176] Important instances of this are also evident in rulings of the ECtHR. For example, many notable cases are found in rulings against Russia. In fact, almost half of all ECtHR cases against Russia are Article 6 cases, regarding violations of the right to a fair trial and access to justice. These include over 750 judgements, including important recent cases concerning access to justice by organizers of gay pride events,[177] arbitrary detention of opposition leaders[178] and inadequate provision of evidence in administrative proceedings against protesters.[179]

Partly because of the importance of these rulings in international courts, domestic courts have also constructed a broad body of case law that accentuates the right to judicial remedy as a primary right, often using international law to support this. Rights of access to justice have been hardened across the spectrum of democratic institutionalization. Jurisprudence concerning such rights has acquired greatest importance in relatively recent democracies, or in states with only partial democratic features. In fact, enforcement of access to justice is often pursued in such contexts as a strategy of democracy reinforcement, and increased popular use of law is seen as a means for heightening the effective accountability of governing bodies. This is exemplified in court rulings during processes of democratic stabilization in Latin America, Africa and Eastern Europe.[180]

---

[175] As basis see IACtHR, Juridical Condition and Rights of the Undocumented Migrants, Mexico, Advisory Opinion, Advisory Opinion OC-18/03; Judicial Guarantees in States of Emergency (Arts. 27.2, 25 and 8 American Convention on Human Rights), Advisory Opinion OC-9/87, 6 October 1987.

[176] IACtHR, Case of the *Pueblo Bello Massacre* v. *Colombia*. Judgment of 31 January 2006.

[177] *Lashmankin and Others* v. *Russia* (Applications nos. 57818/09 and 14 others. Judgment of 17 February 2017).

[178] *Navalnyy* v. *Russia* (Applications nos. 29580/12 and 4 others, Judgment of 2 February 2017); *Nemtsov* v. *Russia* (Application no. 1774/11, Judgment of 31 July 2014).

[179] See, for example, *Kasparov and Others* v. *Russia* (No. 2) (Application no. 51988/07, Judgment of 13 December 2016).

[180] In Ghana for example, Art 2(1) of the 1992 Constitution any person may initiate litigation to defend the constitution. For an important ruling on access to courts in Ghana see *Sam* v. *Attorney-General No 2* [1999–2000] 2 GLR 336. See the later statement of Chief Justice Date-Bah, in *Adofo* v. *Attorney-General* [2003–5] 1 GLR 239:

> The unimpeded access of individuals to the courts is a fundamental prerequisite to the full enjoyment of fundamental human rights. This court has a responsibility to preserve this access in the interest of good governance and

In some such instances, domestic courts have taken international provisions concerning access to justice to initiate legislation in the domestic arena, and to facilitate judicial redress for prospective litigants. In Russia, for example, which was traditionally marked by low confidence in the formal legal order, the Supreme Court has used the ECHR as a basis for introducing measures to heighten judicial transparency, and generally to expand the openness of the judicial system to society.[181] Moreover, the Supreme Court has tied such policies to specific rulings of the ECtHR against Russia. However, this elevation of rights concerning access to justice is also a feature of more established democracies, for example the UK, where in recent years judges have clearly taken pains to reinforce rights of adequate access to courts.[182]

In addition, the right of access to courts has expanded beyond the context of more classical international and national judicial systems, and it is now widely emphasized in international organizations. Increasingly, for example, international organizations are subject to customary norms in this regard, and they are expected to provide access to justice for their employees and for persons affected by their actions. This development in fact began in the 1950s, in the ILO.[183] More recently, employees of

---

constitutionalism. Unhampered access to the courts is an important element of the rule of law to which the Constitution, 1992 is clearly committed. Protection of the rule of law is an important obligation of this court. Accordingly, we are willing to hold that, quite apart from the legal reasoning based on article 140(1) of the Constitution, 1992 which is outlined later in this judgment, it is incompatible with the necessary intendment of chapter 5 of the Constitution, 1992 for a statute to provide for a total ouster of the jurisdiction of the courts in relation to rights which would otherwise be justiciable.

See also the case in Chilean Constitutional Court, Rol 205/1995. The Russian courts have made many rulings on this question, often using Art 6 ECHR. Art 46 of the Russian Constitution protects access to courts, including anti-government litigation and international protection of human rights. Art 46 is cited in well over 26,000 cases of Russian courts. There are almost 16,000 cases in all Russian courts (1998–2016) that refer to Article 6. One of the most important RCC Rulings on merits in which Art 6 ECHR was used is RCC Rulings on merits No. 13-P of 30 July 2001 [Izykskiy mine].

[181]   Supreme Court of the Russian Federation (2012), Plenum Ruling No. 35 of 13 December 2012 'On the Openness and Transparency of Judicial Proceedings and Access to Information on the Activities of Courts'.

[182]   See for example *Leech* v. *Governor of Parkhurst Prison HL* ([1988] AC 533; *FP (Iran)* v. *Secretary of State for the Home Department* [2007] EWCA Civ 13; *R* v. *Secretary of State for the Home Department, ex parte Doody* [1994] 1 AC 531; *R (Osborn)* v. *Parole Board* [2013] UKSC 61.

[183]   See Administrative Tribunal of the International Labour Organization, *Waghorn* v. *ILO* (1957), Judgment No. 28.

other international organizations have been able to seek judicial redress against these organizations.[184] Of course, remedies against international organizations can easily conflict with state immunity provisions, especially in the case of the UN, which means that a categorical right of access to a court is not guaranteed for persons adversely affected by acts of international organizations.[185] However, provisions for protection of such rights in international courts have been discernibly extended. Notably, the ECtHR has recently ruled that domestic implementation of UN directives must be balanced against the obligation to ensure access to court for parties affected by such directives. This has particular importance in decisions regarding governmental classification of persons as terror suspects, in which cases the ECtHR has insisted that decisions must be amenable to legal challenge.[186] Moreover, domestic courts have found ways of reviewing acts of international organizations, in particular the UN. Directives of the UN Security Council implementing asset freezing for persons suspected of terrorist involvement have been declared void by national courts on grounds that the listing of suspects denied the right of legal challenge for those affected.[187] In a case of this kind, the European Court of Justice (ECJ) decided that access to court should be seen as a right with *jus cogens* rank.[188]

Overall, presumptions in favour of a *right to have rights* are now consolidated at different levels of global society. In different ways, the growing width of the protection granted to access to justice affects the form of national democracy, and it has clear constitutional implications.

Most evidently, the growing prominence attached to the right to rights means that international courts produce founding norms for national polities, and they even assume clear legislative functions. In some cases, international courts have used access to justice provisions in international

---

[184] For an important rejection of an international organization's claim to immunity from suit in a national court, see the Belgian Labour Appeal Court case, *Siedler* v. *Western European Union* (2003). See the ECtHR rulings in *Waite and Kennedy* v. *Germany* (1999); *Beer and Regan* v. *Germany* (1999).

[185] See *Mothers of Srebrenica et al* v. *State of The Netherlands and the United Nations,* Supreme Court of The Netherlands (2012); *Delama Georges, et al,* v. *United Nations, et al,* U.S. District Court for the Southern District of New York, No. 1:13-cv-7146 (2014).

[186] ECtHR, *Al-Dulimi and Montana Management Inc* v. *Switzerland* (Application no. 5809/08) (21 June 2016).

[187] *HM Treasury* v. *Ahmed & Ors* [2010] UKSC 2 (27 January 2010).

[188] ECJ, Joined Cases C-402/05 P and C-415/05 P. *Yassin Abdullah Kadi and Al Barakaat International Foundation* v. *Council of the European Union and Commission.*

conventions to intervene directly in domestic policy-making.[189] In other cases, where access to justice is compromised, international courts have recommended far-reaching reform of national court systems.[190] Further, international courts have reasoned that access to justice concerns should prevent recognition of domestic amnesty for perpetrators of breaches of *jus cogens*, so effectively overruling domestic law.[191] Alongside this, the increasing emphasis on the right to rights reflects a process in which different courts can at times disentangle their functions from specific territorial locations, and they create a socially abstracted web of interactions, providing primary norms to regulate actions performed by bodies in other societies. As mentioned, the growing right to rights has led to a presumption that international organizations must provide avenues for legal redress. To some degree, as considered below, this presumption is also reflected in the fact that it is possible to initiate extra-territorial litigation against human rights abusers. Indeed, extra-territorial suits are usually filed where they provide the only effective access to justice for victims of violation:[192] that is, where states in which violations have been perpetrated deny access to justice in domestic judicial fora. In such cases, the broad reading of the right to rights means that courts in one society can hear suits filed for abuses in a different society. Through this, courts are able, to some degree, to position themselves outside their given physical jurisdictional location and they project a fabric of citizenship, based on a primary right to rights, that reaches outside formally constituted territories.[193] As a result, the emphasis on the right to rights transforms judicial bodies into primary law makers, projecting laws beyond their traditional jurisdictional limits.

In some cases, naturally, the expansion of rights of access to justice has extended beyond the recognition of a simple right to seek a formal judicial hearing. Judicial pronouncements on such rights have involved the insistence that courts are required not only to provide judicial redress,

---

[189] IACtHR, *Case of the Constitutional Court v. Peru*, 31 January 2001; IACtHR, *Case of the Dismissed Congressional Employees (Aguado-Alfaro et al) v. Peru*, 24 November 2006.

[190] IACtHR, Case of *Radilla-Pacheco v. Mexico*, 2v November, 2009; Case of *Rosendo Cantú et al v. Mexico*, 31 August 2010.

[191] ECtHR, *Ould Dah v. France*, No. 13113/03 (2009). See comment in Weatherall (2015: 331–8).

[192] For example, in the Pinochet cases in London, one key argument supporting the presumption of Pinochet's liability was that his victims would not find justice in Chilean courts.

[193] See discussion of the 'right to prosecute' in *R v. Bow Street Metropolitan Stipendiary Magistrate and others ex parte Pinochet Ugarte (Amnesty International and others intervening) (No. 3)*, – [1999] 2 All ER 97 179.

but also to offer remedies that meet a certain international threshold. In many cases, judicial directives regarding provisions of effective remedies have had deep-reaching institutional effect in national societies. This is common in the Inter-American system, where the IACtHR has prescribed improved judicial remedies, which at times has led to extensive institutional reform in national political systems.[194] It is also common under the ECHR, where many states have been instructed to improve standards of justice, and domestic courts have then applied these rulings to initiate reforms to domestic judicial and constitutional practice. In Russia, rulings handed down by the ECtHR regarding Art 6 breaches have led to significant judicial reforms, especially regarding the speed of judicial proceedings and the implementation of judicial remedies. For example, following the pilot judgement *Burdov* v. *Russia (No. 2)* of 15 January 2009 new federal legislation was adopted to provide compensation for lengthy trials.[195] Subsequently, the same guarantee was reproduced in the Administrative Litigation Code.[196] One outcome of criticism of the Russian courts in Strasbourg is that the Russian Supreme Court has actively promoted publication of court proceedings.[197] In the UK, famously, the ruling in *Smith and Grady* v. *UK* that the UK military had violated ECHR Art 13 eventually had the outcome that the courts altered more traditional modes of judicial review. In this case, in fact, the courts effectively recognized *a right to remedy by proportionality* for persons claiming abuse of rights defined under ECHR.[198]

The growing protection of the right to an effective remedy has instilled a uniform system of norms across different states, which has profoundly moulded their normative architecture. In many cases, the insistence on the domestic availability of effective remedies has engendered substantively new rights within, and across, domestic legal orders. *Smith and*

---

[194] Far-reaching constitutional reforms in Mexico, which gave higher protection to international human rights law, were conducted against a background marked by IACtHR censure of the Mexican judicial system. See note 192 above. See also IACtHR, Case of *Fernández Ortega et al.* v. *Mexico*, 30 August 2010.

[195] Federal Law No. 68-FZ of 30 April 2010 'On Compensations for Violation of the Right to Justice in Reasonable Time or the Right to Execution of the Judgment in Reasonable Time' [O kompensatsii za narusheniye prava na sudoproizvodstvo v razumnyy srok ili prava na ispolneniye sudebnogo akta v razumnyy srok].

[196] Federal Law No. 21-FZ of 8 March 2015.

[197] See Supreme Court of the Russian Federation (2012). Plenum Ruling No. 35 of 13 December 2012 'On the Openness and Transparency of Judicial Proceedings and Access to Information on the Activities of Courts'.

[198] *Smith and Grady* v. *UK* (1999) 29 EHRR 493.

Grady v. *UK* clearly had this effect in the UK, as it altered the procedural rights guaranteed under the classical system of administrative law and led to a heightened judicial scrutiny of public acts in human rights cases.[199] The Pinochet rulings in London had far-reaching resonance in Chilean law, providing heightened domestic protection against human rights violations.[200] In Mexico, IACtHR rulings on access to justice have led to a wholesale rewriting of the human rights sections in the constitution.[201]

In each case, the protection of judicial rights forms a powerful link in the architecture of the global legal system. The global legal system attaches particular weight to the right to rights, which structurally presupposes the right of access to court. This right, based on a common, globalized concept of citizenship, generates legal obligations that extend beyond regionally defined societies, and it forms the cornerstone for a transnationally extended normative-democratic order, integrating national and international judicial institutions. Within national societies, this right imposes a relatively standardized form on political institutions, it limits the scope of national judicial policies, and it creates an emphasis in favour of particular remedies and particular grounds for administrative action. As discussed more extensively below, moreover, this right also allows new democratic subjects to emerge within the law, which are then able to lay claim to new rights.

3.2.10   *Rights Create Rights*

The increasing linkage between national courts and international courts also releases free-standing processes of law making, because it means that courts, quite generally, acquire the capacity to create new rights, often with *de facto* constitutional effect. Classically, as discussed, rights were created by acts of citizens, acting in their basic political capacity. Now, however, rights are widely created, at least in part, by articulations within the law. This is of course not in itself new. There are many historical instances in which existing rights have been constructed to create further rights. This is especially prominent in the construction of privacy rights, which has

---

[199]   *R* v. *Secretary of State for the Home Department, Ex p Daly*, [2001] UKHL 26 (23 May 2001).
[200]   See Corte Suprema, 28/01/2009, 4691-2007. In this case, the Court used international law to determine that some crimes committed under the dictatorship could not be subject to limitations.
[201]   See note 196 above.

given rise to additional rights, such as sexual and reproductive rights.[202] The construction of rights from other rights, however, has become increasingly detached from acts and demands of citizens, and many rights, often forming basic laws in national societies, are produced through inner-legal actions. In many cases, this occurs because courts are able to extract new rights from the rights that already exist in the legal system, whether expressed in an international instrument or in a domestic constitution, such that existing legal rights can be interpreted expansively, generating new rights *by contagion*. Through this process, basic rights are often created, in purely inner-legal fashion, by other rights.

Above the level of national societies, for example, regional international courts have often argued for an integrated construction of human rights instruments, declaring that primary human rights ought to be interpreted, consequentially, to engender subsidiary or secondary rights, required for the concrete materialization of primary rights. Most notably, the IACtHR has adopted a holistic approach to interpreting human rights, arguing that all human rights are interconnected, and they are defined by 'principles of universality, indivisibility, and interdependence'.[203] As a result, the Court assumes the authority to expand secondary rights, and to promote new rights, because of their linkage to primary rights.

As one important example of this, the IACtHR has strategically amplified provisions for basic rights to produce extended rights for different social groups, and for different ethnic communities. First, the IACtHR has argued that essential rights to life and rights to health necessarily imply rights of land use and even rights to territory for indigenous and other marginalized peoples.[204] Importantly, second, the IACtHR has stated that the right of access to justice for indigenous groups means that they must have access to remedies in cases in which their particular rights – that is, rights distinctively inhering in indigeneity – are violated. On this basis, the Court decided that, given the significance attached by indigenous peoples to communally owned land, these peoples must have access to remedies if communally owned land is forcibly damaged or expropriated: the Court thus found that the indigenous communities, as free-standing legal persons with rights of judicial redress, can necessarily presume possession of a 'right to collectively own property', and they can claim distinct damages

---

[202] *Griswold* v. *Connecticut*, 381 U.S. 479 (1965). See discussion of this process in Germany at p. 317 below.

[203] IACtHR, *Human Rights Defender et al* v. *Guatemala*, 28 August 2014.

[204] IACtHR, *Mayagna (Sumo) Awas Tingni Community* v. *Nicaragua*. 31 August 2001; *Yakye Axa Indigenous Community* v. *Paraguay*. 17 June 2005.

if this right is adversely affected.[205] Perhaps most importantly, third, the IACtHR has determined that the basic right to life should be interpreted not as a mere right to bare existence, but as a right to live life with dignity: as a right to *vida digna*. Indeed, the IACtHR has developed an important body of case law concerning *vida digna*, which has radiated throughout Latin America. The right to *vida digna* was originally construed by the IACtHR as a right of ultra-marginalized persons, living in extreme poverty, and it was conceived as a protective right, expressing an obligation on states that are parties to the ACHR to treat such people with dignity.[206] Later, however, the construction of this right was linked to indigenous rights, and it became a platform on which indigenous communities were granted expansive positive rights, such as rights to use lands with sacred importance to them. In particular, this right was constructed to indicate that indigenous persons have a right to own, or not to be relocated from, their ancestral lands because of the fact that these lands are culturally fundamental to their wellbeing and to their ability to live their lives in dignified fashion.[207]

Within national societies, domestic courts have promoted transformative jurisprudence in order to construct new rights for their populations, sometimes dictating new basic rights through inter-judicial dialogue. As mentioned, in some societies in Latin America, domestic constitutional law is expressly founded in the assumption that the group of rights formally outlined in the constitution is open to interpretive expansion by the courts.[208] In such settings, courts have been able to create quite distinctive rights, and very broadly to expand the catalogue of publicly protected goods. Typically, such expanded rights are consolidated on the grounds that they are seen to flow inevitably from other given rights – for instance, from the right to life – and they are justified on grounds of propinquity to other rights.[209] Usually, such expanded rights include post-classical rights, such as the right to water or the right to health care.[210] In some cases, however, courts have created rights only rather intuitively linked to other core rights, such as, for example *the right to public space*.[211] In fact, some national

---

[205] *Saramaka People* v. *Suriname*. 28 November 2007, para 78.
[206] *Case of the 'Street Children' (Villagran-Morales et al)* v. *Guatemala*. Judgment of 19 November 1999.
[207] See important discussion in Antkowiak (2014).
[208] Colombian Constitutional Court C-1062/2000.
[209] See early use of this argument in Colombian Constitutional Court T-491/92.
[210] Colombian Constitutional Court T-597/93.
[211] Colombian Constitutional Court T-503/92; Bolivian Constitutional Court 0014/2013.

courts have actively elaborated rights that contradict more classical rights, and, especially when addressing claims of distinct population groups, they have established protection for collective property rights, rights to natural resources and rights to use of particular territories, which limit more classically constructed rights of ownership.[212]

An extreme example of this autonomous self-generation of rights is evident in the Constitutional Court in Bogotá. In some instances, this Court has created a chain of rights in which its establishment of one new right has stimulated the emergence of other subsidiary rights, so that the right itself engenders further rights, usually on grounds that subsidiary rights are *necessarily connected with* other, preceding rights.

One key example of this is health rights. The right to health is not recognized as an unqualified right in the Constitution of 1991. However, in the 1990s, the Constitutional Court began to construct health rights using the principle of connectedness, which it had already applied in addressing other rights.[213] Over a longer period of time, the Constitutional Court intensified its protection of health rights to declare that the right to health is a fundamental right.[214] Subsequently, the Court established that the right to health gives rise to secondary rights, and the fundamental guarantee of the right to health created, by a logic of connection, other rights relating to health care. For example, the right to health was declared, in the first instance, to include the right of access to effective and good-quality medical services.[215] This right was then further amplified to incorporate, *inter alia*, rights to continuing treatment for illnesses and to effective diagnosis.[216] Eventually, the right to mental health was also placed under constitutional protection.[217] Through this secondary process, the basic right to health itself acquired a constitutional – or, strictly, constituent – power, radiating through the health care system, and generating connected rights, effectively producing a normative order for health care as a distinct social domain. Ultimately, the principle of connectedness was also used by the Court to rule that rights to health possess correlated environmental implications, so that the right to health produced rights to a clean environment, in cases where pollution poses a risk to health.[218] Notably, principles of

[212] See Colombian Constitutional Court T-257/93; Bolivian Constitutional Court 0572/2014.
[213] T-491/92.
[214] T-760/08.
[215] Ibid.
[216] T-361/14.
[217] T-010/16.
[218] T-046/99.

international law were widely used to consolidate health rights.[219] These rulings also gave rise to important packages of legislation to protect health rights.[220]

Similar examples can be found in Colombian education law. The 1991 Constitution did not guarantee education as a fully enforceable fundamental right. However, the Constitutional Court has established a right to education on the grounds that there exists a 'close linkage' between education and the basic values enshrined in the constitution, notably free development of personality, equal opportunities and access to culture.[221] Later, the Court established the right to education as a fundamental right for all persons under 18 years of age.[222] This right was subsequently expanded to generate more differentiated rights, as the Court placed the government under obligation to offer education that was available, accessible, acceptable and adaptable: the right to education acquired four subsidiary characteristics, generating sub-differentiated rights.[223] Moreover, this right was expanded to include differentiated education rights for disabled persons, who were defined as subjects requiring enhanced constitutional protection.[224] It was also interpreted to determine that indigenous population groups possessed a fundamental right to a 'special system' of education, linked to the right to identity.[225] Notably, principles of international law were widely used to consolidate education rights.[226]

In these examples, primary norms of social life are created through the expansionary judicial construction of rights. The rights structure of society now typically originates in the global normative system, and this structure then evolves at a high degree of autonomy, stimulated by judicial actions. This process forms a parallel to classical patterns of citizenship, in that it marks a widening of the rights structure in society. However, unlike classical patterns of citizenship, it occurs within the law. In such processes, basic laws are produced not as the results of primary societal/political decisions or practical/political acts, but *within the legal system.*

---

[219] See for example very extensive use of international law in T-760-08.
[220] See discussion of this effect in Uprimny and Durán (2014: 8, 13).
[221] T-329/93.
[222] T-775/08.
[223] T-743/13.
[224] T-247/14.
[225] T-907/11.
[226] One leading case on the status of the right to education as a fundamental right (T-775/08) made wide use of international law.

3.3   Inclusion Not Participation

Through this range of processes, a deep and basic alteration to the concept of the democratic citizen and democratic practice has occurred. As discussed, the classical construction of democracy was centred on the idea that the citizen stands at the origin of the law, and, as the interests of citizens are mediated through representative procedures, law obtains legitimacy as a legal enactment of a will originally imputable to citizens. Above all, in the classical construction, citizens assumed a political role by politicizing rights and by articulating claims to rights towards the political system. In contemporary society, however, the underlying reality of democracy is largely determined not by acts of politically identifiable citizens, but by a construction of the person as rights holder, which is stored, consolidated and reproduced, within the legal system, where it acts as a principle for law's production and legitimation. Of course, this model of democracy is marked by variations, and some governmental systems are defined by the tendency, at least in part, to reject it. Indeed, some constitutional democracies have in recent years been created by multi-centric, highly activist processes of foundation, which stress the constitutive role of political participation, and express particular hostility to autonomous judicial norms.[227] Despite this, however, the judicial or inner-legal form of democracy remains much the most dominant pattern of democratic institution building and legal authorization in global society. Even in societies where states avowedly found their legitimacy in specifically and distinctively national modes of justice and political volition, the highest source of normative authority remains based on the self-construction of the law, centred around human rights.[228]

Through the rise of democratic systems with this inner-legal focus, the condition classically known as democracy has been supplanted by a political-systemic order in which, in many respects, the law generates the law, and the citizen as a factual legal agent loses its status as the author of the law. In this process, the citizen does not disappear from the law. Indeed, law conserves a formal model of the citizen as rights holder, which underlies and supports inner-legal acts of law construction. Yet, the citizen loses its status as an external legitimational figure, claiming externally constructed rights. In many situations, the citizen has no obvious reality outside the law, and the law constructs the citizen through its

---

[227] For an account of Bolivia as one example of this see Lazarte (2010: 36).
[228] Bolivian Constitutional Court, 1624/2012, 1422/2012.

own communications. In this system, the concept of material/political participation loses importance as a primary source of legal authority, and many law-creating acts bypass the political system. Instead of a *system of participation*, democracy becomes a *system of inclusion*, and democracy is increasingly defined as a condition in which courts construct generalized norms for the expansive inclusion of society. Basic functions of integration and legislation attached to democratic citizenship are configured around functional equivalents inside the legal system. This condition is not restricted to particular geographical territories, and, given its reference to a generic form of the citizen, it necessarily extends across historical boundaries between states and societies.

3.4   The New Semantics of Legitimacy

These processes, in total, have given rise to a deep transformation in the vocabulary of political legitimacy. Historically, both the political system as a whole and its single legal acts explained their legitimacy in distinctively and generically political categories. As discussed, the idea of a shared political bond, or a shared political decision, was fundamental to democratic enfranchisement, and early democracy was centred on the categorical distinction of political membership from other non-elective social units. More broadly, it is a fundamental feature of the modern political system that it owed its rise to the separation of the vocabulary of political legitimacy from all other functional categories.

First, from the Reformation to the French Revolution, the concept of political legitimacy was formulated in categorically secular political terms, particular to the political system itself, and it was detached from religious vocabulary. Accordingly, political legitimacy was phrased as the result of the positive rational command of a sovereign, whose authority was supported by the idea of the state as a formal secular order, forming an alternative to religious patterns of authority.[229]

Second, after the revolutionary époque, the legitimacy of the political system was phrased as a reflection of citizenship, in which laws were accorded validity as expressions of collective social interests and unifying commitments, and legislation extracted validity from its positive inclusion of the people as sovereign actor. Both these concepts allowed the political system to evolve on free-standing foundations, and to generate quite distinctive reserves of authority and recognition for its functions.

---

[229] See the claims in Koselleck (1959: 101).

As discussed, the legitimational idea of citizenship did not acquire mate-rial political reality for a long time after the French Revolution and the American Revolution. Nonetheless, the revolutionary period spelled out a distinct political norm of legitimacy, based on a mixture of individualism and collective obligations, through which the modern political system was able to explain its authority across society, and on the foundation of which it gradually took shape as a differentiated set of institutions. After 1789, increasingly, the legitimacy of political acts, and especially acts of legis-lation, began to be measured by the extent to which they enacted inter-ests of citizenship or originated in the will of the people, reflected through processes of participation. Through this construction, the people were imagined as the original subjects of the law, and they contributed to the formation of law by extracting political resonance from claims to rights.

To an increasing degree, this classical political vocabulary of legitimacy is now being supplanted by a vocabulary in which the legitimacy of politi-cal acts is defined not by a link to the people, but by the extent to which they accord with human rights norms: that is, with norms which the law itself already contains. As a result, the matrix in which law is legitimated, accepted or challenged is now subject to far-reaching alteration, and law's authority is increasingly either accepted or challenged on the grounds of its conformity, or otherwise, to basic human rights. This is reflected at a national level, as most domestic laws are expected to reflect basic human rights norms. This is even more evident in the international and the trans-national domain, as laws produced outside national societies are increas-ingly susceptible to challenge on human rights grounds.[230] Overall, the contestation of law's legitimacy rarely focuses on the question whether law originates in collective acts of participation. The claim that law is propor-tioned to rights, however, is vital both for law's authorization, and for its contestation. As discussed, in fact, the law now at times recursively pro-duces not only the grounds for its own contestation, but also the citizens who contest its legitimacy. In consequence, the law authorizes itself by referring to a normative construct of the citizen that is actually fabricated within the law, and the real existence of citizens outside the law is dimin-ished. *The subject of law (the citizen) moves from the beginning to the end of law.*

---

[230] For example, human rights norms are now used by the ICJ to address acts in the inter-state arena. See Legal Consequences of the Construction of a Wall in the Occupied Palestinian Territory, ICJ Advisory Opinion, 9 July 2004. As discussed above, further, UN directives are also subject to being struck down on human rights grounds. See above at p. 264.

Underlying this is a deep systemic process, in which the legal system appears as a dominant system in global society. In consequence, national democracy evolves as a secondary outcome of this process of global legal-systemic differentiation.

3.5   Conclusion

At a primary level, of course, there is no contradiction between democracy and human rights law, which is usually pre-figured by international law. Many theorists have argued – with perfect plausibility – that democracy, even in a classical construction, presupposes human rights (Habermas 1992: 124; Beetham 1999: 114). However, the correlation between human rights and democracy rests on the presumption that human rights law creates a set of preconditions for the effective performance of democratic functions, essentially ensuring that members of a *demos* are institutionally able to exercise the degree of participation required to contribute to acts of legislation. On this account, rights need to be perceived as corollaries of some underlying political agreement. In recent decades, however, the political system known as democracy has undergone a quite profound political and conceptual transformation, such that the role of the people in creating laws is subject to constraint, and much law identified as democratic is produced through processes in which the people are only marginally present. At the centre of this transformation is a process in which the subjective author of democratic law has been moved *from a position outside* the legal system *to a position inside* the legal system. As a result, *the law refers to the law as the ground of law's authority*, and processes of legal construction classically pertaining to political actions now widely occur as elements in a process of *secondary constitution making*, in which already defined legal norms are re-articulated. That is to say, the citizen is now constructed, largely, in inner-legal processes, and the rights exercised and laws formed by citizens are often articulations of the law itself. Through this process, the formula of legitimacy is partly disconnected from factual processes of interaction and articulation, and rights of citizenship lose force as lines of social contestation. In this system, the citizen is constructed through interaction between different elements of the global legal system. The citizen is of course still implicated in making laws. However, the citizen contributes to making of laws not through primary non-setting acts or through factual contestation of rights, but either as a secondary agent or as a formal legal construct. The citizen, therefore, evolves in modern society, neither as a concrete source of law nor as an agent engaged in democratic practices, *but as a centre of attribution in a transpersonal process of inclusion*. Although originally conceived as a categorically political order of social organization, in its factual form, democracy has evolved as a *comprehensively and intrinsically legal system of inclusion*. The essential functions of political subjects have been internalized to such a degree within the law that politics and law have become inseparable. As discussed, the classical structure of politics, in which the political system is determined by an external will, did not, conclusively, create an enduring differentiated political system.

Of course, none of this implies that mechanisms of democratic representation have become invalid, or that the people have disappeared from democracy. However, the basic subject of democratic representation (the citizen) has only been established through a coalescence of national agents and global law, and it is only through a process in which the citizen has been partly insulated against its own politicization that the form of democracy has been stabilized. As discussed below, in fact, the political branches of the government have usually proven structurally incapable of solidifying a concept of the citizen to produce legitimacy for laws. Although the classical conception of the citizen imagined the rights of the citizen as enacted through legislatures, in most cases, legislatures could not achieve this objective. On this basis, early sociologists were correct in arguing that democracy evolves as a process of differentiated institutionalization and autonomous legal integration. However, this only occurred as law became fully free-standing, which, in turn, only occurred as law was infused with content extracted from international norms.

Politics Becomes the Law

4.1   Human Rights and the Differentiation of the Legal System

It is necessary to reformulate the inherited conceptual apparatus of democratic legitimacy. The elemental structure of democracy is no longer shaped by the translation of a political will, condensed around the practices of citizens, into legal form. Now, at a basic level, democracy is more usually shaped by the inner-legal projection of obligatory norms and concepts of legal validity, in which primary norm-setting functions are internalized, and recursively produced within the law. In fact, the structure of democracy is no longer founded in processes of norm formation that are discernibly political. Classically, democratic theory revolved around the assumption that a political system possesses distinctive reserves of collectively produced authority, which means that it has primacy *vis-à-vis* other systems in society. The political system is then defined by this primacy, which it invokes to create, to radiate and to enforce generalized norms across society. In contemporary democracy, however, the legal system has acquired clear primacy in relation to interactions classically identified as political.

To understand contemporary democracy, it is essential to approach democratic institutional formation not as a collectively acceded process of political organization, but as the result of the global differentiation of the legal system, which assimilates many classical political functions. To understand modern democracy, we need to abandon ancient antinomies in constructing the foundations of democracy, and we need to observe not societal conflict mediation or will formation, but *legal auto-genesis*, as the origin of democratic law, democratic politics, and democratic integration. In its central normative dimensions, democracy is produced as the secondary political consequence of occurrences within the law, in which classical modes of political agency and norm construction have reduced significance.

The relation between legal-systemic differentiation and democratic formation is visible in the patterns of transnational norm formation examined above. As discussed, the laws of democratic political systems are now widely authorized by concepts and procedures created through the balancing of existing legal norms. At a primary level, democratic law making is framed by a process in which judicial institutions align and connect principles (usually based on human rights) contained in different dimensions of the global legal system. On this foundation, the basic reference of the national political system – the citizen – evolves as a construction of global law, and this construction underpins the legislative acts of national democracies. This pattern of democracy is not simply a reality, in which domestic state institutions act in accordance with international rule-of-law principles. Rather, it reflects a reality in which the global legal system demonstrates and intensifies its own autonomy, and produces democratic norms for national political systems as it does so. Of course, in most national legal systems it remains the case that single actors with judicial duties will show some deference for decisions of a classically political nature, made by classical political branches of government. Such actors may even formally subscribe to some variant on a political-question doctrine, showing restraint in the control of executive decision in some areas of policy making.[1] In fact, it remains that case that, in some societies, national judiciaries are subservient to, or even more reactionary than, executive bodies. An important example of this is contemporary Brazil. In Brazil, the judiciary originally played an important role in aiding the transition to democracy in the 1980s, but it has recently been weak in its support of democratically mandated government.[2] In fact, certain peculiarities in Brazilian constitutional law limit the openness of the domestic legal system to international law.[3] Moreover, it remains the case, with variations from polity to polity, that judges will reject the use of international norms in national legal interpretation.[4] When we talk of the global legal system, therefore, we are not simply talking about an aggregate of judicial

---

[1] See, in the USA *Williams* v. *Suffolk Insurance Company*, 38 U.S. 13 Pet. 415 415 (1839); *Luther* v. *Borden* 48 U.S. 1 (1849); *Pacific States Tel. & Tel. Co.* v. *Oregon* 223 U.S. 118 (1912); *Colegrove* v. *Green*, 328 U.S. 549 (1946). See Frankfurter's classical expression of this doctrine in *Dennis* v. *United States*, 341 U.S. 494 (1951). See the refutation of this doctrine in *Baker* v. *Carr* 369 U.S. 186 (1962), and *Reynolds* v. *Sims*, 377 U.S. 533 (1964).

[2] See, Brazilian Supreme Federal Court, Mandado de segurança N° 34448/DF – Distrito Federal 0058751-32.2016.1.00.0000. Relator: Ministro Roberto Barroso. Judgment: 10 October 2016.

[3] In Brazil, only a small number of actors and organizations can initiate constitutional litigation, and litigation on pure human rights grounds is infrequent. See for discussion Costa and Benvindo (2014: 63, 72).

[4] See pp. 227, 398 below.

figures. The global legal system is constituted as a mass of legal/normative exchanges, based primarily on human rights, which are able to generate authoritative law without political support, and which, outside national borders, connect and encompass different tiers of global society. This mass of norms exists in independence of the decisions of particular judicial actors, and, as discussed, its impact inside national societies is very diffuse. As discussed below, in fact, even where domestic use of international norms is not pronounced or consistent, these norms infiltrate national law in numerous ways.

The correlation between the rights-based differentiation of the global legal system and the stabilization of democracy is not only visible in the *conceptual* apparatus of global law. This correlation is also observable at a more *structural-systemic* or even *concrete-institutional* level. The link between global legal differentiation and the institutional solidification of democracy can be captured in more empirical institutional analysis, focused on the historical formation of different national systems of government. In many national societies, the deepening of democratic government has been driven by a process in which the global differentiation of the legal system has heightened the internal differentiation of the national legal system, and this in turn has acquired formative implications for the development of national democracy as a whole. In such instances, the citizen constructed under international law has often demonstrably facilitated the structural adaption of national political systems, and it acts as a foundation on which they extend their integrational reach into national societies, and complete the process of democratic inclusion and institution building. Although the citizen of international law was projected specifically as a reaction to interwar authoritarianism, it also evolved as a structural norm around which, in a broad range of settings, democracy could be consolidated, and very different impediments to democratic consolidation could be removed. Indeed, the interlocking between global law and national law is the most common precondition for the effective construction of democratic institutions at a national level. Of central importance in this regard is the fact that global law instils a concept of the citizen in national law, so that citizens act as citizens of global law and national law at the same time, and *the global citizen, distinct from the national citizen in its historical construction, forms the foundation for the national citizen.* In many societies, national democracy has only acquired institutional form around the figure of the global citizen, configured within the global legal system. In many settings, this correlation between national and global citizenship facilitates historically precarious processes of democratic legitimacy production and institution building. In fact, most national democracies only obtained stable political institutions, able to reach deep into national societies, as they cemented these systems around global law, and as they constructed their legitimacy around global models of citizenship.

Vital in this connection, first, is the fact that in many societies the global legal system has created a sustainable and generalized model of democratic citizenship in settings where this process, for different sociological reasons, encountered historical obstruction. In particular, second, the global legal system has achieved this, across a range of very different societies and trajectories of democratization, where the 'political' branches of government have not been capable of performing fully inclusive legislative functions. In many societies, classical political institutions have directly impeded the formation of democracy, and they have, for inner-structural reasons, obviated the sustainable construction of the agent from which they extract their own legitimacy – the national citizen. In most cases, the construction of the citizen was a process that could only be initiated, yet not concluded, under national political institutions, and it presupposed the articulation between national and global law for its full realization.

Modern democracy revolves around the paradox that, from the eighteenth century onward, the figure of the citizen opened the national political system to distinctive processes of societal politicization, legitimization and rights attribution, which we associate with democracy. As discussed, the basic legitimacy of modern society was deeply correlated with inclusion of the citizen. Yet, the national-inclusionary claims inherent in these processes only came to conclusion, nationally, as national legal norms were determined by global legal norms – as the citizen became an object of external legal construction.

The sections below address a number of cases in which the correlation between global legal differentiation and the consolidation of national democracy becomes visible, showing how the growth of democracy was prevented by institutions based solely in national citizenship, such that it relied for its completion on global citizenship norms. Each case examined below illuminates this correlation in a distinct setting. For example, the analysis below of the USA and the UK show how the correlation between global law and democracy is visible in societies with a long history of partial, but enduringly selective, democratic institutional formation. The study of the FRG shows how this correlation is visible in democracies, which were created anew in the wave of transitions after 1945. The study of Russia shows how this correlation is visible in societies that are, at present, only partly constructed as democracies. The study of Colombia shows how this correlation is visible in societies in which democratization has been obstructed by weak institutionalization, by low elite commitment to governance and by high levels of social violence. The study of Kenya shows how this correlation is visible in societies in which democratization has necessitated the overcoming of ethnic antagonisms. Overall, the case studies below are designed to illuminate the general correlation between democratic formation and global legal differentiation, covering societies in which democratization occurred in different historical periods, and in which democratic institutions have assumed very different features, on different points of a spectrum between full democracy and authoritarianism. These studies are intended to examine the growth of democracy in societies marked by very different structural resistances to democracy, and the societies that they examine are selected on that basis. These studies do not claim to be exhaustive, but they cover a broad range of patterns of democratization and a broad range of factors that usually impede democratization. Moreover, in different ways, they illustrate how purely national systems of political representation contain attributes that have prevented the stabilization of national democracy, and how, in part, this has been remedied by the impact of global law. Of course, this does not mean that institutionalized procedures for popular representation and political participation have, in these societies, become incidental to democracy. In each case, however, such procedures were not able, without an external global reference, to produce democracy.

Some historians and sociologists have examined the emergence of democracy and democratic citizenship as a relatively general continuous process, building on patterns of political representation that existed quite commonly in pre-modern Europe. For example, Reinhard Bendix describes the 'over-all similarity of the Western European experience' of democratization, in which, he argues, the estate assemblies of the Middle Ages formed a basis for 'the development of modern parliaments and for the conception of a right to representation which was gradually extended to previously unrepresented sections of the population' (1996 [1964]: 122). More typically, however, historians and historical sociologists make sharp distinctions between emerging patterns of democratic citizenship in different societies, often accentuating differences between nineteenth-century states with an authoritarian bias and nineteenth-century states with a democratic emphasis (see Brubaker 1992: 1). Notably, some of the most important historical-sociological research is concerned with the inner-societal forces that gave rise to, or did not give rise to, democratic formation.[5] Moreover, many theorists have reflected on the varying preconditions for the ongoing maintenance of democracy.[6] Using such approaches, many historical accounts of modern democracy have stressed the importance of embedded variations in processes of democratization (Janoski 1998: 174–5). This has even led both historians and sociologists to claim that some national populations, especially in Europe, had an original propensity either for democracy or for authoritarianism,[7] which decisively influenced the formation of democratic government in these societies. Indeed, it is widely claimed that some national societies have been forced by their socially entrenched propensities for authoritarianism onto special paths – *Sonderwege* – towards the construction of democratic institutions (see Wehler 1970: 14; Martin 1987: 37; Kocka 1988). Of course, it was for a long period a sociological commonplace that democracy was an artefact of Western Europe, and other countries in its sphere of influence (Markoff 1996: 79). Some interpreters argue that entire continents have experienced quite distinct, and distinctively troubled patterns of democracy building (Forrest 1988: 423–4; Neves 1992: 108; O'Donnell 1993; Bates 2008: 43).

[5] Classical examples include the following: Lipset (1963: 21), stressing the role of values in supporting democracy; Przeworski (2008: 308), stressing the threat of revolution as impetus for democracy; Tilly (2004: 132; 2007: 33), stressing the importance of contentious movements; Moore (1973 [1966]: 413–52), sketching out alternative paths, democratic and authoritarianism, towards modern societal formation; Downing (1988), stressing importance of early constitutional institutions as conducive to democratization; Downing (1992: 239) seeing protracted warfare as a factor that impeded the rise of constitutional democracy; Luebbert (1987), accentuating the early integration of labour movements as a core part of the path to democratic stability; Rueschemeyer, Stephens and Stephens (1992: 272), claiming that democracy depends on a collaborative middle-class posture; and Markoff (1996: 45), linking democracy to the early prominence of social movements. One influential account has argued that 'transitions from authoritarian rule and immediate prospects for political democracy' were primarily explicable 'in terms of national forces and calculations' (Schmitter 1986: 5).

[6] One common assertion is that democracies presuppose relative affluence amongst citizens (Lipset 1959; Huntington 1991). For a classical cultural explanation of democratic stabilization see Almond and Verba (1989 [1963]). For an account placing emphasis on the importance for democracy of a densely organized civil society see Rueschemeyer, Stephens and Stephens (1992: 215). For an account of civic culture as a precondition of democracy see Putnam et al. (1993: 115). See for syntheses of the literature Beetham (1994); Diamond (1999: 64–116).

[7] For sociological variants on this claim see Parsons (1954: 104–6; 1964: 353); Dahrendorf (1965: 26); Lipset (1960: 138); Fraenkel (1964: 30). Münch is more accurate in identifying different national histories as marked by varying obstructions to the realization of democracy (1984: 194–5). For different positions in historical analysis of this question, see, for example, Winkler (1979: 23; 2000: 648); Martin (1987).

Generally, however, it is difficult to see either deep continuities connecting modern democracy to historical/political conditions or deep causal or cultural variations in the national experiences of democratization. Contrary to established lines of historical sociology, the analyses below claim that the preconditions for democratization and citizenship formation, across the globe, are not to be found within national society. Therefore, the structural propensities of national societies do not allow us to assess the probable success of democratization processes. Democratization has almost invariably resulted from the incursion of global norms within national society, leading to a deep rupture between national and global patterns of norm formation. This does not mean, naturally, there are no regional or socio-structural particularities in the emergence of democracy. But what is striking in this process is not the structurally determined diversity, but the relative uniformity of different histories of democratic integration. Before 1914, many states, especially in Europe, followed variable pathways of nationalization and rudimentary democratization, centred around the construction of national citizenship.[8] Then, after 1918, most states collapsed in face of the pressures induced by the two trajectories (nationalization and democratization) by which their own formation had been accompanied and determined. Before 1945, very few societies had established secure democratic institutions, and very few states had reliably enfranchised their populations. In fact, very few societies had assumed a fully nationalized political form. However, after 1945, most societies, albeit gradually, became democracies. In virtually every case, the establishment of democracy was not induced by processes occurring within national societies, and it is only partially explicable through comparative sociological analysis. It is difficult to explain the formation of democratic systems through the historical-sociological analysis of separate national societies. Instead, a global sociology of democracy is required, which places the origins of democracy in global focus, and which observes democracy as constructed by forces outside national society, gaining intensity after 1945, penetrating into the national legal-political structure, and transfiguring national institutions through global norms.

Globally, the establishment of democracy was linked, most vitally, to the deep interaction between national and international normative systems,

---

[8] Caramani argues that at the time of World War I most societies had reached the endpoint of a process of political nationalization and de-territorialization, caused by urbanization, state formation and communication technology, and reflected in greater political homogeneity and the establishment of organs of mass democracy (2005: 320).

mediated through human rights law, which instilled a set of practices reflecting a *world model of citizenship* within national societies. In virtually every case of democratic formation, the construction of the citizen, which, at a primary and final level, holds together and legitimates national democracy, has been extracted from the global legal system, and it reflects a relatively autonomous interaction between different spheres of global law. Indeed, in nearly every case of democracy building, the reliance of national law on global law is evident at two different levels. First, as discussed, global law constructs the basic legal-normative form of the citizen. Second, global law constructs the national institutional structure in which democratic citizenship is exercisable, facilitating the effective penetration of the political system of society. Consequently in most polities, both the democratization of the political system and the nationalization of society have relied on global norms.

Central to this social phenomenon is the fact that, after 1945, law-making institutions were able to extract some legitimacy for their actions from a construction of the citizen extracted from global law, which meant that they were not required to generate authority for their decisions by mobilizing the will of the people in factually concretized national form. After 1945, gradually, the citizen, to which the national polity owed its legitimacy, was turned outward towards international law, and it was configured around rights defined in international law. This meant that laws applied within national societies could be legitimated without a deep transmission of social antagonisms from society, through the citizen, and then into the institutions of government. In fact, this meant that the global citizen could be imposed onto the national citizen, and the national political system could presume a more stable, controlled form of citizenship around which to order its inclusionary and legitimational functions. The political system thus generated its legitimacy increasingly through outward compliance, and decreasingly through internal conflict management. As a result, the political system became less prone to destabilization through conflicts between its own citizens, and it adopted a model of the citizen as legitimational figure that was more statically constructed, and less inclined to produce and politicize deep-lying societal contests. In this process, notably, legislative institutions lost some of their importance as sources of legitimate will formation. Historically, as discussed, the construction of citizenship was primarily articulated through legislatures. However, in most cases, legislatures on their own proved incapable of galvanizing a generally inclusive idea of the citizen, and they stabilized citizenship around separate group prerogatives. Indeed, in most cases, legislatures were marked by the twofold paradox that, although defined as the institutional fulcrum of democracies, they promoted generalized models of citizenship that could not easily incorporate minorities, and they attached immovable legislative power to the prerogatives of leading social groups. It was only as the acts of legislatures were pre-formed by global citizenship norms that national citizenship, incorporating all society, yet not bound to dominant interests, became possible. In this process, further, the concept of the citizen underlying the legitimacy of the democratic political system was produced *within the legal system*. The citizen first emerged as a figure that politicized society by translating distinct social claims into legal rights. Ultimately, however, it was the fact that international human rights separated the citizen from concrete positional struggles in society that, across variations between national societies, formed the cornerstone of democratic inclusion.

4.2 Global Human Rights and the Construction of the National Citizen

4.2.1 Global Human Rights and National Democracy 1: The USA

The impact of the global legal system on democratic institution building in national societies is strikingly evident in the post-1945 history of the USA.

For a number of reasons, this claim may appear counterintuitive.

First, for example, the USA has a long history of domestic civil rights jurisprudence, and a long history of partial democratic representation. In fact, in the USA, the growth of democracy and the growth of basic civil rights were always very closely connected. The early rise of American democracy, and American national society more widely, were clearly shaped by the enforcement of constitutional rights by federal courts.[9] Indeed, most epochal stages in the long process of nation building in the USA, from the Founding, to the Civil War, to Reconstruction, to the New Deal, to the counter-mobilization of the 1950s and 1960s, were connected to a deepening societal solidification of constitutional rights in American society.[10] Second, the period before and after 1945 is usually seen as a period in which the federal courts enjoyed rather diminished authority,

---

[9] See in particular *Fletcher* v. *Peck*, 10 U.S. (6 Cranch) 87.

[10] Early documents of the American Revolution, including the resolutions of the Stamp Act Congress (1765) and the Continental Congress (1774), the Virginia Declaration of Rights (1776) and the Declaration of Independence (1776) were phrased in the diction of rights.

and in which they displayed heightened deference to Congress and the President (see Leuchtenburg 1995: 219). This is the result of the fact that in the 1930s the Supreme Court had initially obstructed the New Deal policies implemented during the presidency of Roosevelt,[11] which had presupposed a strengthening of executive power. Roosevelt reacted to this by appointing judges to the Court who were sympathetic to executive-led government, and less likely to veto policy making.[12] Third, more generally, the impact of international law never reached the same level in the American legal system as in other national legal systems, and American courts today still reject the use of international human rights law as determining grounds for decisions.[13] Indeed, it is a derisive commonplace that the USA advocates human rights for the global community, yet not for itself (Cohen 2006: 326). The attempt to comprehend democratic institution-making in the USA in the decades following 1945 as the consequence of a deep interaction between national law and global law can thus easily appear implausible.

Despite this, the years following 1945 in the USA can surely be seen, in part, as a period in which the national legal system slowly reached an unprecedented level of autonomy and authority. This was partly caused by the pervasive impact of international legal norms within the domestic legal system. This increasing autonomy of law had far-reaching implications for the structure of national democracy, in some cases causing a penetration of national-democratic norms, especially civil rights, into regions previously only tenuously connected to the federal legal/political order. In consequence, this process also established uniform concepts of citizenship to underpin the democratic order.

To explain this impact of global law on American law, first, it is vital to bear in mind that use of the term *democracy* to describe the mode of political institutionalization in the USA before the 1960s requires, at the very least, some qualification.

Many accounts claim that the 'notion of natural rights' was 'absolutely fundamental' to the American Founding, where it formed a 'Revolutionary Language' (Bradburn 2009: 27).

[11] See *Panama Refining Co.* v. *Ryan*, 293 U.S. 388 (1935); *A.L.A. Schechter Poultry Corp.* v. *United States*, 295 U.S. 495 (1935); *United States* v. *Butler*, 297 U.S. 1 (1936).

[12] By 1945, judges appointed by Roosevelt constituted 67 per cent of the appellate branch and 59 per cent of the district branch (Irons 1982: 291).

[13] Famously, it was decided in a Circuit Court of Appeals that UN rulings could not prevail over federal laws: *Diggs* v. *Schultz* 555 F.2d 461 (DC Cir 1972). See the most emphatic expression of this law of domestic primacy in Rakin (2007). See Scalia's expression of 'fear' concerning the 'accelerating pace' of use of foreign law in the American Supreme Court (2004: 308).

As discussed in the introduction, the USA was originally founded in a spirit of popular democratic citizenship. This was reflected in particular in the first state constitutions created after 1776. However, the Federal Constitution of 1789 also provided for national representation on a broad electoral basis. Later, the Civil War, Reconstruction and the Constitutional Amendments passed at this time were intended to impose universal rights of citizenship across all parts of the polity (Gillette 1979: 25–6). One observer argues that the Civil Rights Act (1866) and the Reconstruction Act (1867) were designed 'to define in legislative terms the essence of freedom', consolidating democratic citizenship as a structural norm for the entire American polity (Foner 1988: 244).

However, from the Founding onwards, American citizenship was only partial and selective in its scope, and in many areas it was only fully accorded to ethnically privileged (white-skinned) social groups. Owing to the loosely coordinated federal system and the weak judicial enforcement of civil rights norms, the provisions for democratic rights guaranteed in the original Constitution of 1789/91 and the Civil War Amendments did not pierce deeply into the legal/political life of all federated states. After the rapid failure of Reconstruction in the southern states after the Civil War, in fact, State Congresses in a number of states successfully mobilized against the imposition of national constitutional law to preserve white political supremacy, often with the acquiescence of the federal judiciary and the presidency.[14] As a result, up to 1964, when the Civil Rights Act was passed, and, perhaps more importantly, to 1965, when the Voting Rights Act was passed, the USA only possessed a quasi-democratic political system. This system was based, to some degree, on an apartheid model, in which, in some regions, non-white population groups were routinely excluded from exercise of the civil rights constitutive of democracy.[15] In many

---

[14] See Gillette (1979: 45). The 'gutting' of the Civil War Amendments by the Supreme Court has of course been widely discussed. Notably, in *Williams* v. *Mississippi*, 170 U.S. 213 (1898), the Supreme Court condoned restrictions imposed on electoral participation of black voters in Mississippi. On judicial responsibility for the failure of Reconstruction see Kruger (1975: 50–83); Forbath (1999: 51); Kousser (1999: 53). Kruger states that by 1900 'the Supreme Court had nullified nearly every vestige of the federal protection that had been cast like a comforting cloak over the black man' (1975: 83). For an important revisionist appraisal of this view, however, see Brandwein (2011: 64, 98).

[15] After 1965, registration of black voters in Mississippi increased from 6.7 per cent to 59.8 per cent. For this analysis and discussion of the 'revolutionary' consequences of the Voting Rights Act of 1965, see Grofman et al. (1992: 16, 23). In agreement with my claim that the USA had not established full democratic suffrage until 1964/5, see the views in Steinfeld (1989: 336). The greatest rise in black electoral enrolment occurred in the years 1965–9

ex-Confederate states, the pre-1964 political system was based on comprehensive exclusion of members of the black population from electoral participation, either by constitutional or para-constitutional discrimination. One account explains that, before the 1960s, franchise restrictions in the south created a 'system which insured the absolute control of predominantly black counties by upper-class whites', effectively suppressing all organized political opposition to dominant social groups (Kousser 1974: 238).[16] 'Apartheid', as one great authority has explained, was, until the 1960s, a 'governing system that pervaded half the country' (Cover 1982: 1316).[17] A different, equally authoritative, commentator has claimed that, until the 1960s, the USA, like South Africa, could only be viewed as a partial democracy, centred on 'a unique socio-economic structure and a political apparatus which was simultaneously racist, stubbornly capitalist, and committed to a limited form of bourgeois democracy: a racist/capitalist state' (Marable 1991: 4). Only from the mid-1960s onwards was it clear that African Americans were to be classed as fully enfranchised citizens of the USA, and that equal inclusion of society was an invariable component of governmental legitimacy. In the USA, therefore, the 1960s were emphatically a period of *democratic transition*.[18]

(Lawson 1976: 334). For use of the term 'American apartheid' see Friedman (2002: 111, 285).

[16] On the Voting Rights Act as the most effective instrument for enforcing universal democracy see Lichtman (1969: 366); Friedman (2002: 300).

[17] On broader similarities between South Africa and the USA after 1945, see Plummer (1996: 192).

[18] Other authors apply the democratic transition paradigm to the USA under the Civil Rights Movement, explaining that this period led government from a non-democratic to a democratic condition. See most notably the outstanding analysis in Mickey (2015: 66). Mickey's account, in itself magnificently illuminating, applies the democratization paradigm to explain the transformation of the southern states alone, which are described as 'enclaves' of authoritarian rule that evaded incorporation in the democratic order of American society as a whole (13). Democratization thus appears to Mickey as the overcoming of 'subnational authoritarianism' (35). On my reading, as the southern states were at least notionally part of the USA, the democratization paradigm should be applied to the USA as a whole. On my account, the disfranchisement of large swathes of the black population after Reconstruction meant that the USA as a whole, having briefly become something close to a democracy in the 1860s, stopped being a democracy after Reconstruction had failed. For analysis that questions the perspective that weak democracy was localized in the USA, see King (2007: 205). One other excellent analysis of the Civil Rights Movement describes the 'exceptional nature of America's development as political democracy', stating that 'no other democracy in the world has ever enfranchised a large group and then disenfranchised it' (Valelly 2004: 148). In this regard, however, the USA appears less than exceptional. Something similar happened repeatedly in France from 1789–1871 and also, recurrently, in Spain up to 1975. A different account argues that, up to the mid-1960s, the USA contained 'two different

The fact that national democracy was only partially evolved in the USA before 1964/65 was due, mainly, to the fact that the political system was not originally founded in a simple definition of citizenship, able to form a centre of normative consistency for the law. At one level, of course, the weak construction of the citizen was simply determined by discriminatory national policies in favour of white communities (see King 2000: 41–6, 124).[19] As early as 1790, Congress itself applied an exclusionary principle to citizenship questions, limiting naturalization to white aliens and restricting enrolment in militias to white citizens (Litwack 1961: 31). However, the weak construction of the citizen was also the result of the federal organization of American government, which led to variations between different federal states in the construction of political rights. This was linked to the founding doctrine of concurrent or even multiple sovereignty, which underpinned the original conception of the American constitution (see Lacroix 2010: 135). Ultimately, this system generated deep contradictions between conceptions of citizenship at state level and at federal level.

Famously, for example, the early formative period of the American Republic was dominated by the polarization between rival concepts of citizenship, in which Federalists and Democrats proposed models of the citizen that defined, respectively, the federal government or the state governments as primary foci of obligation (Smith 1997: 196). To be sure, the 1789 Constitution was called into life by a theoretical vision of a unified nation with normatively unified citizenship. In *Federalist 2*, John Jay argued that the USA was formed by 'one people' with 'each individual citizen everywhere enjoying the same national rights, privileges, and protection' (Madison, Hamilton and Jay 1987 [1787–8]: 91–2). In reality, however, the constitution did not contain a secure construct of the national citizen (see Bickel 1973: 370), and laws were proportioned to multiple, overlapping, but at times highly fragmented, ideas of the citizen, which

---

democracies', separated by divergent attitudes to slavery (Wilentz 2005: 705). If we assume that the USA was, at least legally, a nation after 1789, the coexistence of two democracies cannot be possible: it either *was*, or (more plausibly) *was not* a democracy. Notably, one expert contemporary observer argued that the southern states were marked by a 'struggle against democracy' by 'legal and extralegal restrictions of the right to vote' (Schattschneider 1988: 99). Using standard measurements for the quality of democracy, the USA before 1964 the USA did not meet a core test of democracy, which is not satisfied 'if one or more segments of all adult citizens are excluded from the civil right of universal suffrage' (Merkel 2004: 49).

[19] See, indicatively, the restrictive ruling on non-white naturalization in *Takao Ozawa v. United States*, 260 U.S. 178 (1922).

were located at different points in the national political system. Indeed, the idea of national citizenship in revolutionary America was intrinsically weak – the collective people of the nation were always distinct from the collective peoples in the separate states (Hulsebosch 2005: 229; Fritz 2008: 196). As a result, the Constitution sanctioned a system of dual citizenship, in which the national government and the states exercised sovereignty in different social spheres, which meant that in different parts of national society national citizenship was institutionalized in different ways. This naturally meant that the universal implications of national citizenship were subject to limitation by the states, and states could moderate citizenship in accordance with their own prerogatives, often on ethnic grounds, such that the basic egalitarian implications of national citizenship often fell short of including non-white population groups.

Acceptance of divergent patterns of citizenship, entailing divergent obligations and uneven calibration of inclusionary entitlements, was reflected in early rulings of the Supreme Court.

In some early rulings, the Supreme Court was inclined to identify national citizenship as having primacy over citizenship based in the separate states.[20] This line of reasoning was not uniform, as, in some cases, the Court upheld a concept of twofold citizenship, in which social agents were subject to some obligations as citizens of states and some obligations as citizens of the America Republic.[21] However, the more federalist line of reasoning peaked in *McCulloch v. Maryland* (1819).[22] Indeed, very notably, the early Supreme Court tied its federalist stance to an enthusiasm for international law, and international norms were deployed to expand both the reach and the consistency of federal law in relation to the states.[23] As Chief Justice of the Supreme Court, John Marshall argued for the unrestricted territorial sovereignty of the nation, and he defined the 'jurisdiction of courts' as a 'branch of that which is possessed by the nation as an independent sovereign power'.[24] At the same time, he stated that 'the Court is bound by the law of nations which is part of the law of the land'.[25] In some of the most important cases decided by Marshall, notably *Murray v. Schooner Charming Betsy* (1804), *Rose v. Himely* (1808) and *Brown v. United States* (1814), affirmative reference was made to foreign and

---

[20] *Chisholm v. Georgia*, 2 U.S. 419 (1793)
[21] *United States v. Worrall*. 2 U.S. 384(1798).
[22] *McCulloch v. Maryland*, 17 U.S. 4 Wheat. 316 316 (1819).
[23] For background see Lenner (1996: 73).
[24] *The Schooner Exchange v. M'Faddon, 11 U.S. (7 Cranch) 116, (1812).*
[25] The Nereide, 13 U.S. (9 Cranch) 388 (1815).

international law as the basis for final ruling.[26] National citizenship and international law, consequently, were closely connected from an early stage, and the authority of international law provided a normative basis for the expansion of federal authority and federal citizenship.

By the 1830s, however, the Supreme Court became more protective of the rights of states, ruling that constitutional rights were not enforceable against the states.[27] In *Dred Scott*, most notoriously, the Taney Court asserted the primacy of state citizenship over federal citizenship. Taney used this principle to institutionalize a caste-like hierarchy of citizens, in which people of colour could not be classed as citizens under the federal Constitution.[28] Subsequently, after Reconstruction, the Court again opted for an extremely constrained view of national citizenship (Smith 1999: 332). The Fourteenth Amendment, introduced after the Civil War, declared reasonably clearly that state citizenship should be secondary, or at least closely aligned, to citizenship of the United States.[29] The Fifteenth Amendment gave reality to these principles by establishing universal (male) black suffrage. After this, however, the Supreme Court declared in The *Slaughterhouse Cases* 'that there is a citizenship of the United States, and a citizenship of a State, which are distinct from each other, and which depend

---

[26] For comment on these cases see Calabresi and Zimdahl (2005: 763–71).

[27] *Barron* v. *Baltimore*, 32 U.S. (7 Pet.) 243 (1833),

[28] See the following argument in *Dred Scott*, which still bears repetition as an exercise in stimulating moral revulsion:

> The words 'people of the United States' and 'citizens' are synonymous terms, and mean the same thing. They both describe the political body who, according to our republican institutions, form the sovereignty and who hold the power and conduct the Government through their representatives. They are what we familiarly call the 'sovereign people', and every citizen is one of this people, and a constituent member of this sovereignty. The question before us is whether the class of persons described in the plea in abatement compose a portion of this people, and are constituent members of this sovereignty? We think they are not, and that they are not included, and were not intended to be included, under the word 'citizens' in the Constitution, and can therefore claim none of the rights and privileges which that instrument provides for and secures to citizens of the United States. On the contrary, they were at that time considered as a subordinate and inferior class of beings who had been subjugated by the dominant race, and, whether emancipated or not, yet remained subject to their authority, and had no rights or privileges but such as those who held the power and the Government might choose to grant them.

Dred Scott v. *Sandford* 60 U.S. 393 (1857)

[29] On the primacy of US-citizenship implied by the Fourteenth Amendment see D. Smith (1997: 800). On this aspect of the Civil War legislation more generally see Oakes (2013: 358–9).

upon different characteristics or circumstances in the individual'. Notably, in ruling this, the Court declined to enumerate those rights, privileges and immunities that all citizens of the USA held as inviolable.[30] The principle of divided citizenship was also expressed in cases concerning voting rights for minority populations.[31] This was not a fully consistent line of reasoning; in other cases the Supreme Court argued for a more encompassing notion of citizenship.[32] Yet, these rulings meant that policies to promote national citizenship after the Civil War were weakened, and civil rights norms were not incorporated across all states of the Union. As a result, the consolidation of the single rights-based model of the citizen was postponed;[33] full nationalization of society did not occur until the 1960s.

This splitting of the citizen into partly separate state-based and federal components permitted the persistence of a racist model of citizenship in the USA, and it impeded the full formation of a democratic system, based on a single national democratic people (see Allen 2006: 120–5). Major historical caesura, notably the Civil War, Reconstruction, the New Deal and the Civil Rights Movement reflected politically volatile, essentially revolutionary contestations over the construct of the citizen, attempting to spread, or – conversely – to counteract the spread, of a unifying idea of citizenship to all members of the national community.[34] In such moments, it became clear that the ideals of democratic popular sovereignty declared in the Founding era were not correlated with any socio-material reality, and, especially in the Civil War, the democratic people had to be created through acts of violence. In this respect, importantly, in the Civil War, Reconstruction and the aftermath of World War II, the widening of the reach of black citizenship was strongly linked to experiences of military mobilization, through which black soldiers were reinforced in their demands for the classical rights of political citizenship.[35] Up to the 1960s,

---

[30] The Slaughter-House Cases, 83 U.S. 36 (1873). See also *United States* v. *Cruikshank*, 92 U.S. 542 (1875).

[31] *Giles* v. *Harris*, 189 U.S. 475 (1903).

[32] Ex parte Siebold, 100 U.S. 371 (1879); Ex parte Yarbrough, 110 U.S. 651 (1884).

[33] This of course remained a critical point in American constitutionalism. Eventually, the idea was expressed in the Supreme Court that 'citizens would have two political capacities, one state and one federal, each protected from incursion by the other', but that the national government 'owes its existence to the act of the whole people who created it': *U.S. Term Limits, Inc.* v. *Thornton*, 514 U.S. 779 (1995) (Kennedy).

[34] See for discussion Bradburn (2009: 295). Tellingly, James Garfield described the Civil War and Reconstruction as a 'gigantic revolution', greater even than 1776 (Wang 1997: 140).

[35] Black military service for the Union army in the Civil War had played an important role in propelling the movement for full citizenship (see Foner 1987: 864; Oakes 2013: 378–9).

however, laws shaping different life-contexts were not typically justified through reference to shared rights, to a unified concept of citizenship or to a unified concept of democracy. Up to this point, the American political system can only be characterized as a democracy if a racist definition of democracy is accepted. Democracy needed to be built, incrementally, through the social extension of civil rights, and, as discussed below, this was not established in classical political fashion.

To explain the significance of global law for American democracy, second, it should be noted that, although the composition of the Supreme Court after 1945 was determined by Roosevelt's personal nominations, Roosevelt had generally appointed judges who were sympathetic both to liberal reformism and to the (closely related) widening of federal government. Above all, he had appointed judges who viewed the generalized enforcement of human rights norms (that is, *rights-centred Liberalism*) as a strategy for expanding the power of the federal state across society (Tushnet 1994: 70; McMahon 2004: 25, 73). Tellingly, Roosevelt had argued that the southern states were still dominated by conventional or customary patterns of authority, which resembled the legal order of feudal Europe (McMahon 2004: 17). Like the anti-feudal revolutionaries of the late Enlightenment, therefore, he promoted policies designed, from within the federal government, to impose uniform legal rights across society, especially in social legislation, as a means to construct society in more inclusive fashion, and to extend the basic structure of a national legal system across society in its entirety.[36] After Roosevelt's death, by consequence, the Supreme Court was staffed with judges who were generally committed to the extension of federal power, and who saw the broadened solidification of civil rights across American society as a vital social and political necessity. Notably, before 1945, the Supreme Court had already begun to endorse rigorous intervention in cases of political discrimination against racial minorities.[37] The post-1945 period then saw a deepening shift in the Supreme Court from concern

---

Truman's military desegregation laws (Executive Order 9981, 1948) after World War II had central importance in the background to the Civil Rights Movement in the 1960s.

[36] However, note the argument that racism was not only institutionalized in the states – it was also fundamentally embedded in Federal government (see King 2007: 16).

[37] See the famous footnote 4 in *United States* v. *Carolene Products Co.* 304 U.S. 144 (1938), in which Justice Stone considered 'whether prejudice against discrete and insular minorities may be a special condition, which tends seriously to curtail the operation of those political processes ordinarily to be relied upon to protect minorities, and which may call for a correspondingly more searching judicial inquiry'. As stated in this footnote, laws restricting political citizenship for black people had already been struck down in *Nixon* v. *Herndon*, 273 U.S. 536 (1927) and *Nixon* v. *Condon*, 286 U.S. 73 (1932). One outstanding

with single monetary rights to concern with civil and political rights as the core pillars of American nationhood (Leuchtenburg 1995: 235).

In the process of democratization in the 1960s, notably, leading actors in the American judiciary, who had traditionally been Conservative, outpaced the Presidency in promoting civil rights.[38] Indeed, the judicial system obtained great significance in the extension of rights-based democracy. After World War II, first, the Supreme Court gained a reputation for activism and autonomy, which eventually culminated under the Chief Justiceship of Earl Warren (Barkow 2002: 266). By the early 1960s, certain commonplaces of American jurisprudence had been unsettled by the increasingly activist jurisprudence of the Supreme Court. For example, the Supreme Court launched an attack on the previously entrenched doctrine, supported by Roosevelt's judges,[39] that certain legal questions had political status, falling solely under the powers of Congress and not amenable to control by the courts.[40] In some rulings, the Supreme Court dictated the principle of equal voting rights as a political basis for society.[41] Moreover, the Supreme Court placed restrictions on traditional balances between state rights and national government, and it showed great willingness to issue rulings that extended federal power. Many decisions in the Warren court entailed an intensification of federal authority, at times against the express wishes of the incumbent President.[42] In some cases,

---

observer describes this footnote as both 'a precursor and a precondition' of the Second Reconstruction (Kousser 1999: 68).

[38] Eisenhower was notoriously unsupportive of civil rights cases (see Lichtman 1969: 349). One interpreter claims that he 'refused to show public support' for the ruling in *Brown* v. *Board of Education*, and he regretted the damage done by this case to the cause of Southern Republicanism (Luders 2010: 153). A different account states that he was 'lukewarm if not hostile to Negro aspirations' (Lawson 1976: 140). Further, civil rights legislation often encountered deep resistance in Congress – so it cannot be assumed that these laws expressed a broad popular political will (see Graham 1990: 147, 152).

[39] For this see *Colegrove* v. *Green*, 328 U.S. 549 (1946). See Brandeis's classical statement of judicial reticence in 1936: 'The Court will not pass upon the constitutionality of legislation in a friendly, nonadversary, proceeding, declining because to decide such questions is legitimate only in the last resort, and as a necessity in the determination of real, earnest and vital controversy between individuals. It never was the thought that, by means of a friendly suit, a party beaten in the legislature could transfer to the courts an inquiry as to the constitutionality of the legislative act'. *Ashwander* v. *Tennessee Valley Authority*, 297 U.S. 288 (1936).

[40] See *Baker* v. *Carr*, 369 U.S. 186 (1962): 'The courts cannot reject as "no law suit" a bona fide controversy as to whether some action denominated "political" exceeds constitutional authority'.

[41] *Wesberry* v. *Sanders*, 376 U.S. 1 (1964); *Reynolds* v. *Sims*, 377 U.S. 533 (1964).

[42] Note Eisenhower's opposition to the Supreme Court's position in questions of intrastate transportation (Burk 1984: 170).

federal courts identified instances of egregious unconstitutional behaviour within particular states, and they imposed federal remedies directly to rectify this.[43] For example, the Supreme Court handed down rulings that declared unconstitutional discriminatory practices, notably school and other educational segregation, institutionalized in the wake of *Plessy v. Ferguson*, and restricted voting, institutionalized in state constitutions and by Supreme Court rulings.[44] The centrepieces of this process were the rulings in *Brown v. Board of Education* (1954) and *Cooper v. Aaron* (1958). However, later cases, affirming the primacy of constitutional amendments and congressional civil rights legislation over state rights, also played an important role in this broadening of federal power.[45] Eventually, the elevation of the status of constitutionally guaranteed rights made it possible for federal courts and federal legislation to penetrate more deeply into the traditional jurisdiction of the states, and to ensure that constitutional rights were more fully incorporated in state law.[46] By the 1960s, state-level incorporation of federal civil rights was greatly augmented (Lewis and Trichter 1981: 217). Under the Warren Court, clearly, federal courts began to oversee functions of state-level regulatory agencies, such as education providers, and to scrutinize their adherence to federal court rulings. Increased judicial activism and civil rights enforcement also resulted in the increased imposition of federal norms on state courts.[47] It also led to the creation of new standards on use of evidence in state tribunals.[48] Moreover, heightened protection was established for persons suffering violations of civil rights by public bodies.[49] These developments tightened lines of control between national and state governments, effectively promoting the more complete nationalization of society.

In each of these respects, the mass of legal institutions in American society clearly acquired an unprecedented autonomy in the years after 1945, and they assumed powers that significantly exceeded their traditional

---

[43] *Holt v. Sarver*, 309 F. Supp. 362 (E.D. Ark. 1970).

[44] *Giles v. Harris*, 189 U.S. 475 (1903).

[45] See for example *Heart of Atlanta Motel Inc. v. United States*, 379 U.S. 241 (1964); *South Carolina v. Katzenbach*, 383 U.S. 301 (1966).

[46] See notably *Gideon v. Wainwright*, 372 U.S. 335 (1963), See discussion of the theory of incorporation developed by Hugo Black in Hockett (1996: 113). See historical analysis in Casper (1972: 39).

[47] *Mapp v. Ohio*, 367 U.S. 643 (1961); *Dombrowski v. Pfister*, 380 U.S. 479 (1965).

[48] See for example *Escobedo v. Illinois*, 378 U.S. 478 (1964). On the increased availability of federal habeas corpus in this era see the excellent account in Glennon (1994: 905).

[49] See for example *Monroe v. Pape*, 365 U.S. 167 (1961) see also the district court ruling *Holt v. Sarver*, 309 F. Supp. 362 (E.D. Ark. 1970).

constitutional limits. In important ways, actors within the legal system constructed the foundation for a more inclusive system of democracy, using civil rights jurisprudence to link diffuse parts of society to the national government (see McMahon 2004: 3).[50] Through these processes, above all, the national legal system obtained greater presence and immediacy across different spheres of society, and judges applied civil rights as principles that underscored the societal immediacy of national constitutional law. Ultimately, the consolidation of federal government through judicial practice proved a core precondition for the relative success of the Civil Rights Movement in the 1950s and early 1960s. The fact that the government had extended rights quite broadly across American society meant that, by the 1950s, it possessed sufficient infrastructural power to ensure that southern states could not, as had been the case after Reconstruction, continue to flout constitutional obligations regarding the civil rights of African Americans.[51] Civil rights, in other words, were both the building blocks and effective indicators of national governmental power.

In addition, third, it is widely accepted that, at least at federal level, the American legal system has shown only limited openness to international norms.[52] This is of course true in a restricted sense, as few cases in the American Supreme Court have been decided using international law.[53] However, the years after 1945 witnessed a number of processes, some direct and some more oblique, in which international legal presumptions gained unprecedented authority in the USA, and in which legal procedures were deeply shaped by principles of international law. International law in fact played a core role in the expansion of national democracy, and it acquired distinctive importance in cases with implications for racial exclusion, helping to remedy shortfalls in democratic legitimacy.

The legal order of American democracy underwent a process of redirection after 1945, in part, because of the international rise of human rights

---

[50] This claim has been forcefully disputed in Rosenberg (1991: 343). However, even if Rosenberg's call for a more restrictive view of the power of courts is heeded, it remains the case that the vocabulary of rights (a judicially constructed vocabulary) formed the basis for the general legal/political register of democratization in the USA.

[51] In agreement see Valelly (2004: 1–2).

[52] One account claims that a 'deep strain of U.S. political thought portrays international law as an illegitimate attempt by democratically unaccountable foreigners to interfere with the legit mate self-governance of democratic majorities at home' (Goldsmith and Levinson 2009: 1793). At most, it is argued elsewhere, the American courts may employ international law as 'one element of a complex inquiry into constitutional meaning' (Neuman 2004: 90).

[53] However, see important exceptions in *Lawrence v. Texas*, 539 U.S. 558 (2003) and *Roper v. Simmons*, 543 U.S. 551 (2005).

law, triggered by global horror at the experiences of European fascism. Before the USA entered the World War II, notably, the Supreme Court had already shown implicit awareness of authoritarian practices in societies in Central Europe, and it insisted that American public agents should be held to account by rigid normative standards.[54] Later, Eleanor Roosevelt's role in creating the human rights instruments of the UN, in which prevention of racial discrimination was a deep motivation, gave growing salience to human rights norms in American society.[55] Clearly, this was shaped by the fact that World War II had been inextricably linked to race and racism, and, despite their own openly racist policies, the victorious powers were ideologically committed to the stigmatization of racism.[56] Early Supreme Court rulings after World War II cited the UN Charter in cases concerning discriminatory laws within the USA.[57] Some state courts also began to cite directly from the human rights laws of the UN in cases concerning racial discrimination.[58] Moreover, although judges of the Supreme Court rarely based decisions on international norms, it is well documented that, in hearing civil rights cases, they were attentive to concerns in the international legal community, and that they received amicus curiae briefs, which referred to the UN Charter (see Lockwood 1984: 916, 948).[59] In leading anti-discrimination cases, petitioners brought arguments articulating principles informed by the UN Charter, and the Court expanded protection against discrimination on grounds partly borrowed from international law.[60] In the 1950s, Civil Rights groups also saw growing acceptance of

[54] See the analysis of instruments used by 'tyrannical governments' in *Chambers* v. *Florida*, 309 U.S. 227 (1940). Moreover, the experience of authoritarianism in Europe affected academic perceptions of police practice in the USA, and prominent publications drew parallels between law enforcement in the USA and in interwar Germany (see Hall 1953: 140). Famously, during world war 2 Gunnar Myrdal asked the question: 'Is the South Fascist?' (1944: 458). He decided it was not fascist, not because of insufficient racism, but because it 'lacked the centralized organization of a fascist state'.

[55] Representatives of black civil rights organizations were invited observers at the San Francisco Conference, which gave rise to the UN Charter (see Plummer 1996: 132).

[56] On the symbolic connections between American perceptions of the Nazi holocaust and perceptions of victims of racial violence in the USA see Bradley (2016: 70, 87). After 1945, in promoting democracy in Germany, American troops questioned Germans about their perceptions of black people as a means to measuring the persistence of Nazism (Merritt 1995: 95–6, 258). Perhaps, in so doing, some Americans perceived similarities between themselves and their adversaries, and drew conclusions from this.

[57] *Oyama* v. *California* 332 U.S. 633 (1948).

[58] *Perez* v. *Sharp*, 32 Cal.2d 711; *Kenji Namba* v. *McCourt*, (185 Ore. 579, 204 P. 2d. 569).

[59] *Henderson* v. *United States*, 339 U.S. 816 (1950); *Bolling* v. *Sharpe* 347 U.S. 497 (1954).

[60] See *Shelley* v. *Kraemer*, 334 US 1 (1948). This case, one of the most important of all race-related cases, was strongly influenced by the UN human rights instruments.

international human rights law as a factor that provided openings for protest and strategic agitation, and different groups petitioned the UN to bring Jim Crow laws to an end, once on grounds of genocide.[61] International law thus created a platform for legal activism, and this in turn reinforced the effect of international norms.

Importantly, further, broader international political conjunctures also played a role in ensuring that human rights law acquired increased impact in American society. It is often argued that the Cold War militated against the realization of the human rights ideals spelled out after 1945 (see Chesterman 2004: 34; Madsen 2014: 254). Within American society, however, the opposite is in some respects true, and the realities of the Cold War had far-reaching implications for the solidification of democracy (Lockwood 1984: 916; Borstelmann 2009: 3). Notably, media coverage of American politics in ideologically hostile countries after 1945 widely fixed on racial discrimination as a means of discrediting the USA, whose global international capital was strongly linked to democracy promotion. Moreover, the official support of the USA for decolonization in countries previously under the rule of European Empires sat uneasily with clear support for ethnic privileging within the USA itself (see Luard 1982: 58). Successive Presidents were clearly aware of the sensitivity of this fact. For example, Eisenhower expressed alarm that, owing to American apartheid, the USA could, by its enemies, be 'portrayed as a violator of those standards of conduct which the peoples of the world united to proclaim in the Charter of the United Nations' (Spiro 2003: 2016). Later, Kennedy promoted civil rights in domestic law as a means 'to restore America's relative strength as a free nation' and to regain 'leadership in a fast-changing world menaced by communism' (Brauer 1977: 42). In the proceedings in *Shelley v. Kraemer*, tellingly, the opinion was recorded that 'acts of discrimination taking place' in the USA were proving detrimental to 'the conduct of foreign relations' (Lauren 1983: 25). This meant that advocates promoting civil rights in the USA touched on matters that had great relevance for questions of national security and foreign policy, creating distinct opportunities for effective oppositional mobilization (Skrentny 1998: 242). Ultimately, Johnson's civil rights policies were clearly directed towards an international audience, and he appealed to global human rights norms as authority for legislation regarding civil rights (Jensen 2016: 114).

---

[61] See Martin (1997: 36). Yet, for a discussion of typical UN vacillation on such core issues see Anderson (2003: 82).

This bundle of international factors created a strong imperative for the hardening of civil and political rights for black communities, and for the general deepening of national democracy, in the USA. Political developments in the USA in the longer wake of 1945 are not easily explicable outside this international political constellation. One important account has even declared that the entire culture of minority rights which evolved in the USA in the 1960s resulted from national security concerns, linked to the USA's global exposure to criticism in light of the growing system of international human rights, which the American government had been instrumental in designing (Skrentny 2002: 7, 27). During this time, both legislative and judicial decisions increasingly reflected the emerging international consensus on human rights. Surely not by coincidence, the core pieces of legislation establishing democratic citizenship for all Americans, the Civil Rights Act (1964) and the Voting Rights Act (1965), were passed at the same time as the UN Convention on the Elimination of all Forms of Racial Discrimination (1965).[62] As discussed, in fact, this raft of legislation coincided with a growing tendency amongst international lawyers to view apartheid as a breach of *jus cogens*. This package of civil rights legislation also included important measures to liberalize immigration law, the Immigration and Nationality Act (1965), in which the previous race-based quota system was abolished.[63]

In some ways, the process of democratization in the USA after 1945 brought to conclusion a long process of rights-based nation building, societal transformation and legal citizenship construction.

Most evidently, the Civil War had been a war fought both about rights and about national unity, in which different visions of rights had traced out the fault lines between conflicting visions of nationhood and citizenship. Clearly, the causal background of the Civil War had been determined by the ruling in *Dred Scott*, which denied that black federal citizenship could exist, opening up a line of violent contestation connecting questions of rights, citizenship and federalism. The Civil War Amendments and Reconstruction were then implemented as programmes to create a constitutional reality of universal rights-holding citizenship, connecting

---

[62] In agreement, one excellent account explains that the USA opened the UN General Assembly debates in 1965 on the draft for the Convention on the Elimination of all Forms of Racial Discrimination, and the USA's recent domestic legislation on human rights was discussed extensively (Jensen 2016: 117).

[63] On the significance of this law as a 'civil rights triumph' see Chin (1996: 276). On the discriminatory nature of earlier legislation passed in the 1920s, and its implications for black people in the USA, see King (2000: 164, 224).

and binding the states and the union in equal measure (see Kaczorowski 1987a: 210). One observer asserts, quite plausibly, that the 'United States might have had no true constitution until the Fourteenth Amendment was enacted' and that the constitution in its original form, 'built upon multiple, inconsistent foundations', was not really, in its social consequences, 'a constitution at all' (Eisgruber 1995: 73). In addition, the Civil War had implications for the reach of the judicial branch of government. One outcome of the Civil War amendments was that the Supreme Court was consolidated in its position as a guarantor of rights of federal subjects, and, under the Fourteenth Amendment, it was authorized to review the jurisprudence of state courts (Weinberg 1977: 1199). The Supreme Court was thus expected to distribute rights across state boundaries as a cornerstone of national unity and national citizenship. One analysis explains that this period saw the rise of a 'revolutionary legal theory', establishing the 'primacy of national civil rights' (Kaczorowski 2005: 1), and creating a condition in which the 'fundamental rights of citizens were nationalized' (Kaczoroski 1987b: 57). As late as the 1880s, judges on the Supreme Court insisted that the post-bellum civil rights legislation served 'to protect the citizen in the exercise of rights conferred by the Constitution of the United States, and it was essential to the healthy organization of the government itself.[64]

In the wake of the Civil War, however, the rights obtained through the constitutional amendments and subsequent civil rights legislation were not effectively implemented. These laws were partly blocked by state legislatures, partly allowed to fall into neglect by Congress and the President, partly undermined by the weak administrative capacities of the federal government, and partly stripped of substance by the Supreme Court.[65] Rejection of civil rights was at the centre of the backlash against Reconstruction, reflected in growing support for the Democrats across many states (Gillette 1979: 220–6).[66] As discussed, the Supreme Court played a leading role in such retrenchment, ruling in 1883 that constitutional rights did not offer protection from discriminatory acts of private individuals in the states.[67]

---

[64] Ex parte Yarbrough, 110 U.S. 651 (1884).

[65] The Civil Rights and Slaughterhouse cases are usually seen as exemplary of the Supreme Court's change of direction in applying federal rights provisions against the state. One account claims that in the period 1868–1911 the Supreme Court reached 604 rulings involving the Fourteenth Amendment, but upheld basic principles on only six occasions (see McAdam 1982: 71).

[66] Tellingly, Gillette (1979: 379) argues that after the Civil War 'the nation was reunited, but there had been no national settlement'.

[67] Civil Rights Cases, 109 U.S. 3 (1883).

It was only in the 1960s, a period close to a second national Civil War, in which rival visions of American nationhood again confronted each other in rival visions of civil rights, that a national citizenship took shape, providing substance for a fully national democracy.[68] At this time, the war over rights, citizenship, nation building and judicial power that took place in the 1860s re-emerged in a second war over rights, citizenship, nation making and judicial power. However, this war approached an end because of the impact of global norms, and because a national model of the rights-holding citizen was configured around global norms. Parsons himself provided deeply penetrating commentary on this process. Although he failed to notice the international dimension of American nation-building, he clearly observed that the universal circulation of civil rights in American society played a key role in the final consolidation of the USA as a comprehensively nationalized society.[69]

Of course, the completion of American democracy in the 1960s was not exclusively a legal process. At this time, clearly, the legal system did not disconnect itself from other branches of government, and the courts on their own did not have the capacity to transform the structure of democracy.[70] Democratization in the 1960s was evidently marked both by a process of liberalization in the Presidency and by a liberalization in the Supreme Court. Therefore, the rise of judicial activism was a partly political, partly legal process, reflecting a deep tidal change in social

---

[68] One influential account sees the Civil Rights Movement as a 'Second Reconstruction' (Woodward 1957: 240). Given its nation-building implications, I am more inclined to see the Civil Rights Movement as a Second Civil War.

[69] See both Parsons (1970: 15) and the general argument in Parsons (1965). To support this association between civil rights and national societal formation, see Pole (1978: 264, 289, 326).

[70] Different perspectives in the literature on the role of the Supreme Court place varying emphasis on the importance of its role in transforming inter-ethnic relations in the USA. Most enthusiastic is the claim that the Civil Rights struggle was 'sired', 'succored' and 'defended' by the Supreme Court in Williamson (1979: 3). Similarly one author claims that civil rights litigants played a 'pivotal role in the growth of federal court power', helping federal institutions to 'power-grab from state courts' (Francis 2014: 8). A different account, amidst more reserved pronouncements, states that from the 1950s the courts were 'the most accessible and, often, the most effective instruments of government for bringing about the changes in public policy sought by social protest movements' (Neier 1982: 9). On the limits of judicial power in the Civil Rights era see Tushnet (1994: 231). More cautious about the capacity of litigation for effecting wholesale social change is the analysis in Scheingold (1974: 95); Handler (1978: 232–3); McCann (1986: 26); Klarman (1996; 6, 2004: 457–9); Patterson (2001: 118). See also the more trenchantly critical discussion of the political limitations of courts in Rosenberg (1991: 343); Brown-Nagin (2005: 1439, 1489).

value orientations.[71] Moreover, rights-based legal engagement was only one focus of the Civil Rights Movement as a whole. The legal arm of the movement, the National Association for the Advancement of Colored People (NAACP), although initially the pioneering organization, did not always enjoy an uncomplicated relation with other movement actors and organizations.[72] Very clearly, further, the rights cemented in national society were linked to wider changes in political culture. These rights were galvanized by a new cultural background, in which the cross-cultural spread of radio, jazz and rock and roll had already created equal, radically enfranchised communities through racially integrated aesthetic practices (see Ward 2004: 123; Hale 2011: 49). The promotion of civil rights for black people was thus partly driven by the wider emergence of elective counter-culture patterns of contested citizenship, which also extended demands for rights to other disfranchised minorities, such as women and homosexuals. Importantly, in addition, the inner-societal expansion of democracy took place as Americans perceived themselves, nationally, as a militarized community, engaged externally in war in Vietnam. As in other cases, in the USA in the 1960s, national citizenship was fundamentally redesigned and broadened through the experience of war, and the radicalization of different anti-military protest groups traced out new patterns of citizenship in an as yet not fully unified nation.[73]

Overall, the 1960s witnessed a number of multi-layered nation-building processes, marked by distinct patterns of mobilization, cultural inter-cutting and unified citizenship construction, articulated through claims about different sets of rights. Through this, the USA finally evolved into a basically nationalized society, with a broadly inclusive national democratic government. Indicatively, this process was flanked by a massive growth in the administrative capacities of federal government and with a rapid expansion of its fiscal requirements.[74]

Nonetheless, these political processes were clearly underpinned by the rising authority and autonomy of the law, and it is debatable whether they could have been accomplished by conventional political means. On one hand, access to law was vital to the Civil Rights Movement, and its impact was inseparable from mobilization through the courts. Different important

---

[71] See excellent analysis of this point in Zolberg (2006: 302); Balkin (2009: 576, 597)

[72] On these different points see Morris (1984: 14–15, 125).

[73] For reflections on these points see Anderson (1995: 130, 337).

[74] On increases in fiscal increases in the 1960s and the general expansion of the administrative state see Graham (1990: 463).

analyses have noted how the broad construction of civil rights in the courts created new opportunities for social mobilization, building resonance across different sectors (Tarrow 1994: 128), and eventually leading to an increase of state capacity in law enforcement (Pedriana and Stryker 2004: 718, 752).[75] Moreover, this process always possessed an international dimension. It may be exaggerated to see this as a dominant factor in the Civil Rights Movement. Yet, the growing power of international human rights surely formed a core aspect of its societal context. Clearly, moreover, civil rights could not be easily established by sitting legislatures, as these legislatures, especially at state level, had resolutely introduced policies to withhold them. This was the main reason why political agency was displaced into the courts (Tushnet 1994: 99).

Broadly, the growing salience of global human rights after 1945 created a legal-political diction, shared by different branches of American government, which galvanized, promoted and contributed to the efficacy of, socio-political mobilization in the name of equal democratic rights. Such mobilization was not restricted to the judiciary, but the authorship of the diction of transformation was, to a substantial degree, of diffuse inner-legal origin.[76] Indeed, concerns about loss of electoral support in the southern states had repeatedly impeded purely political – that is, presidential or congressional – solutions for the diminished citizenship of some minorities. In consequence, it was only as global citizenship norms infiltrated national society that the national citizen was established. In the USA, uniform national citizenship was not a construction of the national political system, and its realization under purely national constitutional law was only fitful.

Through these dynamics, judicial institutions in the USA began to assume a position in which they were able not only to strengthen their power in relation to other political organs, but effectively to create new constitutional principles. In fact, the authority that the courts extracted from their revitalized construction of civil rights laws meant that they were able both substantially to expand existing rights, and even, in some cases, to generate quite distinct constitutional rights, to be applied across all parts of society. This was clear enough in the desegregation cases of the 1950s, in which the Supreme Court, to all intents and purposes,

---

[75] One account has construed the basic growth of federal power and the rise in legal mobilization as closely correlated processes (Tobias 1989: 277).

[76] Importantly, the NAACP, the torch bearer for the early Civil Rights Movement, specifically identified litigation as a means of franchise extension (Lawson 1976: 22).

established rights of equal treatment not expressly foreseen in the constitution. Indeed, one observer has implied that the desegregation cases formulated a *right not to be humiliated* as a basic point of American law (Ackerman 2014: 154). Later, the Supreme Court opted for a very broad reading of the 1964 Civil Rights Act, which prohibited actions by employers with discriminatory results for minority groups. In this respect, the Court moved beyond the original construction of discrimination as a matter of *intent*.[77] Further, under Warren, the Supreme Court expanded its civil rights jurisprudence to impute new rights to other groups. For example, in *Griswold* v. *Connecticut* the Court discovered 'penumbral rights' hidden in the constitution.[78] This allowed it to widen given rights of privacy to establish rights concerning sexual preference, and ultimately of bodily integrity and reproductive choice, which added substantially new rights to the constitutional fabric of society. Perhaps most notably of all, the expansion of existing rights under the Warren Court culminated, in *Miranda* v. *Arizona*, in an interpretation of the Fifth Amendment that was designed to ensure procedures against self-incrimination.[79] Tellingly, subsequent cases referred to *Miranda* as a ruling with a *de facto* constitutional standing – as a case that created 'a constitutional rule that Congress may not supersede legislatively'.[80]

As a result of these developments, the high judiciary in the USA was extricated from its habitual position in society, in which, at least from Reconstruction to the new deal, it had tended to obstruct the growth of the power of the federal government. Instead, it began to premise its authority on its ability to define, dictate and construct a system of democratic rights, which widened the national political order as a whole, even in regions and questions not traditionally subject to government control. Of course, after the 1960s, the judiciary eventually retreated, to some degree, from its initial pro-rights and pro-government jurisprudence.[81] The limits to judicial autonomy and judicial democratic consolidation in the USA, therefore,

---

[77] *Griggs* v. *Duke Power Co*, 401 US 424 (1971).
[78] *Griswold* v. *Connecticut*, 381 U.S. 479 (1965).
[79] *Miranda* v. *Arizona* 384 U.S. 436 (1966).
[80] *Dickerson* v. *United States* 530 U.S. 428 (2000).
[81] See excellent early analysis in Weinberg (1977: 1203). In fact, fundamental rights doctrine was limited by the Burger Court as early as 1973, in *San Antonio Independent School District* v. *Rodriguez*, 411 U.S. 1 (1973). State rights were defended in *National League of Cities* v. *Usery*, 426 U.S. 833 (1976). For description of the 'assault on prevailing civil rights policies and constitutional doctrine' under the Reagan administration see Neier (1982: 78); Yarbrough (2000: x).

have become quite apparent. Nonetheless, in the decades after 1945, the legal system of the USA as a whole became centred on rights, partly because of its intensified interaction with the emergent global legal system and the acceptance of global constructions of rights-based citizenship (Layton 2000: 8; Skrentny 2002: 7). Both the legal system and the political system of the USA derived a large share of their legitimacy, both publicly and inter-institutionally, from the inner-societal application of civil rights norms, proportioned to an increasingly salient construction of the citizen as a general rights holder. Once centred on the circulation of rights, then, the legal system began to extend and reproduce itself at an elevated level of autonomy. Litigation over civil rights became an almost self-generative basis for American democracy, and the successes of civil rights litigation led to the proliferation of legal activism in other areas.[82] This led to rising rights-based litigation and a consonant expansion of rights consciousness, in which different persons across society increasingly phrased their relations to government in the register of rights.[83] Once centred on rights, in fact, the legal system acquired a high degree of autonomy *vis-à-vis* other departments of the polity, and it absorbed some functions of primary law making (especially in the production of new rights) originally assigned to the political branches.

The USA is not an exception to the general pattern of democratic formation through the interaction of national and global law. In the USA, in fact, the model of the democratic citizen was created and cemented across national society within the law, as the legal system was attached more firmly to the global legal system. An idea of national democratic citizenship was inchoately implied in the original constitutional order of the USA (see Farber 2003: 38). But it required external impetus from the global

---

[82] One account argues that the spread of legal activism in the 1960s and 1970s, carried forward by the Civil Rights Movement, was an 'expression of American exceptionalism', utilizing new techniques to leverage social transformation (Cummings and Trubeck 2008: 8–9).

[83] On the lessons learned from the Civil Rights Movement by other marginal groups, including women, students, farm workers and native Americans, see Morris (1984: 287). See, emblematically, the penetration of constitutional rights into prisons in the district court case *Holt v. Sarver*, 309 F. Supp. 362 (E.D. Ark. 1970). As one analysis has explained, there was a 'causal' link between the spread of rights in race-related cases and the spread of rights in prison-related cases, and both types of case brought a great extension of federal power (Feeley and Rubin 1998: 159, 175). As a proportion of the total number of cases heard by the Supreme Court, civil rights cases increased exponentially between the mid-1960s and the mid-1970s, sinking then up to the mid-1980s, but by the mid-1990s reaching a higher level than the peak in the mid-1970s (see Cichowski and Stone Sweet 2003: 199).

legal system to become real. Global law triggered an intensified interaction between domestic legal agents and domestic constitutional rights, and this led, finally, to the completion of the democracy-building project that had commenced in the late eighteenth century.

4.2.2   Global Human Rights and National Democracy 2: Federal Republic of Germany (FRG)

The connection between the rise of global human rights law, the differentiation of the legal system, and the institutionalization of democratic citizenship is equally, if not more clearly, evident in the new democratic political system formed in the FRG, in the years following 1945. Like the USA, the FRG can be seen as polity, which, from its initial foundation in 1871 within Imperial Germany, was marked by a highly uncertain definition of the basic source of its authority. Historically, the modern German political system extracted its legitimacy from multiple patterns of citizenship, and it was marked by deeply paradoxical, often unsettling processes of national inclusion, national legitimation and inter-normative conflict. Ultimately, the construct of the global citizen played a core role in resolving these conflicts.

First, the governmental system of Imperial Germany was primarily created not through the acts of a popular sovereign, but through the expansion of Prussian authority across other German territories, which were assimilated in the German Empire (*Reich*) with varying degrees of willingness. Moreover, the essential constitutional order of Imperial Germany was written in peremptory fashion. The constitution of the *Reich* was actually, in basic structure, the constitution of the short-lived North German Federation, which had been written by Bismarck, while on vacation in late 1866, and was carried over onto the *Reich* in 1870–1. For this reason, the originating source of the modern German state was hardly located in a generalized process of legitimation or a uniform articulation of national citizenship.

Second, after the creation of the *Reich*, German citizenship was only weakly nationalized, and the political system did not originally penetrate deeply into society. In observing this, to be sure, we should not be drawn into the trap of assuming that Germany was utterly atypical in this respect, or that its features reflected a wider exceptionalism in its formation as state. In fact, it needs to be noted, as a corrective to some analyses, that, in some respects, the national political system of Imperial Germany permitted a greater degree of socio-political integration than was evident in other major European states.[84] At the level of the *Reich*, manhood suffrage was established in 1871. Importantly, this led to an institutionalization – at least intermittent – of class politics, a vital indicator of political-systemic nationalization more generally. The national political system in Imperial Germany did not impede class-based party-political activism, as was the case, for example, in Britain, and it fostered national citizenship practices across class divisions.[85] Although the SPD was legally suppressed from 1878 to 1890, the Imperial political system clearly enabled the active politicization of particular class interests and class antagonisms, and it promoted robust institutionalization of the SPD in the *Reich* (Nipperdey 1961: 90).[86] As one important account has noted, the electorate of late nineteenth-century Germany, at a national level, was fully politicized, and the universal (male) franchise meant that there occurred a 'penetration of conflictual politics into the state and municipalities': i.e. the government's exposure to political contests of national importance, typically reflecting

[84] Despite the claims of influential observers (see pp. 327 below), Imperial Germany was not an authoritarian state. In some respects, strikingly, the political system was constructed in manner that exposed the governmental executive to certain intense political risks, such as the open politicization of class conflict, which were obviated through franchise restrictions in supposedly more 'liberal' countries, such as the UK. Of course, Imperial Germany had some authoritarian features, but this was not distinctive.

[85] One of the most brilliant interpreters of British labour politics has posed himself the question why the German SPD was historically stronger than the British Labour Party. He observes:

> British working-classes had not suffered active persecution, nor seen their Party driven underground, as the Germans had done. This was a political trauma that shaped the personality of the German labour movement. It welded the German working classes together, probably heightened their political consciousness, and certainly made the SPD the focus for emotional loyalties that the British Labour Party had never received. (McKibbin 1974: 246)

McKibbin's views invariably demand great respect. Yet, it seems to me that the German SPD was more powerful than the British Labour Party for the simple reason that, from the foundation of the *Reich* onward, the SPD was not as adversely affected by restrictive electoral laws as the Labour Party, and it was not forced into the soft but debilitating embrace of an existing Liberal Party. I agree with the (intentionally revisionist – but plainly accurate) claim that Bismarck's introduction of manhood suffrage between 1867 and 1871 was 'far more daring' than simultaneous franchise reforms in Britain (Anderson 2000: 5).

[86] On the connection between suffrage expansion and nationalization of political parties see Caramani (1996: 215). Some theorists have contributed to the broad *Sonderweg* debate by arguing that in Germany political parties had a distinctive position, in that they were weakly institutionalized owing to the fact that they were 'built into the institutional framework' of government as an afterthought (Ritter 1976: 114). This may be true. But German political parties were no more weakly institutionalized than in other countries; in fact, parties of the Left were much more robustly institutionalized.

divergent class prerogatives, was not mitigated by franchise restrictions (Suval 1985: 243). Accordingly, by about 1900, the German SPD was by some distance the most powerful party of the European labour movement, and has been very reasonably described as the 'very model of a mass political party' (Sperber 1997: 19). As early as the 1880s, some major cities in Germany were primarily represented by the SPD in the Imperial parliament (*Reichstag*) (Müller 1925: 79–82).

Nonetheless, Imperial Germany possessed a number of features that militated against systemic nationalization and the full consolidation of national citizenship. Significantly, the competences of the *Reichstag* were limited by the fact that the ministerial executive was not directly accountable to elected politicians, and the organizational force of political parties was reduced by the fact that they could not directly assume occupancy of governmental office (see Weber 1921: 351). The *Reichstag* did not create the government, and its power in shaping government policy was always limited. Moreover, the single states within the *Reich* retained their own state institutions, performing many core political functions. As a result, the *Reich* contained multiple political systems, with multiple electoral regimes, and multiple patterns of representation within the different states, sitting alongside the system of representation institutionalized at the level of the *Reich*. Tellingly, Prussia, by far the largest state, retained a distinctive three-class franchise, in which electoral citizenship was determined in accordance with fiscal contribution, a fact that obviated the political mobilization of working-class constituencies within Prussia. Partly as a result of its composite features, further, the statehood of the *Reich* was fragile and ill-determined, and, at the national level, some systemic characteristics of statehood only evolved very gradually. Notably, a national high court was not created until 1879, a uniform code of civil law was not implemented until 1900, and, vitally, the fiscal system was not fully nationalized until after the collapse of the *Reich*.[87]

In addition, importantly, the basic legal question of citizenship in Germany was historically deeply vexed. The nationalization of citizenship in the *Reich* naturally only took shape after 1870/1. The 1871 Constitution provided a brief definition of legal entitlements ascribed to all Germans, and it established the primacy of Imperial law over regional law in some aspects of citizenship. This was expressed in Article 3 of the constitution, which allowed freedom of movement, employment and acquisition of property across lines between different states. Owing to the complex

---

[87] See expert analysis in Witt (1970).

population of the Empire, however, it was difficult to produce a categorical definition of the preconditions for German citizenship, and to establish in neat categories to whom rights of citizenship should be accorded. In fact, concepts of rights generally had limited importance in the 1871 Constitution, which did not contain a separate catalogue of rights. Legislation was passed in 1913 to give further clarity to the definition of national citizenship. This law has been famously described as an expression of a highly exclusionary, even militarized, model of citizenship, as it linked rights of citizenship to familial membership and military service.[88] However, this law did not distinctively sanction ethnically constructed ideas of citizenship.[89] Indeed, it permitted the naturalization of non-German children, and it clearly combined ethnic and residential criteria to determine citizenship claims. Placed in the broader context of German history, it appears more as a document that testifies to the technical difficulties in defining German citizenship, after the exclusion of Austria from, and the absorption of the smaller German states and former immediate territories of the Holy Roman Empire into, the German nation state.

Eventually, the construction of political citizenship in Germany was further complicated by the fact that the Weimar Republic, founded in 1918–19, was deeply marked by the conviction that Imperial Germany had not been fully consolidated as a nation state. The founders of the Weimar Republic sought to devise quite new models of citizenship, which were strong enough to cement a conclusively nationalized socio-political order in German society. Accordingly, the Weimar Republic was based on the conviction that national (still called *Imperial*) laws had primacy over regional laws. Indeed, in the constitution of 1919, and it was expressly stated that the highest executive functions of the government related immediately to citizens in the single states, and such citizens always owed higher obligation to Imperial laws than to regional laws.[90] Moreover, the 1919 Constitution was designed to restrict the power of Prussia within the Reich, and to ensure that regional counterweights to national government were removed.[91] This nationalizing strategy behind the 1919 Constitution

---

[88] See the famous expression of this view in Brubaker (1992).

[89] I agree with Jan Palmowski's claim that the 1913 law did not reflect a distinctively 'ethno-cultural concept of belonging' (2008: 560).

[90] Notably, Article 48 of the Constitution stated that the categorical and binding source of law, which becomes visible in states of political emergency, is located in the *Reich*. In extreme situations, thus, the citizen of the *Reich* could claim higher normative status than the citizen of the separate states.

[91] Leading architects of the Weimar Constitution despised Prussia, which they saw as responsible for obstructing, for 70 years, the formation both of a German democracy and of a

was flanked by a distinctive conception of the constitutional role to be ascribed to basic rights. The catalogue of rights in the constitution, which included early provisions for socio-economic rights, was initially conceived as a type of national catechism,[92] to bind together different social groups and educate them in the exercise of citizenship (Spael 1985: 198–9). In this respect, the constitution of the Weimar Republic added very distinctive dimensions to standard models of citizenship, and it was shaped by the assumption that laws require authorization by citizens both as political agents and as material agents: it was based on a construct of the citizen as a participant in both the political and the economic dimensions of the national political order. At this time, in consequence, governmental legitimacy was expressly attached to a post-traditional concept of the citizen, founded in the idea that the simultaneous exercise of political and social rights by the citizen could create a fully nationalized, class-transcendent bedrock of legitimacy for the political system.[93]

Ultimately, German citizenship was redefined after 1933, on premises that were simultaneously radically inclusive and radically exclusive. By 1935, an ethnic, expressly racialized model of citizenship was promoted, which incorporated all ethnic Germans. This was flanked by a wider tendency amongst legal ideologues of the National Socialists to replace classical legal concepts of citizenship with a passive construction of legal entitlement, based not on formal rights, but on objective national-historical membership.[94] However, the ethnicization of citizenship under Adolf Hitler actually led to a fragmentation of citizenship, in which, as in premodern societies, different social and ethnic groups acquired calibrated rights of inclusion. As discussed, the political system in the 1930s underwent a deep regionalization, in which, beneath the loud proclamations

---

German national state (Preuß 1897: 96, 105). Hugo Preuß argued that the 'basic idea in the Weimar Constitution' was to enable the 'self-determination of the unified German people', and, thus, to eradicate all 'rights of Prussian hegemony' (1926: 435, 437).

[92] The main author of the basic rights section in the constitution, Friedrich Naumann, tried to translate constitutional rights into a popular vernacular to make them intelligible to all members of society (1919: 156–7).

[93] The Weimar Republic was rooted in the social constitutionalism of Hugo Preuß, whose theory was based on the claim that the state should be seen as 'an organic totality of constituent persons' (1902: 115–16). Later, Preuß saw his organic model of the state realized in the associational structure of the Weimar Republic, which he viewed as 'state formation through comradeship' (1926: 489).

[94] The principle of citizenship was replaced in the 1930s by the principle of national comradeship (*Volksgenossenschaft*) as the source of legal entitlement and obligation (Larenz 1935: 21).

of national unity, local power again became very important.[95] Moreover, the 1930s saw an expulsion of the unifying material elements from the concept of citizenship which had evolved in the Weimar era. This process of national fragmentation was perpetuated under the post-1945 military occupation, as citizenship in occupied Germany, as far it was legally defined, dissolved into a patchwork of externally controlled administrative zones (Gosewinkel 2001: 421).

Overall, the accelerated emergence of German national statehood from 1870 to the 1930s reflected a sequence of rapidly shifting, often conflicting constructions of the citizen, or, indeed, the national people, as the source and focus of law. These shifts were determined, at core, by the fact that Germany was not fully formed as a nation state, and basic integrative features of statehood were not formally solidified. Since 1945, it has become commonplace for even the most educated Germans to observe pre-1945 or even pre-1990 German history as overshadowed by a deep propensity for authoritarianism, and low political engagement (Winkler 1978: 83). Indeed, this seems to be part of the legitimational myth of contemporary Germany, in the same way that (for no obvious reason) British citizens have constructed a legitimational myth of their country as defined by long-standing commitment to democracy.[96] In the period 1930/1933–45, to be sure, Germany's political trajectory deviated dramatically from that of many other states. This deviation is manifest not in the authoritarianism that developed at this time, which marked an extreme point on a quite general spectrum, but in the genocidal nature of the government that developed under Hitler. Otherwise, however, Germany is defined by the same process of incomplete democratization as other societies, and the absence of a solid tradition of political citizenship is not distinctive. Most crucially, the similarity between Germany and other states is evident in the fact that democracy was only secured, at least in the FRG, after 1945, and it was secured on a pattern that confirms the general principle that national citizenship and national political-systemic formation were only stabilized

---

[95] See pp. 149–50 above.

[96] See Eley (1995: 90); Anderson (2000: 6–8). To illustrate this, see the (to my mind utterly unsubstantiated) claim in one of the most famous books on the sociology of democratic behaviour: '[W]hereas the development of political democracy in Britain has had a long history and has added a significant degree of citizen competence to subject competence, political democracy has had a far less orderly and successful development in Germany. While in the nineteenth century the British middle class, followed by the working class, was demanding and receiving political influence over the government, the German middle class accepted the law and order of the German Rechtsstaat, under which it might prosper but have no political influence' (Almond and Verba 1989 [1963]: 182–3).

on the basis of global norms. As in other settings, the institutional design of the democracy created in the FRG after 1945 was defined by a strategic centration of the legal/political system around human rights law, partly of international provenance, by the rapidly growing autonomy of the legal system, and by the supplanting of inner-national legal norms by international legal principles. This played key role in articulating a foundation for the law, and in constructing a model of the citizen around which the political system could finally be stabilized.

First, of course, the institutional arrangements supporting the FRG were partly imposed by occupying military forces, who provided instructions regarding the content of the new constitution of 1949 (*Grundgesetz*). In fact, in overseeing the writing of the *Grundgesetz*, the Allies supressed some elements of public law based on more traditional German constitutional models.[97] As a result, the *Grundgesetz* did not initially enjoy broad-based recognition. It was not created by primary acts of citizenship, and, like the constitution of 1871, it was conceived in perfunctory fashion, as a solution to immediate administrative problems. In fact, it was widely viewed as an imposed, provisional document, lacking organic foundations in society and structural linkage with the national people, and it was only very gradually that it came to be perceived as a permanent normative substructure for the FRG.[98]

Second, constitutional experts in the Parliamentary Council, which drafted the *Grundgesetz* in 1948–9, declared that the new constitution would contain robust guarantees for basic rights, as required by the allied powers. Indeed, it was expected that international human rights law would assume vital importance in the constitutional order of the new German democracy. In particular, constitutionalists attached to the SPD, especially Carlo Schmid and Ludwig Bergsträsser, argued that human rights should be constitutionally entrenched at a higher level than dictated by the occupying forces. The argument in favour of basic rights in the Parliamentary Council was very strongly founded in international law, and draft human rights provisions for the *Grundgesetz* were modelled, in part, on human

---

[97] Between 1945 and 1949, the trade unions in some areas occupied by the Western Allies had pressed for a reconsolidation of concepts of economic democracy promoted in the 1920s, but this had been suppressed by the Allies (see Schmidt 1975: 61–623, 221). The Allies also refused to give effect to some constitutional provisions in the *Länder* constitutions because of their collectivist emphasis (see Rütten 1996: 156).

[98] It was argued by Carlo Schmid in the Parliamentary Council that the *Grundgesetz* would immediately lose validity once a constitution had been approved by a 'freely elected, autonomous national assembly, representing the entire German people' (Feldkamp 1998: 99).

rights norms endorsed by the UN.[99] Very importantly, Schmid stated that the *Grundgesetz* should provide for immediate domestic application of international human rights. He declared that it was vital 'to move away from the previous doctrine of international law, in which international law only addresses states, and not single individuals'. He emphatically rejected the idea of a dualistic constitutional order in which 'the individual person is only bound by provisions of international law, and only obtains rights from them, when norms of international law are transformed into domestic law by national legislators'. Consequently, he demanded, in 1948, that the FRG should be the first country in which international law directly conditions 'domestic legal life' and 'addresses the individual German immediately, imposing rights and obligations' (1949: 65). Very importantly, Schmid's emphasis on international law as a foundation for the state was not solely shaped by humanitarian ideals. It also had its origins in German theories of international law after 1918, which viewed the imputation of high authority to international law as a means of strengthening the German national state.[100] Ultimately, partly because of Schmid's interventions, the *Grundgesetz* had the distinctive feature that it prescribed openness to general international law as an overriding feature of constitutional law (Article 25).

Once constructed, the democratic system in the FRG developed a normative structure, in which, to a greater extent even than in the USA, legal institutions were able to act autonomously in relation to other political institutions. Indeed, owing to American influence, the founders of the *Grundgesetz* were committed to establishing a Constitutional Court, standing separately from the regular judiciary (Laufer 1968: 40). A primary function of this court was to assess the validity of legislation, on referral either from lower courts or from members of the legislature, and to ensure that laws had been passed in procedurally appropriate fashion, and that, substantively, they reflected the provisions for basic human rights contained within the constitution. Progressively, the Constitutional Court was able to consolidate its competence within a governance system in unforeseen manner, and it was able to acquire expansive authority through its position as interpreter and guarantor of basic rights.

In the early years of its operation, the Constitutional Court, which heard its first case in 1951, gradually widened its powers in relation to other

---

[99] For references in the Parliamentary Council to the UN Declaration and to English, American and French legal traditions see Pikart and Werner (1993: 9–10, 11–12).
[100] See the illuminating discussion in Weber (1996: 62).

branches of government.[101] To be sure, such innovations were initially rather tentative. Nonetheless, in one of the first rulings after 1951, the court emphasized that it had authority to define the constitutional parameters for all organs of government.[102] By the later 1950s, leading judges on the Court defined it unreservedly as the 'guardian of the Constitution', with supreme entitlement to interpret the Constitution, and possessing a constitutional status not inferior to other organs of state, including the parliamentary legislature (*Bundestag*) and the President (Leibholz 1957: 11–12).[103] By the late 1950s, the authority of the Constitutional Court was partly reflected in its willingness to strike down legislation. It was partly reflected in its involvement in politically sensitive cases.[104] It was partly reflected in its assertion of primacy over other courts, insisting *inter alia* that constitutional norms, especially basic rights, should be applied in the sphere of private law.[105] Importantly, its authority was also reflected in the fact that the Court elaborated a theory of balancing or proportionality, which implied a high weighting for protective rights. In developing this doctrine, the Court projected a constitutional order in which both legislature and judiciary were obliged actively to promote and dictate rights across society, so that state actions were pre-defined by protective constitutional rights.[106] Eventually, by the 1970s, the Court was able to declare that it possessed a distinctive interpretive power, allowing it to establish meanings for law that exceeded the manifest intentions of the authors of the Constitution.[107] In each respect, the Constitutional Court used the basic rights provisions in the Constitution to cement its independent position within the architecture of the state, producing norms for all legislation. One leading commentary has observed how this enforcement of fundamental rights altered the form of the state itself, such that the Court's responsibility for the 'concretization of fundamental rights' meant that it increasingly functioned as a 'political organ' of state, revising classical

---

[101] Chancellor Adenauer himself expressed alarm and surprise at the growing power of the Constitutional Court (see Vorländer 2006: 9).

[102] BVerfG 1, 208 (1952) – 7, 5% Sperrklausel.

[103] This idea was in fact already established in the founding conception of the Constitutional Court.

[104] See Elfes-Urteil (BVerfGE 6, 32).

[105] BVerfGE 7, 198 – Lüth.

[106] BVerfGE 7, 198 – Lüth. For expert analysis of the implications of this, see Ladeur (2004: 10).

[107] The Court thus declared: 'The law can in fact be smarter than the fathers of the law': BVerfGE 36, 342 – Niedersächsisches Landesbesoldungsgesetz.

provisions for the separation of powers in favour of a 'jurisdictional state' (Böckenförde 1990: 25, 29).

The expansive power of the Constitutional Court in the early FRG was closely linked to the importance of international law. In some respects, to be clear, the eventual standing of international law within the legal system of the FRG remained controversial and ambiguous. Some Articles of the *Grundgesetz*, in particular Article 25, implied that the FRG possessed a monist legal system. Ultimately, however, the interaction between the Constitutional Court and the system of international law did not establish monism as a leading principle in domestic jurisprudence. Some earlier rulings of the Constitutional Court subscribed to lines of reasoning close to classical dualist analysis.[108] Progressively, then, the Constitutional Court developed a line of jurisprudence that accorded high significance to international treaties and acknowledged principles of *jus cogens*, especially in relation to ordinary domestic laws, yet which insisted on the sovereignty of the constitution as the final point of legal attribution.[109] Through this process, the constitution evolved on a hybrid dualist–monist model. International law did not acquire direct supreme authority in

[108] In BVerfGE 6, 290 – Washingtoner Abkommen (1957) it was decided that, because treaties generate rights and duties in domestic law, they are subject to control by the Constitutional Court, and do not have direct effect. On this basis, the Court subscribed to the essential dualistic principle that treaties can be binding between states without having binding effect in domestic law, implying that domestic law and international law have different normative foundations and sources of validity. In a further early ruling, BVerfGE 6, 309 – Reichskonkordat, the Court declared that general rules of international law can have effect in domestic law without any statutory act of transformation, but they remain inferior to provisions of the constitution. For dualist interpretations of the Constitutional Court's jurisprudence see Amrhein-Hofmann (2003: 264); Ohler (2015: 40–1). For more balanced general comment see Schorkopf (2010).

[109] On one hand, in examining the status of international treaties and international human rights law in domestic law, the Court argued that treaties have 'constitutional significance'. This was based on the 'fact that the *Grundgesetz* is friendly towards international law', stipulating that 'the exercise of national sovereignty' should be conducted 'through the international law of treaties and international cooperation' and that conflicts between domestic law and international law should be avoided. However, the Court also argued that the 'opening for international-legal obligations' envisaged by the *Grundgesetz* was not unlimited and that it was 'based in the classical conception' that national law and international law pertain 'to separate legal domains', such that international law cannot claim 'the rank of constitutional law'. On this basis, the principle was set out that the *Grundgesetz* aims to promote the 'integration of Germany in the legal community of free states', but that this does not entail renunciation of the 'sovereignty residing in the German constitution': BVerfGE 111, 307 (2004). On these controversies see Partsch (1964: 41). On the position of global *jus cogens* as part of German public law see Kadelbach (1992: 341).

domestic law. However, the Constitutional Court developed patterns of reasoning designed to integrate international law through its own jurisprudence, and to ensure that international human rights law was given clear domestic recognition.[110] Openness to international law thus formed a key regulatory principle, guiding interpretation of domestic constitutional law.[111] Over a longer period, in fact, the Constitutional Court began to make more expansive declarations about the standing of international law. It arrived at the principle that, although the legal system was essentially dualist, the obligation to 'friendliness to international law' expressed in the *Grundgesetz* promoted 'the integration of general rules of international law'. Consequently, acts of constitutional interpretation should be conducted so as to avoid 'conflict with obligations under international law'.[112] Most significantly, however, basic rights initially defined at an international level were given such strong protection in domestic law that the Constitutional Court of the FRG did not need to develop a formally monist legal system in order to constitutionalize the hard normative core of the international human rights order. Central to the constitutional model of the FRG was the principle articulated by Schmid in the Parliamentary Council – namely, that the Constitution of the FRG should give higher protection to internationally defined basic rights than other states. In many respects, the protection of domestic human rights provisions by the Constitutional Court served to give effect to norms originating in international law.

The position of the Constitutional Court had a series of basic outcomes for the legal and social order of the FRG. First, as in the USA, the Court utilized human rights jurisprudence to establish a unified legal order across different parts of society, thus contributing to the normative nationalization of society as a whole. Notably, some early rulings of the Court had implications for sub-national government bodies, and they hardened the connections between the federal government and the *Länder*.[113] Second, the Court utilized human rights jurisprudence to create a basic order of citizenship for the FRG as a whole. As mentioned, in the early years of the FRG, the *Grundgesetz* was widely perceived as a provisional document, whose mobilizing force was limited.[114] However, the Court extracted a

---

[110] BVerfGE 75, 1.
[111] See BVerfGE 74, 358. See for comment Proelß (2014: 43, 51).
[112] BVerfGE 111, 307.
[113] BVerfGE 1, 208 – 7.5%Sperrklausel (1952).
[114] In opinion polls in the years after 1949 public identification with the democratic political system was low (Merritt 1995: 330).

rights-based legal order from the *Grundgesetz*, which gradually assumed pervasive force as a grammar of social motivation.[115]

Alongside these facts, as in the USA, the early human rights jurisprudence of the Constitutional Court of the FRG was marked by a tendency not only to consolidate existing rights, but to derive new normative principles from such rights. Indeed, the Court soon began to generate new rights, or new ways of applying rights, from provisions established in domestic law and international law. In the first instance, the Court began to express the presumption that the scope of the rights defined in the constitution should be widened beyond their classical restrictive application to vertical interactions between citizen and the state. On this basis, taking the protection of human dignity as a guiding value principle, the Court insisted that all relations in society, including relations traditionally covered by contract, should be bound by objective constitutional values based on human rights, and subject to the jurisdiction of the Court itself. In declaring this principle, the Court extended the purchase of fundamental constitutional rights to cover all areas of society, including lateral relations between private parties, determining that all human interactions should be regulated by legal norms defined as *essential for democracy*.[116] Indeed, the Court decided that basic rights were endowed with the power to radiate, normatively, through all social domains. This radiating effect of rights was promoted by an extensive use of proportionality reasoning, which was also applied to the sphere of private law (Jestaedt 1999: 53; Petersen 2015: 146). Increasingly, this expansive reading of constitutional rights created a foundation on which the Constitutional Court could elaborate further the substantive content of existing constitutional rights.[117] Notably, the court extracted from classical guarantees regarding personal inviolability a body of norms to protect private life and use of private information.[118] Ultimately, these rights were expanded to include rights

---

[115] By the 1980s, the Constitutional Court was amongst the most trusted institutions in the FRG. See Vorländer and Brodocz (2006).

[116] This notion was articulated in *Lüth* (1958) (1 BvR 400/51, BVerfGE 7, 198 – Lüth). See later expansion of this principle (in 1978) in BVerfGE 49, 89 (Kalkar I), stating that fundamental rights are 'objective-legal value decisions', which inform all areas of law and guide functions of government, including legislation, administration and justice. This principle was reinforced in Mülheim-Kärlich-Beschluss (BVerfGE 53, 30) where it was stated that the state had a positive obligation to protect individual persons from violations of their rights caused by third parties.

[117] On the Lüth ruling as an opening for the creation of other subsidiary rights, see Hornung (2015: 183).

[118] BVerfGE 35, 202 Lebach.

to confidentiality[119] and rights to data protection in electronic media.[120] In these rulings, the Court created a range of rights to protect the integrity of persons in the private sphere. Eventually, the Constitutional Court also recognized a right to basic levels of social welfare, which was also based on rights of personal dignity.[121]

In these respects, the Constitutional Court of the FRG imprinted a characteristic form both on the governance system, and on interactions between government and society, which was deeply configured by, and mediated through, human rights norms (Isensee 1976: 232; Aulehner 2011: 131). Progressively, the Court established a condition close to *total rights-based democracy* in the FRG, of which it itself acted as primary guarantor. Judicial actions projected a constitutionally defining model of the citizen, in relation to which the basic normative order of society was constructed. Indeed, by implication, the courts distilled a model of the *total citizen*, which dictated that all laws, in all social domains, obtained legitimacy to the degree that they were proportioned to a notion of the legal subject as a holder of basic rights. In each respect, the high judiciary of the FRG clearly obtained a position of pervasively influential autonomy, both in the political system and in society more widely. Indeed, in key respects, the courts of the FRG began to operate as bodies that were formally distinct from the rest of the political system, and which distributed constitutional norms through society on relatively autonomous, internally constructed principles, producing authoritative higher-order norms without reference to external acts or criteria. Through this process, society as a whole became more cohesively integrated into one normative order, and so more deeply nationalized.

Notable in the FRG is the fact that, as they consolidated the form of national democracy, judicial institutions were progressively integrated into a complex supranational legal system. In fact, the promotion of democracy was underpinned by a deep articulation between national and transnational judicial bodies. On one hand, the principle of openness to international law dictated by the *Grundgesetz* meant that, from the outset, the courts were expected to be receptive to rulings of UN bodies, in particular to those of the ICJ. Indeed, despite upholding a basic dualist stance, the Constitutional Court eventually concluded that it was a constitutional duty of the German courts to show regard for rulings of international

---

[119] BVerfGE 90, 255.
[120] BVerfG, 27.02.2008 – 1 BvR 370/07.
[121] See BVerfGE 125, 175 – Hartz IV.

courts with responsibility for Germany.[122] Increasingly, further, this meant that the courts of the FRG were required to construct a stable relation with the ECtHR, whose rulings acquired great normative significance, albeit not without restriction, for the German legal system.[123] More problematically, however, this meant that the FRG entered a distinctive relation with the judicial apparatus of the EU, in particular the ECJ, to which the government of the FRG was constitutionally connected by the *Grundgesetz* (revised Article 23).

In these linkages, gradually, the German courts began *de facto* to endorse a more general doctrine of *open statehood*. That is, the German governance system was progressively conceived, in distinctive post-classical fashion, as an aggregate of institutions within a wide supranational normative order, in which national and international institutions could interact freely, and in which some classical functions of national norm production could be transferred to external judicial institutions. Of course, a post-classical pattern of statehood first began to emerge in the FRG because, after 1949, the government did not possess full sovereignty, and, owing to its partition, uncertainties persisted as to its territorial limits. Notably, theorists of the early FRG, whose conception of the state was formed in the Weimar Republic, denied critically that the government of the FRG could even be perceived as a state. In 1963, for example, Carl Schmitt claimed pointedly, with a view to the FRG, that 'the age of statehood is approaching its end' (1963: 10). In 1971, Ernst Forsthoff observed that West Germany no longer possessed a state 'in the traditional sense of the word' (1971: 158). Progressively, however, the post-traditional form of the state was deliberately and positively fashioned to produce a theory of transnational inter-judicial or inter-institutional relations, in which national and international elements overlapped (see Häberle 1995: 306). In many respects, in fact, the German governance system only acquired features of national statehood, reflected in deep societal penetration, as it was modelled as an open state. Open statehood became a positive mode of state construction, which actively reinforced national institutions and consolidated national patterns of citizenship.

This process of open state formation had particular importance for the relation between the West German courts and the ECJ, whose rulings, by the early 1970s, were perceived as increasingly intrusive and as imposing unfounded limits on the autonomy of national institutions in the FRG.

---

[122]   BVerfGE 08 July 2010 – 2 BvR 2485/07; 2 BvR 2513/07; 2 BvR 2548/07.
[123]   BVerfGE 111, 307 (2004).

To determine its relation with the ECJ, notably, the Constitutional Court of the FRG spelled out a doctrine of transnational human rights observance. In particular, it declared that it would only endorse and accept compliance with the rulings of courts outside the domestic order *as long as* it was convinced that such courts were sufficiently protective of human rights norms to satisfy domestic standards and thresholds.[124] One immediate consequence of this was that the high judiciary of the FRG made its own authority insolubly contingent on the domestic protection of human rights law, and it defined application of human rights as the immovable foundation of the basic democratic order of the FRG. In projecting a robust grammar of constitutional rights for domestic society, then, the Constitutional Court also turned this grammar outwards, to establish its position in relation to international bodies. National sovereignty was expressly defined through the construction of basic rights, and the court assumed the power to protect the democratic will of West German citizens as *a right to protect rights*: national citizenship in the FRG became inseparable from the exercise of basic rights. As mentioned, this approach can easily be seen as a logical corollary of Carlo Schmid's observations in the Parliamentary Council, demanding that the government of the FRG should establish higher standards of human rights protection than those declared in other legal orders. A longer-term consequence of this was that the Constitutional Court of the FRG, acting in tandem with other national courts, began to promote a constitutional grammar of basic rights for the EU as a whole. In fact, the argument in the Constitutional Court of the FRG that its authority in relation to other courts was founded in its high protection of human rights meant that the ECJ began to support its own rulings with human rights norms, in order to gain acceptance for its rulings in the FRG.[125] As a result, both within and above the member states, the EU itself was defined, gradually, as a community of rights holders. In consequence of this, in fact, the ECHR ultimately became a foundation for public order in the EU, and it was increasingly used as a normative standard to justify decisions of the ECJ. In turn, this eventually meant that the Constitutional Court of the FRG became more willing to accept the jurisprudence of the ECJ, as long as it showed due regard for human rights norms.[126]

---

[124] BVerfGE 37, 271 2 Solange I.
[125] ECJ, *J Nold, Kohlen- und Baustoffgroßhandlung* v. *Commission of the European Communities* (Case 4/73) [1974] ECR 491.
[126] BVerfGE 73, 339 2 Solange II.

The construction of open statehood by the German Constitutional Court was not a linear process, and the Court at times linked its recognition of transnational human rights law to a more traditional defence of national sovereignty.[127] In key judgements, it made the extension of the authority of EU law contingent on the consent of the sovereign organs of national democracies.[128] At times, it advocated qualified enforcement of the ECHR.[129] Over a longer period of time, however, the strict human-rights orientation of the German Constitutional Court had the result that it projected a distinctive legal-democratic design for the German state. In this model, national and transnational institutions were ordered on a pattern of deferential (comity-based) human rights observance, with each institution occupying a distinct position within a human rights landscape and assuming competences, within clear normative constraints, for a particular set of functions.[130] In this model, moreover, legislation was enacted quite freely by actors at different points in a transnational legal order, on the precondition that such legislation was supported by adequate observance of human rights (see Calliess 2016:163). In this model, additionally, observance of human rights was necessarily exported to other actors in the transnational system, whose need for normative recognition in Germany heightened the protection that they gave to basic rights. The German state, centred on the Constitutional Court, thus locked itself into, and in turn, helped to consolidate, a transnational system of human rights. In this regard, territorial boundaries lost some importance as a basis of citizenship, and German citizens were envisioned as actors that are categorically bound by human rights, irrespective of physical location. Ultimately, the founding norms of domestic law were projected as obligatory for all

---

[127] In enumerating the types of review to which the Constitutional Court subjects EU law, see the analysis in Tuori, who explains that 'in fundamental rights review the Court appraises an EU measure in the light of national fundamental rights law' (2015: 90).

[128] See BVerfGE 123, 267 – Lissabon.

[129] See for example BVerfGE 111, 307

[130] As Tuori explains:

> With reference to the principle of conferral, the Court argued that the EU can only exercise such powers as Member States, in accordance with their national constitution, have transferred to it through the Treaties ... The Member States remain Masters of the Treaties and possess ultimate jurisdiction over EU institutions acting within the confines of their transferred competences. The Court reiterated its readiness to exert ultra vires review when needed with regard to acts adopted by EU institutions. However, it also emphasized the ultima ratio nature of this review and announced that it will not be applied as long as – so lange – the EU's internal monitoring is able to prevent or correct excesses of competence (2015: 93).

German citizens, even when acting outside Germany's regular jurisdictional boundaries.[131] To be a German citizen meant, in effect, to be a bearer of transnational rights-based citizenship duties.

In sum, a model of democracy evolved in Germany in which domestic courts, acting either in consort or comity with inter- or supranational courts and norm providers, supplied the basic normative architecture for democratic governance (Voßkuhle 2010). This instilled a comprehensive model of the citizen into the structure of national society. Indeed, the architecture of domestic democracy was underpinned by the principle that the domestic political system as a whole possessed a fluid normative foundation, partly located within and partly located outside the limits of a determinately national legal domain. The classical distinction between national and international law partly disappeared in Germany, and German political institutions eventually came to position themselves within a wider transnational constitutional system. This system as a whole was stitched together through human rights law, and human rights law, originating in international law but constructively produced and controlled by the Constitutional Court, formed an ultimate foundation for all norms, whether national or transnational, creating binding obligations for all Germans and all German institutions. In each respect, German democracy was shaped by the fact that the legal order constructed itself at a high degree of autonomy. Interactions between different legal institutions, supported by the authority ascribed to human rights law, were fundamental to the production and authorization of democratic law, and of democracy more widely. Indeed, the transformative deepening of German democracy can be observed as a process of accelerated legal differentiation, beginning slowly in the 1950s, and gathering pace towards the end of the twentieth century. This process was not originally supported by a strong concept of citizenship; as discussed, the 1949 Constitution was externally imposed. In this process, however, the national legal system began autonomously to generate new inner-legal patterns of sovereign citizenship and national inclusion, partly founded in international norms, which eventually radiated outwards to configure transnational law and transnational citizenship. National citizenship in fact always co-implied transnational citizenship.

---

[131] See Verwaltungsgericht Köln, 3 K 5625/14 (27 May 2015). Arguably, this could also be applied to exchanges in the private-legal domain, which could be captured by the transnational extension of the horizontal effect of basic rights (see Ladeur and Viellechner 2008: 71).

4.2.3   Global Human Rights and National Democracy 3: United Kingdom

A very different, but still analogous, set of processes can be observed in the development of public law and political democracy in the UK. In this setting, the increasing autonomy of the global legal system, linked in part to the growth of human rights law, also contributed substantially to the elaboration of the basic order of democracy.

As in the case of the USA, the association of British democracy with the differentiation of global law may easily sound counterintuitive. Like the USA, the UK had a long tradition of at least partial democratic institutionalization before 1945. Some observers have even been prepared to see the UK as an old democracy, which 'made the transition to democracy' before 1900 (Huntington 1991: 17). Moreover, in the UK, the judicial application of international law is subject to substantial restrictions, and it was traditionally argued that international treaties could not create domestic rights unless enforced by an Act of Parliament.[132] Owing to the traditional sovereignty of the Westminster parliament, international law cannot typically gain direct entry into the domestic legal system. In addition, the constitutional doctrine of parliamentary sovereignty, stating that parliament can change all laws and is not bound by entrenched laws from previous parliaments, means that the power of the judiciary is historically weak (see Wade 1955: 174).[133] Indeed, the public-law functions of judicial institutions are not founded in a distinct system of norms, standing separate from parliament itself. As a result, formally entrenched constitutional rights do not easily fit into the constitutional order.

Despite these qualifications, however, the democratic form of the governance system in the UK has been deeply marked by the global process of legal-systemic differentiation. In this respect, the development of democracy in the UK closely reflects recent patterns of institution building in other countries. Arguably, in fact, the constitutional impact of international law in the UK has been greater than in societies whose constitutions are more programmatically open to interaction with external norm setters.

To explain this, it is vital to note – first – that the assumption that the UK is an old democracy is very questionable. In fact, it is simply not accurate. The account of the UK as an old democracy appears to have been caused by

---

[132] See the classical statement of this in *R v. Chief Immigration Officer, Heathrow Airport and another, ex parte Salamat Bibi* – [1976] 3 All ER 843.

[133] See also note 166 below.

the fact that the British polity had evolved some representative features by the nineteenth century, and by the later nineteenth century it had intensified the democratic element of electoral representation in its constitution. However, the fact that the UK had a number of democratic characteristics by the late nineteenth century does not mean that it was a democracy. In some respects, in fact, the relatively early elaboration of proto-democratic institutions in the British polity ultimately obstructed its conclusive formation as a democratic governance system. Until the middle of the twentieth century, the political system of the UK did not satisfy basic criteria for classification as a democracy.

In the UK, distinctively, democracy developed through a long process of democratic transition, in which the principle of full and equal political inclusion was introduced gradually into the political system, often in *ad hoc*, uncommitted fashion. This transition lasted from the Reform Act of 1832, the first step in a long line of franchise extensions, to the general elections of 1950, when a fully democratic, and evenly inclusive, electoral system was finally established.

To be sure, the first step in this process was modest. The Reform Act of 1832 did not create a system that we would now even begin to recognize as democratic. Indeed, it was not intended to incorporate new social actors in the system of representation, and it may even have reduced political participation for members of the working class (Gash 1977: 12). However, the Reform Act marked the beginning of a process, in which pre- or anti-democratic features were slowly eradicated from the political system, and, very gradually, the single person, in the form of a citizen, became the primary focus of political representation and legitimation.[134] After this early beginning, then, it was not until 1918 that the UK was substantially democratized. Before 1911, parliamentary legislation could be rejected by an unelected second chamber of parliament, comprising persons of inherited wealth and standing. This fact alone indicates that at this point the British political system could not be seen as democratic. Up to 1918, members of the elected chamber (House of Commons) of the UK parliament were placed in office, as mentioned above, by a franchise comprising about 30 per cent of the adult population (roughly 60 per cent of men, and no women), access to which was largely dictated by occupancy

---

[134] One account argues that the Great Reform Act of 1832 first articulated the principle – although surely not one reflected in practice – that 'the individual citizen' is the 'unit to be represented', instead of the 'community or interest' (Birch 1964: 24). Accordingly, a different account explains how an MP elected after 1832 'was exposed to greater pressures both from his constituents and from his party' than before 1832 (Gash 1989: 164).

of property.[135] Well into the twentieth century, the primary unit of political representation remained not the single person or the citizen, but the household, which meant that a property qualification, reflecting domestic authority, was at the centre of representative procedures and electoral participation. In fact, members of the House of Commons were actually elected by multiple distinct franchises, affiliation to which was essentially a matter of private membership and association, reflecting different interests, material qualifications and social positions.[136] Not surprisingly, one account has stated that, up to 1918 the right to vote in the UK was a 'limited and well controlled privilege' (Moorhouse 1973: 347).[137] Due to the role of privilege in regulating access to political rights, further, the political system was not strongly nationalized before 1918, and in many constituencies representatives had a personal monopoly of power, and elections were not competitively contested.[138] Most importantly, owing to the partial exclusion of the working-class vote, specific class-determined interests could not easily be articulated as decisive questions in general elections, and the politicization of class conflicts was not nationally pronounced.[139]

In these respects, a comparison between Britain and Germany is illuminating. Germany is of course widely associated with an authoritarian *Sonderweg* in its progression towards democracy, whereas Britain is sometimes perceived as having followed a characteristic liberal *Sonderweg* (see Blackbourn and Eley 1984: 7; Weisbrod 1990: 236).[140] This commonly proposed dichotomy between Britain and Germany in fact reflects longstanding preconceptions. During World War I, for example, Weber was able to lament, in telling fashion, that working-class servicemen from Prussia fighting at the front were exposed to the terrible injustice that they

---

[135] See excellent analysis in Blewett (1965: 347).

[136] See above at p. 135.

[137] A different account states that 'voting was a trust, not a right' (Kahan 2003: 23).

[138] One calculation claims that, as late as 1910, 25 per cent of parliamentary seats were not contested (Lubenow 1988: 26). On the long survival of local power in the UK see Pole (1966: 389).

[139] In agreement with my claims see Urwin (1982: 41, 43, 47). Like my account, Urwin argues that the nationalization of the British political system was only fully realized after 1945.

[140] This oppositional view is carried over, in much more nuanced form, into Ziblatt's recent account of unsettled democratization in Germany and settled democratization in the UK, stressing the vital democratizing importance of elite accommodation amongst Conservatives in the UK (2017: 10). For all its brilliance, this account overstates the degree of democratization in the UK before 1945. In my view, it also fails to acknowledge that, owing to franchise restrictions, British Conservatives were less threatened by a nationally organized labour movement than their German counterparts, and it was easier for them to be accommodating.

might return home to Berlin to find themselves still subject to a political system with a weighted franchise. As discussed, up to 1918, Prussia had a three-class franchise, so that Prussian citizens voted on state-level questions in an electoral system which greatly privileged people who paid higher taxes.[141] Like others, Weber viewed the existence of the weighted franchise as a fact that vividly underlined the authoritarian nature of the Prussian state (1921: 247). Like other observers, in fact, he viewed the weakness of the elected legislature at the *Reich* level as a sign of under-evolved political culture, defined by *negative politics*, in Germany as a whole (1921: 251). Moreover, Weber himself seems to have considered Britain a relatively liberal society, possessing some features of an advanced rationalized party democracy (1921/2: 862). Important contemporaries of Weber expressly argued that England had followed a liberal special path into modernity (Hintze 1962: 50).

At this point, however, it becomes clear that the conventional contrast between Britain and Germany is very misleading. Tellingly, at the moment when Weber was expressing these claims in World War I, Britain itself still had plural voting, which, albeit not to the same degree as the weighted franchise in Prussia, systematically privileged the interests of wealthy Conservative voters.[142] More importantly, the universal male suffrage established at the level of the *Reich* in Germany in 1871 was not established in the UK until 1918, and then it still was incompletely realized. This means that approximately 50 per cent of the working-class servicemen fighting for Britain against Germany in World War I were not allowed to take part in voting at all (see Close 1977: 893). In fact, one interpreter has argued, quite correctly, that at the time of World War I, 'England (sic) had one of the least democratic national suffrages' amongst all European states (Bartolini 2000: 135). As significant background, moreover, by around 1910 the UK was far more industrialized and urbanized than Germany, and only 9 per cent of the working population were employed in agriculture (Rokkan 1970: 89; Mann 1987: 348). Conditions, thus, were

---

[141] The weighted, three-class franchise in Prussia was a counter-revolutionary constitution, based on the idea that persons paying more tax should have more heavily weighted votes. The franchise provisions were derived from local constitutional arrangements in the Rhineland and were introduced in Prussia as a whole in 1849 (Boberach 1959: 92, 149). Of course, the *Reich*, within which Prussia was situated, had manhood suffrage from 1871, albeit for a weak parliament.

[142] On similarities between plural voting and class-weighted franchises see Goldstein (1983: 11).

substantially more propitious for democratization than in Germany.[143] In fact, other conditions in the UK, such as early territorial unification, small geographical territory and relative confessional uniformity, also created a highly favourable basis for democratization. On balance, therefore, it is difficult to see why the epithet *authoritarian*, which is almost universally applied to Imperial Germany, is not also applied to the UK in the same historical period, and in fact beyond.[144] Britain may have differed from other societies in Europe in the earlier and middle part of the Twentieth Century in that it experienced relatively low levels of social violence, limited domestic militarization and relatively low levels of state repression and official criminality.[145] Yet, this does not amount to non-authoritarian governance. In fact, the generally less repressive nature of the British state

---

[143] On the usual connection between urbanization and working-class mobilization see Bartolini (2000: 122).

[144] Dahrendorf famously claimed simply: 'Imperial Germany was politically authoritarian' (1965: 73). In similar spirit, one of modern Germany's most eminent historians states that Germany became a democracy 'much later' than Britain. I would dispute this claim. On my account, by the 1870s Germany and Britain were both merely partial democracies, and both fell far short of democracy, albeit in very different ways. Germany had full male suffrage from 1871, but it had a weak parliament. The UK had a stronger parliament, although the elected chamber of parliament could be blocked by the House of Lords until 1911. Even after the franchise reforms of 1884, however, Britain only had about 60 per cent male suffrage – before 1867, it had only had about 10 per cent male suffrage. After 1919, Germany was, constitutionally, far more democratic than the UK; under the Weimar Constitution, Germany had universal male and female suffrage, whereas the UK had restricted female suffrage until 1928, and it retained plural voting. Only in the wake of the crisis of 1929/30, did Germany and the UK move in completely divergent directions. After 1933, of course, Hitler established a genocidal quasi-state in Germany. The UK also moved away from competitive democracy in 1931, but to a degree not remotely comparable with Germany. Both the UK and the FRG finally became full democracies within a year of each other, the FRG in 1949, and the UK in 1950. Very noteworthy in this comparison is the fact that Germany permitted mass voting for class interests at a much earlier stage than the government of the UK. This is one key indicator of societal commitment to democratic politics. This meant that in the interwar era working-class opposition parties were far more robustly institutionalized in Germany than in the UK. Representation of working-class interests in the UK was not cemented until Clement Attlee became Prime Minister. One reason for the fragility of German democracy after 1918 was that the political system was suddenly exposed to a highly mobilized Social Democratic Party, with a long history of organizational power. This did not happen in the UK, partly because after 1918 Liberals and Tories colluded to suppress the effective political mobilization of organized labour, and partly because full institutionalization of the Labour Party had been prevented by franchise restrictions before 1918. One important interpretation argues that from 1867 Germany 'consistently maintained its position in the first ranks' of countries allowing expansive suffrage (Bartolini 2000: 215).

[145] Note, however, the analysis of protest against the national government and related political repression in the 1930s, see Ewing and Gearty (2000: 215–75).

may easily have masked the fact that, from an electoral perspective, it was - at least intermittently – less democratic than most other European polities.

Overall, if we accept a fully inclusive definition of democracy, insisting that democracy implies a general subjective right for adults to participate, as equal citizens, in competitive elections, and to define the legitimacy of government, the UK should be seen as a late democracy.[146] Indeed, it should be seen as a democracy that developed late despite very advantageous preconditions for democratic institution building. Universal male suffrage was established in Britain in 1918, and universal female suffrage was established in 1928. However, it was only in the years 1948–50, during the implementation of the 1948 Representation of the People Act, that, after various attempts earlier in the century, the government finally abolished multiple franchise membership and plural voting. Consequently, Britain is the primary exception to Dieter Gosewinkel's claim that 'in all European states' the end of World War I brought 'general, equal male suffrage' (2016: 243). In fact, even if we see the extent of plural voting after 1918 as too slight to prevent the classification of the UK as a democracy, it also fell short of democracy on other counts. Before 1945, elections in the UK were typically not fully competitive, and, after 1928, when the universal franchise was created, Britain was only governed for a very short period (1929–31) by a government that had been elected in genuinely competitive elections. From 1931–45, British governments were created by elections that were, at best, only semi-competitive.[147]

---

[146] For claims in agreement, see Weir and Beetham (1999: 24).

[147] The National Government of 1931 marked a move away from democratic governance, and it effectively eliminated organized electoral opposition from the political system. This government was originally designed as an emergency executive, to last for a few weeks, after Ramsay Macdonald resigned as Labour Prime Minister to form a national government (see Searle 1995: 169; Smart 1999: 11–14). However, it lasted, with varying composition, until 1945. During this time, executive posts were not clearly tied to electoral outcomes, and the government drew its legitimacy primarily from the presumption of national emergency. Although less authoritarian and violent than its equivalents elsewhere, the National Government belongs to the family of supra-party anti-Socialist governments, able to co-opt the more reactionary or compliant elements of the labour movement, which became widespread in all Europe after the Wall Street Crash of 1929. Like its equivalents, it was designed to cut public expenditure and reduce salaries to shore up the public economy amidst the deep economic slump of the 1930s. Like the Brüning Cabinet in Germany, with which it had much in common, the National Government was created because of a fiscal crisis, it was sustained initially by support from the King (Brüning was installed as Chancellor by President Hindenburg in 1930), and it was based on a loose configuration of personalities, drawn from different parties – which were, in any case, not compactly institutionalized. On these points, see Pimlott (1977: 15); Thorpe (1991: 89, 257–8). Like other authoritarian regimes, the National Government also had corporatistic features (see Ritschel 1991: 57).

This means that the UK finally became a democracy after 1945, at approximately the same time as many supposedly 'late' European democracies, such as the FRG and Italy. This means, further, that the UK became a democracy at the same time as some post-colonial states, some of which, such as India, had been British colonies, and were supposedly educated toward democracy by representatives of the British government. This also means that the UK first held fully democratic elections in the same year (1950) that the British government signed the ECHR. The final construction of democratic citizenship in the UK was probably caused by the effects of World War II in promoting social solidarity in British society, reflected in the policies of the resultant Labour government under Clement Attlee.[148] However, it is reasonable to presume that Britain's promotion of democratization in post-1945 Germany and in some former colonies, especially India, and its willingness to support international human rights law, had the consequence that post-1945 governments felt an obligation to complete the process of democratic formation in the UK itself. In any case, it was only in 1948 that, in the UK, legislation was introduced to ensure compliance with Article 21 of the UDHR (also approved in 1948), which stipulated that government should be conducted 'by universal and equal suffrage'. In consequence, national democratic citizenship only began to

---

Very importantly, Neville Chamberlain described the National Government as a 'parliamentary dictatorship', in which all real opposition was incorporated in the government (Williamson 1992: 480). For a different account of the National Government as a 'Party Dictatorship' see Webb (1932: 3). Whether the National Government can be classified as a dictatorship depends on the definition of dictatorship. However, it clearly did create a *de facto* one-party state. Broadly, the British political system did not adjust to the rise of class voting, caused by the franchise reforms of 1918, until after 1945, and it struggled to establish a rhythm of consensual representation adjusted to a society defined by a range of politically organized socio-economic groups. Most British governments formed in the interwar era were based on cross-party collaboration, designed to keep the bulk, and the more radical elements, of the Labour Party out of power. This was clear enough in the Coupon Election of 1918, but it culminated in 1931 when MacDonald extracted himself from his own party to make the anti-Labour coalition, which was the National Government, complete. In my opinion, it was the belated enfranchisement of the working class that was primarily responsible for preventing Britain from assuming fully democratic form until after 1945.

[148] On the transformation of the ethics of citizenship in the UK during the World War II see Rose (2003: 22). This change in political outlook was partly caused by the fact that the Labour Party was incorporated more fully in government during the war. Popular attitudes were also shaped by international events, not least by the staggering military endeavours and sacrifices of the Soviet Union, which led to a more positive perception of Russia (Addison 1975: 138–41).

act as the dominant legitimational principle within the UK as the state was placed within a global legal order.[149]

The slow emergence of democracy in the UK was mirrored in the fact that the concept of the citizen was also solidified very slowly. Indeed, still today, the UK does not possess a fully secure concept of the citizen as a sovereign actor, supplying primary legitimacy for the public order. Instead, historically, the citizen was constructed as a participant in legislative acts through a sequence of electoral reform laws, which inserted provisions for citizenship practices into an existing order of state. The primary constitutional commitments to democracy are articulated in piecemeal form, in the Reform Acts of 1832, 1867, 1884, 1918, 1928 and 1948. Taken together, these Acts of Parliament do not present a strong constitutional definition of democratic citizenship as the legitimational bedrock of government, and they merely served incrementally to expand the popular component of the polity. Above all, however, the weaknesses underlying the construction of political citizenship in British public law are caused by two quite distinct factors, which are close to the core of British constitutional development. Indeed, certain underlying ambiguities in the conception of public authority in the UK obstructed the emergence of a clear, generalized idea of citizenship, and, as a result, they prevented the effective consolidation of democratic order.

For historical reasons, first, the British polity does not contain a strongly articulated concept of the state, defined under a clear corpus of public law. In the UK, bodies with public status evolved gradually, and they were not constructed by clear constitutional decisions, or determined by objectives of a clear public nature. The state has in fact grown out of the crown, which was, in origin, and – arguably – still remains, in essence, a private corporation.[150] In fact, the elected component of the state, the House of Commons, was first constructed as a corporation within a corporation, and its function was not to enact the will of citizens, but to assume a

---

[149] Notably, in parliamentary debates prior to the passing of the 1948 Representation of the People Act, it was stated that the Act was needed in order 'to complete the long evolution of Parliamentary democracy' (Peart, Labour). These debates contained extensive references to the international situation after 1945, showing determination to consolidate the UK's status as 'one of the few free democracies left in the world' (Boyd-Carpenter, Conservative). In this respect, the Act clearly reflected anti-Communist attitudes in the UN and later in the Council of Europe, and it was designed both to denounce the political systems of Eastern Europe and to protect the UK from unfavourable international comparison (HC Deb 23 June 1948).

[150] See the claim in the 1970s that the Crown should be seen as 'a corporation aggregate headed by the Queen'. *Town Investments Ltd* v. *Department of the Environment*. [1978] AC 359.

corporate consultative role in affairs of the crown.[151] In consequence, British public institutions were not originally proportioned to a general construction of the citizen, defined as publicly constitutive agent. This means that the structural correlation between the legitimacy of the state and the rights and obligations of citizens, which is central to other polities, was not fully elaborated in the UK (see Loughlin 1999: 76; Murkens 2009: 434).

At a more conceptual level, second, the concepts of legitimation which historically underpinned the emergence of British government prevented the formation of a clear idea of citizenship. Importantly, although it evolved only belatedly into a *representative democracy*, Britain possessed a system of *representative government* from an early stage. Indeed, before the nineteenth century, the British governance system was centred around a two-pronged constitutional concept of representation.

On one hand, British government was originally founded on the principle that, although very few people could actually vote as enfranchised citizens, interests in society at large were represented through the three organs of parliament (Lords, Commons and Monarch).[152] This principle implied that the legitimacy of government was sustained not by direct representation, election or delegation, but by the *virtual representation* of society through parliamentary members (see Pole 1966: 443). Indeed, as championed (rather implausibly) by Edmund Burke, the idea of virtual representation implied that each Member of Parliament represented the nation in its entirety,[153] and that parliament could speak as 'the abstracted quintessence of the whole community' (Goldsworthy 1999: 97). This doctrine gave rise to the second core principle of classical British constitutionalism – parliamentary sovereignty. On this basis, the principle developed that parliament itself was the sovereign focus of government, such that government was conducted through sovereign acts not of the people, but of parliament in its simple representative capacity, whose objective coincidence

---

[151] On the nature of the House of Commons as a 'corporate body' see Seymour (1915: 199).

[152] Parliamentary rule in the UK context clearly does not of itself imply democracy. It implies a balanced relation between three organs of state – Common, Lords, Monarch – none of which, prior to 1832, had any claim to democratic legitimacy. On the relation between the three constituent organs of parliament see Blackstone (1765: 149).

[153] Burke stated in 1774 that 'Parliament is a deliberative assembly of one nation, with one interest, that of the whole, where, not local purposes, not local prejudices ought to guide, but the general good, resulting from the general reason of the whole' (1854: 446–8). See discussion of the misleading nature of this principle in Langford (1988: 87).

with the people was not a factual precondition of its legitimacy.[154] On this basis, further, parliament acquired a high degree of legislative autonomy, and it was defined by the constitutional presumption that, at any given moment, it could directly transpose the will of society into legislative form. Parliament thus initially emerged as a formidably authoritative legislature, legitimated by its condensed corporate embodiment of societal interests, and able to introduce legislation, both statutory and constitutional, without higher normative restriction.

Many observers have seen great benefits in the British political system, and, historically, it was often viewed as a model for emulation. For example, the doctrine of parliamentary sovereignty meant that Britain was widely seen, throughout pre-democratic, and even nineteenth-century, Europe as possessing a highly evolved system of national representation, which many progressive thinkers in different countries wished to emulate (see Esmein 1903: 46–8; Israel 2006: 356–64). In some cases, this admiration lasted well into the twentieth century (see Hintze 1962: 49–51). In similar spirit, important recent commentators have argued that, in the later early modern era, Britain's parliamentary system established 'foundations for the transition from a monarch-subject relationship to a state-citizen relationship' (Heater 1999: 4). One of the most significant contemporary sociologists has argued that 'institutionalized rights of citizens' were established first in England (Münch 1984: 296).[155] In reality, however, the British system of virtual representation and parliamentary sovereignty had certain very damaging outcomes for the constitutional development of a democratic state, authorized by its citizens. The main tenets of British parliamentary doctrine stood obdurately in the path of the emergence of generalized patterns of citizenship, supporting the growth of democratic institutions, and British institutions persisted for centuries in a condition of half-privatized partial democracy.

First, for example, the British concept of virtual representation had the implication that government was not bound, for its legitimacy, to members of society as a whole. This meant that, beneath the veneer of universal parliamentary accountability, small sets of select interests were easily able to assume a privileged position in the system of political representation (see Pole 1966: 444–57). Indeed, the existence of multiple franchises,

---

[154] This theory was already set out by Blackstone (1765: 143). But see the classic formulation in Dicey (1915 [1885]: 406).

[155] This is also implied in the famous, but also excessively favourable, commentary in Habermas (1990 [1962]: 142).

which still defined the British polity through the nineteenth century, clearly reflected the fact that government was expected to represent the particular prerogatives of designated social groups and communities. Originally, electoral franchises in Britain were close in character to stakeholder groups, based on aggregated overlapping private interests, and they were specifically not engineered to articulate collectively structured obligations for government. Far from guaranteeing national representation, therefore, the doctrine of virtual representation imposed a condition of parcellation on British society, ensuring that society appeared in the political system not as a national collective, but as a series of segmentary interest blocs (Esmein 1903: 69; Pole 1966: 444, 452). The fracturing of society into discrete interests persisted well into the era of large-scale political enfranchisement. Even after 1867, electoral constituencies were expressly created to represent particular professions and particular social sectors (Bentley 1999: 178). The doctrine of virtual representation left a pervasive legacy of political privatism, which sat uneasily alongside the development of generalized concepts of citizenship.

Second, the deepest implication in the concept of parliamentary sovereignty, clearly and emphatically, is that the single citizen is not the primary focus of government, and governmental power is not normatively sustained by a general principle of popular-democratic citizenship.[156] Historically, the fact that parliament (Commons, Lords and Monarch) was defined as the sovereign organ of government restricted the space for the construction of the citizen as a political subject outside parliament. Indeed, the focusing of sovereignty around the corporate powers of parliament prevented citizens from laying claim to generalized political rights, separated from single legal enactments of parliamentary authority.[157] Under the parliamentary constitution, social agents can, through their representatives, claim and enact rights through individual acts of parliament. However, it is essential to the doctrine of parliamentary sovereignty that single acts of parliament create different sets of statutory rights, and they are not strongly shaped by an image of their addressee (the citizen) as a holder of rights, which all law must recognize. This is clearly reflected in the classical parliamentary doctrines that each parliament is sovereign and can repeal acts of previous parliaments, and that, accordingly, there is no relative entrenchment or hierarchy between statutes. This is

---

[156] For analysis close to mine on this point see Judge (1999: 17); Oliver (2009: 150).
[157] On the historical distinction of the English concept of the subject from the more obviously democratic concept of the citizen see Salmond (1902: 50); Price (1997: 88).

also reflected in the fact that, where rights guaranteed under one statute conflict with rights guaranteed under a different statute, the rights deriving from the most recent statute prevail.[158] On this basis, the rights of citizens in British public law cannot easily be seen as separable from single momentary pieces of parliamentary legislation, and statutory rights do not attach to the citizen *per se*, as a generally constructed political subject. Social agents cannot easily appear in the political system as citizens, uniformly implicated in legislation. Moreover, they cannot easily appear as sources of distinctively public legitimacy for the government, tying government to a clear image of its public origins and duties. In the concept of parliamentary sovereignty, the citizen appears, in essence, as an interested party, seeking to translate a particular momentary interest or a series of particular momentary interests into a piece or several pieces of legislation.[159] However, the citizen does not appear as a general source of public authority, possessing rights on whose recognition the legitimacy of the political system in its entirety categorically depends.

In classical British parliamentarism, to be sure, the common law provided some general rights for individual persons, which they were able, notionally, to hold as principles against the acts of government. Persons in society were able to articulate some constant rights in the environment of government. In some famous cases, it was stated that the common law was able to establish clear restrictions to curb the power of government agents.[160] Yet, such rights were traditionally of a private nature, and they lacked the force of statutory rights. Such rights could not provide strong protection for rights of a political nature, required for the consolidation of a modern democracy, especially in times when such rights came under duress (Ewing and Gearty 2000: 13, 20, 323).

---

[158] This is expressed in the rule of implied repeal, which states that 'if Parliament has enacted successive statutes which on the true construction of each of them make irreducibly inconsistent provisions, the earlier statute is impliedly repealed by the later': *Thoburn* v. *Sunderland City Council and other appeals* – [2002] All ER (D) 223 (Feb)

[159] One reason for this is that parliament was originally a judicial body, before which individual parties sought justice, remedy and redress. Until the seventeenth century, parliament was not finally distinct from a judicial institution, and it assumed its authority as the highest court of the realm, limiting the powers of the monarchy by applying the common law (MacKay 1924: 239; Gough 1955: 42; Goldsworthy 1999: 155). To some degree, the echo of this is still audible in parliament's contemporary features and functions.

[160] See Dr. Bonham's Case, 8 Co. Rep. 114 (Court of Common Pleas [1610]). But note that Coke, who ruled in this case, stated more doctrinally that 'all weighty matters in any parliament' 'ought to be determined, adjudged, and discussed by the course of the parliament, and not by the civill law, nor yet by the common law' (1797 [1628–44]: 14). See also *Entick* v. *Carrington* [1765] EWHC KB J98.

Overall, the political subject of British public law appeared, historically, in a form that was divided into two separate parts. The political subject existed as the holder of residual rights of an individual nature, which were protected at common law, but lacked constitutional authority. The political subject also emerged as the *electoral citizen*, who, if permitted, took part in popular elections, and then appeared as the addressee of single separate acts of parliament, whose authority was extracted from the representative functions of the parliamentary system, and which granted rights on that basis. In this dual form, the citizen was not formed as a participant in a stable, normatively cohesive political community, possessing generalized political rights and expectations. In both its dimensions, in fact, the political subject was essentially privatistic, holding separate sets of private rights. As a subject of parliament, the citizen always appeared in doubly privatistic fashion, only possessing political rights through isolated Acts of Parliament, recognizing citizens as momentary stakeholders, and endowed with only marginally relevant private rights to set against governmental encroachments.

The British parliamentary constitution has often been viewed as a markedly political constitution, distinct from the legally entrenched normative orders found in more codified constitutions.[161] In key respects, however, the British constitution is precisely not an eminently political constitution, based on a strict construction of public authority and a strict legitimation of public acts by publicly acceded principles. On the contrary, it is a privatized constitution, directed towards the easy transposition of private interests into legislative form. In fact, it is distinctive for the British parliamentary polity that its structure has militated against the construction of a sustained model of citizenship, it has prevented the establishment of public norms to sustain government functions and it allows the citizen recurrently to lapse into privatism.

In some ways, the weak articulation of the citizen in British public law was directly responsible for the fragmented formation of democracy, discussed above. The fact that governmental legitimacy did not presuppose a solid construct of the citizen was reflected in the emergence of multiple franchises. It was also reflected in the *ad hoc* expansion of the suffrage, and in the extraordinarily protracted persistence of plural voting. Each of these factors implies that the British polity defined its citizens, in essence, as private rights holders. However, the adverse impact of the under-formation of

---

[161] See varying formulations of this view in Griffith (1979: 16); Gee and Webber (2010: 288); Tomkins (2010: 2).

citizenship in British public law became especially acute through the long process of franchise reform, which gathered pace in the 1860s, in which rival interests were incorporated in the legislature. Through this process, the machinery of government became more complex, and the regulatory burdens directed towards the government necessitated production of a rapidly growing volume of law. In this setting, the classical principles of British public law proved singularly ill-suited to the conditions of mass democracy, and they struggled to generate a concept of legitimacy to support governmental functions.

First, the expansion of parliament's regulatory powers in Britain through the twentieth century meant that governmental functions were increasingly centred around the executive branch. In fact, although parliament had originally evolved as the nervous centre of government, by the early twentieth century many legislative functions of parliament migrated to the executive (see Parris 1969; 184; Marsh and Read 1988: 1–2; Daintith and Page 1999: 24). By World War II at the latest, the idea that the elected chamber of parliament might act as a sovereign organ of government was clearly implausible, and the cabinet had become the dominant element of the political system. However, because the political system as a whole was based on the notional primacy of the parliamentary legislature, giving unmediated expression to popular interests, it was not possible, normatively, to institutionalize strong checks on executive power; indeed, the political system was not capable of generating such normative checks. The fact that the government was designed for the momentary enactment of the parliamentary will meant that the norms required to constrain executive actors, which had arrogated parliamentary functions, were very weak (Birch 1964: 166; Woodhouse 1994: 17; Norton 2005: 62, 81).

Overall, this created a rather perverse institutional order. In this system, the legislature was supposed to represent the will of the people, and it was subject to only limited constraint because of its privileged claim to ensure representation of this will. In fact, however, legislative functions were largely performed by the executive, which, because of the lack of horizontal checks on legislative process, was able to function at a very high degree of autonomy. Paradoxically, the British parliament eventually proved to be a very weak legislature, whose function was merely to collaborate with the executive in the daily conduct of government. The underlying reason for this was that parliament obtained legitimacy not from its recognition of citizens as rights holders, but from its enactment of the particular momentary interests of parliamentary majorities.

As a result of this, second, the general system of public accountability in the UK was formed very slowly. Indeed, the weakness of British democracy was reflected in the fact that, for some time after 1945, the obligations of public bodies were imprecisely defined. As late as the 1970s, for example, a clear definition of public law had not been established in the UK,[162] and the basic legal norms governing exchanges between public bodies and citizens were only inchoately articulated. In fact, controversy persisted into the 1960s as to whether the UK actually possessed a system of administrative law, placing formalized checks on acts of public bodies, and ensuring that such bodies act in a fashion proportioned to rights of citizens.[163] This uncertainty was caused by the fact that the parliamentary constitution did not permit the enforcement of fully free-standing normative constraints on acts of government. Indeed, under the parliamentary constitution, courts, as far as they were authorized to regulate public bodies, were only able, in strict terms, to measure the legitimacy of public acts on expanded *ultra vires* grounds, by assessing the compliance of such acts with original momentary decisions of parliament.[164] Indicatively, the use of *ultra vires* as a concept for controlling public acts originated in legal rulings concerned with the scope of public contracts granted to corporations,[165] implying that public bodies and public agencies were perceived, residually, as corporations, and their relation to citizens was construed in analogy to a private legal arrangement.

The importance of *ultra vires* in UK public law meant that a comprehensive corpus of public law, centred in autonomously defined legal principles, was not deemed necessary, and it impeded the emergence of a system of formal and actionable rights to regulate use of public authority. In fact, judicial control of administrative acts developed in English public law as a function of the common law, without any clearly formalized constitutional

---

[162] See the following claims: 'The expressions "private law" and "public law" have recently been imported into the law of England from countries which, unlike our own, have separate systems concerning public law and private law. No doubt they are convenient expressions for descriptive purposes. In this country they must be used with caution, for, typically, English law fastens not on principles but on remedies'. *Davy* v. *Spelthorne Borough Council* – [1983] 3 All ER 278 (Wilberforce LJ). See arguments in agreement with this analysis, though claiming that a strict distinction between private and public law is not desirable, in Harlow (1980: 258).

[163] See discussion of this in *Ridge* v. *Baldwin and others* – [1963] 2 All ER 66.

[164] See discussion in Schwartz and Wade (1972: 210–11); Griffith and Street (1973: 211); Wade and Forsyth (2004: 35); Elliott (2001a: 23, 79).

[165] See *East Anglian Railways Co.* v. *The Eastern Counties Railway Co.*, (1851) 11 C. B. 775.

basis.[166] The essential objective of judicial review, initially, was to preserve a separation of powers arrangement within the governance system, and to make sure that executive bodies did not act beyond the powers bestowed by parliament. By the 1960s, to be sure, the courts had begun to flesh out a set of distinctively public-legal norms, applying free-standing principles to assess the legitimacy of public acts.[167] In fact, the courts had been left to craft a body of administrative law, instilling both general principles of natural justice and private- or common-law concepts of liability into a basic public-law doctrine of *ultra vires*.[168] Before the 1970s, nonetheless, the ability of the courts to impose normatively independent constraints on government remained limited. Tests for proper use of public authority were restricted to vague standards of natural fairness and reasonableness, and courts were not easily able to articulate substantive criteria to assess the use of governmental power.[169] The late twentieth century saw a dramatic expansion of government functions, reflecting the rise of a modern welfare state. Yet, this was not flanked by the emergence of a strict normative order to determine relations between citizens and government, and,

---

[166] See the judicial claim that 'judicial review was an artefact of the common law whose object was to maintain the rule of law' in *R (on the application of Cart)* v. *Upper Tribunal; R (on the application of MR (Pakistan))* v. *Upper Tribunal (Immigration and Asylum Chamber) and another* – [2011] All ER (D) 149 (Jun). On the common-law foundations of judicial review see Schwartz and Wade (1972: 209); Craig (1998: 90).

[167] See the constitutional construction of rules of 'natural justice' in *Ridge* v. *Baldwin and others* – [1963] 2 All ER 66. See the expanded definition of 'lawfulness' in *Padfield and Others* v. *Minister of Agriculture Fisheries and Food and Others* – [1968] 1 All ER 694.

[168] On the role of the courts in creating a public-law doctrine of accountability see the claim that 'ultra vires has replaced the civil law concept of negligence as the test of the legality, and consequently of the actionability, of acts or omissions of government departments or public authorities done in the exercise of a direction conferred on them by Parliament'. *Home Office* v. *Dorset Yacht Co Ltd* – [1970] 2 All ER 294 (Diplock LJ). On the implications of this see Hickman (2011: 13).

[169] See the following claim:

> [A]t a time when more and more cases involving the application of legislation which gives effect to policies that are the subject of bitter public and parliamentary controversy, it cannot be too strongly emphasised that the British Constitution, though largely unwritten, is firmly based on the separation of powers: Parliament makes the laws, the judiciary interpret them. When Parliament legislates to remedy what the majority of its members at the time perceive to be a defect or a lacuna in the existing law (whether it be the written law enacted by existing statutes or the unwritten common law as it has been expounded by the judges in decided cases), the role of the judiciary is confined to ascertaining from the words that Parliament has approved as expressing its intention what that intention was, and to giving effect to it

Duport Steels Ltd and others v. *Sirs and others* – [1980] 1 All ER 529 (Diplock LJ).

as reflected in the importance of *ultra vires*, the simple construct of the citizen as the electoral citizen, represented through single acts of parliament, remained the essential focus of public regulation.

Underneath the classical parliamentary constitution, in short, the British political system was not able to manufacture a concept of the citizen that was clearly separable from single acts of parliament, and that defined the publicly acceded obligations of government. This weak constitutionalization of rights attached to citizens under the British constitution meant, historically, that public law lacked an inherent normative unity. Public law was rooted in the concept of the citizen represented through parliamentary legislation, but it did not provide generalized parameters for the use of public power. The citizen could obtain separate rights under individual acts of legislation. Yet, few rights were implied across the legal/political system as a whole. Government could not be conclusively constructed in the image of the democratic citizen, and, in fact, a basic idea of the citizen could not be supplied to legitimate legislation or to control administrative acts. This was stated quite clearly in a case of the 1990s, where it was explained, fittingly, that in the UK: 'Public law is not at base about rights, even though abuses of power may and often do invade private rights; it is about wrongs – that is to say misuses of public power'.[170] As mentioned, from the 1960s to the 1980s, the British courts established some free-standing norms to determine 'wrong' use of public power. However, this opinion implies that the legitimacy of public power is to be challenged, primarily, on separate, punctual grounds, depending ultimately on the interpretation of the powers granted under a particular statute.

From this relatively unpromising position, from the 1970s onwards, institutions in the legal system eventually conducted a far-reaching, although still only partial, reconstruction of public law in the UK. Through this process, persons subject to law were, to some degree, separated from momentary acts of parliament, and positioned as generalized legal addressees (citizens). This greatly hardened the restrictions on governmental agencies, and it significantly altered the inherited system of parliamentary-constitutional democracy. At this time, in addition, legal institutions in the UK began to articulate and to produce norms in increasingly autonomous fashion, and to insist on some norms as possessing a degree of normative force independent of parliamentary intention. Crucially, legal institutions began to implant an abstracted idea of the democratic citizen in UK public

---

[170]   *R v. Somerset County Council and ARC Southern Ltd*, ex p Dixon (1997) 75 P & CR 175, [1997] NPC 61 (Sedley J).

law. This in turn led to a partial redefinition of democracy in the UK, in which the role of clearly public norms in dictating the conditions for use of governmental power was greatly increased.

In the 1970s, the emergence of new constitutional concepts was reflected, in particular, in the sphere of administrative law. By the 1970s, the courts had begun to formulate certain norms as possessing clearly binding status for public bodies. First, the courts began to develop the idea that there existed independent standards of legality, imposing obligations on all public agents.[171] Progressively, in fact, they began to suggest that there existed certain *constitutional rights*, which the courts were called upon to defend against encroachments of the legislative and executive branches. In so doing, the courts slowly elaborated the idea, very tentatively in the first instance, that the rights enshrined in common law were not entirely distinguishable from rights enshrined in general human rights law,[172] and that parliament was only allowed to encroach on formally held rights to the minimal necessary extent.[173] This meant that the authority of law could be defined and assessed not solely by its origin in parliament, but by its inner proportioning to the rights and interests of democratic citizens. The courts began to propose a supplementary construct of the citizen in public law, to sit alongside the electoral citizen expressed through the doctrine of parliamentary sovereignty. Indeed, the courts promoted the idea that there existed a constitutional idea of the citizen, holding certain relatively entrenched, even *fundamental rights*,[174] recognition of which would

---

[171] See notes 167–8 above.

[172] See the claim that rights that are 'deeply embedded in the common law' and now also 'embodied in the Universal Declaration of Human Rights (1949) (Cmd. 7662) and the European Convention for the Protection of Human Rights and Fundamental Freedoms (1953) (Cmd. 8969)'. The implicit claim in this is that English law *got to rights first*. In any case, the presumption that the common law is a reservoir of basic rights gave rise to the statement that 'it is a firm rule of statutory construction that such construction shall not interfere with such freedoms unless expressly stated': *Wheeler* v. *Leicester City Council* [1985] AC 1054. See the later claim 'that in the field of freedom of speech there was no difference in principle between English law on the subject and art 10 of the convention': *Derbyshire County Council* v. *Times Newspapers Ltd and Others* – [1993] 1 ALL ER 1011 (Keith LJ).

[173] See *Morris* v. *Beardmore* – [1980] 2 All ER 753.

[174] See the growing diction of constitutional rights in the following argument: 'to hold a party up to public obloquy for exercising his constitutional right to have recourse to a court of law for the ascertainment and enforcement of his legal rights and obligations is calculated to prejudice the first requirement for the due administration of justice: the unhindered access of all citizens to the established courts of law'. *Attorney General* v. *Times Newspapers Ltd* – [1973] 3 All ER 54 (Diplock LJ). See use of the concept of the 'fundamental right of a citizen' in *R* v. *Samuel* – [1988] 2 All ER 135.

normally be taken as a primary principle of parliamentary legislation, and whose rights parliament would not violate without good cause and express justification. This did not amount to an obligation for parliament to give effect to the rights of citizens. However, it reflected the more residual principle that legislation should not contravene implied basic rights. On this premise, the courts projected a broad rights-based constitution for public agencies, based on an implied homology between core elements of common law and core elements of general human rights law.

Very indicative in this respect was the fact that the gradual rise of formal human rights in UK public law meant that the courts extended their control of public organs beyond classical questions of *ultra vires* (see Oliver 1987: 567). In particular, the courts began not only to use formal rights to limit functions exercised under statutory powers, but also to conduct review of the exercise of powers that did not originate in statutory provisions, including prerogative powers based on the common law.[175] Through these processes, elements of British public law began to assume the form of a free-standing constitutional order, by which all the functions of the political system, in a generalized sense, were bound. This process was based on the assumption that, with some qualifications, *all public acts* were subject to normative control, and that the original common-law role of courts in policing observance of parliamentary decisions required expansion if courts were effectively to regulate the exercise of power in the modern state, populated by democratic citizens. Indeed, the expansion of judicial review created a more solid definition of the basic characteristics of a public power and a public act. In subjecting prerogative powers to judicial review, the courts implied a concept of public authority as comprising all acts that affect persons (citizens) in their rights. On this basis, the idea was generated, albeit somewhat obliquely, that public agency is defined as such by its reference to citizens, and it acquires legitimacy if applied in a form that recognizes the general rights of citizens.[176] An essential citizen-based

---

[175] See the following claim: 'Seeing that the prerogative is a discretionary power to be exercised for the public good, it follows that its exercise can be examined by the courts just as any other discretionary power which is vested in the executive'. *Laker Airways Ltd v. Department of Trade* – [1977] 2 All ER 182. See also the famous analysis in *Council of Civil Service Unions and others v. Minister for the Civil Service* – [1984] 3 All ER 935. One account – quite correctly – sees this ruling as the end of strict *ultra vires* (Elliott 2001a: 5). A different account – quite correctly – sees this ruling as adding an element of constitutional review to the British constitution (Jacob 1996: 261).

[176] See the opinion expressed obiter that 'If the executive in pursuance of the statutory power does an act affecting the rights of the citizen, it is beyond question that in principle the

construction of public law thus appeared, primarily, through the evolution of administrative law.

During the 1970s, the impact of international human rights law on UK law still remained marginal.[177] Even the most effective international human rights convention, the ECHR, was only accorded a very restricted role in domestic public law. Indeed, as mentioned, it was commonly accepted that international norms could not directly penetrate into UK law.[178] However, this period saw a pronounced change not solely in the self-conception of the courts, but also in classical notions regarding the domestic constitutional authority of international law. The leading cases in which UK courts first extended and systematized their powers of legal control over public bodies were not substantially influenced by international law. Indeed, despite occasional intimations that the ECHR should inform acts of public officials,[179] there is little evidence in such cases to indicate that the courts deviated from classical dualist principles of UK public law. However, there are important cases in this line of reasoning in which judges clearly hardened rights defined at common law by supporting their arguments with reference to international instruments. In particular, it was increasingly argued during the solidification of British public law that common law rights and international human rights were closely related.[180] To a certain degree, therefore, the tentative concretization of a rights-defined constitution in the UK was linked to an increasingly porous or osmotic interaction between the UK legal system and the international legal system.

---

manner of the exercise of that power may today be challenged' in *Council of Civil Service Unions and others* v. *Minister for the Civil Service* – [1984] 3 All ER 935 (Roskill LJ).

[177] The classical dualist reading of the British constitution was tempered by some judges in the 1960s to the degree that it was presumed that 'there is a prima facie presumption that Parliament does not intend to act in breach of international law, including therein specific treaty obligations'. On this basis, it was reasoned that 'if one of the meanings which can reasonably be ascribed to the legislation is consonant with the treaty obligations and another or others are not, the meaning which is consonant is to be preferred': *Salomon* v. *Commissioners of Customs and Excise* [1967] 2 QB 116 (Diplock LJ). See also opinions in *Corocraft* v. *Pan American Airways* (1969) 1 All E.R. 82.

[178] *R* v. *Chief Immigration Officer, Heathrow Airport and another, ex parte Salamat Bibi* – [1976] 3 All ER 843. But see the later claim that judges should 'should have regard to the provisions' of the ECHR in *Attorney General* v. *British Broadcasting Corporation* – [1980] 3 All ER 161. See excellent analysis of use of the ECHR in Feldman (1999: 543).

[179] See claims of Scarman in *Reg.* v. *Secretary of State for the Home Department, Ex parte Phansopkar* [1976] Q.B. 606.

[180] See for example Scarman's joint reading of *Entick* v. *Carrington* and the ECHR in *Morris* v. *Beardmore* – [1980] 2 All ER 753.

This correlation between domestic law and international human rights in British public law became more intense through the 1980s, when legal expectations linked to the implementation of the ECHR became important determinants in domestic legal procedure. At one level, the conviction still persisted into the 1990s that the ECHR was not an incorporated part of domestic law, and that the values and principles derived from the ECHR could not be applied by the courts to evaluate the acts of domestic public bodies. It was accepted that attempts by the courts to 'incorporate the convention' into domestic law would amount to a 'judicial usurpation of the legislative function'.[181] Remedies for violations of ECHR rights, thus, could only be obtained in Strasbourg. Nonetheless, it became a settled notion that 'in construing any provision in domestic legislation which is ambiguous in the sense that it is capable of a meaning which either conforms to or conflicts with the convention, the courts will presume that Parliament intended to legislate in conformity with the convention, not in conflict with it'.[182] Moreover, it became common practice in administrative law for courts to apply particularly exacting standards to assess acts of public bodies in cases in which rights recognized under international law, especially the ECHR, were affected. Judges began independently to accept that their scrutiny of public acts should be calibrated in accordance with the importance of the rights affected by the act under consideration.[183] As a result, they implicitly implemented a standard of proportionality, separate from *ultra vires* review, arguing that proportionately greater justification would be required for a public act that placed limits on core human rights.[184] To this degree, the courts began to assimilate both ECHR norms and norms of general international law into domestic law, and they began to promote a relative weighting for different rights and a more substantive evaluation

---

[181] *Brind and others* v. *Secretary of State for the Home Department* – [1991] 1 All ER 720 (Bridge LJ).

[182] Ibid.

[183] See the following principle 'The most fundamental of all human rights is the individual's right to life and, when an administrative decision under challenge is said to be one which may put the applicant's life at risk, the basis of the decision must surely call for the most anxious scrutiny'. *Bugdaycay* v. *Secretary of State for the Home Department and related appeals* – [1987] 1 All ER 940 (Bridge LJ). It was later argued in the Supreme Court that the effect of this was 'to expand the scope of rationality review so as to incorporate at common law significant elements of the principle of proportionality'. *Pham* v. *Secretary of State for the Home Department* [2015] UKSC 19.

[184] See discussion in *R* v. *Ministry of Defence, ex parte Smith and Grady* and *R* v. *Admiralty Board of the Defence Council, ex parte Beckett and Lustig-Prean*, [1996] QB 517 (CA).

of particular acts, in the scrutiny of government functions.[185] Indeed, even where they rejected the immediate applicability of the ECHR, the courts proposed themselves as custodians of generalized rights and generalized principles of citizenship.[186]

This constitutional interaction between UK courts and the European human rights system was intensified, finally, in a case in which courts encountered the limits of their powers, as defined under the parliamentary constitution. Confronted with a case filed by two homosexuals who claimed discrimination under the ECHR because of their expulsion from the UK military on the grounds of their sexual orientation, the Court of Appeal decided that the tests of public action available in UK public law could not provide for adequate adjudication of the rights implicated in the case, and they could not lead to adequate remedies for persons subject to discrimination in this way. As a result, the case was opened for challenge to the ECtHR. Ultimately, the Strasbourg court declared that persons affected in their convention rights by public decisions were entitled, under ECHR Article 6, to claim remedies not foreseen in more classical provisions for judicial review in UK public law. Effectively, therefore, the ECtHR decided that procedures for judicial review in the UK, classically based on *vires* concerns, did not in all circumstances provide a basis for an effective remedy. Accordingly, it declared that, in certain cases with human rights implications, proportionality review, entailing a substantive evaluation of the public act in question, should replace conventional patterns of judicial control.[187] In response to this, the UK courts established new principles for judicial review in domestic human rights cases, clearly abandoning the assumption that judicial control of administrative acts was limited to policing the separation of powers, on *vires* grounds.[188] The use of proportionality implied the existence of generalized citizens, possessing generalized rights, to be considered as implicated, and requiring recognition, in all public acts.

In these respects, the exchanges between the UK courts and bodies in the transnational legal domain, especially the ECtHR, meant that the

---

[185] In fact, a near-classical proportionality argument was used to protect rights of prisoners in *R* v. *Secretary of State for the Home Department, Ex p Leech* [1994] QB 198. Close to my reading see Hunt (1997: 220). For very extensive use of ECHR see *R* v. *Secretary of State for the Home Department, ex parte McQuillan* – [1995] 4 All ER 400, stressing proximity between ECHR and the common law.

[186] *Brind and others* v. *Secretary of State for the Home Department* – [1991] 1 All ER 720.

[187] *Smith and Grady* v. *UK* (1999) 29 EHRR 493.

[188] *R* v. *Secretary of State for the Home Department, ex parte Daly* – [2001] All ER (D) 280 (May).

national legal system assumed a certain degree of autonomy within the political structure of British domestic society. Over a longer period of time, in fact, courts were able to project and enforce conditions of constitutional control, and to define the legal form of democratic government more widely. This process produced a far-reaching reconstruction of constitutional democracy in the UK, and it gave near-constitutional authority to the presumption that acts of government could be assessed in light of fixed substantive norms, reflecting a hierarchy of human rights. Through the osmotic reception of the ECHR as a basis for judicial review, the higher courts in the UK increasingly perceived their functions in analogy to more conventional constitutional courts.[189] To some degree, in fact, this process served, for the first time, to condense a formal system of public law for the UK government.

On one hand, this process separated judicial control from the simple interpretation of parliamentary statutes; it detached judicial review from its original foundation in the common-law power of the courts, and it elevated judicial review to a position close to the rank of constitutional protection. As a result, the courts projected a separate, public-law construction of legitimacy to determine the limits of public authority, and the ends to which such authority could be used. On the other hand, this process established a series of rights-based norms and rights-based remedies not originally extracted from private law, according to which government functions could be measured, and it crystallized a system of increasingly generic public-law rights, by which public authorities were bound. Ultimately, this meant that the courts became more assertive in insisting that laws needed to be authorized by implied citizens, comprising relatively uniform aggregates of rights, standing separate from, and providing a basis for evaluation of, individual parliamentary acts. Notably, this reinforced the primary claim that any 'power conferred by Parliament' cannot be presumed 'to authorise the doing of acts by the donee of the power which adversely affect the legal rights of the citizen', unless the relevant Act of Parliament 'makes it clear that such was the intention of Parliament'.[190] Most importantly, this meant that the basic political subject of democracy

---

[189] *International Transport Roth GmbH & Ors v. Secretary of State For the Home Department* [2002] EWCA Civ 158 (22 February 2002) 71 (Laws LJ).

[190] *Pierson v. Secretary of State for the Home Department* – [1997] 3 All ER 577 (Browne-Wilkinson LJ). Note also the consideration of treaty obligations, especially in respect of human rights treaties, as authoritative guidance for interpreting the will of parliament in *R v. Secretary of State for the Home Department, ex parte Venables; R v. Secretary of State for the Home Department, ex parte Thompson* – [1997] 3 All ER 97 (Browne-Wilkinson LJ).

was detached from its expression through single parliamentary decisions, and it was distilled as a source of substantive democratic obligation for all acts of public bodies. This process instilled a democratic subject in society that was less immediately implicated in single acts of legislation, but which was more robustly generalized as the primary focus of legal legitimacy and public accountability.

Finally, this process of democratic redesign acquired a foundation in parliamentary authority, through which the normative construction of the democratic citizen was greatly reinforced. This occurred in the Human Rights Act (HRA) (1998), which solidified a number of already existing tendencies in British public law. This Act gave domestic effect to the ECHR as a framework for judicial interpretation of statutes and for regulation of administrative functions. It also led to the establishment of a special committee in parliament, the Joint Committee on Human Rights, to screen draft bills for compliance with the ECHR. Moreover, it translated into hard law the conventional principle that parliament could only legislate in contravention of ECHR rights if it expressly declared this intention (see Kavanagh 2009: 99).

After the entry into force of the HRA in 2000, first, the judicial imposition of constitutional constraints on government became more robust, although it still remained relatively tentative (see Dickson 2013: 16, 98). After 2000, courts routinely applied harder normative criteria to judge the legitimacy of administrative acts, including secondary legislation, in cases with human rights implications.[191] Moreover, courts showed some willingness to challenge primary legislation,[192] and to read new normative meanings into older statutes, to bring existing laws into line with international norms, and with current conceptions of citizenship.[193] In addition, courts began to extend their competence to address questions in the domain of international law and foreign policy.[194] In each respect, the British judiciary entered a closer relation to the ECtHR, as domestic judges increasingly founded their rulings in case law and jurisprudence emanating from

---

[191] Eventually, this established a system of review quite separate from ultra vires. See the following argument: 'The role of the court in human rights adjudication is quite different from the role of the court in an ordinary judicial review of administrative action. In human rights adjudication, the court is concerned with whether the human rights of the claimant have in fact been infringed, not with whether the administrative decision-maker properly took them into account'. *Belfast City Council* v. *Miss Behavin Ltd* – [2007] 1 WLR 1420 (Hale LJ).

[192] *A and others* v. *Secretary of State for the Home Department* [2004] UKHL 56.

[193] See *Ghaidan* v. *Godin-Mendoza* – [2004] All ER (D) 210 (Jun) (Nicholls LJ).

[194] *Bank Mellat* v. *HM Treasury* (No 2) – [2013] 4 All ER 533.

Strasbourg,[195] and they imported Strasbourg norms to articulate hardened constitutional checks on the sovereign power of parliament. In some cases, in fact, the courts decided that, as objective interpreters of legal rights, they could, conceivably, insist upon constitutional rights in order to block primary legislation and to strike down parliamentary acts.[196] In other words, courts perceived themselves as sources of constitutional law. In particular, some judges viewed the HRA as a statute that defied the traditional aversion to vertical privileging of statutes. They interpreted it both *de facto* as a constitutional statute, with transversal force, defining norms for the application of other statutes,[197] and as a statute that entrenches the power of the courts with regard to parliament (see Young 2009: 4). Through the HRA, therefore, the concept of the citizen in British public law was detached from the traditional punctual construction of the electoral citizen, and it was attached, at least in some interpretations, to a more generalized comprehension of law's public authority.

The linking of the UK courts to a supranational judicial order did not solely lead to the simple domestic reinforcement of already established international rights, and it did not mean that the courts became simple passive recipients of ECtHR decisions. On the contrary, this linkage meant that the domestic courts acquired a new spontaneity in the production of rights, and they reconfigured the normative architecture of government in a number of quite distinctive ways.[198] Most importantly, the UK courts began to extract new rights and new modes of rights formation from the substance of the ECHR. On one hand, the courts decided that the principle of proportionality, originally deemed in conflict with the basic principles of UK public law, should be interpreted as compatible with, or even integral to, common law; this significantly expanded the rights fabric of the common law, as far as it applied to public bodies.[199] Additionally, the courts decided that, although nominally bound to recognize Strasbourg rulings as authoritative declarations in human rights questions, they were not formally obliged to accept such rulings, and they could, of their own accord, constructively interpret the ECHR to produce distinctive rights.

---

[195] *R (on the application of Ullah)* v. *Special Adjudicator Do* v. *Secretary of State for the Home Department* – [2004] All ER (D) 153 (Jun).

[196] See the conjectural discussion of this in *R (on the application of Jackson and others)* v. *Attorney General* – [2005] All ER (D) 136 (Oct); *Moohan* v. *Lord Advocate* [2014] UKSC 67.

[197] *Wilson* v. *First County Trust* (No 2) [2003] UKHL 40.

[198] This is perfectly within the scope of the ECHR. See for comment Masterman (2005: 910).

[199] *Pham* v. *Secretary of State for the Home Department* [2015] UKSC 19.

In some cases, this had the result that UK courts were willing to go further than the Strasbourg court in the generation of protective rights and guarantees, and they sometimes established rights above the thresholds set by the ECtHR itself.[200] In this respect, to be sure, the UK courts retained some aspects of the tradition of judicial deference to the political branches.[201] However, they began to assume unprecedented levels of autonomy, and they constructed from international human rights norms a flexible premise for substantive control of government.

Overall, although still relatively closed to the influence of international legal norms, the public legal order of the UK has evolved, almost paradigmatically, through a process in which the domestic legal system has approached a heightened level of differentiation and self-authorization. This differentiation has been caused, in part, by the interaction between domestic courts and supranational institutions, and by the often diffuse entry of international human rights law into the substructure of national law and domestic jurisprudence. As in other cases, the courts emerged as actors with strongly enhanced abilities to create public law, in independence both of their own governments and of the supranational courts, by which they were supposedly determined. Indeed, although, by most reasonable definitions, the political system of the UK had evolved into a democracy by 1950, many normative features of democracy were only consolidated through constructive judicial reasoning, linked to the articulation between national and global law. This was most evident in the construction of principles of administrative accountability. However, this was also evident in the fact that courts compensated for the historically weak construction of the citizen, whose formation had been impeded by the underlying principles of parliamentary constitutionalism. It was only on the grounds of international human rights law that British public law internalized an image of the consistently formed citizen, to whom all acts of parliament owed recognition in similar ways, so that authorship of law was legitimated through a relatively consistent idea of its addressee.[202] In

---

[200] On provision of elevated rights in mental health cases see *Rabone and another* v. *Pennine Care NHS Foundation Trust* – [2012] All ER (D) 59 (Feb).

[201] *R (Lord Carlile of Berriew QC & Ors)* v. *Secretary of State for the Home Department* [2014] UKSC 60.

[202] See the idea of the HRA as allocating generalized rights, beyond the scope of a single statute, in *Wilson* v. *First County Trust (No 2)* [2003] UKHL 40. See the following construction of the prisoner as citizen in the context of a proportionality argument:

> Any custodial order inevitably curtails the enjoyment, by the person confined, of rights enjoyed by other citizens. He cannot move freely and choose

this respect, courts produced a clearly public construction of law's legitimacy, and they separated law from residually privatistic concepts representation that, classically, had dominated British constitutionalism. The new concept of the citizen brought a deep modification of democratic structure, countervailing the traditional dominance of the executive. Underlying this process was not simply a strategic elevation of the role of the judiciary, but rather a construction of the legal system as an autonomous domain of social practice, able to generate constitutional norms and rules of democratic governance on internal premises, without reference to classical political processes. Democratic citizenship was forged through relatively autonomous inner-legal acts, stimulated by the influx of global legal norms.

Self evidently, this does not mean that the entanglement between national and international law in the UK conferred fully secure democratic form on the British polity. The privatistic instability in the concept of the citizen in British public law remains evident in the fact there is diminishing confidence in the parliamentary constitution to create reliable mandates for government, and governments allow popular plebiscites, in which citizens revert to punctual acts of acclamation, to dictate higher-order constitutional norms. This again creates a deeply paradoxical constitutional situation, typical of the British parliamentary system. On one hand, parliament is supposed to be sovereign, and it cannot be constrained by higher norms. Yet, in matters of decisive importance, parliament's sovereignty is suspended, and higher law-making functions are ascribed to individual decisions of the people, in some cases leading to the abrogation, in one decision, of sets of rights generated through complex processes of citizenship formation.[203] In such features, the UK acts, for the sake of

---

his associates as they are entitled to do. It is indeed an important objective of such an order to curtail such rights, whether to punish him or to protect other members of the public or both. But the order does not wholly deprive the person confined of all rights enjoyed by other citizens. Some rights, perhaps in an attenuated or qualified form, survive the making of the order. And it may well be that the importance of such surviving rights is enhanced by the loss or partial loss of other rights.

R v. Secretary of State for the Home Department, ex parte Daly – [2001] All ER (D) 280 (May). On the high symbolic status of the HRA see Feldman (1999: 178).

[203] Notably, in the leading legal judgement regarding the correct procedure for the UK to leave the EU, it was reasoned that EU Treaties had built up a complex store of rights in British law – 'they are a source of domestic legal rights many of which are inextricably linked with domestic law from other sources'. This informed the decision that distinctive legislative authorization was required to take the UK out of the EU: R (on the application of Miller

purported democracy, in rebellion against the process of incremental transnational legal construction that has actually brought democracy into its constitution.

4.2.4   Global Human Rights and National Democracy 4: Colombia

A particularly close correlation between the differentiation of the global legal system, the rising impact of international human rights, and the growth of democracy is observable in Colombia. In fact, Colombia can be seen, in a global perspective, as one of the leading examples of democratic consolidation caused by the systemic differentiation of global law and the systemic construction of the global citizen. Given the extreme obstacles to effective democratization in Colombia, it can be viewed as an extreme exemplification of ways in which global law overcomes structural resistance to effective democratic citizenship.

Examined in a formal perspective, Colombia had a stronger historical record of democratic consolidation than many Latin American countries, and it is sometimes viewed as an outlier amongst Latin American states with weak democratic traditions (see Murillo-Castaño 1999: 47). Notably, Colombia, in the form of Nueva Granada, had a broad male franchise as early as 1853. The Constitution of 1886 then established universal male suffrage at a local level, with literacy and property qualifications for national representation (Rojas 2008: 318). Moreover, in Colombia, pure dictatorship has been a rare phenomenon. Since the late 1950s, overt military involvement in Colombian politics has been rare, elections were held at regular intervals and rotation of governmental executive was partly institutionalized. One commentator observes that Colombia is distinct from other Latin American countries in that, since its first consolidation, it has possessed a 'surprising institutional continuity', and it has generally had 'popularly elected governments and an electoral and parliamentary history without discontinuities or ruptures' (Uribe de Hincapié 1998a: 14). In the 1980s, a leading external commentator observed that Colombia is one of the only countries in Latin America whose political order has had a democratic character, almost without interruption, for a century (Pécaut 1987: 15).

---

and another) v. *Secretary of State for Exiting the European Union*; Re Agnew and others' application for judicial review (reference by the Attorney General for Northern Ireland); Re McCord's application for judicial review (reference by the Court of Appeal (Northern Ireland)) – [2017] 1 All ER 593.

To be sure, such observations need to be assessed with certain qualifications, and Colombian democracy has invariably been marked by unusual features. Even during the period of greatest democratic stability, under the *Frente Nacional* (1958–74), elections in Colombia were not fully competitive. In this period, government took the form of a compacted alternation of executive functions between Presidents from different parties, tellingly described as a 'two-party alliance', with power effectively shared between historical adversaries (Plazas Vega 2011: 57). Moreover, it is widely noted that this system was underpinned by localized patronage networks – indeed, patronage was used both to pacify rival factions and to articulate the government with regional actors, in the absence of broad-based political participation (Leal Buitrago and Dávila Ladrón de Guevara 1990. 10, Martz 1997: 311; Dávila Ladrón de Guevara 1999: 67; Leal Buitrago 2016: 129). Nonetheless, formal governmental structures in Colombia have only rarely deviated categorically from democratic norms. Importantly, except for short interludes, Colombia did not have such a strongly evolved corporatist tradition as many other Latin American countries, and the structural intersection between government bodies and economic organizations was limited (Pécaut 1987: 135, 180). As a result, the corporatist hollowing out of democracy which afflicted many Latin American states was, although not absent, not strongly pronounced in Colombia.

Beneath the formal political arena, however, the governmental order of Colombia was shaped, historically, by a series of profound problems, which meant that national processes of democratic institution building were very precarious.

First, problems in defining basic principles of national citizenship affected the Colombian state from the start, before its final formation as a Republic in 1886. Most obviously, the rise of national citizenship was affected by the fact that Colombia contains a series of very different cultures: the Hispanic urban culture, the Andean culture, the Caribbean culture and the Amazonian culture being the most evident examples. In addition, the pacific region of Colombia contains large African-Colombian populations, comprising descendants of fugitives from the slave trade. After the collapse of the Spanish colonial administration in the early nineteenth century, moreover, the institutionalization of central government was undermined by the complex cultural order of society, which was often reflected in the solidification of local power structures (see Conde Calderón 2009: 271; Márquez Estrada 2011: 68). Initially, notably, definitions of Colombian citizenship in the nineteenth century were not strictly separated from local authority, and local dignitaries acquired privileged rights of citizenship, such that access to the national political sphere was controlled at a local level. One consequence of this was that political coordination between centre and periphery was often dependent on the dispensing of patronage by local actors, who acted as intermediaries between local and national systemic positions (González González 2009: 192). In turn, this meant that the power of central government was restricted by local monopolies and corporate bodies, that national and local elites were not strongly articulated or unified, and that sub-national affiliations and local citizenships were strongly privileged and entrenched (González González 2014: 183, 535). This also meant that citizenship possessed a multi-centric quasi-familial character,[204] and there existed a deep disjuncture between the increasingly urgent demands for nationalized citizenship that became vocal in the middle of the nineteenth century and the factual design of society (Uribe de Hincapié 1998a: 37). For this reason, one important account describes early Colombian citizenship as 'hybrid citizenship', comprising elements of local, clientelistic and national obligation (Uribe de Hincapié 1996: 75). The legacy of this has remained visible into recent history, as clientelistic relations long retained force as important linkages between the political system and society, forming alternatives to popular representation, and political actors not able to dispense patronage still today possess limited mobilizing power.[205]

As a consequence of these factors, the societal penetration of the Colombian state was traditionally very low, and the ability of the government to perform political functions across society (i.e. to raise taxes, to enforce legal norms, to galvanize general support) was routinely obstructed by influential social elites and by the local dispersal of power.[206] In some respects, prominent economic actors in Colombia strategically opposed the emergence of a central government, based on national patterns of citizenship and collective obligation, able to dictate national law and national policy and to establish uniform conditions of entitlement, and they actively boycotted the process of national political institution-

---

[204] See discussion in Márquez Estrada (2012: 301).

[205] For discussion of the importance of clientelism in recent Colombian history, see Martz (1997: 40, 309); Uprimny (1989: 129); Dávila Ladrón de Guevara (1999: 74).

[206] The emergence of the Colombian state as a state with weak capacities was probably shaped by the fact that Colombian elites possessed private power and private security, and they did not want a strong state (see Pécaut 1987: 18; Uribe López 2013: 198). In Colombia, the tax-raising powers of municipal bodies are still variable and their governance capacity is low. See on this García Villegas et al. (2016: 44, 78).

alization (see Uribe López 2013: 145, 287). This meant that the evolution of a fully nationalized political system was always a fitful and deeply contested process, and, historically, the state lacked the capacities to exercise integrative control across society. To be sure, the Constitution of 1886 was, notionally, a very centralizing document, and it instituted a nationalized political and judicial order, to replace pre-existing federal arrangements (see Cajas Sarria 2015a: 64). Yet, the factual structure of society resisted nationalization, and it persisted in its multi-centric form (Leal Buitrago 2016: 115).

Most significantly, however, the obstruction to national democracy in Colombia was caused by the intermittently extremely high levels of social violence and civil conflict, often of a multi-polar nature, which ravaged Colombian society, and blocked societal penetration of state power. To a large degree, of course, social violence was the result of the historical mismatch between government and society that was inherited from the colonial period and was accentuated during the nineteenth century. Through the early period of state formation, the use of violence demonstrated, whether consciously or not, a contest over the conditions of systemic nationalization, elaborating rival accounts of national society and national citizenship, and contesting the terms under which the political arena extended into society.[207] To this degree, violence formed a mode of illegal political participation, alongside more institutionalized articulations between state and society (Leal Buitrago 2016: 137). More contingently, social, violence was exacerbated through the solidification of a strict two-party system of representation in the twentieth century, which led to an intermittently intense politicization of local and traditional conflicts and rivalries (González González 2014: 298). Moreover, violence resulted from the lack of institutional organs strong enough to resolve social conflicts at a national level, especially conflicts relating to agrarian production in rural areas.

Whatever its particular causes, the prevalence of extreme violence in Colombia necessarily weakened the power of the national political system, and it called into question the basic locus of political sovereignty in society (Uribe de Hincapié 1999: 30). This was clearly manifest in the period of acute civil conflict in the 1950s, when it appeared that hostile factions had effectively created separate Republics within the space notionally seen as Colombian national territory (Aguilera Peña 2014: 12–13). From the late 1960s onward, then, Colombia was again increasingly beset by such intense civil conflict, escalating into the 1980s and 1990s, that in some parts

---

[207] See outstanding analysis in Uribe de Hincapié (1998a: 45).

of society political power was not primarily vested in formally ordered state-like institutions. By the 1980s, a number of actors and organizations, including insurgent guerrillas, rightist paramilitaries and drug cartels, rivalled or even replaced state agencies in some regions. In fact, both guerrillas and paramilitaries established alternative modes of relatively cohesive sovereign organization in the particular regions over which they acquired control, even creating local judicial and fiscal systems,[208] thus acting as *de facto* micro-states. These factors meant that Colombian society as a whole was only unevenly centred around identifiably public institutions, and the political system as a whole assumed a highly polycratic form, containing many parallel modes of authority. In many instances, in fact, the formal state structure was not clearly distinct from bodies deploying more obviously privatized resources of violence, as the government had routinely co-opted paramilitaries in order to crack down on Communist militias. Moreover, even regular military forces were not securely under government control.[209]

Overall, until the 1990s, Colombian democracy was not based on a centralized or even coherently defined organizational system. Democratic government institutions were acutely undermined by the localization of power and the privatization of political institutions and by at times extreme levels of social and political violence. Although the Colombian political system was formally democratic, political institutions lacked the robustness and the institutional penetration needed to make democracy a socially meaningful condition, with secure foundations across different societal regions.

The most concerted attempt to remedy problems of state diffusion in Colombia began with the drafting of a new constitution, which entered force in 1991. At this point, the decision to write a new constitution was reached as part of a strategy to pacify society, and to establish institutions able to gain support amongst rival parties in the civil conflict. This was of course an intensely pressing necessity, reflecting the background of

---

[208] For analysis see Uribe de Hincapié (1999: 39–40); González, Bolívar and Vázquez (2003: 31, 198, 231, 250, 257). One deeply illuminating account sets out a periodization of this process, arguing that after 1985 guerrillas began to colonize municipal power in some areas (Aguilera Peña 2014: 129). This is seen as a continuation of the 'fragmentation of sovereignty' which occurred, in a different constellation, in the 1950s (Aguilera Peña 2014: 139). Notably, this policy of dominating municipal executive and legal functions was also pursued by paramilitary organizations (Aguilera Peña 2014: 377). The relation between paramilitaries and the regular state is more problematic, as in many regions the paramilitaries were an informal wing of the government (see Grajales 2017: 88–9).

[209] On these points see Bejarano (2011: 207, 296).

the rapidly escalating violence that marked the 1980s, exemplified in the assassination of leading judges in the Supreme Court in 1985. The 1991 Constitution was conceived as a focus for a wholesale process of political reorientation and even for national re-foundation. Although not a transitional constitution in the strict sense, it was intended to establish new institutional foundations for popular democratic government. Moreover, it was also conceived as a peace treaty, intended to reinforce government institutions by ending the civil war. Indicatively, the convocation of the Constituent Assembly charged with drafting the Constitution originated in an emergency presidential decree (Decree 927 of 1990), which stated that broad exercise of popular constitution-making power was required to solidify state institutions and to overcome the permanent destabilization of public order caused by civil violence. Unusually, in consequence, this Constitution resulted from a relatively open, socially pluralistic process of constitution making, which was not dominated by the historically dominant Liberal and Conservative parties. In fact, different parties in the civil conflict, alongside other social organizations, obtained a position in the Constituent Assembly. The earlier part of the constitution-making process was also influenced by a range of grass-roots initiatives, particularly the student movement, motivated by a commitment to long-term demilitarization.[210]

In its eventual written form, the 1991 Constitution of Colombia anticipated aspects of later constitutions in Bolivia and Ecuador, as it integrated an array of organizations in the political system, giving recognition to NGOs, human rights organizations and indigenous population groups as effective constitutional subjects. In this respect, the constitution was designed to extend the boundaries of the political system beyond the formal political arena, aiming to establish wide consensus across society for the newly founded democratic order. Accordingly, the constitution placed great emphasis on the importance of civil participation in government functions (especially Articles 40–1, 95(5), 103). Moreover, the constitution enacted a policy of partial decentralization, designed to reinforce municipal governments as important subsidiary pillars of the political system, and to increase engagement and participation in political functions at municipal and local levels.

Most notably, the 1991 Constitution accorded high symbolic status to human rights law as the basis for political reorientation. The doctrine of

---

[210] See the interviews regarding this point in Restrepo Yepes, Bocanument Arvelaez and Rojas Betancur (2014: 46, 54).

human rights had a very prominent place in the Constituent Assembly, and the commitment to human rights obligations assumed a rank close to a pre-constitutional law, informing and pre-structuring discussions in the Assembly.[211] Notably, human rights diction had assumed salience in Colombian society in the 1980s, as international organizations had become more involved in the Colombian conflict, and different domestic factions increasingly formulated their positions around human rights claims (Yates 2007: 129; Grajales 2017: 158–60). The constitution in fact strategically utilized human rights to separate the organs of government from previously dominant political stakeholders, and to project a common socio-political language, through which actors in different social formations were able to address and to engage with the state as common interlocutor (Lemaitre Ripoll 2009: 107, 216). In some respects, the Constitution promoted human rights as a unifying *normative* diction to replace the unifying *material* order established by the 1886 Constitution, whose centralizing dimensions had met with deep opposition. More generally, however, the Constitution was intended to rebuild the state through the use of human rights, and even to create a unified model of the citizen, to underpin the state, by borrowing constructs from human rights law. Indeed, a perception that state debility was correlated with a weak articulation of the citizen, which could be rectified through the consolidation of human rights, was pervasive through the constitution-making process.[212] In these respects, the Colombian Constitution of 1991 formed a prototype for later transformative constitutions, in which human rights law was utilized as a hard instrument for societal reconstruction, intensified intergroup articulation, and unified citizenship formation.

In conjunction with this, the 1991 Constitution of Colombia also had the distinction that it established a powerful Constitutional Court. To some degree, this aspect of the Constitution built on already existing elements of Colombian constitutionalism. Notably, before 1991, the Supreme Court had already acquired some features usually associated with a Constitutional Court. It already possessed a chamber with responsibility for constitutional review, which resulted from proposals in the late 1960s to create a Constitutional Court (Cajas Sarria 2015b: 99–104). As early as 1910, in fact, the Supreme Court had obtained the authority to

---

[211] See witness reports in Restrepo Yepes, Bocanument Arvelaez and Rojas Betancur (2014: 287, 304).

[212] For historical-sociological analysis of this three-way nexus in Colombia between weak statehood, weak construction of the citizen and the promotion of human rights, see Uribe de Hincapié (1999: 30–1).

exercise control of statutes (Cajas Sarria 2015a: 16). Then, in the 1970s, the Supreme Court declared some constitutional reforms and electoral laws unconstitutional (Cajas Sarria 2015b: 207, 214, 253). Moreover, the Supreme Court had played a role in creating the constitution-making situation in 1991, as, in face of congressional opposition, it had approved Decree 927 and Decree 1926 (1990), which ultimately authorized the Constituent Assembly to create a new Constitution, insisting that the people have a right to act as 'primary constituent' of the political order (Cajas Sarria 2015b: 406). After 1991, the Court quickly began to develop a very activist line of constitutional review, and it utilized its powers to establish robust lines of articulation between different societal groups and institutions in the governance system. Through this, the Court became a core actor in the promotion of an overarching structure of national citizenship.

After 1991, on one hand, the Constitutional Court strongly upheld the participatory dimensions of the Colombian Constitution. In its early rulings, the Court projected a strong ethic of participatory citizenship, emphasizing the claim that all people possessed a 'fundamental right to participation' in the 'exercise and regulation of political power', and stressing the obligation of the state to ensure the 'participation of the citizenry in the processes of taking decisions of relevance for collective destiny'.[213] Importantly, the Court also ruled that there exists a right to information, to facilitate the right to participate in shaping government decisions.[214] In these respects, the Court supported a classical model of the citizen as participatory political agent, implied in the constitution. Indeed, the Court evidently understood itself as a protagonist in the national endeavour to create strong institutions and to consolidate national support for government through the invigoration of citizenship practices.[215] In parallel to this, however, the Court used supplementary means to integrate societal actors into the political system, and it took particular steps to ensure that all persons in society were constructed in uniform categories of citizenship. The Court in fact devised a normative apparatus in which it could help to eradicate regional and social variations in access to legal inclusion, and to intensify the societal reach of government by cementing a stable legal order of citizenship.

To accomplish this, after 1991, the Constitutional Court began to promote very strong protection for human rights within Colombian society,

---

[213] C-180/94.
[214] C-891/02.
[215] See early discussion in T-479/92.

and it applied human rights as powerful elements in a system of normative integration. In this regard, the jurisprudence of the Court centred on the principle, borrowed from German constitutional law, that the protection of human dignity should be interpreted as a meta-norm in the Constitution, and that the Court had an obligation to 'enlarge' this value, to ensure its enforcement in all constitutional practices, and to give effect to it in the 'social dimension' of human life.[216] As a result, the Court extracted from this principle a commitment independently to expand the rights contained in the Constitution, and to increase enjoyment of rights amongst all social agents, placing particular emphasis on socio-economic rights and minority-group rights, to be protected equally across society.

In this strategy of rights expansion, the Colombian Constitutional Court often supported its rulings through reference to international human rights law. In fact, the growing power of the high judiciary in Colombia was closely linked to the rising authority of the IACtHR, and it clearly reflected a wider tendency towards the concretization of human rights law as a regional supra-national structure in Latin America.[217] Ultimately, the Constitutional Court assumed an unusually constructive approach in the domestic assimilation of international law, and it integrated many principles of international law, possessing varying degrees of formal authority, as binding norms of domestic legal order. As discussed, this was expressed at an early stage in the process of constitutional redirection, as the Court declared in 1992 that international norms with *jus cogens* rank, including international humanitarian law, should be subject to 'automatic incorporation' in the domestic legal order.[218] This was then elaborated in the doctrine of the block of constitutionality, through which the Constitutional Court established the norm that, at the insistence of the Court itself, international treaties could become constitutionally binding elements of domestic law.[219] Moreover, the Court ruled that judgements of the IACtHR should have direct domestic effect,[220] and that they form a 'hermeneutical criterion' for establishing basic rights in domestic law.[221]

---

[216] T-881/02.

[217] This was noted in Inter-American Commission on Human Rights (1993): 'The work being done by the new Constitutional Court, whose magistrates were sworn in as recently as March 1992, deserves a special word of recognition from the Inter-American Commission on Human Rights for the work it is doing to defend, strengthen and consolidate Colombia's constitutional system.'

[218] C-574/92.

[219] C-408/96.

[220] T-275/94.

[221] C-010/00.

Eventually, the Court stated that rulings of the IACtHR should be treated as part of the domestic block of constitutionality.[222]

In this approach, the Constitutional Court promoted a clearly constitutional interpretation of international human rights law, adopting international norms as the essential premise for the legitimacy of governmental acts. Through this, effectively, domestic citizens assumed immediate rights as citizens of international law, and, if so determined by the Court, government bodies were obligated directly to international law. Indeed, this approach was based on the express claim that the sovereignty of state institutions is strictly relativized by international human rights law – that human rights 'are too important for their protection to be left exclusively in the hands of states.'[223] As mentioned, this approach acquired particular importance in the sphere of socio-economic rights, as the Constitutional Court imposed strict obligations on the government for the satisfaction of material rights.[224] However, this approach was also reflected in questions more specific to Colombian society. The Court addressed many structural problems historically characteristic of Colombia in a framework provided by international norms. In particular, this became visible in the Court's jurisprudence in questions linked to problems caused by social violence. Very notably, as discussed below, international human rights norms were used, often in ways not anticipated in international instruments themselves, to construct a rights-based legal regime for internal refugees, to attribute responsibility for violence perpetrated by paramilitary groups, and to suppress regional disorders.[225] International law was thus deployed to attribute enhanced rights to the most vulnerable and marginalized groups in society, and it formed a core medium of societal inclusion and structural formation.

Especially important in the jurisprudence of the Colombian Constitutional Court is the fact that, through its overtly activist, outward orientation, it increasingly utilized international norms not only to impose constraints on, but also to dictate policies to, actors in other branches of the political system. In some cases, in fact, the Constitutional Court constructed international human rights law as a constitutional order in which it, of itself, assumed legislative responsibility, so that it

---

[222] T-1319/01.
[223] C-408/96.
[224] T-426/92.
[225] Notably, the Constitutional Court gave constitutional standing to soft-law norms of the UN concerning displaced populations, the Deng Principles and the Pinheiro Principles. See T-327/01; T-602/03.

could correct the actions or inactions of politically mandated legislators.[226] Owing to the historical weakness of the government, in fact, inaction of government agencies became a particularly frequent ground for judicial intervention. This activist strategy was developed by the Court across a range of different cases, including prison-law cases. However, this strategy ultimately assumed regular prominence as waves of persons displaced by internal violence in rural regions entered Bogotá in the years around 2000, confronting the urban population with the personal consequences of protracted civil conflict. During this period, the Court took a more interventionist stance towards the political branches, especially in cases in which government complicity in civil violence was suspected. In so doing, the Court assumed a highly unusual position in the political system, often demanding legislative authority by claiming that Congress was unable (or unwilling) to address the social problems with which it was confronted and that the Court was obliged to perform legislative functions to fill this gap.[227]

Initially, the Constitutional Court's attempts to control political institutions were mainly oppositional in nature, and the Court expressed harsh criticism of government policy. Over a longer period, however, the Constitutional Court slightly revised its terms of engagement with other governmental institutions, and it began to play a more constructive role in the development of Colombian democracy. Ultimately, the Court adopted a strategy in which it phrased its normative directives as manageable policy guidelines, designed to improve government performance and even to enhance state capacity through recognition of international legal norms.

In the first instance, the Court assumed these remedial functions by aligning its rulings and recommendations to the case law of the IACtHR, which, in a number of cases, had sought to bring pressure to bear upon the Colombian government to avert civil violence. In some cases, the Constitutional Court supported the IACtHR in its criticism, and it deliberately reproduced the criticisms levelled at the national government by the IACtHR. Notable amongst these is the case, *Caballero Delgado and Santana*, heard by the IACtHR in 1995, which concerned the kidnapping and presumed murder of trade unionists by members of the national army and by citizens acting as soldiers (paramilitaries).[228] Initially,

---

[226] See below p. 364.

[227] On the dislike for Congress and the perception of Congress as corrupt amongst judges on the Colombian Constitutional Court, see Landau (2014: 1520).

[228] IACtHR, *Caballero Delgado and Santana v. Colombia*, Judgment of 8 December 1995.

the government of Colombia denied any responsibility for the kidnapping, dismissing evidence to prove that the kidnapping had been conducted by persons acting in a public capacity. This claim was disputed by the IACtHR, which ruled that the government had responsibility for such acts, and it was subject to indictment under the ACHR. In later cases, the IACtHR extended these arguments, stating that even when persons committing human rights violations were not acting under immediate colour of law, or where this was difficult to determine, the state could still be found in breach of its obligations under the ACHR.[229] In so doing, gradually, the IACtHR spelled out an increasingly strict principle of state liability to address problems of private violence in Colombia, insisting that the Colombian state was directly responsible for all acts of violence perpetrated within its territories. Progressively, then, the Colombian Constitutional Court began to replicate this approach, and it endorsed the attribution of political liability proposed by the IACtHR. As a result, it applied these principles to coordinate branches of government, claiming that the government was liable for shortcomings in its provision of protection for its subjects and in its preservation of law and order.[230] On this basis, the Court assumed authority to dictate policy in areas in which the state had proved deficient. This line of jurisprudence was shaped by the principle that the political branches had failed in some of their core functions, notably in territorial pacification and judicial control, such that the Court assumed a distinct duty to *correct state failure*.[231] In this respect, the Court began to construct transnational principles of government obligation in Colombia, and, it invoked international jurisprudence in order to intensify the constitutional structure in which the government was positioned, and its functions were exercised. Indeed, the Court utilized international directives to expand the government's responsibilities across society, and so effectively to build and to extend the national constitutional structure of the state.

Most notably, the Constitutional Court in Colombia gradually elaborated a line of reasoning to the effect that in certain situations, marked by egregious and systemic human rights violations, it was entitled to make a declaration against the executive or against Congress not only regarding one point of law or one particular violation of a right, but about an entire set of social circumstances. Such cases have usually arisen in *tutela*

---

[229] See Case of the *"Mapiripán Massacre" v. Colombia*. Judgment of 15 September 2005.

[230] See the classic examples C-370/2006 and C-334/13, responding to the IACtHR's findings against Colombia in Case of the *"Mapiripán Massacre" v. Colombia*.

[231] See below at pp. 365–6.

litigation. The *tutela* is a distinctive legal instrument in Colombia, established under Article 86 of the 1991 Constitution, and it is designed to enable challenge against public bodies for human rights violations, especially in circumstances in which other causes of action are not available. However, the submission of *tutelas* assumed unforeseen dimensions after the implementation of the 1991 Constitution, and rising use of *tutelas* created a situation in which, owing in part to the weakness of other branches of government, the courts were required to engage immediately with a range of persons, social actors and social movements (Lemaitre Ripoll 2009: 24). In *tutela* rulings, notably, individual proceedings against public bodies have often formed the basis for wholesale remedial measures, reaching far beyond the case at hand. Indeed, in such cases, the Constitutional Court has assumed authority to prescribe remedies that apply not only to the parties that had lodged an application, but to 'all persons placed in the same situation'.[232] This meant that, in some *tutelas*, the Court was able to issue rulings that introduced blanket, open-ended policies, designed to remedy massive systemic failures in public order. Such highly politicized jurisprudence was not unprecedented, and similar examples can be found in the USA in the 1960s.[233] However, this pattern of reasoning assumed great significance in the context of Colombian society, and the Court began to issue declarations that, in some circumstances, it was confronted with an 'unconstitutional state of affairs', which required remedies robust enough to reinstate comprehensive constitutional order. Early examples of declarations of an unconstitutional state of affairs often referred to systemically localized problems, such as social security provisions or prison regulation.[234] Eventually, such rulings were made in a number of critical situations, for example in large-scale environmental crises.[235] However, the primary rulings of this kind were made in situations in which large numbers of the population had been forcibly displaced as a result of guerrilla and paramilitary violence, usually in remote rural areas. In such circumstances, many population groups were exposed to depredation and

---

[232] T-025/04.

[233] See the precedent for this in *Holt* v. *Sarver*, 309 F. Supp. 362 (E.D. Ark. 1970).

[234] See T-153/98. For the first declaration that an entire 'state of affairs', in this instance a complex of problems relating to educational administration, was 'openly unconstitutional' see SU-559/97.

[235] See T-622/16. In this case, pollution of the Atrato basin, near Quibco, caused by illegal mining operations, was seen as the cause of an unconstitutional state of affairs, leading to a violation *inter alia* of the right to life, of rights to a clean environment, rights to food security and rights of indigenous communities.

deprived of core rights, so that, in affected regions, normal legal/constitutional provisions had restricted effect.

In a series of rulings concerning internal displacement beginning in 1997, the Constitutional Court defined the conditions of displaced populations as characterized by the 'repeated and constant infringement of fundamental rights, affecting many people, whose solution necessitates the intervention of various entities to address problems of a structural character'. In such circumstances, the Court decided that it had authority to declare a state of *structural unconstitutionality*: that is, to claim that certain 'structural factors', not solely attributable to one entity or to one public authority, had led to a 'massive abuse' of human rights, resulting, quite generally, in 'an unconstitutional state of affairs'.[236] In such instances, the Court ruled that it was required to provide remedies affecting a number of bodies, not all of which were directly or causally implicated in the instant *tutela*.[237] On this basis, the Court was able to generalize quasi-legislative remedies across society, often claiming authority to do so through international human rights law. In addition, the Court decided that it had the power to monitor governmental implementation of remedies prescribed by the judiciary in situations of this kind. In such cases, therefore, the Constitutional Court sanctioned and encouraged processes of *structural litigation*, in which court cases were expected to produce remedies of broad structural importance, resolving problems of a general societal nature, and creating binding obligations for different government branches. In such cases, the Court declared that judges were obliged to display a 'special dynamism' in the type of decisions which they took.[238] Moreover, judges in lower regional courts identified such cases as containing instructions for their rulings in related or similar cases, such that principles set out by the Constitutional Court were replicated throughout the entire judicial system.[239]

The main ruling of this kind is T-025/2004, one of the most important decisions in the global history of modern public law. In this case, a *tutela* case filed on public-interest grounds, the Constitutional Court established a landmark ruling concerning the violation of the basic rights of large numbers of displaced persons caused by civil violence. In the reasoning

---

[236] T-025/04.

[237] T-153/98.

[238] A-385/10.

[239] For example, T-025/04 is cited in important land restitution cases in regional land courts. See Court for Restitution of Land (Quibdo), Interlocutory Appeal 0035 (24 April 2017); Interlocutory Appeal 006 (30 January 2013).

of the Court, this mass-displacement was taken to indicate the existence of an unconstitutional state of affairs in Colombian society. In response to this, the Court assumed competence to prescribe to responsible authorities a number of policy measures required to remove the unconstitutional state of affairs. Tellingly, the Court saw this power as founded in the principle of 'harmonious collaboration between the distinct branches of power', each of which had the obligation to 'ensure the fulfilment of the duty of effective protection of the rights of all residents in the national territory'.[240] Owing to the large proportion of the population affected, the ruling was accorded *inter comunis* effect, so that it was binding on all persons suffering human rights violations caused by displacement, and applicable to large numbers of people across society. In subsequent related rulings in fact, the Constitutional Court devised the concept of the 'passive subject' in cases of large-scale human rights violations, implying that parties affected by, and requiring remedies in, such cases did not need to be involved in court proceedings, and in fact did not need to have knowledge of them. The Court used this concept to categorize the personality of affected parties as broadly as possible, ensuring that the social extension of rulings with structural significance was maximized and judicial directives relating to egregious human rights violations could acquire the greatest possible resonance across society.[241]

In T-025/04, effectively, the Colombian Constitutional Court argued that, in light of mass displacement, the Colombian state had experienced a wholesale systemic failure, manifest in its inability to secure stability within its borders, and it assumed for itself direct responsibility for overcoming this condition.[242] The Court utilized human rights norms to make this argument, claiming that the deprivation of large swathes of the population of basic rights had proved that the state was not in a position to fulfil its duties as a state. In this respect, the Court used human rights law as an instrument to measure existing state capacity, suggesting that generalized non-fulfilment of human rights obligations was evidence of a broad political-institutional crisis. The Court actually formulated this strategy in consciously 'Weberian terms', arguing that protection of human rights was a means for the state to show its legitimacy by 'monopolizing the exercise of force' in society.[243] Accordingly, the Court concluded that the rising

---

[240]   T-025/04.

[241]   A-385/10.

[242]   Quite correctly, one observer describes the political response to mass displacement as a 'breathtaking failure' (Landau 2012: 223).

[243]   SU-1150/00.

crisis of the state could only be seen as resolved if society as a whole entered a condition in which each person was adequately protected as a rights holder, and where violation of human rights was no longer endemic. As a guarantor of human rights, thus, the Court claimed a particular competence to 'dictate the orders' that appeared 'necessary to secure the effective enjoyment of the human rights of the displaced population'.[244] In particular, the Court declared that the 'seriousness and complexity' of the circumstances brought before it, the 'frequency of the violation of rights', and the number of 'public authorities compromised', meant that judges were required to arrive at rulings that were sufficiently robust and conclusive to re-establish the structural/institutional efficacy of the political system, and to reinstate the population in their rights.[245] As a result, judges assumed authority to issue remedial declarations with full legislative force, giving immediate effect to constitutional law and international human rights law, and filling gaps in the regulatory orders imposed by the government.[246]

In T-025/04, the Colombian Constitutional Court devised a very distinctive line of jurisprudential argument, and it imposed a very distinctive set of obligations for implicated public agencies. First, the Court ordered that relevant authorities should take all necessary steps to improve the circumstances of persons affected by structural problems in society, and, additionally, they should implement programmes to rectify the *weaknesses in institutional capacity* that had led to the crisis.[247] Further, the Court stated that the ruling should form a wide framework for subsequent legislation and policy making. In fact, the verdict issued in T-025/04 was essentially defined as a higher directive, under which the Court reserved authority to introduce further judicial rulings, orders and injunctions on a rolling basis. Most importantly, after the ruling in T-025/2004, the Court issued a large number of subsequent declarations concerning matters incidentally related to the original case (*autos*), in which the Court evaluated the implementation of its directives, often making additional recommendations for their fulfilment. In some *autos*, the Court made provisions for organizing oral hearings between the government and affected parties and stakeholders, and it even insisted that national and international organizations should be co-opted to resolve structural problems.[248] In some *autos*,

---

[244]   A-385/10.
[245]   Ibid.
[246]   Ibid.
[247]   T-025/04.
[248]   T-602/03.

the Court went as far as to recommend alterations to the national fiscal system, arguing that existing revenues were insufficient for the government to regain structural dominance in society and to put an end to the unconstitutional situation. Tellingly, the Court indicated that Congress had been ineffective in its budgetary and fiscal policies, and it implied that fiscal incompetence on the part of the Congress, leading to a basic debility of state structure in society, was a primary cause of human rights violations. Moreover, the Court requested the government to draw up 'indicators' to gauge satisfactory protection of the rights violated through the unconstitutional state of affairs,[249] and the government eventually established standards of compliance, based on international legal norms, by which the Court assessed implementation of its directives.[250] Although the Court's rulings clearly entailed harsh criticism of governmental failings, therefore, the Court also attempted to secure a workable collaboration with Congress. In however strained fashion, it established a basis of consensus between itself and other branches of government. Notably, these rulings and orders resulted in the passing of the *Victims' Law* of 2011 (Law 1448/2011), which placed some of the Court's ordinances on statutory foundations.

In these respects, the measures taken by the Colombian Constitutional Court were clearly focused on the construction of a national governance system, which was seen as a task that Congress itself had not accomplished, or Congress had not wished to accomplish.[251]

For example, one key point of emphasis in the *autos* issued by the Court subsequent to T-025/04 was that they were intended to establish greater coordination between national and regional entities, in addressing which the court aimed to solidify the national governance structure at different levels across society. As a result, human rights norms were implemented as instruments to extend the societal reach of the government. In fact, they were intended to impose a broad order of national citizenship on society, in which inclusion in the legal and political system was more robustly guaranteed. In one highly indicative declaration, the Court stated that the provision of remedies and the protection of human rights for displaced persons were being undermined by the weakness of local government bodies in regions affected by displacement and, above all, by

---

[249] A-266/06.

[250] A-109/07.

[251] See lengthy discussion of these processes in Rodríguez Garavito and Rodríguez Franco (2010: 51, 90, 276).

the 'inadequate co-ordination between the Nation and local government bodies'.[252] Accordingly, the Court announced that heightened cooperation between national government and regional or municipal authorities was required, and it prescribed measures to tighten lines of accountability between central government and the regions. One key claim in this *auto* was that the national government could not use the weakness of local bodies as an 'excuse or pretext' for its own failings in resolving human rights violations, and it was obliged to strengthen regional organs of administration in order to implement the rulings of the Court.[253] Human rights norms thus became, literally, a platform for national democratic institution building,[254] and human rights were used to form core elements in a material constitution, placing linked obligations on all public agencies, both central and local, and binding together different tiers of governance system.[255]

A further key point of focus in these *autos* was that the Court developed a differential theory regarding the implementation of its rulings. Over a longer sequence of declarations, the Court stated that human rights protection should be intensified for social groups whose vulnerability was disproportionately increased by violence and displacement; in particular, for women and indigenous persons (and for indigenous women most especially).[256] In so doing, the Court assumed heightened authority for monitoring government policies in cases in which groups marked by distinctive vulnerability were implicated, and it ordered a heightened degree of structural control – that is, in effect, affirmative action – in such circumstances, often most visible in remote regions.[257] Ultimately, the Court decided that the state had an obligation to use 'affirmative means' to ensure the 'real and effective equality' of persons affected by displacement.[258] In these respects, differential protection of the rights of marginal groups became a central part of a strategy of systemic consolidation and

---

[252] A-385/10.
[253] Ibid.
[254] These policies had limited effect in rural areas, but were successful in larger cities.
[255] See T-602/63; Auto 007/2009.
[256] See A-092/08 in which the Court ordered implementation of special policies to protect displaced women, especially indigenous women.
[257] The Court generally adopted a theory of differential protection. It declared, indicatively, that the 'right to urgent preferential treatment' is a core device for protecting persons in a state of 'defencelessness caused by internal forced displacement' (T-268/03). In the follow-up cases to T-025/04, it identified a number of groups as requiring differential protection. These included (A-004/09) indigenous communities and (A-092/08) women.
[258] T-267/11.

national integration. The Court strategically used human rights law to incorporate vulnerable social constituencies in the domain of state power, and to elevate the power of the state above 'other centres of military power' that existed in Colombian society.[259]

One outcome of these processes was that the Colombian government itself began to accept the principles of liability defined by the Constitutional Court and the IACtHR, and it increasingly acknowledged its responsibility under international law for crimes committed by persons acting in the extended peripheries of the formal governance system. In accepting these rulings, in fact, the government admitted deficiencies both in its constitutional structure and in its societal centrality, and it endeavoured to augment its responsibility across different parts of Colombian society. Notably, the government accepted responsibility for the actions of private persons perpetrating military violence, and it acknowledged that it had a duty to obviate the private assumption of coercive power.[260] To this degree, the government accepted that it had an obligation to improve standards of legal enforcement and legal remedy across different parts of domestic society, thus internalizing international obligations as a basis for its own legal functions.[261] Very significant in this regard is that many of the most important human rights rulings were handed down under the presidency of Uribe, whose commitment to constitutional rule was questionable, and whose vision of state consolidation was emphatically repressive. The fact that its rulings were accepted shows that the Court had acquired an unusual degree of political traction. Finally, it was noted, not lastly by the IACtHR, that standards of accountability increased sharply in Colombia, and that domestic provision for personal security was in some cases sufficient to obviate complaints to the IACtHR.[262]

---

[259] SU-1150/00.

[260] This recognition is reflected in a number of acts of the Colombian government, including acknowledgement of international responsibility, compliance with remedies, creation of permanent education programmes on human rights and international humanitarian law, and administration of criminal trials in response to the reparations ordered by the IACtHR.

[261] The creation of the 'Comisión Nacional de Reparación y Reconciliación' in Law 975/2005 (Ley de Justicia y Paz) and the institution of a domestic programme of integral reparation for victims of the internal armed conflict in Law 1448/2011 (Ley de Victimas) attest to domestic acceptance of international obligations.

[262] In the recent cases, *Case of the Afro-Descendant Communities Displaced from the Cacarica River Basin (Operation Genesis)* v. *Colombia*, Judgment of 20 November 2013 and Case of *Yarce et al.* v. *Colombia*, Judgment 22 November 2016, the IACtHR took into account the existence of domestic reparation mechanisms in Colombia and allowed such mechanisms to fulfil some reparation requirements. For recent discussions of this topic see Lessard (2017); Sandoval (2017).

The most important outcome of these processes was that in the longer wake of the creation of the Constitution in 1991 the basic capacity of the Colombian state increased in tangible ways. Eventually, the strategies of human rights enforcement deployed by the Constitutional Court gave rise to a process of intensified structural formation and increasing legal/political institutionalization. At one level, the growing robustness of state institutions was reflected in certain basic indicators, such as the linkage between national and regional government organs, and in increasing the fiscal capacity of government.[263] However, the increasing robustness of state institutions was also reflected in the fact that government bodies were able to reach more deeply into society, and to build frameworks in which, even in remote areas, individuals and organizations could interact with the national government. This became visible in the fact that, from the earlier 1990s onwards, use of human rights petitions (*tutelas*) against public agencies became geographically widespread, bringing actors across society into a more even relation to central institutions.[264] In this respect, human rights became an important *inter-group vocabulary* of inclusion, establishing hard connections between different social groups, different institutions and different regions. Litigation in *tutelas* began to appear as a distinctive pattern of citizenship practice, and members of society were able both to gain societal integration and even to shape legislative processes through litigation. Indeed, human rights formed a normative web across society that linked social agents, especially those marginalized by class or violence, to governmental institutions. One reason for the promotion of human rights, of course, was that in many regions radical insurgents had created their own governance systems, emphasizing social equality, and human rights law allowed public bodies to mobilize an alternative legitimating register for their functions. In this respect, human rights formed a binding legal/constitutional structure for all persons in society, leading to a deep-reaching constitutionalization of everyday life and a

---

[263] The tax-raising capacity of the state increased by circa 100 per cent between 1970 and 2016. However, it remains very low at about 15 per cent of GDP. See García Villegas et al. (2016: 13).

[264] The geographical spread of *tutela* cases is quite broad, and it seems broadly to reflect the nature of the violations appealed. For example, in 2014, the highest density of *tutelas* regarding human dignity was found in Antioquia (circa 23 per cent), which is also the case for *tutelas* concerning economic, social and cultural rights (circa 42 per cent). The largest number of due process *tutelas* was heard in Bogotá (35 per cent). The greatest overall percentage increases were recorded in more remote areas, Putumayo (14,887 per cent) and Amazonas (4,481 per cent) (Defensoría del pueblo 2015: 75–6).

deep societal penetration of national citizenship, attaching persons across society to the national government.

The web of human rights created by the Constitutional Court intensified not only the geographical and functional penetration of the Colombian legal order, but also its penetration into different social domains. As discussed, the Constitutional Court used international law to create robust rights-based legal norms in order to regulate – or effectively to constitutionalize – different sectors of social exchange, including, in particular, health care,[265] education[266] and the environment.[267] The sectoral constitutions established in this way were not constructed in complete independence of each other, and they were sustained by the transversal value of human dignity, which the Court identified as the meta-normative value in the Constitution. In each domain, however, the Court promoted distinct patterns of *sectoral citizenship*, sustained by overlying values, to sit alongside the uniform patterns of national citizenship which it promoted in addressing outcomes of civil violence and national fragmentation. In some cases, in fact, constitutional formation extended beyond human subjects, and different natural entities, animate and inanimate, were constructed as constitutional subjects.[268] Overall, the Court adopted a two-level approach to citizenship formation, aiming to consolidate citizenship at a national level, but also to embed citizenship practices in different social domains.

The structurally formative role of human rights in Colombia became especially visible in the fact that it provided normative authority for decisions concerning societal conflicts of the most extreme intensity. This has been discussed in relation to mass displacement. This has also been discussed in relation to questions of mass brutality. In these instances, the insistence of the Constitutional Court, linked to rulings of the IACtHR, that the Colombian government should accept legal responsibility for all interactions in Colombian society hardened the material obligations of government in some parts of society. However, this role of human rights also became manifest in questions regarding the peace process that eventually terminated the long-standing civil war. In this context, the Constitutional Court applied international law in cases concerning the

---

[265] The Court established a fundamental right to health in T-760/08.

[266] The Court established a right to education in T-775/08.

[267] The Court argued that the rights to a clean environment belonged to the class of 'rights of constitutional rank' in T-760/07. It also argued that, as part of the environmental constitution, animals had certain constitutional rights. See C-666/10.

[268] For a ruling on the constitutional personality of rivers see T-622/16.

participation of political groups in post-conflict electoral processes,[269] and in cases concerning reparation, and transitional justice.[270] In each respect, the Court applied international law, and especially rulings of the IACtHR, as a basic framework for political inclusion.[271] Ultimately, the consensus engendered by the interaction between domestic actors and international norm providers galvanized different interests and factions in Colombian society, and it created a platform for eventual comprehensive demilitarization. Crucially, even the fact that the peace agreements between parties in the civil war were rejected by popular plebiscite in 2016 did not cause a crisis of the state. In fact, the Constitutional Court approved procedures for holding the plebiscite and for subsequent revision of the original peace agreements,[272] so that the process of peace building did not have to be abandoned.

In total, in the process of democratic consolidation that took place in Colombia after 1991, deep interactions between judicial bodies, situated in a differentiated normative domain between the national and the international sphere, established basic foundations – both normative and institutional – for national democracy. In this regard, it needs to be stated very clearly that the constitution was not initially successful in its transformative goals, and it did not immediately lead to a reinforcement of democratic structure. Excessively optimistic evaluation of the achievements of the 1991 Constitution and the Constitutional Court needs to be avoided. In fact, in the first decade after the constitution took effect, social violence reached unprecedented levels.[273] During this time, moreover, consolidation of private governance regimes became more entrenched (see Aguilera Peña 2014: 379). By other indicators, further, Colombia continued to fall short of the characteristics of a fully nationalized political order. Notably, electoral participation remained very low and regionally variable, and mobilization of the electorate often relied on patronage.[274] Over a longer period of time, however, the legal institutions established by the

---

[269] C-577/14.

[270] See the construction of a right to truth and reparation in C-715/12.

[271] See the Court's citation of the verdict of the IACtHR that there exists a 'strict relation between political participation, the rights that guarantee it, and the construction of a democratic society' (C-577/14).

[272] See C-379/16; C-699/16.

[273] One account argues that the 'greatest geographical expansion of the conflict' occurred in 2002 (González González 2014: 440).

[274] Electoral participation in Colombia is far lower than in Chile, Uruguay, Brazil and Argentina (see Flórez 2011: 173). Key popular votes, such as the elections to the Constituent Assembly in 1990 and the peace plebiscite in 2016, had very low turnout. One important

1991 Constitution assumed great importance in the gradual penetration of a democratic governance system into society, and in the resultant pacification of social antagonisms. In some respects, interactions between legal institutions compensated for the weakness of political institutions, and they played a key role in promoting a basic democratic order for national society.

First, most simply, interactions between legal institutions helped to create a generally enforceable body of constitutional norms, which the national government in Colombia, historically, had not successfully accomplished. Second, these interactions established a basic normative structure that was imposed by public bodies across previously unregulated domains in society. In addition, third, these interactions created a condition of inclusion for many social groups, differentiated in accordance with vulnerability. In each respect, the basic construction of the democratic citizen, as a holder of political, material and ethnic rights, was produced from within the legal system, and it was consolidated, to a large degree, through international human rights law. The model of the citizen around which national society eventually converged was stripped away from the factually existing citizens in the objective structure of society, and it in fact signalled a negation of the existing order of nationhood as a primary form of inclusion.[275] It is of great symbolic importance in Colombia that human rights norms were most emphatically applied to create uniform thresholds of citizenship amongst displaced persons – that is, amongst persons, often originating from historically marginalized areas, who had been deprived of all effective citizenship rights, and forced to inhabit the peripheries of legal citizenship. Tellingly, in one of its earlier cases concerning displacement, the Constitutional Court defined displacement as *absence of citizenship* – in which the affected person 'suffers a dramatic process of impoverishment, loss of liberties, damage to social rights, and deprivation of political participation'.[276] The role of the Constitutional Court in this respect appears as a symbolic response to the most exceptionalist problems of order, nationality and sovereignty in Colombian history, creating and giving effect to principles of citizenship, and so extending the societal reach of the political system, in otherwise normatively evacuated, alegal locations. In fact, in different situations, the Court was particularly attentive

---

account links the low levels of electoral participation to political apathy caused by clientelism (Leal Buitrago and Ladrón de Guevara 1990: 300–2).

[275] On the rejection of classical ideas of nationhood in this context and on the importance of the internationalization of human rights protection see Uribe de Hincapié (1998b: 36).

[276] T-602/03.

to questions of legal exceptionalism, and it insisted that, even under emergency conditions, basic norms of international human rights law had to be guaranteed.[277]

After 1991, the construction of the Colombian citizen was primarily promoted by legal actors, partly on the basis of international human rights law. This occurred in a societal constellation in which, historically, the formation of a unified idea of the citizen, in relation to which public acts could be robustly legitimated, had proved impossible. The national citizen was only formed through the global legal system, and it emerged as a figure that stood directly at the intersection between national and international law. Ultimately, this transnational construct of the citizen reached deep into the recesses of national society, and it acquired emblematic expression in the figure of the domestic refugee, translated by global law into a subject of national legal inclusion.

Colombia appears as the most extreme example of the impact of the growing differentiation of the legal system on democratic institution building. As an extreme example, however, it throws paradigmatic light on a general phenomenon. In Colombia, judicial institutions, positioned at different points in the global legal system, interacted at a high level of autonomy, to create a more robust body of constitutional norms to determine the use of public authority in national society, and even to create foundations for a national legal/political system *per se*. Of course, it would be illusory to claim that this process has created a uniform material structure in society. As explained, one of the two primary objectives of the Constitution – to create a peace settlement – was not realized (if it was realized at all) for over 25 years. In consequence, the essential institutional conditions for democratic consolidation were not immediately established.[278] During this time, however, the legal system itself acted, in some respects, as a surrogate for political democratization. Indeed, engagement of citizens with international human rights replaced, or at least rivalled, engagement with national-political institutions as the primary element of political citizenship, so that international law sometimes reached deep into the most violent and exceptionalist zones in Colombian life. This reflects the deep irony that modern Colombia is based on a constitution that emphatically subscribes to an ethic of participatory citizenship. Such emphasis, of

---

[277] See lengthy discussion of the state of exception in C-802/02. Here, it is striking that the Court insisted on continued enforcement of the block of constitutionality in political emergencies and it quoted extensively from the ACHR and the ICCPR.

[278] See the typology of regional de-institutionalization in Colombia in García Villegas et al. (2016: 95–100).

course, has not been without effect. In some respects, however, use of law and engagement with courts have been the most socially formative mode of citizenship practice.

4.2.5   Global Human Rights and National Democracy 5: Russia

The relative autonomy of the legal system also underlies political and constitutional developments in some societies that have not assumed a fully democratic form. In recent Russian history, for example, the consequences of inter-judicial interaction, especially between national and international bodies, are comparable with those experienced in other settings. Indeed, articulations between legal institutions in Russian society and international legal bodies have pervasively shaped the accountability principles that surround the political system. As a result, the approximation towards democratic citizenship, which exists in some parts of the Russian legal/political system, is primarily generated through inner-legal processes.

Naturally, this claim may, for a number of reasons, appear implausible. First, clearly, the quality of democracy in Russia under Vladimir Putin is widely criticized. It is easily observable that the Russian political system deviates from standard models of democracy, which have the primary feature that the exercise of governmental power depends on the protected institutionalization of opposition parties, which can compete with governing parties for occupancy of office on broadly equal terms.[279] In Russia, the institutionalization of opportunities for opposition to executive or presidential policy is not non-existent, as opposition is articulated through smaller parties in the Duma, and in regional institutions. However, structures facilitating organized opposition are relatively weak; the leading political party is in many respects an adjunct of the state, and it is improbable that it could be replaced by regular democratic rotation of governmental office (Roberts 2012: 98). As a result, the accountability of the government to political groups outside the executive apparatus (broadly defined) is reduced, the openings for the effective exercise of popular citizenship rights are curtailed, and access to the political process is controlled. Moreover, the Russian government is commonly con-

---

[279] See Reuter (2010: 295). See extreme critique of Putin's regime in Hassner (2008); Chandler (2014: 743); Petrone (2011: 168); Gill (2015). Amongst grounds for the classification of Putin's government as straightforwardly authoritarian can be included amendments (2004) to the Law on Political Parties (2001), making restrictive provisions for the formation of political parties. The source of legislation quoted in this chapter, unless otherwise noted, is www.pravo.ru and www.consultant.ru.

demned in international judicial fora, and acts of government are often found in breach of international human rights conventions. For example, the ECtHR has very recently found violations of the ECHR in the Russian government's policies concerning adoption of Russian children by nationals of the USA,[280] in the treatment of HIV-positive aliens[281] and in differential policies regarding male and female military personnel.[282] Further, it is often alleged, although not always in adequately corroborated fashion, that the Russian judiciary is susceptible to external political influence (see Ledeneva 2008: 330; Hendley 2009: 242).

On these counts, the Russian political system cannot easily be aligned to a simple model of democratic formation through differentiation of the legal system. In some respects, nonetheless, political realities in contemporary Russia can be placed on the same spectrum as other patterns of democratic formation through autonomous legal agency. Indeed, given the semi-authoritarian nature of the Russian polity, the legal system has distinct salience as a channel for articulating and enshrining social liberties, and it plays a primary role in upholding and expanding citizenship rights. Albeit in rather unintended manner, the legal system has evolved as an important source of counter-power within the polity as a whole, so that, to some degree, patterns of agency transmitted through the legal system countervail the authoritarian emphases of the political system. As a result, the Russian political system can be observed as possessing a *sui generis* constitutional order, on which certain processes within the legal system have left a very distinctive structural mark, and in which judicial institutions consistently shape the parameters of government. In fact, the legal system has created distinct opportunities for the exercise of citizenship practices and for collective norm production, which are less strongly established within the political branches of the state. The weak institutionalization of opposition parties is partly balanced by practices located in the legal system, and counterweights to governmental power are partly generated within the law. On these grounds, Russia can be seen as a striking example of a polity in which classical democratic citizenship practices have only obtained limited expression, but the law partly compensates for this weakness. Indeed, in certain respects, leading actors in the government

---

[280] *A.H. and Others* v. *Russia* (Applications No. 6033/13, 8927/13, 10549/13 et al., Judgment of 17 January 2017).

[281] *Novruk and Others* v. *Russia* (Applications No. 31039/11, 48511/11, 76810/12 et al., Judgment of 15 March 2016).

[282] *Konstantin Markin* v. *Russia* (Application No. 30078/06, Judgment of 22 March 2012).

consciously utilize the law as a medium that compensates for weaknesses of political institutionalization.

The importance of legal interactions in contemporary Russian politics is closely connected to embedded patterns of institutional formation in Russian history. In fact, the Russian political system is defined in central respects by a deep reliance on the law, and legal institutions have played a vital, albeit unusual, role in the recent development of the Russian polity. This has a long historical tradition, and, since the nineteenth century, Russian leaders have often reached for the law as a means for solving structural problems in the state.[283] The most important immediate reason for this, however, is that, in the 1990s, the Russian political system experienced a process of catastrophic institutional collapse, caused by a variety of factors. In this setting, various strategies of legal reform were promoted to overcome the crisis, so that policies for improving the rule of law acquired core significance as instruments of state construction. Indeed, judicial institutions acquired a structurally formative role within the state, and the legal system assumed an unusual constitutional position because of this.

First, the Russian state approached collapse in the 1990s because, in the wake of the reforms to the Soviet system of political economy introduced by Gorbachev, powerful economic actors stripped the government apparatus of its assets, and they transformed much of the institutional order of the old regime into private spoils.[284] Importantly, prior to Gorbachev, the political apparatus of the Soviet Union was already based in a pattern of indirect rule, in which regional party secretaries acted as dispensers of patrimonial privileges, entailing at times egregious levels of corruption and private arrogation of public goods.[285] As a consequence, government institutions were already marked by deep privatization, especially in remote territories of the Soviet Union, and articulations between citizens and the state were defined by informal interests, motivations and transactions, and they lacked uniform reserves of legitimacy. By the mid-1980s,

---

[283] For earlier examples see Rudden (1994: 56); Wortman (2010: 9).

[284] See discussion in Grzymala-Busse and Luong (2002: 545); Shlapentokh (1996: 394, 396); Tompson (2002); Taylor (2011: 25); Gel'man (2004: 1024); Easter (1996: 602, 606); Garcelon (2005: 221).

[285] See discussion of this system of indirect rule in Central Asia in Mirsky (1997: 3). The Brezhnev era was synonymous with local corruption and monopolization of regional government by 'complex networks of friends, clients, and relatives erected by local party bosses' (Suny 1993: 119). Importantly for the argument set out here, Brezhnev established a loosely regionalized corporatist model of government, in which great trust was placed in local elite cadres, effectively re-institutionalizing semi-autonomous ethnicities (see Shcherbak 2015: 874).

Gorbachev increasingly defined promotion of the rule of law as a priority policy objective, and he saw this as a means to reduce the reliance of government agents on corruption and local (often ethnic) power monopolies (White 1990: 37; Kahn 2002: 87): reform of the legal system, or even *legal revolution*, was perceived as a way to establish public foundations for government and to intensify state capacity (Kahn 2002: 87). Gorbachev's reforms, however, did not achieve this goal. On the contrary, they triggered intense economic crisis and institutional fragmentation, in which existing tendencies towards corruption and resource grabbing were greatly exacerbated, resulting in still more corrosive colonization and debilitation of the governmental order. In consequence of this, state control of society in the Soviet Union and then, later, in the Russian Federation was greatly undermined, and collective confidence in institutions was deeply unsettled. Importantly, social agents commonly showed reluctance to use public institutions for provision of justice, often preferring to approach private actors, including gangs and oligarchs, for redress and remedy in their grievances (Gel'man 2015: 57). Legal institutions, which were already weak in the Soviet Union, were dramatically eroded through its collapse. Putin acknowledged this very clearly when he introduced plans for judicial reform in 2001. He claimed that lack of trust in the state had led to the proliferation of 'shadow justice', which meant that citizens were inclined to seek remedies for legal problems by private means, thus diluting the power of the central government.[286] In fact, he expressly declared that a state not consistently governed by law is a *weak state* (2000), and his own policies were deeply shaped by this observation.

Second, the Russian political system approached collapse in the 1990s because of the fact that Gorbachev's reforms released a surge of separatism in the constituent Republics and in other autonomous entities of the Soviet Union, and, after 1991, in the Russian Federation. This separatism was initially greatly encouraged by Yeltsin, as Chairman of the Russian parliament. In fact, by 1990, Yeltsin strongly encouraged different territorial subjects to assume sovereign powers of government. Subsequently, as President of the Russian Federation, he continued this policy by contracting out government functions to regional subjects, often through bilateral treaties negotiated on an extraconstitutional basis (see Shlapentokh, Levita and Loiberg

---

[286] Annual Address of the President of the Russian Federation to the Federal Assembly, delivered on 3 April 2001. As background to Putin's policies, see the account of shadow justice in Baranov (2002). By 2012, Putin claimed that great success had been achieved in ending shadow justice. This view was expressed in Putin's speech (2012) at the VIII National Congress of Judges, 18 December 2012.

1997: 101; Kahn 2002: 168, 187; Robertson 2011: 109).[287] As a result, the Russian political system was deprived of its basic institutional capacity to legislate and uniformly to enforce law across all parts of national society, and the limited cohesion that it possessed was derived from precarious inter-elite arrangements (Kahn 2002: 234). In turn, this exacerbated the broader problem of endemic privatization in the Russian political system, as sitting elites in different regions often exploited their growing autonomy to monopolize public resources, and to distribute public goods as patrimonial commodities in order to secure their hold on political authority. In many regional units of the Russian Federation, sitting governments became effectively private, semi-sovereign dynasties, whose authority was based on strong patron–client links (Sharlet 2001: 199; Cappelli 2008: 547; Chenankova 2010: 44). From 1991 on, therefore, acute centrifugalism posed a potent threat to governmental cohesion in the Russian Federation. Many regions then further intensified their powers, often in contravention of the formal text of the Russian Constitution, through the latter part of the 1990s (Konitzer and Wergren 2006: 503). Indicatively, some regions, such as the Bashkortostan and Ingushetia Republics, even tried to introduce their own judicial systems (Pavlikov 2004: 85).

For these separate reasons, by the late 1990s, the Russian political system had in many respects forfeited its basic quality as a centre of determinately public order, and the ability of Russian society to rely on a distinctively public domain was clearly curtailed. Owing to powerful tendencies towards centrifugalism and privatism within the political system, society as a whole lacked a basic inclusive normative substructure. Like Colombia, in fact, although Russia possessed a formally democratic system in the 1990s, this formal democracy had limited bearing on society as a whole. Actors within the political system were not able to assert a monopoly of power in society's different functional domains, and many key political institutions were hollowed out thorough the influence of private actors. This period witnessed large-scale societal disengagement from the political system. Indeed, it witnessed an endemic *deconstitutionalization* of both state and society.

---

[287] In 1990, Yeltsin famously instructed subjects of the Republic to 'take as much sovereignty as you can swallow'. His primary motivation in so doing was to build up support amongst the regional leaders (Kahn 2000: 76–7). Later, In the Federation Treaty 1992, Yeltsin claimed authority to appoint regional governors (Moraski 2006: 15, 17). By 1994, Yeltsin began signing power-sharing treaties with subjects of the Federation, as a result of which some assumed powers close to those of nation states (Goode 2011: 8).

Against this twofold background, following his assumption of the Russian presidency in 1999–2000, Putin embarked on a comprehensive process of systemic transformation, implementing a number of far-reaching reforms. This process was oriented towards consolidation of public authority, re-centralization of government functions and restriction of regional and ethnic autonomy. These reforms had various profound implications for the Russian political system, and for the distinctive model of democracy that eventually developed. Central to this wider reform process were packages of judicial reform, which were designed to encourage citizens to address social grievances in a formalized institutional domain, and to use regular courts as means of conflict resolution. Individual elements in these reform policies were intended to increase the quality of jurisprudence in the law courts, to standardize judicial procedure and to bring normative and regional consistency to the legal order, to improve judicial training, and to tighten the articulations between different levels of the court system.[288] These policies were flanked by more specific measures to increase openness of the courts, to raise the transparency of judicial functions, and to ensure that case law and judicial decisions were available for public scrutiny.[289] Also significant in this regard were measures to diminish judicial corruption, including laws to improve salaries and working conditions for judges, creating strong disincentives for professional malfeasance among judges.[290] In each of these respects, Putin's judicial reforms were designed to enhance protection of basic rights in

---

[288] These general objectives were proclaimed in government target programmes on the development of the Russian judicial system. See Decrees No. 805 of 20 January 2001 'On the Federal Target Program "Development of the Russian Judicial System in 2002–2006"'; No. 583 of 21 September 2006 'On the Federal Target Program "Development of the Russian Judicial System in 2007–2012"'; No.1406 of 27 December 2012 'On the Federal Target Program "Development of the Russian Judicial System in 2013–2020"'.

[289] See Federal Law No. 8-FZ of 9 February 2009 'On Ensuring Access to Information about the Functioning of State and Municipal Authorities'; Federal Law No. 262-FZ of 22 December 2009 'On Ensuring Access to Information about Activities of Courts in the Russian Federation'; Supreme Court Plenum Ruling No. 35 of 13 December 2012 'On the Openness and Transparency of Judicial Proceedings and Access to Information on the Activities of Courts'.

[290] See, for example, Decree of the President of the Russian Federation No. 784 of 8 June 2012 'On Increasing the Salaries of Judges in the Russian Federation'. Since 1 January 2013, a new grade-based remuneration system for judges has been introduced, tying salaries to different qualification classes and ensuring upward mobility of judges through the grades. See Federal Constitutional Law of 25 December 2012 No. 5-FKZ and Federal Law No. 269-FZ of 25 December 2012.

the legal system, and to ensure that rights could be more easily activated through litigation.[291]

On one hand, Putin promoted reform of the legal system as a means to eradicate private power from political institutions, and to stabilize a domain of clearly public authority in society, not monopolized by influential private bodies and players. As mentioned, one of Putin's greatest concerns at his accession to the presidency was the prevalence of *shadow justice*, sometimes described as *legal nihilism*, in the political system. He envisaged that increased access to formal law would consolidate the legal order of government, linking people across society directly to the state. On the other hand, Putin pursued reform of the legal system as a means to consolidate a more *uniform legal space* across the different territories in the Russian federation (Sharlet 2001: 203; Kahn, Trochev and Balayan 2009: 330).[292] In this regard, Putin's policies were premised on the assumption that the increased willingness of citizens to litigate would act as a socially integrative practice. In fact, given the weakness of nationally overarching political organizations, litigation was perceived as a social activity in which citizens across the Russian Federation could engage in direct fashion with the political system, and in which nationalized patterns of legal/ political behaviour and interaction could be institutionalized. Notable in this regard was the fact that Putin's early legal reforms were not restricted to civil law, and they included measures to simplify litigation against government agencies, which culminated, first, in the passing of the Civil Procedure Code of 2002.

Overall, the judicial reforms initiated by Putin were intended to remedy a number of separate, yet related weaknesses in public order, and they were designed to connect citizens across society in more immediately integrated fashion to the organs of government. The promotion of legal reform was conceived as a means to ensure that the legal system could be clearly

---

[291] Universal principles and norms of international law are considered an integral part of the Russian legal system, while the priority of international treaty norms over domestic legislation is guaranteed by Article 15(4) of the Russian Constitution. International human rights conventions are directly applied by Russian courts. Such application is encouraged by the Supreme Court and Russian legislation in general. See Supreme Court Plenary Rulings No. 5 of 10 October 2003 'On Application by Courts of General Jurisdiction of Universally Recognised Principles and Norms of International Law and International Treaties of the Russian Federation'; No. 23 of 19 December 2003 'On Judicial Decision'; No. 21 of 27 June 2013 'On Application by Courts of General Jurisdiction of the ECHR'.

[292] Promotion of a 'unified legal space' is one of the priorities of the legal reforms of the 2000s. One of Putin's most important early orders was Decree No. 1486 of 10 August 2000: 'On Additional Measures to Ensure the Unity of the Legal Space in the Russian Federation'.

perceived and consolidated as a relatively autonomous system of interaction in society, in which publicly authorized actors and organizations could be factually and symbolically differentiated from more private sources of interest, prerogative and authority. In fact, these policies were designed to promote a *re-constitutionalization of society*, and especially to impose a stricter constitutional diction on the lines of interaction between citizens and state. Implementation of legal reform was thus clearly observed as a vital element in a broad strategy of state building.[293]

In addition, the legal reforms promoted by Putin were designed to imprint a particular unifying pattern of citizenship in the Russian Federation. Notably, like other countries considered here, the Russian political system had not, historically, been centred around simple or unified models of national citizenship. As a result, the political system was not supported by strong structures of political obligation and legitimation, and its inclusionary force was patchy and variable. Against this background, one intended function of Putin's legal initiatives was to address enduring problems in the institutionalization of national citizenship in Russia.

The complexity of citizenship in Russia was caused, historically, by the multinational character of the Russian Empire and then of the Soviet Union. First, in the Tsarist Empire, citizenship had a variable quality, as many citizens were incorporated in the Empire by military annexation, and they acquired citizenship as collective subjects (see Hessen 1909: 203; Ponisova 2011). Moreover, the legal category of citizenship was only generalized after the reforms of 1864 and the military conscription law of 1874 (Sanborn 2003: 4).[294] The polity of the Soviet Union, then, contained many different autonomous or semi-sovereign subjects, and a very pluralistic construction of citizenship was accepted in order to hold the different subjects together. Self-evidently, the Soviet Union witnessed periods of aggressive Russification, especially in the 1930s.[295] Moreover, inhabitants of the Soviet Union were often either fully or partly excluded from the exercise of citizenship rights on ideological grounds, which sometimes coincided with ethnic categorizations. The late 1920s

---

[293] On the nexus between constitutional implementation and state-building in Russia see Sharlet (1999: 98).

[294] On these points see Lohr (2012: 34, 123).

[295] Initially, Lenin had opted for pragmatic recognition of separate nationalities as a means to hold the Soviet Union together (see Namaylo and Swoboda 1990: 58–9; Martin 2001: 23). Stalin supported recognition of indigenous nationalities in the 19290s, but changed policy in the 1930s (Martin 2001: 177). This culminated in violent ethnic cleansing (Martin 2001: 311; Gosewinkel 2016: 184). In 1937–8, leaders of all ethnic Republics except Azerbaijan and Georgia were purged (Smith 2013: 119).

in particular saw large-scale disfranchisement of class aliens and unde-
sirables, including peripheral ethnic groups (Alexopoulos 2003: 25–8,
57). Nonetheless, both before and after Stalin, the Soviet government
promoted affiliation to Soviet ideology, or Soviet citizenship, in a fashion that did not preclude recognition of separate national and cultural
identities. On the contrary, the government usually actively encouraged
national feeling and national autonomy within the constituent entities of
the Soviet Union, providing incentives for indigenous elites to identify
with the Communist Party, presumably to avoid the patterns of nationalist sabotage that had unstitched other European Empires (Roeder 1991:
207; Suny 1993: 102–3; Beissinger 2005: 28). As a result, the Soviet Union
established an ethno-federal order, in which units within the Union were
organized around ethnically homogeneous populations, and institutions of autonomous ethnic groups were highly structured and deeply
legitimated (Brubaker 1996: 23; Gorenburg 2003: 77). One account even
states that the Soviet Union was based in 'chronic ethnophilia' (Sleznine
1994: 415).

Consequently, in the Soviet Union, the Communist Party promoted a
complex, multi-level institutionalization of citizenship. At the surface level
of society, Soviet identity, linked to Communist ideology, was established
as a primary, albeit rather thin, stratum of obligation, which all inhabitants of the Soviet Union were expected to recognize.[296] However, beneath
this layer of obligation, it was perfectly possible for separate nationalisms
to flourish, so that affiliation to the Soviet Union could coexist with subsidiary modes of national attachment (Grebenok 2011). Indeed, separate
ethnic groups were organized in Republics, and their representatives
were accorded priority treatment, beneath the formal affiliation to the
Union, partly because this helped to strengthen loyalties to the central
government (see Silver 1974: 46; Zaslavsky 1992: 98, 102; Brubaker 1994:
61).[297] In the Soviet system of ethno-federalism, above all, legal rights
of citizenship were not congruently linked to nationhood. Constituent
subjects of the Union possessed nationalities that did not fully overlap with citizenship: rights of citizenship, as a legal-political construct,
were concentrated around the Soviet Union, whereas claims to nationality were embedded in the Republics and other autonomous entities.

---

[296] The idea of a 'Soviet people' was promoted in the 1960s, but with limited effect (see Raffass
2012: 66).

[297] One brilliant analysis of this process states that the Soviet government utilized the 'local
indigenous population' as sources of support in the geographical expansion of the political
system, so that particular ethnic groups appeared as 'valuable colonists' (Hirsch 2005: 91).

Importantly, moreover, the Soviet Union did not promote an overarching Soviet nationality as a basis for citizenship. This had particular significance for Russia itself, whose nationhood, arguably, was deprived of institutional distinction because of Russia's leading political position in the Soviet Union (Tolz 1998: 1004; Beissinger 2002: 397).[298] Of course, further, the Soviet Union also propagated, generally, a distinct pattern of social citizenship (Mann 1987: 349).

These different dimensions of citizenship became acutely problematic during the collapse of the Soviet Union. In fact, some authors suggest that the Soviet identity crisis had become, by 1980s, the Union's 'gravedigger', and one of the main triggers of its eventual implosion (Turaev 2016: 76). At this time, obviously, the idea of social citizenship, ideologically integral to the Soviet Union, was dissolved. Moreover, the trans-regionally unifying element of Soviet citizenship became extremely fragmented, and the quasi-states already created by the Soviet Union began to assume institutionalized national form.[299] In this process, inherited multi-level models of Soviet citizenship were rivalled by citizenship demands in emergent successor states, challenging the primacy of obligations towards the Soviet government, and replacing generalized patterns of Soviet citizenship with nationally and often ethnically reinforced constructions. After the formation of the Russian Federation under Yeltsin, then, models of citizenship continued to coalesce around separate nationality claims, and these demands contested the territorial boundaries of the Russian state, and the primacy of obligations towards the Russian government.[300] Through the transition from the Soviet Union to the Russian Federation, therefore, it became difficult to construct a clearly national government and a clearly

---

[298] One account describes Russian nationality as the 'great taboo' of the Soviet Union (Martin 2001: 39). Other authors connect this with the idea of the Soviet state as a higher value, to which the population of the Russian Republic owed particular obligation (Plotnikova 2016: 15). One interpreter explains that the Russian Republic in the Soviet Union was 'the least distinctly and cohesively constituted of all the federal units' and that little effort was made to construct a Russian ethnic consciousness separate from the Soviet Union (Roshwald 2001: 179). See also Riga (2012: 22).

[299] See the account of how the 'segment-states' created in the Soviet Union became independent after 1991 in Roeder (2007: 255).

[300] Notably, some constituent Republics of the Russian Federation tried to claim their own regional citizenship based on ethnic composition. See, for example, RCC Ruling on Admissibility No. 250-O of 6 December 2001 on regional citizenship of Bashkortostan Republic. In this ruling, the Court stated that only unified federal citizenship is possible in the territory of the Russian Federation. A similar decision was reached by the Court in its Ruling on Merits No. 2-P of 22 January 2002 in respect of the regional citizenship of Tatarstan Republic.

national foundation of citizenship to sustain the government. Indeed, the longer wake of the dissolution of the Soviet Union was marked by repeated and protracted problems in the creation and institutional consolidation of a genuinely national political system.[301] At the same time, given the multinational composition of the Soviet Empire, the actual legal parameters of Russian citizenship were difficult to define, and early citizenship laws (1991) in Russia were expansive in recognizing non-Russian citizens of the Soviet Union as citizens of Russia (Shevel 2012: 117–20). Both ideologically and systemically, in sum, the 1990s witnessed an acute fracturing of the order of balanced loyalties and dual obligations around which the Soviet Union had been built.

Putin's legal reforms formed, in part, a reaction to this condition of extreme legal and structural fragmentation. As mentioned, these reforms were designed to stimulate litigation, to generate a demand for law,[302] and to reinforce legal order across society.[303] At the same time, however, the reforms also promoted particular citizenship practices, which responded to the increasing conflicts between different models of citizenship in the Russian Federation. Most notably, the reforms implicitly fostered a concept of the citizen as litigant or a concept of *inner-legal citizenship*,[304] in which use of the law, expressed in acts of litigation, was imputed a

---

[301] On weak political nationalization in Russia see Golosov (2015: 401).

[302] All early judicial reform programmes were aimed at ensuring wider access to court throughout the country. See, for example, Government of the Russian Federation Decree No. 805 of 20 January 2001 'On the Federal Target Program "Development of the Russian Judicial System in 2002–2006"'; Government of the Russian Federation Decree No. 583 of 21 September 2006 'On the Federal Target Program "Development of the Russian Judicial System in 2007–2012"'; Government of the Russian Federation Decree No. 1406 of 27 December 2012 'On the Federal Target Program "Development of the Russian Judicial System in 2013–2020"'. Moreover, all new procedural codes were adopted during the early years of Putin's presidency: Civil Procedure Code No. 138-FZ of 14 November 2002; Arbitrazh Procedure Code No. 95-FZ of 24 July 2002; Code of Administrative Offenses No. 195-FZ of 30 December 2001.

[303] For example, some authors suggest that establishment of justices of the peace in all regions, including the Chechen Republic, has created more opportunities for litigation, helping to include the Republic in the unified legal space of the Russian Federation (Saydumov 2010).

[304] Litigation against actions and decisions violating human rights is a constitutional right in Russia (Articles 45–6). This right was further expanded in the Federal Law No. 4866-1 of 27 April 1993 'On Judicial Review of Actions and Decisions Violating Rights and Freedoms of Citizens'. This legislative act was actively used in litigation. Annually, approximately 300,000 claims of this type are considered by Russian courts (statistical data available from www.cdep.ru). This Federal Law was replaced in 2015 by the Administrative Litigation Code (Federal Law No. 21-FZ of 8 March 2015). The Code, in turn, contains special provisions in which judicial review is defined as a protected activity of any citizen.

quasi-constitutional force.[305] In these reforms, legal practices were expected to lock society and public institutions more closely together, and to articulate a general normative grammar to frame and to regulate exchanges between citizen and government. Central to this was the idea that heightened engagement with the law would promote patterns of affiliation that would connect citizens more directly to the national political system, so that regional identities and memberships could once again be configured within a construct of all-Russian citizenship. Indeed, it was imagined that litigation would assume a distinctive role in establishing a national normative domain, in which persons at different locations in society were to be integrated in a shared normative order, formed by acts of citizens. Of course, litigation was not the only means used to promote a nationalization of the political system. Putin's legal reforms were flanked by alternative mechanisms to offset national fragmentation. For example, the introduction of legal reforms coincided with the introduction of measures to impose controls on gubernatorial elites in the regions and Republics of the Federation (Reuter and Robertson 2012: 1027, 1031; Golosov 2015: 415; Saikkonen 2017: 58). These reforms were also flanked by the establishment of *United Russia* as a national political party. However, at a normative level, the legal reforms introduced by Putin formed an important element in a strategic process of national political system building and societal integration. Arguably, in fact, litigation was specifically promoted in Russia as an instrument of nationalization because political organizations that typically serve to heighten the national reach of the political system, such as democratically galvanized political parties, were not fully evolved. The law was thus used to obtain the systemic benefits of citizenship practices in a context in which classical expressions of political citizenship were curtailed. In each respect, litigation was actively encouraged as a technique for the re-constitutionalization of the sphere of interaction between citizens and government, and the legal element of citizenship assumed particular prominence as part of a wider process of national integration.

---

[305] The transformative effect of litigation is visible through important decisions of both Supreme Court and the RCC, establishing new legal practices without recourse to the traditional route of the legislative process. For example, proportionality has become 'a constitutional principle' of jurisprudence (RCC Ruling on Merits No. 2-P of 10 February 2017).

Putin's reforms to the Russian legal system meant that a very distinctive and important position was assigned, within the national legal system, to international law, including, most particularly, international human rights law. Importantly, international law had already played an important part in the early attempted consolidation of the Russian legal system before and after 1991. The impetus towards the constitutional recognition of international law was already evident in pre-transitional legal and constitutional reforms, beginning in the 1980s. For example, in 1990, the Declaration of State Sovereignty of the Russian Soviet Federative Socialist Republic (RSFSR) announced that the reformed state had a strong 'commitment to the universally recognized principles of international law'.[306] The same principle was reflected in the Declaration of Human Rights and Freedoms of the Soviet Union (1991),[307] which, as the final act of the USSR Congress of People's Deputies, proclaimed that international covenants should be used as the basis for domestic human rights. In turn, the RSFSR Declaration of the Rights of Man and Citizen made provision for the primacy of 'international law, particularly human rights norms' above RSFSR legislation.[308] Significantly, the year 1991 also saw the adoption of the *Concept of Judicial Reform*,[309] which identified international law as an important source of law in Russia, regardless of whether it had been formally incorporated in the domestic legal system. This *Concept* prescribed that the 'universally recognized principles' of international law (interpreted at that time as *jus cogens*) should have higher authority than domestic legislation.[310] Moreover, a new constitution for the Russian Federation was created in 1993, which, in Article 15(4), dictates that international law must be directly applied in court practice.[311] Even before the constitution

---

[306] Declaration of State Sovereignty of the Russian Soviet Federative Socialist Republic (RSFSR) of 12 June 1990.

[307] Declaration of Human Rights and Freedoms of the Union of Soviet Socialistic Republics (USSR) No. 2393-I of 5 September 1991.

[308] Declaration of the Rights of Man and Citizen of the Russian Soviet Federative Socialist Republic (RSFSR) adopted by the RSFSR Supreme Soviet's Resolution No. 1920-1 of 22 November 1991.

[309] Supreme Soviet of RSFSR Decision No. 1801-1 of 24 October 1991 'On the Concept of Judicial Reform in RSFSR'.

[310] Ibid.

[311] Supreme Court Plenary Rulings No. 5 of 10 October 2003 'On Application by Courts of General Jurisdiction of Universally Recognized Principles and Norms of International Law and International Treaties of the Russian Federation'; No. 21 of 27 June 2013 'On Application by Courts of General Jurisdiction of the Convention for Protection of Human

was enacted, Russia had obtained a Constitutional Court, one of whose responsibilities was to enforce international law in the domestic domain.[312]

Consequently, the first process of democratic formation in Russia was partly driven by an intersection between the national legal system and the international legal order. The initial results of this interaction remained limited, since, as discussed, the Russian legal/political system as a whole entered a period of intense crisis in the 1990s. After 1998, however, when Russia acceded to the ECHR, the domestic penetration of international law was intensified, and it began to impact more substantially on the domestic legal and political system. Tellingly, Putin's endeavour to establish the legal system as an autonomous, socially consolidated set of institutions was guided by the assumption that use of international law by judges would instil a corpus of free-standing principles within the law, raising the consistency of legal finding and elevating public confidence in the law.[313] In Putin's first presidency, international law was consciously assimilated in domestic law, and international norms were viewed as instruments for establishing legal uniformity across society, for consolidating the 'unity of legal space' across the Russian Federation,[314] and for constructing reliable constitutional principles to support new legislation, especially in legally unstable areas of social practice.[315] The general policies to encourage wider use of the law were thus inextricably linked to the assimilation of international law. In 2001–2, all of the major procedural codes were renewed in accordance with the new constitution, in conformity with Russia's international obligations.[316]

Of course, since the onset of Putin's reforms, the integrity of the legal system in Russia has often been questioned, and many observers, for different reasons, dispute whether the courts exercise their functions without

---

Rights and Fundamental Freedoms of 4 November 1950 and the Protocols thereto'; No. 23 of 19 December 2003 'On Judicial Decision'.

[312] The requirement to apply international law is the same for all Russian courts, including the RCC, see Article 3 of the Federal Constitutional Law No. 1-FKZ 'On the Judicial System of the Russian Federation'.

[313] The importance of international law as a foundation for legal consistency was accentuated in Article 3 of the Federal Constitutional Law No. 1-FKZ of 31 December 1996 'On the Judicial System of the Russian Federation'.

[314] Presidential Decree No. 1486 of 10 August 2000: 'On Additional Measures to Ensure the Unity of the Legal Space in the Russian Federation'.

[315] For comment see Tiunov (2011).

[316] These Codes are: Criminal Procedure Code of the Russian Federation No. 174-FZ of 18 December 2001; Code of the Russian Federation on Administrative Offenses No. 195-FZ of 30 December 2001; Arbitration Procedure Code No. 95-FZ of 24 July 2002; Civil Procedure Code of the Russian Federation No. 138-FZ of 14 November 2002.

political or monetary influence (Thorson 2012: 152; Mazmanyan 2015: 214).[317] Some observers argue that the Russian legal system is defined by a formal dualism, in which legally ordered institutions co-exist with informal patterns of social control, so that primary modes of authority are really constructed through personal arrangements, and formal law has limited purchase in society.[318] Other observers assert that much of the legal reform in Russia is little more than shadow play, and that vital decisions of the executive and the President are removed from judicial scrutiny (Fish 2005: 45).

Clearly, such accusations cannot simply be dismissed. There is clear evidence to indicate that public-law litigation is very predominantly focused on the acts of lower-level agencies, and some elements of the political system are outside the scope of the law.[319] Moreover, judges have been subject to political pressure in some high-profile cases.[320] Most alarmingly, recent years have seen an increasing politicization of criminal law. For example, recently, charges for treason have been pressed against persons found sending text images of Russian military equipment, or making telephone contact with the Ukrainian embassy. Importantly, since the Russian–Georgian war of 2008, cases concerning terrorism, treason and espionage do not require trial by jury.[321] Furthermore, in 2012, federal treason laws were re-worded to prohibit not only publicization of state secrets, but also provision of 'any assistance to a foreign country, international organisation or a foreign organisation if their activity is aimed against Russia'.[322]

---

[317] This view is less strongly endorsed in research of the highest calibre (see Trochev 2008: 185).

[318] See the account of 'practices of para-constitutionalism' in Sakwa (2011: 47). Sakwa's claim, in simple terms, is that: 'Contemporary Russian politics can be characterized as a struggle between two systems: the formal constitutional order, what we call the normative state; and a second world of informal relations, factional conflict, and para-constitutional political practices, termed in this article the administrative regime' (2010: 185).

[319] Indeed, among more than a hundred cases of judicial review of presidential decrees considered by the RCC since 2000, none have resulted in declaring a decree unconstitutional, see www.ksrf.ru.

[320] For example, in July 2016, all the judges in a district court in Kazan, in the Tatarstan Republic, refused to consider criminal accusations regarding a large-scale fraud allegedly committed by a local very influential banker. The court of higher instance – Supreme Court of the Republic of Tatarstan – had to rule on changing the jurisdiction of the case to avoid possible pressure.

[321] Federal Law No. 321-FZ of 30 December 2008.

[322] Article 275 of the Criminal Code (as amended by Federal Law No. 190-FZ of 12 November 2012).

Despite these qualifications, Putin's promotion of legal and judicial consistency has substantially altered the linkage between citizen and state, and his reforms have had discernible impact on the structure of government. Indeed, these reforms have resulted in the creation of a legal/political order that is demonstrably marked, in some of its features, by a relatively high degree of judicial autonomy, and by a strong capacity of judicial bodies to produce independent norms to frame and regulate governmental power. Moreover, these reforms have generated important, relatively autonomous domains of political practice, and they have institutionalized elements of citizenship within the legal system.

These processes are visible in a variety of ways. To some degree, of course, the increased autonomy of the Russian legal system is simply the result of presidential legislation (either formally introduced or informally solicited by the President), designed to ensure openness and transparency in court proceedings, and to reduce judicial corruption.[323] Notably in this respect, policies of judicial reform have had significant impact on public perceptions of judicial functions, and public confidence in the courts, in different fields of litigation, has increased significantly.[324] At the same time, however, the growing autonomy of the legal system is reflected in certain more pervasive, less strategically ordained processes, which take place outside immediate political control. In some respects, the legal system has evolved a quite differentiated, spontaneous capacity for norm production, which impacts in rather contingent fashion on the constitutional order of government. In particular, increasing litigation caused by judicial reform now acts as an important source of constitutionally effective legal principles, analogous to the acts of citizens in more typical democratic polities. In some respects, as mentioned legal processes often play an important role in substituting the nation-building functions of full political citizenship, and they help to institutionalize patterns of national membership

---

[323] See above p.379.

[324] The increase of trust has been documented by academics, politicians and judges. Opinion polls also show a growing satisfaction with the work of the judiciary among those respondents who have experienced personal interactions with courts. For example, a 2008 survey by the All-Russia Centre for Public Opinion Research (WCIOM) reported that of those respondents who had themselves participated in the legal process 56 per cent were satisfied with the result and more than half positively evaluated the professionalism of judges and believed that an average person could expect a just resolution of their problems (WCIOM. ru 2008). Both the Chairman of the Constitutional Court and former president of the Higher Arbitration Court agree that growing litigation is a sign of an improving legal culture of the Russian people and of 'increasing trust, especially in the period of crises' (see Zorkin 2006, 2011; Yakovlev 2010).

in the absence of a strong solidified national party apparatus.[325] Both normatively and systemically, therefore, legal functions partly compensate for weak institutionalization of citizenship practices in the political system.

First, for example, the relative autonomy of the legal system in Russia is evident in the impact of international law on the legal and political system as a whole. As mentioned, use of international law was originally promoted during the earlier stages of the post-Soviet transition, primarily as a means for improving judicial consistency. However, at different levels of the legal/political system, international law has acquired a relatively independent authority, and it has created a foundation for distinct patterns of norm construction. International law is now widely used, both by judges and by advocates, to buttress jurisprudential argument, especially in public-law cases, and it plays a significant role in defining the obligations of public bodies. This is especially the case with citations from the ECtHR.[326] Notably, the reception of international law is typically strong in relatively minor administrative law cases, in which local or regional authorities are held to account by internationally standardized norms.[327] To this degree, Putin's strategy in assimilating international law to increase the domestic penetration of the legal system as a whole was a success, as implementation of international law clearly serves to instil relatively uniform lines of accountability into Russian society.[328] At the same time, however, courts

---

[325] On the weakness of political parties at a national level see Hale (2006); Moraski (2006: 25); Goode (2011: 8). Importantly, Putin has tried to use the dominant party, *United Russia*, as an instrument of political nationalization, but with only limited success (see Easter 2008: 218).

[326] By 2015, the annual number of citations of the ECHR in regional courts exceeded 8,000. In the short period between 2012 and 2015, the number of rulings of regional courts referring to the ECHR increased from 3,800 to 8,000. Source of the data: www.consultant.ru.

[327] Successful judicial review cases are seen in different areas of practice. Examples are challenges to illegal refusals to issue construction permits (Appellate Decision of Rostov Oblast court No. 33a-17585/2016 of 17 October 2016); challenges to illegal interference with the work of a lawyer in prison (Appellate Decision of Sverdlovsk Oblast Court No. 33a-17636/2016 of 12 October 2016); challenges to illegal prevention of immigration for persons with family members in Russia (Appellate decision of Moscow Oblast Court No. 33a-21367/2016 of 26 September 2016); challenges to other decisions made by immigration officers on the basis of Article 8 ECHR (Appellate Decision of Saratov Oblast Court No. 33-2071/2017 of 23 March 2017).

[328] Notably, international law is often utilized in appeal cases to overturn lower-court judgements, thus helping to instil uniformity across the whole legal system. In 40 per cent of

have shown some willingness to use international law, and especially norms based on the ECHR, to prescribe remedies against higher-level public bodies, and even to declare government acts unconstitutional.

In addressing these issues, caution is required. As mentioned, courts are not always robust in their scrutiny of executive and presidential acts. In the very recent past, moreover, the domestic effect of international law has been weakened.[329] Despite this, the Russian courts have applied international law to oppose public policy in important functional spheres, and even to suggest remedial legislation in areas in which international human rights norms have been inadequately acknowledged.[330] Indeed, use of international law against public bodies has resulted in the adoption of important pieces of legislation. At different societal levels, governmental compliance with judicial prescriptions is high, and the government has even established a monitoring system for controlling implementation of judicial recommendations for new legislation.[331] In these respects, judicial institutions, partly locked into a transnational legal system, have acquired important constitutional, even quasi-legislative, functions.

---

appellate rulings of regional courts referring to ECHR, the result of the appeal was positive for the applicant.

[329] See p.232 above.

[330] For example, a 2009 ruling of the Supreme Court Plenum and a 2012 Constitutional Court Ruling both used international law to expand the scope of responsibility for agents performing public functions. In these rulings, it was insisted that private organizations with a special public status could be subject to standard norms of public liability (see item 5 of the Supreme Court of the Russian Federation Plenary Ruling No. 2 of 10 February 2009 (void since 27 September 2016 when a new Plenary Ruling No. 36 clarified the application of similar provisions of the Administrative Litigation Code); and RCC Ruling on Merits No. 19-P of 18 July 2012). In 2013, this principle was solidified in a federal law, Federal Law No. 80-FZ of 7 May 2013 'On Amendments to Article 5.59 of the Code of Administrative Offences and Articles 1 and 2 of the Federal Law "On Regulations Concerning Consideration of Russian Citizens' Petitions"'.

[331] For example, since 2009, all rulings of the RCC requiring legislative changes are communicated to the State Duma. Compliance with such rulings is monitored and reported annually. Similarly, the Supreme Court communicates most important decisions requiring legislative attention through dedicated publications and through a special representative of the Duma in the Supreme Court (see State Duma Resolution No. 1050-6 of 26 October 2012 'On the Plenipotentiary Representative of the State Duma of the Federal Assembly of the Russian Federation in the Supreme Court of the Russian Federation'). Both the RCC and the Supreme Court have the right to introduce draft legislation to the Duma (Article 103(1) of the Constitution).

Second, the relative autonomy of the legal system in Russia is visible in the fact that general use of the law across society has increased, and litigation has become an increasingly institutionalized mode of conflict resolution. This is a general development, and it is manifest in all areas of litigation. However, increasing use of courts is particularly striking in litigation involving the filing of suits against public bodies, which was notably simplified in 2002. After the beginning of Putin's reforms, administrative litigation increased substantially. By way of example, judicial review of secondary legislation rose in the period 2002–7 from 4,000 to 6,000 cases per year, with a 76 per cent success rate. Judicial review of non-normative decisions of public bodies (illegal actions and inaction) rose in the period 2006–11 from 50,000 to 150,000 cases per year, with a 63 per cent success rate. Individual claims against all organizations with a legal personality, including state bodies, rose in the period 2008–15 from 1,300,000 to 2,100,000 cases, with an average 90 per cent success rate. Significantly, the number of straightforward anti-government cases, filed by individuals against state bodies, has declined in the period 2007–16 from over 500,000 to 220,000 cases per year, with an average 85 per cent success rate. This decline may be due to measures introduced by the government to cut the workload of the courts. Importantly, the government has introduced instruments to facilitate extra-judicial dispute resolution.[332] In 2015, it introduced a requirement for professional legal representation in administrative litigation, and it simplified procedures for judicial review of small individual administrative claims and civil claims.[333] It has also implemented procedures to filter out frivolous claims,[334] to incentivize

---

[332] Chapter 2.1 on the Pre-Judicial and Extra-Judicial process of challenging actions and decisions of public bodies providing state or municipal services was introduced into the Federal Law No. 210-FZ of 27 July 2010 'On the Organization of Provision of Federal and Municipal Services' by the Federal Law No. 383-FZ of 3 December 2012.

[333] For administrative claims see Article 227(1)(2) of the Arbitrazh Procedure Code, as amended by Federal Law No. 86-FZ of 25 June 2012. Since 2016, small civil claims are considered in a simplified procedure. Importantly, this procedure was introduced with reference to regional international law. In particular, the explanatory note to the law refers to the Council of Europe Committee of Ministers Recommendation No. R(81)7 'On Measures Facilitating Access to Justice', and, paradoxically, the Regulation (EC) No 861/2007 of the European Parliament and of the Council of 11 July 2007 establishing a European Small Claims Procedure. See Federal Law No. 45-FZ of 2 March 2016 and Explanatory Note to the Draft Federal Law No. 725381-6.

[334] For example, the concept of the new Unified Civil Procedure Code approved by the State Duma in December 2014 proposes the introduction of compulsory representation by a professional lawyer in all civil claims.

private arbitration, conciliation and mediation,[335] and to promote the use of specialised tribunals.[336] Importantly, the introduction of compulsory pre-judicial conflict resolution for some categories of cases has been a priority state policy since 2006.[337] Overall, however, recent years have seen growing willingness amongst citizens of the Russian Federation to seek redress through the courts against public agencies. This is especially notable because increases in judicial caseload are substantial in potentially sensitive areas of the law, such as immigration and housing.[338] This increase in administrative litigation has been strongly encouraged by the government, and recent acts of legislation, in particular the Administrative Litigation Code of 2015, have facilitated administrative litigation.

Significant in this regard is the fact that increasing litigation in Russia is partly linked to the incorporation of international law, and especially human rights law, in Russian domestic law. In fact, generally, international law has been used to provide the underlying normative framework, in which measures to facilitate litigation have been introduced. Importantly, new procedural codes introduced by Putin instruct the courts to resolve disputes by referring to international treaties, alongside relevant domestic legislation.[339] Moreover, both the regular courts and the Supreme Court systematically take into account relevant practice of the ECtHR, including judgements concerning access to courts.[340] The Supreme Court also regularly refers to the ECHR in order to establish normative uniformity in Russian courts.[341] Pilot judgements of the ECtHR concerning access to courts are

---

[335] Federal Law No. 193-FZ of 27 July 2010 'On Alternative Dispute Resolution Procedure Involving a Mediator (Mediation Procedure)'.

[336] An example is the Intellectual Property Court, established as an independent type of arbitrazh court in 2011. See Federal Law No. 4-FKZ of 6 December 2011.

[337] See Federal Law No. 137-FZ of 27 July 2006 amending the Tax Code to include compulsory pre-judiciary administrative consideration of disputes related to tax offenses.

[338] For example, administrative cases regarding provision of free housing, housing benefits, and conditions of social housing increased from 2,558 in 2012 to 6,877 in 2015. Administrative deportation cases increased in the same period from 30,767 to 97,691.

[339] Article 11(1) of the Civil Procedure Code; Article 13(1) of the Arbitrazh Procedure Code; Article 15(1) of the Administrative Litigation Code.

[340] In 2007, the Supreme Court applied Article 6 ECHR to overturn decisions of lower courts as violating the principle of legal certainty in matters of substantive law. See Supreme Court Ruling No. 6-V07-28 of 2 November 2007. See for more detail on application of Article 6 (Burkov 2010).

[341] See Supreme Court Plenary Rulings No. 8 of 29 May 2014 'On the Practice of Application by Courts of Legislation on Military Duty and Military Service and the Status of Servicemen'; No. 41 of 19 December 2013 'On the Practice of Application by Courts of Legislation on Preventive Measures in the Form of Detention, House Arrest and Bail'.

implemented on a national scale.[342] Further, international obligations concerning access to courts have led to important procedural developments in the Russian judicial system. For example, legislation regarding the transparency of judicial proceedings has resulted from Russian cooperation with the Council of Europe.[343] Indicatively, the explanatory note accompanying the draft for the 2015 Administrative Litigation Code expressly mentioned that the Code was intended to establish principles of administrative judicial process reflecting the UDHR, the ICCPR and the ECHR, taking into account best practices of administrative proceedings in other countries.[344] Adoption of the Code was encouraged by the UN Special Rapporteur on the Independence of Judges following her visit to Russia in 2013, and she eventually described the Code 'as one of the means of strengthening mechanisms to effectively fight corruption and ensuring liability of state officials' (Special Rapporteur on the Independence of Judges and Lawyers 2014: 14).

In parallel to this increase in the use of law, recent years have seen a widening of options for litigation in Russian society. Since 2001, litigation with a public interest dimension has become more widespread.[345] Moreover, laws on standing before court have been relaxed, and procedures for representing general social interests have diversified. In Russia, rules concerning public interest litigation are generally restrictive, and they still reflect

---

[342] For example, following the pilot judgement *Burdov* v. *Russia* (No. 2) of 15 January 2009, new federal legislation was adopted to provide compensation for lengthy trials. The same guarantee was reproduced in the Administrative Litigation Code. See Federal Law No. 68-FZ of 30 April 2010 'On Compensation for Violation of the Right to Justice in Reasonable Time or the Right to Execution of the Judgment in Reasonable Time'.

[343] See Federal Law No. 262-FZ of 22 December 2009 'On Ensuring Access to Information about Activities of Courts in the Russian Federation'.

[344] Draft Administrative Litigation Code and Related Federal Laws are Submitted to the State Duma, 27 March 2013.

[345] The previously strict rules of standing for public interest cases are being relaxed, and new proxies have been designated that can bring cases to court that reflect a public interest. Such proxies include federal and regional ombudspersons, the state agency for protection of personal data, the federal bar association, associations of citizen's oversight, and even certain state corporations and foundations. See, respectively, Article 40(1) of the Administrative Litigation Code and the Federal Constitutional Law No. 1-FKZ of 26 February 1997 'On Ombudsman of the Russian Federation' as amended by the Federal Constitutional Law No. 1-FKZ of 8 March 2015; Article 23(1) of the Federal Law No. 152-FZ of 27 July 2006 'On Personal Data' as amended by the Federal Law No. 261-FZ of 25 July 2011; Article 35(2) of the Federal Law No. 63-FZ of 31 May 2002 'On Advocacy and the Legal Profession in the Russian Federation', as amended by the Federal Law No. 160-FZ of 2 February 2016; Federal Law No. 212-FZ of 21 July 2014 'On the Basics of Citizens' Control'; Article 8(6) of the Federal Law No. 473 of 29 December 2014 'On Territories of Advanced Socio-Economic Development' as amended by the Federal Law No. 213-FZ of 13 July 2015.

traces of Soviet-era political paternalism. Recent legislation, however, has widened legal opportunities for public interest litigation, and it allows a number of proxies to file suit. In 2014, most importantly, a new Federal Law 'On Citizens' Oversight' was adopted, which authorizes different associations, including NGOs, 'to submit claims to court in the interests of an unidentifiable number of persons against public bodies'.[346]

In these different respects, Putin's reforms to the judicial system have triggered an intensified use of law, or even, to some extent, a broad process of selective legal mobilization. The increased use of law in Russia has a rather distinctive significance, as it is primarily stimulated by systemic actors, and it is facilitated through strategic reform processes. The use of law to express spontaneous challenges to public institutions is less common, although not unknown.[347] However, increased use of the law in Russia has the outcome, as in other national settings, that it promotes collective engagement with the legal system, it solidifies and expands existing rights, and it hardens legal obligations placed on public bodies. As in other settings, moreover, litigation forms an important sluice through which international law enters the national legal system, creating more robust constitutional rights through this process.[348] In each respect, engagement with the legal system through litigation practices forms a functional equivalent to more classical citizenship practices.

The constitutional outcomes of litigation in Russia are visible in two separate dimensions.

In one dimension, the constitutional impact of litigation is evident in Russia in the fact that Russian courts have issued rulings that tighten the constraints on government bodies, intensifying the regulatory order in which such bodies function. This occurs, significantly, in controversial areas of government activity. For example, courts have taken action to challenge federal immigration policy, especially concerning deportation of aliens. In particular, the courts have done this by insisting that immigration policies must show regard for the family ties, the health condition and the risks to the life of persons subject to deportation by public officials.[349]

---

[346] Articles 10(1)(7), Federal Law No. 212-FZ of 21 July 2014 'On the Basics of Citizens' Control'.

[347] See below pp. 476–8.

[348] After introduction of the new Administrative Litigation Code in 2015, the percentage of rulings referring to the ECHR increased to just under 10 per cent. After adoption of the Administrative Litigation Code in 2015, an average of 8 per cent of cases challenging the legality of public decisions referred to the ECHR (with a 63 per cent success rate).

[349] See for example Supreme Court Decision No. 18-AD14-58 of 7 November 2014; Abinskiy District Court of Krasnodarsky Krai Decision No. 5-116/14 of 11 April 2014.

The Supreme Court summarized judicial practice in this regard in its
2013 guidelines, advising lower courts to take Article 8 ECHR into consideration in all cases concerning administrative deportation of foreign
citizens.[350] Furthermore, the willingness of courts to expand constitutional
law is exemplified by cases in which the RCC has intervened in questions
regarding taxation policy, a domain traditionally reserved exclusively
for governmental decision-makers. In the period 2007–14, the Court
invalidated several provisions of the federal Tax Code,[351] which meant
that important aspects of taxation policy were amended. In cases of legal
uncertainty, moreover, courts have applied international law, even in cases
where it places additional restrictions on public agencies. For example, in
February 2017 a regional court in Voronezh applied the constitution and
international law to declare legal a protest against the war in Syria and
against lack of direct elections in the appointment of the city's mayor. In
this case, the Court referred to Article 11 ECHR and the ECtHR jurisprudence.[352] Alongside this, cases of strategic litigation have also generated constitutionally significant outcomes. In one such case, the Court
invalidated a norm of the Russian Prison Code prohibiting long visits by
relatives of some detainees, and it made reference to Article 8 ECHR in so
doing.[353] Following this ruling, the Ministry of Justice prepared a draft federal law to address the suspended norm (Kulikov 2016). Strategic litigation
thus also shapes sensitive areas of public policy, and its outcomes are partly
determined by international law. In such respects, strategic litigation in
Russia is close to the model of contentious norm formation documented
in other polities (Burkov 2010: 172–222).

In a different dimension, widening legal engagement appears to diminish extreme variations between regional and all-Russian citizenship, and
it transplants nationally consolidated norms across all society. Notably,
increasing litigation constructs integrative patterns of citizenship by virtue

---

On deportation of HIV-infected migrants see RCC Ruling on Merits No. 4-P of 12 March
2015; RCC Ruling on Admissibility No. 155-O of 12 May 2006.

[350] Supreme Court Plenum Ruling No. 5 of 24 March 2005 'On Some Issues Arising from
Application of the Code on Administrative Offenses by Courts'. (amended on 19 December
2013): Para. 23.1.

[351] Tax Code of the Russian Federation: Part One, No. 146-FZ of 31 July 1998; Part Two, No.
117-FZ of 5 August 2000.

[352] Tsentralny District Court of Voronezh City, Decision on Administrative Misconduct No.5.
Judgement 8 February 2017.

[353] RCC Ruling on Merits No. 24-P of 15 November 2016. The ruling invalidated Articles 125
and 127 of the Penitentiary Code of the Russian Federation No. 1-FZ of 8 January 1997.

of the fact that it helps to draw together all members of Russian society in the same system of norm construction, establishing the legal dimension of citizenship as a nationally encompassing form. At one level, the simple fact that Russian citizens are increasingly willing to use the law implies that the formal legal order has pierced deeply into society, inserting itself both into lateral relations between private citizens and into vertical relations between citizens and government. Still more importantly, however, willingness to litigate is becoming widespread across all parts of the Russian Federation, even in regions where use of formal legal instruments is not strongly institutionalized. Even in regions with strong traditions of informal legal culture and equally strong anti-Russian traditions, the use of formal legal methods of dispute resolution is spreading. For example, in the Chechen Republic unofficial petitions to the president of the Republic still remain the primary mode of dispute resolution. However, reportedly, the number of Chechen residents using the federal judicial system in the Republic has increased,[354] and other means of informal dispute resolution are losing importance. This trend has become particularly pronounced since 2003, when full-time judicial bodies were formed in the Republic (Bogomolov 2003).

In both these respects, litigation now assumes some functions usually attached to more classical expressions of citizenship. It acquires a key role in societal norm production, in the enforcement and expansion of constitutional laws, and in the normative nationalization of political system. As a result, some core aspects of political citizenship practice appear to have been transferred to litigation procedures, such that, increasingly, litigation can be seen as a functional equivalent to political citizenship.

Third, the growing autonomy of the Russian legal system is manifest in the fact that, from 2000 onward, the judiciary became a more evidently self-regulating entity. Initially, as mentioned, the growth of judicial autonomy was a primary focus of government policy, and it reflected Putin's measures to reduce judicial colonization by private actors. In parallel to this, however, the autonomy of the judiciary has been strengthened through internal policies, and senior figures in the judiciary have regularly introduced measures to heighten consistency and uniformity in judicial procedure. The use of international law to support judicial rulings, initially linked to government policy, is now strongly promoted by judges themselves, and

---

[354] The number of administrative cases considered by courts of the Chechen Republic has increased from 107 in 2012 to 201 in the first half of 2017.

application of international law is widely supported through authoritative case law and plenary rulings of the superior courts.[355] Moreover, the courts have begun, without legislative instruction, to adopt new modes of judicial argumentation, such as precedential reasoning and proportionality reasoning, which augment the autonomous authority of the judiciary, and allow the courts to impose intensified constraints on the actions of public bodies. The use of proportionality in particular reflects a deep interaction between domestic law and international law, and the growing importance of proportionality means that norms to regulate acts of government are extracted from an implied set of transnational norms.[356]

In consequence, the form of the political system in contemporary Russia is very closely linked to the growing autonomy of the judiciary, which is itself connected to the deepening engagement between national and international legal norms. Of course, the commitment of the Russian presidential executive to judicial autonomy is not unrestricted. As mentioned, there are high-profile instances, and even acts of legislation, in which the government has tried to weaken the line of obligation between domestic courts and supranational courts.[357] Generally, however, the Russian legal system is defined by a surprising homology between national and international legal structures, and by an unusually deep commitment to the assimilation of international law by national courts. As a result, actions within the legal system constitute a primary source of norms to check

---

[355] For example, the Supreme Court in Plenum Ruling No. 21 of 27 June 2013 'On Application by Courts of General Jurisdiction of the ECHR' reiterated the binding nature of ECtHR judgements against Russia. Most importantly, the Supreme Court ordered the lower courts to use the principle of proportionality in cases of marked by conflicting human rights. The Supreme Court stated that in such cases the factual circumstances of the case should always be taken into account in order to counter a more traditional strictly positivist approach.

[356] In a recent case, the RCC referred to proportionality as a constitutional principle, although there is no mention of it in the text of the Russian Constitution. The RCC used the classical proportionality argument in a case on criminal liability for multiple violations of the rules of public assembly (See note 305 above). The court has also ordered the Duma to take necessary legislative measures to address this problem.

[357] As discussed above, the RCC Ruling on Merits No. 21-P of 14 July 2015 proclaimed 'the supremacy of the Constitution' over conflicting rulings of international court and tribunals. Subsequently, Federal Constitutional Law No. 7-FKZ of 14 December 2015 was adopted, which solidified the right of the RCC to rule on the constitutionality of a Strasbourg judgement. Later, this law was used to check the constitutionality of two ECtHR judgements, *Anchugov and Gladkov* v. *Russia* (Applications nos. 11157/04 and 15162/05, Judgment of 4 July 2013) in RCC Ruling on Merits No. 12-P of 19 April 2016 and OAO *Neftyanaya Kompaniya Yukos* v. *Russia* (Application no. 14902/04, Judgment of 15 December 2014) in RCC Ruling on Merits No. 1-P of 19 January 2017.

government acts, and legal engagement is an important surrogate form of citizenship practice, in a societal setting in which the scope for the traditional exercise of citizenship is diminished.

In light of this background, it is possible to conjecture, on one hand, that leading actors in the Russian state have promoted legal/judicial autonomy for obvious systemic benefits. It appears that the President and actors in the governmental executive have endeavoured to utilize judicial reform in order to obtain international recognition and credibility, showing partial compliance with international human rights norms. Moreover, it appears that judicial reform has been used to ensure the enhanced societal penetration of government functions, especially in the context of a political system marked historically by intolerably high levels of state privatization. As discussed, Putin and his allies in the courts have repeatedly declared a mission to combat *legal nihilism*, and to raise confidence in the law in order to intensify connections between the political system and society more widely. Owing to the historically debilitating privatism of the political system, persons positioned in the high executive extract distinctive systemic advantages from the rising autonomy of the legal system, linked to increasing use of international law. Notably, both the President and the government are increasingly able to presuppose normative uniformity across society, to diminish private authority and local corruption, to bind society more closely to central institutions, and generally to establish central institutions as reliable centres of societal control.

In addition to this, however, the growing autonomy of the judicial system is not simply steered by imperatives of leading actors in the political system. On the contrary, the growing autonomy of the legal system has been driven by a set of processes that are relatively free of political control, and the judiciary is able independently to generate norms that are not merely dictated by actors in the political branch of government. In fact, the promotion of judicial autonomy in Russia means that legal practices, especially acts of litigation, have assumed clear quasi-constitutional functions, and, quite independently, they even construct a distinctive pattern of constitutional democracy. At one level, the Russian courts have elaborated a legal framework for the exercise of public power which extends original guarantees and securities contained in the formal text of the 1993 Constitution. In some instances, moreover, the courts have solidified constitutional obligations in a fashion not foreseen by the constitutional text, and they have created stricter and expanded normative duties for public bodies.[358] In addition, the day-to-day mobilization of citizens through increasing litigation acts as a source of norm production, which in some respects counterbalances the reduced degree of governmental account-ability in the political domain. The growth of legal mobilization is evident both in regular administrative litigation, but also in the emergence of pub-lic interest litigation. In each respect, the legal system forms a channel of norm-constitutive engagement in settings in which other lines of demo-cratic responsibility are not fully evolved.

As in other cases, Russia has evolved a system of democracy, or at least a system of qualified, managed democracy, in which the evolution of a relatively differentiated legal system has assumed an important, norm-constitutive role. As in other cases, the legal system distils a model of citi-zenship, which spills over into the political arena, creating a normative order that frames for the exercise of political power and intensifies the gen-eral penetration of the political system. This model of citizenship is not fully reproduced in the Russian context, as democracy is weakly institu-tionalized at the national political level. Nonetheless, legal engagement cre-ates practices of citizenship which, to some degree, compensates for the weaknesses of formally institutionalized democratic organs, partly replac-ing classical democratic processes in generating norms of public account-ability. Moreover, legal engagement has central importance in facilitating the social extension of the polity. As in other cases, this partial democratic model has been propelled by the fact that the national legal system and the international legal system have become structurally interwoven through reference to international human rights law. The legal system as a whole, fus-ing aspects of domestic and international law, has acquired a certain degree of constitutional autonomy because of this, and it independently produces core elements of the normative order in which government is positioned. Indeed, the legal system itself has projected the most sustained image of a citizen to support the political order and its integrational functions, and it has created openings for the exercise of democratic citizenship, which are relatively uniform across different parts of the Russian Federation. As in Colombia and the USA, in fact, legal developments in Russia reflect a process in which the rising autonomy of the global legal system has acted to secure not only certain elements of democracy, but, in some aspects, the basic national substructure of the governmental system itself. Even in a state with clear tendencies towards classical political authoritarianism, the reliance on global law as a source of citizenship functions remains strong.

[358] See p. 396 above.

4.2.6   Global Human Rights and National Democracy 6: Kenya

Analogies to the cases discussed above can be found in the recent process of democratic formation in Kenya. In the Kenyan setting, the historical evolution of democracy had been afflicted by problems not dissimilar to those observed in some of the societies discussed above. In this context, the global differentiation of the legal system again assumed distinctive importance, and interaction between national institutions and global norms played a central role in constructing national citizenship, and in forming basic premises for national democracy.

Most notably, first, the establishment of democratic institutions in Kenya was obstructed, historically, by the fact that the central organs of state possessed weak foundations, so that these institutions struggled to exercise generalized power across society. This problem itself was caused by the pluralistic form of Kenyan society, which obstructed the articulation of unified patterns of citizenship to sustain and legitimate governmental functions.

Problems of democratic formation in Kenya were linked, originally, to the fact that state institutions were partly rooted in the institutions created by British colonial authorities, who imposed a centralized coercive order on society, with little broad-based support. Importantly, under colonial rule, the universal rule of law was not established, and parallel legal systems were used for different sectors of the population and different categories of case (Ghai and McAuslan 1970: 130). Moreover, British rulers deliberately encouraged tribalism and chieftaincy, as they relied on chiefs and local notables to uphold the system of indirect rule, based on the devolution of administrative powers from centrally imposed colonial institutions to local and tribal governmental bodies, which they imposed on Kenyan society (Throup 1988: 144, 238; Bates 1989: 47–8; Joireman 2011: 36). The system of indirect rule meant, clearly, that governmental authorities did not possess immediate obligations towards actors in society, and that the direct relation between government and citizen required for national democracy could not be established. In this respect, colonial society closely mirrored pre-modern political structures in Europe, in which governmental force was mediated through local potentates.[359]

---

[359] See for analysis Tilly (2004: 165). Imperial spokespersons saw indirect rule, widely adopted in the later stages of European Imperialism in Africa, as a benign governance system, in which 'the tutelary power' granted statutory powers to local organizations, facilitating self-administration by 'a chief in council' or 'a council of elders' and offering recognition for customary law (Perham 1934: 690–1). As in pre-modern Europe, however, this system

The system of indirect rule also meant that the legal-political order could not be extended into a nationalized form, and that the legal structure of society remained parcellated and deeply pluralistic (see Kamoche 1981: 199). As a result, indirect rule instilled a factionalized, intensely divisive political system into the heart of Kenyan society.

More immediately, second, problems of democratic construction in Kenya were caused by the fragmented ethnic composition of Kenyan society, itself an outcome of colonial rule. Notably, the process of decolonization in Kenya in the 1950s and 1960s was not driven by a single national people, seeking to replace the British colonial administration with a simple nation of citizens. Under British rule, pervasive societal nationalization had traditionally been obstructed, and colonial authorities had originally opposed the formation of national political organizations able to integrate different social groups (Kamoche 1981: 233; Maxon 2011b: 30).[360] By the 1950s, the British colonists looked more sympathetically at moderate, orderly nationalist movements, which were perceived as providing a potentially useful basis for post-colonial reorganization and social management.[361] But the political mechanisms for nation construction were not elaborate. To be sure, Kenyan society had become partly nationalized in the Mau Mau uprising of the 1950s, during which colonial rule was severely unsettled (see Gordon 1986: 113–14).[362] In fact, the Mau Mau revolt spelled the beginning of the end of British occupation in Kenya. However, the Mau Mau revolt did not easily fit the simple nationalist template – it was largely driven by conflicts over land, resulting from a history of racist land administration, reflected in colonial expropriation and reallocation.[363] As well as expressing hostility towards the British

---

created a dualistic legal system, marked by variable obligations and patterns of affiliation. It prevented the rise of unified constructions of society and promoted the entrenchment of highly particularized ethnicities (see Mamdani 1999: 868). On the inevitable localization of society under indirect rule see Berman and Lonsdale (1992: 277).

[360] Such organizations were legalized in 1959 (see Bates 1989: 52).

[361] Sir Andrew Cohen, Governor of Uganda, argued that 'successful working with nationalists is the smoothest way of helping a country to self-government' (1959: 61).

[362] Debate persists as to whether Mau Mau was a nationalist movement, an anti-colonial uprising, or, in part, a civil war between factions of the Kikuyu. For the former view see Berman (1991: 200). For the latter view see Throup (1985: 426); Branch (2007: 300). For a mixed account see Gordon (1986: 114). One author claims that Mau Mau was a 'complex symbiotic interaction of Kenyan nationalism, Kikuyu cultural mobilization and internal strife within the Kikuyu community' (Young 1976: 128).

[363] For discussion of the importance of contest over land in the period of the Mau Mau uprising, see Sorensen (1967: 80); Leo (1984: 44); Bates (1987: 20); Kanogo (1987: 136); Berman and Lonsdale (1992: 245).

administration, Mau Mau created inter- and inner-group conflicts, and it left a long legacy of division between different ethnic population groups and between different factions in the same tribal communities.[364] The rise of political consciousness in the 1950s, therefore, was not necessarily identical with the rise of a national consciousness. Overall, a clearly national foundation to support government was not established in Kenya before independence.

This lack of national cohesion was reflected in the writing of the Kenyan Independence Constitution (1963). In this process, different ethnic groups promoted sharply divergent models of political organization for the new post-colonial state.[365] In particular, constitutional designs during the period of decolonization were split between distinct conceptions of citizenship and statehood, reflecting deep-rooted conflicts between groups committed to building a centralized unitary state and groups defending local interests and tribal affiliations. In this setting, non-dominant tribal groups tended to advocate a quasi-federal polity, in which separate ethnic interests would be protected at a local level.[366] This was reflected in the fact that some groups promoted the creation of a *majimbo* constitution, emphasizing the importance of tribal identities, and seeking to protect tribal autonomy through strong provincial governments (see Maxon 2011b: 18, 77, 105). In addition, of course, many European members of Kenyan society were deeply sceptical about Kenyan nationhood altogether, and they were reluctant to accept Kenyan citizenship (Rothchild 1973: 316, 371). In fact, up to 1960, the British administration had favoured a policy of *multiracialism* for the emergent Kenyan polity, in which different ethnic groups would share power. It was only as the constitution took shape that it became clear that it would be a fully Kenyan constitution (Maxon 2011a: 180, 255). Generally, the first constitution of Kenya evolved in unpropitious circumstances. It was not driven by any uniform construction of the polity. It was shaped by a background in which colonial forces had launched a violent crackdown on Kenyan nationalism, so that the first steps towards the construction of the post-colonial polity occurred in a state of emergency.

---

[364] For analysis of this, see Oucho (2002: 114). Bates also argues that the Mau Mau uprising was a broad conflict over land tenure, and not primarily a conflict between white and black people (1987: 26). On the importance of conflicts over land in this period see also Rosberg and Nottingham (1966: 136–7);

[365] One observer states that by 1962 the 'nationalist struggle was characterized by ethnic parochialism', in which each group sought to avoid Kikuyu dominance (Kanogo 1987: 173).

[366] During the 1960s, the Kikuyu were the dominant ethnic group, and Kenyatta was supported by Kikuyu elites and he actively promoted Kikuyu dominance.

It was also accompanied by controversy over policies addressing the ultra-sensitive and highly divisive issue of land apportionment.

Initially, the Kenyan constitution established a semi-federal political order, reflecting some *majimbo* ideas, in which minority ethnic constituencies preserved some autonomy, and favourable conditions were established for minority groups (Ndegwa 1997: 605; Maxon 2011b: 265). In this respect, the Constitution was conceived as a technical instrument for the peaceful transfer of governmental functions, providing sufficient benefits for each societal groups to avert intense inter-ethnic conflict.[367] Immediately after independence, however, the Kenyatta government abandoned the *majimbo* components of the constitution, and imposed a unitary state on society, in stark opposition to the model of decentralized government that had been endorsed by other stakeholders in the decolonization process (Gertzel 1970: 28; Rothchild 1973: 140; Lynch 2011: 66–8).[368]

In this shift towards political centralism, Kenyatta was guided by nationalist prerogatives. At one level, he promoted a number of strategic nation-building initiatives, with both political and economic emphases, oriented towards comprehensive Africanization of government, citizenship and economic resources.[369] Despite this, however, Kenyatta's governmental regime was a unitary state in name alone; it did not possess full integrational force amongst different social groups, and it did not effectively overarch or integrate different ethnicities. Politically, in fact, Kenyatta's policies directly obstructed the rise of national political citizenship, as, in the late 1960s, the democratic constitution was replaced and Kenya became a de facto one-party state. Moreover, his economic policies failed to impose a uniform political order across the ethnic fissures in society.[370] Beneath the facade of national unity, the state that emerged in Kenya in the 1960s was dominated by small, ethnically privileged elites.

---

[367] This claim is made in Munene (2002: 140). Notably, the writing of the constitution coincided with policies for the consolidation of land tenure, and it was followed by policies for reallocation of land. It was framed by great uncertainty over land tenure (Sorrensen 1967: 118).

[368] One account claims that the 'dismantling of regionalism', partly caused by inter-ethnic clashes, was the main policy concern in the immediate aftermath of independence (Okoth-Ogendo 1972: 18).

[369] On the promotion of African citizenship after independence, on terms initially designed to include non-African minorities, see Rothchild (1968: 421, 428).

[370] Notably, a uniform model of political affiliation was proclaimed through the policy of promoting African socialism, which, beginning in the mid-1960s, declared a self-sufficient, responsible semi-socialist economy as a framework for galvanizing national citizenship (Harbeson 1973: 172–6).

Successive governments sustained their hold on political authority not by appealing to persons in society as national citizens, but by building up coteries of support amongst distinct ethnic contingents, or by designing alliances between different population groups (see Withroup 1987: 48, 67; Ajulu 2002: 263; Murunga and Nasong'o 2006: 10). In this respect, Kenyan politicians simply established a model of government, based on privatistic social alliances and unrepresentative executive power, that partly replicated patterns of British domination under the colonial order.

Owing to the growing linkage between government and ethnicity in Kenya, successive governments from the 1960s onwards justified their hold on the instruments of political authority by claiming that the holding of democratic national elections would trigger uncontrollable ethnic rivalry and intensified conflict over land (see Ndegwa 1997: 610). Anxiety about the politicization of ethnic fissures in society was intermittently intense, and it prevented the promotion of national citizenship practices. As a result, social integration took place primarily through selective material allocation and distribution of offices as privileges, but these were not tied to the uniform distribution of rights or to unifying experiences of citizenship.[371] A core feature of post-colonial Kenyan government, in fact, was that patrimonial distribution of goods, often linked to particular ethnic privileges, formed a primary pillar of state authority. This also meant that national political institutionalization, entailing the expression of national patterns of will formation and the national exercise of sovereignty, was strategically impeded.

A further cause of problems of democratic formation in Kenya, third, was that different organs of state were not securely institutionalized, and the extent to which political organs could impose and legitimate control on actors in the executive was limited. Due to the prevalence of patrimonialism, different organs of the polity were not easily separated from sitting executives. In particular, judicial institutions had an ingrained tradition of patrimonialism, corruption and deference, and the reluctance of judges to hold government bodies to account was widely acknowledged (Ojwang and Otieno-Odek 1988: 45, 49; Nowrojee 2014: 37–9). By the late 1980s, judges had devised a number of innovative excuses for not applying the precise normative provisions of the constitution to restrict government

---

[371] Indicatively, Kenyatta's support was based on distribution of patronage to the Kikuyu. Later, President Moi 'dismantled Kikuyu privilege and replaced it with a Kalenjin cohort' (Ndegwa 1998a: 360; Lynch 2011: 108, 133).

actions, so that the constitution had clearly been relegated to dead-letter status.[372]

Overall, in post-independence Kenya, the legal and political conditions for the expression of national democratic citizenship and the recognition of laws as products of a national will were weakly consolidated. A clear and abiding legacy of colonial rule was that institutions were precariously structured, and their ability to claim representative attachment to national citizens and national society was limited, as offices of state were often perceived as the property of one ethnic group. Dual institutionalization of legal and political obligations, divided between nation and ethnicity, remained a primary hallmark of Kenyan society.[373] An enduring outcome of this was that members of Kenyan society conceived their position as citizens in parallel categories – in 'dual and competing citizenships' – in which local ethnic loyalties often prevailed, and loyalties towards national institutions were purchased by material patronage (Ndegwa 1997: 613).

Eventually, Kenya began a gradual passage to democracy and a gradual renewal of constitutionalism in the 1990s and the early 2000s. A first transition to multi-party democratic elections occurred, formally, in 1992, but, in the first instance, inter-ethnic bargaining meant that elections held at this time were not fully competitive. In fact, these elections were followed by a period of authoritarian repression, in which basic political liberties were again curtailed (Ndegwa 1998b: 188). After 2000, then, the momentum towards more effective institutional reorientation increased; in 2004, a new draft democratic constitution was written; in 2005, a constitutional referendum was held, in which a revised constitution was rejected; in 2010, a new constitution was finally approved by referendum. Notable in the background to this process was the fact that the public economy in Kenya had been deflated as a result of structural adjustment policies implemented by the International Monetary Fund, which meant that the resources of patronage at the disposal of the government were diminished (Berman 2010: 19; Mati 2013: 247). The traditional pattern of social integration through selective allocation of material entitlements was thus replaced, in part, by an attempt to promote integration through the distribution of broadened political rights and the solidification of constitutional

---

[372] In 1989, in *Maina Mbacha and 2 Others* v. *The Attorney General*, the High Court ruled 'inoperative' Section 84 of the Constitution, which provided for the judicial protection of fundamental rights (see discussion in Kuria and Vazquez 1991: 142; Ross 1992: 424). In fact, in the late 1960s the Court had ruled that the constitution should be interpreted in the same way as any regular statute. See *Republic* v. *El Mann* (1969) E.A 357.

[373] On this phenomenon in general see Mamdani (1996: 22, 26, 113, 189).

rule (see Ndegwa 1998a: 364; Onalo 2004: 193). The constitution approved in 2010 was designed both to establish democracy and to transform the foundation of the state from patrimonialism to citizenship.

During the long democratic transition in Kenya, the different draft constitutions, as well as the final ratified constitution of 2010, all placed great emphasis on the importance of mass-political engagement in the consolidation of democracy. All promoted a strongly participatory, transformative concept of the democratic citizen, designed to galvanize and express the will of the nation. This was expressed most especially in Articles 174(c) of the final version of the 2010 Constitution, which stressed the importance of local participation. However, this principle runs like a thread through the whole constitution. Clearly, this participatory impulse in Kenyan constitution writing was intended, for symbolic reasons, to create a constitution that was decisively separated from colonial influence. The constitution of 1963 had been written under the eyes of British officials, and it did not result from the decisive acts of the Kenyan population. Moreover, this aspect of the 2010 Constitution was intended to increase the sense of public identity with the state, encouraging citizens to step outside traditional, post-colonial perceptions of the state as an alien body, and to engage directly and formatively with the domain of public authority. Further, in its participatory dimensions, the Kenyan 2010 Constitution was designed to articulate the political system with actors at different points in society, to weaken the historical influence of sub-national groups in the political system, and to underpin the formation of a political system not immediately susceptible to colonization by one particular ethnic population group and its elite representatives. This clearly reflected a very pressing exigence, as the longer constitution-making process was punctuated by ethnic violence, stimulated by contests over different draft constitutions, and by attempts of different groups to monopolize the content of the constitution.[374] In each respect, the constitution was an endeavour to solidify a national population of citizens, and the emphasis that it placed on active participation was designed to incorporate different social groups into the state in a form, that of the national citizen, that was decisively detached from their personal or ethnic affiliation.

At the same time, all the draft constitutions written during the transitional interim in Kenya contained clauses that were intended to intensify the authority of the legal system, and all attempted to separate the legal

---

[374] See discussion in Bannon (2007: 1854); Berman, Cottrell and Ghai (2009: 495–6); Kramon and Posner (2011: 97).

system from private control. In each instance, the promotion of a political system based on even national citizenship was inextricably linked to the promotion of a differentiated, relatively autonomous legal order. Indeed, the legal system was accorded great importance in establishing national patterns of citizenship, and the legal system had particular responsibility for institutionalizing direct lines of articulation between citizen and state. This was ultimately reflected in the judicial provisions in the 2010 Constitution; the constitution established the right to institute proceedings in cases where a human right had been violated (Article 22(1)), it created a separate procedure for human rights appeals (Article 23(1)) and it encouraged public interest litigation (Article 22(2)(c)). In each respect, the constitution encouraged citizens to engage directly with the legal system, and to utilize the law as a medium of social agency. Moreover, the implementation of the constitution was flanked by subsidiary policies to safeguard judicial autonomy – notably, by frameworks for improving judicial quality, for elevating levels of judicial education and for reducing judicial corruption.[375]

The transition to democracy in Kenya remained affected by traditional factors that had impeded democratic formation. Notably, in the years after 2010, ethnic monopoly of office-holding remained rife, patrimonialism and related corruption remained embedded, and official disregard for constitutional norms remained a recurrent, although not invariable, phenomenon. Most importantly, the formal political organs of the Kenyan state have not been fully detached from ethnic factionalism, and in popular elections, which still risk generating inter-population violence, voting attachments are very strongly determined by group affiliation. This can be seen in the conduct of the 2017 elections, in which ethnic violence was commonplace, and sub-national affiliation was a strong determinant in voting practices. The extent to which the Constitution has created a nation of political citizens, therefore, is a matter of dispute. As discussed above, moreover, the relation between courts and executive since 2010 has often assumed an attritional and personalized character, marked by intermittent political pressure on legal appointments. This culminated, of course, in the initial decision of the Supreme Court in 2017 that the national election results were invalid, and that new elections had to be held.[376]

---

[375] Central to this was the implementation of the Judiciary Transformation Framework, initiated in 2012.

[376] *Raila Amolo Odinga & another* v. *Independent Electoral and Boundaries Commission & 2 others* [2017] eKLR.

In the Kenyan setting, however, the formation of national citizenship, to the extent that it exists, has proved strikingly dependent on the societal penetration of global norms. Indeed, legal institutions have assumed particular importance because of their ability to project generalized patterns of integration, and to outline modes of political obligation that are not linked to ethnicity and particular membership. The legal system, articulated to the global normative order, forms a vital store of democratic norm formation and a vital focus of national inclusion.

To illustrate this, for instance, Willy Mutunga, appointed Chief Justice in 2011, assumed an important role in placing the judiciary at the centre of the reformed Republic in Kenya. In particular, he attempted to consolidate the Supreme Court as a fully national court, in which judges acted to protect the sovereignty of the people from regional or organic fragmentation, and to use judicial powers as a core element in the broader construction of a national popular will. To this end, he endeavoured to establish a categorically national body of constitutional jurisprudence, separate from English common law, through which he sought to project a robust construction of integrative national values. In an important opinion, Mutunga explained the practical realities of democratic self-rule in Kenya, asserting that courts are bound in 'indestructible fidelity to the value and principle of public participation'. To this degree, he viewed the courts as core organs of national citizenship, creating a medium for the direct expression of the popular will, separate from ethnic particularities. However, he also accorded to the courts a distinctive constructive role in this process, claiming that the courts needed to bring together a range of 'rich ingredients', including judicial analysis of scholarly works and use of 'comparative jurisprudence from other jurisdictions',[377] to stabilize democratic participation and collective/popular self-expression. In particular, he argued that a constructive judicial approach was required 'to deconstruct and demystify the participation of the people', translating the ideal of popular sovereignty into an implementable value.[378] Implicitly, this approach presupposed that popular participation had to be moderated through judicially constructed principles, and judicial institutions had a strong responsibility for ensuring that the popular will was expressed as a general set of national norms, distinct from the interests of large influential ethnic groups.

Significant in the process of constitutional redirection in Kenya was a debate about the role and authority of international law in the new Kenyan

---

[377] In the Matter of the National Land Commission [2015] eKLR at para 355.
[378] In the Matter of the National Land Commission [2015] eKLR at para 321.

democracy. Indicatively, leading judges in pre-transitional Kenya had interpreted the role of international law in strict conformity with common-law dualist principles, and it had been declared in leading cases that international conventions and instruments could not impact directly on domestic rulings (see Okuta 2009: 1068; Wabwile 2013: 171).[379] As mentioned, further, by the late 1980s, judges had abdicated responsibility for enforcing the basic rights provisions inscribed within domestic law. During the constitutional transition, however, the push for increased judicial autonomy was shaped, not coincidentally, by the increasing, albeit initially tentative, openness of the legal system to international norms. During the transition, a number of important rulings gave cautious protection to internationally defined rights within the national legal order,[380] and citation of principles derived from international law became part of the broad constitution-making situation. This was strongly reinforced in the 2010 Constitution, which acknowledged international norms as important sources of domestic law (Articles 2(5), 21(4)). After 2010, much debate ensued in Kenya about the relative standing of international law in the domestic legal system, and different rulings pulled in different directions in this regard.[381] In general, however, senior figures in the judiciary became increasingly resolute in arguing that the Kenyan legal system needed to be construed in monist categories, and that international law should be used as an immediate source of authority for legal rulings (Mutunga 2015b: 8).

Against this background, Kenya forms the most vivid example of society in which the national substructure of democracy has been strategically created on global legal premises. In Kenya, international law was used to abstract and construct a counter-factual idea of the national citizen, in a form indifferent to inner-societal attachments, and external legal sources were specifically configured to impose a system of uniform legal/political inclusion on society. The nation-building role of international law in Kenya then became visible in a number of different processes.

At a purely normative level, Kenyan judges have used international law in order to separate a legal form for the national citizen from traditional ethnic monopolies, and to generate equal rights and equally binding legal protection for all sub-communities within national society. In this respect, recent rulings in cases concerning the most contested and divisive issues

---

[379] The classic case is *Okunda* v. *Republic* [1970] EA 453.
[380] See for example In Re the Estate of Andrew Manunzya Musyoka (2005), eKLR. For discussion see Kabau and Ambani (2013: 40); Oduor (2014: 98).
[381] See for a summary Kabau and Ambani (2013).

have often contained extensive reference to international law, to underline the objective authority of the decision. For example, the courts have used international law to give recognition for rights of minority populations.[382] In establishing such rights, importantly, the courts have often simply expanded other rights, for example the right to water, the right to housing, or the broader right to a dignified life, in order to protect minority and marginalized population groups, using international law to define such rights.[383] In such processes, collective actors defined by ethnic affiliation have been able to pursue legal inclusion through reference to norms of citizenship based on international principles. As a result, courts have been able to guarantee access to national goods for ethnically constructed communities without premising such recognition on legal acknowledgement of group affiliation as a source of rights. In this way, ethnic groups have been able to acquire and exercise group rights in categories not linked expressly to ethnicity, and unlikely to induce destabilizing political conflict. Inclusive patterns of national citizenship have thus, to some degree, been constructed because international law is able to express a generalized abstract concept of the citizen, which can be articulated to establish multiple rights and obligations above the fissures in national society, without reference to historical realities and divisions. The fact that citizenship can be centred around a global model facilitates the construction of the basic form of national citizenship, and it makes it possible to overcome the classical division between national and ethnic citizenship, simplifying the factual inclusion of particular social groups within a single and socially overarching normative order.

At a more structural level, judicial actors in Kenya have insisted on the importance of international law because of its importance in the campaign against judicial corruption and ethnic monopoly of judicial functions, reflecting a concern that renewed judicial office trading would derail the process of democratic consolidation (see Mutunga 2015a). In this respect, judges have attempted to link Kenyan case law to international standards in order to ensure that case rulings are visibly underwritten by normative principles that are relatively immune to personal manipulation or ethnic bias. Use of international law is promoted as a policy to

---

[382] See extensive use of international covenants to recognize political rights of the Il Chamus people in *Lemeiguran and Others* v. *Attorney-General and Others* (2006) AHRLR 281 (KeHC 2006).

[383] See important use of international human rights law and other international instruments in protecting indigenous land rights in *Charles Lekuyen Nabori & 9 others* v. *Attorney General & 3 others* [2007] eKLR; *Joseph Letuya & 21 others* v. *Attorney General & 5 others* [2014] eKLR.

uphold the basic differentiation and the general autonomy of the legal system within Kenyan society, and to preserve clearly national principles to sustain legal authority. Indeed, although high levels of judicial corruption persisted in Kenya after 2010, international law has provided a solid basis for litigation against government bodies, and rulings in contentious political cases have been supported by reference to international norms.[384]

In Kenya, however, perhaps the most important impact of the internalization of international norms became visible in the fact that, following the implementation of the constitution, the volume of litigation increased significantly, including a steady rise in the filing of constitutional petitions.[385] Moreover, in this period, patterns of litigation underwent marked diversification. In recent years, actors from different social and regional positions in society have used the courts as instruments both for general conflict resolution and for proceedings against the government. Importantly, this has been reflected in the growing use of courts by socially disadvantaged groups; the post-transitional period has seen a wave of public-interest litigation over social-economic rights, often referring to international or comparative law.[386] Through this process, the courts have opened up new opportunities for mobilization and political subjectivization, again using international norms to imprint unified models of citizenship on society. At the same time, this internalization of international norms has been reflected in the use of the law as a medium for presenting claims by different ethnic population groups. Notable in post-2010 Kenyan legal history, in fact, is the growing tendency for members of minority populations to utilize the law, and for such groups to reach into the domain of international law to assert legal claims within national society. This should not be seen as a linear or incremental process. The Kenyan government has not shown itself consistently sympathetic to such claims, and it has been subject to international sanction for failure to recognize indigenous rights.[387]

---

[384] See *Mitu-Bell Welfare Society* v. *Attorney General & 2 others* [2013] eKLR.

[385] The number of constitutional petitions increased from 341 in 2011 to nearly 600 in 2012 (Mukaindo 2013).

[386] See relaxation of standing in *Priscilla Nyokabi Kanyua* v. *Attorney General & another* [2010] eKLR. This ruling used Indian case law.

[387] See the case against Kenya before the African Commission, *276/03 Centre for Minority Rights Development (Kenya) and Minority Rights Group (on behalf of Endorois Welfare Council) / Kenya*. See the resultant case heard by the African Court on Human and Peoples Rights, *African Commission on Human and Peoples' Rights* v. *Republic of Kenya*, Application 006/2012, Judgment of 26 May 2017.

Nonetheless, strategic litigation for minority groups has become partly institutionalized, both in law and in practice.[388]

In different respects, in consequence, the Kenyan constitution has created a legal/political order in which new patterns of inclusion, mobilization, participation and citizenship have been generated. As mentioned, this is a precarious condition; the web of national citizenship shaped by the constitution is very fragile, and it remains uncertain whether the legal construction of citizenship will cut deep enough into society to sustain a full democracy. However, the interpenetration of domestic law and international law is a core aspect of Kenyan democracy, and it creates an overarching focus for democratic integration which is unmistakeably separate from legally parcellated or traditionally dominant ethnic groups. In some instances, paradoxically, the fact that the state is founded on a unified construct of the citizen, established under global norms, means that members of the people can factually present themselves in pluralistic modes of citizenship to the legal/political system. In particular, the use of human rights derived from international law in domestic law means that recognition can be given for particular group claims in relatively abstract principles and in relatively neutralized procedural fashion, such that recognition of ethnic particularity does not necessitate a politicization of ethnic interests around the political system. The pluralistic form of society, thus, can be represented by democratic means specifically because the essential rights and principles of citizenship originate outside national society. For these reasons, further, the rights-based abstraction of the national legal system has begun to form an important parallel system of democratic agency and will formation, sitting alongside more classical political institutions and forms of interest representation. Indeed, the capacity of the legal system to reflect global models of citizenship remains a key counter-weight to the particularistic tendencies that affect the composition of the political branches.

4.3   Human Rights and the Transformation of Politics

In most settings, the general spread of national democracy has been driven by a process in which the legal system and legal constructions of political agency have assumed a position of relative autonomy in national societies. In this process, judicial bodies have acquired relatively independent capacities for producing law, for establishing constraints on the power of governments, and for underpinning complex, multi-focal forms of

---

[388] See further discussion below at p. 412.

democratic agency, citizenship and inclusion. Generally, national political systems became democratic, or at least acquired some democratic features, through their integration in a global system of norms, leading to the partially virtual inner-legal construction of citizenship. Moreover, political systems usually remain democratic to the extent that they preserve their basic contiguity with a global normative system. At the core of modern democracy is the fact that patterns of citizenship are created above the factual interactions in society, and political institutions refer for their legitimacy to norms that are not really embedded in society. The legitimational detachment of the political system from material agents in society is the most typical precondition for national citizenship and national democracy.

A number of political theorists have argued that democratic citizenship presupposes national identity, and that the practices of citizenship risk being devalued if located outside national contexts and national processes of legislation.[389] In reality, however, few national societies generated secure concepts of citizenship. In virtually all societies, national political institutions ensured that the rights of citizenship could not be equally claimed by all social groups. National legislatures almost invariably failed to create national citizenship. In fact, legislatures failed to create national citizenship for a range of different reasons – sometimes, because they entrenched class dominance; sometimes because they solidified ethnic hegemony; sometimes because they were enmeshed in private conventions in society; sometimes simply because they were unable to form normative articulations with all social groups. It was only as the central content of citizenship was designed within a global normative order that the exclusionary pathologies of citizenship became less pronounced.[390] Quite generally, the national citizen had to be incorporated in national legislation from an external, international source.

A number of sociologists have noted how the deepening interpenetration between national legal structures and global law, including globally defined human rights, has contributed to a solidification of democracy

---

[389] Some argue that citizenship is essentially linked to national territories or at least to distinct cultural identities (Walzer 1994; Canovan 1996: 44; Sandel 1996: 343–5; Miller 2000; Schuck 2000: 225). Others argue that democratic citizenship is already in principle, or at least in part, decoupled from national territory (see Soysal 1994: 165; Jacobson 1996: 106; Delanty 2000: 136; Sassen 2002b: 5; Höffe 2004: 171; Colliot-Thélène 2010b: 178). For critical reflections on the bounded construction of the citizen, see Benhabib (2000: 24); Stokes (2004: 128); Linklater (2007: 16); Isin (2012: 5).

[390] From a different angle, see the account of the correlation between the global diffusion of certain basic rights, the rising robustness of state institutions and the nationalization of citizenship practices in Meyer et al. (1977: 251).

and democratic citizenship in national societies.[391] Moreover, a number of sociologists have argued that the extension of inclusive rights to traditionally excluded social groups has resulted from the emergence of a 'world model' of political citizenship.[392] The analysis set out above affirms these insights. However, the analysis offered here also extends such hypotheses, claiming that national citizenship itself was only rarely fully consolidated before global norms began to define the grammar of national political inclusion. Indeed, such claims are widened here to incorporate the secondary claim that democratic citizenship has almost invariably depended on the formation of a world model of citizenship, constructed through the dense articulation between national and global legal domains. Even the basic formation of a generalized national political community, supposedly the constitutive political core of citizenship, has only been possible through the penetration of international law into domestic legal practices. Most societies did not succeed in establishing a distinctive political domain, separated from dominant private bonds in national society, without international normative support.

These processes possess particular significance for the sociology of law. In recent decades, the process of integration through the law, and through rights contained in the law, which classical sociologists located at the heart of modern democracies has, at least partially, become reality. Indeed, integration through the functions of a differentiated legal system became a core founding dimension of modern democratic systems. But this only occurred in societies as they were lifted above their national form, and the integrational functions of law were not realized on national foundations. Classical sociologists looked in vain for a higher set of norms, within national societies, to support law's functions. They also looked in vain for rational processes of will formation to support the law. Law's integrational force only became real as international human rights supplanted national systems of rights as the foundations of social integration, and as these rights were separated from national populations.[393] Only as international

---

[391] For such analysis see Boli, Ramirez and Meyer (1987: 167); Meyer, Ramirez and Soysal (1992); Meyer et al. (1997: 157–9); Ramirez, Soysal and Shanahan (1997).

[392] See for one use of this concept Ramirez, Soysal and Shanahan (1997: 743).

[393] It is extraordinary that the leading sociologists writing after 1945 who examined processes of legal integration in modern democratic society omitted to observe the importance of international law. For example, Parsons (1965), Luhmann (1965) and Habermas (1990 [1962]) all identified the construction of constitutional rights as vital for democratic inclusion, and all were working in nations whose formation as democracies was inseparable from the pervasive force of international law. Yet, none of them noticed this proces – or at least, in the case of Habermas, not until much later.

rights penetrated into patterns of interaction in national society did rights act as a means of comprehensive integration, able to mediate the inter-group conflicts which had historically impeded the realization of demo-cratic citizenship.

In key respects, across different lines of democratic polity building, national democracies have been formed through complex patterns of *inter-legality*. This term is usually reserved to describe volitional or activist pro-cesses of legal mobilization (Sousa Santos 2002: 437, 2006: 70; Sierra 2005: 310). However, this term also captures the essential foundation of modern democracy, as democracy widely evolves not through the strict exercise of political agency, but through overlapping trajectories in which legal institutions, at different global positions, construct overarching norms, which are then assimilated and configured in socio-political practice. This normally occurs because the national legal system uses global norms to separate citizenship practices from factual modes of agency and affiliation, and, on this basis, it creates general premises for inner-societal interaction between citizens themselves and between citizens and the political system. This assumes different form in different societies. But, typically, democ-racy has only taken shape as the construction of citizenship has been dis-placed from the national political system into the global legal system. As a result, the ongoing globalization of democracy over recent decades is inseparable from a process in which the primary norms of society, and the primary procedures of citizenship, are constructed not by political actions, but by actions and interactions performed *within the law*. The globaliza-tion of democracy is thus part of a wider process – namely, the globaliza-tion of the legal system. *The globalization of democracy is one consequence of a broader globalization of the legal system, in which the legal system has attained a high level of differentiation and influence in relation towards other systems through reference to human rights law.* Democracy was classically understood as a pattern of national political self-legislation, and it is not easy conceptually to separate democracy from national polities. As men-tioned, there is much controversy about transnational citizenship, and the question is often posed whether the substance of citizenship can extend beyond national boundaries. However, democracy only became a globally widespread factual reality through a process that profoundly contradicted the traditional conception of democracy. The national citizen only evolved on a transnational basis, and democracy depended on constructions of political obligation, binding on both citizens and institutions, that were secured outside national societies, and outside the realities of national social structure. The deep democratic nexus between citizen and state, which necessarily underpins political democracy, had to be interposed between state and citizen in a form extracted from the global domain. As discussed, interactions in the global legal system formed surrogates for more classical citizenship practices, and the basic inclusionary implications of citizenship could only be realized through the translation of citizenship into global functional equivalents. In the cases examined, the transposition of democratic norms into functional equivalents articulated the process in which the original norms of democracy approached reality.

Through these processes, both nationally and globally, the differentiation of the legal system has created a reality in which much that was once political is now simply law. The growing autonomy of the global legal system effectively means that, at different societal levels, the legal system has acquired primacy over the political system. At a global level, it is difficult to identify any phenomena close to an overarching political system; global political functions are more typically performed by judicial bodies. At a national level, similarly, political institutions are deeply reliant on, and enmeshed within, legal institutions. Overall, the globalization of democracy has occurred as part of a process in which society as a whole has been stripped of its distinctive political subjectivity, or its political subjectivity has been translated into functional equivalents. The idea that the institutional form of democratic society can be defined by categorically political decisions, reflecting political agency separate from the law, has disappeared. The politics of modern society as a whole is underpinned by an increasingly asymmetrical relation between politics and law, as result of which, at different points in society, law integrates the functions of politics: law, not politics, makes the law, and law institutionalizes the modes of social inclusion in which law is made.

In some respects, the depletion of politics has acted as the constitutive precondition for the emergence of democracy as a global political-institutional form. As mentioned above, the classical idea of democracy hinged on two conjoined principles: the principle of full legal inclusion (in a system of rights) and the principle of national political participation, attached to citizenship.[394] Classically, the first principle was seen as contingent on the second principle. However, these two principles proved internally conflictual, and democracies legitimated by participation failed to establish full legal inclusion. In fact, democracies legitimated by mass participation remained structurally exclusionary, and they failed to establish a pattern of citizenship able to penetrate deep into society. Democracy

---

[394] See pp. 37–8 above.

was only realized as legal inclusion replaced participatory politics as the mainstay of democracy. For this reason, the essential normative subject of democracy – the political citizen – needs to be abandoned, or at least re-imagined in a system of equivalence. As discussed, the fact that the differentiation of the global legal order has implanted an autonomous legal structure in national societies, even generating the basic subjective forms of citizenship practice, is often a primary reason why democracy is able to take hold. Often, paradoxically, the political desubjectivization of society through the global differentiation of the legal system forms the main ground for the generalization of democracy. Through the global differentiation of the legal system, the law began to absorb within itself both principles of democracy – integration and participation – and it was only as a result of law's double democratic function, promoting rights-based inclusion and participation as inner-legal functions, that democracy could be broadly institutionalized. Democracy began to evolve as a global political form as it was separated from the *demos*. Indeed, democracy was only stabilized as the citizen, as a participatory source of norms, was transformed into an inner-legal figure. If democracy is founded on both the legal integration and the political participation of citizens, it depended historically both on the construction of external normative premises for integration and on the assimilation of many participatory practices within the law. Through this process, in effect, the law internalized the source of its own integrational authority, providing integrational functions to underpin democracy by translating the citizen into functional equivalents. This paradox formed the core of modern democracy.

In the 1920s, Carl Schmitt argued that legislatures could not create democracies. More specifically, he argued that legislatures were in thrall to particular interests in society, and they could not generate broad or group-transcendent foundations to bring legitimacy to legislation (1923: 19–20). As a remedy for this, he advocated that legislatures should, in some circumstances, be suspended in favour of plebiscitary patterns of acclamation, distilling the national will into single homogenous decisions, enacted directly by national executives (1927: 38).

On one count, Schmitt was right. Legislatures did not create democracy. Indeed, across a range of societal environments, it is visible that national political systems, notionally centred on legislatures, prevented the final realization of democracy. Accounts of democracy that prioritize the role of legislatures usually present highly idealized, counter-factual pictures of legislative bodies (Waldron 2006: 1361). In most cases, models of democracy focused on national legislatures obstructed the comprehensive inclusion of society and they failed to generate overarching and fully inclusive constructions of citizenship. In the examples examined above, we can see that legislatures failed in these respects for many different reasons.

On one count, however, Schmitt was clearly wrong – in fact, he was wrong in rather spectacular fashion. Eventually, democracy did not evolve in a form that relied on any regress to a pure national will. To be sure, Schmitt would not have accepted the ultimate prevalent form of democracy as true democracy. However, the form finally taken by democracy depended on the fact that the will of the people, which was supposed to be channelled through the acts of legislatures, was separated, by global law, from the factual will of the people, and stabilized through inner-legal exchanges, in a global system of functional equivalence. Only through this process was it possible to separate law's source from dominant groups in national societies, and only through this process was a variable form created within which, however imperfectly, all persons in society could assume a position in a national system of inclusion. International law provided a construction of the citizen that avoided both the excessive particularism and the excessive homogeneity that characterizes democratic polities centred on legislatures.[395] The precondition for this shift was that the form of the citizen was extracted from outside national society, and detached from the factual reality of the national citizen.

Of course, this does not mean that legislatures play no role in contemporary democracy. However, the global legal system instils the form of the citizen in society, and it pre-structures the legislative functions of democracy. In fact, democracies increasingly rely on two lines of legal/political communication, one representative, and one judicial, both of which play a role in actively articulating the state and society. In most instances, as discussed, it is the legal/judicial line of communication, partly elevated above the interests of factual citizens, that plays the deepest, most constituent role in shaping the form of democracy.

---

[395] See above pp. 287–92, 324–5, 403–6.

5

The Reconstruction of Democratic Agency

5.1 New Forms of Democratic Agency: Multiple Articulations

On the basis of the above analyses, many of the classical principles that underlie democratic politics and its theoretical constructions now appear invalid, or require substantial qualification. In particular, the essential focus of normative authority, which supports the legitimacy of laws (both primary and statutory), is now widely extracted not from the concrete acts of citizens or from processes of popular will formation, but, to a large degree, from human rights norms, which are preserved and enacted within an existing transnational legal order. As a result of this, the original sources of authority for legislation have been – in part, at least – relocated from a position *outside* the legal system (the political will of the citizens, or the constituent power) to a position *inside* the legal system (basic rights, usually declared at an international level, and then internalized within domestic legal systems). At a most fundamental level, a model of democracy has begun to emerge in which *legal procedures* have dislodged *political procedures* as the defining focus of democratically legitimated legislation, such that, in a pattern of functional equivalence, the articulation of global legal norms appears as a primary mode of democratic agency. In Chapter 3, it was observed that the conceptual structure of classical democracy has been partly translated into a normative order in which legal procedures, conducted either within national courts, or in the interaction between international norm providers and domestic courts, perform core legitimational functions. In Chapter 4, it was observed that, across a range of different political systems, the factual-institutional form of national democracy has been engendered, at least in part, by procedures that take form within the law, reflecting a broad interpenetration between the national legal system and the global legal system. The essential concepts of democracy – such as people, nation, popular sovereignty and collective self-legislation – cannot now be used to capture this condition. Even the factual form of the national citizen only acquired full reality within the system of global law. In democratic polities, the acts that establish authority for laws, both constitutional and statutory, are procedures in which human rights norms, already consolidated within the legal system, are articulated and reproduced as a normative framework for legislation. The fact that the legal system is centred on human rights, and that human rights project an overarching norm of legitimacy for legal/political acts, means that the legal system itself becomes a primary constitutional subject in modern democracy, and its internal procedures now form functional equivalents to classical acts of democratic formation, citizenship and constitution making.

In contemporary democracy, legitimacy for national legislation is constructed through multiple lines of communication around the political system, many of which are focused on the recursive reproduction and re-expression of existing global legal norms. In this setting, the citizen typically approaches the political system in a form mediated by global law, so that the claims to legal rights and legislative recognition made by citizens articulate principles of global law, and they link the political system directly to the global legal order. Classically, the citizen was a source of agency that channelled inner-societal claims directly into the political system, and the citizen generated legislation on that basis. Now, the citizen is partly translated from a political figure into a formal legal figure, and, as it engages with citizens, the political system also engages with global legal norms. In raising claims to rights, the citizen transmits claims towards the political system by linking such claims to global law, and especially to human rights established in global law. In so doing, the citizen connects the national political system directly to the global legal system, constructing a cycle of transmission between the national political system and the global legal system. The citizen was once the external societal environment of the political system. But the citizen now appears to the political system as part of the global legal system, partly detached from the realities of national society, such that, refracted through the citizen, the global legal system becomes the defining outer environment of the national political system. Indeed, in contemporary democracy, the citizen is partly separated from its factual social position, and it assumes law-making force by instilling globally formed norms into national legal orders and by locking national law into global law. This means that both in its global external orientation and in its national internal orientation, the national political system has become part of the global legal system, and, both nationally and globally, the political system is internalized within the law. Through the reconstruction of the citizen, in short, the political system of national society has become part of global law.

In consequence, democracy now assumes the form of a complex system of legal inclusion. In this system, naturally, the organs of classical legislative bodies still play an important role in articulating society's legislative functions to social agents. It is clearly not possible to have a democracy without a functioning legislature, and some interactions between polity and citizens run specifically through legislatures. However, contemporary democracy has evolved as a complex law-making system, in which the legislature loses its dominance as the primary channel for the translation of social claims into law, and legislative acts now take place in a number of different cycles of communication around the political system. In contemporary democracy, in fact, the political system is usually marked by three lines of communication with its societal environment, so that social claims assume legal form through separate processes. In each line of communication, interaction between national law and global law has assumed defining importance.

First, as mentioned, legislative functions are still performed by legislatures, mandated by popular elections. In such contexts, the citizen still appears as a primary political agent. However, the interactions between legislatures and their societal environments are pre-structured by global legal norms, and the content of legislation, even if produced in classical form, is broadly subject to global legal constraint.[1] As a result, global law predefines the normative form in which citizens can appear to legislative bodies, and standard legislative processes are configured through global law. Democratic legislation is never separate from global law, and classical legislative processes usually express, and give effect to, principles of global law.

Second, legislation is often produced through processes in which legislatures play a more marginal role, and many acts of legislation result from exchanges between national governments and persons in national society that occur within the legal system – through legal claims, legal mobilization, litigation and human rights activism. Law thus loses its status and particular dignity as an 'offshoot of politics' (Waldron 1999: 166). In such instances, legal exchanges act, alongside legislatures, as a second communication loop around the political system, and they assume core legislative functions. As discussed, such exchanges are often centred on articulations between national law and global law. In such contexts, the citizen appears as a legal agent.

Third, interactions between national legal bodies and global legal institutions are capable of creating legislation in autonomous fashion, so that

---

[1] See examples above at pp. 221–31.

global law can, *of itself,* create law, which is recognized as democratic, on autonomous foundations. As will be discussed below, in fact, articulations between bodies situated at different positions in the system of global law often create not only law, but the persons to whom laws are attached and attributed, and they allow new legal subjects to appear. The production of law now occurs in an increasingly autonomous domain, marked by highly contingent processes of subject formation. In such contexts, the citizen appears as an internal construction of the law.

On this basis, the reliance of democracy on functional equivalents means that that democratic citizen assumes a divided shape. At one level, the citizen still interacts directly through political procedures with legislative institutions. At a different level, however, the citizen interacts with the political system through more contingent processes and lines of exchange. The citizen is divided into a political form and a legal form, each of which communicates with the political system in a distinctive dimension. The political citizen remains vital for the formation of legislation. However, the legal citizen acquires underpinning legitimational functions, and it usually sets the leading norms for the political system as a whole, so that legislation that extends the societal frontiers of the political system is triggered by the citizen in its legal dimension. Society may acquire robustly enforceable legislation from classical legislatures, representing citizens in the political dimension of communication. Yet, it is the legal form of the citizen that communicates at the boundaries of the political system, and underpins new processes of normative integration and construction. This is usually caused by the fact that the citizen in its legal form attaches inner-societal exchanges to global norms, and it expands the structure of the political system on that basis. As discussed, in classical democracy, the political citizen extended the boundaries of the political system by communicating through rights. This function now falls primarily to the citizen in its legal form.

Overall, the contemporary model of political democracy is not fully centred on exchanges between the political system and factually existing citizens, and citizens, in their concrete/material form, have forfeited their original status as the primary authors of law. The democratic system is underpinned by a basic legitimational switch from the citizen to human rights, and communications that assume the form of law increasingly do so because they are articulated with the system of global human rights. Such communications produce legislation in multiple ways, splitting the citizen into multiple inner-legal forms, and they often do not require a foundation in physical acts of citizens.

What emerges through these processes is a reorientation of democracy towards a pattern of democratic practice in which democracy is no longer perceived as a *total form*, giving expression to freedoms in which citizens are comprehensively implicated. The citizen loses some of its reality as a factual actor, and it becomes, itself, a construct of law. The fact that the citizen as legitimational figure is split apart from the citizen as a factual collective agent means that the freedoms that the citizen is able to exercise are detached from deep-lying private/societal contests. The freedoms of citizenship are now often defined externally, in particular by judicial bodies applying international law. Further, democracy is no longer based on acts of political participation which imply an integral correlation between the collective will of citizens and decisions made within the political system.[2] The external stabilization of the citizen limits the contestation over the most basic normative order of society, and it often reduces the intensity attached to the exercise of citizenship rights. As the legitimation of the political system is linked to a formally determined subject, the total politicization of society becomes improbable, even impossible. In fact, as the citizen is constructed as part of global law, citizenship often loses connection with a fully material reality – it is primarily a figure through which the political system articulates itself with global law. In each respect, the main stimulant of legislation is provided by interactions between different norms within the global system, and the primary subject of law is the global citizen, located, in abstract legal form, outside national society.

This progressive translation of democracy into a sub-system of global law is widely treated with derision, as a political order that entails deep attenuation of human political potentials. Of course, such contempt for the construction of democracy as an inner-legal system is sometimes expressed in momentary political acts, in which governments or national populations act against global norms and external judicial institutions, especially those with transnationally founded authority.[3] However, some more refined legal observers claim that contemporary democracy reflects a socially compliant formalism, that it negates more effective patterns of democratic will formation, and that it eradicates basic political experiences of contestation

---

[2] Here I agree with the argument set out by Helmut Willke, stating that in contemporary democracy we need to give up the idea that 'all people participate in all areas' (2014: 158). However, Willke imagines alternative patterns of participation through specialized competence. My theory would also accommodate this, although I place greater emphasis on legal mobilization.

[3] Recent examples are the Brexit referendum in the UK and attacks on the Constitutional Court in Poland.

and grounded demands for emancipation from society.[4] In such instances, the inner-legal construction of democracy and democratic citizenship is observed as an illegitimate deviation from a political ideal type. In addition, some sociological analyses suggest that, partly owing to the growing power of international institutions, we have now moved beyond the realm of classical democracy, into a pattern of *post-democratic* political administration, in which democracy again loses its original meaning (see Crouch 2004: 104–6; Willke 2014: 49, 97). Alongside this, some theorists argue that the recent relative stabilization of democracy depends on a model of low-intensity democracy (Marks 2000: 57; Brunkhorst 2014: 460), or 'low-intensity citizenship' (O'Donnell 1993: 1367), even giving rise to a new global brand of monetary imperialism, in which the basic rights of citizens are constrained (Gills, Rocamora and Wilson 1993: 21). Across all these lines of research, the view is now commonplace, with variations, that the global form of society has reduced the basic autonomy and capacity of nation states, weakening classical resources of democracy.[5]

It is difficult fully to deny the justification of such claims. Clearly, the global intensification of inner-legal power has led to the institutionalization of systems of legal-political inclusion that only remotely resemble classical democratic ideals. As discussed, the current form of democracy is not easily combined with a theory of constituent power, and the principle, central to classical democracy, that the legitimacy of democratic institutions can be radically recast, through some regress to the original will of the people, becomes submerged in this system.[6] It has become difficult to understand democracy as a mode of political organization that is founded on substantial norms, prescribed by acts of collective agreement. It is difficult see the legitimacy of political institutions as a phenomenon generated by primary volitional acts of a people. In particular, it is difficult to see democracy as a governance system in which legitimacy is produced through a simple factual chain of communication between political institutions and the citizens of a given national society. It is difficult to understand democracy as a system of political organization that is centred around single institutions, with deeply representative decision-making functions. It is also difficult to view democracy as a mode of social administration, in which single decisions can radically redirect existing political

---

[4] For different expressions of these claims see Tushnet (1984: 1384, 1394, 1989: 421, 438); McCann (1986: 188); Kennedy (2002); Douzinas (2007); Hirschl (2007).
[5] See a notable formulation of this claim in Markoff (1999b).
[6] See discussion above at pp. 36–7.

institutions. Under the recent form of democracy, moreover, citizens generally assume rights in uniform procedures, dictated by a global model, and rights are not constructed through deep-rooted lines of societal contest. Indeed, as the rights of citizens are increasingly defined in an external normative order, there are usually limits to the extent to which society can be politicized through legal claims and by mobilized legal actors.[7] In contemporary democracy, there is no obvious political citizen beneath the legal citizen, and the citizen is positioned in society by legal acts that are constructed through global norms. As mentioned, democracy widely presupposes the detachment of the citizen, as a focus of political rights and obligations, from real citizens in society.

In some respects, however, the inner-legal construction of democracy only appears deficient if democracy is observed through the literalistic lens of classical democratic theory, assuming the material presence of the citizens in government, and defining the factual politicization of society as the basic foundation of the political system. Indeed, critiques of inner-legal patterns of democratic formation can easily be seen as measuring the object of their criticism against false historical standards. As discussed, it is not easy to find a historical period in which more classical models of democracy actually existed, at least in moderately enduring form. Consequently, the assumption that democracy is in a state of decline or that we can speak of an endemic crisis of democratic politics is difficult to verify. If we were to accept the theory that we are witness to the rise of post-democracy or low-intensity democracy, the period between pre- and post-democratic societies or high-intensity and low-intensity democracies would have to appear very brief. We can, therefore, pose the question: *When was the era of full or high-intensity democracy?* More generally, the theory that national democracy has been brought to crisis by global forces is also very simplified. As discussed, national democracy was only created by global forces, and *national societies did not create democracy*: the dominant political form of national society was *incomplete democracy*, in which legislatures typically obstructed full democratization. It is difficult,

---

[7] For example, indigenous rights are obviously produced through social politicization (See below pp.437–42). Yet, owing to the international legal framework, this politicization takes place within pre-defined constraints, and it can be authoritatively controlled. Similarly, more individualized rights, such as health rights, land rights and medical rights, are evidently constructed through social mobilization. However, such mobilization is widely proportioned to rights that already exist, in international law. The granting of such rights in national law is, therefore, often a process that is controlled by pre-established legal norms.

therefore, to find a period of national democracy that was not deeply determined by global forces.

If democracy is viewed through the eyes of legal sociology, the fact that democracy was finally stabilized in a form that did not presuppose the active exercise of a popular political will ought not to appear surprising, and it ought not to be perceived as an indication of democratic crisis. Democracy has widely emerged as a political system in which the basic construction of law's origin, classically attached to the idea of the citizen, has been displaced from the political system into the legal system. Through this displacement, the paradoxical problem of law's original authority is translated into a legal problem, in which the legal system provides its own normative constructions, largely based on international law, to sustain the authority of the political system. To a sociological perspective, this might easily appear as a quite expected outcome of the essential fictionality of democracy, which early sociology identified, and the inner-legal construction of the figure of the citizen, acting as the primary author of laws, might seem a necessary resolution of the historical difficulty in solidifying the political source of law's integrational obligatory force. The fact that democracy became global through the displacement of the citizen from the political system in fact provides deep corroboration for the primary intuitions of legal sociology. The argument proposed in classical legal sociology – that democracy itself contains insoluble paradoxes, that many of its core constructions are fictitious, and that the term democracy overlies very contingent processes of social inclusion and political-systemic construction – might appear much more plausible than theories of endemic political-democratic crisis in explaining why contemporary democracy is centred on weakly formed political agency. On this basis, there is nothing surprising in the fact that democracy developed around a model that reduced the participatory role of the citizen.

For more practical reasons, further, the reconfiguration of democracy described above should not be observed solely as a process that diminishes society's capacities for collective self-legislation and decisive legal authorization. The fact that the growing autonomy of the law separates political agency from monolithic concepts of peoplehood, sovereignty and nationhood means that the legal system can establish categories of political agency more attuned to the factual, pluralistic reality that characterizes most societies. In freeing society from the fictitious expectation that laws can have their legitimational origins in founding acts of collective will formation, the contemporary democratic model splits democratic agency, communication or citizenship into a multiplicity of forms. Through this process, the basic quality of citizenship – participation in the political system through the shaping of legislation – experiences a process of diffusion, and many actors, in different dimensions of society, acquire legislative force. The inner-legal proceduralization of political agency, therefore, often gives rise to a more pluralistic form of citizenship, at least within the secondary dimension of the global constitution. As such proceduralization separates the form of the citizen from actual material agents in national society, it allows the citizen to assume multiple forms and multiple roles, and it avoids the compulsive homogeneity that, as discussed, easily inheres in citizenship models centred around legislatures. Consequently, it is not necessarily the case that the rising differentiation of the legal system eradicates classical expressions of politics (dispute, will formation, conflict, deliberation, contested agency) from society, or that such expressions lose articulation with legislative processes. Dispute, contest and conflict clearly remain salient dimensions of societal exchange. Such patterns of politicality are widely internalized within the law, and their transmission through legislative processes occurs inner-legally, through the law, using procedures constructed through the global legal system. In some ways, however, this generates an intensification of political practice.

Overall, we can see the following process at the core of modern democracy. It is now established that the citizen that authorizes law is, at least partly, a fiction, separated from the real people, and stabilized as an internal reference within the legal system. However, this stabilization of the citizen as a fiction has real implications for the interactions that connect the political system and persons in its social environment. In particular, the fact that the citizen that underpins the political system is distinct from physical citizens means that the rights of citizens, and rights to shape legislation, can be claimed by many agents, in many different domains and procedures, and in many lines of legal-political communication. Global rights soak into the fabric of national law, and these rights are able to configure new forms of citizenship, sometimes detached from real material subjects, in highly contingent ways. This allows the emergence of new partial or *segmentary* patterns of citizenship, in which many actors outside the legal/political system can assume legal/political subjectivity, often of a momentary nature. On this basis, in contemporary democracy a rapid multiplication of citizenship occurs: persons in society can enter into interaction with the legal/political system in many ways, and the legal/political system opens itself to exchanges with societal actors through many different rights. Persons exercise citizenship rights by communicating with the political system through the rights that exist in its environment, in the system of global law. This means that citizens can communicate immediately with political institutions, phrasing their communication in relation to global rights. This then gives rise to a legal/political system which has multiple articulations with citizens in its environments, both national and global. In some cases, the legal/political system communicates, through global rights, with citizens that exist, factually and materially, in society. In some cases, as discussed below, the legal/political system communicates with citizens that it itself engenders, so that the citizen itself appears as a construct of the law.

The emergence of a political system on this global design was partly anticipated in the social theory of Niklas Luhmann, who imagined the modern political system – the political system of *world society* – as a system that is able to sustain flexible and pluralistic interactions with different social domains. As discussed, Luhmann rejected the idea that the political system has a dominant position amongst other social systems or that it concentrates a total will or a total rationality for all societal interaction (1981b: 22–3). Importantly, he argued that the political system translates social impulses into law through multiple channels, and it relies on the institutionalization of complex and contingent interactions between the political system and individual citizens (1983 [1969]: 34). Moreover, he observed how human rights act as media of inclusion, connecting the political system to actors in its societal environments in measured, differentiated fashion.[8] In each respect, he suggested that the political system communicates with social agents through a wide range of procedures, implying that the production of legitimate law is perceived in deeply simplified form in classical accounts of democracy. Similar concepts have been carried over into the thought of sociologists influenced by Luhmann, who view the claim that the state contains a cognitive intelligence that is valid for all society as illusory (Willke 1998: 14; Ladeur 2006: 5). Indeed, the multiplication of society's political procedures has already been observed, in more normative fashion, in theories of democracy that stress the mismatch between classical democracy and the complex and acentric form of society as a whole. Important examples of such theories argue that the political system should limit its functions to supervisory oversight of the relations between different social systems (Willke 1996: 335), even advocating the formation

---

[8] In particular, Luhmann claimed that the conception of persons as holders of rights of freedom and dignity creates a generalized basis for 'communicative behaviour' and for the 'generalization of communication', which the political system itself presupposes (1965: 70–1).

of a decentred political system, containing organs of representation in different functional domains (Willke 2016: 109, 137).[9]

However, Luhmann's theory was not finally adequate for understanding the contemporary political system, and he struggled to describe the concrete features of the political system of global society that, conceptually, he imagined. In particular, Luhmann did not evaluate the transformation of the political system through its position in a global environment. Strikingly, he paid little attention to the emergence of international organizations or the effects of international norms, and he viewed the multi-articulated exchanges of the political system as occurring within a regionally delineated society. In fact, he envisioned the political system, finally, as a classically ordered social system, extracting legitimacy from conventional processes of political communication, focused on the production of simple acts of legislation, directed towards aggregated groups of people (1971: 62). As discussed, in Luhmann's thought the classical construction of law's collective authorship is preserved.

The political system of global society is now assuming concrete shape in a way that Luhmann had not anticipated. A fact that requires stronger emphasis in analysis of the global form of the political system is that the political system is itself no longer the sole site of political practice, and functions of legitimate legislation are not ordered solely in procedures that pertain to politics. An adequately multi-centric construction of the political system needs to observe ways in which the legal system itself has become a domain of legislation, and more pluralistic patterns of interest articulation result from the centration of politics around the legal system. Indeed, the heightened differentiation of the law means that the legal system often becomes the domain in which social agency presents itself in political form. The law itself, increasingly, becomes the site in which a society channels its primary conflicts, in which it contests underlying grammars of legitimacy, in which it produces experiences of participatory citizenship, and in which it establishes and renews its primary norms.

The differentiation of the global legal system through the inner reference to human rights marks, at one level, the end of classical democracy and the weakening of classical democratic agency. Of course, classical political procedures still exist in democratic societies, and, as discussed,

---

[9] Willke's work is one of the most important attempts to configure a sociologically refined model of the contemporary political system. However, like Luhmann, he proceeds from the view that legislation is the 'core of politics' (1997: 27), and he retains a neo-classical view of the role legislation in managing the interaction between social systems.

legislatures still possess a central role as organs of legislation. However, the overarching, norm-founding scope of such procedures is limited; they do not express the basic political will of society; they do not have a monopoly of society's legislative acts. At a different level, however, the differentiation of the legal system releases and helps to institutionalize new modes of legal/political agency and subjectivity, and it projects a pervasive legal grammar for society, in which political contests can be transposed into law (or refracted through law) in a number of different ways, and by a plurality of different subjects. In many societies, although originally distilled at an international level, human rights norms now form a deeply ingrained part of social structure, and they establish a variety of normative channels, in which social agents, as citizens, are able to form legally constitutive articulations with each other, with their governments, and with other norm providers. In some cases, human rights law forms a normative system, which is able to obtain recognition across very diffusely connected regions within national societies, even amongst actors and groups originally marginalized from national societies, and which allows a direct articulation between these actors and the legal/political system. As discussed, in many societies, human rights form a normative system of inclusion that penetrates much deeper into national societies than more classical, vertically ordered state institutions.[10]

As a result, the global conversion to self-referential or inner-legal democracy that has defined the recent globalization of democracy has been marked by a conversion to a model of *multi-centric* democracy. In this model, law can be contested, defined, legitimated and produced within parameters internally constructed by human rights law, by many different procedures, by many different interactions, and by many different actors.[11] As the global legal system constructs the *primary norms* for legal acts, the range of subjects able to construct *secondary norms* for legal acts necessarily increases. Such subjects are typically able to engage formatively in the production of law by explaining their interests in relation to partial rights: secondary subjects are able to assume a norm-giving role in contemporary society to the extent that they translate particular social interactions and particular disputes into the primary systemic diction of

---

[10] See discussion of the impact of human rights law on complex societies above at pp. 350–419.
[11] For a conception that parallels this view, see the theory of subjective rights in Colliot-Thélène (2010b: 197), which also argues for a multiple politics of rights as a socially adequate pattern of citizenship. To my perspective, Colliot-Thélène is inadequately attentive to the transformation of subjective rights through the domestic penetration of global human rights.

human rights. The splitting of the primary form of the citizen from real persons generates multiple *secondary patterns* of citizenship, in which citizens can engage with the legal/political system and shape legislation through a growing range of rights. This process does not suppress political conflict. On the contrary, it creates new figures of multiple citizenship and new political subjects.

This multiplication of democratic agency naturally occurs in a range of different ways in different societies, and it can be placed at diverse points on a spectrum of democratic organization. In many cases, as discussed, this conversion to multi-centric democratic formation occurs as a process that sits alongside and reinforces more classical patterns of political democracy.[12] In some cases, this occurs as a process that creates quite distinct modes of democratic inclusion. For example, this can occur as a process that compensates for the weakness of more classical democratic institutions, or that progressively transforms existing democratic organs. However, the inner-legal splitting of democratic subjectivity is now a universal feature of democracy. This is widely reflected in the fact that, in most political systems, legislation is triggered by pressures on the system of global law, often linked to different patterns of legal mobilization.

Important in this regard is the fact that the formation of the inner-legal citizen creates the most expansive openings for the exercise of transnational citizenship. Despite the projected ideals of some theorists, to be sure, we cannot identify institutions of an evolved world polity or transnational democracy in contemporary society.[13] Even in more consolidated transnational political entities, such as the EU, transnational citizenship is not fully established beyond a relatively thin tier of formal personal rights.[14] Citizenship does not exist at the global level in the sense of legal affiliation to a distinct community, and it does not exist globally as a claim to democratic participation.[15] However, as discussed, in some of its dimensions, democratic citizenship is of itself intrinsically transnational. As a focus of

---

[12] See in particular the discussion of Colombia at pp. 270–1 above.

[13] See p. 181 above. See the most expansive claim for the existence of a 'system of cosmopolitan governance', in which people might 'enjoy multiple citizenships' in Held (2003: 524).

[14] For sample attempts to bridge the divide between the given construction of EU citizens as legal subjects, with market-based rights, and the construction of citizens as political agents see Shaw (1998: 316); Wiener (1998: 252, 290). Experiences in the UK show that rights (putatively) held by EU citizens can be easily removed by national governments, and they do not fully qualify as citizenship rights.

[15] Some theorists have tried, rather fancifully, to imagine a model of global 'discursive democracy', which does not necessarily presuppose 'electoral democracy': i.e. a democracy in which it is not necessary to vote (see Dryzek 2006: 25, 154). Purely discursive patterns of

legal agency, the citizen is palpably capable of participating in transnational law-making processes, and many legal acts of citizens help to stabilize rights that have a transnational character. In fact, the primary rights attached to the citizen in national society can easily be transferred either to the global domain or into other polities – many such rights originate in the global domain, and core normative elements of citizenship converge between the national and the global dimensions of society.[16] If the citizen is conceived, in the global context, not as a political actor, but as a legal actor, transnational citizenship can easily develop as a set of practices with a participatory, politically formative content.[17] Through legal engagement, people can easily shape law in contexts in which they do not have state-conferred political rights, so that political citizenship acquires a form that is distinct from national citizenship. If the world citizen is to emerge as more than an agent demanding protective rights, the form of the world citizen is likely to develop through acts of legal engagement and legal mobilization. Indeed, it is as a legal agent that the world citizen becomes politically manifest: the world citizen assumes political form not through a world polity, but through engagement in world law.

In each respect, the increasing autonomy of the global legal system has, in its subsidiary dimensions, created multiple pluralistic patterns of democratic subjectivity, citizenship and legal/political norm construction. In some ways, this remedies the exclusionary dimension of citizenship discussed above, as it offsets the focus on homogeneous rights that citizenship necessarily implies.[18] The renunciation of the democracy of the total national citizen in favour of the democracy of the partial world citizen has created new patterns of segmentary political agency and liberty. To appreciate this, it is necessary to renounce classical constructions of politics.

---

democracy can easily exist at the global level. Currently, however, global equivalents to electoral democracy do not exist.

[16] For different accounts of the movement of rights from the global to the domestic level see Linklater (1998: 34); Delanty (2000: 80); Bosniak (2000: 491); Soysal (1994: 165); Münch (2001: 190–1); Cohen (1999: 262, 2012: 216–7); Weinstock (2001: 59); Sassen (2002a: 287); Stokes (2004: 133); Goodhart (2005: 133); Habermas (2005: 240); Benhabib (2009); Sikkink (2011); Ramirez and Meyer (2012: 21); Glenn (2013: 197); Brunkhorst (2014).

[17] In agreement with this, see the theory of Kapczynski (2008). Kapczynski argues that through strategic use of law 'coalitions, political identifications, and publics can be built across national boundaries and among geographically dispersed communities' (880). I would go further – as mobilized litigant, the citizen is almost of necessity a member of a global public. See the account of different patterns of transnational public community in Fox (2005: 193–4), which also identifies legal activism as a mode of citizenship. For similar views see Bader (1995: 235).

[18] See p. 20.

5.2   New Democratic Subjects: Formal Persons

The emergence of more pluralistic patterns of citizenship and norm formation is visible in the construction of primary norms for national democracies. The creation of democratic constitutions and the consolidation of democratic institutions now widely occurs as a process in which many participants engage, often exercising very atypical resources of political agency. Usually, this is due to the fact that the underlying preconditions of national political systems are defined through reference to international human rights law, which, at a *primary* level, creates prior immovable constitutional limits for the political system as a whole. The underlying institutional form and legitimacy of national democracy are thus pre-defined, as one part of the global legal system. On this foundation, however, a range of *secondary* democratic subjects are able to appear and to assume a role in processes of constitutional norm formation and institution building. Such subjects do this, typically, by claiming to represent and to enact interests related to human rights, by correlating social claims with already established rights and by intensifying the standing of international norms (usually linked to human rights) in national societies. Human rights, accordingly, form a line of articulation in which different actors across society can acquire constitution-making and constitution-reinforcing authority. In so doing, such actors express social prerogatives and contests in a form to which the political system, as part of the global legal system, is already sensibilized, and they present multiple claims in the register of human rights, which then have a possibility of being translated into law. As national laws lose their status as primary laws, the range of actors engaged in the making of constitutional law can easily be expanded, and such actors exercise extensive constituent power, within pre-stabilized limits.

This is seen, first, in cases in which new democratic actors possess a quite clearly defined legal/political personality, and such actors acquire relatively conventional recognition for rights of constitutional participation.

5.2.1   New Democratic Subjects: NGOs and Social Movements

One example of this multiplication of democratic agency is seen in the activities performed by NGOs, which in recent years have assumed an important position as political norm setters. At a most obvious level, it is now increasingly widespread for NGOs to appear as distinct legal agents during constitution-making processes. In the drafting of some constitutions, different organizations, typically claiming a stake in constitutional foundation through their interest in the protection of human rights law, have been able to act as factual constituent subjects.[19]

Still more widely, NGOs act as subjects that implement and give firm reality to established constitutional provisions, assuming authority either to ensure recognition of constitutional rights in national societies, or directly to enforce international human rights as *de facto* constitutional principles. This can occur in many different ways. For example, this sometimes occurs as NGOs enter formal consultative relations with national government bodies about enforcement of human rights norms, often acting as norm-setters with transnational effect (see Schuppert 2006: 212). This also occurs as NGOs pressurize national governments to recognize constitutional or international norms through media engagement, through monitoring activities, participation in meetings with supranational organs, or submission of reports to the UN or to other supranational bodies (see Merry 2006: 58; Simmons 2009: 32–5; Sikkink 2011: 64). This occurs, most importantly, as NGOs engage or assist in litigation against government agencies. In many societies, NGOs now play a leading role in initiating human rights cases against national governments, often securing recognition of established rights, and, in some cases, creating new constitutional rights.[20] In each instance, the realm of democratic agency is markedly broadened by the fact that NGOs can articulate a personality for themselves through reference to international human rights law. By claiming a legal personality in this way, many such organizations assume positions at least analogous to that of more classical political-constitutional subjects.

Less securely, the same can also be said of social movements, whose political position has become increasingly institutionalized through their role in solidifying human rights law. Like NGOs, in some settings, social movements have been partly co-opted in constitution-making processes.[21] More generally, social movements have been able to acquire a direct articulation with national governments through pressure-group activities,

---

[19] Cases of this can be found in Bolivia, Colombia, South Africa and Kenya. By way of example, for analysis of the role of human-rights activists in creating a constitution-making situation in Colombia, see Tate (2007: 129); Grajales (2017: 160–2); on similar processes in South Africa, see Klug (2000: 59).

[20] The classic example in Latin America is the Centre for Justice & International Law (CEJIL). Founded in 1991, in its first two decades CEJIL represented over 13,000 victims of human rights violations in more than 300 cases and proceedings for protective measures within the Inter-American System of Human Rights. In the early 1990s, CEJIL monopolized the System, being responsible for almost 90 per cent of the cases decided by the IACtHR.

[21] See discussion of Colombia above at p. 355.

focused on human rights questions, so that they perform constitution-reinforcing functions. Clearly, the emergence of social movement politics is very closely linked to the importance of human rights as a constitutive political vocabulary, which creates a shared diction for political agency outside conventional procedures and even across the boundaries between national states and their constituencies.[22] The fact that human rights define particular themes in society as demanding political attention projects a normative order in which political agency can be concentrated around single questions or relatively free-standing demands for recognition, which are not necessarily correlated with universal socio-political outlooks or holistic ideas of citizenship. As a result, society is able to mobilize around particular social interests, such as gender politics, ethnic politics, educational politics, sexual politics, environmental politics, health politics and reproductive politics, and such mobilization is often channelled through social movements. In such processes, the vocabulary of rights forms a medium in which actors in different spheres of agency can aim to obtain authoritative recognition, exercising sectoral/segmentary citizenship or even sectoral/segmentary constituent power. The vocabulary of rights creates a network of articulations around the political system, in which social actors can emerge in relatively spontaneous fashion and intensify constitutional norms across distinct spheres of society. Often, this means that social actors can circumvent formal political procedures, and they can gain immediate access to political influence (i.e. they can make laws) by interacting directly with the political system through rights.

In these examples, the fact that human rights law frames the legitimacy of the legal/political system means that democratic institutions obtain a widened periphery, in which many groups and many citizens can gain inclusion in constitutional and legislative procedures. Moreover, the prominence of human rights law means that diverse societal claims can be transmitted directly into the legal system, and the legal system is centred on norms that permit the rapid translation of originally diffuse societal claims into formal law. The freeing of political agency from unitary subjects creates new openings for the politicization of society. Indeed, it creates opportunities for the emergence of new modes of sectoral, or even

---

[22] Foweraker and Landman (1997: 42, 227); Keck and Sikkink (1999: 91); Tsutsui and Wotipka (2002: 613); Tarrow (2005: 188). Some observers see the growth of social movements as a process that challenges the power of thinly rooted, rights-based democracies (Gills, Rocamora and Wilson 1993: 24). This may of course be true. But social movements are also products of this system and its segmented patterns of citizenship.

segmentary, citizenship, in which political acts of citizens refer to functionally distinct experiences.

5.2.2 New Democratic Subjects: Ethnic Population Groups

A further example of this transformation of democratic agency is visible in the fact that recent processes of democratic foundation and democratic solidification have brought heightened recognition for ethnic communities as political-constitutional subjects.

This is particularly visible in Latin America. In some societies in Latin America, indigenous communities have obtained legal recognition as collective participants in constitution-making processes. In Bolivia, for example, the present constitution, in force since 2009, was created through the exercise of a multi-centric constituent power, of which indigenous groups formed a core part, and indigenous groups now occupy a distinct, elevated position under the constitution. In some settings in Latin America, further, superior courts have independently ascribed formal legal or even ius-generative personality to indigenous populations. In Colombia, the Constitutional Court has declared that indigenous communities form a distinct 'collective subject', which is not simply to be viewed as the sum of 'individual subjects that share the same rights or diffuse or collective interests'.[23] In consequence, the rights that are asserted by indigenous groups, unless they are contrary to higher constitutional norms, are viewed as having greater force than those asserted by less clearly authorized subjects.[24] In addition, some constitutions have been established in Latin America, in which indigenous communities obtain formal protection for customary rights and even for the administration of communal justice, so that, within higher-order constraints, powers of self-determination and sub-national citizenship are allotted to ethnic groups. Constitutional provisions for indigenous rights of self-determination have had far-reaching impact in some societies, notably in Bolivia and Colombia. In Colombia, the right to self-determination of indigenous groups includes, formally, the right to select communal government, the right to determine the form of political institutions, the right to create laws in conformity with inherited customs and the right to determine procedures for election of indigenous authorities.[25] As mentioned, the Colombian Constitutional Court has adopted

---

[23] T-380/93.
[24] T-143/10.
[25] T-601/11.

a policy of maximization to secure indigenous rights of self-determination. Such constitutional provisions clearly represent a multiplication of democratic agency, establishing multi-level patterns of citizenship, and, in some cases, ensuring that the societal form of the constitution, even after ratification, remains open to impulses from a range of constitutional subjects.

In most Latin American societies, the construction of indigenous groups as distinct political subjects was partly shaped by the fact that, prior to the emergence of the particular constitution-making situation, these groups had been able to claim rights and protective guarantees under international law, notably under Convention 169 (1989) of the ILO (ILO 169). ILO 169, which was quickly ratified in many Latin American societies, includes provisions to ensure that indigenous communities can assume governmental influence and rights of consultation in matters affecting their livelihood. In states that ratified ILO 169, these provisions often acquired great authority in domestic law, and they immediately altered the normative hierarchy of society. In Colombia, ILO 169 was incorporated as part of domestic higher law, and it was integrated in the block of constitutionality.[26] This implies that the constitutional subjectivity of indigenous populations was established under international human rights law *before* it became part of domestic law. In fact, the agency asserted by indigenous groups in helping to create, or in seeking recognition under, multi-centric national constitutions entailed the concrete exercise of rights that had already been defined within the system of international law. Such acts of constituent agency involved the realization and consolidation of rights that *already existed*, and they assumed constituent force, in part, because they transposed rights from the transnational level of the global legal system onto the national level, extracting political resonance from these rights within domestic locations.

One illuminating case of articulation between ILO 169 and domestic constitutional processes is evident in Colombia, where the 1991 Constitution was written during ratification of ILO 169. The growing international concern with indigenous rights at this time meant that indigenous groups could utilize the vocabulary of rights to position themselves in the national constitution-making process.[27] This was facilitated by the

---

[26] Colombian Constitutional Court SU-039/97.

[27] Indigenous groups had three representatives in the Assembly that wrote the 1991 Constitution, and they obtained rights of representation and self-governance. Most of these rights were already envisaged in existing international norms and instruments.

fact that Colombia had a long tradition of protecting indigenous rights,[28] and many indigenous leaders were trained in law. International human rights instruments thus created distinct mobilizational opportunities for indigenous organizations, whose rights were more robustly secured in the 1991 Constitution.

An alternative case in which indigenous rights acquired political strength through international law is visible in Bolivia. In Bolivia, indigenous communities obtained an important position in the Constituent Assembly that wrote the 2009 Constitution under Evo Morales. They justified this position, in part, by extracting authority from a pre-existent normative structure, largely based on international human rights provisions. To be sure, indigenous communities in different parts of Bolivia had a long history of spontaneous social mobilization, and the decades prior to the writing of the 2009 Constitution had seen intensified activism focused on claims to indigenous rights (see Van Cott 2000: 207; Yashar 2005: 55; Blomberry 2008). This was partly caused by the fact that the traditional corporatist mechanisms for promoting national integration of indigenous communities, based on vertically ordered peasant trade unions, had been weakened in the 1980s,[29] and indigenous affiliations, distinct from the centralized apparatus of formal trade unions, assumed greater significance as a focus of contestation. This was also partly caused by decentralization laws passed in 1994, which created a more stable municipal framework for indigenous political representation (K. O'Neill 2005: 63; Postero 2007: 5–6; Bazoberry Chali 2008: 171). Moreover, indigenous populations in Bolivia do not form a united political subject, and the vocabulary of indigenous rights is not a universally accepted formula of mobilization. Many indigenous groups, especially larger communities located around the Andean plateau, construct their identity in more general terms, as members of the *first nations* (*naciones originarias*) of Bolivia; this term is clearly distinct from the concept of indigenous peoples (*pueblos indígenas*). In fact, even the most successfully mobilized indigenous populations are not ethnically homogeneous. In consequence, generalized pronouncements about indigenous mobilization and political subject formation in Bolivia are to be avoided. Nonetheless, the process in which, under different self-constructions, indigenous peoples became active political subjects in Bolivia intersected formatively with the rising grammar of indigenous rights in international

---

[28] Law 89 of 1890 established some rights for indigenous communities – although it also referred to them as 'savages'.
[29] For background see Liendo (2009: 109–10); Balenciaga (2012: 147–8).

law. Indeed, in a number of respects, the principles of ILO 169 sank deeply into the daily logic of indigenous constitutional politics in Bolivia, and this created a distinct pattern of constitutional-political agency.

The impact of ILO 169 in Bolivia is visible in the fact that, first, generally, the indigenous groups that assumed positions of influence in the Bolivian constitution-making process utilized it as an important foundation on which they were able to justify their position and to assert collective rights.[30] Indeed, the constitution-making process was supported by the assumption that the constitution would give effect to ILO 169, so that internationally defined norms were located from the outset at the centre of the constitutional order.[31] This meant that some norms concerning rights of sub-national subjects were already taken for granted during the constitution-making process, such that elements of the eventual constitution were separated out from factual contest. As a result, the constitution that came into force in 2009 contained extensive provisions for the autonomy of indigenous communities and rights of consultation in matters affecting them. Article 269 of the Bolivian Constitution states that Bolivia is to be organized into departments, provinces, municipalities and rural native indigenous territories. Article 30 established cultural rights and rights of consultation for indigenous peoples. Articles 289 and 296 provide for certain powers of indigenous self-government and the creation of autonomous indigenous regions. Moreover, it is generally axiomatic in the constitution that indigenous law stands on equal footing with ordinary law. These provisions of the constitution should not be taken too literally; the constitutional order created under Morales has not delivered on all its promises, and hard restrictions have been placed on the exercise of political, jurisdictional and even civil rights by indigenous communities. In particular, the principle in the constitution that indigenous law and ordinary law should have equal status in the legal hierarchy of society has not been

---

[30] Before the writing of the 2009 Constitution in Bolivia, ILO 169 had already inspired constitutional reforms in 1994. One account argues that international instruments regarding human rights and indigenous rights were the 'direct source' for the recognition of indigenous communities as distinct actors at this time (Tamburini 2012: 250). On the importance of international precedents for the growing autonomy of indigenous communities see Molina Saucedo (2015: 278).

[31] One critical account states that ILO 69 was one of the most important points of reference as the constitution was bring written, but argues that indigenous leaders used ILO 169 to gain rights of autonomy far more extensive than those that it actually foresaw (Lazarte 2015: 69). A different account lists ILO 169 first amongst legal precedents, national and international, for the constitutional provisions for indigenous autonomy in Bolivia (Molina Saucedo 2015: 278).

fully honoured.[32] Nonetheless, the wording of the Bolivian Constitution is not entirely fictional, and it has instituted certain forms of ethno-political pluralism and multiple subject formation.

Most notably, second, the interaction between domestic and international law in Bolivia is expressed in constitutional provisions for the creation of autonomous communities (*autonomías*) by indigenous peoples (Articles 271, 290, 304). In this respect, communities seeking autonomy are required to draw up a statute to determine their governance arrangements, and so, in essence, to establish a secondary constitutional form for regional self-determination, within the broader constitution of the state. On completion of the draft statute, communities seeking autonomy are expected to secure authorization for their legal order by submitting their statute to the national Constitutional Court. If endorsed by the Constitutional Court, the statute needs to be approved by means of a local plebiscite. Notably, the first indigenous community to constitute itself as an autonomous region – that is, the Guarani people in Charagua, which is located close to the Paraguayan border – achieved this, in part, by positioning its statutory order within the hierarchy of international norms.[33] Other communities that have endeavoured to obtain autonomy have also given high standing to international law in their founding statutes.[34] The Statute of Charagua reflects this hierarchy in that it specifically defines indigenous self-governance institutions as elements in a system of international law, authorized by ILO 169 (Article 3). Moreover, it recognizes all obligations of the Bolivian government enforced by international treaties (Article 13, Article 29). In assessing the compatibility of the Statute of Charagua with the constitution, the Bolivian Constitutional Court stated that assumption of autonomy by indigenous peoples is justified under international law, especially ILO 169. Moreover, it declared that any recognition of the *autonomía* as a self-governing region presupposes its formal acceptance of the hierarchy of constitutional law and international law. The Court declared as a point of procedure that 'indigenous autonomy must be subordinate not only to ratified treaties and conventions that address indigenous peoples, but also to ratified treaties and

---

[32] This provision was cut down severely in Law 073 of 2010, which set out a long list of matters that could not be subject to indigenous jurisdiction. See Nuñez del Prado (2015: 219).

[33] See the Estatuto de la Autonomia Indígena Guarani Charagua Iyambae, ratified in 2015.

[34] See Article 89(2) of the Estatuto Autonómico Originario de Totora Marka, which was not approved by local plebiscite.

conventions that address the nation more widely'.[35] By implication, therefore, the Court stated that the autonomous powers of the Charagua community were both constituted and circumscribed by norms of international
law, and they were legitimated by a balance between different international-
legal provisions.

In both Colombia and Bolivia, membership of indigenous groups
has emerged as a distinct source of constituent agency at different societal
levels. This is due, in large part, to the fact that such agency is authorized,
or even partly pre-formed, under international law. This process of subject
formation became visible, in both societies, in the creation of the national
constitution. However, this remained visible in subsidiary constitutional
processes, in which the constituent position of ethnic membership groups
was articulated – expressly – as a secondary enactment of primary, originally international, norms. Notably, contemporary Bolivia is often observed
as a site of radical democratic experimentation, in which sub-national population groups are granted far-reaching powers of autonomy. This is often
presented as a process that depends on the recuperation of political sovereignty through the autonomous mobilization of pluralistic communities
within the national population itself, entailing an at times express negation,
or at least relativization, of international norms (Sousa Santos 2012: 12–14).
In many respects, however, the patterns of agency that are constitutive of
contemporary Bolivian democracy are pre-determined by international
law, and they assume and explain their legitimacy, in part, as secondary
articulations of principles already established in the global legal system. In
fact, these patterns of agency appear as points in a complex constitutional
loop, in which primary rights, established in the global legal system, are singularly concretized at a secondary, national level. In each respect, human
rights permit a multiplication of constitutional subjects and a proliferation
of new modes of citizenship. Indeed, political acts of citizens acquire distinctive emphasis because they give emphasis to rights that are conserved in
the global legal system, and because they mediate directly between national
and global law. Citizenship, in other words, becomes a contingent practice
of articulation between national and global legal norms.

5.3   New Democratic Subjects: From Citizens to Litigants

In the cases discussed above, the transformation of democratic agency
through the differentiation of global law is observable in the fact that new

---

[35] Declaration of the Constitutional Court 0013/2013 p. 30

constitutional subjects are emerging that, although in fact exercising secondary constituent power, appear in some respects as analogues to more classical constitutional subjects. Notably, social movements, NGOs and indigenous community representatives are capable of organizing themselves in a fashion similar to conventional constituent actors, and they can assume relatively ordered organizational form within constitution-making processes. Although their access to constitutional power is usually determined by prior inner-legal norms, these subjects can sometimes claim, and indeed appear, to process a distinct legal identity that enables them to act *before the law*, as *primary democratic norm setters*.

Alongside this, however, the general shift to inner-legal democratic agency has meant that some actors that have little resemblance to classical constitutional subjects now assume authority to make laws, and even substantially to define the basic order of government. In particular, the fact that primary norm-setting acts occur partly within the legal system means that functions of legislation classically accorded to political actors and to processes of democratic will formation are now often imputed to persons acting not as legislators or as citizens, but as *litigants*. In many settings, litigation has become a core mode of law production, and litigation in relation to human rights often replaces political participation, or more institutionalized modes of citizenship, as a foundation for law-making. Much law, both constitutional and statutory, is now generated through *litigation loops*, in which legal claims are filed in national societies, which forge a link between national litigation and international legal norms, ultimately leading to the permeation of international norms into domestic law, at times with clear constitutional effect. Often, in consequence, it is in their quality, not, in the classical sense, *as political citizens*, but *as litigants*, that members of society acquire their greatest political importance, and their greatest impact on legislation. The global solidification of the rights around which social conflicts congregate means that litigation over rights becomes a core pattern of citizenship, which is able to create laws with close to constitutional rank in particular national societies, and in particular social spheres.

5.3.1   *Litigants as Citizens 1: Individual Litigation*

The role of litigation as a surrogate for classical expressions of democratic agency can be seen in litigation initiated by single persons. One consequence of the differentiation of the global legal system is that, under certain circumstances, individual persons can mobilize legal claims around global human rights norms, and, in so doing, they can substantially alter the part of the legal-political order to which their acts of litigation relate.

This can be observed in many ways.

First, the legislative effect of litigation is most manifest in national societies that are tightly integrated into supranational human rights systems. In societies in this position, the attempts by single persons to obtain redress in acts of litigation, especially in those acts relating to the exercise or withdrawal of internationally sanctioned human rights, can easily transform the existing order of democracy. Examples of this can be found in Europe, in which cases brought from national societies before both the ECtHR and the ECJ have led to deep alterations in the fabric of national democracies, and at times created new rights in domestic law.[36] Far-reaching examples of this can be seen in Latin America, in which cases brought before the Inter-American Commission on Human Rights and the IACtHR have had substantial implications for national societies. In some cases, single acts of litigation have led to the establishment of new rights and new guarantees. For instance, acts of litigation have led to the establishment of new categories of crimes, especially for vulnerable social groups,[37] and new rights of property ownership.[38] Indeed, in some cases, national courts have used norms of international law that are not domestically incorporated to create new rights, and they have utilized authority implied in international law to acquire legislative functions. For example, the Argentine Supreme Court has ruled that there is a right to health on the basis of international treaties.[39] The Colombian Constitutional Court has declared that it can give 'binding effect' to rights that 'are not expressly included in international treaties ratified by Colombia'.[40] As mentioned, it has also integrated international soft-law rights for displaced persons in the domestic constitution.[41]

---

[36] See discussion of the right to proportionality and the right to substantial judicial review in the UK at p. 266.

[37] In Brazil, a special law, Law 11.340/2006, or Law Maria da Penha, was created to address violence against women as a response to the Report published by the Inter-American in 2001 in consideration of a petition filed before the Inter-American Commission in 1998. See Inter-American Commission on Human Rights, *Fernandes* v. *Brazil (Maria da Penha)*, Case 12.051, Report N. 54/01, OEA/Ser.L./III.111.

[38] IACtHR, *Mayagna (Sumo) Awas Tingni Community* v. *Nicaragua*. Merits, Reparations and Costs. Judgment of 31 August, 2001.

[39] Causa A.186 XXXIV "Asociación Benghalensis y otros c/ Ministerio de Salud y Acción Social – Estado Nacional s/ amparo ley 16.986"; causa C 823. XXXV. "Recurso de Hecho – Campodónico de Beviacqua Ana Carina c/ Ministerio de Salud y Acción Social – Secretaría de Programas de Salud y Banco de Drogas Neoplásicas".

[40] T-477/95.

[41] T-967/09.

In many countries, further, litigation concerning human rights has led judges to create new rights not by assimilating international law in domestic law, but by expanding on the existing jurisprudence of international courts, and by spontaneously giving broader scope to rights than international courts.[42] In all such cases, litigation has been able to initiate a complex chain of interaction between domestic law and international law, leading directly to the production of laws, sometimes with constitutional standing, whose primary authority is extracted *from the law itself.*

In close relation to this, second, some constitutions specifically institutionalize provisions for human rights litigation, in which single agents are clearly entitled to expand existing constitutional rights. In India, notably, Article 32 of the Constitution allows individuals to file suit against the government on human rights grounds, and the Supreme Court has sought innovative ways of allowing parties to use this facility.[43] Some cases of this kind have had far-reaching constitutional consequences.[44] Perhaps the most important example of this can be found in Colombia. As mentioned, an important aspect of the Colombian Constitution is that its basic rights texture is open and subject to expansion. Moreover, in Article 86, the 1991 Constitution provides for the submission of *tutelas* to the Constitutional Court: that is, it establishes procedures for challenges to decisions of public agencies that are perceived to violate human rights in cases in which legal redress is not procedurally guaranteed. Taken together, these features create potent instruments, which allow litigants to construct new rights. Notably, after 1991, the Constitutional Court in Colombia rapidly expanded the range of rights that could be addressed by *tutelas*, and, in so doing, it expanded the range of rights accorded constitutional rank. *Tutelas* were first conceived as mechanisms for the protection of fundamental constitutional rights that are 'abused or at risk' and for the provision of orders against the persons perpetrating the violation.[45] However, the Court soon widened its *tutela* jurisdiction, claiming that it could also hear *tutelas* in cases in which rights were affected that, by connection, had implications for more strictly defined and protected

---

[42] See examples above at pp. 227–8.
[43] See the submission by informal letter of a third party in the prison-rights case: *Sunil Batra* v. *Delhi Administration* on 20 December 1979, Equivalent citations: 1980 AIR 1579, 1980 SCR (2) 557.
[44] See pp. 251–2. Note more sceptical reflections on this in Shankar (2009: 154), stating that most constitutional rulings relied on prior laws.
[45] T-597/93.

fundamental rights.[46] Within a short period, the Court developed a *tutela* jurisprudence that revolved around the principle that the state had positive obligations to promote conditions in which basic rights could be broadly enjoyed, and state actions were subject to petition by *tutela* if they did not positively facilitate exercise of rights by as many social actors as possible. In particular, this implied that the government had expanded responsibilities towards socially marginalized persons, and that the 'adoption of measures favouring marginalized groups' was a primary duty of the state.[47] As a result, the range of matters open to challenge by *tutela* extended rapidly, and courts were able to hear *tutelas* in cases in which the government was expected to fulfill social obigations, defined by the Constitutional Court itself. *Tutelas*, in fact, soon formed a very important line of socio-political communication between the government and a broad range of persons and social groups, traditionally located outside the reach of state power.

The widespread use of *tutelas* in Colombia has led to the consolidation of core constitutional rights, and it has helped give reality to formal human rights provisions. Equally importantly, as discussed, litigation through *tutelas* has substantially altered the range of rights that are given constitutional protection.[48] In Colombia, judges initially established a doctrine of *connectedness* to expand the reach of *tutela* jurisprudence, and this soon led to a widening of existing constitutional rights, and to the establishment of guarantees for supplementary rights. Notably, for example, the 1991 Constitution did not fully guarantee health rights as fundamental rights. However, in an early *tutela*, the Constitutional Court declared that, although rights to health benefits are not in principle protected by *tutelas*, *tutelas* could be used to claim these rights if violation of such rights affected, or was *necessarily connected to*, primary rights, such as the right to life or the right to dignity.[49] On this basis, the Court ruled that there exists both a right to health and a right to health care assistance, because such rights form a precondition of the right to life.[50] In parallel, further,

---

[46] This expansion meant that *tutelas* could be used, for example, to claim health rights (e.g. T-597/93) or rights to a clean environment (T-257/96; T-046/99).

[47] Sentencia T-025/04.

[48] At an early stage, the Constitutional Court argued that it is not only fundamental rights that can be protected by *tutela*. This can also apply to rights obtaining less than fundamental protection – for example, the right to social security. On this account, the extent to which a right is classifiable depends on the given case; if absence of a non-fundamental right (e.g. welfare) jeopardizes other rights (e.g. the right to life), such a right may be seen as fundamental by contagion. See for example T-491/92.

[49] T-597/93.

[50] T-485/92.

the Constitutional Court applied the logic of connectedness to determine that citizens possess a fundamental right to education. This right was constructed on the ground that education is closely connected to other established fundamental rights contained in the constitution, and it is connected, constitutively, to the right to the development of personality, to civil and political rights, to rights of personal self-determination, and to the right to work and to equality.[51] A similar logic has been applied to rights of protection from environmental damage. Even the Supreme Administrative Court (*Consejo de Estado*) in Colombia, whose human rights jurisprudence was originally more restrictive than that used by the Constitutional Court,[52] has greatly widened the existing corpus of constitutional rights in order to reinforce environmental rights.[53] In the most far-reaching administrative law case in this domain, the *Rio Bogotá* pollution case (2014), the *Consejo de Estado* replicated aspects of *tutela* jurisprudence, and it established generalized collective environmental rights.[54] In most spheres, in fact, the Constitutional Court ultimately moved beyond its reasoning that promoted the expansion of rights owing to *connectedness*. For example, it ultimately established rights to health and to education as free-standing fundamental rights.[55]

Overall, it is difficult to see Colombian *tutelas* as categorically distinct from a mode of constituent action. *Tutelas* often secure more effective inclusion of marginalized citizens in society in law-making processes than is possible in more classically centralized patterns of constitution making and political engagement. As discussed, judges in *tutela* cases have also established differential categories of human rights protection, creating special rights for designated vulnerable constitutional subjects.[56] Through *tutelas*, therefore, a pluralization of legal/political subjectivity

---

[51] T-1227/05.

[52] See discussion in López Cuéllar (2015: 51).

[53] On the complex relation between the superior courts in Colombia, with the Constitutional Court favouring a less formalist, more individual-centred approach see López Martínez (2015: 103–4).

[54] Sentencia n° 25000-23-27-000-2001-90479-01(AP) de Consejo de Estado – Sección Primera, 28 March 2014. In this case, the *Consejo de Estado* actually amplified environmental rights guaranteed by the Constitutional Court, and it set out a list of directives for public agencies to secure environmental rights, and especially rights to clean water, for persons affected by pollution of the Bogotá river. This case can be seen as the equivalent in administrative law to T-025/04 in constitutional law. Notably, the *Consejo de Estado* has also implicitly interpreted international biodiversity treaties to create rights for animals. See 25000-23-24-000-2011-00763-01 (2013).

[55] For an early leading case concerning this principle see T-491/92.

[56] See p. 271 above.

occurs, which is proportioned to the sectorally complex structure of society. Naturally, litigation associated with *tutelas* is widely related to international law, and new rights substantiated through *tutelas* are commonly supported by reference to international norms.[57] In an important early statement concerning questions which could be brought before the Constitutional Court as *tutelas*, it was argued that the protection of a right under international law was a core ground for its designation as subject to *tutela* protection.[58] New lines of political articulation and subject formation are thus directly stimulated by the autonomy of the global legal system.

Third, at a more general level, there is an increasing tendency, in many societies, for litigation to fix on questions of rights, and the establishment of human rights as central principles of legal argumentation almost inevitably means, in different national societies, that legal claims gravitate around rights. As a result of this, litigation now widely involves the translation of separate social disputes into a common normative vocabulary (rights), which is generally accepted as democratically necessary, and through which legal claims can easily be transposed into legislative acts. As litigation is increasingly phrased in relation to rights, moreover, separate acts of litigation produce norms with relevance for all society, across different functional spheres, and litigation has an increasingly broad capacity for creating and solidifying uniformly binding norms. In many settings, the growing convergence of legal disputes around claims over basic rights means that single legal claims intensify a common grammar of constitutional normativity in society.

One important example of this broad constitutional impact of litigation is the USA, where, as discussed, the expansion of basic rights jurisprudence in the 1950s and 1960s led to deep processes of constitutional transformation. Notably, the increasing prominence of rights as a normative register in the USA at this time meant that claimants were able to present single cases in a normative diction that could be easily elevated to a high degree of formal abstraction, across different legal spheres and different geographical regions. As discussed, the fact that the salience of human rights was linked to the rise in federal power created a situation in which single acts of litigation could both harden existing rights and generate new rights, which were then expanded, across the entire federal polity, as parts

---

[57] The right to environmental protection was constructed on the basis of a number of international norms and agreements (T-154/13). The right to housing also presupposed citation of international instruments (T-239/13).

[58] T-002/92.

of the constitutional architecture of democracy. In some ways, accordingly, litigation became constitutionally formative of the USA as a national state, and it extended the reach, and supplemented the relatively weak regulatory capacities, of the federal government (Friedman 2002: 480; Kelemen 2009: 1). This is visible in leading civil rights cases, which greatly impacted on the material constitution of national society as a whole. This is perhaps most clearly exemplified by *Griswold* v. *Connecticut* (1965), in which a ruling on reproductive liberties implied the existence of a system of corollary rights, applicable across all states, required to give effect to primary rights set out in the constitution itself.[59] Notably, further, the increasing importance of civil rights jurisprudence gave rise to an intensified culture of litigation, in which new legal actors assumed prominence and new issues, articulated through new rights claims, could be brought to the attention of the courts, and translated into recognized legal norms (see Epp 1998: 69; Friedman 2002: 460–7).

An alternative example of the wider constitutional impact of litigation is the UK. As, in the 1970s, British public law slowly began to assimilate formal human rights law from the ECHR, litigants increasingly raised questions relating to formal human rights law, and claimants endeavoured to present cases in a register that was open to rights.[60] As a result, as discussed, the courts began to harden the status of human rights in UK law, aligning common-law rights to international human rights. After the passing of the HRA (1998), then, it was increasingly accepted that human rights imposed normative uniformity on UK law, dictating principles to be applied across all parts of the judicial and legislative systems.[61] Ultimately, the view became prevalent that the courts were required actively to develop a shared system of rights, suffusing all spheres of law, reflecting a growing cross-fertilization between the common law and the ECHR. Accordingly, it was reasoned in leading judicial rulings that human rights derived from the ECHR should not be seen as forming 'a discrete body of domestic law derived from the judgments of the European court'. Instead, it was argued, ECHR rights should be observed as norms that soak through and permeate all relevant areas of the law,[62] and courts had a particular duty to

---

[59] See analysis in Luban (1999: 37).
[60] See discussion of this tendency by Ackner LJ in *Wheeler* v. *Leicester City Council* [1985] AC 1054, [1985] 2 All ER 1106.
[61] *Wilson* v. *First County Trust* (No 2) [2003] UKHL 40 (Earlsferry LJ).
[62] *R (Osborn) v Parole Board* [2013] UKSC 61.

expand the general reach of and elaboration of human rights.[63] In other words, human rights assumed a dynamic pervasive force within the UK legal order, and, in all areas, single acts of litigation were able to circulate and entrench generalized norms across society. In some cases, notably, rights that had only been tentatively acknowledged in common law were more strictly formulated through the fusion of ECHR norms and common law principles.[64]

Perhaps the most striking illustration of this diffuse impact of human rights litigation can be observed in the FRG, gaining particular momentum in the 1950s and 1960s. During this time, the presumption was progressively reinforced in the courts that the basic rights expressed in the constitution were co-implied in all legal exchanges, and that all legal cases brought before the courts were subject to basic rights, originally extracted from international human rights.[65] This principle was explained, most famously, with reference to the distinction between public law and private law. In this regard, it was decided in the Constitutional Court that basic constitutional rights implied an overarching constitution for all society, binding both on vertical interactions between persons and the state and lateral exchanges between individual persons. This principle instilled a deep dynamic of subjectivization in the domestic legal order, in which each person was constructed, in all social relations, both as a holder, and as an active interpreter, of constitutional rights, and all legal relations, vertical and horizontal, were defined on that basis.[66] In this setting, acts of litigation became a mainspring in promoting the construction of a relatively uniform rights-based constitution, and litigation necessarily deepened the penetration of constitutional norms into society.

A very distinctive example of the widening constitutional implications of human rights litigation can be found in Russia. In Russia, the assimilation of international human rights law in domestic law has been a complex, contested and tortuous process, at times obstructed, but generally encouraged, by actors in the political executive. As discussed, however, as domestic law became articulated with international law, individual acts of litigation began to acquire a distinctive force in the wider legal order. In a society marked historically by extreme institutional diffuseness, the fact that citizens were able to articulate legal claims through the relatively

---

[63] See also *A v. British Broadcasting Corporation* – [2014] All ER (D) 65 (May).

[64] See the creation of a strengthened, effectively constitutionalized guarantee of a right to appeal a judicial ruling in *FP(Iran) v. Secretary of State* [2007] EWCA Civ 13.

[65] See discussion above at p. 317.

[66] See for theoretical articulation of this Häberle (1975).

universal diction of human rights linked agents in society more directly and more uniformly to the institutions of the federal state, and it expanded a relatively consistent legal order across society. In fact, human rights litigation was clearly promoted by government bodies as an activity that instilled greater legal uniformity across society, and which established a basic normative structure to stabilize society around the political system. For this reason, litigation was officially activated as an instrument for institutionalizing national patterns of citizenship, and litigation was deliberately constructed as a practice that promoted systemic nationalization. Striking in this respect, above all, is the fact that in Russia citizens were particularly encouraged to initiate litigation on grounds linked to international human rights norms. As discussed, after 2000, the citation of international human rights law in Russian court hearings became more frequent, and court reforms and reforms to procedural codes were introduced to bring domestic courts into line with international standards. This meant that legal cases related to internationally defined rights came to act as a primary source of public legal and even political-systemic construction, placing stricter constraints on acts of public agencies, and correcting the historical weaknesses in the linkage between state and society. In each respect, the broad translation of legal disputes into a register of rights acted to spread a formally constituted legal order across all parts of the law and across all parts of society. In each respect, this process was driven by the fact that domestic law became more permeable to international law, which meant, over time, that single acts of litigation linked individual agents more immediately to the global system.

In each of the above respects, the growing autonomy of the legal system means that the basic constitutional-political form of society is produced through multiple processes, in which single acts of litigation, initiated by many different subjects, have a primary position. Often, in fact, human rights law promotes a radical multiplication or segmentarization of democratic citizenship, creating openings for law-making practices in a number of different roles, social dimensions and functional spheres.

5.3.2   Litigants as Citizens 2: Collective Litigants

Rights-based litigation has had the most profoundly transformative effect on the nature of democratic practice, not through the actions of singular persons as litigants, but rather through the emergence of new collective litigants. In some cases, engagement of collective actors in litigation is clearly equivalent to political or even constituent practice. For example, it is now commonplace for some collective litigants to assume signifi-cant positions in longer processes of democratization. Many processes of political democratization have been partly propelled by collective agents pursuing human rights litigation against oppressive governments.[67] In addition, some processes of political democratization have been immedi-ately stimulated by mobilization around demands for particular collective rights – for example, for health rights.[68] In such instances, human rights have created a focus of collective mobilization, located within the law, which has initiated wider political-systemic changes. However, the impor-tance of collective litigation is not specific to democracies prior to, or in, a process of transition, and the importance of collective litigation does not only appear prior to, or in, classical constitution-making processes. On the contrary, collective litigation forms a mode of inner-legal political prac-tice in which many groups, in both new and (nominally) more established democracies, can engage. In some settings, collective litigation constitutes a *sui generis* practice, in which international norms penetrate deep and fluidly into society, articulating with hidden groups and hidden subjects, at times unearthing new political agents. The fact that law is not anchored in fixed political subjects means that, in litigation, new subjects can appear within national societies, and new political personalities can be made vis-ible within historically formed constitutional structures. Indeed, in some cases, collective litigation facilitates the emergence of new citizen groups, especially amongst actors traditionally excluded from legal personality and effective citizenship rights. In collective litigation, therefore, global law acquires constitutive political force at a unique level of autonomy.

5.3.2.1 Indigenous Peoples and Other Collectives

The role of litigation as a pattern of collective practice and collective sub-ject formation is visible in legal actions relating to indigenous peoples. In different settings, indigenous groups have begun to act as distinct political subjects, with distinct reserves of politically formative agency. Historically, of course, indigenous groups were often invisible amongst dominant pop-ulation groups in national societies. In many cases, moreover, indigenous peoples have a specific transnational character, as they claim identities that pre-exist national societies, often inhabiting territories that cross state

---

[67] See discussion of Argentina above at p. 211.

[68] Note for instance the democratizing impact of popular campaigns for health rights in Bolivia in the 1980s, in which mobilization around health care rights led, ultimately, to a broader deepening of democracy as a whole. See on this Torres-Goitia Torres, Torres-Goitia Caballero and Lagrava (2015: 116–24).

boundaries. On both grounds, indigenous population groups have struggled to assert a distinctive legal subjectivity, and to acquire recognition as holders of collective rights. In some cases, however, the recent differentiation of the law's authority from the will of factual populations has begun to disarticulate indigenous groups within their societal settings. In such cases, indigenous groups emerge as new political subjects, and the fact that the legal system is not bound to a factual material citizen means that such groups can assert new modes of collective citizenship. Litigation has central importance in this process.

Even in societies in which plural rights attached to ethnicity have long-standing protection, ethnic membership has been consolidated as a distinct category of legal/political subjectivity. Examples of this can be found in parts of the former Soviet Union: that is, in the Republics and constituent units of the Russian Federation. In Russia, Federal Law No. 82-FZ (1999), 'On Guarantees of the Rights of Indigenous Peoples of the Russian Federation', recognizes distinct rights of indigenous populations, and it makes special provision for their legal representation and standing before the courts. However, the construction of indigenous groups as collective democratic subjects is most striking in Latin America. As discussed, a number of Latin American societies now designate indigeneity as a distinctively protected legal title. In consequence, indigenous communities possess elevated status as claimants to constitutional protection, and they engage directly with the political system, as free-standing political subjects, as they pursue litigation for separate rights. Successful rights claims in Latin America made by indigenous groups are widely sustained either by reference to ILO 169 or by reference to rulings of the IACtHR, which has proactively supported indigenous rights.

A significant feature in litigation regarding indigenous rights in Latin America is that this is not a static process, in which already established rights are ascribed to already existing and categorized legal subjects, or in which formalized rights are simply moved from one legal domain to another. On the contrary, litigation for indigenous rights often involves the inner-legal construction of new rights, and, in some cases, of quite new, contingent collective subjects. Significantly, in many cases, rights ascribed to indigenous communities have not been primarily established on the grounds that the claimants are indigenous, and rights granted to indigenous groups are not defined as rights of an absolutely unique nature, pertaining exclusively to indigenous communities for some material-anthropological reason. To be sure, it is now quite common for Latin American courts to acknowledge a series of distinct rights that are specific to indigenous communities. For example, one core right amongst the set of rights assigned to indigenous groups is the right to occupy ancestral land.[69] A further core right imputed to indigenous communities is the right to consultation in matters affecting occupancy of ancestral lands – for example, road building and extractivist activities.[70] In securing such rights, litigation for indigenous rights has clearly assumed legislative force, and indigenous groups, as litigants, have evolved as concrete democratic subjects, able, through litigation, to expand and intensify formal provisions for their rights. Important in this respect, however, is the fact that most indigenous rights have been created not as free-standing rights, or as rights that are generically attached to indigenous subjects, but as rights derived from other rights, which are more generally protected. In such processes, indigenous groups often emerge as rights-holding subjects, in more spontaneous fashion, through the actual practice of litigation. As a result, litigation by indigenous groups appears as a mode of democratic agency, or even as a mode of democratic subject formation, in which new rights are formulated, and in which new legal/political subjects are transformed, or become visible, through the act of claiming rights. To this degree, such rights have been elaborated on inner-legal foundations, as relatively contingent outcomes of litigation processes.

To illustrate this, leading cases of litigation concerning the land rights of indigenous peoples in Latin America have established indigenous rights through the extension of other private and civil rights, and especially through an amplificatory reading of the right to life.[71] Similarly, indigenous rights to consultation are not of a fully *sui generis* nature. In some countries, for example, the right of a group to be consulted about matters affecting its wellbeing is not exclusive to indigenous population groups, but has been extended to other groups affected by extractivist or similar activities.[72]

---

[69] See the Peruvian case: *Comunidad Nativa Tres Islas Y Otros* EXP. N° 01126-2011-PHC/TC (9/11/2011); and see the Bolivian case SCP 0572/2014. In fact, this right is protected in Article 231, § 3° of the Brazilian Constitution.

[70] See the Peruvian case: Constitutional Court (Grand Chamber), STC N° 06316-2008-PA/TC (11/12/2009). See also the Chilean case: Supreme Court Rol 10.090-2011 (22/03/2012). In one case, C-030/2008, the Colombian Constitutional Court invalidated an entire piece of legislation because there had been no prior consultation with indigenous communities.

[71] See above p. 269.

[72] See the Brazilian case, JFPA, Sentença na Ação Civil Pública n° 3883-98.2012.4.01.3902, UHE São Luiz do Tapajós. Decision of 15 June 2015. The right to free, prior and informed consultation to indigenous population affected by the construction of the São Luiz do Tapajós dam is upheld in this decision. This ruling also advocates an expansion of the right to be consulted to other traditional communities. This case established the very important concept of 'traditional communities' to create rights for populations with some

In most cases, the recognition of indigenous rights becomes possible because legal rights are severed from entitlements that are materially attached to ethnicity as an objective social quality, and indigenous groups acquire rights, constitutively, as they are legally separated from their material social form. In each respect, the subject of the indigenous citizen is constructed within the law itself, and the law itself produces conditions of multi-centric citizenship. In most cases, indigenous rights have resulted from the expansion of rights already consolidated in international law, and the legal subjectivity of indigenous peoples has been partly formed through inner articulations between national and global law.[73]

Similar patterns of political subject formation can be seen in Africa. In many African countries, legal claims attached to ethnicity have a particularly sensitive position, and contests over indigeneity can easily trigger very delicate political and constitutional reactions. This is the case, above all, because of the ethnic composition of governing elites in most African societies. Latin American societies are still primarily governed by elites of Hispanic extraction, and the category of indigeneity can easily be applied to non-Hispanic population groups to produce rights as a means of supporting societally disadvantaged sectors. By contrast, in much of Africa, government functions are almost exclusively vested in persons with strong claims to membership in indigenous groups, and it is usually impossible to make a distinction between various social groups by differentiating between

---

similarities to indigenous groups. Recently, in SU-133/17, the Colombian Constitutional Court has extended rights accorded to indigenous communities to professional groups, in particular miners, attributing to them a distinct personality on the basis of their 'mining identity'.

[73] As discussed above (p. 269), line of reasoning that expanded the rights to life to create rights for indigenous peoples was cemented in the IACtHR. Notably, judges in the IACtHR initially created land rights for indigenous peoples through a broad interpretation of the right to life, enshrined in Article 4 of the ACHR. In particular, they expanded this right to argue that the right to life entails a notion of *vida digna* – the right to live in dignity. In essence, the concept of *vida digna* indicates that the fundamental right to life is not exhaustively defined as the simple negative right not to be deprived of life. On the contrary, the right to life is seen to contain, by inference or by necessary extension, a cluster of positive rights, including the right to gain access to the conditions (broadly defined) that guarantee a dignified existence (see Pasqualucci 2006: 299). This concept can be traced to earlier decisions in India and Colombia. For the key Indian precedent, see *Francis Coralie Mullin v. The Administrator, Union Territory of Delhi*, AIR 1981 SC 746. But this concept first appeared in the IACtHR in decisions such as *Villagran Morales (Street Children) v. Guatemala*, 19 November 1999, and *Instituto de Reeducación del Menor v. Paraguay*, 2 September 2004, which addressed legal claims of marginalized social groups, especially vulnerable children. However, this concept is now often applied in cases involving indigenous people.

them on grounds of indigeneity or non-indigeneity. As a result, reference to indigeneity as a legal designation can easily be seen to promote special treatment for particular communities, and even to justify a privileging of one population group over others. Indeed, in distinguishing between different populations groups on the same territory, the concept of indigeneity can even give rise to separatist claims. In consequence, this concept is often opposed in Africa because it might appear to legitimate demands amongst distinct population groups for secession from existing nation-states, causing further depletion of already weak state institutions.[74] In the longer period of decolonization, significantly, African states routinely adopted very defensive conceptions of state sovereignty, and both single governments and inter-state agreements refused to acknowledge claims to autonomy or partial autonomy by ethnically distinct communities (see Ndahinda 2011: 171).

Not surprisingly, therefore, recent processes of democracy-building in Africa have been marked by great reticence in the acknowledgement of claims to rights made by ethnic collectives. Few African constitutions make strict and express provision for the protection of indigenous people. Such rights are recognized in the Preamble to the Constitution of Cameroon and in Articles 6 and 148 of the 2015 Constitution of the Central African Republic. Other constitutions, such as those of Mali, Burundi and South Africa, provide more general protection for indigenous groups, especially under clauses and declarations acknowledging rights of linguistic, cultural and epistemic diversity. In 2011, the Congo introduced a new national law on the rights of indigenous peoples. The Ethiopian Constitution is based on a model of power-sharing ethno-federalism, which gives clear powers of autonomy to different ethnic groups, in sub-national units. Also, in many cases, protective provisions for minorities implicitly cover indigenous peoples. For instance, the Kenyan Constitution (2010) does not specifically protect indigenous peoples. However, it prescribes affirmative action for minorities and marginalized groups (Article 56). In many African societies, further, the collective rights of indigenous communities are quite broadly protected under constitutional and statutory guarantees for the validity of customary law (Ndahinda 2011: 93; Ibhawoh 2000: 847). Notable examples of this are found in the constitutions of Kenya (Article 63),[75]

---

[74] Following the UN Human Rights Council's adoption of the Declaration of the Rights of Indigenous Peoples in June 2006, a group of African States reacted with caution. They expressed concerns that, considering 'Africa is still recovering from the effects of ethnic based conflict', the concept of indigenous presented might be 'threatening the political unity and the territorial integrity of any country' (African Group 2006: paras 2.2, 3.2).

[75] The Kenyan Constitution (Article 63) protects community land held under customary law. Kenyan legislation also protects African customary law as a valid source of law in civil cases.

and South Africa (Articles 211–12).[76] Under the 1992 Constitution of Ghana, the institution of chieftaincy and traditional systems of administration as established by customary law and usage are recognized (Article 270).[77] In fact, in Article 11(3), the Constitution recognizes and supports patterns of customary law in Ghana as practised and applied by the various ethnic groups. In Ghana, further, ethnic rights relating to land ownership are constitutionally protected.[78] More generally, however, even the most progressive African constitutions usually avoid attaching strict legal titles to indigenous groups, and they tend to protect indigenous groups by more implicit provisions. Generally, models of democracy have been promoted that are based on overarching patterns of national affiliation and popular sovereignty.

Alongside this, acceptance of international norms regarding indigeneity in Africa is limited. For example, most African states have refused to ratify established international instruments for guaranteeing indigenous rights in domestic politics. At the time of writing, the Central African Republic is the only state in Africa that has ratified ILO 169. Even in cases before international tribunals, where judges have recognized claimants as possessing collective rights as peoples, the formal recognition of indigeneity has been very cautious, and subject to clear qualifications.[79] For a long time, the African Commission on Human and Peoples' Rights was very reluctant to recognize indigeneity as a meaningful term to describe African peoples (see Bojosi and Wachira 2006: 390, 394). Notably, important cases heard by the African Commission regarding indigenous groups have been processed without cooperation of the respondent states.[80]

In recent years, to be sure, there have been changes in international recognition of indigeneity. A majority of African states recognized the (non-binding) UN Declaration on Indigenous Rights (2007). The African

---

[76] For debates see note 87 below.

[77] On chieftaincy as institution in Ghana see Ray (1996); Brydon (1996).

[78] On the constitutional creation of an enforceable trust in relation to skin and stool lands see *Owusu* v. *Adjei* (1991) 2 GLR 493 at 516.

[79] In an important early ruling concerning indigenous peoples, the word 'indigenous' was not used. See African Commission, (SERAC) and *Center for Economic and Social Rights (CESR)* v. *Nigeria*.

[80] The Commission heard Centre for Minority Rights Development (Kenya) and Minority Rights Group International on behalf of *Endorois* v. *Kenya* without Kenya's full cooperation. It referred the next case against Kenya (*African Commission on Human and Peoples' Rights* v. *the Republic of Kenya*, filed 2012) directly to the African Court on Human and Peoples' Rights.

Commission has begun to promote a progressive construction of indigeneity, and, in its rulings, it has recognized indigenous communities as claimants to specific collective rights. This attitude has now also been replicated in the recent case law of the African Court on Human and Peoples' Rights.[81] In fact, the African Commission created a Working Group on Indigenous Populations/Communities, which cautiously promoted recognition of indigeneity within established states.[82] Cases heard by the African Commission have seen a progressive elaboration of the concept of an indigenous people, bearing collective legal rights, and based on common history, identity and tradition.[83] Nonetheless, in accepting the existence of such rights, the African Commission has declared that subnational self-determination can only be exercised in a fashion that fully acknowledges 'principles such as sovereignty and territorial integrity'.[84] In fact, wide endorsement of the UN Declaration in Africa resulted partly from the observation of the African Commission that its provisions should be applied in a fashion commensurate with general international norms concerning territorial integrity (see Crawhall 2001: 26). The Working Group of the African Commission declared that recognition of indigeneity can only occur if 'due regard' is shown for the sovereignty of national states (2005: 75). Overall, therefore, even in accepting indigenous rights, the African Commission has expressed caution about the implementation of the UN Declaration in African societies,[85] and it has shown wide respect for anxieties regarding secession and the destabilization of national boundaries attached to the establishment of such rights.[86] Notably, the Working Group Report stressed that the African Commission should only acknowledge indigeneity in the 'analytical form of the concept', to be applied to 'marginalized groups' in order 'to draw attention to and alleviate the particular form of discrimination they suffer from' (2005: 88). On

---

[81] See African Court on Human and Peoples' Rights, *African Commission on Human and Peoples' Rights v. the Republic of Kenya*, Application No. 006/2012 (2013), Judgment 26 May 2017 at para 107.

[82] This Report stated that the title of indigeneity can be justified by groups claiming 'a special attachment to and use of their traditional land' (African Commission's Working Group of Experts on Indigenous Populations/Communities 2005: 93).

[83] *Kevin Mgwanga Gunme et al./Cameroon* Comm. No. 266/03 (2009) at para 179.

[84] *Katangese Peoples' Congress v. Zaire*, African Commission on Human and Peoples' Rights, Comm. No. 75/92 (1995).

[85] See Advisory Opinion of the African Commission on Human and Peoples' Rights on the United Nations Declaration on the Rights of Indigenous Peoples.

[86] *Kevin Mgwanga Gunme et al./Cameroon* at para 1999.

this basis, indigenous communities are partly defined in terms that are unlikely to fuel secessionist movements or claims to political autonomy.

Despite this, however, ethnic groups have recently emerged as constitutional-political subjects in Africa in several quite distinct ways. First, in some national cases, indigenous communities in Africa have been allowed to assert a claim to certain collective rights, such as privileged access to land and resources. Indigeneity has been used as a distinctive explanation for such rights.[87] Second, international judicial bodies in Africa have begun to establish indigeneity as specific grounds for legal claims. This has also led to international recognition of rights to land and resources.[88] Notable in such cases, both in national and supranational law, is the fact that, as in Latin America, collective claims to rights by distinct ethnic communities in Africa are often secured through reference to other more generally recognized rights, which already enjoy national and international protection. For example, the rights of indigenous groups are often established through litigation over rights to land, to water or to cultural integrity, and these rights create a situation in which rights particular to the life of ethnic communities can be recognized and preserved. Even in cases where indigeneity is admitted as the ground for an entitlement, rights attached to indigeneity are usually constructed through the expansion of other primary rights, often on the basis of international instruments.[89] Moreover, rights granted to indigenous communities in Africa, as in Latin America, are not categorically bound to indigeneity as a

[87] See the Botswanan case *Sesana and Others* v. *Attorney-General* (2006) AHRLR 183 (BwHC 2006) 117. For comment on the taboo-breaking nature of this ruling see Zips-Mairitsch (2013: 346). See the South African cases *Richtersveld Community and Others* v. *Alexkor Ltd and Another* (488/2001) [2003] ZASCA 14; [2003] 2 All SA 27 (SCA) (24 March 2003) 26 and *Alexkor Ltd and Another* v. *Richtersveld Community and Others* (CCT19/03) [2003] ZACC 18; 2004 (5) SA 460 (CC); 2003 (12) BCLR 1301 (CC) (14 October 2003). See the Kenyan case *Joseph Letuya and 21 Others* v. *Attorney General and 5 Others* [2014] eKLR.

[88] See the following rulings of the African Commission, *Social and Economic Rights Action Centre (SERAC) and Another* v. *Nigeria* (2001) AHRLR 60 (ACHPR 2001); *Katangese Peoples' Congress* v. *Zaire*, Comm. No. 75/92 (1995); *276/03 Centre for Minority Rights Development (Kenya) and Minority Rights Group (on behalf of Endorois Welfare Council)/ Kenya*.

[89] See the Kenyan case *Charles Lekuyen Nabori and 9 Others* v. *Attorney General and 3 Others* [2008] eKLR, p. 78. See the Botswanan case *Mosetlhanyane and Others* v. *Attorney General of Botswana*, Civil Appeal No. CACLB-074-10. Judgement 27.1.2011 This ruling overturned the far more restrictive ruling of the High Court, delivered in *Mosetlhanyane and Another* v. *the Attorney General* [2010] 3 BLR 372 HC.

material or extra-legal substrate. Indeed, these rights are often widened so that they can be exercised by other subjects that are exposed to analogous deprivations.[90]

In these processes in Latin America and Africa, opportunities created through litigation focused on human rights law have enabled ethnic communities to become political or even constitutional subjects in many different ways. In a range of settings, indigenous populations now form important democratic actors, partly separate from national constituencies, often shaping the institutional structure of democracy by expanding and solidifying a spectrum of specific collective rights claims. In such cases, however, the emergence of indigeneity as a source of political subjectivity occurs mainly as an articulation of a prior, given legal structure, and factual group membership is not essentially constitutive of group rights. Indeed, ethnic populations usually appear as political subjects through the constructive mobilization of rights that are already established at a primary (that is, global) constitutional level. As discussed, in many cases, these rights do not pertain generically to indigenous subjects, and they are attached to indigenous subjects through an inner-legal process of secondary rights generation. In many cases, the legal substance of indigeneity evolves through the course of litigation itself, and the legal personality of indigenous groups is generated through the amplification of existing rights. It is habitual for theorists of indigenous law to see indigenous rights as an element of legal pluralism that is asserted by concretely embedded subjects, which resist incorporation in the formal legal system of society (see Merry 1988: 873; Tamanaha 2008: 399). In most cases, however, autonomous indigenous rights are established through the secondary enforcement of increasingly unified global norms, and such rights become real, not as the attributes of factual anthropological subjects, but as determinate instantiations of a primary system of global human rights.

5.3.2.2   Displaced Peoples

Analogies to the formation of indigenous peoples as litigants capable of exercising political agency can be found in legal cases regarding internally displaced persons, forced into inner-societal migration by, for example, violence, ethnic conflict or environmental crises. In such cases, patterns of inner-legal interaction have created fora for the substantiation of displaced

---

[90] The Kenyan courts have constructed rights of indigenous communities and rights of displaced communities on the same grounds. See *Satrose Ayuma and 11 Others v. Registered Trustees of the Kenya Railways Staff Retirement Benefits Scheme and 3 Others* para 15.

persons as visible political subjects, sometimes acting to modify the basic structure of national democratic systems. In fact, the emergence of displaced communities as distinct legal-political subjects provides particular evidence of the constituent force of interactions between different spheres of global law, and it illuminates the capacity of litigation to supplement democratic agency as a constitutive source of legal norm construction. Notably, the legal position and constitutional impact of indigenous communities was originally defined and protected under international law, agreed in inter-state treaties, so that they progressively gained constitutional protection because of this. By contrast, internally displaced persons possess a much weaker personality under international law, and much more precarious claims to effective citizenship, and they have been forced to establish legal personality without clear formal international protections. As a result, legal protection for displaced populations has been created in much more contingent processes, in which acts of litigation play a key role.

The relatively weak legal protection of displaced peoples is due, first, to the fact that the presence of internally displaced persons often presents a threat to established national legal systems, defined by the primacy of sovereign state institutions. Internally displaced persons are typically victims of violence, in which domestic political institutions have some degree of complicity, or, at least, which they lack the power or will to prevent (see Phuong 2005: 209). Indeed, states may themselves be in breach of international treaty norms by virtue of the fact that displaced persons exist within their territories (Vidal López 2007: 107). Consequently, persons in a condition of displacement find it difficult to channel legal claims towards domestic state institutions, and they are usually only able to obtain weak remedies under domestic law (Geissler 1999: 467). Some societies that have recent experience of large numbers of internally displaced persons, notably Kenya and Colombia, have introduced legislation to protect them.[91] Moreover, displaced persons are of course covered by general human rights law. However, the robustness of such provisions is questionable, especially as many displaced persons specifically wish to preserve invisibility in face of public authorities, in order to avoid exposure to renewed persecution.

[91] For Kenya, see The Prevention, Protection and Assistance to Internally Displaced Persons and Affected Communities Act (2012). For Colombia, see Law 387 on Internal Displacement (1997), Decree 173 of 1998 adopting the National Plan for Comprehensive Assistance to Populations Displaced by Violence (1998), and, above all, the Victims' Law (Law 1448, 2011).

The weak protection for displaced persons is due, second, to the fact that, unlike cross-border refugees, whose legal position is defined and determined by a complex and well-entrenched corpus of international law, internally displaced communities are not easily visible to international norm setters, and their claims are primarily directed to national state organs. International protection regimes do not easily accommodate displaced persons (see Luopajärvi 2003: 686; Deng 2009: 250). UN guidelines on internally displaced persons, notably the Deng principles and the Pinheiro principles, are viewed by some states as *de facto* binding, and some states use them in domestic law (Cohen 2004: 469). However, these guidelines only have soft law status, or even, as one commentary observes, mere *secondary soft law status* (Luopajärvi 2003: 708). Regional instruments regarding displaced persons also have variable and patchy application. To be sure, the jurisprudence of the IACtHR contains clear norms for treatment of displaced persons,[92] and it has articulated an effective *right not to be displaced.*[93] Some states in East Africa have also acceded to the Great Lakes Protocol on Internally Displaced Persons. However, the only international convention with binding force that is specifically concerned with internally displaced persons is the Kampala Convention of the African Union. Notably, the application of these documents remains uneven; the Kampala Convention, although formally binding, is difficult to enforce (Kidane 2011: 77–84). In Africa, moreover, the African Charter has not generated hard protection for internally displaced persons. Notably, the African Commission has established certain norms in this regard, but it has encountered obstacles in implementation.[94]

One obvious consequence of their lack of recognition in international law is that internally displaced persons have limited significance for the international community. Indeed, they are not widely seen as persons of relevance for states beyond the affected state, and other states have limited legal or humanitarian interest in their welfare. One further consequence of this is that internally displaced persons are located in a very uncertain legal environment, in which the normative framework for their rights is unclear and necessarily in flux. Indeed, in many cases, the causes of internal displacement often destroy the institutions capable of providing legal protection for displaced persons. Countries with large internally displaced

---

[92] *Case of the Afro-Descendant Communities Displaced from the Cacarica River Basin (Operation Genesis) v. Colombia* (2013).
[93] *Case of the 'Mapiripán Massacre' v. Colombia.* Judgment of 15 September 2005.
[94] For comment see Abebe (2009: 164).

populations, such as Somalia and Sudan, also have very weak judicial systems (see Maru 2008: 2).

Partly owing to such uncertainly, however, legal cases addressing the rights of internally displaced persons have given rise to a complexly structured body of transnational law, integrating elements of international hard law, elements of international soft law and elements of domestic human rights law (Orchard 2010: 286). In fact, internally displaced persons often require international legal assistance within their own states, which means that acts of litigation in support of internally displaced persons result in transnational norm production, creating laws that incorporate international norms immediately within national sovereign states. In some respects, accordingly, internally displaced persons have emerged as *transnational constitutional subjects*, which have established rights in a legal zone between the domestic and the international domains, in the consolidation of which judicial actions have played a crucially formative role.

Some examples of this are evident in Kenya. In recent years, the Kenyan government has been required to accommodate large groups of internally displaced persons. These groups included persons uprooted by inter-population violence following the 2007 elections, but they also included numbers of people exposed to mass eviction for other reasons. In the aftermath of 2007, remedies for displacement were mainly provided by the political branches of government, notably in legislation of 2012, *The Prevention, Protection and Assistance to Internally Displaced Persons and Affected Communities Act*. Moreover, Kenyan courts have in the main been unwilling to ascribe liability for displacement to government agencies, arguing that inter-ethnic conflict after the 2007 elections 'was in many ways spontaneous', so that the 'State cannot be said to have be aware in advance just how widespread and how destructive the violence would be'.[95] Nonetheless, displacement has emerged in Kenya as an issue around which national and international norms coalesce, and in which litigation articulates new legal norms with far-reaching impact.

First, for example, the legislation of 2012 was partly prompted by legal activists, and it involved the domestic incorporation of both the UN Guiding Principles on Internally Displaced Persons and the Great Lakes Protocol on Internally Displaced Persons. Alongside this, although persons uprooted in 2007 have been reluctant to file cases, Kenyan courts have independently used international norms to establish basic rights in

---

[95] *Paul K. Waweru & 4 others* v. *Attorney General & 2 others* [2016] eKLR at p. 4.

cases regarding displacement of persons caused by ethnic conflict.[96] As discussed, moreover, they have also used international law in other cases relating to mass internal displacement, determining that large-scale forcible evictions entail a violation of the right to accessible and adequate housing. Such arguments have been underpinned by reference to the ICCPR, to the UDHR and to other UN guidelines with soft law status. Moreover, such arguments have been backed by reference to rulings on the right to housing in the South African Constitutional Court.[97] In a number of cases, Kenyan courts have used international norms to define the rights of persons in a state of displacement caused by eviction, stipulating access to health care and resources, and 'legal security of tenure' as norms for treating displaced population groups.[98] In one recent Court of Appeal case concerning mass eviction, the Court tried to weaken the effect of international law in Kenya,[99] and it attempted to re-establish a political question doctrine, to restrict judicial intervention in and supervision of political decisions.[100] The legal position of displaced persons thus appears as a prism for deep-lying conflicts around the sources of law, and the displaced person forms a highly contested figure of constitutional agency.

The most important examples of the emergence of displaced persons as legal/political subjects are evident in Colombia, the state with the largest number of persons displaced by civil conflict. To be sure, the normative framework in Colombia for addressing internally displaced persons is now based on a substantial body of legislation, especially in Law 387 (1997) and Law 1448 (2011) (see Lemaitre Ripoll and Sandvik 2014: 387). However, the rights of displaced persons have been substantially constructed through judicial practices, notably through the *tutela* jurisprudence of the Colombian Constitutional Court. In fact, Colombian law is distinctively able to address the claims of displaced population groups, who may of themselves be reluctant to file suit, because it permits representation of marginal groups in *tutelas* by proxies – that is, by *agencia oficiosa*.[101] Notably, Law 2591 of 1991 specifically declares that, where social groups affected in their basic rights are legally undefended or disadvantaged,

---

[96] *Florence Amunga Omukanda & another* v. *Attorney General & 2 others*, [2016] eKLR.

[97] *Ibrahim Sangor Osman* v. *Minister of State for Provincial Administration & Internal Security*. eKLR [2011].

[98] *Kepha Omondi Onjuro & others* v. *Attorney General & 5 others* [2015] eKLR.

[99] *Kenya Airports Authority* v. *Mitu-Bell Welfare Society & 2 others* [2016] eKLR at para 118.

[100] *Kenya Airports Authority* v. *Mitu-Bell Welfare Society & 2 others* [2016] eKLR at para 141.

[101] The Constitutional Court specifically ruled that *agencia oficiosa* could be used to represent displaced persons in T-267/11.

legal representatives distinct from these immediately affected, and without any legal contract with such persons, may submit *tutelas* to defend them. *Agencia oficiosa* may thus be used in contexts in which applicants lack linguistic skills, or are prohibited by geographical, educational or monetary factors from effective petition, a fact which creates important litigation opportunities for internally displaced persons.[102]

Especially notable in Colombia, first, is the fact that, in leading *tutela* cases lodged by representatives of internally displaced persons, the Constitutional Court has decided that groups of internally placed persons are defined by a 'condition of extreme vulnerability'. On this basis, displaced persons form a separate legal subjects, requiring 'particular protection', and demanding interventionist remedial measures from the judiciary.[103] As discussed, extensive legislation concerning displaced persons was dictated by the Court in *tutela* T-025/04,[104] in which, and in subsequent *autos*, the Court ordered a thorough 'structural reform of the government's humanitarian response to internal displacement' (Lemaitre Ripoll and Sandvik 2015: 7). Importantly, second, the courts have made extensive use of international norms in seeking to stabilize society in the wake of the mass population movements. As mentioned, the Constitutional Court decided that international soft law principles, especially the Deng principles and the Pinheiro principles, should be applied as a binding source of domestic rights. Through this process, relevant soft law was incorporated within Colombia as part of the *block of constitutionality*,[105] and displaced persons are able to acquire immediate constitutional rights from international soft law. Moreover, third, the Court has used norms based on international humanitarian law to measure and improve the government's progress in remedying the displacement crisis.[106] As discussed, the Court observed the mass violation of the rights of displaced persons as a generic failing of the state – as an unconstitutional state of affairs – which required exceptional judicial supervision of the government and strict interventions to ensure satisfaction of basic rights. In this respect, the Court used international law to spell out distinctive sets of rights for displaced persons, including the right to truth and justice, the right to full restitution of property and the right to protection from repeated displacement.

[102] See T-342/94; T-380/93.
[103] T-239/13.
[104] T-025/2004.
[105] See T-327/01; T-068/10. On the hardening of soft law in the Colombian Constitutional Court see Vidal López (2007: 79).
[106] See A-178/05, A-109/07.

Moreover, it struck down sections of laws relating to the displaced population that did not adhere to these principles.[107]

In such cases, litigation conducted by or on behalf of displaced persons forms a practice in which, in a social and legal situation defined by acute socio-political instability and extreme institutional weakness, a new subject of rights has been able to take shape and gain recognition, constructing hard rights from a fluid mix of normative sources (see Vidal López 2007: 107). In this setting, rights-determined litigation itself gives rise to new legal persons, to new articulations of democratic practice, and to more robustly defined constitutional norms. Subjects with no obvious political or representative status become important sources of law, often replacing or acting alongside classical patterns of citizenship. In each respect, constitutional agency, and indeed the basic form of the constitutional-political subject, emerges as a construction *of* and *within* the law, outside or between the politically formalized domains of national and international law.

5.3.3   Litigants as Citizens 3: Public Interest Litigation

The most striking example of ways in which litigation act alongside more classical modes of democratic agency appears in the realm of public interest litigation.[108] That is, the potential of litigation for supplanting standard citizenship practices is most evident in third-party litigation against public bodies concerning collective interests, which are defined as separate from the constitutionally defined rights of particular persons or groups. Such litigation usually has a strategic character, and it often reflects collective or group-led mobilization around particular claims, aimed at the prevention of future violation of collective rights. It is a characteristic of such litigation that classical private-law restrictions on rights of standing are relaxed, and litigation can be initiated by a widened set of parties, claiming an interest in the case on the grounds that it represents a broad public concern or that a wide public interest has been violated. In some cases, public interest litigation has necessitated revision of deep-seated constitutional principles.[109]

---

[107] C-715/12.

[108] The transformation of the legislative process through public interest cases was noted early by Chayes, who argued that it necessitated a 'transformed appreciation of the whole process of making, implementing and modifying law', and that, owing to this, representation is no longer conducted 'alone through the voter or by representation in the legislature' (1976: 1315–16).

[109] See below pp. 472–5.

Public interest litigation is not new. In fact, the origins of such litigation can be traced to Roman law. More recently, precursors of contemporary public interest rules can be found in much civil legislation in Latin America, for example the Brazilian Class Action Law of 1965 (Law 4.717/1965). Indeed, provision for public-interest cases acquired constitutional standing in the Spanish Constitution of 1978. Moreover, such litigation is not universal. In some countries, it is not formally foreseen by the constitution, but it exists at a more informal level, and is currently in a process of expansion. In Germany, for example, where strict rules on standing apply, there are currently legislative initiatives designed formally to introduce collective litigation. In some countries, public interest litigation is suppressed, at least intermittently, for political reasons.[110] In some countries, it is technically possible, but it is restricted by traditional rules on standing.[111] Furthermore, as discussed, public interest litigation is not always separable from other modes of litigation by collective legal subjects. As a result, in different jurisdictions, it overlaps with class action cases, with *tutelas* and with general administrative litigation.[112]

In recent years, however, public interest cases, in a range of variations, have begun to form a very important legal domain. In most countries, rules on standing have been liberalized, and the widening of access to justice for third-party litigants has assumed an important role in most processes of democratic polity-building. In such cases, litigation is initiated not by persons claiming to suffer measurable damages, but by persons claiming to protect public interests, in their general role as defenders of collective interests – *as citizens*. Such cases, therefore, are shaped by socially generalized interests, in which individual persons engage with law in generic categories of political agency. Moreover, such cases often entail a societal deepening of the public domain, in which citizens are able to impose intensified principles of constitutionality on different social spheres, and private actors and organizations can also be bound by norms pertaining to

---

[110] See discussion of Egypt below at p. 472.

[111] For the UK, see the widening of standing rules in *R* v. *HM Inspector of Pollution* ex p. Greenpeace (No 2) [1994] 4 All ER 329. Historically, the UK had narrow rules on standing. This flows from the fact, as discussed, that UK public law construed rights as rights of individuals, either based in common law or asserted against single abuses of the powers conferred under particular statutes. Under this scheme, it is naturally difficult to accept a violation of rights held collectively by all citizens. Accordingly, many defenders of the classical model of the political constitution are hostile to public interest litigation (see Harlow 2002: 5).

[112] In Colombia, one commentator speaks of a 'necessary overlap' between the *tutelas* and public interest cases (Borrero Restrepo 2008).

public law, often based on human rights (see Vining 1978: 180–1; Fletcher 1988: 225). In such cases, the separation between litigation, constitutional norm formation and general democratic practice has become very blurred, and legal activism manifestly shapes the form of democracy. In fact, we can see a variety of ways in which litigants exercise legislative and quasi-constituent power, and they often generate new constitutional rights. Naturally, as outlined below, public interest litigation leads to different constitutional outcomes in different polities, and its efficacy is often determined by the degree to which democratic governance is already formally entrenched. Although its outcomes are contingent on polity type, however, public interest litigation has acquired an almost global constitutional force. Across different polity types, public interest litigation is closely linked to the assimilation of international law, and collective litigants often establish premises for action on global legal foundations.

5.3.3.1   Public Interest Litigation and the Strengthening of Democracy

As one example, we can find cases of litigation with a public interest element, in which litigation serves to consolidate the position, and, above all, to extend the societal reach, of provisions for rights contained in an existing constitution. Such litigation commonly possesses a clearly anti-systemic dimension, mobilizing norms implied within the domestic constitution against the existing governance system. However, in such cases, anti-systemic litigation occurs within already relatively secure normative parameters, so that litigation acts democratically to solidify constitutional norms across society, and to intensify the penetration of established democratic norms. In such cases, public interest litigation serves the reinforcement, or the deepening, of democracy.

Early examples of such public interest litigation can of course be found in litigation connected to the Civil Rights Movement in the USA. *Brown v. Board of Education* (1954) is widely recognized as the result of a long strategy of contestation devised by civil rights advocates, dedicated to deploying litigation as an instrument of social/constitutional transformation, and promoting the enforcement of new constitutional rights of social equality.[113] As discussed, this case occurred in a setting marked by the expanding impact of human rights law in American society (Dudziak 1988: 94). This case reflected the beginnings of a pattern of legal practice, in which

---

[113]   See Yeazell (2004: 1976); Klarman (2004: 344–442). For an account that more broadly contextualizes the role of the courts in this process see Mack (2005: 258).

lawyers began to pursue litigation as a means of structural transformation for all society, pursuing litigation as part of a long 'social process', with ramifications and implications reaching far beyond any particular case (see Tushnet 1987: 144). The contemporary model of public interest litigation in the USA was established in the Circuit Court case, *Scenic Hudson Preservation Conference* v. *Federal Power Commission* (1965), in which provisions for standing were extended to collective organizations with interests in particular cases.[114] Laws on standing were then relaxed in amendments to federal rules on civil procedure. Over a longer period, subsequently, public interest lawyers in the USA made increasing use of human rights law as an instrument for shaping judicial rulings and sharpening obligations placed on public agencies (see Cummings 2008: 985). Eventually, public interest litigation gave rise to a series of landmark court rulings, with deep impact on American constitutional law and American society more broadly. In this process, public interest cases were pursued to trigger legislation in a number of different areas, notably with regard to prison law, gender equality, health law and reproductive law. One account calculates that in the early 1970s public interest groups stimulated over 30 pieces of significant legislation (McCann 1986: 125).

Similar consequences of public interest litigation can be found in Canada. Laws on standing were widened in Canada in the 1970s, notably in *Thorson* v. *Canada (AG)* (1974), and *Nova Scotia Board of Censors* v. *McNeil* (1975).[115] Broad standing was eventually established in *Canada (Attorney General)* v. *Downtown Eastside Sex Workers United Against Violence Society*, in which the Supreme Court strategically promoted widened access to justice. The reasoning in this case was specifically intended to secure social and political rights for marginalized professional groups, in this instance prostitutes.[116] Moreover, analogies to the democracy-reinforcing role of public interest litigation can be found in Brazil, where, at an early stage in the process of constitutional reform beginning in 1984/85, a law enabling the filing of class action claims was introduced, with the symbolic design of heightening public engagement with the political system. This law was the Civil Class Action Law of 1985, which simplified collective legal actions against government bodies. In Brazil, there now exists an array of provisions for defending collective

---

[114] *Scenic Hudson Preservation Conference* v. *Federal Power Commission*, 354 F.2d 608 (2d Cir. 1965).

[115] *Nova Scotia Board of Censors* v. *McNeil*, [1976] 2 S.C.R. 265.

[116] *Canada (Attorney General)* v. *Downtown Eastside Sex Workers United Against Violence Society* [2012] SCC 45.

rights of groups and diffuse collective interests, enabling diverse groups to promote social interests through the law. The Brazilian Constitution of 1988 (Article 5, LXXIII) provides guarantees for the filing of public interest suits by citizens (*ação popular*), although these guarantees are more restrictive than in some other countries in Latin America, and rulings in such cases do not necessarily have *erga omnes* effect.[117] Moreover, in Article 129 (III), it enables filing of public-interest cases through the public prosecutor's office (*ação civil pública*). The constitution thus contains two distinct mechanisms for the channelling of public interest litigation, the *ação popular* granting *locus standi*, and *ação civil pública* covering a more comprehensive set of rights.[118] In some countries, where relatively tight laws concerning *locus standi* still prevail, courts have recognized the democratic importance of public interest litigation and shown some willingness to relax conventions determining which person, and with what type of interest in the outcome of proceedings, might be a party to a case.[119] In all such examples, public interest litigation was perceived as an instrument of democratic enhancement.

The 1991 Constitution of Colombia has created particularly strong protections for public interest litigation. Colombia had a strong tradition of protecting collective interests in private law long before 1991, and the right to litigate for public interests was secured in Articles 1005 and 2359 of the Civil Code of 1887. The expansion of public interest litigation (*acciones populares*) was then a particular objective of the Constituent Assembly in 1991, which clearly observed such ligation as a core democratic practice, and enshrined it in the constitution (Article 88) (Londoño Toro 1999: 109). In Colombia, some cases with a public interest dimension are obviously filed as *tutelas*, under Article 86. As discussed, the most important *tutela*, T-025/04, was a public-interest case. In the wake of this case, the Constitutional Court gradually elaborated the concept of the 'subject of

---

[117] See the principle set out in the landmark case 'Raposa Serra do Sol' that decisions issued in a suit of *ação popular* do not have *erga omnes* force, although a decision of the Supreme Court necessarily possesses strong persuasive force: Pet 3.388 ED, rel. min. Roberto Barroso, j. 23-10-2013, P, DJE de 4-2-2014.

[118] Although *ação civil pública* is subject to a restricted *locus standi*, the Public Prosecutor's Office has employed it to litigate on a wide range of matters, including readjustment in tuition fees (Súmula 643); rights of children and adolescents (AI 698.478, rel. min. Joaquim Barbosa, decisão monocrática, j. 18-5-2012, DJE de 28-5-2012.); environmental rights (RE 464.893, rel. min. Joaquim Barbosa, j. 20-5-2008, 2ª T, DJE de 1º-8-2008.); public transport ([RE 379.495, rel. min. Marco Aurélio, j. 11-10-2005, 1ª T, DJ de 20-4-2006]. = RE 228.177, rel. min. Gilmar Mendes, j. 17-11-2009, 2ª T, DJE de 5-3-2010); fees for public street lighting (RE 213.631, rel. min. Ilmar Galvão, j. 9-12-1999, P, DJ de 7-4-2000).

[119] See the liberalization of standing in the UK in *R v. Secretary of State for Foreign Affairs, ex parte World Development Movement Ltd* – [1995] 1 All ER 611.

special constitutional protection', to designate groups requiring intensified legal support to obtain full enjoyment of rights.[120] In the longer implementation of T-025/04 a large number of social groups were identified that, owing to the *inter comunis* standing of the initial ruling, were able to claim distinct collective rights, and to demand inclusion in legislation aimed at remedying the cause of the *tutela*. In such litigation, the courts have effectively widened the lines of articulation between state and society, allowing a range of collective actors in society to enter an immediate relation to the government, and to acquire collective rights. One account describes such collective litigation in Colombia as a form of 'juridical experimentalism' which creates a political dialogue between new collective actors in society and the state and even, in so doing, forms a primary 'mechanism of political legitimation' (Latorre Iglesias 2015: 12, 116).

Alongside *tutelas*, however, provisions for public-law litigation in Colombia also allow for filing of public interest cases in a stricter definition of the term. Unlike *tutelas*, public interest litigation is placed in the sphere of administrative law, under the jurisdiction of the *Consejo de Estado*. Notably, in Article 88, the constitution allows litigation in cases in which members of the public, not necessarily organized as an identifiable legal person, experience a threat to acknowledged collective interests – regarding, for example, the environment, the quality of public space, or administrative morality. These constitutional provisions were later solidified in legislation of 1998 (Law 472), which, in Article 12, defines the categories of person, including single persons and NGOs, which are authorized to initiate public interest cases. Importantly, in Article 35, this law states that rulings in public interest cases are binding both for the particular parties and for the public as a whole, so that case rulings have *erga omnes* force. In fact, this principle has been consolidated in the *Consejo de Estado* to the effect that judicial decisions in public interest cases have equal effect for the entire 'interested community', and the 'holders of an interest' in the case, to whom rulings are applicable, do not need to be identical with the actual claimant. The protected interest in public interest cases, thus, is distinct from the persons actually filing the case, and, as in *tutelas*, rulings can easily obtain broad structural impact.[121]

The formative democratic importance of public interest litigation in Colombia has been accentuated in case law of the Constitutional Court, which has accorded to such litigation a clearly political, constitutive

---

[120] A-073/14.
[121] Consejo de Estado, 18001 23 31 00 2011-00256-01 (AP) 22 January 2015.

force. In leading opinions of the Court, which define the scope of public interest litigation, it has been declared that public interest cases should be encouraged as an instrument for promoting 'law based in participation and solidarity'. Moreover, the Court has sharply distinguished public interest cases from class action litigation. In this respect, public interest litigation is construed as a practice for protecting interests of a very strictly collective nature, of relevance for all citizens, not attached to specific subjects, and not registered through damages to clearly identified rights.[122] Notably, in leading relevant case law, it is stated that, in public interest cases, matters should be treated that do not have a 'subjective or individual content', and which do not relate to a 'damage that can be repaired subjectively'.[123] In consequence, such cases are focused on 'collective rights, in contrast to individual rights': on rights that 'belong to the entire community', and whose holder 'is a plurality of persons'.[124] Standing for filing such cases, accordingly, depends solely on membership in the national community, and no other interest is required to justify legal proceedings.[125] Through this, collective litigation becomes a core expression of democratic citizenship.

5.3.3.2   Public Interest Litigation and Disruptive Citizenship

In parallel to the democracy-enhancing force of litigation, we can find cases of public interest litigation in which such actions have a more challenging or constitutionally disruptive impact on the order of government. Such cases reflect a more emphatically contentious constitutional practice, which is often only tolerated because of the precarious legitimacy of the regime in which it is exercised.

A very informative example of this is Egypt in the years before the end of the Mubarak regime, in which cases with a public interest element formed an important domain of contestation, often with very unsettling implications for the government. Notably, in Egypt, formal rules regarding *locus standi* were historically restrictive. By way of example, Article 12(1) of the State Council Law (Law 47/1972) prohibited the administrative courts from hearing claims brought by people with no personal interest in the matter. Moreover, under the Mubarak regime, the courts themselves at times used restrictive criteria to address questions of standing. Such formal

---

[122] C-215/99.
[123] T-528/1992.
[124] T-254/1993.
[125] T-528/1992.

restrictions notwithstanding, however, administrative litigation emerged as an important avenue of legal/political opposition under Mubarak, and much administrative litigation possessed a public interest dimension. It is widely documented that contention expressed through such litigation proved very destabilizing for the regime, as it opened up an alliance between anti-regime activists and the courts, at times supported by transnational human rights groups (see Moustafa 2003: 884; El-Ghobashy 2008: 1613; Odeh 2011: 996). Prior to 2011, in fact, litigation played an important role in creating a new constitution-making situation, in which global norms acquired high directive authority. Since the collapse of the Mubarak regime, judicial policies have been introduced in Egypt in order to restrict public interest litigation, reflecting the progressive renewed turn to authoritarianism. This is notable in Law 32/2014, which limits standing in challenges to the probity of government contracts. This clearly reflects the volatility attached to such litigation. Despite this, however, the disruptive potential of public interest cases has not entirely vanished. Indicatively, the legality of Law 32/2014 has been publicly challenged.[126]

The politically disruptive role of public interest litigation is also salient in the case law of the Kenyan superior courts. Kenyan rules on standing were historically restrictive.[127] However, they were liberalized under President Moi, before the establishment of the new democratic constitution, in the Environment Management and Co-ordination Act of 1999. Now, the democratic constitution of 2010 gives particular protection, in Articles 22(1)(c) and 258(2)(c)), to rights of public-interest litigation (Sang 2013: 40). After 2010, public interest litigation, although often following *ad hoc* strategies, acquired an important role in the process of embedding the new 2010 Constitution in society, and in bringing reality to the rights contained in the constitution. On one hand, since 2010, public interest litigation in Kenya has clearly followed the Indian model, discussed below, as a legal practice aimed to promoting social rights jurisprudence, and public interest cases have been instrumental in hardening legal recognition of social rights.[128] At the same time, however, public interest cases have also been initiated to ensure that public bodies act within constitutional parameters, and to ensure the integrity of public officials.[129] Notable

---

[126] See for discussion of this case and relevant matters Hazzaa and Kumpf (2015).
[127] See *Maathai* v. *Kenya Times Media Trust Ltd* [1989] eKLR.
[128] See above p. 247.
[129] See *Mumo Matemu* v. *Trusted Society of Human Rights Alliance & 5 others* [2014] eKLR.

in the post-2010 Kenyan setting, above all, is the fact that public interest litigation often occurs in an attritional environment; it encounters resistance both from the government and judicial actors, and litigators and litigants often face implementation gaps in respect of remedies. The degree of democratic consolidation in Kenya is often measurable by the outcomes of public interest cases, and government retrenchment against the legal implications of the democratic transition can clearly be seen in restrictive rulings in such cases.[130]

Even before ratification of the 2010 Constitution, public interest litigation had assumed a distinctive constitutional significance in Kenya, and it played an important role in setting the basic form of democracy. In fact, the new constitution was cemented in a setting that was deeply marked by public interest litigation, and it was discernibly shaped by relevant court rulings. During the process of constitution writing, for example, public interest litigation was used to obtain rights of political representation for minority groups, allowing minorities to 'articulate their distinct concerns and seek redress and thereby lay a base for deliberative democracy'.[131] Unusually for the public law of African states, in some cases, distinct ethnic communities were able to secure recognition of unincorporated international instruments (especially ILO 169) regarding minority or indigenous rights in domestic law.[132]

Especially noteworthy in the Kenyan setting, is the famous case *Njoya and Others* v. *Attorney General and Others* (2004).[133] In this case, a Presbyterian pastor, together with other applicants, challenged the authority of the National Constitutional Conference (an adjunct to the sitting parliament) to approve a new constitution. Significantly, the applicants argued that the sitting parliament was not entitled to claim the right to exercise constituent power, and a new constitution could not be accorded validity by an already elected government. In addition, the applicants protested against the division of the Kenyan nation into separate districts during the writing of the constitution, claiming that this accorded undue privilege to distinct ethnic groups, and generally impeded the formation of a nationally legitimated constitution. Ultimately, the court found

---

[130] See *Kenya Airports Authority* v. *Mitu-Bell Welfare Society & 2 others* [2016] eKLR.

[131] *Lemeiguran and Others* v. *Attorney-General and Others*. This case was initiated by representatives of the Il Chamus community, relying on a wide grant of standing. The ruling was extensively supported by the African Charter and general international human rights law.

[132] *Lemeiguran and Others* v. *Attorney-General and Others*.

[133] *Njoya and Others* v. *Attorney-General and Others* (2004) AHRLR 157 (KeHC 2004).

in favour of the applicants, declaring that a new constitution could only acquire legitimacy if established by a higher-order political will, and that it needed to extract its authority from the single and sovereign national people, acting not as part of a parliamentary assembly, but as a primary constituent power. Decisively, the Court ruled that 'every person in Kenya' had an 'equal right to review the constitution' and even to participate 'in writing and ratifying the Constitution'. It concluded that a referendum was required to endorse the constitution, and it declared that the applicants possessed a 'constituent right' to 'adopt and ratify a new Constitution', and even that this right was the 'centre-piece of a people-driven constitutional review process'.[134] The collective right to exercise constituent power assumed particular weight, the court argued, because of the regionalistic bias of the institutions responsible for drafting and approving the constitution, which, allegedly, sought to 'fragment and balkanize the Republic of Kenya into ethnic mini-states'.[135] In marked contrast to conventional jurisprudence in Kenya, which had usually accentuated the primacy of domestic law in over international law, the Court also cited Article 21 of the UDHR to reject the apparent discriminatory composition of the constitution-making body. The eventual practical result of this case was that a new constitution was drafted, which in 2010 was approved by referendum. The theoretical result of this was that, to all intents and purposes, public interest litigation acted as a source of constituent power, and the basic form of the national polity was distilled by the courts in the course of a litigation procedure. In fact, public interest litigation generated a *right to constituent power*.

Overall, the longer constitution-making process in Kenya was punctuated by important cases, in which public interest litigation had palpable impact on the basic normative fabric of the political system, effectively setting out new constitutional rights in parallel to the writing of the constitution itself. In each respect, litigation challenged the limits of the constituent form of the people, and it supplemented the more regular expression of constituent power. Notably, during the Kenyan transition, public litigation was increasingly underpinned by international law, which, as discussed, eventually became an important part of the constitution and subsequent constitutional jurisprudence.

---

[134] Kenya Law Reports [2004] 1 KLR 238.
[135] Kenya Law Reports [2004] 1 KLR 239.

5.3.3.3   Public Interest Litigation and
Compensatory Democracy

As a further alternative, there are also a number of polities that did not traditionally, in the strictest sense, permit public interest litigation, but which have established analogues to such proceedings, and which have increasingly allowed, or even encouraged, litigation on grounds of public interest concern. This is widespread in societies in which formal opportunities for political agency are curtailed, so that collective litigation acts as a distinct sluice for articulations of social interest and opposition. This can be observed in China, where, despite restrictions on political agency, public interest litigation is now tolerated.[136]

A most illuminating case in this regard is Russia, where, in recent years, opportunities for public interest litigation have been markedly extended. On one hand, the Russian legal system follows the traditional German model in preventing private parties from litigating on behalf of collective public interests. The Russian legal system still requires a state agent – the public prosecutor – to bring cases in the public interest, or, in Russian terminology, cases that are filed 'on behalf of an unidentified number of persons'.[137] In such cases, the number of suits filed by the public prosecutor is not insignificant. In fact, public prosecutors initiate on average 700,000 cases of this type per year, with very high levels of success (about 90 per cent).

Alongside this more classical mode of public interest litigation, however, recent years have seen the liberalization of Russian laws concerning public interest litigation. As mentioned above, rules on standing for individuals and associations are in the process of being relaxed. In particular, laws have been introduced which make it possible for proxies, including *inter alia* ombudspersons, data protection agencies and the Federal Chamber of Lawyers, to file cases with a public interest element. One of the most visible recent changes in the Russian public law landscape is that the federal ombudsman and the regional ombudspersons have the right to initiate cases in the interest of an unidentifiable number of persons. Before 2015, an ombudsman could only represent individuals in court, including the Constitutional Court, if their rights and freedoms had been violated by a public body and if they requested legal representation.

---

[136] For example, environmental NGOs have been admitted as plaintiffs (see Mingde and Fengyuan 2011: 232). Public interest lawyering has also become quite widespread (see Fu and Cullen 2008).

[137] See clarification of this principle in Plenum of the Supreme Court Resolution No. 25 of 23 June 2015 'On Application by the Courts of Some of the Provisions of Section I of the First Part of the Civil Code of the Russian Federation'.

The new Administrative Litigation Code of 2015 now names the federal ombudsman and regional ombudspersons in the list of proxies that are authorized to bring administrative cases in the interests of unidentifiable number of persons. The Federal Law 'On the Ombudsman' was also altered in 2015, stating in Article 29(1) that the federal ombudsman can bring such cases against a public body or any other organisation performing public functions.[138] In 2014, as mentioned, a new Federal Law 'On Citizens' Oversight' was adopted.[139] Under this law, any public association or NGO can perform *functions of citizens' oversight* prescribed by the federal law: i.e. any association is permitted 'to submit claims to court in the interests of an unidentifiable number of persons against public bodies' (Article 10(1)(7) of the Federal Law). Citizens' oversight can take various forms. For example, individuals can inspect the activities of state agencies, or offer expert services, while public associations and NGOs can carry out monitoring functions or engage in public discussions of governmental initiatives. Through the law 'On Citizens' Oversight', the government has created a significant opening for a new form of anti-government litigation, available to a wide circle of subjects, in order to motivate individuals to bring public authorities to court and to raise the legal accountability of the state.

Such revisions to classical rules on standing in Russia have been initiated as part of a wider reform process, discussed above, which has been promoted in order to comply with constitutional requirements and the international obligations of Russia. Like the rise of litigation more widely, the expansion of public interest litigation in Russia can be viewed as one element in a political strategy for linking organs of state and agents in society more closely together. Consequently, public interest litigation in Russia is not strictly, or at least not exclusively, of an anti-systemic nature. It is promoted, in part, by the government as a means of socio-constitutional inclusion, in which individual agents are integrated more immediately into the governance system. In some ways, in fact, litigation compensates for the relatively weak consolidation of other patterns of political agency, especially as litigation has increased at a time of broad political retrenchment. Nonetheless, a growing range of subjects can acquire standing in Russian law, thus also acquiring increased degrees of legal recognition, entitlement, and constitutional force. There are important public interest cases in which groups previously excluded from standing have been able

---

[138] As amended by the Federal Constitutional Law No. 1-FKZ of 8 March 2015.
[139] Federal Law No. 212-FZ of 21 July 2014 'On the Basics of Citizens' Control'.

to gain recognition as collective subjects. This has occurred, for instance, in cases regarding pensioners of a particular autonomous region,[140] and recipients of benefits relating to the Chernobyl disaster.[141]

5.3.3.4   Public Interest Litigation and New Rights

Alongside such cases, we can also find polities in which courts, on their own initiative, have deliberately facilitated public interest litigation in order to expand and transform the sets of constitutional rights existing in society. In such polities, courts themselves acquire a constitutionally form-ative position, and they deliberately promote the multiplication of demo-cratic agency. In such instances, the courts have often strategically decided to relax laws on standing in order to simplify access to law for classically marginalized legal actors, consciously allocating ius-generative force to new subjects, across a range of socio-economic variations,[142] and increas-ing the number of social agents assuming formative relevance for law. In fact, courts have intentionally utilized litigation to open the perimeters of the legal system, to intensify lines of articulation between government and its social environment, and to link the legal system more conclusively to its addressees (its constituents), especially those in marginal social locations. In consequence, in polities of this kind, public interest cases are able to give rise to many new rights, allocated to newly personified legal interests, such that public litigation over rights, actively encouraged by the judiciary, creates new founding norms, and it alters the basic constitutional struc-ture of society. In such cases, international law is widely used to support the creation of new rights.

The *locus classicus* for such promotion of public interest litigation as a source of new rights can be found in the case law of the superior courts in India (see Sathe 2001: 71–2, 2002: 17, 202). In such rulings, the Indian Supreme Court has linked its jurisprudence very directly to interna-tional human rights law, and, on this foundation, it has greatly expanded

---

[140] Supreme Court Ruling No. 51-V08-13/2008.

[141] Supreme Court Ruling No. 77-V07-10/2007.

[142] The cases discussed below occurred in common-law settings, and they saw a liberalization of standing rules partly because this permitted a shift away from English metropolitan law, towards a more decidedly post-colonial constitution. English laws on standing were tra-ditionally very restrictive, as expressed in the following: 'a private person could only bring an action to restrain a threatened breach of the law if his claim was based on an allegation that the threatened breach would constitute an infringement of his private rights or would inflict special damage on him'. *Gouriet* v. *Union of Post Office Workers and others* – [1977] 3 All ER 70.

provisions for constitutional rights.[143] At the core of this approach is a constructive reading of Article 32 of the Constitution, through which the principle was established that constitutional rights can give rise to broad interests, and that persons other than immediately aggrieved parties can file suit to claim such rights.

In leading public interest cases, first, the Indian Supreme Court emphasized the importance of access to law for all persons in society. It expressly identified widened standing as a means for reconfiguring the constitutional domain of public law, and, in particular, for establishing Indian public law on free-standing foundations, separate from the legal legacy of colonialism. The implications of such cases are illustrated most notably by the Supreme Court case, *S.P. Gupta* v. *President of India and ors* (1981). In this case, the Court rejected classically restrictive rules on standing derived from English law, and it concluded that, in human rights cases, the courts had a duty to help 'to democratise judicial remedies'. Accordingly, the Court pledged to 'promote public interest litigation so that the large masses of people belonging to the deprived and exploited sections of humanity may be able to realise and enjoy the socio-economic rights granted to them'.[144] In a series of subsequent cases, the Supreme Court amplified these principles, and judges made grants of standing, in which the Supreme Court assumed authority to hear cases concerning human rights violations as a result of notification by concerned, yet otherwise unaffected, individuals.[145] In later public interest cases, standing was granted on the basis of 'bare interest', and it was presumed that a simple concern for the preservation of human rights could provide grounds to warrant standing.[146]

In such instances, the Indian Supreme Court created new categories of legal/political subject, and it widened the peripheries of the political system to allow these new subjects to impact on legislation. In so doing, the Supreme Court also created new sets of rights. In particular, it established

---

[143] The basic structure doctrine, asserting the absolute entrenchment of certain elements of the constitution, provided the original premise for the subsequent rise of public interest litigation. This doctrine was worked out through reference to international human rights law. See arguments in *His Holiness Kesavananda Bharati Sripadagalvaru and Ors.* v. *State of Kerala and Anr.* (1973) 4 SCC 225). Here it was reasoned that 'this Court must interpret language of the Constitution, if not intractable, which is after all a municipal law, in the light of the United Nations Charter and the solemn declaration subscribed to by India'.

[144] *S.P. Gupta* v. *President of India and ors.* (1982 (2) SCR 365) (Bhagwati J).

[145] See *Bandhua Mukti Morcha* v. *Union of India* (1984) 3 SCC 161 (Bhagwati J). See excellent commentary on these points in Susman (1994: 57–9).

[146] *Chairman, Railway Board* v. *Chandrima Das* (2000) 2 SCC 465.

protective rights against class-based discrimination, rights against gender discrimination and rights against harassment.[147] It also established positive rights to legal services,[148] the right to a healthy environment,[149] the right to eat,[150] and the right to medical treatment.[151] In parallel to this, further, the Court began to devise expansive remedies to address the matters covered in public interest cases, often providing, through the innovation of continuing mandamus, for ongoing monitoring of the implementation of its rulings.[152] In this respect, the Court effectively supplanted normal legislative functions.[153] Notably, many new rights created by the Court were extracted from international law. The right to food was based on international law,[154] as were rights against sexual discrimination.[155] More generally, the Court adopted the principle that the UDHR should be read into domestic law,[156] and it has at times constructively interpreted constitutional clauses to give effect to international norms (Sathe 2002: 135).

Following these Indian examples, similar principles have been spelled out in cases in other jurisdictions, especially in countries influenced by Indian law, where courts have used public interest cases to promote a distinctive post-colonial jurisprudence. One primary example of this is Tanzania, where public interest litigation over social rights is widespread and often programmatically endorsed.[157] In Ghana, whose judicial

[147] See *Vishaka and others* v. *State of Rajasthan and others* (1997) 6 SCC 241, AIR 1997 SC; *Madhu Kishwar and others* v. *The State of Bihar and others* (AIR 1996 5 SCC 125).

[148] *Hussainara Khatoon* v. *State of Bihar*, AIR 1979 SC 1377.

[149] *Rural Litigation and Entitlement Kendra Dehradun and ors.* v. *State of Uttar Pradesh*, 985 SCR (3) 169.

[150] *PUCL* v. *Union of India and Ors*, Writ Petition (civil) 196/2001.

[151] *Paschim Banga Khet Mazdoor Samity & Ors* v. *State of West Bengal & Anor.* (1996) 4 SCC 37.

[152] See above p. 251.

[153] Strikingly, one analysis explains that the reinforcement of the Court was caused by the weakening of the legislative and executive branches, owing to corruption scandals (Mate 2015: 216–17).

[154] See the ruling of the Supreme Court in *Chameli Singh and Ors.* v. *State of U.P. and Anr.* [1996] 2 SCC 549 referring to Article 11 of the International Covenant on Economic, Social and Cultural Rights, 1966. The Court declared that the State parties recognize 'the right to everyone to an adequate standard of living for himself and for his family including food, clothing, housing and to the continuous improvement of living conditions'.

[155] *Vishaka and others* v. *State of Rajasthan and others* (1997) 6 SCC 241.

[156] *Chairman, Railway Board* v. *Chandrima Das* (2000) 2 SCC 465.

[157] See the Tanzanian case *Christopher Mtikila* v. *Attorney General*, Civ. Case. No, 5 of 1993 (High Court, Dodoma, 1993). Here the argument runs as follows:

> The relevance of public interest litigation in Tanzania cannot be over-emphasized. Having regard to our socio-economic conditions, this development

system is relatively closed to international influence, public interest litigation has played an important role in expanding the range of given constitutional rights. In a line of Ghanaian case law from the 1990s, it is recognized that the 1992 Constitution grants relatively wide standing to plaintiffs acting on public interest grounds.[158] In one notable public interest case, it was decided that 'every Ghanaian, natural artificial, had *locus standi* to initiate an action in the Supreme Court to enforce any provision of the Constitution'. This case proved a breakthrough for recognition of social rights, rights to personal dignity and rights at the place of work.[159] Famous public interest cases in South Africa have had very wide-ranging implications for the protection of social rights, both in South Africa and beyond.[160] Most notably, strategic litigation for health rights in *Treatment Action Campaign (2002)*, which created rights of access to HIV retrovirals, led to a situation in which a collective litigator (an NGO) was integrated into policy-making procedures.[161]

In Colombia, public interest litigation has also been promoted as a legal practice in which new rights are established. Collective litigation in

---

promises more hope to our people than any other strategy currently in place. First of all, illiteracy is still rampant ... Secondly, Tanzanians are massively poor. Our ranking in the world on the basis of per capita income has persistently been the source of embarrassment. Public interest litigation is a sophisticated mechanism which requires professional handling. By reason of limited resources the vast majority of our people cannot afford to engage lawyers even where they were aware of the infringement of their rights and the perversion of the Constitution. Other factors could be listed but perhaps the most painful of all is that over the years since independence Tanzanians have developed a culture of apathy and silence. This, in large measure, is a product of institutionalized mono-party politics which in its repressive dimension, like detention without trial, supped up initiative and guts.

My thanks are due to Elizabeth O'Loughlin for drawing my attention to this case.

[158] *New Patriotic Party* v. *Attorney General* [1997–98] 1 GLR 378.

[159] *Adjei-Ampofo (No 1)* v. *Accra Metropolitan Assembly & Attorney General* (No 1) [2007–2008] SCGLR. This reasoning ultimately, in *Adjei-Ampofo (No 2)* v. *Accra Metropolitan Assembly & Attorney General* (No 2) [2007–2008] SCGLR, allowed the plaintiff to defend rights of night soil carriers (excrement transporters from latrines) to work under dignified conditions.

[160] See especially *Minister of Health* v. *Treatment Action Campaign (TAC)* (2002) 5 SA 721 (CC).

[161] This process resulted in a policy document on Aids and sexual illnesses. See for comment on the policy implications of this case Heywood (2009).

Colombia has formed a core constitutional strategy for securing rights, especially historically unconsolidated rights, such as environmental rights and health care rights.[162] Justifications for such rights have usually been strongly backed by international law. As mentioned, the principle is pervasive in Colombian constitutional law that the list of rights formally enumerated in the constitution is not exhaustive, and both the Constitutional Court and the *Consejo de Estado* can develop new rights, reacting to legal claims through interpretation and adaption of existing provisions.[163] As a result, public interest cases act as a testing ground for the assertion of new rights and new collective subjectivities, and courts hearing such cases are able to assess whether the interests articulated in hearings warrant formal legal protection through more solidly guaranteed constitutional rights. Indicatively, in one leading case, the Constitutional Court ruled that collective interests actually only become concrete through the course of a legal hearing, and procedures relating to public interest cases make it possible for potential rights and potential collective legal personalities to appear before the law, and, if acknowledged, to assume legally elaborated form.[164] The actual process of public litigation thus forms a procedure in which the law experiences an intensified opening to constitutional claims, and new modes of agency and newly articulated collective concerns assume potential constitutional force.

In certain respects, the use of public interest litigation, combined with the overlapping use of *tutelas*, has led, across Colombian society, to the formation of a legal order that promotes participatory legal/political engagement in distinct spheres of social exchange. Indeed, it has stimulated rising legal/political activism in domains such as health care, service provision and environmental protection, which were historically not eminent objects of political will formation. Over a longer period, such litigation helped to establish, within the broad scope of the classical order of the constitution, a set of subsidiary or *sectoral* constitutional rights, focused on distinct societal domains: that is, a set of rights close in standing to a health constitution; a set of rights close to an environmental constitution, and even a set of rights close to a constitution of indigeneity. As discussed, the right to health was not originally established in the Constitution, and the right to a healthy environment was not classified as fundamental. However, it was established in the courts that these rights could be asserted through

---

[162] See analysis in Coral-Díaz, Londoño-Toro, Muñoz-Ávila (2010).
[163] C-1062/00.
[164] C-251/99.

public interest litigation, and they were constructed as fundamental rights because of their connection to other guaranteed rights – i.e. the right to life, the right to health and the right to physical integrity.[165] Analogously, the *Rio Bogota* public interest case has played perhaps the greatest role in solidifying hard environmental rights across Colombian society, instituting (and insisting on finance for) an integrated and coordinated system for decontaminating and managing water supplies around Bogotá.[166] In subsequent constitutional Court cases, nature itself, and even natural entities such as rivers, have also been accorded separate rights.[167] In each respect, litigation fleshed out a series of secondary, partial constitutions within the overarching normative system of national public law. In this respect, Colombian law is again emblematic of wider tendencies in global public law, and its emphasis on collective litigation stimulates segmented, legally constructed patterns of citizenship, through which new sets of rights are created.

Across this range of examples, generally, it is clear that public interest litigation can be used not only to give legal articulation to the will of the people, but also, in different ways in different settings, deeply to shape the legal architecture of democratic life.

5.3.3.5   Public Interest Litigation and New Constitutional Subjects

In public interest litigation, quite generally, democratic practice is condensed into a legal process, in which a number of subjects play legally formative roles. In such litigation, self-evidently, litigants and their advocates assume a leading position in the creation of new legal norms and new constitutional laws. This is particularly the case because broad laws on standing and the relatively informal consultative procedures typical of public interest cases encourage an expansionary construction of given constitutional rights,[168] and they generate opportunities in which litigants can articulate new interpretations of existing constitutional norms. This is also the case because public interest cases are often focused on rights that are still ill-defined, not restricted to single social domains, and exercise of

---

[165] T-1527/00. This case was supported by the ombudsman.

[166] Consejo de Estado, 25000-23-27-000-2001-90479-01. Note that in Colombia lack of resources cannot excuse a public body for not fulfilling the terms of a ruling in a public-interest case. See Consejo de Estado 18001-23-31-000-2011-00256-01 AP (2015).

[167] See T-080/15; T-622/16.

[168] Close to this view see the account of public interest litigation as a source of 'destabilization rights' in Sabel and Simon (2004: 1020).

which is not the province of simply defined subjects. For these reasons, public interest cases do not only translate interests into law – they allow such interests constructively to articulate themselves, and they even allow new legal rights and new legal subjects slowly to assume effective shape. Additionally, in public interest litigation, members of the judiciary acquire a share in the process of constitutional construction, as the relaxation of rules of procedure enables judges to play a more proactive fact-finding role in hearing cases, simplifying communication between the legal system and its addressees and establishing new openings for cognitive norm construction (see Tobias 1989: 281).[169]

In both respects, public-interest litigation provides a forum in which political agency is both procedurally reconstructed and activated in precise form, proportioned to a clear legislative objective – the creation of new rights. Indeed, public interest litigation is at times capable of enacting a more integrally national mode of democratic agency than is possible in more classical, delegatory expressions of democratic mobilization: in open-ended processes of litigation, multiple actors, not historically classified as possessing distinct legal personality, assume inclusion in primary law-making acts, and they act to define the deep constitutional fabric of society. Not coincidentally, one key development in public interest litigation is that it often acts as a mechanism in which exchanges usually determined as belonging to private law are transferred into the domain of constitutional law, and it concretizes rights with a wider scope and with wider reach than is typical of either classical public law litigation or classical constitutional processes.[170] As a result, public interest litigation is able to constitutionalize new spheres of society, and it deepens the societal penetration of laws with strictly constitutional character. In one leading case in Colombia, it was specifically claimed that public interest litigation serves to 'overcome the traditional division between public law and private

---

[169] See the following comment about public interest litigation (here, PIL) in India:

> PIL cases must be based on constitutional claims and can be brought only against the government, not private parties. Unlike traditional litigation, PIL has looser procedural requirements, particularly in regard to legal standing. Furthermore, in a PIL case there is no trial; the governmental respondents are expected to cooperate with the petitioners, rather than act as opponents; objective third parties, such as amici curiae and expert committees, are often involved in the litigation; and the Court plays a particularly active role in directing the proceedings and monitoring the implementation of its orders (Sood 2006: 4).

[170] See for example the Indian cases above at pp. 479–80. In some cases, as discussed, public interest litigation has also been used to secure new rights regarding environmental protection, rights of recognition for sexual minorities and welfare rights.

law', altering the parameters of productive activities and market practices, and moving beyond the classical construction of human rights as a 'closed system' of public law norms.[171]

Especially notable in the rising importance of public interest litigation is the fact that it dramatically expands the range of social groups that constitute themselves as recognized political subjects. Indeed, it is an essential aspect of public interest cases that the law creates a normative environment in which new subjects, often minorities with limited political recognition, can acquire momentary legal/constitutional personality, as their interests are concretized through legal proceedings and reflected as relevant for society as a whole. In such cases, subjects claim to represent rights of collective reach and scope, and they differ markedly from persons assuming legal rights that are already clearly defined: collective actors in fact often acquire and enhance their legal personality *through the procedural act of claiming new rights*, and their emergence visibly expands law's sensitivity to new legal claims.

This was clear enough in the leading earlier public interest cases in the USA, in which minority groups secured heightened legal status and personality through strategic litigation. In other settings, distinctive political subjects have been able to coalesce, often momentarily, around litigation over sexual and reproductive rights. Important examples of this are found in India, in which groups with unifying interests owing to sexuality or position in the system of social stratification have been able to acquire collective legal force.[172] In South Africa and Latin America, health care users have been formed as distinct political subjects, often through of use of elements of international law.[173] Even in legal systems, such as that of the UK, that place questions of standing firmly in the discretion of the courts, there has been a relaxation of attitudes to the personality of applicants, especially in cases regarding environmental litigation.[174] For each reason, claims to rights in public interest cases are formative of new political subjects, and human rights distil a vocabulary around which, within the law, new, pluralistic subjectivities are able to crystallize. Often, this creates a pattern of *sectoral subjectivization*, in which subjects are constructed in relation to distinct spheres of social exchange and to particular rights. Indeed, such

---

[171] Constitutional Court, C-377/02.
[172] See above p. 480.
[173] See examples above at p. 481.
[174] See discussion of the UK above at p. 467.

subjects often have no reality prior to their claim to rights, and they are formed through inner-legal procedures.

In many contexts, in sum, litigation has assumed a legally and constitutionally formative role far beyond its classical compass as a process framed by the already acknowledged norms of a constitution or a given democratic order. Across different societies and different legal traditions, litigation has now internalized a powerful democratic force, and it shapes the constitutional order of national societies in a number of different ways. The constitutional power of litigation illustrates the rising autonomy of the global legal system as a source of primary norms, and it usually assumes secondary constituent force because it elaborates and amplifies norms already stored, at a primary level, in the system of global law. In particular, the growing importance of rights-based litigation reflects a situation in which, through its relative differentiation, the law has institutionalized multiple channels between the political system and its addressees, so that the law now permits a *multi-centric, parallel proceduralization of democratic activity*. The fact that some communication between the political system and the citizen loops through the system of global law, granting high protection for certain rights, creates new configurations in the basic form of the citizen. Indeed, the fact that law is produced autonomously within the law, and that the law does not rely for its authority on an immediate homology with a single existing *people*, means that the law can construct, and form articulations with, the people in procedurally diverse fashion. This allows members of society to appear as citizens in multiple fashion, in multiple subjectivities, often of a contingent nature. The growing differentiation of the law as a realm of political practice has created new, pluralistic patterns of political agency, and it has enabled multiple democratic actors to emerge, beneath or alongside more homogeneous national political subjects. In some cases, the exercise of political agency through inner-legal actions often guarantees more refined representation to complex, multi-focal societies than is possible in democracies centred on political institutions as organs of societal mediation. On each count, the rising differentiation of the legal system means that society's responsiveness to political claims is not diminished. In fact, owing to the differentiation of the law and the inner-legal fabrication of new political subjects, society's capacity for phrasing political demands is transferred onto a more partial, acentric foundation, permitting multiple actors to promote the politicization of societal phenomena, to link sectoral concerns to the political domain, and so to shape the construction of legislation.

5.3.4 Citizens as Litigants 4: Human Rights and Segmentary Citizenship

The increasing importance of the political role of the litigant implies, at an immediate level, that political agency becomes centred around the form of *the segmentary citizen*. That is to say, as politically formative litigation usually focuses on global human rights, and global human rights usually refer to quite specific positive values or protective concerns in society, the growing force of litigation tends to fragment society into segments of citizenship, in which the exercise of citizenship is oriented towards the realization of rights located in a distinct functional domains.

This tendency towards segmentary citizenship is clearly evident in the fact, as discussed, that, in many societies, patterns of collective legal personality are beginning to emerge, which are focused on the contestation of particular, functionally specific rights. This means, for example, that groups such as indigenous communities, other minorities, collectives affected by environmental problems, health care users, displaced persons and homeless persons, have acquired consolidated legal personalities in recent years. In the exercise of such personality, these groups have been able to harden rights, through litigation, within different spheres of society, or for different spheres of human interest. Indeed, in some societies, it is now possible to speak of a process of parallel constitutionalization, in which different rights have been cemented in different social spheres, and the construction of these rights has acquired dimensions not prescribed by a formal overarching constitution.[175] To this degree, the differentiation of the legal system as a site of citizenship has promoted processes of segmentary norm production and segmentary constitutionalization, in which citizens tend to detach their claims from the structure of society as a whole and construct them around functionally segmented experiences. Indeed, in some respects, this process generates transnational communities of segmentary citizens, as persons in different territories are connected by shared exposure to legal questions pertaining, for example, to health care, to the environment and to medicine. Increasingly, these persons are bound together across national frontiers by similar legal frameworks and even by similar jurisprudence regarding segmentary concerns.[176]

---

[175] This phenomenon was identified in the FRG in the 1970s in Scholz (1978: 219). For a more evolved example, see the discussion of Colombia above at p. 482.

[176] For example, we can see a global community of health-care users, engaged in similar patterns of litigation, using global health norms in similar ways. Displaced persons also form

At the same time, the growth of segmentary citizenship through litigation does not mean, exclusively, that the impact of citizenship practices remains restricted to discrete functional spheres. On the contrary, the functionally focused exercise of citizenship rights can also be seen as enhancing the quality of national democracy in its entirety, and even as creating conditions for the development of democracy *tout court*. Indeed, in key respects, litigation over fractional or domain-specific rights has a transfer effect in the general dimension of society, and it establishes a system of inclusion that promotes democracy in more universal terms. The rise of litigation might be seen, thus, as establishing a pattern of democratic agency in which the political emphasis on particular claims both consolidates functionally specific rights, and, by extended impact, solidifies the strength of democracy as a whole.

The general democracy-building role of litigation is seen, first, in the systemic dimension of democracy: that is, in the infrastructural capacity of democratic institutions. As discussed, for example, it is widely observable that litigation concerning specific rights serves to extend the penetration of democratic institutions into society, and it heightens the immediacy between citizens in society and the political system more widely. In some cases, such as Russia and Colombia, this occurs because litigation quite generally underscores the national penetration of democratic institutions, and weakens the effect of local or extra-systemic authority. In some cases, this occurs because litigation over a distinct set of rights forces national government to intensify its hold on society. The key example of this is civil rights litigation in the USA in the 1950s and 1960s. However, litigation over prison rights in the USA, in Colombia and in Brazil has had similar consequences.[177] In such cases, the exercise of citizenship rights in focused litigation has clearly had a spill-over effect, and it has helped to stabilize the foundations of democracy more widely. In each case, the inner-legal construction of the citizen has acquired functions not limited to law, and it has hardened the fabric of democracy more widely. As discussed, in such cases, litigation has usually been shaped by the reception of international law.

The general democracy-building role of litigation is seen, second, in the normative dimension of democracy: that is, in the extent to which legal norms promote wider democratic practice. For example, sectoral

a global community. Even internet users may constitute a global community, whose legal order is likely to be formed, primarily, through litigation.

[177] As discussed, *tutelas* regarding prison conditions in Colombia led to the declaration of prison conditions as demonstrating an 'unconstitutional state of affairs', demanding the blanket imposition of human rights norms.

litigation over gender rights has far-reaching normative implications for national society as a whole, increasing social mobility access to educational resources, and widening professional opportunities for half of the population. Gender rights litigation might be seen as a process that eradicates obstacles to democratic participation, and which is normatively formative of democratic institutionalization as a whole. Similarly, litigation concerning minority or migrant rights promotes social, geographical and educational mobility, and it enhances access to processes of political inclusion.[178] Litigation over information rights can be seen to have similar outcomes, as it enhances discursive opportunities and cognitive qualifications for political engagement. Litigation over resources can also be seen as having similar results. Indeed, in many cases, litigation over resources, especially health care resources, is deeply interlinked with the quality of democracy as a whole, as effective exercise of citizenship rights clearly presupposes, or it is at least enhanced by, certain general health entitlements. In each respect, the singularity of rights claims plays a core role in creating qualifications for citizenship at a general societal level.

In these respects, the political significance of litigation resides in the fact that it can distil highly localized claims into a general political medium: that is, into rights, often linked to global norms. Litigation can construct patterns of agency that articulate the political system with single actors or small distinct groups of actors for whom more comprehensive multi-issue communication with the political system, for instance through political parties or broad social movements, would be difficult to establish. In some ways, litigation allows the citizen to appear to the political system in a functionally disaggregated form, it relieves the citizen of the need to assert a broad set of interests in entering political exchanges, and it gives voice to claims specific to distinct sectoral domains. As a result, where the citizen appears as litigant, the political system becomes sensibilized to different aspects of its multi-centric environment. Indeed, the very fact that the focus of courts is narrower than that of legislatures means that litigation is able to pick up societal contents that evade legislatures.[179] In some

---

[178] In important example is case 0260/2014 heard by the Bolivian Constitutional Court, in which a law fixing a minimum size for policemen was found to discriminate against indigenous people, so creating enhanced professional opportunities for a large number of population groups. Note the impact of litigation in UK regarding professional exclusion on grounds of sexual orientation. This is discussed above at p. 267.

[179] See the classical analysis in Friedman (1975: 233). Nothing, therefore, seems more inaccurate than the radical claim that rights embody a 'one-size-fits-all emancipatory practice' (Kennedy 2004: 13).

respects, this simply results in the distinctive constitutionalization of different social spheres. At the same time, however, litigation re-articulates a more comprehensive construct of the citizen at the general level of national democracy, providing a basis for broader processes of inclusion.

It is sometimes argued, for various reasons, that litigation, especially for resources, is unreliable in achieving collectively beneficial goals. Indeed, some observers claim that it is inherent in the individualized remedies imposed by courts that they do not gain broad effect.[180] Others even argue that such remedies disproportionately benefit wealthier social agents, who are able to avail themselves effectively of expertise required for litigation procedures.[181] This claim is of course, also, widely refuted.[182]

Even if such critique has some validity, however, it slightly misses the point about the sociological or systemic function of litigation. The political outcomes of litigation are not solely defined by single remedies and their efficacy. Such outcomes are defined, more widely, by the fact that litigation configures, and adds new rights to, constructions of political citizenship, and it builds up, from everyday activities and requirements, a complex evolving profile of the claims and expectations that can be attached to citizenship. In particular, litigation is able to align legal claims to international norms, and it is able to graft new rights onto given legal expectations on this basis. Moreover, in changing the rights profile of persons in society, litigation is able to generate new legal subjects, and to bring into visibility legal persons that had historically not been recognized. As discussed, this process is at the core of the formation of national societies. Litigation thus creates models of citizenship that step beyond the limits of the aggregated rights defined and conferred by national bodies, to identify new legal/political subjects, and to trace out new potentials for broader legal-political mobilization and recognition. Outcomes of litigation need to be perceived, not only in terms of particular remedies, but in the fact that litigation projects leading norms for society as a whole. As a result, litigation intersects with, and often pre-defines, other patterns of agency, such as protest, lobbying, and policy promotion, to create multifocal experiences of citizenship.[183] Crucially, litigation often reinforces

---

[180] The classic objection to the claim that litigation solidifies citizenship is that litigation outcomes do not easily extend beyond single cases, and they cannot acquire the broad effect or the broad legitimacy of legislative packages (see Stoddard 1997: 991).

[181] For this claim in different contexts see Dugard and Roux (2006: 119); Landau (2012: 201, 229–30); Gotlieb, Yavich and Báscolo (2016: 7–8).

[182] See discussion of the expansion of rights through litigation in Gauri and Brinks (2008: 303); Uprimny and Durán (2014: 42).

[183] See excellent analysis of this in Barkan (1979: 955).

other patterns of agency, establishing initial and anticipatory recognition for rights that subsequently undergo political expansion.[184] In this respect, too, the growing autonomy of the global legal system constructs new patterns of citizenship in national societies, and it creates opportunities for complex, sectoral democracies and for complex articulations between the political system and society. In most settings, it is only as the citizen enters the political system through two parallel communication loops, one based in common patterns of political representation, and one based in litigation attached to global norms, that the citizen acquires a form that is fully adequate to societal reality.

5.4 Democracy and Legal Mobilization

In the large body of research on democracy, only relatively few publications examine the role of legal mobilization in the development and consolidation of democracy. Generally, outlooks in this body of research suggest that the willingness of social agents to engage in litigation, especially regarding human rights, acts both to elevate public trust in democratic institutions, and to increase the collective legitimacy enjoyed by these institutions. In other words, in this body of research, legal engagement through litigation is perceived as a core reflection of democratic confidence, which stands alongside political engagement as a source of strong democratic culture.[185] Of course, this body of research has also come under fire from authors who believe the transformative force accorded to legal practices to be exaggerated, and who stress the privileging of elite actors in legal process (see Rosenberg 1991; Brown-Nagin 2005: 1439, 1489). It is also common amongst radical legal theorists to question the extent to which rights obtained through litigation reinforce democracy more broadly, and such theorists often prefer instead a more holistic register of social critique and action.[186] However, the arguments set out above emphatically concur with the analysis that accentuates politically transformative role of litigation. It is becoming clear that legal mobilization through law, expressed in different patterns of litigation, is a practice that has far-reaching implications for the

---

[184] For very prominent examples, see the discussion above of civil rights in the USA, and health rights in Colombia. Recently, Krajewska and Cahill-O'Callaghan (2018) have observed, at a micro-level, how litigation over reproductive and surrogacy rights in the UK has invoked the ECHR to instil new rights into constructions of citizenship, ultimately leading to legislation to mirror and reinforce the rights intimated through litigation.

[185] See discussion in Zemans (1983); Eskridge (2001: 454–8); Yeazell (2004: 1990); Siegel (2006: 1333); Simmons (2009: 139).

[186] See, prominently, Tushnet (1989); Kennedy (2002), (2004: 9–11).

development of democracy, and the preparedness of citizens to pursue litigation typically indicates both deepening democratic institutionalization and socially proportioned multiplication of democratic agency.

In general, legal mobilization *supplements* classical patterns of political organization, centred around legislatures, and, in so doing, it creates more complete, more deeply articulated democracies than those focused solely on conventional legislative functions. It is sometimes claimed that the assumption of a political role by litigants contradicts the majoritarian principles of democracy (Harlow 2002: Redish 2003: 74, 125). However, this stance depends on a mono-centric conception of society's political system, and it is not adapted to a societal order in which political communication, by necessity, occurs through multiple channels. First, democracies in which legal mobilization has a prominent role make it possible for persons to enter the legislative system through multiple channels and multiple personalities, which legislatures, on their own, struggle to permit and recognize. Legal mobilization thus adds dimensions of lateral and vertical porosity to the political system, and it creates new legislative mechanisms in the state. Second, as discussed, the reinforcement of sectoral or segmentary rights generally helps to solidify democracy as a whole. Segmentary rights asserted through litigation usually have a tendency to transcend their segmentary or fractional nature, and they usually help to reinforce democracy more widely. In each respect, legal mobilization reflects the emergence of a new pattern of democracy, in which social claims are transmitted through separate openings into the political system.

In some instances, further, legal mobilization actually *stands in for* democratic agency, and it assumes a primary role in the process of creating legislation, both constitutional and statutory. In many of the cases discussed above, litigation forms a procedural order in which different legal collectives emerge as political subjects, directly expanding the rights fabric of society, outside their more regular position within institutionalized political-democratic procedures. Such legal collectives then engage in classical political acts, usually through litigation over rights. In some cases discussed above, the subjectivization of persons as litigants makes it possible for society as a whole to construct new reserves of political agency, proportioned to its factual pluralistic structure. Often, the system of political representation is articulated with society more comprehensively where political subjects are constructed, pluralistically, through reference to rights claims, via inner-legal procedures, than when they rely solely on more conventional patterns of political categorization and mobilization. The fact that democratic agency is relocated from a position *outside* to a position *inside* the legal system thus provides, in some cases, for the emergence of patterns of political agency that more fully reflect the complex modes of subjectivity that actually exist in different societies. Paradoxically, the fact that the national citizen enters the political system through global law means that, in some ways, political order becomes more democratically representative than simple patterns of national will formation.

5.5   The Beginnings of Global Citizenship

Despite the transformation of democracy through the emergence and increasing autonomy of the global legal system, the above analyses of modified patterns of democratic agency do not imply that we are witnessing the formation of political subjects of a conclusively transnational nature. Global law clearly shapes new expressions of political agency, which often cut through the boundaries of national political orders, creating rights of transnational nature. However, the recognition of transnational subjects and the rights that they may create or exercise is, in the final analysis, still determined by national jurisdictions. In other words, although the practice of citizenship has an increasingly global nature, the effective exercise of citizenship still depends, to a large degree, on the conferral of political rights by nation states, whose institutions can, ultimately choose the subjects to which they accord rights of inclusion. New patterns of citizenship may arise from the integration of global law in national law, but states still act as the primary filters for this process. Nonetheless, in the above processes, certain emergent patterns of transnational citizenship can be observed: that is, we can see aspects of citizenship, in which legal practices generate rights and shape laws beyond the strict limits of nationally constructed legal orders. We can identify the beginnings of a domain of citizenship that stands independently of the acts of states, and this domain is formed, primarily, *through litigation* – through acts not of political engagement, but of legal articulation.

Such developments can be seen, first, in interactions between different international courts. As discussed, for example, the IACtHR has openly defined itself as the interpreter and producer of a corpus of international human rights law, which freely borrows from other courts, both national and international, in order to create rights for individual persons subject to its jurisdiction (see Neuman 2008: 109–110).[187] Human rights litigation

---

[187] The Court has reiterated that 'human rights form a single, indivisible, interrelated and interdependent corpus iuris', of which the Court as one interpreter: IACtHR, Juridical Condition and Rights of the Undocumented Migrants, Mexico, Advisory Opinion, Advisory Opinion OC-18/03, 17 September 2003.

before other courts contributes directly to the construction of rights in the IACtHR, and it applies rights originating outside its own regional jurisdiction. More specifically, distinctive human rights norms often migrate across global and regional jurisdictions in cases in which courts are confronted with new subjects and new claims, especially where these are of a transnational nature. To illuminate this, recent rulings in the African Court on Human and Peoples' Rights have, albeit without extensive citation, established both cultural and collective property rights for indigenous peoples very similar to those guaranteed in the IACtHR.[188] Litigation for particular rights in Latin America has thus, indirectly, generated similar rights in Africa.

Such developments can be seen, second, in legal communities marked by high levels of interaction between different courts. As discussed, legal cases in regionally influential courts generate norms that acquire higher-order status in other states, especially when these states are confronted with similar problems. As discussed, we can see examples in which litigation in Colombia has created rights in Chile, and litigation in India or South Africa has created rights in Kenya.

Third, such developments can be seen in the fact that human rights law is increasingly endowed with extra-territorial force. For example, Canadian citizens and German citizens are bound by domestic human rights law when acting outside their own societies.[189] Moreover, until recently, courts in the USA often heard alien tort cases against public officials and private actors responsible for human rights violations outside their national territory.[190] In the Pinochet cases, UK courts also asserted extra-territorial jurisdiction for crimes against humanity.[191] In these instances, the bonds between national citizenship and global citizenship have been strengthened, and, in acts of litigation, both persons and collective actors have been able to transport the political practices of citizenship to a global level.

To a lesser degree, fourth, such developments have also become manifest in the emergence of transnational sectoral communities. Increasingly, for example, persons engaged in transnational scientific practices create rights and regulatory frameworks in their specific domain, and it is possible

---

[188] See discussion at p.412 above.
[189] *Canada (Justice)* v. *Khadr* 2008 SCC 28; Verwaltungsgericht Köln, 3 K 5625/14 (27 May 2015).
[190] See the leading alien tort case concerning company liability for human rights violations, *Doe* v. *Unocal*, 395 F.3d 932 (9th Cir. 2002).
[191] See p. 265 above.

to see an aggregate of practices close in quality to transnational scientific citizenship. Similarly, persons engaged in transnational sporting activities create and presuppose normative structures which reach outside and across national boundaries.[192] Internet users may also, in some respects, be viewed as a transnational community, with growing capacity for establishing a functionally specific normative order. In such cases, it is important not to overstate the solidity of transnational legal protection. Notably, rights that are commonly subject to transnational violation, such as intellectual property rights, are not easily protected outside the country where the right is held.[193] However, to the extent that it exists, the basic order of a transnational functional domain results, at least in part, from litigation, and litigation is a core practice of transnational citizenship in this context. For example, transnational sporting regulation is likely to be driven by litigation about players' transfers, mobility, corruption, use of performance enhancers, reputation, etc.[194] The community of internet users is also, demonstrably, inclined to construct its normative order through litigation regarding defamation, intellectual property, censorship and promotion of violence.[195]

Overall, it is still fanciful to imagine global citizenship as a condition that involves the exercise of a fully evolved set of political rights. However, as litigants, citizens are able to extend some conventional powers of citizenship into the global domain, and they are able to create and define rights and legislation without state-conferred entitlements. As agents in the system of world law, therefore, citizens are able to gain entry to national political systems other than their own, and they are able to shape legislation both across and beyond national boundaries.

5.6   Conclusion

The contemporary political system is marked by multiple articulations with the societal actors in its environment, and it channels social claims into law through a series of different openings. It is now simply illusory

---

[192] This argument is the property of Gunther Teubner. See discussion above at pp. 198–201.

[193] See *Starbucks (HK) Ltd* v. *British Sky Broadcasting Group Plc* [2015] UKSC 31.

[194] The ECJ ruling in *Union Royale Belge des Sociétés de Football Association ASBL* v. *Jean-Marc Bosman* (1995) C-415/93 had a deep impact on the sub-constitution of football. Currently, three Russian cyclists have taken legal action against the World Anti-Doping Agency (WADA) and Canadian doping investigator because of their exclusion from participation in the Olympic Games in Brazil. This has the potential significantly to alter core practices in sporting regulation.

[195] See the Australian High Court ruling in *Dow Jones & Company Inc* v. *Gutnick* [2002] HCA 56), addressing questions of global defamation.

to envision the political system as a volitionally constructed set of institutions for producing legislation. In the contemporary political system, to be sure, the citizen gains reality through regular processes of national political representation, which play a key role in creating legislation. But the citizen also gains reality through segmented or sectoral lines of communication, linked to demands for globally established rights, which also generate legislation. The citizen appears to the political system as a member of a national society, communicating through classical political procedures. However, the citizen also appears as a holder of global rights, and, in the second capacity, political exchanges between the citizen and the political system often bypass classical legislative processes, and they generate norms by linking the national political system directly to the global legal system. As discussed, national democratic political systems were not founded in solely national constructions of citizenship; they presupposed global additions to construct national citizenship. Once established, national democracies only partially structure their political systems around national citizenship, and they now conduct many processes of legislation and rights construction by articulating themselves with the differentiated system of global rights, through the global citizen, and by producing legislation through reactions to communications articulated around these rights. In key respects, it is the citizen as a construct of global law that underpins the legitimational and legislative functions of modern democracy, and this citizen is defined specifically by the fact that it is not identical with national citizens.

This transformation of the citizen into a global legal construct has implications for the political substance of democracy. In particular, it means that the primary political norms of the political system are not set by volitional political acts. As discussed, however, this does not erode the basic political substance of society. Within the normative order of global law, national political systems generate pluralistic patterns of political agency and citizenship, often achieving more socially proportioned patterns of political inclusion and engagement than under systems defined by highly politicized constructs of national citizenship. This is expressed in new modes of political participation, and even in new modes of political subjectivization, usually linked to inner-legal interactions between national and global human rights law. To capture this, we need a multi-focal construct of politics, adapted to the reality of a political system that generates society's laws through multiple articulations with social actors.

Conclusion

It is central to the idea of democracy that it is associated with the self-legislative acts of a group of national citizens. Moreover, it is central to the idea of democracy that it forms a political system in which members of a national society exercise their collective faculties to establish laws that guarantee a condition of generally maximized freedom. On this basis, democracy is viewed as a political system in which members of society progressively form a public order which is rationally acceptable for all, or in which all members of society at least find some subjective grounds for recognizing the laws that are applied to them as objectively reasonable. As discussed, democracy is widely seen both as the result of a process of nationalization, and as the result of a process of rationalization, through both of which processes members of society construct the political system as a focus of general obligations. In each respect, further, the normative core of democracy resides in the figure of the participatory citizen, such that citizens authorize democratic law by actively engaging in its formation.

This book argues, however, that there is no obvious rational foundation for democracy. Democracy was not typically brought into life by self-legislative collective subjects, and it often evolved on highly contingent, contradictory premises, which had little to do with collective demands for autonomy or freedom. Even more importantly, democracy was not created through the national construction of society, or by the formation of a national body of citizens. In fact, the converse was commonly the case. Almost without exception, national societies, or national groups of citizens, did not create democracies. In many cases, national societies created partial, selective or incomplete democracies, in which, typically, leading social groups obstructed the admission of other social groups to the full exercise of citizenship rights. Generally, it was only when societies stopped constructing their citizens in terms based solely on national law that they began effectively to establish democracy as a system of equal inclusion. Widely, it was only as global norms, typically linked to international human rights law, entered national political systems that these systems began to approach their domestic constituencies as aggregates of democratically entitled, legally equal citizens. Democracy became a real material form in national societies as national political institutions integrated their populations through normative constructions extracted from global models of citizenship, based on concepts of international human rights law that became widespread after 1945. Prior to this, virtually all national societies contained embedded constituencies that obstructed the societal generalization of citizenship practices, and prevented the growth of democratically mandated political institutions. The classical concept of the national citizen, based on the expectation of general freedoms, normally resulted in the creation of very particularistic political systems. For this reason, the idea of the participatory citizen had to be renounced, or at least substantially revised, before democracy could be created as an inclusive legal/political order.

As a result of this, national democracy has typically evolved on a pattern in which the political system extracts its essential reserves of legitimacy from a construct of the citizen that does not factually exist – which is separated from the formative political locations of national society, and which is primarily defined outside national society, under international law. In the first emergence of proto-democratic political systems, organs of government acquired legitimacy by institutionalizing a legitimational cycle of communication with citizens within national societies, and, as this cycle became more expansive, societies became more nationalized and more democratic. However, it was only as the national political system began to correlate its legitimational exchanges with a construct of the citizen located not in national society, but in the global legal domain, that it finally obtained fully democratic legitimacy and finally included its population in equal, even, democratic fashion. Typically, the national political system became democratic as it institutionalized a cycle of communication with its citizens through the formal medium of global human rights law, so that the citizen appeared to the political system as a holder of globally defined rights. The establishment of democracy occurred, thus, through the effective differentiation of the global legal system, which, often quite contingently, created the conditions in national societies in which inclusive democratic institutions could be constructed and gain societal purchase. It is vital to democracy that it extracts legitimacy from a citizen that is constructed within the globally differentiated legal system, and which is not identical with real citizens in society: usually, it is only where it is separated from the citizens to which it is accountable that a political system becomes fully democratic. Consequently, the paradigmatic core of national democracy – the citizen – only became real as it merged with a global legal system. This involved the splitting of the citizen into two figures, one political and the other legal, which communicated with the political system through different lines of articulation. Today, democracy is not yet established at a global level, and we cannot identify, even in outline, a political system that stands above national societies. In some respects, however, every national democratic polity has global foundations, and some element of global law stands, constitutively, at the core of every democratic political order.

What is particularly striking in these processes is that through the rise of democracy, the principle that democracy is a political system focused on simple acts of legislation, mediated through an elected legislature, has become very questionable. Only very few national legislatures have been able to overcome structural opposition to complete the process of inner-societal democratization. In most cases, judicial institutions, closely aligned to global norm setters, have played a leading role in the construction of democracy, and in fact they have promoted the formation of national political institutions more widely. One reason for the dependence of national democracy on global law is that global law weakens the exclusive political monopoly of nationally constructed legislatures, populated by national citizens, and it places alternative sources of legitimacy alongside legislative bodies, allowing social actors to engage with the legislative process through new avenues. The role of legal institutions in creating democracy means, above all, that social actors can use legal patterns of norm construction to shape legislation, often through actions and exchanges quite specific to the legal system.

As discussed, the global structure of contemporary democracy has transformed our basic understandings of politics, as many classical political functions are now essentially internalized within the legal system. However, the fact that the legitimacy of the national political system is partly detached from real citizens does not mean that the cycles of political exchange around the political system have become less vital. On the contrary, by displacing its primary source of legitimacy into the global legal system, the national political system has, in many instances, become better equipped to integrate its addressees in forms and procedures that are adequate to the complexity of their factual societal locations. In fact, once legitimated by the global citizen, the political system is able to evolve multiple articulations with the persons (citizens) in its environment, and citizens are able to exercise political agency and shape the legislative outputs of the political system in many different ways. In many instances, this gives rise to new political subjects, often of a transnational character, as transnational human rights norms separate new subjects out from the uniform body of national populations. New patterns of political agency and political subjectivity, linked outwardly to the global normative system, have become commonplace in contemporary democracies, and the basic category of political-democratic practice has been expanded. The global-legal pre-construction of democracy does not only reinforce classical patterns of democracy; it engenders decentred models of democracy, in which legislation can be stimulated by multiple actors in society.

The core insights of legal sociology have particular value for interpreting the distinctive global form of contemporary democracy. As discussed, classical legal sociology understood democracy as a political system that evolves relatively independently of the citizens that it incorporates, and which cannot be seen as the expression of a collective political subject, endowed with faculties of rational volition. Legal sociology also accorded a core role to law itself, and to rights stored in the law, as media of integration formative of democracy. These founding insights in fact persisted into the core canon of more recent legal sociology. Notably, classical legal sociology viewed the growth of democracy as a process that occurs as the political system and the legal system extend their own societal penetration, such that persons are constructed as citizens as part of a process of autonomous institutional formation, adapted to relatively expansive, individualized, differentiated societies. Most crucially, leading outlooks in classical legal sociology intuited the fabric of contemporary democracy by observing democracy as a political system that cemented itself not by solidifying general freedoms, but by reacting to plural demands for freedom, and by contributing to their distinct local institutionalization. In each of these respects, in reacting against the rationalist philosophy of the Enlightenment, early legal sociology anticipated many basic characteristics and formative processes underlying contemporary democracy.

Contra the intuitions of classical legal sociology, however, the patterns of institutional formation that underpin democracy only finally approached reality as national political systems internalized an idea of the global citizen, and as they generated a legal construction of the national citizen through global human rights law. Early legal sociology viewed the construction of democracy as a process in which an institutional system was created that was capable of performing integrational functions for modern society, after the dissolution of the local patchwork form of early modern social orders. Most sociologists concluded, then, that democracy had to be held together by distinctively political patterns of rationality, expressed by the state, so that the state became the integrational fulcrum of society. In fact, democracy was constructed as the political system looped its exchanges through the global legal system, so that the primary addressee of the political system – the citizen – was partly formed in global law. Broadly, the institutional shift from the political system to the legal system, in which the political system becomes a secondary component of the legal system, is the most essential precondition of contemporary democracy.

Paradoxically, in consequence, although classical legal sociologists clearly perceived the contingent premises of democracy, they did not perceive the centrality of the legal system in creating democracy. As discussed, most classical legal sociologists intuited the autonomous role of law in establishing democracy, but all, at some point, renounced the *legal* dimension of sociology, and they opted instead for a strongly *political* focus, attaching democratic legitimacy and democratic stability to more classical political concepts of collective rationality and will formation. Classical legal sociologists almost invariably emerged as deeply political theorists of social formation. As a result, they partly effaced the greatest explanatory achievements of their own academic discipline.

Now, however, the reality of contemporary democracy invites us to think through the categories of classical legal sociology to understand democracy in terms which were closed to classical sociologists themselves – that is, to understand democracy, in a global sociological perspective, as a construction of the legal system, in which even core political subjects and practices are produced by law. If we accentuate the strictly legal implications of classical sociology, we acquire a much clearer framework for comprehending the global rise of democracy than if we adhere to its political principles: legal sociology comprehends democracy most accurately where it ceases to be political sociology and becomes, resolutely, legal sociology.

Some influential lines in political theory have expressed awareness of the deep linkage between the national citizen and the global citizen. As discussed, this insight is common among theorists associated with cosmopolitan outlooks. However, legal sociology, where it develops a global focus, is able to provide quite compelling, empirically reinforced insights into the overlayered relation between national and global citizenship. As a theory of democracy, legal sociology provides the basis for a refined realistic cosmopolitanism, which is able to perceive and reconstruct the essentially global foundations of national societies and their democratic institutions.

In this spirit, global legal sociology is likely to differ very sharply from more conventional cosmopolitan views. As a theory of democracy, first, global legal sociology is unlikely to show enthusiasm for the democratically expansive ideals of some cosmopolitan theorists, assuming the existence of highly evolved deliberative procedures or even state-like structures, close to a *world polity*, at the supranational level. In fact, global legal sociology may make very uncomforting observations about the decreasing centrality of real people in the final construction of democracy. As a theory of democracy, second, legal sociology is likely to reject the cosmopolitan claim that democratic institutions above nation states grow out of, and so extend, democratic structures established at a national level. The sociological approach outlined above implies that the contrary is the case – national democracies do not precede global citizenship norms. Overall, legal-sociological variants on cosmopolitanism are likely to emphasize the primary sociological intuition that democracy is constructed without a subject and that democracy results from contingent, fragile patterns of autonomous institutional formation and integration, which are now inextricably linked to the global arena.

Despite its natural caution about democracy, however, global legal sociology may move close to cosmopolitan thinking by indicating that democracy requires a condition in which the national citizen, normatively, is as close as possible to the global citizen, to the citizen of *world law*. Here again, to be sure, global legal sociology can only offer a very sceptical variant on cosmopolitan ideals. For the legal-sociological outlook, the proximity between national and global citizenship is required not to transfer given democratic practices to the global level, but to remedy weaknesses of democratic formation that are inherent in national polities. Nonetheless, a basic claim of cosmopolitan theory – namely, that national and global citizenship are not separable – is deeply corroborated by empirical legal-sociology inquiry, where it thinks in a global dimension. Most importantly, global legal sociology may concur with more conventional inquiry in suggesting that it is impossible to cut through the abstracted transnational norms that surround contemporary democracy, that there is no intensified political idyll behind the plural, filtered reality of global democracy, and that the price paid for any substantial move away from the global form of democracy is – in all probability – the price of democracy itself.

BIBLIOGRAPHY

Abebe, Allehone Mulugeta (2009), 'Legal and Institutional Dimensions of Protecting and Assisting Internally Displaced Persons in Africa'. *Journal of Refugee Studies* 22(2): 155–76.

Abendroth, Wolfgang (1967), *Antagonistische Gesellschaft und politische Demokratie: Aufsätze zur politischen Soziologie*. Neuwied: Luchterhand.

Achaintre, Christophe (2008), *L'instance legislative dans la pensée constitutionelle révolutionaire (1789–1799)*. Paris: Dalloz.

Ackerman, Bruce (1991), *We the People, I: Foundations*. Cambridge, MA: Harvard University Press.

——— (2007), 'The Living Constitution'. *Harvard Law Review* 120(7): 1737–812.

——— (2014), *We the People, III: The Civil Rights Revolution*. Cambridge, MA: Harvard University Press.

Adams, John (1979), 'Letter to James Sullivan, May 1776' in Robert J. Taylor (ed), *The Adams Papers, Papers of John Adams, vol. 4, February–August 1776*, Cambridge, MA: Harvard University Press, pp. 208–13.

Addison, Paul (1975), *The Road to 1945: British Politics and the Second World War*. London: Cape.

Adler, Max (1922), *Die Staatsauffassung des Marxismus: Ein Beitrag zur Unterscheidung von soziologischer und juristischer Methode*. Vienna: Verlag der Wiener Volksbuchhandlung.

——— (1926), *Politische und soziale Demokratie: Ein Beitrag zur sozialistichen Erziehung*. Berlin: Laub.

African Commission's Working Group of Experts on Indigenous Populations/ Communities (2005), *Report*. Copenhagen: Eks/Skolens Trykkeri.

African Group (2006), *Draft Aide Memoire on the United Nations Declaration on the Rights of Indigenous People*, New York, 9 November 2006, available at: www.ipacc.org.za/images/reports/human-rights/Africa_Group_Aide_ Memoire_2006.pdf.

Aguilera Peña, Mario (2014), *Contrapoder y justicia guerrillera, fragmentación política y orden insurgente en Colombia (1952–2003)*. Bogotá: IEPRI.

Ahlhaus, Svenja and Markus Patberg (2012), 'Von der verfassunggebenden zur konstituierenden Gewalt – Die demokratische Legitimität völkerrechtlicher Konstitutionalisierung' in Bardo Fassbender and Agelika Siehr (eds),

Suprastaatliche Konstitutionalisierung: Perspektiven auf die Legitimität, Kohärenz und Effektivität des Völkerrechts. Baden-Baden: Nomos, pp. 23–56.

Ajulu, Rok (2002), 'Politicised Ethnicity, Competitive Politics and Conflict in Kenya: A Historical Perspective'. *African Studies* 61(2): 251–68.

Albert, Mathias (2002), *Zur Politik der Weltgesellschaft: Identität und Recht im Kontext internationaler Vergesellschaftung*. Weilerszwist: Velbrück.

(2014), 'World State: Brunkhorst's "Cosmopolitan State" and Varieties of Differentiation'. *Social & Legal Studies* 23(4): 517–31.

Albertin, Lothar (1974), 'Faktoren eines Arrangements zwischen industriellem und politischem System in der Weimarer Republik' in Hans Mommsen et al. (eds), *Industrielles System und politische Entwicklung in der Weimarer Republik*. Düsseldorf: Droste, pp. 658–74.

Albrecht, Eduard (1837), 'Rezension über Maurenbrechers Grundsätze des heutigen deutschen Staatsrechts'. *Göttingische gelehrte Anzeigen* 150–2: 1489–503, 1508–515.

Alexander, Jeffrey C. (2006), *The Civil Sphere*. Oxford University Press.

Alexopoulos, Golfo (2003), *Stalin's Outcasts: Aliens, Citizens, and the Soviet State, 1926–1936*. Ithaca, NY: Cornell University Press.

Allen, Austin (2006), *Origins of the Dred Scott Case: Jacksonian Jurisprudence and the Supreme Court 1837–1857*. Athens: University of Georgia Press.

Almond, Gabriel A. (1991), 'Capitalism and Democracy'. *Political Science and Politics* 24(3): 467–74.

Almond, Gabriel A. and Sidney Verba (1989 [1963]), *The Civic Culture: Political Attitudes and Democracy in Five Nations*. Newbury Park, CA: Sage.

Althusius, Johannes (1614), *Politica*, third edition. Herborn: Corvinus.

Aminzade, Roland (1993), *Ballots and Barricades: Class Formation and Republican Parties in France, 1830–1871*. Princeton University Press.

Amrhein-Hofmann, Christine (2003), *Monismus und Dualismus in den Völkerrechtslehren*. Berlin: Duncker und Humblot.

Andenaes, Mads and Eirik Bjorge (2013), 'The Norwegian Court Applies the ECHR by Building upon its Underlying Principles'. *European Public Law* 19(2): 241–46.

Anderson, Carol (2003), *Eyes off the Prize: The United Nations and the African American Struggle for Human Rights, 1944–1955*. Cambridge University Press.

Anderson, Margaret Lavina (2000), *Practicing Democracy: Elections and Political Culture in Imperial Germany*. New York, NY: Princeton Unversity Press.

Anderson, Terry H. (1995), *The Movement and the Sixties: Protest in America from Greensboro to Wounded Knee*. Oxford University Press.

Anter, Andreas (1995), *Max Webers Theorie des modernen Staates: Herkunft, Struktur und Bedeutung*. Berlin: Duncker und Humblot.

Antkowiak, Thomas (2014), 'Rights, Resources, and Rhetoric: Indigenous Peoples and the Inter-American Court'. *University of Pennsylvania Journal of International Law* 35(1): 113–87.

Aranovskiy, Konstantin and Sergey Knyazev (2013), 'Sudba sudebnogo pretsedenta v romano-germanskom prave' [The Destiny of Judicial Precedent in Roman-Germanic Law]. *Zhurnal konstitutsionnogo Pravosudiya* 4(34): 30–9.

Arato, Andrew (2000), *Civil Society, Constitution, and Legitimacy*. Lanham/Oxford: Rowman and Littlefield.

Archibugi, Daniele (2008), *The Global Commonwealth of Citizens: Toward Cosmopolitan Democracy*. Princeton University Press.

Arendt, Hannah (1951), *The Origins of Totalitarianism*. London: André Deutsch.

(1958), *The Human Condition*. Chicago, IL: University of ChicagoPress.

Ariel, Yehoshua (1964), *Individualism and Nationalism in American Ideology*. Cambridge, MA: Harvard University Press.

Attard Bellido, María Elena (2014), *Sistematización de jurisprudencia y esquemas jurisprudenciales de pueblos indígenas en el marco del sistema plural de control de constitucionalidad*. La Paz: Konrad Adenauer Stiftung.

Auchterlonie, Mitzi (2007), *Conservative Suffragists: The Women's Vote and the Tory Party*. London: Tauris.

Aulehner, Josef (2011), *Grundrechte als Gesetzgebung*. Tübingen: Mohr.

Austin, John (1832), *The Province of Jurisprudence Determined*. London: Murray.

Backes, Uwe (2000), *Liberalismus und Demokratie – Antinomie und Synthese: Zum Wechselverhältnis zweier politischer Strömungen im Vormärz*. Düsseldorf: Drostre.

Bader, Veit (1995), 'Citizenship and Exclusion: Radical Democracy, Community and Justice. Or, What is Wrong with Communitarianism?' *Political Theory* 23(2): 211–46.

Balenciaga, Aitor Iraegui (2012), *La democracia en Bolivia*. Cochabamba: Plural.

Balibar, Étienne (2008), 'Historical Dilemmas of Democracy and their Contemporary Relevance for Citizenship'. *Rethinking Marxism* 20(4): 522–38.

(2011), *Citoyen sujet et autres essais d'anthropologie philosophique*. Paris: Presses universitaires de France.

Balkin, Jack M. (2009), 'Framework Originalism and the Living Constitution'. *Northwestern University Law Review* 103(2): 549–614.

Ball, Stuart (1988), *Baldwin and the Conservative Party: The Crisis of 1929–1931*. New Haven, CT: Yale University Press.

Bannon, Alicia L. (2007), 'Designing a Constitution-Drafting Process: Lessons from Kenya'. *The Yale Law Journal* 116(8): 1824–72.

Baranov, Vladimir (2002), 'O tenevom prave' [On the Shadow Law]. *Novaya Pravovaya Misl* 1: 13–20.

Barbalet, J.M. (1988), *Citizenship: Rights, Struggle and Class Inequality*. Milton Keynes: Open University Press.

Barber, Benjamin (1984), *Strong Democracy: Participatory Politics for a New Age*. Berkeley, CA: University of Califonia Press.

Barkan, Steven E. (1979), 'Political Trials and Resource Mobilization: Towards an Understanding of Social Movement Litigation'. *Social Forces* 58(3): 944–61.

Barkow, Rachel E. (2002), 'More Supreme than Court? The Fall of the Political Question Doctrine and the Rise of Judicial Supremacy'. *Columbia Law Review* 102(2): 237–336.

Barthélemy, Joseph (1904), *L'Introduction du regime parlementaire sous Louis XVIII et Charles X*. Paris: V. Giard & E. Brière.

Bartolini, Stefano (2000), *The Political Mobilization of the European Left 1860–1980*. Cambridge University Press.

Bassiouni, M. Cherif (1996), 'Accountability for International Crimes and Serious Violations of Fundamental Human Rights'. *Law and Contemporary Problems* 59(4): 63–74.

Bastid, Paul (1954), *Les Institutions politiques de la monarchie française (1814–1848)*. Paris: Sirey.

Bates, Robert H. (1987), 'The Agrarian Origins of Mau Mau: A Structural Account'. *Agricultural History* 61(1): 1–28.

   (1989), *Beyond the Miracle of the Market: The Political Economy of Agrarian Development in Kenya*. Cambridge University Press.

   (2008), *When Things Fall Apart: State Failure in Late-Century Africa*. Cambridge University Press.

Bauer, Otto (1980), 'Das Gleichgewicht der Klassenkräfte' in Otto Bauer, *Werkausgabe*, edited by Arbeitsgemeinschaft für die Geschichte der österreichischen Arbeiterbewegung. Vienna: Europaverlag, 9, pp. 55–71.

Bazoberry Chali, Oscar (2008), *Participación, poder popular y desarrollo: Charagua y Moxos*. La Paz: CIPCA.

Beaud, Olivier (1994), *La Puissance de l'état*. Paris: Presses universitaires de France.

Beck, Ulrich (1998), 'Wie wird Demokratie im Zeitalter der Globalisierung möglich?' in Ulrich Beck (ed), *Politik der Globalisierung*. Frankfurt: Suhrkamp, pp. 7–66.

Beetham, David (1993), 'Liberal Democracy and the Limits of Democratization' in David Held (ed), *Prospects for Democracy*. Cambridge: Polity, pp. 53–73.

   (1994), 'Conditions for Democratic Consolidation'. *Review of African Political Economy* 21: 157–72.

   (1999), *Democracy and Human Rights*. Cambridge: Polity Press.

Beissinger, Mark R. (2002), *Nationalist Mobilization and the Collapse of the Soviet State*. Cambridge University Press.

   (2005), 'Rethinking Empire in the Wake of Soviet Collapse' in Zoltan Barany and Robert G. Moser (eds), *Ethnic Politics after Communism*. Ithaca, NY: Cornell University Press, pp. 14–45.

Bejarano, Ana María (2011), *Democracias precarias: Trayectorias políticas divergentes en Colombia y Venezuela*. Bogota: Universidad de los Andes.

Bell, David A. (1994), *Lawyers and Citizens: The Making of a Political Elite in Old Regime France*. Oxford University Press.

Bellamy, Richard (2007), *Political Constitutionalism: A Republican Defence of the Constitutionality of Democracy*. Cambridge University Press.

(2011), 'Citizenship' in George Klosko (ed), *The Oxford Handbook of the History of Political Philosophy*. Oxford University Press, pp. 586–99.

Bendix, Reinhard (1996 [1964]), *Nation-Building and Citizenship: Studies of our Changing Social Order*, new and enlarged edition. New Brunswick: Transaction Press.

Benhabib, Seyla (1999), 'Citizens, Residents, and Aliens in a Changing World: Political Membership in the Global Era'. *Social Research* 66(3): 709–44.

(2000), *Transformations of Citizenship: Dilemmas of the Nation State in the Era of Globalization*. Assen: Koninklijke Van Gorcum BV.

(2004), *The Rights of Others: Aliens, Residents and Citizens*. Oxford University Press.

(2009), 'Claiming Rights across Borders: International Human Rights and Democratic Sovereignty'. *American Political Science Review* 103(4): 691–74.

(2012), 'Is There a Human Right to Democracy? Beyond Interventionism and Indifference' in Claudio Corradetti (ed), *Philosophical Dimensions of Human Rights: Some Contemporary Views*. Dordrecht: Springer, pp. 191–213.

Bentham, Jeremy (2002), *Rights, Representation, and Reform: Nonsense upon Stilts and Other Writings on the French Revolution*, edited by Philip Schofield, Catherine Pease-Watkin, and Cyprian Blamires. Oxford University Press.

Bentley, Michael (1999), *Politics without Democracy 1815–1914*. Oxford: Blackwell.

Benvenisti, Eyal and Alon Harel (2017), 'Embracing the Tension between National and International Human Rights Law: The Case for Discordant Parity'. *International Journal of Constitutional Law* 15(1): 36–59.

Berman, Bruce J. (1991), 'Nationalism, Ethnicity and Modernity: The Paradox of Mau Mau'. *Canadian Journal of African Studies* 25(2): 181–206.

(2010), *Ethnicity and Democracy*, JICA-RI Working Paper, JICA Research Institute, 22, available at: www.jica.go.jp/jica-ri/publication/workingpaper/ ethnicity_and_democracy_in_africa.html.

Berman, Bruce J., Jill Cottrell and Yash Ghai (2009), 'Patrons, Clients, and Constitutions: Ethnic Politics and Political Reform in Kenya'. *Canadian Journal of African Studies* 43(3): 462–506.

Berman, Bruce J. and John Lonsdale (1992), *Unhappy Valley: Conflict in Kenya and Africa*. Oxford: Curry.

Bermbach, Udo (1967), *Vorformen parlamentarischer Kabinettsbildung in Deutschland: Der interfraktionelle Ausschuß 1917/18 und die Parlamentarisierung der Reichsregierung*. Cologne: Westdeutscher Verlag.

Bernstein, Eduard (1899), *Die Voraussetzungen des Sozialismus und die Aufgaben der Sozialdemokratie*. Stuttgart: Dietz.

Berry, Mary Frances (1977), *Military Necessity and Civil Rights Policy: Black Citizenship and the Constitution, 1861–1868*. Port Washington, NY: Kennikat Press.

Berton, Henry (1900), *L'Évolution constitutionelle du Second Empire*. Paris: Alcan.

Best, Heinrich (1990), *Die Männer von Bildung und Besitz: Struktur und Handlung parlamentarischer Führungsgruppen in Deutschland und Frankreich 1848/49*. Düsseldorf: Droste.

Biagini, Eugenio F. (1992), *Liberty, Retrenchment and Reform: Popular Liberalism in the Age of Gladstone 1860–1880*. Cambridge University Press.

Bickart, Roger (1932), *Les Parlements et la notion de la souveraineté nationale au XVIIIe siècle*. Paris: Félix Alcan.

Bickel, Alexander M. (1973), 'Citizenship in the American Constitution'. *Arizona Law Review* 15: 369–87.

Billaud-Varenne, Jacques Nicolas (1794), *Rapport fait a la convention sur la théorie du gouvernmement démocratique*. Paris: Imprimerie du tribunal révolutionnaire.

Birch, A.H. (1964), *Representative and Responsible Government: An Essay on the British Constitution*. London: Allen & Unwin.

Blackbourn, David and Geoff Eley (1984), *The Peculiarities of German History: Bourgeois Society and Politics in nineteenth-century Germany*. Oxford University Press.

Blackstone, Willam (1765), *Commentaries on the Laws of England*. Oxford: Clarendon.

Blewett, Neal (1965), 'The Franchise in the United Kingdom 1885–1918'. *Past & Present* 32: 27–56.

(1972), *The Peers, the Parties and the People: The General Elections of 1910*. Basingstoke: Macmillan.

Blomberry, Victoria (2008), 'Refounding the Nation: A Generation of Activism in Bolivia'. *American Behavioural Scientist* 51(12): 1790–800.

Blum, Carol (1986), *Rousseau and the Republic of Virtue: The Language of Politics in the French Revolution*. Ithaca, NY: Cornell University Press.

Boberach, Heinz (1959), *Wahlrechtsfragen im Vormärz: Die Wahlrechtsanschauung im Rheinland 1815–1849 und die Entstehung des Dreiklassenwahlrechts*. Düsseldorf: Droste.

Böckenförde, Ernst-Wolfgang (1958), *Gesetz und gesetgebende Gewalt: Von Anfängen der deutschen Staatsrechtslehre bis zur Höhe des staatsrechtlichen Positivismus*. Berlin: Duncker und Humblot.

(1990), 'Grundrechte als Grundsatznormen: Zur gegenwärtigen Grundrechtsdogmatik'. *Der Staat* 29(1): 1–31.

(1991), *Staat, Verfassung, Demokratie: Studien zur Verfassungstheorie und zum Verfassungsstaat*. Frankfurt am Main: Suhrkamp.

Boehm, Christopher (2001), *Hierarchy in the Forest: The Evolution of Egalitarian Behavior*. Cambridge, MA: Harvard University Press.

Bogomolov, Alexander (2003), 'Ukaz prezidenta – bolshoy podarok' [The Presidential Decree is a Great Gift] *Izvestia*, 23 March 2003, available at: https://iz.ru/news/274524.

Bojosi, Kealeboga N. and George Mukundi Wachira (2006), 'Protecting Indigenous Peoples in Africa: An Analysis of the Approach of the African Commission on Human and Peoples' Rights'. *African Human Rights Law Journal* 6: 382–406.

Boli, John (1989), *New Citizens for a New Society: The Institutional Origins of Mass Schooling in Sweden*. Oxford: Pergamon.

Boli, John, Francisco O. Ramirez and John W. Meyer (1985), 'Explaining the Origins and Expansion of Mass Education'. *Comparative Education Review* 29(2): 145–70.

Boli, John and George M. Thomas (1997), 'World Culture in the World Polity: A Century of International Non-Governmental Organization'. *American Sociological Review* 62(2): 171–90.

Bollmeyer, Heiko (2007), *Der steinige Weg zur Demokratie. Die Weimarer Nationalversammlung zwischen Kaiserreich und Republik*. Frankfurt am Main: Campus.

de Bonald, Louis Gabriel Ambroise (1843 [1796]), *Théorie du pouvoir politique et religieux dans la société civile*, 3 vols. Paris: Adrien le Clere, vol. I.

   (1847 [1802]), *Législation primitive, considerée dans les derniers temps par les seules Lumières de la raison*. Paris: Andrien le Clerc.

Bonini, Francesco (2004), *Storia della pubblica amminstrazione*. Florene: Le Monnier.

Borrero Restrepo, Gloria María (ed) (2008), *Balance de los 10 años de las acciones populares y de grupo*. Bogotá: Corporación Excelencia en la Justicia.

Borstelmann, Thomas (2009), *The Cold War and the Color Line: American Race Relations in the Global Arena*. Cambridge, MA: Harvard University Press.

Bosniak, Linda (2000), 'Citizenship Denationalized'. *Indiana Journal of Global Legal Studies* 7(2): 447–509.

Bouglé, Célestin (1896), 'Sociologie et démocratie'. *Revue de métaphysique et de morale* 4(1): 118–28.

   (1910), 'Proudhon sociologue'. *Revue de métaphysique et de Morale* 18(5): 614–48.

Bourricaud, François (1977), *L'Individualisme institutionnel: Essai sur la sociologie de Talcott Parsons*. Paris: Presses universitaires de France.

Bradburn, Douglas (2009), *The Citizenship Revolution: Politics and the Creation of the American Union 1774–1804*. Charlottesville, VA: University of Virginia Press.

Bradley, Mark Philip (2016), *The World Reimagined: Americans and Human Rights in the Twentieth Century*. Cambridge University Press.

Branch, Daniel (2007), 'The Enemy Within: Loyalists and the War against Mau Mau'. *The Journal of African History* 48(2): 291–315.

Brandwein, Pamela (2011), *Rethinking the Judicial Settlement of Reconstruction*. Cambridge University Press.

Brauer, Carl M. (1977), *John F. Kennedy and the Second Reconstruction*. New York, NY: Columbia University Press.

Breuer, Stefan (1991), *Max Webers Herrschaftssoziologie*. New York, NY: Campus.

(1994), *Bürokratie und Charisma: Zur politischen Soziologie Max Webers*. Darmstadt: Wissenschaftliche Buchgesellschaft.

Brockmöller, Annette (1997), *Die Entstehung der Rechtstheorie im 19: Jahrhundert in Deutschland*. Baden-Baden: Nomos.

Brown-Nagin, Tomiko (2005), 'Elites, Social Movements and the Law: The Case of Affirmative Action'. *Columbia Law Review* 105(5): 1436–528.

Brubaker, Rogers (1992), *Citizenship and Nationhood in France and Germany*. Cambridge, MA: Harvard University Press.

(1994), 'Nationhood and the National Question in the Soviet Union and post-Soviet Russia: An Institutionalist Account'. *Theory and Society* 2: 47–78.

(1996), *Nationalism Reframed: Nationhood and the National Question in the New Europe*. Cambridge University Press.

Brudner, Alan (1985), 'The Domestic Enforcement of International Covenants on Human Rights: A Theoretical Framework'. *The University of Toronto Law Journal* 35(3): 219–54.

Brunkhorst, Hauke (1994), *Demokratie und Differenz: Vom klassischen zum modernen Begriff des Politischen*. Frankfurt: Fischer.

(1998), 'Demokratischer Experimentalismus' in Hauke Brunkhorst (ed), *Demokratischer Experimentalismus: Politik in der komplexen Gesellschaft*. Frankfurt: Suhrkamp, pp. 7–12.

(2002), *Solidarität: Von der Bürgerfreundschaft zur globalen Rechtsgenossenschaft*. Frankfurt: Suhrkamp.

(2007), 'Die Legitionationskrise der Weltgesellschaft: Global Rule of Law, Global Constitutionalism und Weltstaatlichkeit' in Mathias Albert and Rudolf Stichweh (eds), *Weltstaat und Weltstaatlichkeit: Beobachtungen globaler politischer Strukturbildung*. Wiesbaden: Verlag für Sozialwissenschaften.

(2010), 'Düstere Aussichten – Die Zukunft der Demokratie in der Weltgesellschaft: Sieben Thesen'. *Kritische Justiz* 43(1): 13–21.

(2012), *Legitimationskrisen: Verfassungsprobleme der Weltgesellschaft*. Baden-Baden: Nomos.

(2014), *Critical Theory of Legal Revolutions: Evolutionary Perspectives*. London: Bloomsbury.

(2017), 'Sociological Constitutionalism – An Evolutionary Approach' in Paul Blokker and Chris Thornhill (eds), *Sociological Constitutionalism*. Cambridge University Press, pp. 95–131.

Brunnée, Jutta and Stephen J. Toope (2000), 'International Law and Constructivism: Elements of an Interactional Theory of International Law'. *Columbia Journal of Transnational Law* 39: 19–74.

Brunner, Otto (1942), *Land und Herrschaft: Grundfragen der territorialen Verfassungsgeschichte Südostdeutschlands im Mittelalter*, second edition. Brünn: Rohrer.

Bryce, James (1923), *Modern Democracies*, 2 vols. London: Macmillan, Vol. II.

Brydon, Lynne (1996), 'Women Chiefs and Power in the Volta Region of Ghana'. *Journal of Legal Pluralism & Unofficial Law*, 37/38: 227–47.

Buonarroti, Philippe (1957), *Conspiration pour l'égalité dite de Babeuf*. Paris: Éditions sociales.

Burbank, Jane (2003), 'An Imperial Rights Regime: Law and Citizenship in the Russian Empire'. *Kritika: Explorations in Russian and Eurasian History* 7(3) (2003); 397–431; 422–4.

Burk, Robert Fredrick (1984), *The Eisenhower Administration and Black Civil Rights*. Knoxville, TN: University of Tennessee Press.

Burke, Edmund (1854), *The Works of the Right Honourable Edmund Burke*. 6 vols. London: Henry G. Bohn, Vol. I.

(1910 [1790]), *Reflections on the Revolution in France*. London: Dent.

Burke, Roland (2010), *Decolonization and the Evolution of International Human Rights*. Philadelphia, PA: University of Pennsylvania Press.

Burkov, Anton (2010), *Konventsiya o zashchite prav cheloveka v sudakh Rossii [Convention for Protection of Human Rights in Russian Courts]*. Moscow: Wolters Kluwer.

(2017), 'V borbe za pravo obnyat muzha, otsa, syna' [Fighting for the Right to Hug a Husband, a Father, a Son] in M. A. Mityukov, S. V. Kabyshev, V. K. Bobrova and A. V. Sychyeva (eds), *Kak polozhit chinovnika na lopatki, ili strategicheskiye tyazhby: opyt raboty amerikanskikh i rossiyskikh sutyazhnikov po obshchestvenno znachimym delam [How to Put an Officer on the Blades, or Strategic Litigation: The Experience of American and Russian Litigants in Public Interest Cases]*. Moscow: NP, pp. 73–86.

Bury, J.P.T. (1973), *Gambetta and the Making of the Third Republic*. London: Longman.

Cajas Sarria, Mario Alberto (2015a), *La historia de la Corte Suprema de Justicia de Colombia, 1886–1991, I: De la Regeneración al régimen militar, 1886–1958* (Bogota: Ediciones Uniandes).

(2015b), *La historia de la Corte Suprema de Justicia de Colombia, 1886–1991, I: Del Frente Nacional a la Asamblea Constituyente, 1958–1991* (Bogota: Ediciones Uniandes).

Calabresi, Steven and Stephanie Dotson Zimdahl (2005), 'The Supreme Court and Foreign Sources of Law: Two Hundred Years of Practice and the Juvenile Death Penalty Decision'. *William and Mary Law Review* 47(3): 743–909; 763–71.

Calliess, Christian (2016, 'Die Rolle des Grundgesetzes und des Bundesverfassungsgerichts' in Katrin Böttger and Mathias Jopp (eds), *Handbuch zur deutschen Europapolitik*. Baden-Baden 2016, pp. 149–170.

Calvin, Jean (1939 [1536]), *Institution de la religion chrestienne, in Oeuvres completes,* in 4 vols. Paris: Societé de belles lettres, IV.

Canovan, Margaret (1996), *Nationhood and Political Theory.* Cheltenham: Elgar.

Cappelli, Ottorino (2008), 'Pre-Modern State Building in Post-Soviet Russia'. *Journal of Communist Studies and Transition Poutics* 24(4): 531–72.

Caramani, Daniele (1996), 'The Nationalization of Electoral Politics: A Conceptual Reconstruction and Review of the Literature'. *West European Politics* 19(2): 205–24.

(2003), 'The End of Silent Elections: The Birth of Electoral Competition, 1832–1915'. *Party Politics* 9(4): 411–43.

(2004), *The Nationalization of Politics: The Formation of National Electorates.* Cambridge: Cambridge University Press.

(2005), 'The Formation of National Party Systems in Europe: A Comparative-Historical Analysis'. *Scandinavian Political Studies* 28(4): 295–322.

Carré de Malberg, Raymond (1920–22), *Contribution à la théorie générale de l'État, in 2 vols.* Paris: Sirey, Vol. II.

Carter, April (2001), *The Political Theory of Global Citizenship.* London: Routledge.

Casper, Jonathan D. (1972), *Lawyers befor the Warren Court: Civil Liberties and Civil Rights, 1957–66.* Chicago University Press.

Cassese, Antonio (1979), 'Political Self-Determination – Old Concepts and New Developments' in Antonio Cassese (ed), *UN Law and Fundamental Rights: Two Topics in International Law.* Alphen aan den Rijn: Sijthoof & Noordhoff, pp. 175–95.

(1995), *Self-Determination of Peoples: A Legal Reappraisal.* Cambridge University Press.

Cerna, Christina M. (1995), 'Universal Democracy: An International Legal Right or the Pipe Dream of the West? *NYU Journal of International Law and Politics* 27: 289–329.

Chandler, Andrea (2014), 'Citizenship, Social Rights and Judicial Review in Regime Transition: The Case of Russia'. *Democratization* 21(4): 743–66.

Chaube, Shibanikinkar (2000), *Constituent Assembly of India: Springboard of Revolution,* second edition. New Delhi: Manohar Publishers.

Chayes, Abram (1976), 'The Role of the Judge in Public Law Litigation'. *Harvard Law Review* 89(7): 1281–316.

Chebankova, Elena A. (2010), *Russia's Federal Relations: Putin's Reforms and Management of the Regions.* London: Routledge.

Chesterman, Simon (2004). *You, The People: The United Nations, Transitional Administration, and State-Building.* Oxford University Press.

Chin, Gabriel J. (1996), 'The Civil Rights Revolution Comes to Immigration Law: A New Look at the Immigration and Nationality Act of 1965'. *North Carolina Law Review* 75: 273–345.

Chute, Marchette (1969), *The First Liberty: A History of the Right to Vote in America 1619–1850.* New York, NY: Dutton.

Cichowski, Rachel A. and Alex Stone Sweet (2003), 'Participation, Representative Democracy, and the Courts' in Bruce E. Cain, Russell J. Dalton and Susan E. Scarrow (eds), *Democracy Transformed? Expanding Political Opportunities in Advanced Democracies*. Oxford University Press, pp. 192–220.

Close, David H. (1977), 'The Collapse of Resistance to Democracy: Conservatives, Adult Suffrage, and Second Chamber Reform, 1911–1928'. *The Historical Journal* 20(4): 893–918.

Cohen, Andrew (1959), *British Policy in Changing Africa*. London: Routledge and Kegan Paul.

Cohen, Jean L. (1999), 'Changing Paradigms of Citizenship and the Exclusiveness of the Demos'. *International Sociology* 14(3): 245–68.

Cohen, Jean L. (2008), 'Rethinking Human Rights, Democracy, and Sovereignty in the Age of Globalization'. *Political Theory* 36(4): 578–606.

  (2012), *Globalization and Sovereignty: Rethinking Legality, Legitimacy and Constitutionalism*. Cambridge University Press.

Cohen, Roberta (2004), 'The Guiding Principles on Internal Displacement: An Innovation in International Standard Setting'. *Global Governance* 10: 459–80.

Cohen, Harlan Grant (2006), 'Supremacy and Diplomacy: The International Law of the U.S. Supreme Court'. *Berkeley International Law Journal* 24(1): 273–329.

Coke, Edward (1797 [1628–44]), *Institutes of the Laws of England*, in 4 parts. London: Brooke, part. 4.

Collier, Ruth Berins (1999), *Paths Toward Democracy: The Working Class and Elites in Western Europe and South America*. Cambridge University Press.

Colliot-Thélène, Catherine (2010a), 'Durkheim: Une Sociologie d'État'. *Durkheimian Studies* 16: 77–93.

  (2010b), *La Démocratie sans »Demos«*. Paris: Presses universitaires de France.

Colón-Ríos, Joel (2010), 'The Legitimacy of the Juridical: Constituent Power, Democracy, and the Limits of Constitutional Reform'. *Osgoode Hall Law Journal* 48: 199–245.

Comte, Auguste (1975), *Physique sociale: Cours de philosophie positive, leçons 46 à 60*. Paris: Hermann.

Conaghan, Catherine M. and James M. Malloy (1994), *Democracy and Neoliberalism in the Central Andes*. Pittsburgh, PA: University of Pittsburgh Press.

Conde Calderón, Jorge (2009), *Buscando la Nación: Ciudadanía, clase y tension social en el Caribe colombiano, 1821–1855*. Medelin: La Carreta.

Condorcet, Nicolas de (1797), *Esquise d'un tableau historique des progress de l'esprit humain*, third edition. Paris: Agasse.

  (1847), 'La nation française à tous les peuples' in Nicolas de Condorcet (ed), *Oeuvres in 12 vols*. Paris: Firmin Didot frères, XII, pp. 507–27.

  (1994 [1791]), *Cinque Mémoires sur l'instruction publique*. Paris: Flammarion.

Congar, Yves M.-J. (1958), 'Quod omnes tangit, ab omnibus tractari et approbari debet'. *Revue historique de droit française et étranger* 35: 210–59.

Constant, Benjamin (1997 [1819]), 'De la liberté des anciens comparée à celle des modernes' in Benjamin Constant *Écrits politiques*. Paris: Gallimard, pp. 589–619.

Constitutional Commission of the Conference of Minister Presidents of the Western Occupation Zones (1948), *Bericht über den Verfassungskonvent auf Herrenchiemsee vom 10. Bis 23. August*. Munich: Richard Pflaum.

Coral-Díaz, Ana Milena, Beatriz Londoño-Toro and Lina Marcela Muñoz-Ávila (2010), 'El concepto de litigio estratégico en América Latina: 1990–2010'. *Vniversitas* 121: 49–75.

Costa, Alexandre Araújo and Juliano Zaiden Benvindo (2014), *A Quem Interessa o Controle Concentrado de Constitucionalidade? O Descompasso entre Teoria e Prática na Defesa dos Direitos Fundamentais*, Working Paper available at: www.ufjf.br/siddharta_legale/files/2014/07/Alexandra-Costa-e-Juliano-Zaiden-a-quem-interessa-o-controle.pdf.

Cotterrell, Roger (1977), 'Durkheim on Legal Development and Social Solidarity'. *British Journal of Law and Society* 4(2): 241–52.

(2008), 'Transnational Communities and the Concept of Law'. *Ratio Juris* 21(1): 1–18.

Cover, Robert (1982), 'The Origins of Judicial Activism in the Protection of Minorities'. *The Yale Law Journal* 91(7): 1287–316.

Craig, Paul (1983), *Administrative Law*. London: Sweet and Maxwell.

(1990), *Public Law and Democracy in the United Kingdom and the United States of America*. Oxford: Clarendon.

(1998), 'Ultra Vires and the Foundations of Judicial Review'. *Cambridge Law Journal* 57(1): 63–90.

Crawford, James (1994), 'Democracy and International Law'. *British Yearbook of International Law* 64(1): 113–33.

Crawhall, Nigel (2001), 'Africa and the UN Declaration on the Rights of Indigenous Peoples'. *The International Journal of Human Rights* 15(1): 11–36.

Crouch, Colin (2004), *Post-Democracy*. Cambridge: Polity.

Cummings, Scott L. (2008), 'The Internationalization of Public Interest Law'. *Duke Law Journal* 57(4): 891–1036.

Cummings, Scott L. and Louise G. Trubeck (2008), 'Globalizing Public Interest Law'. *UCLA Journal of International Law and Foreign Affairs* 13: 1–53.

Currie, Robert (1979), *Industrial Politics*. Oxford: Clarendon.

Dahl, Robert (1989), *Democracy and its Critics*. New Haven, CT: Yale University Press.

(1998), *On Democracy*. New Haven, CT: Yale University Press.

Dahrendorf, Ralf (1965), *Gesellschaft und Demokratie in Deutschland*. Munich: Piper.

Daintith, Terence and Alan Page (1999), *The Executive in the Constitution: Structure, Autonomy and Internal Control*. Cambridge University Press.

Dávila Ladrón de Guevara, Andres (1999), 'Clientelismo, intermediación y representación politica en Colombia: que ha pasado en los noventa?' *Estudios Politicos* (15): 61–78.

Defensoría del pueblo (2015), *La tutela y los derechos a la salud y a la seguridad social*. Bogota: Defensoría del Pueblo de Colombia.

De Grand, Alexander J. (1978), *The Italian Fascist Association and the Rise of Fascism in Italy*. Lincoln, NE: University of Nebraska Press.

Delanty, Gerard (2000), *Citizenship in a Global Age: Society, Culture, Politics*. Buckingham: Open University Press.

De Maistre, Joseph (1847 [1797]), *Considérations sur la France*. Lyon: J.B. Pélagand.

Deng, Francis M. (2009), 'Frontiers of Sovereignty: A Framework of Protection, Assistance and Development for the Internally Displaced'. *Leiden Journal of International Law* 8(2): 249–86.

Deslandres, Maurice (1937), *Histoire constitutionelle de la France: L'Avènement de la Troisième République: La Constitution de 1875*. Paris: Colin.

Dezalay, Yves and Bryant Garth (2002), *Internationalization of Palace Wars: Lawyers, Economists and the Contest to Transform Latin American States*. Chicago, IL: University of Chicago Press.

Dhavan, Rajeev (1994), 'Law as Struggle: Public Interest Law in India'. *Journal of the Indian Law Institute* 36(3): 302–38.

Diamond, Larry (1999), *Developing Democracy: Toward Consolidation*. Baltimore, MD: Johns Hopkins Press.

Dicey, Albert Venn (1915 [1885]), *Introduction to the Study of the Law of the Law of the Constitution*, eighth edition. London: Macmillan.

(1962 [1905]). *Lectures on the Relation between Law and Public Opinion in England during the nineteenth Century*. London: Macmillan.

Dickson, Brice (2013), *Human Rights and the United Kingdom Supreme Court*. Oxford University Press.

Donnelly, Jack (1999), 'Human Rights, Democracy and Development'. *Human Rights Quarterly* 21(3): 608–32.

Douzinas, Costas (2007), *Human Rights and Empire: The Political Philosophy of Cosmopolitanism*. Abingdon: Routledge-Cavendish.

Downing, Brian (1988), 'Constitutionalism, Warfare, and Political Change in Early Modern Europe'. *Theory and Society* 17: 7–56.

(1992), *The Military Revolution and Political Change: Origins of Democracy and Autocracy in Early Modern Europe*. Princeton University Press.

Droysen, Johann Gustav (1846), *Vorlesungen über die Freiheitskriege*, in 2 vols. Kiel: Universitäts-Buchhandlung, volume II.

Dryzek, John S. (2006), *Deliberative Global Politics: Discourse and Democracy in a Divided World*. Cambridge: Polity.

Duclos, Pierre (1932), *La notion de constitution dans l'oeuvre de l'assemblee constituante de 1789*. Paris: Dalloz.

Dudden, Faye E. (2011), *Fighting Chance: The Struggle over Women Suffrage and Black Suffrage in Reconstruction America*. Oxford Universirty Press.

Dudziak, Mary L. (1988), 'Desegregation as a Cold War Imperative'. *Stanford Law Review* 41(1): 61–120.

Dugard, Jackie and Theunis Roux (2006), 'The Record of the South African Constitutional Court in Providing an Institutional Voice for the Poor 1995–2004' in Roberto Gargarella, Pilar Domingo and Theunis Roux (eds), *Courts and Social Transformation in New Democracies: An Institutional Voice for the Poor?* Aldershot: Ashgate, pp. 35–59.

Duguit, Léon (1889), 'Le Droit constitutionnel et la sociologie'. *Revue internationale de l'enseignement* 18: 484–505.

(1923a), *Manuel de Droit constitutionenel*. Paris: Boccard.

(1923b), *Traité de droit constitutionnel*, second edition, in 5 vols. Paris: Boccard, II.

Dulitzky, Ariel E. (2015), 'An Inter-American Constitutional Court? The Invention of the Conventionality Control by the Inter-American Court of Human Rights'. *Texas International Law Journal* 50(1): 45–93.

Durkheim, Émile (1890), 'Les principes de 1789 et la sociologie'. *Revue International de l'enseignement* 19: 450–56.

(1898), 'L'individualisme et les intellectuels'. *Revue Bleue* 4(10): 7–13.

(1902), *De la division du travail social*, second edition. Paris: Alcan.

(1918), 'Le «Contrat Social» de Rousseau'. *Revue de métaphysique et de morale* 25(2): 129–61.

(1928), *Le Socialisme*. Paris: Presses universitaires de France, 1928.

(1930 [1897]), *Le Suicide: Étude de sociologie*. Paris: Presses universitaires de France.

(1950), *Leçons de sociologie*. Paris: Presses universitaires de France.

(1953), *Montesquieu et Rousseau: Précurseurs de la sociologie*, introduced by Georges Davy. Paris: M. Rivière.

Durkheim, Émile and Paul Fauconnet (1903), 'Sociologie et sciences sociales'. *Revue Philosophique de la France et d l'Étranger* 55: 465–97.

Easter, Gerald M. (1996), 'Personal Networks and Postrevolutionary State Building: Soviet Russia Reexamined'. *World Politics* 48(4): 551–78.

(2008), 'The Russian State in the Time of Putin'. *Post-Soviet Affairs* 24(3): 199–230.

Echeverria, Durand (1985), *The Maupeou Revolution: A Study in the History of Libertarianism*. Baton Rouge, LA: Louisiana State University Press.

Eckstein, K. (2004), 'Priznaniye obshchikh printsipov prava: Doktrina pravovogo gosudarstva' [Recognition of General Principles of Law: The Doctrine of the Rule of Law State] in Todd Brower and Anton Burkov (eds), *Obshchepriznannyye printsipy i normy mezhdunarodnogo prava, mezhdunarodnyye dogovory v praktike konstitutsionnogo pravosudiya [The Generally Recognized Principles and Norms of International Law, International Treaties in the Practice of Constitutional Justice]*. Moscow: International Relations, pp. 36–9.

Edling, Max M. (2003), *A Revolution in Favor of Government: Origins of the U.S. Constitution and the Making of the American State*. Oxford University Press.

Egret, Jean (1970), *Louis XV et l'opposition parlementaire, 1715–1774*. Paris: Colin.

Ehrlich, Eugen (1989 [1913]), *Grundlegung der Soziologie des Rechts*, fourth edition. Berlin: Duncker und Humblot.

Eichengrün, Fritz (1935), *Die Rechtsphilosophie Gustav Hugos: Ein geistesgeschichtlicher Beitrag zum Problem von Naturrecht und Rechtspositivismus*. Haag: Nijhoff.

Eisgruber, Christopher L. (1995), 'The Fourteenth Amendment's Constitution'. *Southern California Law Review* 69: 47–103.

Eley, Geoff (1995), 'The Social Construction of Democracy in Germany' in George Reid Andrews and Herrick Chapman (eds), *The Social Construction of Democracy, 1870–1990*. New York, NY: New York University Press, pp. 90–117.

(2002), *Forging Democracy: The History of the Left in Europe, 1850–2000*. Oxford University Press.

El-Ghobashy, Mona (2008), 'Constitutionalist Contention in Contemporary Egypt'. *American Behavioral Scientist* 51: 1590–610.

Elkins, Zachary (2010), 'Diffusion and the Constitutionalization of Europe'. *Comparative Political Studies* 43(8/9): 969–99.

Elliott, Mark (2001a), *The Constitutional Foundations of Judicial Review*. Oxford: Hart.

(2001b), 'The Human Rights Act 1998 and the Standard of Substantive Review'. *The Cambridge Law Journal* 60(2): 301–36.

Engelstein, Laura (2009), *Slavophile Empires: Imperial Russia's Illiberal Path*. Ithaca, NY: Cornell University Press.

Epp, Charles R. (1998), *The Rights Revolution: Lawyers, Activists, and Supreme Courts in Comparative Perspective*. Chicago, IL: University of Chicago Press.

Eskridge, William N. (2001), 'Channeling: Identity-Based Social Movements and Public Law'. *University of Pennsylvania Law Review* 150(1): 419–525.

Esmein, Adhémar (1903), *Éléments de droit constitutionnel français et comparé*, third edition. Paris: Larose.

Ewing, K.D. and C.A. Gearty (2000), *The Struggle for Civil Liberties: Political Freedom and the Rule of Law in Britain, 1914–1945*. Oxford University Press.

Ezetah, Reginald (1997), 'The Right to Democracy: A Qualitative Inquiry'. *Brook Journal of International Law* 22: 495–534.

Fahrmeir, Andreas (2000), *Citizens and Foreigners: Foreigners and the Law in Britain and the German States 1789–1870*. New York, NY: Berghahn.

Falk, Richard A. (1964), *The Role of Domestic Courts in the International Legal Order*. Syracuse University Press.

Farber, Daniel (2003), *Lincoln's Constitution*. Chicago University Press.

Fatton, Robert (1992), *Predatory Rule: State and Civil Society in Africa*. Boulder, CO: Lynne Riener.

Feeley, Malcolm M. and Edward L. Rubin (1998), *Judicial Policy Making and the Modrn State: How the Courts Reformed America's Prisons*. Cambridge University Press.

Feldkamp, Michael F. (1998), *Der Parlamentarische Rat 1948-1949: Die Entstehung des Grundgesetzes*. Göttingen: Vandenhoeck & Ruprecht.

Feldman, David (1999), 'The Human Rights Act 1998 and Constitutional Principles'. *Legal Studies* 19(2): 165–206.

(2009), 'Human Rights' in Louis Blom Cooper, Brice Dickson and Gavin Drewry (eds), *The Judicial House of Lords*. Oxford University Press, pp. 541–73.

Ferneuil, Thomas (1889), *Les principes de 1789 et la science sociale*. Paris: Hachette.

Fish, M. Steven (2005), *Democracy Derailed in Russia: The Failure of Open Politics*. Cambridge University Press.

Fishkin, James S. (2009), *When the People Speak: Deliberative Democracy and Public Consultation*. Oxford University Press.

Fitzmaurice, G.G. (1958), 'Third Report on Law of Treaties'. *Yearbook of the International Law Commission* 2: 20–46.

Fitzsimmons, Michael P. (2010), *From Artisan to Worker: Guilds, the French State and the Organization of Labor, 1776–1821*. Cambridge University Press.

Fletcher, William A. (1988), 'The Structure of Standing'. *The Yale Law Journal* 98(2): 221–91.

Flórez, Javier Andrés (2011), 'Democracia y Abstencionismo Electoral' in Rocio Araújo Oñate and María Lucía Torres Villarreal (eds), *Retos de la democracia y participación ciudadana*. Bogota: Editorial Universidad del Rosario, pp. 153–78.

Foner, Eric (1987), 'Rights and the Constitution in Black Life during the Civil War and Reconstruction'. *The Journal of American History* 74(3): 863–83.

(1988), *Reconstruction: America's Unfinished Revolution 1863–1877*. New York, NY: Harper Row.

Forbath, William E. (1999), 'Caste, Class, and Equal Citizenship'. *Michigan Law Review* 98(1): 1–91.

Forrest, Joshua B. (1988), 'The Qust for State "Hardness" in Africa'. *Comparative Politics* 20(4): 423–42.

Forsthoff, Ernst (1971), *Der Staat der Industriegesellschaft*. Munich: Beck.

Fortescue, John (1942 [Written c. 1470]), *De Laudibus Legum Anglie*, edited by S. B. Chrimes. Cambridge University Press.

Foweraker, Joe and Todd Landman (1997), *Citizenship Rights and Social Movements: Comparative and Statistical Analysis*. Oxford University Press.

Fox, Gregory H. (1992), 'The Right to Political Participation in International Law'. *Yale Journal of International Law* 17: 539–607.

Fox, Jonathan (2005), 'Unpacking "Transnational Citizenship"'. *Annual Review of Political Science* 8: 171–201.

Fox, Gregory H. and Brad R. Roth (2001), 'Democracy and International Law'. *Review of Internatinal Studies* 27(3): 327–52.

Fraenkel, Ernst (1964), *Deutschland und die westlichen Demokratien*. Stuttgart: Kohlhammer.

Fralin, Richard (1978), *Rousseau and Representation: A Study of the Development of his Concept of Political Institutions*. New York, NY: Columbia University Press.

Francis, Megan Ming (2014), *Civil Rights and the Making of the Modern American State*. Cambridge University Press.

Franck, Thomas M. (1992), 'The Emerging Right to Democratic Governance'. *The American Journal of International Law* 86(1): 46–91.

   (1994), 'Democracy as a Human Right' in Louis Henkin and John L.H. Hargrove (eds), *Human Rights: An Agenda for the Next Century*. Washington, DC: American Society of Interational Law, pp. 73–101.

   (1995), *Fairness in International Law*. Oxford University Press.

Free, Laura E. (2015), *Suffrage Reconstructed: Gender, Race, and Voting Rights in the Civil War Era*. Ithaca, NY: Cornell University Press.

Freeman, John R. and Duncan Snidal (1982), 'Diffusion, Development and Democratization: Enfranchisement in Western Europe'. *Canadian Journal of Political Science* 15(2): 299–329.

Freyer, Hans (1930), *Soziologie als Wirklichkeitswissenschaft: Logische Grundlegung des Systems der Soziologie*. Leipzig: B.G. Teubner.

   (1935), 'Gegenwartsaufgaben der deutschen Soziologie'. *Zeitschrift für die gesamte Staatswissenschaft* 95(1): 116–44.

   (1955), *Theorie des gegenwärtigen Zeitalters*. Stuttgart: Deutsche Verlags-Anstalt.

   (1976 [1957]), 'Das soziale Ganze und die Freiheit des Einzelnen unter den Bedingungen des industriellen Zeitalters' in Ernst-Wolfgang Böckenförde (ed), *Staat und Gesellschaft*. Darmstadt: Wissenschaftliche Buchgesellschaft, pp. 199–200.

Friedman, Lawrence M. (1975), *The Legal System: A Social Science Perspective*. New York, NY: Russell Sage Foundation.

   (2002), *American Law in the 20th Century*. New Haven, CT: Yale University Press.

Fritz, Christian G. (2008), *American Sovereigns: The People and America's Constitutional Tradition before the Civil War*. Cambridge University Press.

Fu, Hualing and Richard Cullen (2008), 'Weiquan (Rights Protection) Lawyering in an Authoritarian State: Building a Culture of Public-Interest Lawyering'. *The China Journal* 59: 111–27.

Fuller, Lon L. (1969), *The Morality of Law*, revised edition. New Haven, CT: Yale University Press.

Gadjiyev, Gadis (2013), 'Metodologicheskiye problemy «pretsedentnoy revolyutsii» v Rossii' [Methodological Problems of the"Precedent Revolution"in Russia]. *Zhurnal Konstitutsionnogo Pravosudiya* 4(34): 5–8.

Gagel, Walter (1958), *Die Wahlrechtsfrage in der Geschichte der deutschen liberalen Parteien 1848–1918*. Düsseldorf: Droste.

Gall, Lothar (1976), 'Bismarck und der Bonapartismus'. *Historische Zeitschrift* 223: 618–37.

Garaud, Marcel (1953), *La Révolution et l'égalité civile*. Paris: Sirey.

Garcelon, Marc (2005), *Revolutionary Passage: From Soviet to Post-Soviet Russia, 1985–2000*. Philadelphia, PA: Temple University Press.

García Linera, Álvaro (2014), *La condícion obrera en Bolivia: Siglo XX*. La Paz: Plural.

García Villegas, Mauricio, Nicolás Torres Echeverry, Javier Revelo Rebolledo and José R. Espinosa Restrepo (2016), *Los territorios de la paz: La construcción del Estado local en Colombia*. Bogota: Dejusticia.

Garrard, John (2002), *Democratisation in Britain: Elites, Civil Society and Reform since 1800*. Basingstoke: Palgrave.

Garrigou, Alain (2002), *Histoire du suffrage universel en France. 1848–2000*. Paris: Éditions du Seuil.

Gash, Norman (1977), *Politics in the Age of Peel: A Study in the Technique of Parliamentary Representation, 1830–1850*, second Edition. Hassocks: Harvester.

(1989), *Aristocracy and People: Britain 1815–1865*. London: Arnold.

Gauchet, Marcel (1995), *La Révolution des pouvoirs: La Souveraineté, le peuple et la représentation 1789–1799*. Paris: Gallimrd.

(2007), *L'avènement de la démocratie, I: La révolution moderne*. Paris: Gallimard.

Gauri, Varun and Daniel M. Brinks (2008), 'A New Policy Landscape: Legalizing Social and Economic Rights in the Developing World' in Varun Gauri and Daniel M. Brinks (eds), *Courting Social Justice: Judicial Enforcment of Social and Economic Rights in the Developing World*. Cambridge University Press, pp. 303–52.

Gautier, Claude (1994), 'Corporation, société et démocratie chez Durkheim'. *Revue française de science politique* 44(5): 836–55.

Gee, Graham and Grégoire C.N. Webber (2010), 'What is a Political Constitution?' *Oxford Journal of Legal Studies* 30(2): 273–99.

Gehlen, Arnold (1963), *Studien zur Anthropologie und Soziologie*. Neuwied am Rhein: Luchterhand.

Geissler, Nils (1999), 'The International Protection of Internally Displaced Persons'. *International Journal of Refugee Law* 11(3): 451–78.

Geldenhuys, Deon (1990), *Isolated States: A Comparative Analysis*. Cambridge University Press.

Gel'man, Vladimir (2004), 'The Unrule of Law in the Making: The Politics of Informal Institution Building in Russia'. *Europe-Asia Studies* 56(7): 1021–40.

(2015), *Authoritarian Russia: Analyzing Post-Soviet Regime Changes*. Pittsburgh, PA: Pittsburgh University Press.

Gentz, Friedrich von (1979 [1819]), 'Über den Unterschied zwischen den landständischen und Repräsentativ-Verfassungen' in Hartwig Brandt (ed), *Restauration und Frühliberalismus*. Darmstadt: Wissenschaftliche Buchgesellschaft, pp. 218–22.

Gephart, Werner (1993), *Gesellschaftstheorie und Recht: Das Recht im soziologischen Diskurs der Moderne.* Frankfurt: Suhrkamp.

Gerber, Carl Friedrich Wilhelm (1852), *Ueber öffentliche Rechte.* T ber öf: Laupp. (1865), *Grundzüge eines Systems des deutschen Staatsrechts.* Leipzig: Tauchnitz.

Gerlich, Rudolf (1980), *Die gescheiterte Alternative: Sozialisierung in Österreich nach dem ersten Weltkrieg.* Vienna: Wilhelm Braumüller.

Gertzel, Cherry (1970), *The Politics of Independent Kenya 1963–8.* Nairobi: East African Publishing House.

Ghai, Y.P. and J.P.W.B. McAuslan (1970), *Public Law and Political Change in Kenya.* Oxford University Press.

Gill, Graeme (2015), *Building an Authoritarian Polity: Russia in Post-Soviet Times.* Cambridge University Press.

Gills, Barry, Joel Rocamora and Richard Wilson (1993), 'Low Intensity Democracy' in Barry Gills, Joel Rocamora and Richard Wilson (eds), *Low Intensity Democracy: Political Power in the New World Order.* London: Pluto, pp. 3–34.

Gillette, William (1965), *The Right to Vote and the Passage of the Fifteenth Amendment.* Baltimore, MD: Johns Hopkins Press. (1979), *Retreat from Reconstruction 1869–1879.* Baton Rouge, LA: Louisiana State University Press.

Gironda, Vito Francesco (2010), *Die Politik der Staatsbürgerschaft: Italien und Deutschland im Vergleich 1800–1914.* Göttingen: Vandenhoeck und Ruprecht.

Gleditsch, Kristian Skrede and Michael D. Ward (2006), 'Diffusion and the International Context of Democratization'. *International Organization* 60: 911–33.

Glenn, H. Patrick (2013), *The Cosmopolitan State.* Oxford University Press.

Glennon, Robert Jerome (1994), 'The Jurisdictional Legacy of the Civil Rights Movement'. *Tennessee Law Review* 61: 869–932.

Godkin, Edwin Lawrence (1898), *Unforeseen Tendencies of Democracies.* Westminster: Constable.

Goldoni, Marco (2012), 'Two Internal Critiques of Political Constitutionalism'. *International Journal of Constitutional Law* 10(4): 926–49.

Goldsmith, Jack and Daryl Levinson (2009), 'Law for States: International Law, Constitutional Law, Public Law'. *Harvard Law Review* 122(7): 1791–868.

Goldstein, Robert J. (1983), *Political Repression in 19th Century Europe.* London: Croom Helm.

Goldsworthy, Jeffrey (1999), *The Sovereignty of Parliament.* Oxford University Press.

Golosov, Grigorii V. (2015), 'The Idiosyncratic Dynamics of Party System Nationalization in Russia'. *Post-Soviet Affairs* 31(5): 397–419.

González González, Fernán Enrique (2009), 'Espacio, conflicto y poder: las dimensiones territoriales de la violencia y la construcción del Estado en Colombia'. *Sociedad y Economía* 17: 185–214. (2014), *Poder y violencia en Colombia.* Bogota: Odecofi-Cinep.

González, Fernán E., Ingrid J. Bolívar and Teófilo Vázquez (2003), *Violencia política en Colombia: De la nación fragmentada a la construcción del Estado*. Bogota: CINEP.

Goode, J. Paul (2011), *The Decline of Regionalism in Putin's Russia: Boundary Issues*. Abingdon: Routledge.

Goodhart, Michael (2005), *Democracy as Human Rights: Freedom and Equality in the Age of Globalization*. London: Routledge.

Goodin, Robert E. (2000), 'Democratic Deliberation Within'. *Philosophy & Public Affairs* 29(1): 81–109.

(2010), 'Global Democracy: In the Beginning'. *International Theory* 2(2): 175–209.

Gordon, David F. (1986), *Decolonization and the State in Kenya*. Boulder, CO: Westview Press.

Gorenburg, Dmitry P. (2003), *Minority Ethnic Mobilization in the Russian Federation*. Cambridge University Press.

Gosewinkel, Dieter (1995), 'Staatsbürgerschaft und Staatsangehörigkeit'. *Geschichte und Gesellschaft* 21(4): 533–56.

(2001), *Einbürgern und Ausschließen: Die Nationalisierung der Staatsangehörigkeit vom Deutschen Bund bis zur Bundesrepublik Deutschland*. Göttingen: Vandenhoeck und Ruprecht.

(2016), *Schutz und Freiheit? Staatsbürgerschaft in Europa im 20. und 21. Jahrhundert*. Frankfurt: Suhrkamp.

Gotlieb, Verónica, Natalia Yavich and Ernesto Báscolo (2016), 'Litigio judicial y el derecho a la salud en Argentina'. *Cadernos de Saúd pública* 31(1): 1–11.

Gough, J.W. (1955), *Fundamental Law in English Constitutional History*. Oxford: Clarendon.

Gourevitch, Peter Alexis (1978), 'The Second Image Reversed: The International Sources of Domestic Politics'. *International Organization* 32(4): 881–911.

(1984), 'Breaking with Orthodoxy: The Politics of Economic Policy Responses to the Depression of the 1930s'. *International Organization* 38(1): 96–129.

Graham, Hugh Davis (1990), *The Civil Rights Era: Origins and Development of National Policy 1960–1972*. Oxford University Press.

Grajales, Jacobo (2017), *Gobernar en medio de la violencia: Estado y paramilitarismo en Colombia*. Bogota: Editorial Universidad del Rosario.

Gramsci, Antonio (1966), *Socialismo e fascismo: L'ordine nuovo, 1921–1922*. Turin: Einaudi.

Granat, Nina (1998), 'Istochniki prava' [Sources of Law]. *Yurist* 9: 6–12.

Grandmaison, Olivier Le Cour (1992), *Les citoyennetés en revolution (1789–1794)*. Paris: Presses universitaires de France.

Grebenok, Margarita (2011), 'Sovetskiy narod: gosudarstvenno-politicheskiy konstrukt' [Soviet People: A State-and-Political Construct]. *Analitika Kulturologii* 21(2011): 115–18.

Greenhill, Brian (2010), 'The Company you Keep: International Socialization and the Diffusion of Human Rights Norms'. *International Studies Quarterly* 54(1): 127–45.

Greer, Stephen (2000), *The Margin of Apprecation: Interpretation and Discretion under the European Convention on Human Rights.* Strasbourg: Council of Europe Publishing.

Grewe, Willhelm (ed) (1988), *Fontes Historiae Iuris Gentium.* Berlin: de Gruyter, Vol. II.

Griffith, J.A.G. (1979), 'The Political Constitution'. *The Modern Law Review* 42(1): 1–21.

Griffith, J.A.G. and H. Street (1973), *Principles of Administrative Law.* London: Pitman.

Grimm, Dieter (1972), 'Verfassungsfunktion und Grundgesetzreform'. *Archiv des öffentlichen Rechts* 97: 189–637.

——— (2012), *Die Zukunft der Verfassung II: Auswirkungen von Europäisierung und Globalisierung.* Frankfurt am Main: Suhrkamp.

Grinberg, Martine (1997), 'La redaction des coutumes et les droits seigneuriaux: Nommer, classer, exclure'. *Annales. Histoires, Sciences Sociales* 52(5): 1017–38.

Grofman, Bernard, Lisa Handley and Richard G. Niemi (1992), *Minority Representation and the Quest for Voting Equality.* Cambridge University Press.

Gruder, Vivian R. (1984), 'Paths to Political Consciousness: The Assembly of Notables of 1787 and the "Pre-Revolution" in France'. *French Historical Studies* 13(3): 323–55.

Grzymala-Busse, Anna and Pauline Jones Luong (2002), 'Reconceptualizing the State: Lessons from Post-Communism'. *Politics and Society* 30(4): 529–54.

Gueniffey, Patrice (2000), *La politique de la terreur: Essai sur la violence révolutionnaire 1789–1794.* Paris: Fayard.

Guerra, François-Xavier (1992), *Modernidad e independencias: Ensayos sobre las revoluciones hispánicas.* Madrid: MAPFRE.

Guilhot, Nicolas (2005), *The Democracy Makers: Human Rights and the Politics of Global Order.* New York, NY: Columbia University Press.

Gurvitch, Georges (1929), 'Le principe démocratique et la démocratie future'. *Revue de métaphysique et de morale* 36(3): 403–31.

——— (1939), 'La sociologie juridique de Montesquieu'. *Revue de métaphysique et de morale* 46(4): 611–26.

——— (1940), *Élements de sociologie juridique.* Paris: Aubier.

Gutmann, Amy and Dennis Thompson (2004), *Why Deliberative Democracy?* Princeton University Press.

Haack, Stefan (2007), *Verlust der Staatlichkeit.* Tübingen: Mohr.

Häberle, Peter (1972), *Die Wesenheitsgarantie des Art: 19 Abs. 2 Grundgesetz.* Karlsruhe: Müller.

(1975), 'Die offene Gesellschaft der Verfassungsinterpreten'. *Juristenzeitung* 30: 297–305.

(1995), 'Die europäische Verfassungsstaatlichkeit'. *Kritische Vierteljahresschrift für Gesetzgebung und Rechtswissenschaft* 78(3): 298–312.

Habermas, Jürgen (1968), *Erkenntnis und Interesse*. Frankfurt: Suhrkamp.

(1973), *Legitimationsprobleme im Spätkapitalismus*. Frankfurt am Main: Suhrkamp.

(1976), *Zur Rekonstruktion des Historischen Materialismus*. Frankfurt am Main: Suhrkamp.

(1990 [1962]), *Strukturwandel der Öffentlichkeit: Untersuchungen zu einer Kategorie der bürgerlichen Gesellschaft*, new edition. Frankfurt am Main: Suhrkamp.

(1992), *Faktizität und Geltung: Beiträge zur Diskurstheorie des Rechts und des demokratischen Rechtsstaats*. Frankfurt am Main: Suhrkamp.

(1994), 'Über den internen Zusammenhang von Rechtsstaat und Demokratie' in Ulrich K. Preuß (ed), *Zum Begriff der Verfassung: Die Ordnung des Politischen*. Frankfurt: Fischer, pp. 83–94.

(1998), *Die postnationale Konstellation*. Frankfurt am Main: Suhrkamp.

(2005), 'Eine politische Verfassung für die pluralistische Weltgesellschaft?' *Kritische Justiz* 38(3): 222–47.

(2012), 'Die Krise der Europäischen Union im Lichte einer Konstitutionalisierung des Völkerrechts – Ein Essay zur Verfassung Europas'. *Zeitschrift für ausländisches öffentliches Recht und Völkerrecht* 72: 1–44.

Häfelin, Ulrich (1959), *Die Rechtspersönlichkeit des Staates*. Tübingen: Mohr.

Hale, Henry E. (2006), *Why not Parties in Russia? Democracy, Federalism and the State*. Cambridge University Press.

Hale, Grace Elizabeth (2011), *A Nation of Outsiders: How the White Middle Class Fell in Love with Rebellion in Postwar America*. Oxford University Press.

Halévy, Élie (1938). *L'ère des tyrannies: études sur le socialisme et la guerre*, with a preface by C. Bouglé. Paris: Gallimard.

Halisi, C.R.D. (1997), 'From Liberation to Citizenship: Identity and Innovation in Black South African Political Thought'. *Comparative Studies in Society and History* 39(1): 61–85.

Hall, Jerome (1953), 'Police and Law in a Democratic Society'. *Indiana Law Journal* 28(2): 133–77.

Hall, Constance Margaret (1971), *The Sociology of Pierre Joseph Proudhon 1809–1865*. New York, NY: Philosophical Library.

Hamel, Ernest (1865), *Histoire de Robespierre d'après des papiers de famille: La constituante*. Brussels: A. Lacroix, Verboeckhoven & c.

Hamerow, Theodore S. (1983), *The Birth of a New Europe: State and Society in the Nineteenth Century*. Chapel Hill, NC: University of North Carolina Press.

Handler, Joel F. (1978), *Social Movements and the Legal System*. New York, NY: Academic Press.

Hanham, H.J. (1959), *Elections and Party Management: Politics in the Time of Disraeli and Gladstone*. London: Longmans.

Harbeson, John W. (1973), *Nation-Building in Kenya: The Role of Land Reform*. Evanston, IL: Northwestern University Press.

(2012), 'Land and the Quest for a Democratic State in Kenya: Brining Citizens Back in'. *African Studies Review* 55(1): 15–30.

Hardenberg, Karl August Freiherr von (1931 [1807]), 'Rigaer Denkschrift' in Georg Winter (ed), *Die Reorganisation des Preussischen Staates unter Stein und Hardenberg: Erster Teil. Allgemeine Verwaltungs- und Behördenreform, vol. I: Vom Beginn des Kampfes gegen die Kabinettsregierung bis zum Wiedereintritt des Ministers von Stein*. Leipzig: Hirzel, pp. 302–63.

Hardie, Keir (1894), 'The Independent Labour Party' in Andrew Reid (ed), *The New Party*. London: Hodder, pp. 375–86.

Harlow, Carol (1980), '"Public" and "Private" Law: Definition without Distinction'. *The Modern Law Review* 43(3): 241–65.

(2002), 'Public Law and Popular Justice'. *Modern Law Review* 65(1): 1–18.

Hart, Michael (1982), 'The Liberals, the War, and the Franchise'. *The English Historical Review* 97(385): 820–32.

Hassner, Pierre (2008), 'Russia's Transition to Autocracy'. *Journal of Democracy* 19(2): 5–15.

Hause, Steven C. with Anne R. Kenney (1984), *Women's Suffrage and Social Politics in the French Third Republic*. Princeton University Press.

Hawkins, Darren G. (2002), *International Human Rights and Authoritarian Rule in Chile*. Lincoln, NE: University of Nebraska Press.

Hazzaa, Heba and Silke N. Kumpf (2015), 'Egypt's Ban of Public Interest Litigation in Government Contracts: A Case Study of "Judicial Chill"'. *Stanford Journal of International Law* 51(2): 147–71.

HC Deb (1948) (23 June 1948) (Representation of the People Act) vol 452, avaliable at:http://hansard.millbanksystems.com/commons/1948/jun/23/representation-of-the-people-bill#column_1435.

Heater, Derek (1999), *What is Citizenship?* Cambridge: Polity.

Hegel, G.W.F. (1970 [1820]), *Grundlinien der Philosophie des Rechts*, in *Werke*, edited by E. Moldenhauer and K. Michel in 20 vols. Frankfurt am Main: Suhrkamp, Vol. VII.

(1970 [1830]), *Enzyklopädie der philosophischen Wissenschaften, part 3*, in *Werke*, edited by E. Moldenhauer and K. Michel in 20 vols. Frankfurt am Main: Suhrkamp, Vol. X.

Held, David (1991), 'Democracy, the Nation-State and the Global System'. *Economy and Society* 20(2): 138–72.

(1996), *Models of Democracy*, second edition. Cambridge Polity.

(1997), 'Democracy and the new International Order' in Daniele Archibugi and David Held (eds), *Cosmopolitan Democracy: An Agenda for a New World Order*. Cambridge: Polity Press, pp. 96–120.

(2003), 'The Transformation of Political Community: Rethinking Democracy in the Context of Globalization', in Robert Dahl, Ian Shapiro, and José Antonio Cheibub (eds), *The Democracy Sourcebook*. Cambrudge, MA: MIT Press, pp. 516–25.

Hendley, Kathryn (2009), '"Telephone Law" and the "Rule of Law": The Russian Case'. *Hague Journal on the Rule of Law* 1(2): 241–62.

Herrick, Francis H. (1948), 'The Second Reform Movement in Britain 1850–1865'. *Journal of the History of Ideas* 9(2): 174–92.

Hessen, V.M. (1909), *Poddanstvo, yego ustanovleniye i prekrashcheniye [Citizenship, its Establishment and Termination]*. St. Petersburg: Pravda, Vol. I.

Heywood, Mark (2009), 'South Africa's Treatment Action Campaign: Combining Law and Social Mobilization to Realize the Right to Health'. *Journal of Human Rights Practice* 1(1): 14–36.

Hickman, Tom (2011), *Public Law after the Human Rights Act*. Oxford: Hart.

Hilferding, Rudolf (1910), *Das Finanzkapital: Eine Studie über die jüngste Entwicklung des Kapitalismus*. Vienna: Verlag der Wiener Volksbuchhandlung.

Himmelfarb, Gertrude (1966), 'The Politics of Democracy: The English Reform Act of 1867'. *Journal of British Studies* 6(1): 97–138.

Hintze, Otto (1962), *Staat und Verfassung: Gesammelte Abhandlungen zur allgemeinen Verfassungsgeschichte*, Gerhard Oestreich (ed), second edition. Göttingen: Vandenhoeck & Ruprecht.

Hippler, Thomas (2002), 'Service militaire et integration nationale pendant la revolution française'. *Annales historiques de la Révolution française* 3: 1–16.

(2006), *Soldats et citoyens: Naissance du service militaire en France et en Prusse*. Paris: Presses universitaires de France.

Hirsch, Francine (2005), *Empire of Nations. Ethnographic Knowledge and the Making of the Soviet Union*. Ithaca, NY: Cornell University Press.

Hirschl, Ran (2007), 'The New Constitutionalism and the Judicialization of Pure Politics Worldwide'. *Fordham Law Review* 75(2007): 721–53.

Hobbes, Thomas (1914 [1651]), *Leviathan*. London: Dent.

Hockett, Jeffrey D. (1996), *New Deal Justice: The Constitutional Jurisprudence of Hugo L. Black, Felix Frankfurter, and Robert H. Jackson*. Lanham, MD: Rowman & Littlefield.

Höffe, Ottfried (1999), *Demokratie im Zeitalter der Globalisierung*. Munich: Beck.

(2004), *Wirtschaftsbürger: Staatsbürger. Weltbürger. Politische Ethik im Zeitalter der Globalisierung*. Munich: Beck.

Honneth, Axel (1992), *Kampf um Anerkennung: Zur moralischen Grammatik sozialer Konflikte*. Frankfurt: Suhrkamp.

Horne, John N. (1991). *Labour at War: France and Britain 1914–1918*. Oxford: Clarendon.

Hornung, Gerrit (2015), *Grundrechtsinnovationen*. Tübingen: Mohr.

Horowitz, Irving Louis (1982), 'Socialization without Politicization: Emile Durkheim's Theory of the Modern State'. *Political Theory* 10(3): 353–77.

Howell, David (2002), *MacDonald's Party: Labour Identities and Crisis 1922–1931*. Cambridge University Press.

Hugo, Gustav, (1823) *Lehrbuch eines Civilistischen Cursus: Lehrbuch der juristischen Encyclopädie*. Berlin: Mylius, Vol. I.

Hulsebosch, Daniel J. (2005), *Constituting Empire: New York and the Transformation of Constitutionalism in the Atlantic World, 1664–1830*. Chapel Hill, NC: University of North Carolina Press.

Hunt, Murray (1997), *Human Rights Law in English Courts*. Oxford: Hart.

Huntington, Samuel P. (1991), *The Third Wave: Democratization in the Late Twentieth Century*. Norman, OK: University of Oklahoma Press.

Hutchings, Kimberley (1999), 'Political Theory and Cosmopolitan Citizenship' in Kimberley Hutchings and Roland Dannreuther (eds), *Cosmopolitan Citizenship*. Basingstoke: Macmillan, pp. 3–32.

Ibhawoh, Bonny (2000), 'Between Culture and Constitution: Evaluating the Cultural Legitimacy of Human Rights in the African State'. *Human Rights Quarterly* 22(3): 838–60.

Inter-American Commission on Human Rights (1993), Second Report on the Situation of Human Rights in Colombia, Chapter III: The Legal and Political System in Colombia, OEA/Ser.L/V/II.84. Doc. 39 rev. www.cidh.org/countryrep/Colombia93eng/chap.3.htm.

Irons, Peter H. (1982), *The New Deal Lawyers*. Princeton University Press.

Isensee, Josef (1976), 'Der Dualismus von Staat und Gesellschaft' in Ernst-Wolfgang Böckenförde (ed), *Staat und Gesellschaft*. Darmstadt: Wissenschaftliche Buchgesellschaft, pp. 317–29.

Isin, Engin F. (2002), *Being Political: Genealogies of Citizenship*. Minneapolis, MN: University of Minnesota Press.

(2009), 'Citizenship in Flux: The Figure of the Activist Citizen'. *Subjectivity* 29(1): 367–88.

(2012), *Citizens without Frontiers*. New York, NY: Bloomsbury.

Israel, Jonathan (2006), *Philosophy, Modernity, and the Emancipation of Man 1670–1752*. Oxford University Press.

(2014), *Revolutionary Ideas: An Intellectual History of the French Revolution from the Rights of Man to Robespierre*. Princeton University Press.

Ivanov, Anton (2010), 'Rech o pretsedente' [The Speech on Precedent]. *Pravo* 2: 3–11.

Jacob, Joseph M. (1996), *The Republican Crown*. Aldershot: Dartmouth.

Jacobson, David (1996), *Rights Across Borders: Immigration and the Decline of Citizenship*. Baltimore, MD: JohnsHopkins University Press.

Janoski, Thomas (1998), *Citizenship and Civil Society: A Framework of Rights and Obligations in Liberal, Traditional, and Social Democratic Regimes*. Cambridge University Press.

Janowitz, Morris (1976), 'Military Institutions and Citizenship in Western Societies'. *Armed Forces & Society* 2(2): 185–204.

(1980), 'Observations on the Sociology of Citizenship: Obligations and Rights'. *Social Forces* 59(1): 1–24.

Jansen, Nils (2010), *The Making of Legal Authority: Non-Legislative Codifications in Historical and Comparative Perspective*. Oxford University Press.

Jaume, Lucien (1989), *Le discourse Jacobin et la démocratie*. Paris: Fayard.

(1997), 'La souveraineté montagnarde: République, peuple et territoire' in Jean Bart, Jean-Jacques Clere, Claude Courvoisier and Michel Verpeaux (eds), *La Constitution du 24 juin 1793: L'utopie dans le droit public français*. Dijon: Editions Universitaires de Dijon, pp. 115–39.

Jefferson, Thomas (1899), *Writings of Thomas Jefferson*, edited by Paul Leicester Ford. New York, NY: G.P. Putnam's Sons, Vol. 10.

Jensen, Steven L.B. (2016), *The Making of International Human Rights: The 1960s, Decolonization and the Reconstruction of Global Values*. Cambridge University Press.

Jessup, Philip (1956), *Transnational Law*. New Haven, CT: Yale University Press.

Jestaedt, Matthias (1999), *Grundrechtsentfaltung im Gesetz: Studien zur Interdependenz von Grundrechtsdogmatik und Rechtsgewinnungstheorie*. Tübingen: Mohr.

Jhering, Rudolf (1852), *Geist des römischen Rechts auf den verschiedenen Stufen seiner Entwicklung*, in 3 vols. Leipzig: Breitkopf und Härtel, Vol. I.

Joireman, Sandra F. (2011), *Where there is no Government: Enforcing Property Rights in Common Law Africa*. Oxford University Press.

Jonas, Friedrich (1980), *Geschichte der Soziologie I: Aufklärung, Liberalismus, Idealismus, Sozialismus. Übergang zur industriellen Gesellschaft*. Opladen: Westdeutscher Verlag.

Joyce, Patrick (1994), *Democratic Subjects: The Self and the Social in Nineteenth-Century England*. Cambridge University Press.

Joyner, Christopher C. (1999), 'The United Nations and Democracy'. *Global Governance* 5(3): 333–57.

Judge, David (1999), *Representation: Theory and Practice in Britain*. London: Routledge.

Kabau, Tom and J. Osogo Ambani (2013), 'The 2010 Constitution and the Application of International Law in Kenya: A Case of Migration to Monism or Regression to Dualism'. *Africa Nazarene University Law Journal* 1(1): 36–55.

Kaczorowski, Robert J. (1987a), *The Nationalization of Civil Rights: Constitutional Theory and Practice in a Racist Society 1866-1883*. New York, NY: Garland.

(1987b), 'To Begin the Nation Anew: Congress, Citizenship, and Civil Rights after the Civil War'. *The American Historical Review* 92(1): 45-68.

(2005), *The Politics of Judicial Interpretation: The Federal Courts, Department of Justice, and Civil Rights, 1866-1876*. New York, NY: Fordham University Press.

Kadelbach, Stefan (1992), *Zwingendes Völkerrecht*. Berlin: Duncker und Humblot.

Kahan, Alan S. (2003), *Liberalism in Nineteenth-Century Europe: The Political Culture of Limited Suffrage*. Basingstoke: Palgrave.

Kahn, Jeffrey (2000), 'The Parade of Sovereignties: Establishing the Vocabulary of the New Russian Federalism'. *Post-Soviet Affairs* 16(1): 58-89.

(2002), *Federalism, Democratization, and the Rule of Law in Russia*. Oxford University Press.

Kahn, Jeffrey, Alexei Trochev and Nikolay Balayan (2009), 'The Unification of Law in the Russian Federation'. *Post-Soviet Affairs* 25(4): 310-46.

Kahn-Freund, Otto (1932), 'Der Funktionswandel des Arbeitsrechts'. *Archiv für Sozialwissenschaft und Sozialpolitik* 67: 146-74.

Kalyvas, Andreas (2008), *Democracy and the Politics of the Extraordinary: Max Weber, Carl Schmitt, and Hannah Arendt*. New York: Cambridge University Press.

Kamoche, Jidlaph G. (1981), *Imperial Trusteeship and Political Evolution in Kenya, 1923-1963: A Study of the Official Views and the Road to Decolonization*. Washington, DC: University Press of America.

Kanogo, Tanitha (1987), *Squatters and the Roots of Mau Mau 1905-63*. London: Curry.

Kant, Immanuel (1977a [1795]), *Zum ewigen Frieden* in *Werkausgabe*, edited by Wilhelm Weischedel, in 12 vols. Frankfurt am Main: Suhrkamp, 6: 195-251.

Kant, Immanuel (1977b [1797]), *Metaphysik der Sitten*, in *Werkausgabe*, edited by Wilhelm Weischedel, in 12 vols. Frankfurt am Main: Suhrkamp, 8, 432-33.

(1977c [1793]). 'Über den Gemeinspruch: Das mag in der Theorie richtig sein, taugt aber nicht für die Praxis', *Werkausgabe* edited by Wilhelm Weischedel in 12 vols. Frankfurt am Main: Suhrkamp, XI: 127-72.

Kapczynski, Amy (2008), 'The Access to Knowledge Mobilization and the New Politics of Intellectual Property'. *The Yale Law Journal* 117: 805-85.

Kautsky, Karl (1918), *Nationalversammlung und Räteversammlung*. Berlin: Hermann.

Kavanagh, Aileen (2009), *Constitutional Review und the UK Human Rights Act*. Cambridge University Press.

Keck, Margraet E. and Kathryn Sikkink (1999), 'Transnational advocacy networks in international and regional politics'. *International Social Science Journal* 51(159): 89-101.

Kelemen, R. Daniel (2009) 'The Strength of Weak States: Adversarial Legalism in the US and the EU'. Last accessed online 12 October 2017, available at: www.unc .edu/euce/eusa2009/papers/kelemen_10B.pdf.

Kelsen, Hans (1911a), *Über Grenzen zwischen juristischer und soziologischer Methode*. Tübingen: J.C.B. Mohr.

(1911b), *Hauptprobleme der Staatsrechtslehre*. Tübingen: J.C.B. Mohr.

(1962), 'Naturrechtslehre und Rechtspositivismus'. *Politische Vierteljahresschrift* 3(4): 316–27.

(1920), *Das Problem der Souveränität und die Theorie des Völkerrechts: Ein Beitrag zu einer reinen Rechtslehre*. Tübingen: Mohr.

(1925), *Allgemeine Staatslehre*. Berlin: Julius Springer.

(1929), *Vom Wesen und Wert der Demokratie*, second edition. Tübingen: J.C.B. Mohr.

(1933), *Staatsform und Weltanschauung*. Tübingen: J.C.B. Mohr.

(1934), *Reine Rechtslehre*. Vienna: Deuticke.

(2007[1906]), 'Wählerlisten und Reklamationsrecht' in *Werke, I: Veröffentlichte Schriften 1905–1910 und Selbstzeugnisse*, edited by Matthias Jestaedt. Tübingen: Mohr, pp. 301–31.

Kennedy, Duncan (2002), 'The Critique of Rights in Critical Legal Studies' in Wendy Brown and Janet Halley (eds), *Left Legalism/Left Critique*. Durham, NC: Duke University Press, pp. 178–227; 190, 219.

Kennedy, David (2004), *The Dark Sides of Virtue: Reassessing International Humanitarianism*. New York, NY: Princeton University Press.

Kestnbaum, Meyer (2000), 'Citizenship and Compulsory Military Service: The Revolutionary Origins of Conscription in the United States'. *Armed Forces & Society* 27(1): 7–36.

Kettner, James H. (1974), 'The Development of American Citizenship in the Revolutionary Era: The Idea of Volitional Allegiance'. *The American Journal of Legal History* 18(3): 208–42.

(1978), *The Development of American Citizenship 1608–1870*. Chapel Hill, NC: University of North Carolina Press.

Khazanov, Anatoly M. (1995), *After the USSR: Ethnicity, Nationalism, and Politics in the Commonwealth of Independent States*. Madison, WI: University of Wisconsin Press.

Kloppenberg, James T. (2016), *Toward Democracy: The Struggle for Self-Rule in European and American Thought*. Oxford University Press.

Klotz, Audie (1995), *Norms in International Relations: The Struggle against Apartheid*. Ithaca, NY: Cornell University Press.

Kidane, Won (2011), 'Managing Forced Displacement by Law in Africa: The Role of the New African Union IDPs Convention'. *Vanderbilt Journal of Transnational Law* 44(1): 1–85.

King, Desmond (2000), *Making Americans: Immigration, Race, and the Origins of the Diverse Democracy*. Cambridge, MA: Harvard University Press.

(2007), *Separate and Unequal: African Americans and the US Federal Government*, revised edition. Oxford University Press.

Kirchheimer, Otto (1981), *Politik und Verfassung*. Frankfurt: Suhrkamp.

Kirsch, Martin (1999), *Monarch und Parlament im 19. Jahrhundert: Der monarchische Konstitutionalismus als europäischer Verfassungstyp – Frankreich im Vergleich*. Göttingen: Vandenhoeck und Ruprecht.

Klarman, Michael J. (1996), 'Rethinking the Civil Rights and Civil Liberties Revolutions'. *Virginia Law Review* 82(1): 1–67.

(2004), *From Jim Crow to Civil Rights: The Supreme Court and the Struggle for Racial Equality*. Oxford University Press.

Klug, Heinz (2000), *Constituting Democracy: Law, Globalism and South Africa's Political Reconstruction*. Cambridge University Press.

Knauft, Bruce M. (1991), 'Violence and Sociality in Human Evolution'. *Current Anthropology* 32(4): 391–428.

Knox, MacGregor (2007), *To the Threshold of Power, 1922/33: Origins and Dynamics of the Fascist and National Socialist Dictatorships*, Vol. I. Cambridge University Press.

Kocka, Jürgen (1988), 'German History before Hitler: The Debate about the German Sonderweg'. *Journal of Contemporary History* 23: 3–16.

Koh, Harold Hongju (1999), 'How is International Human Rights Law Enforced?' *Indiana Law Journal* 74: 1397–417.

Könke, Günter (1987), *Organisierter Kapitalismus, Sozialdemokratie und Staat: Eine Studie zur Ideologie der sozialdemokratischen Arbeiterbewegung in der Weimarer Republik (1924–1932)*. Stuttgart: Franz Steiner.

König, Matthias (2002), *Menschenrechte bei Durkheim und Weber: Normative Dimensionen des soziologischen Diskurses der Moderne*. Frankfurt am Main: Campus.

Konitzer, Andrew and Stephen K. Wergren (2006), 'Federalism and Political Recentralization in the Russian Federation: United Russia as the Party of Power'. *Publius* 36(4): 503–22.

Koo, Jeong-Woo and Francisco O. Ramirez (2009), 'National Incorporation of Global Human Rights: Worldwide Expansion of National Human Rights Institutions, 1966–2004'. *Social Forces* 87(3): 1321–53.

Koselleck, Reinhart (1959), *Kritik und Krise: Ein Beitrag zur Pathogenese der bürgerlichen Welt*. Freiburg: Alber.

(1979), *Vergangene Zukunft: Zur Semantik geschichtlicher Zeiten*. Frankfurt: Suhrkamp.

Kousser, J. Morgan (1974), *The Shaping of Southern Politics: Suffrage Restriction and the Establishment of the One-Party South, 1880–1910*. New Haven, CT: Yale University Press.

(1999), *Colorbind Injustice: Minority Voting Rights and the Undoing of the Second Reconstruction*. Chapel Hill, NC: University of North Carolina Press.

Krajewska, Atina and Rachel Cahill-O'Callaghan (2018), 'When a Single Man Wants to be a Father- The Invisible Subjects in the Law Regulating Fertility Treatment'. Unpublished Manuscript.

Kramon, Eric and Daniel N. Posner (2011), 'Kenya's New Constitution'. *Journal of Democracy* 22(2): 89–103.

Kruger, Richard (1975), *Simple Justice: The History of Brown v. Board of Education and Black America's Struggle for Equality*. New York, NY: Vintage.

Kühne, Thomas (1994), *Dreiklassenwahlrecht und Wahlkultur in Preussen 1867– 1914: Landtagswahlen zwischen korporativer Tradition und politischem Massenmarkt*. Düsseldorf: Droste.

Kulikov, Vladislav (2016), 'Minyust vystupil za dlitelnyye svidaniya dlya pozhiznenno osuzhdennykh' [The Ministry of Justice Argues for Extended Family Visits for Lifetime-Prisoners.] *Rossiyskaya Gazeta*, available at: https:// rg.ru/2016/06/03/miniust-predlozhil-razreshit-dlitelnye-svidaniia-dlia-pozhiznenno-osuzhdennyh.html.

Kuria, Gibson Kamau and Algeisa M. Vazquez (1991), 'Judges and Human Rights: The Kenyan Experience'. *Journal of African Law* 35(1–2): 142–73.

Kymlicka, Will (1995), *Multicultural Citizenship*. Oxford University Press.

Kymlicka, Will and Wayne Norman (1994), 'Return of the Citizen: A Survey of Recent Work on Citizenship Theory'. *Ethics* 104(2) (1994): 352–81; 353;

Laband, Paul (1911), *Das Staatsrecht des deutschen Reiches*, fifth edition, in 4 vols. Tübingen/Leipzig: J.C.B. Mohr, Vol. II.

Lacroix, Bernard (1981), *Durkheim et la politique*. Paris: Presses de la fondation des sciences politiques.

Lacroix, Alison L. (2010), *The Ideological Origins of American Federalism*. Cambridge, MA: Harvard University Press.

Lacuée, Jean Gérard, Count de Cessac and Joseph Servan (1790), *Projet de constitution par l'armée des François*. Paris: Badouin.

Ladeur, Karl-Heinz (2004), *Kritik der Abwägung in der Grundrechtsdogmatik: Plädoyer für eine Erneuerung der liberalen Grundrechtstheorie*. Tübingen: Mohr.

(2006), *Der Staat gegen die Geesellschaft: Zur Verteidigung der Rationalität der "Privatrechtsgesellschaft"*. Tübingen: Mohr.

Ladeur, Karl-Heinz and Lars Viellechner (2008), 'Die transnationale Expansion staatlicher Grundrechte: Zur Konstitualisierung globaler Privatrechtsregimes'. *Archiv des Völkerrechts* 46(1): 42–73.

Lafon, Jacqueline Lucienne (2001), *La révolution française face au système judiciaire d'ancien régime*. Geneva: Droz.

Laing, Edward A. (1991), 'The Norm of Self-Determination, 1941–1991'. *California Western International Law Journal* 22(2): 209–308.

Landau, David (2012), 'The Reality of Social Rights Enforcement'. *Harvard International Law Journal* 53(1): 189–247.

(2014), 'A Dynamic Theory of the Judicial Role'. *Boston College Law Review* 55(5): 1501–62.

Landauer, Karl (1925), 'Die Ideologie des Wirtschaftsparlamentarismus' in M.J. Bonn und M. Palyi (eds), *Festgabe für Lujo Brentano: Die Wirtschaftswissenschaft nach dem Kriege, vol. I: Wirtschaftspolitische Ideologien*. Munich: Duncker und Humblot, pp. 153–93.

Landshut, Siegfried (1969), *Kritik der Soziologie und andere Schriften zur Politik*. Neuwied am Rhein: Luchterhand.

Lang, Anthony (2017), 'Global Constituent Power: Protests and Human Rights' in Aidan Hehir and Robert W. Murray (eds), *Protecting Human Rights In the 21st Century*. Abingdon: Routledge, pp. 19–33.

Langford, Paul (1988), 'Property and "Virtual Representation" in Eighteenth-Century England'. *The Historical Journal* 31(1): 83–115.

Lapa, Yekaterina (2010), 'Voprosy reformirovaniya gosudarstvennoy sluzhby Rossiyskoy Federatsii: o vozmozhnosti primeneniya opyta Germanii' [On the Issues of Reforming Russian State Civil Service: On the Possibility to use German Experience]. *Sibirskiy yuridicheskiy vestnik* 3: 34–9.

Laquièze, Alain (2002), *Les origines du régime parlementaire en France (1814–1848)*. Paris: Presses Universitaires de France.

Larenz, Karl (1935). *Rechtsperson und subjektives Recht: Zur Wandlung der Rechtsbegriffe*. Berlin: Juncker und Dünnhaupt.

Lassalle, Ferdinand (1892 [1862]), *Ueber Verfassungswesen*. Berlin: Verlag der Expedition des "Vorwärts" Berliner Volksblatt.

Latorre Iglesias, Edimer Leonardo (2015), *Litigio estructural y experimentalismo jurídico: Análisis sociojurídico a los cambios generados por la sentencia T-025 en la población desplazada*. Santa Marta: Universidad Sergio Arboleda.

Laufer, Heinz (1968), *Verfassungsgerichtsbarkeit und politischer Prozeß: Studien zum Bundesverfassungsgericht der Bundesrepublik Deutschland*. Tübingen: Mohr.

Lauren, Paul Gordon (1983), 'First Principles of Racial Equality: History and the Politics and Diplomacy of Human Rights Provisions in the United Nations Charter'. *Human Rights Quarterly* 5(1): 1–26.

Lauterpacht, Hersch (1945), *An International Bill of the Rights of Man*. New York, NY: Columbia University Press.

Lauth, Hans-Joachim (2015), 'The Matrix of Democracy: A Three-Dimensional Approach to Measuring the Quality of Democracy and Regime Transformations', *Würzburger Arbeitspapiere zur Politikwissenschaft und Sozialforschung*, 6. Available at: https://opus.bibliothek.uni-wuerzburg

.de/opus4-wuerzburg/frontdoor/deliver/index/docId/10966/file/WAPS6_
Lauth_Matrix_of_Democracy.pdf.

Laws, Sir John (1995), 'Law and Democracy'. *Public Law* (1995): 72–93.

Lawson, Steven F. (1976), *Black Ballots: Voting Rights in the South 1944–1969.*
New York, NY: Columbia University Press.

Laybourn, Keith and Jack Reynolds (1984), *Liberalism and the Rise of Labour.*
London: Croom Helm.

Layton, Azza Salama (2000), *International Politics and Civil Rights Policies in the
United States, 1941–1960.* Cambridge University Press.

Lazarte, Jorge (2010), *Nuevos códigos del poder en Bolivia.* La Paz: Plural.

(2015), *Reforma del "experimento" Constitucional en Bolivia.* La Paz: Plural.

Leal Buitrago, Francisco (2016), *Estudios sobre el Estado y la política en Colombia.*
Bogota: Universidad de los Andes.

Leal Buitrago, Francisco and Andrés Dávila Ladrón de Guevara (1990), *Clientelismo:
El Sistema politico y su expression regional.* Bogota: Transversal.

Lechner, Frank J. (1998), 'Parsons on Citizenship'. *Citizenship Studies* 2(2):
179–96.

Ledeneva, Alena (2008), 'Telephone Justice in Russia'. *Post-Soviet Affairs* 24(4):
324–50.

Lefort, Claude (1986), *Essais sur le politique.* Paris: Éditions du Seuil.

Lehmann, W.C. (1930), *Adam Ferguson and the Beginnings of Modern Sociology.*
New York, NY: Columbia University Press.

Leibholz, Gerhard (1957), 'Einleitung: Der Status des Bundesverfassungsgerichts'.
Jahrbuch des öffentlichen Rechts Neue Folge 6: 110–221.

Leibniz, Gottfried Wilhelm (1885), 'Initium Institutionem Juris Perpetui', in Georg
Mollat (ed), *Rechtsphilosophisches aus Leibnizens ungedruckten Schriften.*
Leipzig: Robolsky, pp. 1–7.

Lemaitre Ripoll, Julieta (2009), *El derecho como conjuro: Fetichismo legal, violencia y
movimientos sociales.* Bogota: Universidad de los Andes.

Lemaitre Ripoll, Julieta and Kristin Bergtora Sandvik (2014), 'Beyond Sexual
Violence in Transitional Justice: Political Insecurity as a Gendered Harm'.
Feminist Legal Studies 22: 243–61.

(2015), 'Shifting Frames, Vanishing Resources, and Dangerous Political
Opportunities: Legal Mobilization among Displaced Women in Colombia'.
Law & Society Review 49(1): 5–38.

Lenner, Andrew (1996), 'A Tale of Two Constitutions: Nationalism in the Federalist
Era'. *The American Journal of Legal History* 40(1): 72–105.

Leo, Christopher (1984), *Land and Class in Kenya.* Toronto: University of Toronto
Press.

Lepsius, M. Rainer (1993), *Demokratie in Deutschland. Soziologisch-historische
Konstellationsanalysen: Ausgewählte Aufsätze.* Göttingen: Vandenhoeck und
Ruprecht.

Lessard, Geneviève (2017), 'Preventive Reparations at a Crossroads: The Inter-American Court of Human Rights and Colombia's search for peace'. *International Journal of Human Rights*, online first, 1–20.

Leuchtenburg, William E. (1995), *The Supreme Court Reborn: The Constitutional Revolution in the Age of Roosevelt*. Oxford University Press.

Lewis, Peter W. and Joseph Gary Trichter (1981), 'The Nationalization of the Bill of Rights: History, Development and Current Status'. *Washburn Law Journal* 20: 196–240.

Lichtman, Allan (1969), 'The Federal Assault against Voting Discrimination in the Deep South 1957–1967'. *The Journal of Negro History* 54(4): 346–67.

Liendo, Roxana (2009), *Participación Popular y el Movimiento Campesino Aymara*. La Paz: Cipca.

Linklater, Andrew (1996), 'Citizenship and Sovereignty in the Post-Westphalian State'. *European Journal of International Relations* 2(1): 77–103.

(1998), 'Cosmopolitan Citizenship'. *Citizenship Studies* 2(1): 23–41.

(2007), *Critical Theory and World Politics: Citizenship, Sovereignty and Humanity*. London: Routledge.

Linz, Juan (1993), 'State Building and Nation Building'. *European Review* 1(4): 355–69.

Lipset, Seymour Martin (1959), 'Some Social Requisites of Democracy: Economic Development and Political Legitimacy'. *The American Political Science Review* 53(1): 69–105.

(1960), *Political Man*. London: Heinemann.

(1963), *The First New Nation: The United State in Historical and Comparative Perspective*. New York, NY: Norton.

Littré, Émile (1880), *De l'Établissement de la Troisième République*. Paris: Aux Bureaux de la Philosophie Positive.

Litwack, Leon F. (1961), *North of Slavery: The Negro in the Free States, 1790–1860*. Chicago University Press.

Locke, John (1999 [1690]), *The Second Treatise of Government*, edited by T.P. Peardon. New Jersey: Library of Liberal Arts.

Lockwood, Bert B. (1984), 'The United Nations Charter and United States Civil Rights Litigation: 1946–1955'. *Iowa Law Review* 69: 901–56.

Lockwood, David (1996), 'Civic Integration and Class Formation'. *The British Journal of Sociology* 47(3): 531–50.

Loewenstein, Karl (1922), *Volk und Parlament nach der Staatstheorie der französischen Nationalversammlung von 1789: Studien zur Dogmengeschichte der unmittelbaren Volksgesetzbegung*. Munich: Drei Masken Verlag.

Lohr, Eric (2012), *Russian Citizenship: From Empire to Soviet Union*. Cambridge, MA: Harvard University Press.

Londoño Toro, Beatriz (1999), 'Las acciones colectivas en defensa de los derechos de tercera generación'. *Revista Estudios socio-juridicos* 1(2): 103–22.

López Cadena, Carlos Alberto (2015), *Mutación de los derechos fundamentales por la interpretación de la Corte*. Bogota: Universida Externado.

López Cuéllar, Nelcy (2015), *Pluralismo jurídico estatal: Entre conflicto y diálogo*. Bogota: Editorial Universidad de Rosario.

López Martínez, Miguel Andrés (2015), *Responsibilidad del estado frente al desplazamiento forzado: Una exploración conceptual para consolidar el vínculo entre jueces y académicos*. Bogota: Editorial Universidad del Rosario.

López Martínez, Mario and Rafael Gil Bracero (1997), *Caciques Contra Socialistas: Poder y Conflictos en los Ayuntamientos de la República: Granada 1931-1936*. Granada: Diputación Provincial de Granada.

López, Medina, Diego, Eduardo (2004), *Teoría impura del derecho. La transformación de la cultura jurídica latinoamericana*. Bogotá: Legis.

Lorwin, Val. R. (1954). *The French Labor Movement*. Cambridge, MA: Harvard University Press.

Loughlin, Martin (1999), 'The State, the Crown and the Law' in Maurice Sunkin and Sebastian Payne (eds), *The Nature of the Crown: A Legal and Political Analysis*. Oxford University Press, pp. 33–76.

(2010), *Foundations of Public Law*. Oxford University Press.

(2014), 'The Concept of Constituent Power'. *European Journal of Political Theory* 13(2): 218–37.

Lousse, Émile (1958), 'Absolutisme, droit divin, despotisme éclairé'. *Schweizer Beiträge zur Allgemeinen Geschichte* 16: 91–106.

Low, Sidney (1904), *The Government of England*. London: Fischer Unwin.

Luard, Evan (1982), *A History of the United Nations, I: The Years of Western Domination, 1945-1955*. London: Macmillan.

Luban, David (1999), 'The Warren Court and the Concept of a Right'. *Harvard Civil Rights-Civil Liberties Law Review* 34: 7–37.

Lubenow, W.C. (1988), *Parliamentary Politics and the Home Rule Crisis: The British House of Commons in 1886*. Oxford: Clarendon.

Luders, Joseph E. (2010), *The Civil Rights Movement and the Logic of Social Change*. Cambridge University Press.

Luebbert, Gregory M. (1987). 'Social Foundations of Political Order in Interwar Europe'. *World Politics* 39(4): pp. 449–78.

Luhmann, Niklas (1965), *Grundrechte als Institution. Ein Beitrag zur politischen Soziologie*. Berlin: Duncker und Humblot.

(1967), 'Soziologische Aufklärung'. *Soziale Welt* 18(2–3): 97–123.

(1969a) 'Klassische Theorie der Macht: Kritik ihrer Prämissen'. *Zeitschrift für Politik* 10(2–3): 314–25.

(1969b), 'Komplexität und Demokratie'. *Politische Vierteljahresschrift* 1: 314–25.

(1971), *Politische Planung: Aufsätze zur Soziologie von Politik und Verwaltung*. Opladen: Westdeutscher Verlag.

(1973), 'Politische Verfassungen im Kontext des Gesellschaftssystems, I'. *Der Staat* 12(2): 1–22.

(1981a), 'Selbstlegitimation des Staates' in *Archiv für Rechts- und Sozialphilosophie.* Beiheft: Legitimation des modernen Staates, pp. 65–83.

(1981b), *Politische Theorie im Wohlfahrtsstaat.* Munich/Vienna: Olzog.

(1981c), 'Machtkreislauf und Recht in Demokratien'. *Zeitschrift für Rechtssoziologie* 2(2): 158–67.

(1983 [1969]), *Legitimation durch Verfahren.* Frankfurt am Main: Suhrkamp.

(1984a), 'Staat und Politik: Zur Semantik der Selbstbeschreibung politischer Systeme', *Politische Vierteljahresschrift. Sonderheft 15: Politische Theoriengeschichte. Probleme einer Teildisziplin der Politischen Wissenschaft* 99–125.

(1984b), 'Widerstandsrecht und politische Gewalt', *Zeitschrift für Rechtssoziologie* 5: 36–45.

(1988), *Macht*, second edition. Stuttgart: Enke.

(1990), 'Verfassung als evolutionäre Errungenschaft'. *Rechtshistorisches Journal* 9: 176–220.

(1993a), *Das Recht der Gesellschaft.* Frankfurt am Main: Suhrkamp.

(1993b), 'Was ist der Fall, was steckt dahinter? Die zwei Soziologien und die Gesellschaftstheorie'. *Zeitschrift für Soziologie* 22(4): 243–60.

(1994a), 'Partizipation und Legitimation: Die Ideen und die Erfahrungen' in Niklas Luhmann, *Soziologische Aufklärung, 4: Beiträge zur funktionalen Differenzierung der Gesellschaft.* Opladen: Westdeutscher Verlag, pp. 152–60.

(1994b), 'Die Zukunft der Demokratie' in Niklas Luhmann (ed), *Soziologische Aufklärung, 4: Beiträge zur funktionalen Differenzierung der Gesellschaft.* Opladen: Westdeutscher Verlag, 126–32.

(1997), *Die Gesellschaft der Gesellschaft.* Frankfurt am Main: Suhrkamp.

(2000), *Politik der Gesellschaft.* Frankfurt am Main: Suhrkamp.

(2009), 'Der Wohlfahrtsstaat zwischen Evolution und Rationalität' in Niklas Luhmann, *Soziologische Aufklärung 4.* Wiesbaden: VS Verlag für Sozialwissenschaften, pp. 108–20.

Luopajärvi, Katja (2003), 'Is there an Obligation on States to Accept International Humanitarian Assistance to Internally Displaced Persons under International Law?' *International Journal of Refugee Law* 15(4): 678–714.

Luther, Martin (1883a), 'Von weltlicher Oberkeit' in Martin Luther (ed), *Weimarer Ausgabe*, in 120 vols. Weimar: Böhlau, 11, pp. 245–81; 252.

(1883b), 'Von der Freiheit eines Christenmenschen' in Martin Luther (ed), *Weimarer Ausgabe*, in 120 vols. Weimar: Böhlau, 7, pp. 20–38.

Lutz, Donald S. (1980), *Popular Consent and Popular Control: Whig Political Theory in the Early State Constitutions.* Baton Rouge, LA: Louisiana University Press.

Lynch, Gabrielle (2011), *I Say to You: Ethnic Politics and the Kalenjin in Kenya.* Chicago University Press.

de Mably, Gabriel Bonnot (1972), *Des droits et des devoirs du citoyen*, edited by Jean-Louis Lecercle. Paris: Marcel Didier.

MacDonald, R.St.J. (1987), 'Fundamental Norms in Contemporary International Law'. *Canadian Yearbook of International Law* 25: 115–49.

Mack, Kenneth W. (2005), 'Rethinking Civil Rights Lawyering in the Era before "Brown"'. *The Yale Law Journal* 115(2): 256–354.

MacKay, R.A. (1924), 'Coke: Parliamentary Sovereignty or the Supremacy of the Law? *Michigan Law Review* 22(3): 215–47.

Macklem, Patrick (2015), *The Sovereignty of Human Rights*. Oxford University Press.

Maddicott, J.R. (2010), *The Origins of the English Parliament 924–1327*. Oxford University Press.

Madison, James, Alexander Hamilton and John Jay (1987 [1787–88]), *The Federalist Papers*. London: Penguin.

Madsen, Mikael Rask (2014), 'International Human Rights and the Transformation of European Society: From "Free Europe" to the Europe of Human Rights' in Mikael Rask Madsen and Chris Thornhill (eds), *Law and the Formation of Modern Europe: Perspectives from the Historical Sociology of Law*, Cambridge University Press, pp. 245–73.

Maine, Henry Sumner (1886), *Popular Government: Four Essays*. third edition, London: John Murray.

Mamdani, Mahmood (1996), *Citizen and Subject: Contemporary Africa and the Legacy of Late Colonialism*. Princeton University Press.

(1999), 'Historicizing Power and Responses to Power: Indirect Rule and Its Reform'. *Social Research* 66(3): 859–86.

Manin, Bernard (1997), *The Principles of Representative Government*. Cambridge University Press.

Manji, Ambreena (2014), 'The Politics of Land Reform in Kenya 2012'. *African Studies Review* 57(1): 115–30.

Mann, Michael (1987), 'Ruling Class Strategies and Citizenship'. *Sociology* 21(3): 339–54.

Manville, Philip Brook (1990), *The Origins of Citizenship in Ancient Athens*. Princeton University Press.

Marable, Manning (1991), *Race, Reform and Rebellion: The Second Reconstruction in Black America, 1945–1990*. Jackson, MS: University of Mississippi Press.

Markoff, John (1996), *Waves of Democracy: Social Movements and Political Change*. Thousand Oaks, CA: Pine Forge Press.

(1999a), 'Where and When Was Democracy Invented?' *Comparative Studies in Society and History* 41(4): 660–90.

(1999b), 'Globalization and the Future of Democracy'. *Journal of World-Systems Research* 5(2): 277–309.

Marks, Susan (2000), *The Riddle of All Constitutions: International Law, Democracy and the Critique of Ideology*. Oxford University Press.

Márquez Estrada, José Wilson (2011), 'La Infancia de la nación: Estrategias políticas y culturales en el proceso de formación de la ciudadanía en Colombia: 1810–1860'. *Clío América* 5(9): 63–84.

(2012), 'De vecinos a ciudadanos: Las estrategias políticas y culturales en el proceso de formación de la ciudadanía en Colombia'. *Anuario de Historia Regional y de las Fronteras* 16: 295–316.

Marsh, David and Mervyn Read (1988), *Private Members' Bills*. Cambridge University Press.

Marshall, T.H. (1992 [1950]), *Citzenship and Social Class*, introduced by Tom Bottomore. London: Pluto.

Martin, Bernd (1987), 'Japans Weg in die Moderne und das deutsche Vorbild: Historische Gemeinsamkeiten zweier »verspäteter Nationen« 1860–1960' in Bernd Martin (ed), *Japans Weg in die Moderne: Ein Sonderweg nach deutschem Vorbild*. Frankfurt: Campus, pp. 17–44.

Martin, Charles F. (1997), 'Internationalizing "The American Dilemma": The Civil Rights Congress and the 1951 Genocide Petition to the United Nations'. *Journal of American Ethnic History* 16(4): 35–61.

Martin, Terry (2001), *The Affirmative Action Empire: Nations and Nationalism in the Soviet Union, 1923–1939*. Ithaca, NY: Cornell University Press.

Martz, John D. (1997), *The Politics of Clientelism: Democracy and the State in Colombia*. New Brunswick: Transaction.

Maru, Mehari Taddele (2008), 'The Future of Somalia's Legal System and its Contribution to Peace and Development'. *Journal of Peacebuilding & Development* 4(1): 1–15.

Marx, Karl (1852), 'Free Trade and the Chartists', *New-York Daily Tribune*, 25 August 1852.

(1855), Article in *Neue Oder-Zeitung*, 261, 8 June 1855.

(1956 [1844]), *Zur Judenfrage*, in: Karl Marx and Friedrich Engels, *Werke*, in 43 vols (Berlin: Dietz), I: 347–77.

(1960 [1852]), *Der achtzehnte Brumaire des Louis Napoleon* in Karl Marx and Friedrich Engels (eds), *Werke*, in 43 vols (Berlin: Dietz), VIII: 113–207.

(1962 [1932]), *Ökonomisch-philosophische Manuskripte*, in *Frühe Schriften*, edited by J. Lieber and P. Furth. Stuttgart: Cotta, pp. 506–665.

Marx, Karl and Friedrich Engels (1987 [1848]), *Manifest der Kommunistischen Partei*. West Berlin: Verlag das europäische Buch.

Marx, Stephen (1974), 'Durkheim's Theory of Anomie'. *American Journal of Sociology* 80(2): 329–63.

Masterman, Roger (2005), 'Taking the Strasbourg Jurisprudence into Account: Developing a "Muncipal Law of Human Rights" under the Human Rights Act'. *International and Comparative Law Quarterly* 54(4): 907–31.

Mate, Manoj (2015), 'The Rise of Judicial Governance in the Supreme Court of India'. *Boston University International Law Journal* 33: 168–222.

Mati, Jacob Mwathi (2013), 'Antinomies in the Struggle for the Transformation of the Kenyan Constitution (1990–2010)'. *Journal of Contemporary African Studies* 31(2): 235–54.

Matthew, H.C.G. (1973), *The Liberal Imperialists: The Ideas and Politics of a post-Gladstonian Élite*. Oxford University Press.

Matthias, Erich (1970), *Zwischen Räten und Geheimräten: Die deutsche Revolutionsregierung*. Düsseldorf: Droste.

Maxon, Robert M. (2011a), *Britain and Kenya's Constitutions 1950–1960*. Amherst, MA: Cambria Press.

(2011b), *Kenya's Independence Constitution: Constitution-Making and End of Empire*. Lanham, MD: Fairleigh Dickinson University Press.

Mayeur, Jean-Marie (1984), *La Vie politique sous la troisième République, 1870–1940*. Paris: Seuil.

Mayhew, Leon (1984), 'In Defense of Modernity: Talcott Parsons and the Utilitarian Tradition'. *American Journal of Sociology* 89(6): 1273–305.

Mazmanyan, Armen (2015), 'Judicialization of Politics: The Post-Soviet Way'. *International Journal of Constitutional Law* 13(1) (2015): 200–18.

Mbote, Patricia Kameri and Migai Akech (2011), *Kenya: Justice Sector and the Rule of Law*. Johannesburg: Open Society Initiative for Eastern Africa.

McAdam, Doug (1982), *Political Protest and the Development of Black Insurgency 1930–1970*. Chicago University Press.

McCann, Michael W. (1986), *Taking Reform Seriously: Perspectives on Public Interest Litigation*. Ithaca, NY: Cornell University Press.

McCorquodale, Robert (1994), 'Self-Determination: A Human Rights Approach'. *The International and Comparative Law Quarterly* 43(4): 857–85.

McCrillis, Neal (1998), *The British Conservative Party in the Age of Universal Suffrage: Popular Conservatism, 1918–1929*. Columbus, OH: Ohio State University Press.

McKibbin, Ross (1974), *The Evolution of the Labour Party 1910–1924*. Oxford University Press.

(1990), *The Ideologies of Class: Social Relations in Britain 1880–1950*. Oxford: Clarendon.

(2010), *Parties and People: England 1914–1951*. Oxford University Press.

McMahon, Kevin J. (2004), *Reconsidering Roosevelt on Race: How the Presidency Paved the Road to Brown*. Chicago, IL: University of Chicago Press.

McPherson, James M. (1964), *The Struggle for Equality: Abolitionists and the Negro in the Civil War and Reconstruction*. Princeton University Press.

Meier, Christian (1970), *Entstehung des Begriffs ›Demokratie‹: Vier Prolegomena*. Frankfurt: Suhrkamp.

(1980), *Die Entstehung des Politischen bei den Griechen*. Frankfurt: Suhrkamp.

Meister, Rainer (1991), *Die große Depression: Zwangslagen und Handlungsspielräume der Wirtschafts- und Finanzpolitik in Deutschloand 1929–1932*. Regensburg: Transfer Verlag.

Menke, Christoph (2015), *Kritik der Rechte*. Frankfurt: Suhrkamp.

Merkel, Wolfgang (2004), 'Embedded and Defective Democracies'. *Democratization* 11(5): 33–58.

Merritt, Richard L. (1995), *Democracy Imposed. U.S. Occupation Policy and the German Public, 1945–1949*. New Haven, CT: Yale University Press.

Merry, Sally Engle (1988), 'Legal Pluralism'. *Law & Society Review* 22(5): 869–96.

(2006), *Human Rights and Gender Violence: Translating International Law into Local Justice*. Chicago University Press.

Meyer, Georg (1901), *Das parlamentarische Wahlrecht*. Berlin: O. Haering.

Meyer, John (1980), 'The World Polity and the Authority of the Nation-State' in Albert Bergesen (ed), *Studies of the Modern World-System*. New York, NY: Academic Press, pp. 109–37.

Meyer, John W., John Boli, George M. Thomas and Francisco Ramirez (1997), 'World Society and the Nation-State'. *American Journal of Sociology* 103(1): 144–81.

Meyer, John W., Francisco O. Ramirez, Richard Rubinson and John Boli-Bennett (1977), 'The World Educational Revolution, 1950–1970'. *Sociology of Education* 50(4): 242–58.

Meyer, John W., Francisco O. Ramirez and Yasemin Soysal (1992), 'World Expansion of Mass Education, 1870–1980'. *Sociology of Education* 65(2): 128–49.

Michels, Robert (1911), *Zur Soziologie des Parteiwesens in der modernen Demokratie: Untersuchungen über die oligarchischen en Tendenzen des Gruppenlebens*. Leipzig: Werner Klinkhardt.

Mickey, Robert (2015), *Paths out of Dixie: The Democratization of Authoritarian Enclaves in America's Deep South, 1944–1972*. Princeton University Press.

Middlemas, Keith (1979), *Politics in Industrial Society: The Experience of the British System since 1911*. London: Deutsch.

Mill, John Stuart (1861), *Considerations on Representative Government*. London: Parker, Son and Bourn.

(1864), *Principles of Political Economy, with some of their Applications to Social Philosophy*. New York, NY: Appleton.

Miller, David (1995), *On Nationality*. Oxford University Press.

(1999), 'Bounded Citizenship' in Kimberley Hutchings and Roland Dannreuther (eds), *Cosmopolitan Citizenship*. Basingstoke: Macmillan, pp. 60–80.

(2000), *Citizenship and National Identity*. Cambridge: Polity Press.

Miller, Russell A. (2003), 'Self-Determination in International Law and the Demise of Democracy'. *Columbia Journal of Transnational Law* 41: 601–48.

Miller, Susanne (1964), *Das Problem der Freiheit im Sozialismus: Freiheit, Staat und Revolution in der Programmatik der Sozialdemokratie von Lassalle bis zum Revisionismusstreit*. Frankfurt: Europäische Verlagsanstalt.

Mingde, Cao and Wang Fengyuan (2011), 'Environmental Public Interest Litigation in China'. *Asia Pacific Law Review* 19: 217–34.

Mirsky, Georgiy (1997), *On Ruins of Empire. Ethnicity and Nationalism in the Former Soviet Union*. Westport, CO: Greenwood Press.

Molina Saucedo, Carlos Hugo (2015), *De la participación al estado de las autonomías*. Santa Cruz: CEPAD.

Möllers, Christoph (2000), *Staat als Argument*. Munich: Beck.

Mommsen, Hans (1990), *Die verspielte Freiheit: Der Weg der Republik von Weimar in den Untergang 1918 bis 1933*. Frankfurt: Propyläen.

Mommsen, Wolfgang J. (1963) 'Zum Begriff der "plebiszitären Führerdemokratie" bei Max Weber'. *Kölner Zeitschrift für Soziologie und Sozialpsychologie* 15(2): 295–322.

——— (1975), 'Wandlungen der liberalen Idee im Zeitalter des Imperialismus' in Karl Holl and Günther List (eds), *Liberalismus und imperialistischer Staat: Der Imperialismus als Problem liberaler Parteien in Deutschland 1890–1914*. Göttingen: Vandenhoeck & Ruprecht, pp. 109–49.

Moore, Barrington, Jr. (1973 [1966]), *Social Origins of Dictatorship and Democracy: Lord and Peasant in the Making of the Mdern World*. London: Penguin.

Moorhouse, H.F. (1973), 'The Political Incorporation of the British Working Class: An Interpretation'. *Sociology* 7(3): 341–59.

Moraski, Bryon (2006), *Elections by Design: Parties and Patronage in Russia's Regions*. Dekalb, IL: Northern Illinois University Press.

Morgan, Kenneth O. (1979), *Consensus and Disunity: The Lloyd George Coalition Government 1918–1922*. Oxford: Calrendon.

Morris, Aldon D. (1984), *The Origins of the Civil Rights Movement: Black Communities Organizing for Change*. New York, NY: Free Press.

Morsey, Rudolf (1966), *Die deutsche Zentrumspartei, 1917–1923*. Düsseldorf: Droste.

Mouffe, Chantal (2005), *On the Political*. London: Routledge.

Moustafa, Tamir (2003), 'Law versus the State: The Judicialization of Politics in Egypt'. *Law & Social Inquiry* 28: 883–930.

Mugdan, Benno (ed) (1899), *Die gesammten Materialien zum Bürgerlichen Gesetzbuch für das Deutsche Reich*. Berlin: Decker, Vol. I.

Mühlhausen, Walter (2006), *Friedrich Ebert 1871–1925: Reichspräsident der Weimarer Republik*. Berlin: Dietz.

Mukaindo, Petronella (2013), 'A case of mistaken identity? Demystifying the "Constitutional Court" in Kenya'. Available at: http://kenyalaw.org/kenyalawblog/a-case-of-mistaken-identity-demystifying-the-constitutional-court-in-kenya-2/.

Müller, Theodor (1925), *Die Geschichte der Breslauer Sozialdemokratie, II: Das Sozialistengesetz*. Breslau: Verlag des Sozialdemokratischen Vereins Breslau.

Müller, Friedrich (1995). *Fragment (über) Verfassunggebende Gewalt des Volkes: Elemente einer Verfassungstheorie V*. Berlin: Duncker und Humblot.

Münch, Richard (1984), *Die Struktur der Moderne: Grundmuster und differentielle Gestaltung des institutionellen Aufbaus der modernen Gesellschaften*. Frankfurt: Suhrkamp.

(2001), *Nation and Citizenship in the Global Age: From Nations to Transnational Ties and Identities*. Basingstoke: Palgrave.

Munck, Gerardo L. (2016), 'What is Democracy? A Reconceptualization of the Quality of Democracy'. *Democratization* 23(1): 1–26.

Munene, Anthony Wambugu (2002), 'The Bill of Rights and Constitutional Order: A Kenyan Perspective'. *African Human Rights Law Journal* 2: 135–59.

Murkens, Jo Erik Khushal (2009), The Quest for Constitutionalism in UK Public Law Discourse'. *Oxford Journal of Legal Studies* 29(3): 427–55.

Murillo-Castaño, Gabriel (1999), 'Representación, ciudadanía y nueva Constitución en Colombia'. *Nueva Sociedad* 160: 47–55.

Murunga, Godwin R. and Shadrack W. Nasong'o (2006), 'Bent on Self-Destruction: The Khibaki Regime in Kenya'. *Journal of Contemporary African Studies* 24(1): 1–28.

Musgrave, Thomas D. (1997), *Self-Determination and National Minorities*. Oxford University Press.

Mutunga, Willy (2015a), 'Human Rights States and Societies: A Reflection from Kenya'. *The Transnational Human Rights Review* 2: 63–102.

(2015b), 'The 2010 Constitution of Kenya and its Interpretation: Reflections from the Supreme Court's decisions'. *Speculum Juris* 1: 1–20.

Myrdal, Gunnar (1944), *An American Dilemma: The Negro Problem and Modern Democracy*. New York, NY: Harper & Row.

Najemy, John (1979), 'Guild Republicanism in Trecento Florence: The Successes and Ultimate Failure of Corporate Politics'. *The American Historical Review* 84(1): 53–71.

Nahaylo, Bohdan and Victor Swoboda (1990), *Soviet Disunion: A History of the Nationalities Problem in the USSR*. London: Hamish Hamilton.

Naumann, Friedrich (1900), *Demokratie und Kaisertum: Ein Handbuch für innere Politik*. Berlin: Buchverlag der "Hilfe".

(1919), Versuch volksverständlicher Grundrechte'. *Die Hilfe* 13: 156–7.

Ndahinda, Felix Mukwiza (2011), *Indigenousness in Africa: A Contested Legal Framework for Empowerment of 'Marginalized' Communities*. The Hague: Asser.

Ndegwa, Stephen N. (1997), 'Citizenship and Ethnicity: An Examination of Two Transition Moments in Kenyan Politics'. *The American Political Science Review* 91(3): 599–616.

(1998a), 'Citizenship amid Economic and Political Change in Kenya'. *Africa Today* 45(3/4): 351–67.

(1998b), 'The Incomplete Transition: The Constitutional and Electoral Context in Kenya'. *Africa Today* 45(2): 193–211.

Neier, Aryeh (1982), *Only Judgment: The Limits of Litigation in Social Change*. Middletown, CO: Wesleyan University Press.

Nelson, William E. (1975), *Americanization of the Common Law: The Legal Impact of Change on Massachusetts Society, 1760–1830*. Athens: University of Georgia Press.

Neuburg, Clamor (1880), *Zunftgerichtsbarkeit und Zunftverfassung in der Zeit vom 13. bis 16 Jahrhundert*. Jena: Gustav Fischer.

Neuman, Gerald L. (2004), 'The Uses of International Law in Constitutional Interpretation'. *The American Journal of International Law* 98(1): 82–90.

(2008), 'Import, Export, and Regional Consent in the Inter-Ameican Court of Human Rights'. *The European Journal of International Law* 19(1): 1010–123.

Neumann, Franz (1937), 'Der Funktionswandel des Gesetzes im Recht der bürgerlichen Gesellschaft'. *Zeitschrift für Sozialforschung* VI: 542–96.

Neves, Marcelo (1992), *Verfassung und Positivität des Rechts in der peripheren Moderne: Eine theoretische Betrachtung und eine Interpretation des Falls Brasilien*. Berlin: Duncker und Humblot.

Nicolet, Claude (1982), *L'Idée républicaine en France (1789–1924): Essai d'histoire critique*. Paris: Gallimard.

Nipperdey, Thomas (1961), *Die Organisation der deutschen Parteien vor 1918*. Düsseldorf: Droste.

Nisbet, Robert A. (1943), 'The French Revolution and the Rise of Sociology in France'. *The American Journal of Sociology* 49(2): 156–64.

Nogueira Alcalá, Humberto (2013), 'El uso del derecho y jurisprudencia constitucional extranjera y de tribunales internacionales no vinculantes por el Tribunal Constitucional chileno en el período 2006–2011'. *Estudios Constitucionales* 11(1): 221–74.

Nollkaemper, André (2009), 'The Internationalized Rule of Law'. *Hague Journal on the Rule of Law* 1(1): 74–8.

Norton, Philip (2005), *Parliament in British Politics*. Basingstoke: Palgrave.

Nowrojee, Pheroze (2014), 'The Legal Profession 1963–2013: All This Can Happen Again – Soon' in Yash Pal Ghai and Jill Cottrell (eds), *The Legal Profession and the New Constitutional Order in Kenya*. Nairobi: Strathmore Universityy Press, pp. 33–58.

Nozick, Robert (1974), *Anarchy, State, and Utopia*. New York, NY: Basic Books.

Nuñez del Prado, José (2015), *Utopía indígena truncada: Proyectos y praxis de poder indígena en Bolivia Plurinacional*. La Paz: CIDES-UMSA.

Oakes, James (2013), *Freedom National: The Destruction of Slavery in the United States, 1861–1865*. New York, NY: Norton.

Odeh, Lama Abu (2011), 'The Supreme Constitutional Court of Egypt: The Limits of Liberal Political Science and CLS Analysis of Law Elsewhere'. *American Journal of Comparative Law* 59 (2011): 985–1008.

O'Donnell, Guillermo (1993), 'On the State, Democratization and Some Conceptual Problems: A Latin American View with Glances at Some Postcommunist Countries'. *World Development* 21(8): 1355–69.

Oduor, Maurice (2014), 'The Status of International Law in Kenya'. *Africa Nazarene University Law Journal* 2(2): 97–125.

Oertzen, Peter von (1976), *Betriebsräte in der Novemberrevolution: Eine politikwissenschaftliche Untersuchung über Ideengehalt und Struktur der betrieblichen und wirtschaftlichen Arbeiterräte in der deutschen Revolution von 1918/19*. Berlin: Dietz.

Ohler, Christoph (2015), 'Die Rückkehr in die internationale Gemeinschaft: Das Bundesverfassungsgericht als Türhüter des offenen Staates' in Christian Fischer and Walter Pauly (eds), *Höchstrichterliche Rechtsprechung in der frühen Bundesrepublik*. Tübingen: Mohr, pp. 27–42.

Ojwang, J.B. and J.A. Otieno-Odek (1988), 'The Judiciary in Sensitive Areas of Public Law: Emerging Approaches to Human Rights Litigation'. *Netherlands International Law Review* 35(1): 29–52.

Okoth-Ogendo, H.W.O. (1972), 'The Politics of Constitutional Change in Kenya since Independende'. *African Affairs* 71: 9–34.

Okuta, Antonina (2009), 'National Legislation for Prosecution of International Crimes in Kenya'. *Journal of International Criminal Law* 7: 1063–76.

Oliver, Dawn (1987), 'Is the ultra vires Rule the Basis of Judicial Review?' *Public Law*: 543–69.

(2009), 'The United Kingdom Constitution in Transition: From Where to Where?' in Mads Andenas and Duncan Fairgreave (eds), *Tom Bingham and the Transformation of the Law*. Oxford University Press, pp. 147–62.

O'Loughlin, Elizabeth (2018), 'Decolonising Jurisprudence: Public Interest Standing in New Constitutional Orders' in Mark Elliott, Jason N.E. Varuhas, and Shona Wilson Stark (eds), *The Unity of Public Law? Doctrinal, Theoretical and Comparative Perspectives*. Oxford: Hart.

Onalo, P.L. Agweli (2004), *Constitution-Making in Kenya*. Nairobi: Transafrica Press.

O'Neill, Johnathan (2005), *Originalism in American Law and Politics: A Constitutional History*. Baltimore, MD: Johns Hopkins University Press.

O'Neill, Kathleen (2005), *Decentralizing the State: Elections, Parties, and Local Power in the Andes*. Cambridge University Press.

Oppler, Alfred C. (1976), *Legal Reform in Occupied Japan: A Participant Looks Back*. Princeton University Press.

Orchard, Phil (2010), 'Protection of Internally Displaced Persons: Soft Law as a Norm-Generating Mechanism'. *Review of International Studies* 36(2): 281–303.

Osipenkova, Ekaterina (2014), 'Stanovleniye zakonodatelstva o grazhdanstve v Rossii (oktyabr 1917 g. –1922 g.)' [Formation of the Legislation on Citizenship in Russia (October 1917–1922)]. *Teoriya i Praktika Obshchestvennogo Razvitiya* 15: 165–7.

Otis, James (1764), *The Rights of the British Colonies asserted and proved*. London: Almon.

(1769), *A Vindication of the British Colonies*. London: Almon.

Ott, Walter (1976), *Der Rechtspositivismus: Kritische Würdigung auf der Grundlage eines juristischen Pragmatismus*. Berlin: Duncker & Humblot.

Otto, Volker (1971), *Das Staatsverständnis des Parlamentarischen Rates: Ein Beitrag zur Entstehungsgeschichte des Grundgesetzes für die Bundesrepublik Deutschland*. Bonn-Bad Godesberg: Rheinisch-Bergische Druckerei und Verlagsgesellschaft.

Oucho, John (2002), *Undercurrents of Ethnic Conflict in Kenya*. Leiden: Brill.

Packer, Ian (2001), *Lloyd George, Liberalism and the Land: The Land Issue and Party Politics in England, 1906–1914*. Woodbridge: Boydell.

Paine, Thomas (2003 [1791]), *Common Sense and the Rights of Man*. New York, NY: Signet Classics.

Palmowski, Jan (2008), 'In Search of the German Nation: Citizenship and the Challenge of Integration'. *Citizenship Studies* 12(6): 547–63.

Park, Susan (2006), 'Theorizing Norm Diffusion within International Organizations'. *International Politics* 43(3): 342–61.

Parker, Karen and Lyn Beth Neylon (1989), 'Jus Cogens: Compelling the Law of Human Rights'. *Hastings International and Comparative Law Review* 12: 411–63.

Parkinson, Charles O.H. (2007), *Bills of Rights and Decolonization: The Emergence of Domestic Human Rights Instruments in Britain's Overseas Colonies*. Oxford University Press.

Parris, Henry (1969), *Constitutional Bureaucracy: The Development of British Central Administration since the Eighteenth Century*. London: Allen & Unwin.

Parsons, Talcott (1942), 'Max Weber and the Contemporary Political Crisis'. *The Review of Politics* 4(2): 155–72.

(1949 [1937]), *The Structure of Social Action*. New York, NY: The Free Press.

(1951), *The Social System*. Glencoe, IL: The Free Press.

(1954), *Essays in Sociological Theory*, revised edition. New York, NY: Free Press.

(1960), 'Social Structure and Political Orientation'. *World Politics* 13(1): 112–28.

(1962), 'Review: Hurst's Law and Social Process in U.S. History'. *Journal of the History of Ideas* 23(4): 558–64.

(1964), 'Evolutionary Universals in Society'. *American Sociological Review* 29(3): 339–57.

(1965), 'Full Citizenship for the Negro American? A Sociological Problem'. *Daedalus* 94(4): 1009–54.

(1969), *Politics and Social Structure*. New York, NY: Free Press.

(1970), 'Equality and Inequality in Modern Society, or Social Stratification Revisited'. *Sociological Inquiry* 40: 13–72.

(1977), 'Law as an Intellectual Stepchild'. *Sociological Inquiry* 47(3–4): 11–58.

Partsch, Karl Josef (1964), *Die Anwendung des Völkerrechts im innerstaatlichen Recht: Überprüfung der Transformationslehre*. Karlsruhe: Müller.

Pasqualucci, Jo M. (2006), 'The Evolution of International Indigenous Rights in the Inter-American Human Rights System'. *Human Rights Law Review* 6(2): 281–322.

Pateman, Carole (1970), *Participation and Democratic Theory*. Cambridge University Press.

Patemann, Richard (1964), *Der Kampf um die preußische Wahlreform im Ersten Weltkrieg*. Düsseldorf: Droste.

Patterson, James T. (2001), *Brown v Board of Education: A Civil Rights Milestone and its Troubled Legacy*. Oxford University Press.

Pavlikov, Sergey (2004), 'Rossiyskiy federalizm: vliyaniye novykh aspektov na razvitiye sudebnoy sistemy' [Russian Federalism: Impact of New Aspects on the Development of the Judicial System] *Rossiya i sovremennyy mir* 1(15): 82–89; 85.

Pécaut, Daniel (1987), *L'Ordre et la violence: Évolution socio-politique de la Colombie entre 1930 et 1953*. Paris: Éditions de l'École des Hautes Études en Sciences Sociales.

Pedriana, Nicholas and Robin Stryker (2004), 'The Strength of a Weak Agency: Enforcement of Title VII of the 1964 Civil Rights Act and the Expansion of State Capacity, 1965–1971'. *American Journal of Sociology* 110(3): 709–60.

Perham, Margery (1934), 'Some Problems of Indirect Rule in Africa'. *Journal of the Royal Society of Arts* 82: 689–710.

Peters, Bernhard (1993), *Die Integration moderner Gesellschaften*. Frankfurt: Suhrkamp.

Petersen, Niels (2015), *Verhältnismäßigkeit als Rationalitätskontrolle: Eine rechtsempirische Studie verfassungsrechtlicher Rechtsprechung zu den Freiheitsgrundrechten*. Tübingen: Mohr.

Petrone, Laura (2011), 'Institutionalizing Pluralism in Russia: A New Authoritarianism?' *Journal of Communist and Transition Politics* 27(2): 166–94.

Petzina, Dietmar (1985), 'Soziale und wirtschaftliche Entwicklung' in Kurt G.A. Jeserich, Hans Pohl and Georg-Christoph von Unruh (eds), *Deutsche Verwaltungsgeschichte, 4: Das Reich als Republik und in der Zeit des Nationalsozialismus*. Stuttgart: Deutsche Verlags-Anstalt, pp. 39–66.

Pevehouse, Jon C. (2002), 'Democracy from the Outside-In? International Organizations and Democratization'. *International Organization* 56(3): 515–49.

Phuong, Catherine (2005), *The International Protection of Internally Displaced Persons*. Cambridge University Press.

Pikart, Eberhard and Wolfram Werner (eds) (1993), *Der Parlamentarische Rat 1948–1949: Akten und Protokolle*, in 14 vols. Boppard am Rhein: Harald Boldt, Vol. 5/I.

Pimlott, Ben (1977), *Labour and the Left in the 1930s*. Cambridge University Press.

Pitkin, Hanna Fenichel (1967), *The Concept of Representation*. Berkeley, CA: University of California Press.

Plazas Vega, Mauricio A. (2011), *El Frente Nacional*. Bogota: TEMIS.

Plummer, Brenda Gayle (1996), *Rising Wind: Black Americans and U.S. Foreign Affairs, 1935–1960*. Chapel Hill, NC: University of North Carolina Press.

Plotnikova, Olga (2016), 'Krizis natsionalnoy samoidentifikatsii v sovremennoy Rossii' [National Self-Identification Crisis in Contemporary Russia]. *Sotsialniye Issledovania* 2: 13–18.

Pocock, J.G.A. (1975), *The Machiavellian Moment: Florentine Political Thought and the Atlantic Republican Tradition*. Princeton University Press.

(1995), 'The Ideal of Citizenship since Classical Time' in Ronald Beiner (ed), *Theorizing Citizenship*. Albany, NY: State University of New York, pp. 29–52.

Pole, J.R. (1966), *Political Representation in England and the Origins of the American Republic*. Berkeley, CA: University of California Press.

(1978), *The Pursuit of Equality in American History*. Berkeley, CA: University of California Press.

Pomeranz, William and Max Gutbrod, (2012), 'The Push for Precedent in Russia's Judicial System'. *Review of Central and East European Law* 37: 1–30.

Ponisova, Elena (2011), 'Institut grazhdanstva v monarkhicheskoy Rossii' [The Institution of Citizenship in Monarchical Russia]. *Trudy Instituta Gosudarstva i Prava Rossiyskoy Akademii Nauk* 3: 57–73.

Ponteil, Félix (1968), *Les Classes bourgeoises et l'avènement de la démocratie*. Paris: Albin Michel.

Porritt, Edward (1899), 'The Barrier between England and Democracy'. *Political Science Quarterly* 14(4): 628–52.

Postero, Nancy Grey (2007), *Now we are Citizens: Indigenous Politics in Postmulticultural Bolivia*. Stanford University Press.

Prager, Jeffrey (1981), 'Moral Integration and Political Inclusion: A Comparison of Durkheim's and Weber's Theories of Democracy'. *Social Forces* 59(4): 918–50.

Prak, Maarten (1997), 'Burghers into Citizens: Urban and National Citizenship in the Netherlands during the Revolutionary Era'. *Theory and Society* 26: 403–20.

Preller, Ludwig (1949), *Sozialpolitik in der Weimarer Republik*. Stuttgart: Franz Mittelbach.

Preuß, Hugo (1897), *Die Junkerfrage*. Berlin: Rosenbaum & Hart.

(1902), 'Über Organpersönlichkeit: Eine begriffsgeschichtliche Studie'. *Jahrbuch für Gesetzgebung und Volkswirtschaft im Deutschen Reich* 22(2): 103–42.

(1926), *Staat, Recht und Freiheit: Aus 40 Jahren deutscher Politik und Geschichte*. Tübingen: Mohr.

Price, Polly J. (1997), 'Natural Law and Birthright Citizenship in Calvin's Case'. *Yale Journal of Law and the Humanities* 9: 73–145.

Price, Roger (2001), *The French Second Empire: An Anatomy of Political Power*. Cambridge University Press.

Procacci, Giovanna (1968), 'Italy from Interventionism to Fascism, 1917–1919'. *Journal of Contemporary History* 3(4): 153–176.

Proelß, Alexander (2014), *Bundesverfassungsgericht und überstaatliche Gerichtsbarkeit: Prozedurale und prozessuale Mechanismen zur Vermeidung und Lösung von Jurisdiktionskonflikten*. Tübingen: Mohr.

Proudhon, Pierre-Joseph (1865), *De la Capacité politique des classes ouvrières*. Paris: Dentu.

 (1927 [1861]), *La Guerre et la paix: Recherches sur le principe et la constitution du droit des gens*, new edition. Paris: Marcel Rivière.

 (1936), *La Révolution sociale*, in *Œuvres complètes*, edited by C. Bouglé and H. Moysset Paris: Marcel Rivière.

 (1966 [1840]), *Qu'est ce que la propriété? ou Recherches sur le principe du droit du gouvernement*. Paris: Garnier-Flammarion.

Przeworski, Adam (2000), 'Conquered or Granted? A History of Suffrage Extension'. *British Journal of Political Science* 39: 291–321.

Puchta, Georg Friedrich (1828), *Das Gewohnheitsrecht*. Erlangen: Palm.

Pugh, Martin (1978), *Electoral Reform in War and Peace 1906–18*. London: Routledge.

Putin, Vladimir (2000), 'Open Letter from Vladimir Putin to the Russian Voters'. *Kommersant* 32: 25.

 (2012), 'Speech of the President of the Russian Federation at the VIII National Congress of Judges, 18 December 2012'. Available (in Russian) at: www.ssrf .ru/page/9097/detail/.

Putnam, Robert D, with Robert Leonardi and Raffaella Y. Nanetti (1993), *Making Democracy Work: Civic Traditions in Modern Italy*. Princeton University Press.

Quigley, John (1988), 'Perestroika and International Law'. *The American Journal of International Law* 82(4): 788–97.

Rabkin, Jeremy (2007), *Law without Nations? Why Constitutional Government requires Sovereign States*. Princeton University Press.

Raffass, Tania (2012), *The Soviet Union: Federation or Empire?* Abingdon: Routledge.

Ramirez, Francisco O. and John W. Meyer (2012), 'Toward Post-National Societies and Global Citizenship'. *Multicultural Education Review* 4(1): 1–28.

Ramirez, Francisco O. and Rennie Moon (2012), 'From Citizenship to Human Rights to Human Rights Education' in Mikael Rask Madsen and Gert Verschraegen (eds), *Making Human Rights Intelligible: Towards a Sociology of Human Rights*. Oxford: Hart, 191–213.

Ramirez, Francisco O., Yasemin Soysal and Suzanne Shanahan (1997), 'The Changing Logic of Political Citizenship: Cross-National Acquisition of Women's Suffrage Rights, 1890 to 1990'. *American Sociological Review* 62(5): 735–45.

Ramos, Joseph (1986), *Neoconservative Economics in the Southern Cone of Latin America, 1973–1983*. Baltimore, MD: John Hopkins Press.

Ramsay, David (1789), *Dissertation on the Manner of Acquiring the Character and Privileges of a Citizen of the United States*. Charleston, SC.

Ranke, Leopold von (1833), 'Politisches Gespräch'. *Historisch-politische Zeitschrift*, II: 775–807.

Rathbone, Richard (2000), *Nkrumah and the Chiefs: The Politics of Chieftaincy in Ghana, 1951–60*. Athens, OH: Ohio University Press.

Rawls, John (1971), *A Theory of Justice*. Oxford University Press.

Ray, Arun (2003), *Public Interest Litigation and Human Rights in India*. New Delhi: Radha Publications.

Ray, Donald I. (1996), 'Divided Sovereignty: Traditional Authority and the State in Ghana'. *Journal Legal Pluralism and Unofficial Law*, 37/38: 181–202;

Rebentisch, Dieter (1989), *Führerstaat und Verwaltung im Zweiten Weltkrieg: Verfassungsentwicklung und Verwaltungspolitik 1939–1945*. Stuttgart: Franz Steiner.

Redish, Martin H. (2003), 'Class Actions and the Democratic Difficulty: Rethinking the Intersection of Private Litigation and Public Goals'. *The University of Chaicago Legal Forum* (2003): 71–140.

Redslob, Robert (1916), 'Völkerrechtliche Ideen der französischen Revolution' in *Festgabe für Otto Mayer: Zum siebzigsten Geburtstage dargebracht von Freunden, Verehrern und Schülern*. Tübingen: Mohr, pp. 273–301.

Remmert, Barbara (1995), *Verfassungs- und verwaltungsrechtsgeschichtliche Grundlagen des Übermaßverbotes*. Heidelberg: Müller.

Restrepo Yepes, Olga Cecilia, Mauricio Bocanument Arvelaez and Miltón Andrés Rojas Betancur (2014), *Voces de la Asamblea Nacional Constituyente de 1991*. Medellin: Selo Editoral.

Reuter, Ora John (2010), 'The Politics of Dominant Party: United Russia and Russia's Governors'. *Europe-Asia Studies* 62(2): 293–327.

Reuter, Ora John and Graeme B. Robertson (2012), 'Subnational Appointments in Authoritarian Regimes: Evidence from Russian Gubernatorial Appointments'. *The Journal of Politics* 74(4) (2012): 1023–37.

Riedel, Manfred (1982), *Zwischen Tradition und Revolution: Studien zu Hegels Rechtsphilosophie*. Stuttgart: Klett-Cotta.

Riga, Liliana (2012), *The Bolsheviks and the Russian Empire*. Cambridge University Press.

Riley, Patrick (1986), *The General Will Before Rousseau: The Transformation of the Divine into the Civic*. Princeton University Press.

Riser, R. Volney (2010), *Defying Disfranchisement: Black Voting Rights Activism in the Jim Crow South, 1890–1908*. Baton Rouge, LA: Louisiana State University Press.

Risse, Thomas and Kathryn Sikkink (1999), 'The Socialization of International Human Rights Norms into Domestic Practices: Introduction' in Thomas Risse, Stephen C. Ropp and Kathryn Sikkink (eds), *The Power of Human*

Rights: International Norms and Domestic Change. Cambridge University Press, pp. 1–38.

Ritschel, Daniel (1991), 'A Corporatist Economy in Britain? Capitalist Planning for Industrial Self-Government in the 1930s'. *The English Historical Review* 106(418): 41–65.

Ritter, Gerhard A. (1976), *Arbeiterbewegung, Parteien und Parlamentarismus*. Göttingen: Vandenhoeck und Ruprecht.

Ritter, Joachim (1957), *Hegel und die französische Revolution*. Cologne: Westdeutscher Verlag.

Roberts, Anthea (2011), 'Comparative International Law? The Role of National Courts in Creating and Enforcing International Law'. *International and Comparative Law Quarterly* 60(1): 57–92.

Roberts, Sean P. (2012), *Putin's United Russia Party*. London: Routledge.

Robertson, Graeme B. (2011), *The Politics of Protest in Hybrid Regimes: Managing Dissent in Post-Communist Russia*. Cambridge University Press.

Robespierre, Maximilien (1789), *Moniteur universel*, 22–26 October 1789, nr.77: 81.

(1791), *Discours sur la nécessité de révoquer les décrets qui attachent l'exercise des droits du citoyen à la contribution du marc d'argent ou d'un nombre determiné de journées d'ouvriers*. Paris: Calixte Volland.

(1793a), *Discours sur la Constitution*. Paris: Imprimerie Patriotique et Républicaine.

(1793b), *Rapport sur la situation politique de la République*. Paris Imprimerie Nationale.

(1793c), *Rapport sur les rapports des idées réligieuses et morales avec les principes républicains, et sur les fêtes nationales*. Paris: Imprimerie Nationale.

(1793d), *Rapport sur les principes du gouvernement révolutionnaire*. Paris: Imprimerie Nationale.

(1794), *Rapport sur les principes de morale politique qui doivent guider la Convention nationale dans l'adminstration intérieure de la République*. Paris: Imprimerie nationale.

Rocher, Guy (1989), 'Le droit et la sociologie du droit chez Talcott Parsons'. *Sociologie et sociétés* 21(1): 143–63.

Rodríguez Garavito, César and Diana Rodríguez Franco (2010), *Cortes y cambio social – Cómo la Corte Constitucional transformó el desplazamiento forzado en Colombia*. Bogota: Dejusticia.

Roeder, Philip G. (1991), 'Soviet Federalism and Ethnic Mobilization'. *World Politics* 43(2): 196–232.

(2007), *Where Nation-States Come From. Institutional Change in the Age of Nationalism*. Princeton University Press.

Rojas, Cristina (2008), 'La construcción de la ciudadanía en Colombia durante el gran siglo diecineuve 1810–1919'. *Poligramas* 29: 295–333.

Rokkan, Stein (1961), 'Mass Suffrage, Secret Voting and Political Participation'. *European Journal of Sociology* 2(1): 132–52.

(1970), *Citizens, Elections, Parties: Approaches to the Comparative Study of the Processes of Development*. Oslo: Universitetsforlaget.

(1975), 'Dimensions of State Formation and Nation-Building: A Possible Paradigm for Research on Variations within Europe in Charles Tilly (ed), *The Formation of National States in Western Europe*. Princeton University Press, pp. 562–600.

Romanelli, Raffale (1979), *L'Italia liberale*. Bolgna: Mulino.

Rosanvallon, Pierre (1985), *Le moment Guizot*. Paris: Gallimard.

(1992), *Le Sacre du citoyen*. Paris: Gallimard.

(1994), *La Monarchie impossible: Les Chartes de 1814 et de 1830*. Paris: Fayard.

(1998), *Le people introuvable: Histoire de la répresentation démocratique en France*. Paris: Gallimard.

(2000), *La démocratie inachevée: Histoire de la souveraineté du people in France*. Paris: Gallimard.

(2008), *La légitimité démocratique: Impartialité, réflexivité, proximité*. Paris: Seuil.

Rosberg, Carl G. and John Nottingham (1966), *The Myth of "Mau Mau": Nationalism in Kenya*. New York, NY: Praeger.

Rose, Sonya O. (2003), *Which People's War? National Identity and Citizenship in Britain 1939–1945*. Oxford University Press.

Roshwald, Aviel (2001), *Ethnic Nationalism and the Fall of Empires. Central Europe, Russia and the Middle East, 1914–1923*. London: Routledge.

Ross, Stanley D. (1992) 'The Rule of Law and Lawyers in Kenya'. *The Journal of Modern African Studies* 30(3): 421–42.

Rosenberg, Gerald N. (1991), *The Hollow Hope: Can Courts bring about Social Change?* Chicago University Press.

Rosenblatt, Helena (1997), *Rousseau and Geneva: From the First Discourse to the Social Contract, 1749–1762*. Cambridge University Press.

Rothchild, Donald (1968), 'Kenya's Minorities and the African Crisis over Citizenship'. *Race* 9(4): 421–37.

(1973), *Racial Bargaining in Independent Kenya: A Study of Minorities and Decolonization*. London: Oxford University Press.

Rousseau, Jean-Jacques (1966 [1762]), *Du contrat social*. Paris: Flammarion.

Roussellier, Nicolas (2015), *La force de gouverner: Le pouvoir exécutif en France. XIX-XXI siècles*. Paris: Gallimard.

Rudden, Bernard (1994), 'Civil law, Civil Society and the Russian Constitution'. *Law Quarterly Review* 110: 56–83.

Rueschemeyer, Dietrich, Evelyn Huber Stephens and John D. Stephens (1992), *Capitalist Development and Democracy*. Cambridge: Polity.

Ruggie, John Gerard (1982), 'International Regimes, Transactions, and Change: Embedded Liberalism in the Postwar Economic Order'. *International Organization* 36(2): 379–415.

Rütten, Wilhelm (1996), 'Gewerkschaften und Arbeitsrecht nach dem Zweiten Weltkrieg (1945–1950/52' in Bernhard Diestelkamp, Zentarô Kitagawa, Josef Kreiner, Junichi Murakami, Knut Wolfgang Nörr and Nobuyoshi Toshitani (eds), *Zwischen Kontinuität und Fremdbestimmung: Zum Einfluß der Besatzungsmächte auf die deutsche und japanische Rechtsordnung 1945 bis 1950.* Tübingen: Mohr, pp. 149–66.

Sabel, Charles F. and William H. Simon (2004), 'Destabilization Rights: How Public Law Litigation Succeeds'. *Harvard Law Review* 117: 1016–101.

Säcker, Horst (1987), 'Die Verfassungsgerichtsbarkeit im Konvent von Herrenchiemsee' in Walther Fürst, Roman Herzog und Dieter C. Umbach (eds), *Festschrift für Wolfgang Zeidler.* Berlin: De Gruter, pp. 265–80.

Saikkonen, Inga A-L. (2017), 'Electoral Mobilization and Authoritarian Elections: Evidence from Post-Soviet Russia'. *Government and Opposition* 52(1) (2017): 51–74.

Saint-Just, Louis Antoine Léon de (1791), *Esprit de la Révolution et de la Constitution de France.* Paris: Beuvin.

(1793), *Discours sur la Constitution de la France.* Paris: Imprimerie Nationale.

Saint-Simon, Claude-Henri de (1966), *L'industrie*, in *Oeuvres*, in 6 vols Paris: Anthropos, 1966, I.

Sajó, András (1995), 'Reading the Invisible Constitution: Judicial Review in Hungary'. *Oxford Journal of Legal Studies* 15(2): 253–67.

Salmond, J.W. (1902), 'Citizenship and Allegiance II'. *The Law Quarterly Review* 18: 5–63.

Sanborn, Joshua A. (2003), *Drafting the Russian Nation: Military Conscription, Total War, and Mass Politics, 1905–1925.* Dekalb: Northern Illinois University Press.

Sandel, Michael J. (1996), *Democracy's Discontent: America in Search of a Public Philosophy.* Cambridge, MA: Harvard University Press.

Sandoval, Clara (2017), 'Two Steps Forward, One Step Back: Reflections on the Jurisprudential Turn of the Inter-American Court of Human Rights on Domestic Reparation Programmes'. *International Journal of Human Rights*, online first: 1–17.

Sang, Y.K.Brian (2013), 'Tending towards Greater Eco-Protection in Kenya: Public Interest Environmental Litigation and its Prospects within the New Constitutional Order'. *Journal of African Law* 57(1): 29–56.

Sakwa, Richard (2010), 'The Dual State in Russia'. *Post-Soviet Affairs* 26(3): 185–206.

(2011), *The Crisis of Russian Democracy: The Dual State, Factionalism and the Medvedev Succession.* Cambridge University Press.

Sassen, Saskia (2002a), 'Towards Post-National Citizenship and Denationalized Citizenship' in Engin F. Isin and Bryan S Turner (eds), *Handbook of Citizenship Studies.* London: Sage, pp. 277–91.

(2002b), 'The Repositioning of Citizenship: Emergent Subjects and Spaces for Politics'. *Berkeley Journal of Sociology* 46: 4–26.

Sathe, S.P. (2001), 'Judicial Activism: The Indian Experience'. *Washington University Journal of Law & Policy* 6: 29–107.

(2002), *Judicial Activism in India*. Oxford University Press.

Saunders, Robert (2011), *Democracy and the Vote in British Politics, 1848–1867: The Making of the Second Reform Act*. Farnham: Ashgate.

Savigny, Friedrich Carl von (1840a), *System des heutigen römischen Rechts*. Berlin: Veit & Comp, Vol. I.

(1840b), *Vom Beruf unserer Zeit für Gesetzgebung*. Heidelberg: J.C.B. Mohr.

(1850), *Vermischte Schriften*. Berlin: Veit und Comp.

Saydumov, Jambulat (2010), 'Mirovyye sudy v Chechenskoy Respublike kak sostavnaya chast sudebnoy sistemy Rossiyskoy Federatsii' [Justices of the Peace in the Chechen Republic as a Composite Part of the Judicial System of the Russian Federation]. *Vestnik Severo-Osetinskogo Gosudarstvennogo Universiteta Imeni Kosta Levanovicha Khetagurova* 3: 65–68.

Scalia, Antonin (2004), 'Foreign Legal Authority in the Federal Courts'. *Proceedings of the Annual Meeting (American Society of International Law)* 98: 305–10.

Scally, Robert J. (1975), *The Origins of the Lloyd George Coalition: The Politics of Social Imperialism, 1900–1918*. Princeton University Press.

Scelle, Georges (1932), *Précis de droit des gens. Principes et systématique*. Paris: Sirey.

Schaefer, Rainer (1990), *Die SPD in der Ära Brüning: Tolerierung oder Mobilisierung? Handlungsspielräume und Strategien sozialdemokratischer Politik 1930–1932*. Frankfurt: Campus.

Schattschneider, E.E. (1988), *The Semisovereign People: A Realist's View of Democracy in America*, new edition. Fort Worth: Harcourt Brace.

Scheingold, Stuart (1974), *The Politics of Rights: Lawyers, Public Policy, and Political Change*. New Haven, CT: Yale University Press.

Schelsky, Helmut (1973), *Systemüberwindung – Demokratisierung – Gewaltenteilung*. Munich: Beck.

Schieck, Hans (1972), 'Die Behandlung der Sozialisierungsfrage in den Monaten nach dem Staatsumsturz' in Eberhard Kolb (ed), *Vom Kaiserreich zur Weimarer Republik*. Cologne: Kiepenheuer & Witsch, pp. 138–64.

Schiffers, Reinhard (1971), *Elemente direkter Demokratie im Weimarer Regierungssystem*. Düsseldorf: Droste.

Schluchter, Wolfgang (1979), *Die Entwicklung des okzidentalen Rationalismus: Eine Analyse von Max Webers Gesellschaftsgeschichte*. Tübingen: Mohr.

Schlumbohm, Jürgen (1975), *Freiheit: Die Anfänge der bürgerlichen Emanzipationsbewegung in Deutschland im Spiegel ihres Leitwortes (ca.1760–ca.1800)*. Düsseldorf: Schwann.

Schmalz-Bruns, Rainer (1999), 'Deliberativer Supranationalismus: Demokratisches Regieren jenseits Nationalstaats'. *Zeitschrift für Internationale Beziehungen* 6(2): 185–44.

Schmid, Carlo (1949), Speech of 18.11.1948 in *Parlamentarischer Rat, Verhandlungen des Hauptausschusses*. Bonn: Bonner Universitäts-Buch druckerei Scheur.

Schmidt, Christian Hermann (2000), *Vorrang der Verfassung und konstitutionelle Monarchie*. Berlin: Duncker und Humblot.

Schmidt, Eberhard (1975), *Die verhinderte Neuordnung 1945–1952: Zur Auseinandersetzung um die Demokratisierung der Wirtschaft in den westlichen Besatzungszonen und in der Bundesrepublik Deutschland*. Frankfurt: Europäische Verlagsanstalt.

Schmitt, Carl (1919), *Die Diktatur, von den Anfängen des modernen Souveränitätsgedanken bis zum proletarischen Klassenkrieg*. Berlin: Duncker und Humblot.

(1922), *Politische Theologie*. Berlin: Duncker und Humblot.

(1923), *Die geistesgeschichtliche Lage des heutigen Parlamentarismus*. Berlin: Duncker und Humblot.

(1927), *Volksentscheid und Volksbegehren: Ein Beitrag zur Auslegung der Weimarer Verfassung und zur Lehre von der unmittelbaren Demokratie*. Berlin and Leipzig: Duncker und Humblot.

(1928), *Verfassungslehre*. Berlin: Duncker und Humblot.

(1932a), *Der Begriff des Politischen*. Berlin: Duncker und Humblot.

(1932b), *Legalität und Legitimität*. Berlin: Duncker und Humblot.

Schmitt, Eberhard (1969), *Repräsentation und Revolution: Eine Untersuchung zur Genesis der kontinentalen Theorie und Praxis parlamentarischer Repräsentation aus der Herrschaftspraxis des Ancien Régime in Frankreich*. Munich: Beck.

Schmitter, Philippe C. (1986), 'An Introduction to Southern European Transitions from Authoritarian Rule: Italy, Greece, Portugal, Spain and Turkey' in Guillermo O'Donnell, Philippe C. Schmitter and Laurence Whitehead (eds), *Transitions from Authoritarian Rule: Southern Europe*. Baltimore: Johns Hokins, pp. 3–10.

Schnorr, Stefan-Georg (1990), *Liberalismus zwischen 19. und 20. Jahrhundert: Reformulierung liberaler politischer Theorie in Deutschland und England am Beispiel von Friedrich Naumann und Leonard T. Hobhouse*. Baden-Baden: Nomos.

Scholz, Rupert (1971), *Die Koalitionsfreiheit als Verfassungsproblem*. Munich: Beck.

(1978), *Pressefreiheit und Arbeitsverfassung: Verfassungsprobleme um Tendenzschutz und innere Pressefreiheit*. Berlin: Duncker und Humblot.

Schönberger, Christoph (1997), *Das Parlament im Anstaltsstaat: Zur Theorie parlamentarischer Repräsentation in der Staatsrechtslehre des Kaiserreichs (1871–1918)*. Frankfurt am Main: Klostermann.

(2005), *Unionsbürger: Europas föderales Bürgerrecht in vergleichender Sicht*. Tübingen: Mohr.

Schorkopf, Frank (2010), 'Völkerrechtsfreundlichkeit und Völkerrechtsskepsis in der Rechtsprechung des Bundesverfassungsgerichts' in Thomas Giegerich (ed), *Der offene Verfassungsstaat des Grundgesetzes*. Berlin: Duncker & Humblot, pp. 131–58.

Schuck, Peter H. (2000), 'Citizenship in Federal Systems'. *The American Journal of Comparative Law* 48(2): 195–226.

Schuppert, Gunnar Folke (2006), 'The Changing Role of the State in the Growing Importance of Non-State Actors' in Gunnar Folke Schuppert (ed), *Global Governance and the Role of Non-State Actors*. Baden-Baden: Nomos, pp. 203–44.

Schwartz, Bernard and H.W.R. Wade (1972), *Legal Control of Government: Administrative Law in Britain and the United States*. Oxford: Clarendon.

Sciulli, David (1988), 'Foundations of Societal Constitutionalism: Principles from the Concepts of Communicative Action and Procedural Legality'. *The British Journal of Sociology* 39(3): 377–5408.

Searle, G.R. (1995), *Country before Party: Coalition and the Idea of 'National Government' in Modern Britain, 1885–1987*. London: Longman.

Sellin, Volker (2001), *Die geraubte Revolution: Der Sturz Napoleons und duie Restauration in Europa*. Göttingen: Vandenhoeck und Ruprecht.

Semmel, Bernard (1960), *Imperialism and Social Reform: English Social Imperial Thought 1895–1914*. London: Allen & Unwin.

Sewell, William Hamilton (2008), *Work and Revolution in France: The Language of Labor from the Old Regime to 1848*. Cambridge University Press.

Seymour, Charles (1915), *Electoral Reform in England and Wales: The Development of the Parliamentary Franchise, 1832–1885*. New Haven, CT: Yale University Press.

Shankar, Shylashri (2009), *Scaling Justice: India's Supreme Court, Anti-Terror Laws, and Social Rights*. Oxford University Press.

Shany, Yuval (2006), 'How Supreme is the Supreme Law of the Land? Comparative Analysis of the Influence of International Human Rights Treaties upon the Interpretation of Constitutional Texts by Domestic Courts'. *Brook Journal of International Law* 31(2): 341–404.

  (2007), *Regulating Jurisdictional Relations between National and International Courts*. Oxford University Press.

Shapiro, Ian (2003), *The State of Democratic Theory*. Princeton University Press.

Sharlet, Robert (1999), 'Constitutional Implementation and State-Building: Progress and Problems of Law Reform in Russia' in Gordon Smith (ed), *State-Building in Russia: The Yeltsin Legacy and the Challenge of the Future*. Armonk, NY: Sharpe, pp. 81–100.

  (2001), 'Putin and the Politics of Law in Russia'. *Post-Soviet Affairs* 17(3): 195–234.

Shaw, Jo (1998), 'The Interpretation of European Union Citizenship'. *The Modern Law Review* 61(3): 293–317.

Shaw, Martin (2000), *Theory of the Global State: Globality as an Unfinished Revolution*. Cambridge University Press.

Shaw, Timothy (1993), *Reformism and Revisionism in Africa's Political Economy in the 1990s*. New York, NY: St Martin's Press.

Shcherbak, Andrey (2015), 'Nationalism in the USSR: A Historical and Comparative Perspective'. *Nationalities Papers. The Journal of Nationalism and Ethnicity* 43(6): 866–85.

Shevel, Oxana (2012), 'The Politics of Citizenship Policy in Post-Soviet Russia'. *Post-Soviet Affairs* 28(1): 111–47.

Shklar, Judith N. (1991), *American Citizenship: The Quest for Inclusion*. Cambridge, MA: Harvard University Press.

Shlapentokh, Vladimir (1996), 'Early Feudalism – The Best Parallel for Contemporary Russia'. *Europe-Asia Studies* 48(3): 393–411.

Shlapentokh, Vladimir, Roman Levita and Mikhail Loiberg (1997), *From Submission to Rebellion: The Provinces versus the Centre in Russia*. Boulder, CO: Westview.

Siegel, Reva B. (2006), 'Constitutional Culture, Social Movement Conflict and Constitutional Change: The Case of the De Facto Era'. *California Law Review* 94(5): 1323–419.

Sierra, María Teresa (2005), 'Derecho indígeno y acceso a la justicia en México: Perspectivas desde la interlegalidad'. *Revista IIDH* 41: 287–314.

Sieyès, Emmanuel Joseph (1789), *Moniteur universel*, 15–20 October 1789, Nr 75.

(1795), *Moniteur universel*, 13 August 1795.

(1839 [1789]), *Qu'est-ce que le tiers-état?* Paris: Pagnerre.

Sikkink, Kathryn, (2011), *The Justice Cascade: How Human Rights Prosecutions are Changing World Politics*. New York, NY: Norton.

Silver, Brian (1974), 'Social Mobilization and the Russification of Soviet Nationalities'. *The American Political Science Review* 68(1): 45–66.

Simma, Bruno (2013), 'Human Rights before the International Court of Justice: Community Interest Coming to Life?' in Christian J. Tams and James Sloan (eds), *The Development of International Law by the International Court of Justice*. Oxford University Press, pp. 577–603.

Simmons, Beth A. (2009), *Mobilizing for Human Rights: International Law in Domestic Politics*. Cambridge University Press.

Sinopoli, Richard C. (1992), *The Foundations of American Citizenship: Liberalism, the Constitution, and Civic Virtue*. Oxford University Press.

Sintomer, Yves (2011), 'Émile Durkheim, entre républicanisme et démocratie délibérative'. *Sociologies* 4(2): 405–16.

Sismondi, J.C.L. Simonde de (1836), *Études dur les constitutions des peuples libres*. Brussels: Dumont.

Skovoroda, Yegor (2014), '3 dela v chechenskom sude:Reportazh iz Groznogo' [Three Cases in the Chechen Court:Reporting from Grozny]. *Snob.ru*, 16 April 2014, available at: https://snob.ru/selected/entry/74946.

Skrentny, John David (1998), 'The Effect of the Cold War on African-American Civil Rights: America and the World Audience, 1945–1968'. *Theory and Society* 27: 237–85.

(2002), *The Minority Rights Revolution*. Cambridge, MA: Harvard University Press.

Sleznine, Yuri (1994), 'The USSR as a Communal Apartment, or How a Socialist State Promoted Ethnic Particularism'. *Slavic Review* 53(2) (1994): 414–452.

Small, Albion (1907), *Adam Smith and Modern Sociology: A Study in the Methodology of the Social Sciences*. Chicago University Press.

Smart, Nick (1999), *The National Government, 1931–1940*. Basingstoke: MacMillan.

Smend, Rudolf (1955), *Staatsrechtliche Abhandlungen und andere Aufsätze*. Berlin: Duncker und Humblot.

Smith, Douglas G. (1997), 'Citizenship and the Fourteenth Amendment'. *San Diego Law Review* 34: 681–808.

Smith, Rogers M. (1997), *Civic Ideals: Conflicting Visions of Citizenship in U.S. History*. New Haven, CT: Yale University Press.

Smith, Jeremy (2013), *Red Nations: The Nationalities Experience in and after the USSR*. Cambridge University Press.

Smyth, J.J. (2000), *Labour in Glasgow, 1896–1936: Socialism, Suffrage, Sectarianism*. East Linton: Tuckwell.

Snyder, Sarah B. (2011), *Human Rights Activism and the End of the Cold War: A Transnational History of the Helsinki Network*. Cambridge University Press.

Sohm, Rudolf (1892), *Kirchenrecht, I: Die geschichtlichen Grundlagen*. Leipzig: Duncker und Humblot.

Somers, Margaret R. (2008), *Markets, Statelessness, and the Right to have Rights*. Cambridge University Press.

Sood, Avani Mehta (2006), *Litigating Reproductive Rights: Using Public Interest Litigation and International Law to Promote Gender Justice in India*. New York, NY: Center for Reproductive Rights.

Sorensen, M.P.K. (1967), *Land Reform in the Kikuyu Country: A Study in Government Policy*. Nairobi: Oxford University Press.

Sousa Santos, Boaventura de (2002), *Toward a New Legal Common Sense*, second edition. Cambridge University Press.

    (2006), 'The Heterogenous State and Legal Pluralism in Mozambique'. *Law & Society Review* 40(1): 39–75.

    (2012), 'Cuando los excluidos tienen derecho: justicia indígena, plurinacionalidad e interculturalidad' in Boaventura de Sousa Santos and José Luis Exení Rodríguez (eds), *Justicia indígena, plurinacionalidad e interculturalidad en Bolivia*. Quito: Abya-Yala, pp. 11–48.

Soysal, Yasemin Nuhoğlu (1994), *Limits of Citizenship: Migrants and Postnational Membership in Europe*. Chicago University Press.

Spael, Wilhelm (1985), *Friedrich Naumanns Verhältnis zu Max Weber*. Sankt Augustin: Liberal Verlag.

Special Rapporteur on the Independence of Judges and Lawyers (2014), *Report on the Mission to the Russian Federation*, A/HRC/11/41/Add.2 of 30 April 2014.

Special Rapporteur for the topic of jus cogens (2017), Second report on jus cogens, A/CN.4.706.

Sperber, Jonathan (1997), *The Kaiser's Voters: Electors and Elections in Imperial Germany*. Cambridge University Press.

Spiro, Peter J. (2003), 'Treaties, International Law, and Constitutional Rights'. *Stanford Law Review* 55(5): 1999–2018.

Starilov, Yuriy (2005), 'Administrativnoye pravo kak sredstvo razrusheniya "sindroma bespraviya" v sovremennom pravovom gosudarstve' [Administrative Law against the "Lawlessness Syndrome" in the Contemporary Rule of Law State]. *Zhurnal rossiyskogo prava* 4(100): 29–45.

Steinfeld, Robert J. (1989), 'Property and Suffrage in the Early American Republic'. *Stanford Law Review* 41(2): 335–76.

Stoddard, Thomas B. (1997), 'Bleeding Heart: Reflections on Using the Law to Make Social Change'. *New York University Law Review* 72(5): 967–91.

Stokes, Geoffrey (2004), 'Transnational Citizenship: Problems of Definition, Culture and Democracy'. *Cambridge Review of International Affairs* 17(1): 119–35.

Stolleis, Michael (1990), *Staat und Staatsräson in der frühen Neuzeit: Studien zur Geschichte des öffentlichen Rechts*. Frankfurt am Main. Suhrkamp.

Strasser, Hermann (1976), *The Normative Structure of Sociology: Conservative and Emancipatory Themes in Social Thought*. London: Routledge.

Strauss, David A. (2010), *The Living Constitution*. Oxford University Press.

Stürmer, Michael (1973), 'Bismarckstaat und Cäsarismus'. *Der Staat* 12(4): 467–98.

Sunstein, Cass (1993), 'Constitutions and Democracies: An Epilogue' in Jon Elster and Rune Slagstad (eds), *Contitutionalism and Democracy*. Cambridge University Press, pp. 327–53.

Suny, Richard Grigor (1993), *The Revenge of the Past: Nationalism, Revolution, and the Collapse of the Soviet Union*. Stanford University Press.

Susman, Susan D. (1994), 'Distant Voices in the Courts of India:Transformation of Standing in Public Interest Litigation'. *Wisconsin International Law Journal* 13: 57–103.

Suval, Stanley (1985), *Electoral Politics in Wilhelmine Germany*. Chapel Hill, NC: University of North Carolina Press.

Tamanaha, Brian Z. (2008), 'Understanding Legal Pluralism: Past to Present, Local to Global'. *Sydney Law Review* 30: 375–411.

Tamburini, Leonardo (2012), 'La jurisdicción indigena y las autonomías indígenas' in Bouventura de Sousa Santos and José Luis Exení Rodríguez (eds), *Justicia indígena, plurinacionalidad e interculturalidad en Bolvia*. Quito: Abya-Yala, pp. 249–74.

Tanner, Duncan (1990), *Political Change and the Labour Party 1900–1918*. Cambridge University Press.

Tarrow, Sidney (1994), *Power in Movement: Social Movements, Collective Action and Politics*. Cambridge University Press.

(2005), *The New Transnational Activism*. Cambridge University Press.

Tate, Winifred (2007), *Counting the Dead: The Culture and Politics of Human Rights Activism in Colombia*. Berkeley, CA: University of California Press.

Taylor, Brian (2011), *State Building in Putin's Russia: Policing and Coercion after Communism*. Cambridge University Press.

Teubner, Gunther (1983), 'Substantive and Reflexive Elements in Modern Law'. *Law & Society Review* 17(2): 239–85.

    (2004), 'Societal Constitutionalism: Alternatives to State-Centred Constitutioonal Theory' in Christian Joerges, Inger-Johanne Sand and Gunther Teubner (eds), *Transnational Goverrnance and Constitutionalism*. Oxford: Hart, pp. 3–28.

    (2011), 'Verfassungen ohne Staat? Zur Konstitutionalisierung transnationaler Regimes' in Klaus Günther and Stefan Kadelbach (eds), *Recht ohne Staat*. Frankfurt: Campus, pp. 49–100.

    (2012), *Constitutional Fragments: Societal Constitutionalism and Globalization*. Oxford University Press.

    (2017), 'Nine Variations on a Theme by David Sciulli' in Paul Blokker and Chris Thornhill (eds), *Sociological Constitutialism*. Cambridge University Press, pp. 313–40.

    (2018), 'Quod omnes tangit: Transnational Constitutions Without Democracy'. *Journal of Law & Society* 45(4).

't Hart, Marjolein C. (1993), *The Making of a Bourgeois State: War, Politics and Finance during the Dutch Revolt*. Manchester University Press.

Thiry, Jean (1949), *Le sénat de Napoléon (1800–1814)*, second edition. Paris: Berger-Levrault.

Thomas, Daniel C. (2007), 'Constitutionalization through Enlargement: The Contested Origins of the EU's Democratic Identity' in Berthold Rittberger and Frank Schimmelfenig (eds), *The Constitutionalization of the European Union*. Abingdon: Routledge, pp. 43–63.

Thompson, Dennis F. (1970), *The Democratic Citizen: Social Science and Democratic Theory in the Twentieth Century*. Cambridge University Press.

Thornberry, Patrick (1989), 'Self-Determination, Minorities, Human Rights: A Review of International Instruments'. *The International and Comparative Law Quarterly* 38(4): 867–89.

Thorpe, Andrew (1991), *The British General Election of 1931*. Oxford: Clarendon.

Thorson, Carla L. (2012), *Politics, Judicial Review and the Russian Constitutional Court*. Basingstoke: Palgrave.

Throup, David W. (1985), 'The Origins of Mau Mau'. *African Affairs* 84: 399–433.

    (1988), *Economic and Social Origins of Mau Mau 1945–1953*. London: Currey.

Tilly, Charles (1990), *Coercion, Capital, and European States, AD 990–1990*. Oxford: Blackwell.

    (1995), 'The Emergence of Citizenship in France and Elsewhere'. *International Review of Social History* 40(3): 223–36.

    (2000), 'Processes and Mechanisms of Democratization'. *Sociological Theory* 18(1): 1–16.

    (2004), *Contention and Democracy in Europe, 1650–2000*. Cambridge University Press.

    (2007), *Democracy*. Cambridge University Press.

Tiunov, Oleg (2011), 'Mezhdunarodnoye pravo i pravovyye pozitsii konstitutsion-nogo suda RF' [International Law and Legal Positions of the Constitutional Court of the Russian Federation]. *Zhurnal Rossiyskogo Prava* 10(178): 82–96.

Tobias, Carl (1989), 'Public Law Litigation and the Federal Rules of Civil Procedure'. *Cornell Law Review* 74: 270–356.

Tocqueville, Alexis de 1886 [1835]. *De la démocratie en Amérique*. Paris: Charles Gosselin, Vol. I.

Tolz, Vera (1998), 'Forging the Nation: National Identity and Nation Building in Post-Communist Russia'. *Europe-Asia Studies* 50(6): 993–1022.

Tomkins, Adam (2010), 'The Role of the Courts in the Political Constitution'. *University of Toronto Law Journal* 60: 1–22.

Tompson, William (2002), 'Putin's Challenge: The Politics of Structural Reform in Russia'. *Europe-Asia Studies* 54(6): 933–37.

Torres-Goitia Torres, Javier, Javier Torres-Goitia Caballero and Maria Lagrava Burgoa (2015), *La Salud como derecho: Conquista y evaluación en Bolivia*. La Paz: Plural.

Touraine, Alain (1994), *Qu'est-ec que la démocratie?* Paris: Fayard.

Trochev, Alexei (2008), *Judging Russia: Constitutional Court in Russian Politics 1990–2006*. Cambridge University Press.

Troper, Michel (1973), *La Séparation des pouvoirs et l'histoire*. Paris: Richon et Durand-Auzias.

Tsutsui, Kiyoteru and Christine Min Wotipka (2002), 'Global Civil Society and the International Human Rights Movement: Citizen Participation in Human Rights International Nongovernmental Organizations'. *Social Forces* 83(2): 587–620.

Tuck, Richard (2015), *The Sleeping Sovereign: The Invention of Modern Democracy*. Cambridge University Press.

Tuori, Kaarlo (2015), *European Constitutionalism*. Cambridge University Press.

Turaev, Vadim (2016), 'Krizis Sovetskoy identichnosti kak faktor raspada SSSR' [Soviet Identity Crisis as a Factor in the Collapse of the Soviet Union]. *Izvestiya Irkutskogo Gosudarstvennogo Universiteta. Seriya: Geoarkheologiya. Etnologiya. Antropologiya* 15: 64–76.

Turner, Bryan S. (1990), 'Outline of a Theory of Citizenship'. *Sociology* 24(2): 189–217.

 (1993), 'Contemporary Problems in the Theory of Citizenship' in Bryan S. Turner (ed), *Citizenship and Social Theory*. London: Sage, pp. 1–18.

Turner, John (1992), *British Politics and the Great War: Coalition and Conflict 1915–1918*. New Haven, CT: Yale University Press.

Tushnet, Mark (1984), 'An Essay on Rights'. *Texas Law Review* 62(8): 1363–403.

 (1987), *The NAACP's Legal Strategy against Segregated Education, 1925–1950*. Chapel Hill, NC: University of North Carolina Press.

(1989), 'Rights: An Essay in Informal Political Theory'. *Politics & Society* 17(4): 403–51.

(1994), *Making Civil Rights Law: Thurgood Marshall and the Supreme Court, 1936–1961*. Oxford University Press.

Tyrell, Hartmann (1994), 'Max Webers Soziologie – eine Soziologie ohne Gesellschaft' in Gerhard Wagner and Heinz Zipprian (eds), *Max Webers Wissenschaftslehre*. Frankfurt am Main: Suhrkamp, pp. 390–414.

Uprimny, Rodrigo (1989), 'Legitimidad, clientelismo y política en Colombia: Un ensayo de interpretación'. *Cuadernos de Economía* 10(13): 113–64.

Uprimny, Rodrigo and Juanita Durán (2014), *Equidad y protección judicial del derecho a la salud en Colombia*. Santiago de Chile: Naciones Unidas.

Urbinati, Nadia (2006), *Representative Democracy: Principles and Genealogy*. Chicago University Press.

Uribe de Hincapié, María Teresa (1996), 'Proceso histórico de la configuración de la ciudadanía en Colombia'. *Estudios políticos* (9): 67–76.

(1998a), 'Órdenes complejos y ciudadanías mestizas: una mirada al caso colombiano'. *Estudios políticos* (12): 25–46.

(1998b), 'Las soberanías en vilo en un contexto de guerra y paz'. *Estudios políticos* 13: 11–39.

(1999), 'Las soberanías en disputa: conflícto de identidades o de derechos?' *Estudios políticos* (15): 23–45.

Uribe López, Mauricio (2013), *La nación vetada: Estado, desarrollo y Guerra civil en Colombia*. Bogota: Universidad Externado de Colombia.

Urwin, Derek W. (1982), 'Territorial Structures and Political Developments in the United Kingdom' in Stein Rokkan and Derek W. Urwin (eds), *The Politics of Territorial Identity: Studies in European Regionalism*. London: Sage, pp. 19–73.

Valelly, Richard M. (2004), *The Two Reconstructions: The Struggle for Black Enfranchisement*. Chicago University Press.

Van Cott, Donna Lee (2000), 'A Political Analysis of Legal Pluralism in Bolivia and Colombia'. *Journal of Latin American Studies* 32(1): 207–34.

Van der Vyver, J.D. (1991), 'Statehood in International Law'. *Emory International Law Review* 5: 9–102.

Van Eyll, Klara (1985), 'Berufsständische Selbstverwaltung' in Kurt G.A. Jeserich, Hans Pohl and Georg-Christoph von Unruh (eds), *Deutsche Verwaltungsgeschichte, 4: Das Reich als Republik und in der Zeit des Nationalsozialismus*. Stuttgart: Deutsche Verlags-Anstalt, pp. 66–77.

Vardi, Liana (1988), 'The Abolition of the Guilds during the French Revolution'. *French Historical Studies* 15(4): 704–17.

Vergne, Arnaud (2006), *La Notion de constitution d'après les cours et assemblées à la fin de l'ancien regime (1750–1789)*. Paris: De Boccard.

Vidal López, Roberto Carlos (2007), *Derecho global y desplazamiento interno: Creación, uso y desaparición del desplazamiento forzado por la violencia en el Derecho contemporáneo*. Bogota: Pontificia Universidad Javeriana.

Vincent, J.R. (1976), *The Formation of the British Liberal Party 1857–1868*, second edition. Hassocks: Harvester.

Vining, Joseph (1978), *Legal Identity: The Coming of Age of Public Law*. New Haven, CT: Yale University Press.

Vorländer, Hans (2006), 'Deutungsmacht – Die Macht der Verfassungsgerichtsbarkeit' in Hans Vorländer (ed), *Die Deutungsmacht der Verfassungsgerichtsbarkeit*. Wiesbaden: Verlag für Sozialwissenschaften, pp. 9–33.

Vorländer, Hans and André Brodocz (2006), 'Das Vertrauen in das Bundesverfassungsgericht: Ergebnisse einer repräsentativen Umfrage' in Hans Vorländer (ed), *Die Deutungsmacht der Verfassungsgerichtsbarkeit*. Wiesbaden: Verlag für Sozialwissenschaften, pp. 259–95.

Voßkuhle, Andreas (2010) 'Multilevel Cooperation of the European Constitutional Courts: Der Europäische Verfassungsgerichtsverbund'. *European Constitutional Law Review* 6. 175–90.

Wabwile, Michael (2013), 'The Emerging Juridical Status of International Law in Kenya'. *Oxford University Commonwealth Law Journal* 13(1): 167–89.

Wade, William (1955), 'The Basis of Legal Sovereignty'. *The Cambridge Law Journal* 13(2): 172–97.

Wade, William and Christopher Forsyth (2004), *Administrative Law*, ninth Edition. Oxford University Press.

Wahnich, Sophie (1997), *L'impossible citoyen: L'étranger dans le discours de la Révolution française*. Paris: Albin Michel.

Waldron, Jeremy (1999), *The Dignity of Legislation*. Cambridge University Press.
(2006), 'The Core of the Case against Judicial Review'. *The Yale Law Journal* 115: 1346–406.

Waluchow, W.J. (2001), 'Democracy and the Living Tree Constitution'. *Drake Law Review* 59(2001): 1001–46.

Walzer, Michael (1994), *Thick and Thin: Moral Argument at Home and Abroad*. Notre Dame: University of Notre Dame Press.

Wang, Xi (1997), *The Trial of Democracy: Black Suffrage and Northern Republicans, 1860–1910*. Athens, GA: University of Georgia Press.

Ward, Brian (2004), *Radio and the Struggle for Civil Rights in the South*. Gainesville, FL: Florida University Press.

WCIOM (Russian Public Opinion Research Center) (2008), *Nizhegorodtsy v bol'shinstve svoyem veryat v spravedlivyye sudy, khotya mnogiye znakomy s nimi tol'ko po televizoru* [*The Majority of Residents in Nizhny Novgorod Believe in Just Courts, Although Many are Familiar with Them Only via TV*]. Available at: http://wciom.ru/index.php?id=241&uid=9872.

Weatherall, Thomas (2015), *Jus Cogens: International Law and Social Contract*. Cambridge University Press.

Webb, Sidney (1932), *What happened in 1931? A Record*. London: The Fabian Society.

Webber, Grégoire (2009), *The Negotiable Constitution: On the Limitation of Rights.* Cambridge University Press.

Weber, Max (1920), *Gesammelte Aufsätze zur Religionssoziologie,* in 3 vols. Tübingen: Mohr.

(1921), *Gesammelte Politische Schriften.* Tübingen: Mohr.

(1921/22), *Wirtschaft und Gesellschaft: Grundriß der verstehenden Soziologie.* Tübingen: Mohr.

Weber, Petra (1996), *Carlo Schmid 1896–1979: Eine Biographie.* Munich: Beck.

Webster, R.A. (1975), *Industrial Imperialism in Italy 1908–1915.* Berkeley, CA: Univesity of California Press.

Wehler, Hans-Ulrich (1969), *Bismarck und der Imperialismus.* Cologne: Kiepenheuer & Witsch.

(1970), *Krisenherde des Kaiserreichs 1871–1918: Studien zur deutschen Sozial- und Verfassungsgeschichte.* Göttingen: Vandenhoeck und Ruprecht.

(1973), *Das deutsche Kaiserreich 1871–1918.* Göttingen: Vandenhoeck und Ruprecht.

Weichlein, Siegfried (2007), 'Max Weber, der moderne Staat und die Nation' in Andreas Anter und Stefan Breuer (eds), *Max Webers Staatssoziologie: Positionen und Perspektiven.* Baden-Baden: Nomos, pp. 103–17.

Weihnacht, Paul-Ludwig (1969), '"Staatsbürger": Zur Geschichte und Kritik eines politischen Begriffs'. *Der Staat* 8(1): 41–68.

Weinberg, Louise (1977), 'The New Judicial Federalism'. *Stanford Law Review* 29(6): 1191–244.

Weinstock, Daniel M. (2001), 'Prospects for Transnational Citizenship and Democracy'. *Ethics & International Affairs* 15(2): 53–66.

Weir, Stuart and David Beetham (1999), *Political Power and Social Control in Britain: The Democratic Audit of the United Kingdom.* London: Routledge.

Weisbrod, Bernd (1978), *Schwerindustrie in der Weimarer Republik: Interessenpolitik zwischen Stabilisierung und Krise.* Wuppertal: Peter Hammer.

(1990), 'Der englische "Sonderweg" in der neueren Geschichte'. *Geschichte und Gesellschaft* 16(2): 233–52.

Wendt, Alexander (2003), 'Why a World State is Inevitable'. *European Journal of International Relations* 9: 491–542.

Weyland, Kurt (2014), *Making Waves: Democratic Contention in Europe and Latin America since the Revolutions of 1848.* Cambridge University Press.

Wheatley, Steven (2002), 'Democracy in International Law: A European Perspective'. *International and Comparative Law Quarterly* 50(2): 225–47.

(2005), *Democracy, Minorities and International Law.* Cambridge University Press.

(2010), *The Democratic Legitimacy of International Law.* Oxford: Hart.

White, Luise (2015), *Unpopular Sovereignty: Rhodesian Independence and African Decolonization.* Chicago University Press.

White, Stephen (1990), *Gorbachev in Power*. Cambridge University Press.

Wiener, Antje (1998), *'European' Citizenship Practice: Building Institutions of a Non-State*. Boulder, CO: Westview.

(2014), *A Theory of Contestation*. Berlin: Springer.

Wilentz, Sean (2005), *The Rise of American Democracy: Jefferson to Lincoln*. New York, NY: Norton.

Willke, Helmut (1996), *Ironie des Staates: Grundlinien einer Staatstheorie polyzentrischer Gesellschaft*. Frankfurt: Suhrkamp.

(1997), *Supervision des Staates*. Frankfurt: Suhrkamp.

(1998), 'Soziologische Aufklärung der Demokratietheorie' in Hauke Brunkhorst (ed), *Demokratischer Experimentalismus: Politik in der komplexen Gesellschaft*. Frankfurt: Suhrkamp, pp. 13–32.

(2014), *Demokratie in Zeiten der Konfusion*. Frankfurt: Suhrkamp.

(2016), *Dezentrierte Demokratie: Prolegomena zur Revision politischer Steuerung*. Frankfurt am Main: Suhrkamp.

Williamson III, J. Harvie (1979), *From Brown to Bakke: The Supreme Court and School Integration*. Oxford University Press.

Williamson, Philip (1992), *National Crisis and National Government: British Politics, the Economy and Empire, 1926–1932*. Cambridge University Press.

Winkler, Heinrich August (1964), *Preussischer Liberalismus und deutscher Nationalstaat: Studien zur Geschichte der Deutschen Fortschrittspartei*. Tübingen: Mohr.

(1978), *Revolution, Staat, Faschismus*. Göttingen: Vandenhoeck und Ruprecht.

(1979), *Liberalismus und Antiliberalismus: Studien zur politischen Sozialgeschichte des 19. und 20. Jahrhunderts*. Göttingen: Vandenhoeck und Ruprecht.

(2000), *Der lange Weg nach Westen II: Deutsche Geschichte*. Munich: Beck.

Withroup, David (1987), 'The Construction and Destruction of the Kenyatta State' in Michael G. Schatzberg (ed), *The Political Economy of Kenya*. New York, NY: Praeger, pp. 33–74.

Witt, Peter-Christian (1970), *Die Finanzpolitik des Deutschen Reiches von 1903 bis 1913: Eine Studie zur Innenpolitik des Wilhelminischen Deutschland*. Lübeck: Matthiesen.

Wohlgemuth, Kathleen L. (1959), 'Woodrow Wilson and Federal Segregation'. *The Journal of Negro History* 44(2): 158–77.

Wolff, Christian (1751), *Vernünftige Gedanken von Gott der Welt und der Seele des Menschen*, second edition. Halle: Renger.

(1756), *Vernünftige Gedanken von dem gesellschaftlichen Leben der Menschen und insonderheit dem gemeinen Wesen*, second edition. Halle: Renger.

Wood, Gordon S. (1992), *The Radicalism of the American Revolution*. New York, NY: Knopf.

(2008), *Representation in the American Revolution*, revised edition. Charlottesville, VA: University of Virginia Press.

Woodhouse, Diana (1994), *Ministers and Parliament: Accountability in Theory and Practice*. Oxford: Clarendon.

Woodward, C. Vann (1957), 'The Political Legacy of Reconstruction'. *The Journal of Negro Education* 26(3): 231–40.

Worley, Matthew (2005), *Labour inside the Gate: A History of the British Labour Party between the Wars*. London: Tauris.

Wortman, Richard S. (2010), *The Development of a Russian Legal Consciousness*. Chicago University Press.

Wotipka, Christine Min and Kiyoteru Tsutsui (2008), 'Global Human Rights Treaties and State Sovereignty: State Ratification of International Human Rights Treaties, 1956–2001'. *Sociological Forum* 23(4): 724–54.

Wrigley, Chris (1976), *David Lloyd George and the British Labour Movement*. Hassocks: Harvester.

Wylde, Christopher (2012), *Latin America after Neoliberalism: Developmental Regimes in Post-Crisis States*. Basingstoke: Palgrave.

Yakovlev, Veniamin (2010). *Zachem sledstviyu nuzhny aresty? [Why Does the Investigation Need Arrests?]*. Available (in Russian) at: http://pravo.ru/review/view/26363/.

Yampara Huarachi, Simón (2011), 'Cosmovivencia Andina: Vivir y convivir en armonía integral – Suma Qamaña'. *Bolivian Studies Journal* 18: 1–22.

Yarbrough, Tinsley E. (2000), *The Rehnquist Court and the Constitution*. Oxford University Press.

Yashar, Deborah (1998), 'Contesting Citizenship: Indigenous Movements and Democracy in Latin America'. *Comparative Politics* 31(1): 23–42.

(2005), *Contesting Citizenship in Latin America: The Rise of Indigenous Movements and the Postliberal Challenge*. Cambridge University Press.

Yeazell, Stephen C. (2004), 'Brown, the Civil Rights Movement and the Silent Litigation Revolution'. *Vanderbilt Law Review* 57(6): 1974–2003.

Yellin, Eric S. (2013), *Racism in the Nation's Service: Government Workers and the Color Line in Woodrow Wilson's America*. Chapel Hill, NC: University of North Carolina Press.

Yershov, Valentin (ed), *Samostoyatelnost i nezavisimost sudebnoy vlasti Rossiyskoy Federatsii [Autonomy and Independence of the Judicial Power of the Russian Federation]*. Moscow: Russian Academy of Justice, Jurist.

Young, Alison (2009), *Parliamentary Sovereignty and the Human Rights Act*. Oxford: Hart.

Young, Crawford (1976), *The Politics of Cultural Pluralism*. Madison, WI: University of Wisconsin Press.

Young, Iris Marion (1989), 'Polity and Group Difference: A Critique of the Ideal of Universal Citizenship'. *Ethics* 99(2): 250–74.

(2000), *Inclusion and Democracy*. Oxford University Press.

Zalten, Erich (2006), 'Staatslehre und Verfassungstheorie im Licht der Soziologie' in Philippe Mastronardi and Denis Taubert (eds), *Staats- und Verfassungstheorie im Spannungsfeld der Disziplinen*. Stuttgart: Steiner, pp. 223–40.

Zängle, Michael (1988), *Max Webers Staatstheorie im Kontext seines Werkes*. Berlin: Duncker und Humblot.

Zaslavsky, Victor (1992), 'Nationalism and Democratic Transition in Postcommunist Societies'. *Daedalus* 121(2): 97–121.

Zemans, Frances Kahn (1983), 'The Neglected Role of the Law in the Political System'. *The American Political Science Review* 77(3): 690–703.

Ziblatt, Daniel (2006), 'How did Europe Democratize?' *World Politics* 58: 311–38.

(2017), *Conservative Parties and the Birth of Democracy*. Cambridge University Press.

Zips-Mairitsch, Manuela (2013), *Lost Lands? (Land) Rights of the San in Botswana und the Legal Concept of Indigeneity in Africa*. Münster: Lit.

Zolberg, Aristide (2006), *A Nation by Design: Immigration Policy in the Fashioning of America*. Cambridge, MA: Harvard University Press.

Zorkin, Valeriy (2004), 'Pretsedentnyy kharakter resheniy Konstitutsionnogo Suda Rossiyskoy Federatsii' [The Precedential Nature of Constitutional Court Rulings in the Russian Federation]. *Zhurnal rossiyskogo prava* 12: 3–9.

(2006). *Zakonnyy brak: Za oshibki zakonodatelya rasplachivayutsya grazhdane [Legal Defect: Citizens Pay for Mistakes of Lawmakers]* [Online] 7 July 2006. Available (in Russian) at: Rossiiskaya Gazeta, www.rg.ru/2006/07/07/zorkin .html.

(2007), *Rossiya i Konstitutsiya v XXI veke: Vzglyad s Ilyinki [Russia and the Constitution in the XXI Century: View from Ilyinka]*. Moscow: Norma.

(2011), Valeriy *'Konstitutsionnyy sud v istoricheskom kontekste: Razmyshleniya k yubileyu Konstitutsionnogo suda [The Constitutional Court in its Historical Context: Reflections on the Anniversary of the Constitutional Court]'*. Available (in Russian) at: Rossiiskaya Gazeta, www.rg.ru/2011/10/28/sud-site.html.

Zunkel, Friedrich (1974), *Industrie und Staatssozialismus: Der Kampf um die Wirtschaftsordnung in Deutschland 1914–18*. Düsseldorf: Droste.

Zverev, D.V. (2006), 'Novyye istochniki grazhdanskogo protsessualnogo prava v svete Yevropeyskoy konventsii o zashchite prav cheloveka i osnovnykh svobod' [New Sources of Civil Procedural Law in the Light of the European Convention on Human Rights] in R. F. Kallistratova and M. A. Fokin (eds) *Yevropeyskaya integratsiya i razvitiye tsivilisticheskogo protsessa v Rossii: Sbornik nauchnykh statey [The European Integration Process and the Development of the Civil Law in Russia: Collection of Articles]*. Moscow: RAP, pp. 17–22.

INDEX